A Compendium of Rhea and Meigs Counties Tennessee

1808 through 1850

Compiled by
Bettye J. Broyles

Rhea County Historical and Genealogical Society

Heritage Books
2024

HERITAGE BOOKS
AN IMPRINT OF HERITAGE BOOKS, INC.

Books, CDs, and more—Worldwide

For our listing of thousands of titles see our website
at
www.HeritageBooks.com

A Facsimile Reprint
Published 2023 by
HERITAGE BOOKS, INC.
Publishing Division
5810 Ruatan Street
Berwyn Heights, MD 20740

First printing: 1980

Revised and reprinted: 1996
Rhea County Historical and Genealogical Society

International Standard Book Number
Paperbound: 978-0-7884-9122-1

INTRODUCTION

NOTE: Most of the following Introduction was written in 1980. A few additional comments have been added in brackets, as well as new sections on the Tax Lists and the 1850 Census . B.J.B.

When I first thought of doing something with the Rhea County records, I had in mind a compilation of only the marriage records. This was to include the records from the Courthouse in Dayton and those copied by Penelope J. Allen in 1932 from official licenses and bonds in the possession of Mr. George Barnes of Dayton [the Barnes Papers are presently housed in the Special Collections Room at the University of Tennessee Library in Knoxville]. There were many marriages recorded in this transcription that were not in the Courthouse records.

Several years ago I discovered that the Rhea County 1850 Census had never been transcribed. Since then, the Sistler compilation of the entire State of Tennessee has been published, but it is difficult to identify a specific county in these volumes. It seemed logical to combine the marriage and census records of Rhea County into one publication. It soon became apparent that many of the couples married in Rhea County were either living in the portion that became Meigs County or had moved there by 1850.

While doing research in the Meigs County Courthouse in Decatur, I found that Volume II of the marriage records (1846-1857) were not available, having been destroyed by a fire in 1902. Fortunately, many, if not all, of the marriages were copied from licenses and bonds and are on file in the McClung Room of the Knoxville Public Library. Therefore, the Meigs County records also needed to be consolidated into one publication. [The Meigs County marriages from 1836 and 1837 have never been located]

The solution was to do a compendium of both Rhea and Meigs counties using all of the marriges from 1808 through 1850, the 1830, 1840, and 1850 census, and several early Rhea County Tax lists (the early census was destroyed).

Names of early settlers also have been extracted from the minutes of the Board of Commissioners for the Town of Washington (1812-1833) and the Meigs County Commissioners (1836-1840). Additional notes on several families were added from Campbell's ***Records of Rhea*** (1940), Goodspeed's ***History of East Tennessee*** (1887), and Lillard's ***Meigs County, Tennessee*** (1975). [see References on page 241 of this publication]

The next problem was how to organize such a gigantic undertaking so that it could be easily used. After some trial and error, I decided to do it by family names. Sometimes a name appeared in only one record, but many were present in all three (census, tax, and marriage). Each of the married couples who did not appear on either the Rhea or Meigs 1850 Census were looked up in the Sistler compilation of the 1850 Tennessee census.

Since several of the early settlers of Rhea County had been married prior to 1808, those who appeared in the Roane County reords have been noted (Hutcherson and McCuen, 1973). Additional marriages were taken from the McMinn County records (Boyer 1964).

TAX LISTS

Only three Tax Lists from Rhea County were available at the time the Compendium was compiled. In 1989, the Rhea County Historical and Genealogical Society published the Tax Lists from 1819 to 1829, and several lists from 1809 to 1818 have been included in varous issues of ***Rhea Notes***. The 1808 list has been published several times and can be found in the ***History of Rhea County*** published by the Historical Society in 1991.

The Tax Lists are an important indicator of when a person arrived in the County. They provide information on where the person lived and the number of acres owned, the number of lots (TL) in the Town of Washington, the number of White Polls (WP), the number of Black Polls (BP), and the tax paid on stud horses.

1830 AND 1840 CENSUS

The 1830 and 1840 census may take a few words of explanation for new-comers to the research field. The numbers that appear to the right of the names indicate the number of males (first set of numbers) and females (second set of numbers) by age in the household. The first four numbers are in incruments of 5 years, while the remainder are in 10-year spans. Using one of the first families in the Compendium, we have the following:

John Able 010101 - 01200011

John had in his household 1 male and 1 female 5 to 10 years of age, 2 females 10 to 15, 1 male 15 to 20, 1 male 30 to 40, 1 female 40 to 50, and 1 female 50 to 60. Since this record was taken from the 1830 Census, John had a household composed of 1 male and 1 female born between 1820 and 1825, 2 females born between 1815 and 1820, etc.

The 1840 census figures are read in the same way, except the numbers are subtracted from 1840.

The free colored entries on the 1830 and 1840 census were recorded differently. Reading from left to right, the numbers indicate individuals between 0 and 10, 10 to 24, 24 to 36, 36 to 55, and 55 to 100.

Page numbers (and household numbers on the 1850 census) are given for all census records except the 1840 Rhea County census. Unfortunately, it was arranged alphabetically by the enumerator and, since the page numbers would serve no useul purpose, they have not been included.

1850 CENSUS

In 1850, the Government's method of recording the census was changed to include the names and ages of all the household members. For the records included in this publication, all of the pertinent information was transcribed.

The place of birth has been noted (in parenthesis) for each individual born <u>outside</u> of the State of Tennessee. This follows the persons age. The persons occupation (in parenthesis) follows the age and/or the place of birth. Other miscellaneous information includes Deaf and Dumb, Idiot, Student, etc.

Occasionally, it is difficult to know from the name whether the person was a male or female. Since the sex of each individual is specified on the census, the questionable names have been identified by an (m) or (f) between the name and the age.

The free colored people in Rhea and Meigs counties were identified on the 1850 census as black or mulatto. This designation (in parenthesis) follows the age.

MARRIAGE RECORDS

The marriage records also need explaining. Some records have the date of the license as well as the marriage date. The name of the minister or justice of the peace who performed the ceremony appears on some records and not on others. Most of the earlier records also include the name of the bondsman or surety.

In order to conserve space, the records will be written thusly: the name of the groom and bride followed by the license date, the marriage date if given (in parenthesis), the person performing the ceremony (JP = Justice of the Peace; MG = Minister of the Gospel), and the Bondsman (Bm) or Surety (Sur).

The following is an excellent example:
John Atchley to May Genoe, 10 Dec 1825 (12 Dec), Thomas Cox JP, John Davis Bm.

The brides have been cross-referenced as follows: May Genoe to John Atchley q.v.

The biggest problem encountered during transcription of the Rhea County marriages was spelling. The variations are shown for each family name and the names are spelled as they appear in the records. Where alternate spellings appear for a name in the Rhea County records, the first spelling is from the Courthouse marriage book and the second from the Allen transcription of the bonds.

The following is an example:
Jonathan Barnes or Burns to Polly or Patsy Richards, 16 Dec or Nov 1815.

The Courthouse record reads Jonathan Barnes to Polly Richards, 16 Dec 1815; while the Allen transcription is as follows: Jonathan Burns to Patsy Richards, 16 Nov 1815. Since it is impossible to ascertain which is correct, both will be shown. The source of the Rhea County marriage record is indicated by code letters at the end of the individual entry (A = Allen only; AR = Allen and Rhea Courthouse; R = Rhea Courthouse only).

NOTES FROM 1996

The original 1980 publication of the Compendium was privately printed by the University of Mississippi Press in Oxford, Mississippi. In 1991, the publication rights were granted to the Rhea County Historical and Genealogical Society. Several corrections were made with the assistance of Seth Tallent, but the contents were basically unchanged. The pages were reduced in size and positioned side-by-side in order to reduce the thickness. Almost 100 copies of the reduced version have been sold since 1991.

In 1996, when it became necessary to reprint the Compendium, it was decided to retype the entire publication on the computer in order to reduce the number of pages. Although a few corrections have been made, none of the original publication has been omitted.

One change in format has been made to save space. In several instances, a person with a different last name was living in a household (1850 census). In the original Compendium, these were shown as follows:
Jane Hodges 17: living with C. Whitehouse Able q.v.
In this reprinted version, these entries now read:
Jane Hodges 17: see C. Whitehouse Able

Three appendicies appear at the end of this retyped version of the Compendium. Appendix A and Appendix B contain a complete listing of the heads of household on the 1850 Rhea and Meigs county census arranged by page and household number. This will enable a researcher to quickly identify the neighbors of an individual. The third appendix contains all of the statistics included with the 1830, 1840, and 1850 census.

Bettye J. Broyles

A COMPENDIUM OF RHEA AND MEIGS COUNTIES, TENNESSEE, 1808 THROUGH 1850

ABEL / ABLE

TAXES (RHEA)
1808 (Joseph Brooks' List):
Cain Able 1 WP, 121a W Branch Richland Cr (entered by John Able)
John Able 1 WP, 200a
1819 (Capt. McGill's Co.):
Cain Abel 1 WP, 200a
John & Able Able 2 WP, 377a
1823 (Capt. Howard's Co.):
Cain Able 1 WP, 200a

1830 RHEA CENSUS
Cain Able 03020001 - 00010001 p. 381
John Able 010101 - 01200011 p. 381
1840 RHEA CENSUS
Cain Able 00012 - 00010001
James J. Able 00001 - 0002
1850 RHEA CENSUS
C. Whitehouse Able 29 (Farmer), Esther E. 25, Susan E. 2, Mary J. 4/12, Jane HODGES 17, Allison MORGAN 23 p. 628-602
Cain Able 75 (NC)(Farmer), Margaret 72 (Pa), Mary W. 37, James K.P. WOODBY 6 p. 628-600
James J. Able 35 (Tanner), Lucretia 37 (SC), Margaret 11, Myra J. 9, Elizabeth McFARLAND 25, James NASH 24 (Apprentice Tanner), Joseph PEARCE 20 (NC)(Apprentice Tanner) p. 628-599
John R. Able 34 (Farmer), Mary M. 27 p. 628-601
Robert P. Able 32 (Farmer), Mary A. 29, James M. 7, Margaret A. 4, Susan S. 2, Elizabeth FOUST 12, William HODGES 16 (Farmer) p. 630-611
1850 MEIGS CENSUS
William Abel 39 (Merchant), Malinda 26 p. 774-483

MARRIAGES (RHEA)
C.W. Abel to Ester E. Fouste, 21 Sept 1847, John S. Evans JP (R)
Cain Able to Margaret Buice, 2 Oct 1810 (AR)
David Able to Lively Hudleston, 11 Feb 1839 (5 Mar), S.B. Dyer JP, M.W. Smith Bm (AR)
John R. Able to M.M. Alexander, 17 Oct 1849, no return (R)
Linsey or Junsey Able to Dimsey Hilburn q.v.
MARRIAGES (MEIGS)
William J. Abel to Malinda H. Guinn, 21 May 1850, C.R. Smith Sur

MISCELLANEOUS (RHEA)
David Able: Bondsman for Jesse Huddleston, 1849
John Able: On first Grand Jury
" " John & Isabel (McClure) Abel had three sons (Cain, John, and Phillip) and one daughter (Christine) (see Campbell 1940:109)
William Jefferson Abel: Taught mathematics, 1834

- - - - - - - - - - - - -

ACRE / ACREE
(see also AGEE)

1840 RHEA CENSUS
John W. Acre 1211001 - 00101
1850 RHEA CENSUS
Albert N. Acre 7: see Phillip Foust
Asbury Acre 16: see Elias Morgan
John Acre 47: see William B. Johnson
Rachael Acre 6: see Phillip Foust
William Acre 20: see Elijah Largen
MARRIAGES (RHEA)
George Washington Acre to Polly Kinnon, 5 July 1822 (7 July), John Robinson JP, John Parker Bm (AR)
James Acree to Esther Jones, 1 Jan 1823 (same) John Farmer MG (AR)
John Acre to Cinthia Jenkins, 11 Sept 1819, John Witt and Lewis Peterson Bm (A)
Lewis Acre to Rhoda Wigginton, 24 Aug 1825 (25 Aug), Jno Bowman PEMEC, Edmund Bean Bm (AR)

- - - - - - - - - - - - -

ADAMS

1840 MEIGS CENSUS
Abednego Adams 00001 - 21001 p. 240
Phillip Adams (free colored) 00001 - 00101 p. 232
Samuel Adams 10000101 - 00000001 p. 240
Thomas Adams 210001 - 201001 p. 235
1850 MEIGS CENSUS
Phillip Adams 70 (Va)(black), Sidney 70 (Va)(black), Hannah 41 (Va)(black) p. 748-287
Robert Adams 24 (SC)(Farmer), Pricilla 27 (SC), Sarah Ann 10, William J. 5, John D. 3 p. 740-213
Samuel Adams 71 (NC)(Farmer), Elizabeth 67 (NC) p. 819-814
Wm L. Adams 41 (NC)(Farmer), Felix G. 13 p. 819-817
MARRIAGES (RHEA)
Betsey Elizabeth Adams to Henry Dowten q.v.
Elizabeth E. Adams to Elephus Holt q.v.
Joseph Adams to Elizabeth Tigner, 16 Nov 1820 (same), John Chambers Bm (A)
Thomas Adams to Mary Witt, 22 Dec 1846 (23 Dec), E.P. Childress MG (R)
William Adams to Darcus Blackwell, 4 Aug 1831 (16 Aug), L.R. Russell MG, George W. Blackwell Bm (AR)
MARRIAGES (MEIGS)
James Adams to Harriet Caps, 20 Jan 1849 (21 Jan), Jesse Grisham JP [1850 Hamilton Census: James Adams 50, Harriet 26, Robert 16, Ann 10]
Polly Adams to John Davis q.v.
MISCELLANEOUS (RHEA and MEIGS)
William Adams: Bondsman for Henry Dowten, 1834
" " Lived at Cottonport
Wm L. Adams: JP 1843, 1846, 1848-49; Chairman, Meigs County Court 1844, 1848, 1850; Mexican War, 1st Lt.

- - - - - - - - - - - - -

ADDISON / ADISON

MARRIAGES (RHEA)
Dicy Adison to James Stewart q.v.
MISCELLANEOUS (MEIGS)
Jackson Addison: Cherokee Removal muster roll, 1836

- - - - - - - - - - - - -

ADKINS / ATKINS

TAXES (RHEA)
1819 (Capt. Wm. McCray's Co.): Aaron Adkins 1 WP
Samuel Adkins 1 WP
1830 RHEA CENSUS
William Atkins 01001 - 1001 p. 394
1840 RHEA CENSUS
Bartlet Adkins 200001 - 0001
MARRIAGES (RHEA)
Bartley Atkins to Elizabeth Mahaffee, 14 July 1835, William A. Reece Bm (A)
Charles Adkins to Sally Ann Brewer, 6 Mar 1830 (same) Robert Cooley JP, Nathan Brewer Bm (AR)
Sarah Adkins to John Miller q.v.
Susan Adkins to James P. Rector q.v.
MARRIAGES (MEIGS)
Sanford Adkins to Mary Stanley, 29 Jan 1850, John Stanley Sur
MISCELLANEOUS (RHEA)
Aaron Atkins: Bondsman for Warren Rhea, 1819

- - - - - - - - - - - - -

AGEE
(see also ACRE / ACREE)

MISCELLANEOUS (RHEA AND MEIGS)
Calvin Agee: Cherokee Removal muster roll, 1836
James Agee: Bondsman for Joseph Burns, 1828

- - - - - - - - - - - - -

AHART
(see also AIRHART / AIRHEART / AYREHART)

1850 RHEA CENSUS
Adam Ahart 53 (Va)(Farmer), Mary 52, George W. 25 (Va)(Farmer), Adam or Adair (letters have been written over) J. 22 (Va)(Farmer), Elizabeth 18, Jacob 15, Jacob 14 [sic] p. 575-255
[Adam Ahart married Polly Hartley on 1 Nov 1840 in Roane County]
MARRIAGES (MEIGS)
Geo. W. Ahart to Frances Robertson, 24 Sept 1850, Andrew Robertson Sur

- - - - - - - - - - - - -

AIKEN / AIKENS / AKINS / EAKEN / EAKIN

1830 RHEA CENSUS
Jas. Aikens 1011 - 00001 p. 371
Jas. Aikens 000110001 - 111221 p. 368
Henry Aikens 10001 - 0 p. 371
1840 MEIGS CENSUS
James Eakin 122011 - 111002 p. 225
James Eakin Sr. 0000000001 - 000100001 p. 225
1850 MEIGS CENSUS
Isaac Aiken 43 (Va)(Farmer), Mahala 42, James 21 (Farmer), Andrew 20 (Farmer), Allen 18 (Farmer), Elizabeth 12, Margaret 8, Rhoda 4, Samuel 1 p. 800-678
MARRIAGES (RHEA)
James Aikens or Eaken to Milly Whitmore, 23 Dec 1828, Gilbert Kennedy Bm (A)
Jane Akin to Robert E. Singleton q.v.
Samuel Akins to Annis Hobbs, 20 Dec 1834, James Akin Bm (A)
MARRIAGES (MEIGS)
Andrew Eakin to Mary Ann Fitch, 13 Nov 1850, John Fitch Sur
Caty Eaken to Hugh Baker q.v.
MISCELLANEOUS (RHEA)
James Akin: Bondsman for Samuel Akins, 1834

- - - - - - - - - - - - -

AIKMAN

1840 MEIGS CENSUS
John L. Aikman 1200001 - 1110001 p. 245
1850 MEIGS CENSUS
John L. Aikman 57 (Va)(Tanner), Nancy 55 (Va), Mary Jane 20, Manda M. 18, William F. 17 (Farmer), James A. 16 (Farmer), Margaret E. 13, John S. 12, Levina Jane 9, Nancy A. 6, James PAUL 87 (Va) p. 818-806
MISCELLANEOUS (MEIGS)
J.L. Aikman: JP 1848-1849

- - - - - - - - - - - - -

AIRHART / AIRHEART / AYREHART
(see also AHART)

TAXES (RHEA)
1808 (John Henry's List): Henry Airhart 1 WP, 1 BP
1819 (Capt. McGill's Co.): Henry Airhart 1 WP, 600a
1823 (Capt. Howard's Co.): ----- Airhart 1 WP, 420a
1830 RHEA CENSUS
Henry Airheart 10232001 - 0101101 p. 394
[1850 Bradley Census: Henry Airhart 75, Jane 51, Elizabeth 39, Daniel 31, Anna 28, Spencer 6, Samuel 5, Henry 4, Mary S. 2, James 1, Robert READ 16]
1850 MEIGS CENSUS
Michael Ayrehart 36 (NC)(Farmer), Almira 32, Mary Ann 9, Louisa Jane 8, James H. 6, Sarah M. 5 p. 772-471
MARRIAGES (RHEA)
Ann Airhart to Abner Witt q.v.
Caty Airheart to John Buchannon q.v.
James C. Airhart to Nancy Taylor, 3 Feb 1831 (same), John Henninger MG, Wm. K. Alexander Bm (AR)
[1850 Bradley Census: James C. Airhart 43, Nancy 42, Mary S. 15, William 11, Myra L. 8, James L. 3; Nancy was dau of Robert and Catharine Sevier Taylor]

Peter Airheart to Nancy Gillott, 2 Sept 1819 (same), A. David JP, Adam Shell Bm (AR) [1850 Bradley Census: Peter Airhart 50, Nancy 53, Onslow 17, Alexander 15, Moses 13, James 11]
Polly Airheart to John Whaley q.v.

MISCELLANEOUS (RHEA)
George C. Airhart: Bondsman for William Kelly, 1831
Henry Airheart: Bondsman for John Bird, 1809
" " Bondsman for Elisha Parker, 1818
" " Bondsman for Samuel Carr, 1810
James C. Airhart: Bondsman for Larkin Gothard, 1830

- - - - - - - - - - - - -

ALBERT

MARRIAGES (MEIGS)
John M. Albert to Eliza M. Galloway, 4 Sept 1845 (same), D.L. Godsey MG

- - - - - - - - - - - - -

ALEXANDER

TAXES (RHEA)
1808 (John Henry's List): Joseph Alexander 1 WP
1819 (Capt. McGill's Co.): Joseph Alexander 1 WP
William Alexander 1 WP 100a

1830 RHEA CENSUS
John Alexander 20001001 - 001000001 p. 379
John Alexander 112001 - 111001 p. 392
T. J. Alexander 000001 - 100011 p. 393
Wm. Alexander 000010001 - 00000001 p. 387

1840 RHEA CENSUS
William Alexander 011010001 - 001001
William K. Alexander 11001 - 1

1850 RHEA CENSUS
Harvey Alexander 18: see Joshua S. Green

MARRIAGES (RHEA)
Anne Alexander to Joshua S. Green q.v.
James J. Alexander to Katherine Stewart, 17 May 1838 (same), Benj. F. Jones JP, Chas. Morgan Bm (R)
John Alexander to Jemimah Sweet, 11 July 1810, James Hanse Bm (A) [1850 Tipton Census: Jemimah Alexander 51, Thadius A. 17, Mary R. 3]
John H. Alexander to Zerinah W. Jackson, 19 July 1827 (same), Wm. Smith JP, Joshua Green Bm (AR) [1850 Hamilton Census: John Alexander 42, Zerona 41, William 22, Reuben 20, Eliza 18, Thomas 16, Nancy 4, George 11, Mary 9, America 7, John 5, Harriet 9, Margaret 17, Charlotte 16, Prudence 12]
Joseph Alexander to Nancy Hughes, 18 Feb 1818 (same), Abraham Howard JP, Thomas Coulter Bm (AR)
M. M. Alexander to John R. Able q.v.
Thomas J. Alexander to Polly Myors, 23 Oct 1828 (same), John Henninger MG, Andrew Jack Bm (AR) [1850 White Census: Thomas Alexander 42, Polly 42, William 35, George 32, Mary 18, Sally 16, Mary Ann 14, Caroline 12, Eliza 8, Thomas 7]
William K. Alexander to Isabella Johnson, 4 Aug 1831 (same), William Smith JP (AR)
William K. Alexander to Harriet T. Brock, 3 Jan 1841, Lewis Morgan Bm (R) [1850 Hamilton Census: Wm Alexander 40, Harriet 30, Joseph 16, William 14, James 9, Caroline 7, Sarah 3, George 1]

MARRIAGES (MEIGS)
William Alexander to Melsina McAdams, 5 Jan 1847 (6 Jan), W.C. Groves MG

MISCELLANEOUS (RHEA)
John H. Alexander: Bondsman for William Lea, 1831
Wm K. Alexander: Bondsman for James C. Airhart, 1831

- - - - - - - - - - - - -

ALFORD
(see also ALBERT)

1850 MEIGS CENSUS
Alexander D. Alford 23 (Farmer), Mathew 22 (Farmer) p. 810-747
John Alford 37 (Farmer), Hanah 24, Robert 9, William 6, Pleasent 1 p. 817-797

MARRIAGES (RHEA)
James C. Alford to Rhoda Baldwin, 6 June 1835 (7 June), Stephen Winton JP, James A. Winton Bm (AR)

MARRIAGES (MEIGS)
John M. Alford to Hannah Holloman, 13 Apr 1847 (same), William Green MG

MISCELLANEOUS (MEIGS)
R. C. Alford: Surety for Samuel Deatherige, 1850

- - - - - - - - - - - - -

ALLEN

TAXES (RHEA)
1821 (Capt. Smith's Co.): Benjamin Allen 1 WP

1830 RHEA CENSUS
Andrew Allen 200001 - 02001 p. 366
Andrew Allen 200001 - 2001 p. 392
James Allen 1200001 - 102101 p. 357
Mark Allen 202001 - 022001 p. 357
Matthew Allen 20001 - 2001 p. 388

1840 MEIGS CENSUS
Robert Allen 2100001 - 021101 p. 237

1850 RHEA CENSUS
Benjamin Allen 55 (NC)(Farmer), Frances 53 (NC), Martha 24 (NC), Joseph 21 (NC)(Farmer), Emily 19 (NC), William 8 (NC)(Farmer), John 6 (NC)(Farmer), Missouri (m) 4 (NC) p. 600-409
Samuel Allen 21 (Farmer), Dicy A. 21, Martha 1 p. 560-165
Valentine Allen 41 (Ky)(Farmer), Ann 36, Wm G. 15, Thomas A. 12, Geo W. 10, Valentine 8, Barbary 6, Abner 4, Robert S. 2, Nicholas Q. 6/12 p. 616-512
William Allen 19: see Thomas J. Gillespie

1850 MEIGS CENSUS
Dolly Allen 50 (SC), William 19 (Farmer), David 15, Jesse 13 p. 808-729
Robert Allen 56 (Va)(Millwright), Margaret 49 (Va), Elen 24 (Va), Nancy 20, Sarah 18, Samuel 14, Peter 11, Jehue 8 (Idiot), John 5 p. 761-384
Robert J.D.W. Allen 23, Levina Jane 21, Margaret Ann 3, Elender E. 1 p. 754-335
William Allen 31 (Blacksmith), Delphia 31 (NC), Thomas B. 8, Robert A. 7, Elizabeth 6, Christopher C. 4, Margaret 3 p. 751-311

MARRIAGES (RHEA)
Benjamin Allen to Sally Slover, 7 Sept 1823, Thomas Cox JP, Kensey Moore Bm (AR)
George W. Allen to Frances Anderson, 19 Aug 1817 (same), J. Fine JP, John Ramsey Bm (AR)
Joseph Allen to Nancy Bottom, 1 Oct 1834 (2 Oct), Wm Green JP, Charles Bottom Bm (AR)
Samuel Allen to Dicey Dodson, 30 Mar 1848 (same), James Smith JP (R)
Sarah Allen to Fleming C. Pugh q.v.
Valentine Allen to Ann Frazier, 18 Jan 1836 (19 Jan), T. Sullins MG (R)
MARRIAGES (MEIGS)
Jane C. Allen to James F. Melton q.v.
R.J.D.W. Allen to Lavina McMullen, 29 July 1847 (same), D.L. Godsey MG
William Allen to Delpha Blankenship, 13 July 1841 (same), D.L. Godsey MG
MISCELLANEOUS (RHEA)
John Allen: Bondsman for Flemming C. Pugh, 1826
Matthew Allen: Bondsman for Elijah Bell, 1832
MISCELLANEOUS (MEIGS)
James Allen: Mexican War, 1846-47 (died in service)
John Allen: Cherokee Removal muster roll, 1836

\- - - - - - - - - - - -

ALLEND

1830 RHEA CENSUS
Robert Allend 110001 - 11001 p. 376

\- - - - - - - - - - - -

ALLISON / ELLISON / ELISON

1830 RHEA CENSUS
Burch Ellison 3010001 - 100001 p. 388
Peter Ellison 110001 - 11101 p. 358
1840 RHEA CENSUS
Burch Ellison 001400001 - 111001
1840 MEIGS CENSUS
Peter Elison 2211001 - 1011001 p. 241
1850 RHEA CENSUS
James D. Allison 34 (NC)(Farmer), Eliza 39 (NC), Francis W. 16 (NC)(Farmer), Mary M. 10, Clerissa A. 7, Nancy E. 4, Willis R. 2 p. 623-566
John Ellison 22 (Unk)(Hammerman), Alice 18, Mary E. 2/12 p. 582-308
Lyda Allison 64 (NC), Ary 38 (NC), Emeline 24 (NC), Winney BELL 28 (NC), Joseph J. 7 p. 623-570
Thomas Allison 30 (NC)(Farmer), Eliza 25 (NC), Mary 10 (NC), Curtis 8 (NC), Rebecca A. 4 (NC), Nancy M. 1/12, Barbary 19 (NC) p. 625-582
Thomas K. Ellison 26 (Farmer) p. 548-102
William D. Ellison 32 (Farmer), Elender 23 (NC), Eliza J. 6, John Z.T. 2, Sarah C. 1 p. 533-3
1850 MEIGS CENSUS
George W. Allison 30 (Merchant) p. 713-6
Peter Allison 55 (Pa)(Cooper), Susanna 51, Elisha 20 (Farmer), David 18 (Farmer), Francis 15 (Farmer), Peter 13, Jane 11 p. 802-692
MARRIAGES (RHEA)
C.M. Elison to Stephen H. Dyer q.v.
Robert Elison to Zannah Godby, 2 Sept 1821 (13 Sept), Thomas Price JP (AR)
Stacy M. Allison to John M. Furgusson q.v.
MARRIAGES (MEIGS)
Elenor Elison to John Ford q.v.
Elizabeth Elison to W.S. Maples q.v
John Allison to Alsie Butler, 7 Nov 1847 (same) T.B. McElwee JP.
MISCELLANEOUS (RHEA and MEIGS)
David Ellison: Private, Mexican War
David H. Ellison, 2nd Sgt., Mexican War
John Ellison: Private, Mexican War
Peter Allison: Hiwassee District
Robert B. Ellison: Private, Mexican War
Thomas K. Ellison: Private, Mexican War

\- - - - - - - - - - - -

ALOON

MARRIAGES (MEIGS)
Noah Aloon(?) to Mary J. Francisco, 1 Sept 1845 (same), D.L. Godsey MG

\- - - - - - - - - - - -

ALTON or ALTUM

1850 RHEA CENSUS
Martha A. Alton or Altum 19: see Dudley Dismany

\- - - - - - - - - - - -

AMBERS

1850 MEIGS CENSUS
Zachariah Ambers 26 (Farmer), Emaline 26 (NC), John 7, William 2, James Wesley 1 p. 716-31

\- - - - - - - - - - - -

ANDERSON

TAXES (RHEA)
1819 (Capt. W.S. Bradley's District):
Joseph Anderson Esq. 2500a
(Capt. John Ramsey's Company):
Thomas Anderson 1 WP, 150a
1823 (Capt. Brown's Company):
Joseph Anderson, 1800a on Tenn River (part of 5000a grant to Outlaw & Lewis)
(Capt. Brazelton's Co.): Thomas Anderson 1 WP
1830 RHEA CENSUS
Jno. Anderson 011001 - 120101 p. 371
Lath Anderson 00001 - 1 p. 371
Thomas Anderson 2100001 - 0022001 p. 387
1840 MEIGS CENSUS
John Anderson 10001 - 0001 p. 233
1850 RHEA CENSUS
John Anderson 20 (mulatto): see Spencer J. Tedder
Thomas Anderson 32: see Abraham Bryson
MARRIAGES (RHEA)
Andrew Anderson to Elizabeth Walker, 21 Feb 1836 (same), Thomas Cox JP, William Lillard Bm (AR)
Ann Anderson to Joseph Mullins q.v.
Frances Anderson to Alexander Sapp q.v.

Frances Anderson to George W. Allen q.v.
Polly Anderson to Robert Gamble q.v.
Rufus Anderson to Sarah Conner, 2 Dec 1844 (no return), William Wilson Bm (AR)
[1850 Lawrence Census: Rufus Anderson 24, Sarah 24, Elenor 2, Elizabeth 68]
Susan Anderson to Lewis Thornberry q.v.
Vandaman Anderson to Jane Ragsdale, 11 May 1821 (same), John Day Bm (A)
Winny Anderson to John Sapp q.v.
MISCELLANEOUS (RHEA and MEIGS)
Isaac Anderson: MG, organized Monmouth Presbyterian Church in Washington, 1820
Thomas Anderson: Bondsman for Presley Rector, 1812
" " Bondsman for William Davenport, 1832
William Anderson: Hiwassee District

- - - - - - - - - - - - -

ANGLEN

TAXES (RHEA)
1823 (Capt. Smith's Co.): John Anglen 1 WP

- - - - - - - - - - - - -

APPLEGATE

TAXES (RHEA)
1819 (Capt. Wm McCray's Co.):
Samuel Applegate 1 WP, 130a
1823 (Capt. Howerton's Old Co.):
Samuel Applegate 130a W Fork Whites Creek
MARRIAGES (RHEA)
Kesiah Applegate to John H. Hamilton q.v.
MISCELLANEOUS (RHEA)
Samuel Applegate: Bondsman for John H. Hamilton, 1826

- - - - - - - - - - - - -

ARMSTRONG

TAXES (RHEA)
1819 (Capt. John Robinson's Co.):
Andrew Armstrong 1 WP
Daniel Armstrong 100a
Elihu Armstrong 1 WP
1823 (Capt. Brazelton's Co.): Barefoot Armstrong 1 WP
Daniel D. Armstrong 1 WP, 100a Clear Creek
Elihu D. Armstrong 1 WP
1830 RHEA CENSUS
Abel Armstrong 00001 - 10001 p. 357
[Abel Armstrong married Tabitha Rowdon or Roudan on 1 May 1822 in Roane County]
B. D. Armstrong 320001 - 10001 p. 369
Benj. Armstrong 00101 - 12001 p. 372
D. D. Armstrong 12100001 - 0011001 p. 383
1840 MEIGS CENSUS
Benjamin Armstrong 00010001 - 222101 p. 233
William Armstrong 00002 - 100001 p. 233
1850 MEIGS CENSUS
Nancy Armstrong 44 (NC), Altemany 6, Sidney E. (f) 4, Mahala 12, Paulina 10, Alfred F. 7 p. 752-318
William T. Armstrong 35 (Ky)(Farmer), Sarah 29, Martha 7, Martin 6, Cynthia 4, Parthenia 3, Benjamin 63 (Ky) p. 733-163
MARRIAGES (RHEA)
Bearfoot Armstrong to Mary Lewis, 2 May 1820, Miller Francis Bm (A)
Benjamin Armstrong to Betsy Cres, 21 Feb 1827, Peter Fine Bm (A)
Cynthia Armstrong to Peter Minich q.v.
John Armstrong to Elizabeth Mills, 10 Nov 1819, John Collison and Thomas Owens Bm (A)
Margaret Armstrong to John McDonough q.v.
Margaret Armstrong to James Piper q.v.
Tabitha Armstrong to Richard Clifton q.v.
William Armstrong to Flora McDaniel, 17 May 1834 (20 May), James Blevins JP, Wm S. Russell Bm (AR)
MARRIAGES (MEIGS)
Eliza Armstrong to Elgin Brightwell q.v.
Mary Ann Armstrong to Newton Lawson q.v.
Sarah Armstrong to George Gross q.v.
Wm T. Armstrong to Sarah Bell, 29 Mar 1842 (same), John Taff JP
MISCELLANEOUS (RHEA and MEIGS)
Daniel D. Armstrong: Resident, Town of Washington, 1812
William T. Armstrong: Bondsman for Robert Davis, 1836
" " " JP(?) Meigs County, 1840-41, 1844

- - - - - - - - - - - - -

ARNOLD

MARRIAGES (RHEA)
William Arnold to Matilda Kimbrell, 1 Sept 1832 (6 Sept), John Farmer JP, John Kimbrell Bm (AR)

- - - - - - - - - - - - -

ARON

MISCELLANEOUS (RHEA)
Berryman Aron: Bondsman for John Buster, 1833

- - - - - - - - - - - - -

ARRENTS

MARRIAGES (MEIGS)
William Arrents to Artemisa Cross, 13 Feb 1844, Drury L. Godsey MG [Artemisa dau of Zachariah and Sarah]
MISCELLANEOUS (MEIGS)
William Arrents: JP 1848-1849

- - - - - - - - - - - - -

ARRINGTON

1830 RHEA CENSUS
Abel Arrington 1111001 - 0110001
MISCELLANEOUS (MEIGS)
Abel and John Arrington: Hiwassee District

- - - - - - - - - - - - -

ASBELL

MISCELLANEOUS (RHEA)
Allen Asbell: Bondsman for James Elliott, 1814
[In 1850, Allen Asbell, 60, and his family were living in Henderson Co. Tenn.]

- - - - - - - - - - - - -

ASHBURN

MARRIAGES (MEIGS)
John Ashburn to Elizabeth Harrid, 24 Oct 1844 (same), B.F. McKenzie JP

- - - - - - - - - - - - -

ASKINS / ASKIN

1840 MEIGS CENSUS
Harry Askins 111011 - 1120011
1850 MEIGS CENSUS
Henry Askins 45 (SC)(Farmer), Nancy 44, Harriet 19, Anna 18, Christopher 15, Henry 13, Oretha 11, Phebe 3, John T. 1 p. 734-169
Sandford Askins 22 (Farmer), Mary Jane 22 p. 733-161
MISCELLANEOUS (RHEA)
Henry Askin: Bondsman for Benjamin McKenzie, 1830

- - - - - - - - - - - - -

ASTON

MISCELLANEOUS (RHEA)
Samuel M. Aston: V.D.M., 1827

- - - - - - - - - - - - -

ATCHLEY / ATCHLY / ACHLY / ACHLEY

TAXES (RHEA)
1823 (Capt. Smith's Co.): Joshua Atchley 1 WP
(Capt. Wilson's Co.): Joseph Atchley 1 WP
Joshua Atchley 1 WP
Martin Atchley 240a Sewee Cr.
Thomas Atchley 1 WP
1830 RHEA CENSUS
Abram Atchley 0012000001 - 00000001 p. 391
Armistead Atchley 00001 - 01001 p. 353
Hannah Atchley 00001 - 0000001 p. 353
John Atchley 10001 - 10001 p. 353
John Atchley 1001 - 0001 p. 353
Joshua Atchley 00000001 - 00000001 p. 353
Martin Atchley 0101000001 - 00000001 p. 353
Thomas Atchley 0221001 - 001001 p. 364
Tousy(?) Atchley 1001011 - 110101 p. 353
1840 MEIGS CENSUS
Armsted Atchly 001001 - 11 p. 243
Bird P. Atchly 100001 - 20001 p. 238
Christina Atchly 001 - 000000001 p. 243
John Atchly 11101 - 02001 p. 243
John S. Atchly 0 - 0 [sic] p. 243
Joseph Atchly 3222001 - 0000201 p. 242
Joshua Atchly 000000001 - 000000001 p. 243
Thomas Atchly 11111001 - 0000101 p. 243
Thomas V. Atchly 00001 - 20001 p. 244
Washington Atchly 11001 - 11001 p. 244
1850 MEIGS CENSUS
Bird P. Atchly 35 (Farmer), Rebecca 34, Nancy E. 16, Telitha Jane 14, George W. 8, James M. 7, Stanton L. 6, William 1, Lydia Ann 0 p. 784-561
Christenia Atchly (f) 80 (Va) p. 788-588
Elizabeth Atchly 53 (Va), Joshua 25 (Farmer), Robert 16 (Farmer), James A. 12 p. 788-592
George W. Atchly 38 (Farmer), Louisa 38, Nancy Ann 17, Elizabeth 9, Pryor N. 13, Miles 11, Louisa Jane 7, Leander 6 p. 790-604
Hannah Atchley 6: see Leodocia Richards
Joseph Achly 52 (Ky)(Farmer), Mary 52 (Ky), Elijah 26 (Farmer), William 23 (Farmer), John R. 21 (Farmer), George W. 19 (Farmer), Daniel P. 14, Noah R. 11, Joseph A. 7 p. 777-508
Thomas V. Atchley 36 (Blacksmith), Elizabeth 36, Sarah E. 14, Nancy M. 12, Rachael C. 6, Joshua M. 2 p. 818-803
MARRIAGES (RHEA)
Abraham Atchley to Elizabeth Styres, 22 July 1809 (same), Richard Chilton Bm (A)
Bessy Atchley to James Richards q.v.
Bird P. Atchley to Rebecca Tate, 24 July 1834 (29 July), Dan Briggs MG (AR)
Catherine Atchley to Jacob Price q.v.
Cissie Atchley to Joseph H. Thrailkill q.v.
Esther Atchley to George W. Gibson q.v.
John Atchley to Elizabeth W. Banks [Eubanks?], 11 Dec 1825 (14 Dec), John Farmer MG, Ware Runnian Bm (AR)
John Atchley to May Genoe, 10 Dec 1825 (12 Dec), Thos Cox JP, John Davis Bm (A)
John Atchley to Sarah Eubanks, 21 Nov 1827 (same), John Farmer MG, Wear Runnion Bm (AR)
Joshua Atchley to Rhoda Atterley, 19 Apr 1825 (same), Thos Cox JP, Andrew Kincannon Bm (AR)
Mahala Atchley to Michael Wilson q.v.
Moses Atchley to Elizabeth Sutherland, 29 Dec 1831 (31 Dec), Daniel Briggs MG, David Buster Bm (AR)
Nancy Atchley to Alexander Wasson q.v.
Polly Atchley to Moses Wyatt q.v.
Rebecca Atchley to David Hanna q.v.
Ruth Atchley to Cedar Murphrie q.v.
Thomas V. Atchley to Elizabeth Wasson, 26 Dec 1836 (1 Jan 1837), Az. Barton JP, S.R. Hackett Bm (AR)
Washington Atchley to Eliza Gordon, 9 July 1831 (14 July), John Farmer MG, Zoreballe Tankersley Bm (AR)
MARRIAGES (MEIGS)
Abegail Atchley to James Wilhelms q.v.
Mary Atchley to Henson T. Johns q.v.
Metes Achley(?) to Elizbeth Mitchell, 21 July 1845 (same) Joshua Atchley, C.(?), T.B. McElwee JP
Seth Atchley to E.M. Francisco, 18 Feb 1840 (5 Mar), Richard Simpson MG
MISCELLANEOUS (RHEA and MEIGS)
Bird P. Atchley: Resident of Washington, 1812 (lots 54,78)
" " " Hiwassee District
Joseph Atchley: Common School Com., Districk 6, 1836
M. C. Atchley: MG 1845, 1847, 1849
Martin Atchley: Hiwssee District
Miles Atchley: Cherokee Removal muster roll, 1836
Price Atchley: Hiwassee District
Thomas Atchley: Cherokee Removal muster roll, 1836
" " Hiwassee District, Sewee Creek area
" " Bondsman for George W. Gibson, 1827
Thomas V. Atchley: Cherokee Removal muster roll, 1836
" " " JP 1842-48
Washington Atchley: Constable, District 6, 1836

- - - - - - - - - - - - -

ATKINSON / ATCHENSON / AKISON / ACKINSON

1840 MEIGS CENSUS
James Atkinson 0220001 - 220001 p. 232
John Atchenson 000001 - 320001 p. 243
William Atchenson 002001 - 111001 p. 243
1850 MEIGS CENSUS
Calvin Atkinson 22, Adaline 19, John N. 2 p. 741-229
John Atkinson 45 (Farmer), Elizabeth 45 (Va), Clarissa 20, Lucinda 18, Betsy Ann 16, Sarah 13, Martha Ann 10, Mary 8, Louisa 5, John 3, Hugh 1, Calvin Thorp Bound 19 (Farmer), James Leander Bound 16 p. 764-401
MARRIAGES (RHEA)
Jane Akison to John Casey q.v.
Wm L. Atkinson of Washington married Miss Elizabeth Cobb of Grainger Co., Thursday, 20 Sept 1821 (*Knoxville Register*, Vol. VI, No. 272)
MARRIAGES (MEIGS)
Calvin B. Atkinson to Elizabeth A. Masoner, 27 Dec 1847 (30 Dec), B.F. McKenzie JP
Emily Atkinson to James Carter q.v.
MISCELLANEOUS (MEIGS)
C. B. Atkinson: JP(?) 1844
Ezekiel Atkinson: Surety for John C. George, 1850
James Atkinson: JP(?) 1841
John Ackinson: Lived at Cottonport; JP(?) 1840
William Atkinson: JP(?) 1839

- - - - - - - - - - - - -

ATTERLY

MARRIAGES (RHEA)
Rhoda Atterley to Joshua Atchley q.v.

- - - - - - - - - - - - -

ATTLEY

1830 RHEA CENSUS
Thomas Attley 10001 - 2002 p. 387

- - - - - - - - - - - - -

ATWOOD

TAXES (RHEA)
1823 (Capt. Braselton's Co.): Jesse Atwood 1 WP
1840 MEIGS CENSUS
Winna Atwood 0-001001 p. 246
1850 MEIGS CENSUS
Winny Atwood 41, Elizabeth 21 p. 797-658
MISCELLANEOUS (RHEA)
Jesse Atwood: Bondsman for Benjamin Putnam, 1823
" " Bondsman for Baldwin H. Fine, 1827

- - - - - - - - - - - - -

AULT

1840 RHEA CENSUS
Coonrod Ault 02100001 - 0000001
Thomas Ault 0000 - 001
1850 RHEA CENSUS
Charles W. Ault 26 (Farmer), Leah E. 26, Albion 5, Mary J. 3, George W. 1 p. 580-287
Savannah Ault 55, Willie N. 21 (Farmer), George W. 18 p. 572-235
Thomas Ault 31 (Farmer), Jeston E. 26, Patrick H. 8, James C.J. 6, Vesta E. 4, Arthur F. 11/12 p. 565-180
MARRIAGES (RHEA)
Charles W. Ault to Leah E. Smith, 27 June 1844 (same), Nelson H. Chase Bm (AR)
M. A. Ault to Wm G. Smith q.v.
Thomas Ault to Jeston Emaline Creed, 12 Nov 1839 (13 Nov), Wm Bowers MG, Wm F. Smith Bm (AR)
MISCELLANEOUS (MEIGS)
Coonrod Ault: Built jail in Decatur, 1836

- - - - - - - - - - - - -

AUSTON / AUSTIN

MARRIAGES (RHEA)
Jane Auston or Austin to John Garr or Gann q.v.

- - - - - - - - - - - - -

AVERY

1830 RHEA CENSUS
Silas Avery 00001001 - 10010001

- - - - - - - - - - - - -

BAILEY / BAILY / BALEY

TAXES (RHEA)
1819 (Capt. John Ramsey's Co.): James Bailey 1 WP 350a
1823 (Capt. McCall's Co.): Jas Bailey WP, 350a Whites Cr
(Capt. Lewis' Co.): John Bailey 1 WP, 70a
1830 RHEA CENSUS
James Baily 220201 - 100101 p. 388
1850 RHEA CENSUS
Pitser M. Bailey 26 (Sadler), Mary L. 19 (Ala), Elvira 3, Blackstone 1, Susan WATERHOUSE* 35, Susan 16 p. 612-435 [*widow of Blackstone]
Narcissa Bailey 54: see Henry H. Miller
MARRIAGES (RHEA)
Eliza Bailey to Jeremiah Farmer q.v.
John Bailey to Narcissa Ferguson, 8 Apr 1844, Benj. D. Smith Bm (AR)
Joshua Bailey to Malinda Riggle, 24 Oct 1841, James Cole Bm (A)
Margaret Bailey to James Cole q.v.
Pitser M. Bailey to Mary L. Waterhouse, 28 Dec 1846 (same), John Wyott JP (R)

- - - - - - - - - - - - -

BAKER

TAXES (RHEA)
1819 (Capt. John Ramsey's Co.): Isaac Baker 1 WP
John Baker 1 WP
1823 (Capt. Piper's Co.): John Baker 1 WP, 160a
Isaac Baker 1 WP 409a
Samuel Baker 1 WP, 28a

1830 RHEA CENSUS
Isaac Baker 201001 - 210001 p. 361
John Baker 0000011 - 21001 p. 362
John Baker 232001 - 01001 p. 385
Samuel Baker 00011 - 000100001 p. 361
Uriah Baker 200001 - 00011 p. 362
William Baker 1100001 - 012001 p. 380
1840 RHEA CENSUS
John Baker 2000001 - 002001
Uriah Baker 10200001 - 002001
[1850 Dyer Census: Uriah 57, Mariah 21]
1840 MEIGS CENSUS
Hugh Baker 000*0001 - 000000**
[* lower portion of page 225 ragged]
Jane Baker 11022 - 120101 p. 247
Matilda Baker 1 - 10001 p. 236
Samuel Baker 000011 - 000000001 p. 247

1850 RHEA CENSUS
John Baker 36 (Farmer), Mary E. 29, Rhoda J. 10, John F. 9, George W. 7, Thomas J. 5, Jacob W. 3, James W. 1 p. 630-617
1850 MEIGS CENSUS
Benjamin Baker 30 (Farmer), Elizabeth 25, William 2, Infant (m) 0 p. 783-555
Hugh Baker 53 (Va)(Farmer), Catharin 40 (Va), Alexander 17 (Farmer) p. 726-102
Jane Baker 52, Samuel 23 (Farmer), Harriet 22, Mary 21, James 20 (Farmer), Preston 18 (Farmer), Isaac 11 p. 808-732
John Baker 27 (Farmer), Nancy C. 23 (NC), William L. 0 p. 808-733
Samuel Baker 48 (Farmer), Mary 43, John 23 (Farmer), William 21 (Farmer), Samuel 19 (Farmer), Abigal 15, Martha 12, Thomas 8, George W. 5, James D. 2 p. 807-723
William Baker 30 (Farmer), Mary 25, Jane 8, Martha 7, John 5, Elizabeth 2 p. 808-734
[William Baker married Mary Allen on 4 Aug 1840 in Roane County]

MARRIAGES (RHEA)
Isaac Baker to Jane Looney, 6 Mar 1817 (same), J. Fine JP, James Preston Bm (A)
John Baker to Elizabeth Rector, 28 Nov 1821 (30 Nov), Jesse Thompson JP, Landon Rector Bm (AR)
John Baker to Jane Fowler, 21 Apr 1841, no return, William Sims Bm (AR) [1850 Bradley Census: John Baker 24, Jane 20, Frances 9/12]
Mary Baker to Josiah Higgins q.v.
Polly Baker to Thomas McCarty q.v.
MARRIAGES (MEIGS)
Champanius Baker to Elizabeth Baker, 30 Sept 1847 (same), T.B. McElwee JP
Hugh Baker to Caty Eaken, 21 May 1840 (18 June), Richard Simpson MG
John Baker to Nancy Caroline Meadaris, 9 Jan 1850, Samuel Baker Sur
Nancy Baker to Arthur Robinson q.v.
Samuel Baker to Polly Renfrow, 26 Aug 1850, Leroy Looney Sur
Sarah Baker to Alford Gibson q.v.
Wilson Baker to Loucinda Jolly, 20 Dec 1850, Green Gregory Sur

MISCELLANEOUS (RHEA)
Isaac Baker: Bondsman for Greenbury J. Parker, 1827
Isaac Baker: JP 1832-1835
MISCELLANEOUS (MEIGS)
A. J. Baker: JP(?) 1840
Hugh Baker: Cherokee Removal muster roll, 1836
Isaac Baker: Circuit Court, 1836; JP 1836, 1838; Common School Commissioner, 1838; Hiwassee District
John Baker: Hiwassee District
Samuel Baker: Surety for John Baker, 1850; Hiwassee Dist.

\- - - - - - - - - - - - -

BALDWIN / BALDEN / BALDIN

TAXES (RHEA)
1819 (Capt. McGill's Co.):
William Baldwin & Jesse Witt, 3 BP, 200a
1823 (Capt. Jackson's Co.):
William Balden 1 WP, 81a Tennessee River

1830 RHEA CENSUS
Nancy Baldin 2001 - 001001 p. 391
William Baldwin 1201101 - 102101 p. 360
1840 MEIGS CENSUS
Hugh L. Baldwin 100101 - 1120101 p. 241
James Baldwin 10101 - 1001 p. 241
William Baldwin 02120001 - 00101001 p. 241
1850 MEIGS CENSUS
John L. Baldwin 29 (Farmer), Salina 20, James W. 2 p. 800-680
William Baldwin 70 (Va)(Farmer), Elizabeth 62, Rhoda Ann 28, Nancy E. 21, Stephen 19 (Farmer), Charles 17 (Farmer), Elizabeth 13, Jane 12, Caroline 10, Joseph L. 1, Amanda J. DOWDEN 22 p. 774-491
William H. Baldwin 26 (Farmer), Robert S. 24 p. 774-490

MARRIAGES (RHEA)
Hugh L. Baldwin to Betsy S. Wilson, 15 July 1832 (17 July), James Wilson JP, Wm G. English Bm (AR) [Betsy Stockton Wilson was widow of William C. Wilson and dau of Robert and Nancy Blakey Stockton of Kentucky. 1850 Bradley Census: H.L. Baldwin 40, Elizabeth S. 52, Nancy E. 16, Robert W. 13 Malinda C. 12, Hugh W. 10, Malisa J. KENNEDY 6, Rhoda OXFORD 34, James COX 11]
Elizabeth E. Baldwin to Jackson F. Box q.v.
Rhoda Baldwin to James C. Alford q.v.
Sarah M.D. Baldwin to M.D. Thompson q.v.
MARRIAGES (MEIGS)
John L. Baldwin to Salina Griffith, 10 Mar 1847 (11 Mar), Thos Whitten MG
Nancy Baldwin to James W. McDowell q.v.
Sarah Baldwin to M. P. Hail q.v.

MISCELLANEOUS (RHEA and MEIGS)
James C. Baldwin: Bondsman for Peter M. Jacques, 1834
John L. Baldwin: JP(?) Meigs County, 1845
Robert Baldwin: Private Mexican War, 1847
William H. Baldwin: Private, Mexican War, 1847

\- - - - - - - - - - - - -

BALL

1840 RHEA CENSUS
James Ball 1020001 - 130201
1840 MEIGS CENSUS
David Ball 11001 - 10001 p. 239
1850 MEIGS CENSUS
David Ball 36 (Farmer), Darden 34, William 17 (Farmer), Samuel 15 (Farmer), Sarah 13, Nancy 10, Thomas 8, George 6, Mary Ann 4, Martha E. 1 p. 798-666 [David Ball married Darny Davis on 31 Dec 1833 in Roane County]
MARRIAGES (RHEA)
Edney Ball to Pleasant Davis q.v.
Mahala Ball to Alexander Carr q.v.

\- - - - - - - - - - - -

BANDY / BUNDY

1830 RHEA CENSUS
David Bandy 10001 - 0001 p. 378
Dempsy Bandy 110001 - 21200101 p. 394
George Bandy 1111101 - 001001 p. 372
Jesse Bandy 010200001 - 01101201 p. 379
William Bandy 012101 - 1101001 p. 372
1840 RHEA CENSUS
David Bandy 22100 - 1000
Jonathan Bandy 11001 - 11001
1840 MEIGS CENSUS
Bright Bandy 0001 - 0011 p. 229
Reuben E. Bandy 00001 - 00001 p. 229
1850 RHEA CENSUS
Jonathan Bundy 39 (NC)(Farmer), Hester 38 (SC), Francis M. 18 (Farmer), Mary A. 16, Elizabeth 13, John 10, Jane 8, James P. 6 p. 620-544
1850 MEIGS CENSUS
Reuben Bandy 35 (Farmer), Mary 30, Nancy E. 8, John W. 5, David 3, Joseph A. 1 p. 745-260
MARRIAGES (RHEA)
David Bandy to Margaret Casteel, 5 Aug 1828 (7 Aug), John Henninger MG, John W. Wood Bm (AR)
Jonathan Bandy to Hethey Bolin, 5 Apr 1831 (6 Apr), John Cozby JP, John Bolin Bm (AR)
Nancy Bandy to Joseph Casteel q.v.
MARRIAGES (MEIGS)
Reuben E. Bandy to Mary Williams, 15 Feb 1840 (16 Feb), B.F. McKenzie JP
MISCELLANEOUS (MEIGS)
Briant Bandy: JP(?) 1840

\- - - - - - - - - - - -

BANKS

TAXES (RHEA)
1819 (Capt. W.S. Bradley's Co.): Eli Banks 1 WP
MARRIAGES (RHEA)
Elizabeth Banks [Eubanks?] to John Atchley q.v.

\- - - - - - - - - - - -

BANKSTON

1850 MEIGS CENSUS
Grimes Bankston 24 (Farmer), Polly Ann 23, Mary Jane 5, Thomas 2 p. 738-201
MARRIAGES (MEIGS)
Grimes Bankston to Polly Ann Falls, 17 Feb 1844 (same), Wm Johns JP

\- - - - - - - - - - - -

BARE

MARRIAGES (MEIGS)
Henry Bare to Malinda Frie, 2 Apr 1838
MISCELLANEOUS (MEIGS)
Henry Bare: Lived in Ocoee District

\- - - - - - - - - - - -

BARKLEY

MARRIAGES (RHEA)
Joseph Barkley to Polly Leadbeater, 12 Apr 1810 (same), Thomas Kelly Bm (A)
MISCELLANEOUS (RHEA)
Willim Barkley: Signed petition to move Indian Agency

\- - - - - - - - - - - -

BARKSDALE

1840 RHEA CENSUS
Douglas Barksdale 000000001 - 000211001

\- - - - - - - - - - - -

BARMON

MARRIAGES (MEIGS)
N. J. Barmon to Rufus Ferguson q.v.

\- - - - - - - - - - - -

BARNES / BARNS / BURNES / BURNS / BURRIS

TAXES (RHEA)
1823 (Capt. Wilson's Co.): Horatio Burns 1 WP
(Capt. Howerton's Co.): Isaac Burns 1 WP
1830 RHEA CENSUS
A. Barnes 210001 - 010001 p. 383
Mahalal Barnes 00001 - 100001 p. 380
MARRIAGES (RHEA)
Absalom Barnes to Polly Murphrie or Murphree, 10 Nov 1819 (same), David Hanna Bm, returned with papers of D. Walker (AR)
John Gulford Burris or Burns to Elizabeth Bird, 9 Aug 1818 (same), John Moore JP, Sally Whitney Bm (AR)
Jonathan Barnes or Burns to Polly or Patsy Richards, 16 Nov 1815 (same), David Murphree JP, John Handy Bm (AR)
Martin Burns or Burris to Eliza or Edith Dawson, 30 Jan. or June 1816, J. Fine JP, Martin Burroughs and Joseph Carr Bm (AR)

Nathaniel Barnes to Allis Romines, 28 Jan 1828 (29 Jan), D.M. Stockton JP, Thomas Romines Bm (AR)
Silas F. Barns to Catherin Bell, 21 Mar 1825 (26 Mar), A. David JP, Evan Evans Bm (AR)
William A. Burns to Louisa Hughes, 13 Sept 1828, Gilford Burns Bm (R)

MISCELLANEOUS (RHEA and MEIGS)

Absolom Burns: Bondsman for John Owens, 1819
Gilford Burns: Bondsman for William A. Burns, 1828
James Burns: Private, Mexican War
Jonathan Burns/Barnes: Bondsman for Chas Richards, 1815
Pleasant Barnes: Bondsman for Matthew Russell, 1818

- - - - - - - - - - - - -

BARNETT / BARNET / BURNETT / BURNET

TAXES (RHEA)

1823 (Capt. Braselton's Co.): John Barnett 1 WP, 250a

1830 RHEA CENSUS

Jno Barnett 2002 - 12001 p. 394

1840 RHEA CENSUS

Harrison Barnet 10001 - 1000101
James Barnet 101001 - 11001
Nathaniel Barnet 012101 - 210001
William Burnet 0000000001 - 000000001

1850 RHEA CENSUS

George W. Barnett 29 (Farmer), Matilda 29, Juli E. 3, Leonedas 1, Sarah 70 p. 570-229
James R. Barnett 40 (Blacksmith), Charlotte 35, Harriet 16, Isaac 14, Alwisa or Aloise 11, Elvina 9, Horatio 6, no name (m) 4, no name (m) 1 p. 601-413
Margaret Barnett 48, Andrew J. HENRY 7 p. 603-424
Thomas F. Barnett 50 (Va)(Saddler), Mary 43, Wm F.D.C. 20 (School Teacher), Robert F.J.F. 19, Harriet S. 17, Nancy F. 14, Mary E. 11, Martha J.R. 7, Eliza A.C. 7 p. 597-389
William L. Burnett 22 (Blacksmith), Thomas J. 20 (Farmer): see Lavina Scott

MARRIAGES (RHEA)

George Barnett to Matilda Henry, 23 Mar 1843 (same), T.P. Creede JP, Solomon Henry Bm (A)
Harrison Barnet to Jane Robinson, 28 Jan 1835 (29 Jan), Matthew Hubbert JP, Elijah Murphree Bm (AR)
Harrison Barnett to Mariah H. Hosler, 9 Dec 1841 (same), Samuel Frazier JP, Peter Minack Bm (AR)
Hiram Burnett to Viney Mondy or Munday, 21 Oct 1822 (23 Oct), John Rice JP, John Edmondson Bm (AR)
John R. Barnett to Matilda West, 26 July 1827 (same), Matthew Hubbert JP, John W. Hill Bm (AR) [1850 White Census: John Barnett 43, Matilda 38, Charlotte J. 19, Elija L. 17, Sarah Ann 15, John T. 12, Lycurgus 10, Savina M. 8, Mary Ann 8, Bluford T.J. 2]
Polly Barnett to Randolph Harwood q.v.
Sarah Barnett to Joshua Goad q.v.
William Barnett to Peggy Montgomery, 10 Dec 1822 (11 Dec), H. Collins JP, Elijah Rice Bm (AR)

MISCELLANEOUS (RHEA and MEIGS)

Harrison Barnett: Bondsman for Harvey Montgomery, 1834
" " Bondsman for Peter Minich, 1836
" " Bondsman for Edward M. Robertson, 1839
John Barnett: Bondsman for David Lewis, 1823
" " Bondsman for John Hickey, 1832
Nathaniel Barnett: MG 1842, 1849
William Barnett: Bondsman for Henry Morris, 1811

- - - - - - - - - - - - -

BARNHART

MARRIAGES (MEIGS)

Felix Barnhart to Manervy J. McKeon, 18 Dec 1845 (same), D.L. Godsey MG
Henry Barnhart to Jane Wilson, 21 Apr 1847 (22 Apr), D.L. Godsey MG
Mary J. Barnhart to George Kincannon q.v.

- - - - - - - - - - - - -

BARNWELL

1830 RHEA CENSUS

John Barnwell 01011001 - 00010001 p. 382

- - - - - - - - - - - - -

BARR

MARRIAGES (RHEA)

Daniel Barr to Betsy Newmon, 13 Jan 1813, Nathaniel Newmon Bm (A)
Joseph Barr to Patsy Davidson, 5 June 1811, Jesse Davidson Bm (A)

- - - - - - - - - - - - -

BARTON / BURTON / BURTEN

TAXES (RHEA)

1823 (Capt. Piper's Co.): Fielding Burton 1 WP
(Capt. McCall's Co.): Squire Burton 1 WP

1830 RHEA CENSUS

David Burton 003201 - 221001 p. 354
Fielding Burton 1200101 - 11001 p. 358
Nancy Burton 001 - 11101101 p. 386
Sarah Burton 10101 - 010101 p. 362
Squire Burton 11001 - 20001 p. 362

1840 RHEA CENSUS

Azariah Burten [Barton] 112001 - 1001001
Elijah Barton 010001 - 10001
Nancy Burton 01001 - 012200101

1850 RHEA CENSUS

Alfred Barton 11 (NC), Mary 11 (NC), Pincney 10 (NC), Sarah 9 (NC), Martha 8 (NC), James 6 (NC): see Bailey Clifton
Azariah Barton 49 (NC)(Farmer), Susan 50, Calvin 25 (Farmer), Thomas J. 17 (Farmer), Elizabeth B. 15, John N. 12, Oscar 10, Sarah J. 6 p. 541-55
Elijah Barton 38 (Farmer), Caroline 29, John E. 18 (Farmer), William A. 16, Luisa A. 12 p. 581-302
Pryor Barton 23 (Farmer), Mary A. 17 p. 584-320

MARRIAGES (RHEA)

Ann Burton to John Johnston q.v.
Elizabeth Burton to Bailey Clifton q.v.
Hezekiah Burton to Rebecca Shadwick, 10 Aug 1832, John Silkerk Bm (A)

John Burton to Sally Bradey, 22 June 1822 (23 June), J. Fine JP, Thomas Snelson Bm (AR)
Louisa Barton to Addison Locke q.v.
Melvana Barton to John W. Rector q.v.
Pryor Barton to Mary Ann Wassum, 6 Nov 1849 (7 Nov), Snelson Roberts MG (R)
Royal Barton or Ryal Burton to Nancy Harwood, 23 Dec 1818 (same), Michael S. Jones Bm, found among papers of Daniel Walker (AR)
Squire Burton to Rebecca Rhea, 31 July 1822 (same), J. Fine JP, Arthur Pierce Bm (AR) [1850 Hardin Census: Squire Burton 64, Rebecca 44, Sterling 18, Charles 16, Squire 14, Henrietta 12, Royal 10, Willshire 8]

MARRIAGES (MEIGS)
Lydia Burton to William J. Gray q.v.

MISCELLANEOUS (RHEA and MEIGS)
Azariah Barton: JP 1837
" " Bondsman for William Cobb, 1834
" " Bondsman for Jesse Paton, 1842
Fielding Burton: Purchased Lot 2 in Decatur, 1836
Presley Burton: Bondsman for Thomas Lucas, 1812

- - - - - - - - - - - - -

BASS

MISCELLANEOUS (RHEA)
Samuel Bass: Bondsman for Edward Henson, 1830

- - - - - - - - - - - - -

BATES

1830 RHEA CENSUS
Ezekiel Bates 112001 - 201001 p. 370
[On 17 May 1847, Ezekiel Bates of Bradley Co. married Elizbeth Jane Douglas, dau of John Douglas, in McMinn Co.; 1850 Bradley Census: Ezekiel 55, Elizabeth J. 29, Cicero M. 18, Margaret 16, Hannah A. 14, Creade F. 2]

MISCELLANEOUS (MEIGS)
Ezekiel Bates: Hiwassee District, Burkett Chapel area

- - - - - - - - - - - - -

BATTLES / BATTLE / BOTTLES

MARRIAGES (RHEA)
Jane Battles to John Jacobs q.v.
Lucy Bottles to John Harris Smith q.v.
Nelson Battle to Rhoda Winton, 25 Jan 1813 (same), William Davidson Bm (AR)

- - - - - - - - - - - - -

BAVINS

TAXES (RHEA)
1808 (Jonathan Fine's List): Elija Bavins 1 WP

- - - - - - - - - - - - -

BAYLESS

1840 RHEA CENSUS
Joseph Bayless 10001 - 00101

1840 MEIGS CENSUS
William W. Bayless 11001 - 10001 p. 239

MARRIAGES (RHEA)
Joseph Bayless to Patheny Clough, 5 June 1828 (same), James A. Darwin JP, Abraham Miller Bm (AR)

MARRIAGES (MEIGS)
Marthey Bayless to William Blythe q.v.

- - - - - - - - - - - - -

BEAGLE / BEEGLES

1840 MEIGS CENSUS
David D. Beegles 1010001 - 011001001 p. 236

MISCELLANEOUS (MEIGS)
David D. Beegles or Beagle: JP(?) 1842-44
Theophilus W. Beegles: 1st Corp., Mexican War

- - - - - - - - - - - - -

BEAL

1830 RHEA CENSUS
Nancy Beal 0 - 110000001 p. 383 [see also BELL]

- - - - - - - - - - - - -

BEAN / BEENE

TAXES (RHEA)
1819 (Cpt. W.S. Bradley's Dist.):
Edmond Bean 1 WP, 2 Town Lots
1823 (Capt. Brown's Co.): Edmund Bean 1 WP, 1 BP, 2 TL

1830 RHEA CENSUS
Edmond Beene 010101 - 11001 p. 384
Hark Beene 0211301 - 2021001 p. 384
Hazard Bean 100001 - 00001 p. 395

1840 RHEA CENSUS
Charles Bean 210001 - 0101
Edmond Bean 0101001 - 100101
Geo. M. Bean 00021 - 00210001
Hazard Bean 011001 - 21001

1850 RHEA CENSUS
Charles D. Bean 45 (Va)(Farmer), Mary 35 (Va), John 15 (Va), William 13 (Va), Jacob 11 (Va), Sidnah A. 9 (Va), Susan 7 (Va), Charles 5 (Va), Elizabeth 3 (Va) p. 629-607
Edmund Bean 53 (Blacksmith), Elizabeth 20, Onslow 18 (Farmer), James K.P. 9, Franklin 7 p. 608-494
Mary Bean 55 (Md), Jesse 23 (Farmer), Mary C. 19, Sarah E. 18, Benjamin QUALLS 15 p. 542-63
Nancy Bean 17: see John Foote

MARRIAGES (RHEA)
Edmund Bean to Eliza B. Haley, 25 Apr 1820 (same), Matthew Donald MG (AR)
Edmund Bean to Lucretia Locke, 10 Apr 1828 (same), John Henninger MG, Gideon B. Thompson Bm (AR) [Lucretia was dau of Thomas and Susanna Henry Locke]
Elizabeth Bean to P. L. Eaves q.v.
Elizabeth Bean to William Lowery q.v.
Hazard Bean to Isabell Jack, 23 Sept 1828 (same), William Smith JP, Andrew Jack Bm (AR) [1850 Bradley Census: Hazard Bean 44, Isabela 40, Luke 20, John 18, Mary 16, Nancy 14, Martha 12, Thomas 10, Francis 7, James 5, William 3, Eliza 2]

James Bean to Minerva Paine, 17 Apr 1821 (same), Alexander Coulter Bm (A)
Nancy Bean to John Nash q.v.
MARRIAGES (MEIGS)
Manerva Bean to John McKinley q.v.
Margaret D. Bean to Jefferson Matthews q.v.
Mary Ann Bean to Miles P. Penny q.v.
MISCELLANEOUS (RHEA)
Caswell Bean: Bondsman for William Carter, 1825
Edmund Bean: Bondsman for John Henry, 1816
" " Bondsman for Lewis Acre, 1825
" " Bondsman for Benjamin White, 1829
" " Surety for Joseph Williams, 1826
Hazard Bean: Bondsman for James Lauderdale, 1827

\- - - - - - - - - - - -

BEAR

MARRIAGES (MEIGS)
Eliza Jane Bear to John Gross q.v.
Hannah Bear to James Johnson q.v.

\- - - - - - - - - - - -

BEARD

MARRIAGES (RHEA)
H. E. L. Beard to A. G. Hail q.v.
Robert Beard to Polly Dunlap, 24 Jan 1841, Jesse Rector Bm (A) [probably 1850 Bledsoe Census: Robert Beard 56, Mary 32, James H. 7, Joseph S. 5, Zachary T. 3, Elizabeth A. 4/12]
MISCELLANEOUS (MEIGS)
Welcome Beard: Ocoee District

\- - - - - - - - - - - -

BEARDEN

MARRIAGES (RHEA)
Mary E. Bearden to Washington John Dewitt q.v.

\- - - - - - - - - - - -

BEARMAN / BEERMAN

TAXES (RHEA)
1823 (Capt. Wilson's Co.):
William Beerman 1 WP, 15a Tennessee River
MISCELLANEOUS (RHEA)
William Bearman: Bondsman for Thos Lois [Lewis], 1817

\- - - - - - - - - - - -

BEAVERS
(see also BENSON)

MARRIAGES (RHEA)
Spencer Beavers or Benson to Ruth Colville, 10 Nov 1819 (same), Simon Geren Bm, John Walker JP (AR) [1850 McMinn Census: Spencer Beavers 60, Mary 50, etc.; Spencer Beavers married Mrs. Mary Cobbs on 11 Feb 1841 in McMinn Co]

\- - - - - - - - - - - -

BECK / BICK

TAXES (RHEA)
1819 (Capt. John Lewis' Co.): Jacob Beck 1 WP, 131a
1823 (Capt. Lewis' Co.): Jacob Beck 1 WP, 132a
1830 RHEA CENSUS
J. H. Bick 30001 - 00001 p. 357
Jacob Beck 02000001 - 10300001 p. 365
MARRIAGES (RHEA)
Betsy Beck to Hugh Rhea q.v.
Catherine Beck to Aaron Ferguson q.v.
James E. Beck to Elizabeth Ferguson, 17 Sept 1823 (25 Sept), Fred Fulkerson JP, John C. Ferguson Bm (AR)
John H. Beck to Frances H. Smith, 19 July 1825, John Parker Bm (AR)
Milla Beck to Randel Brown q.v.
Susan Beck to William Smith q.v.
MISCELLANEOUS (MEIGS)
John H. Beck: Purchased Lots 54,57,71 in Decatur, 1836
Samuel M. Beck: Cherokee Removal muster roll, 1836

\- - - - - - - - - - - -

BEDDESVILLE

1830 RHEA CENSUS
Squire Beddesville 20001 - 100011 p. 359

\- - - - - - - - - - - -

BEDDIX / BITTIX

1850 RHEA CENSUS
John Bittix 22, Mary J. 19: see Jefferson Moore
MARRIAGES (RHEA)
John B. Beddix to Mary J. Moore, 14 June 1850 (same), James A. Mitchell JP (R)

\- - - - - - - - - - - -

BEDDO

1850 RHEA CENSUS
Albert W. Beddo 27 (Farmer), Margaret K. 26, Asabel R. 6, Daniel J. 4, Phebe E. 1 p. 603-462

\- - - - - - - - - - - -

BEDFORD

1840 MEIGS CENSUS
Joseph Bedford 110101 - 112201 p. 224

\- - - - - - - - - - - -

BEDWELL / BIDWELL

1830 RHEA CENSUS
Arsted Bidwell 00001 - 20001 p. 374
Caleb Bidwell 10001 - 00001 p. 356
Leroy Bedwell 00001 - 0001 p. 353
MARRIAGES (RHEA)
Caleb Bedwell to Polly Newkirk, 13 Sept 1828, Hazlet Hines Bm (A) [1850 Bradley Census: Caleb Bedwell 40, Mary 40, Hiram 18, Amos 16, Adaline BURTON 10]

Leroy Bedwell to Margaret Lackey, 9 Mar 1830, Isaac D. Stockton Bm (A)
Matilda Bedwell to John Buster q.v.
Rebecca Bedwell to James Cahill q.v.

- - - - - - - - - - - - -

BELCHER

MISCELLANEOUS (MEIGS)
John Belcher: JP(?) 1845

- - - - - - - - - - - - -

BELL

TAXES (RHEA)
1823 (Capt. Lewis' Co.): John Bell 4 BP
(Capt. Brown's Co.): Robert Bell 7 BP, 466a Richland
(Capt. Wilson's Co.): Thomas Bell 1 WP
1830 RHEA CENSUS
Lucinda Bell 00100001 - 0 p. 393
Robert Bell 100001 - 20001 p. 367
Robert Bell 001000001 - 1 p. 379
1840 RHEA CENSUS
Elijah Bell 20001 - 00001
Sophia Bell (free colored) 1201 - 20011
William H. Bell 100011 - 11001
1840 MEIGS CENSUS
William Bell 110001 - 211111 p. 246
1850 RHEA CENSUS
David Bell 25 (Wagoner): see Harvey Sanders
Pleasant Bell 14: see Stephen Breeding
William H. Bell 46 (C.P. Clergyman), Nancy 37 (NC), Martha J. 15, David R. 13, Clarissa E. 11, Catharine M. 6, Robert N. 3, Margaret SYKES 15, Crawford McDANIEL 18 (Farmer) p. 599-405
Winney Bell 28 (NC), Joseph 7: see Lydia Allison
1850 MEIGS CENSUS
Eliza Bell 40 (NC), Jessee 17 (Farmer), Plesant 15 (Farmer), Polly 12, Elizabeth 11, Sarah 9, Clarissa 6 p. 811-753
MARRIAGES (RHEA)
Catherin Bell to Silas F. Barns q.v.
Catherine Bell to Henry Griffith q.v.
David Bell to Sarah Simcox, 22 Mar 1842, James W. Gillespie Bm (A)
Elijah Bell to Malinda Miller, 12 Dec 1832 (20 Dec), Isaac Baker JP, Matthew Allen Bm (AR)
[1850 Roane Census: Elija Bell 43, Malinda 30, Robert 13, David 10, James 8, Henry J. 6, William T. 4, Samuel H. 2]
John Bell to Anna Miller, 2 Dec 1840 (3 Dec), A.D. Paul JP (AR)
Rebecca Bell to Oliver Miller q.v.
Robert Bell to Elizabeth Goodwin, 23 Oct 1813 (same), Thomas Nolan Bm (A)
William C. Bell to Eliza Stone, 8 Jan 1831 (same), George Preston JP, Benjamin G. Parker Bm (AR)
MARRIAGES (MEIGS)
Sarah Bell to William T. Armstrong q.v.
Susan M. Bell to Daniel Robertson q.v.

MISCELLANEOUS (RHEA and MEIGS)
Elija Bell: Bondsman for John Miller, 1837
Robert Bell: Board of Commissioners to supervise construction of new jail in Washington, 1825-26
" " Bondsman for William B. Russell, 1826
" " Bondsman for Eliphius Holt, 1831
" " Hiwassee District
William Hutson Bell: MG 1832-1848
" " " Bondsman for Jas M. Cunningham, 1843

- - - - - - - - - - - - -

BENCH

MARRIAGES (MEIGS)
Mary Bench to Martin Farless q.v.

- - - - - - - - - - - - -

BENNEN

1830 RHEA CENSUS
Peter Bennen 000001 - 000000001 p. 392

- - - - - - - - - - - - -

BENNETT

TAXES (RHEA)
1819 (Capt. John Ramsey's Co.): John Bennett 1 WP
1823 (Capt. Wilson's Co.): George Bennett 1 WP
John Bennett 1 WP
1830 RHEA CENSUS
George Bennett 00001 - 30001 p. 359
John Bennett 1001 - 2001 p. 352
William Bennett 21001 - 00001 p. 388
1840 RHEA CENSUS
William Bennett 103001 - 320001
1840 MEIGS CENSUS
Jane Bennet 01 - 0111001 p. 245
John Bennet 011001 - 31001 p. 247
1850 MEIGS CENSUS
Christinia Bennett 45, Sarah 20, Elizabeth 18, Jane 17, William 15 p. 815-792

MARRIAGES (RHEA)
David Bennett or Barnett to Rachel Rhineheart or Rinehart, 16 Apr 1832 (same), Robert Cooley JP, Stephen Moore Bm (AR)
George Bennett to Tinsy Lockmiller, 2 June 1824 (3 June), John Farmer MG, Henry Jones Bm (AR)
John Bennett to Patsy Thrailkill, 31 Mar 1824 (1 Apr), John Farmer MG, Thomas Williams Bm (AR)
[1850 Roane Census: John Bennett 60, Martha 45, William 16, John 14, Margaret 9, James 21]
MARRIAGES (MEIGS)
Elizabeth Bennett to William Davis q.v.
Jane Bennett to Wm R. Sears q.v.

MISCELLANEOUS (RHEA and MEIGS)
George Bennett: Bondsman for William Lockmiller, 1825
John Bennett: Bondsman for Joseph J. Thrailkill, 1821
James W. Bennett: Private, Mexican War

- - - - - - - - - - - - -

BENNICK / BINNICH

1840 RHEA CENSUS
Norris Bennick 1110001 - 111201
MISCELLANEOUS (MEIGS)
S. Binnich: Hiwassee District, Sewee Creek area

- - - - - - - - - - - - -

BENSON / BENSAN / BINSON / BENZON

TAXES (RHEA)
1819 (Capt. W.S. Bradley's Dist.): Gabriel Benson 2 TL
(Capt. McGill's Co.): John Benson 1 WP, 30a
Matthias Benson 1 WP, 85a
Spencer Benson 200a
1823 (Capt. Howard's Co.): Benjamin Benson 1 WP
Isaac Benson 1 WP
John Benson 1 WP, 30a
(Capt. Howard's Co.): Robert Benson 1 WP
Spencer Benson 1 WP, 80a
Spencer Benson Jr. 1 WP, 81a
(Capt. Jackson's Co.): Matthias Benson 1 WP, 81a TR
1830 RHEA CENSUS
Benjamin Benson 101101 - 2211 p. 368
Isaac Binson 0100001 - 00001 p. 379
Robert Binson 20001 - 00001 p. 380
Spencer Benson 100000001 - 0000000001 p. 381
Spencer Benson 110021 - 2001 p. 381
1840 RHEA CENSUS
Barda Benson 100001 - 11001
Isaac Benson 1001001 - 00001
1840 MEIGS CENSUS
Benjamin Benson 0110001 - 1112101 p. 231
1850 RHEA CENSUS
Margaret Benson 10, Mary 12: see Charles Morgan
1850 MEIGS CENSUS
Isaac Benson 28 (Honner), Elizabeth Jane 26, John C. 8, Sarah Ann 7, Martha E. 3, Mathias K. 1 p. 765-414 [Isaac Benson married Jane Collier on 22 Mar 1842 in McMinn Co]
Maddison S. Benson 31 (Tailor) p. 773-480
Mathias Bensan 64 (Del), Hannah 66 (Va) p. 765-415
MARRIAGES (RHEA)
B.F. Benson to Nancy Bryson, 26 June 1842, John Johnson Bm (A)
Isaac Benson to Naomi Bryson, 20 Jan 1819 (same), Abraham Howard JP, John Benson Bm (AR)
Isaac Benson to Rebecca McDonald, 21 Sept 1838 (25 Sept), Benj. Wallace MG, R.N. Gillespie Bm (AR)
Martha Benson to Eliphius Holt q.v.
Matthias Benson to Jane Bryson, 9 Feb 1818 (same), Abraham Howard JP, William Benson Bm (AR)
Nancy Benson to Joseph H. France q.v.
Rosannah Benson to David Stephenson q.v.
Spencer Benson or Beavers to Ruth Colville, 10 Nov 1819 (same), John Walker JP, Simeon Geren Bm (AR)
Spencer Benson Jr. to Fanny Jackson, 3 Oct 1822 (same), John Cozby JP (AR)
William Benson to Catherine Shell, 18 Apr 1815, Spencer Benson Bm (A)
MARRIAGES (MEIGS)
Benjamin F. Benson to Sarah F. Gourley, 16 July 1844 (same), J.P. Fryar MG
Sarah F. Benson to John L. Ellis q.v.
MISCELLANEOUS (RHEA)
Barkley S. Benson: Bondsman for Charles Morgan, 1840
Gabriel Benson: Resident, Washington, Lots 69,70, 1816
Isaac Benson: Bondsman for George Gothard, 1818
" " Bondsman for Jacob Bryson, 1820
" " Bondsman for Michael J. Bulger, 1828
John Benson: Bondsman for Isaac Benson, 1819
Robert Benson: Bondsman for David Stephenson, 1829
Spencer Benson: Bondsman for William Benson, 1815
" " Revolutionary War Pensioner, 1835 list
William Benson: Bondsman for Matthias Benson, 1818
MISCELLANEOUS (MEIGS)
Isaac Benson: JP(?), 1846
J. F. Benson: Surety for John W. Cozby, 1830
William Benson: Surety for Isaac Widows 1850
" " Surety for James W. McDowell, 1850
" " Surety for Samuel Stockton, 1850

- - - - - - - - - - - - -

BENTON

1850 MEIGS CENSUS
John Benton 29 (NC)(Farmer), Sarah 20, Eliza C. 4, William T. 3, John J. 1 p. 764-402
[John Benton married Sarah David on 2 Oct 1845 in McMinn Co]
Lewis Benton 22 (Farmer), Rebecca 22, Martha C. 5, Susannah 4, Nancy 2 p. 782-546
MARRIAGES (MEIGS)
Grover M. Benton to Mary Hudson, 10 July 1840 (12 July), John Seaborn JP
Lewis Benton to Rebecca Smith, 28 May 1849 (same), Ezekiel Ward MG

- - - - - - - - - - - - -

BERRY / BARRY / BAREY / BARRAY

TAXES (RHEA)
1808 (Jonathan Fine's List): Jesse Barey 1 WP
1819 (Capt. W.S. Bradley's Co.): Hugh Berry 1 WP
Berry & Haslerig 1 WP
1823 (Capt. Brown's Co.): James Berry 1 WP
1830 RHEA CENSUS
James Berry 101001 - 000001 p. 384
[James married Mrs. Elizabeth Shoun on 21 May 1812; 1850 Bradley Census: James Berry 61, Elizabeth 51, Francis STOUT 32]
MARRIAGES (RHEA)
Mary Ann Barray to Nicholas Starnes q.v.
MISCELLANEOUS (RHEA)
Berry & Haselrig: Early merchants in Washington
Hugh Berry: Bondsman for William Lewis, 1816
" " Bondsman for Abraham Grimmett, 1816
James Berry: Bondsman for James C. Mitchell, 1812
" " Bondsman for George Mayberry, 1816
" " Bondsman for Rezin Rawlings, 1826
" " Registrar of Deeds, 1821-1823
" " County Court Clerk, 1823-1836
" " Commissioner, Town of Washington, 1826-28

- - - - - - - - - - - - -

BICE / BISE / BIAS / BYCE / BUISE / BUIS / BUISE / BUYSE

TAXES (RHEA)
1808 (Joseph Brooks' List): William Buis 1 WP
1819 (Capt. McGill's Co.): William Buise 1 WP, 161a
1823 (Capt. Howard's Co.): William Buyse 1 WP, 161a
1830 RHEA CENSUS
William Bice 22210001 - 100010001 p. 381
1840 RHEA CENSUS
William Bice 012110001 - 1111001
1840 MEIGS CENSUS
Rily Bias 100001 - 11001 p. 247
1850 RHEA CENSUS
Robert W. Byce 22 (Shoemaker), Eveline 22, Wm D. 2, Catharine FOUST 14 p. 634-644
William Byce 74 (SC)(Farmer), Mary A. 23, Martha J. 19, Sarah E. 16, Margaret S. 12 p. 633-643
1850 MEIGS CENSUS
Riley Bise 40 (SC), Mary 36 (SC), Tappemeer (f) 20 (SC), Martha 12, Drury 10, Charity 7, Rhoda 4, Susan 3, Elizabeth 1 p. 805-707
MARRIAGES (RHEA)
Margaret Buise to Cain Able q.v.
R.W. Bise to Aleminter Wilhim, 17 Dec 1813, David Brown Bm (A)
MISCELLANEOUS (RHEA)
William Buce: Bondsman for Jonathan Williams, 1814

\- - - - - - - - - - - -

BICKNELL / BECKNAL

1840 MEIGS CENSUS
Winna Becknal 1021 - 0101101 [Winney Bicknell married Turner Sharp on 9 Aug 1845 in McMinn Co]
MARRIAGES (RHEA)
Thomas Bicknell or Bedknell to Winney Holmes, 28 Aug 1835 (1 Sept), Daniel Briggs MG, James Tate Bm (AR)

\- - - - - - - - - - - -

BILLINGS

MISCELLANEOUS (RHEA)
J.R. Billings: JP 1848

\- - - - - - - - - - - -

BILLINGSLEY

1840 MEIGS CENSUS
James Billingsley 2111001 - 011001 p. 228
MARRIAGES (RHEA)
Nancy Billingsley to Robert Moore q.v.

\- - - - - - - - - - - -

BINGHAM / BINGON / BINYON

1840 RHEA CENSUS
Benjamin Bingham 0121001 - 1110101
Isaac S. Bingon 11001 - 11001
1850 RHEA CENSUS
Benjamin Bingham 53 (Va)(Wagonmaker), Nancy 51 (NC), Nelson 20 (Carpenter), James 18 (Farmer), Nancy J. 16, Edna C. 13, Harriet T. 8 p. 549-105
Isaac S. Binyon 45 (Md)(Farmer), Susan 49 (Va), Ishum R. 17 (Saddler), Amanda E. 13, Thomas B. 9 p. 585-330
Polly Bingham 75 (Unk), Elizabeth WOODBY 12 (Unk) p. 601-415
Thomas Bingham27 (NC)(Farmer), Emeline M. 30, Charles 13, Minerva F. 4, Nancy E. 2 p. 560-166
William Bingham 27 (Farmer), Charlotte 22, Nancy E. 1 p. 354-124
MARRIAGES (RHEA)
Caroline Bingham to Calvin G. Dudley q.v.
Elizabeth Bingham to William Ford q.v.
Isaac S. Binyon to Nancy Hill, 17 July 1828 (same), Matthew Hubbert JP, Alexander M. Galbraith Bm (AR)
Isaac Binyon to Susan Woodward, 20 Sept 1831 (same), James A. Darwin JP, Allen Kennedy Bm (AR)
Thomas Bingham to Emiline Wiles or Wilds, 21 Mar 1844 (same), J.P. Thompson JP (AR)
MARRIAGES (MEIGS)
Richard Binyon to Nancy E. Woods, 21 Nov 1850, E.D. Gilbert Sur
MISCELLANEOUS (RHEA)
Isaac S. Bingham: Sheriff 1842-1848
Isaac S. Binyon: Bondsman for Saml T. Whittenburg, 1843

\- - - - - - - - - - - -

BIRD

MARRIAGES (RHEA)
Elizabeth Bird to Sutton Green q.v.
Elizabeth Bird to John G. Burris or Burns q.v.
John Bird to Betsey Greene, 12 May 1809, Henry Airheart Bm (A)
MISCELLANEOUS (MEIGS)
Joseph Bird: Hiwassee District

\- - - - - - - - - - - -

BIRDSONG

TAXES (RHEA)
1819 (Capt. W.S. Bradley's Dist.): John Birdsong Sr. 1a
John Birdsong Jr. 1 WP
MARRIAGES (RHEA)
John Birdsong to Catherine Huddleston, 25 Apr 1822 (same), John Cozby JP, Josiah Birdsong Bm (R)
Josiah Birdsong to Nancy Huddleston, 2 Sept 1819 (3 Sept), John Rice JP, William Blimpie Bm (AR)
Polly Birdsong to Reuben Freemn q.v.
Sarah Birdsong to Robert Moore q.v.
MISCELLANEOUS (RHEA)
John Birdsong: Early resident of Washington, Lots 12,13, and 42, 1812
" " Bondsman for Sylus Shoat, 1816
" " Bondsman for Simon Everett, 1820
Josiah Birdsong: Bondsman for John Birdsong, 1822

\- - - - - - - - - - - -

BIRLY / BYERLEY

1840 RHEA CENSUS
Jacob Birly 211001 - 22000
1850 RHEA CENSUS
Jacob Byerley 51 (SC)(Farmer), Sarah 47, Jasper 24 (Farmer), Eliza J. 21, Mariah 19, Margaret 17, William D. 15, Lucy 13, James 11, Sarah 9, Nancy 7, Samuel 2 p. 597-386

- - - - - - - - - - - - -

BISHOP

1840 MEIGS CENSUS
John D. Bishop 110001 - 110001 p. 228
1850 MEIGS CENSUS
Hannah Bishop 43 (NC), Mary Ann 18, James 15, Mary Ann [sic] 13 p. 785-570
MARRIAGES (RHEA)
Nancy Bishop to Samuel Stokes q.v.

- - - - - - - - - - - - -

BLACK / BLACKE

1840 RHEA CENSUS
George W. Black 131001 - 11001
1850 MEIGS CENSUS
George W. Black 54 (Va)(Blacksmith), Frances 40 (NC), Marshall 15, John 14, James 13, Harriet 4 p. 818-809
MARRIAGES (RHEA)
Delila Blacke to Martin Rigg q.v.
George W. Black to Elizabeth Dunken, 11 Jan 1823 (12 Jan), John Robinson JP, Byrum Breeding Bm (AR)
G. W. Black to Sary or Fanny McNutt, 31 Dec 1839 (no return), Isaac Penzer Bm (AR)
Gilford Black to Margaret Frie or Free, 11 Mar 1836 (13 Mar), Eli M. Sutherland --(?), William Chaist --(?) (AR)
Henry Black to Lucinda Hamintree, 6 Aug 1835, John Crawford Bm (A)
Louisa Black to William Clements q.v.
Mary Blacke to Eli Sykes q.v.
Mary D. Black to Benjamin F. Jennings q.v.
Polly Black to James Clemons q.v.
MISCELLANEOUS (RHEA and MEIGS)
Tarlton E. Black: Private, Mexican War (died during war)
William R. Black: Bondsman for Thomas C. Thomas, 1828

- - - - - - - - - - - - -

BLACKBURN

MARRIAGES (RHEA)
Thomas Blackburn to Mary Rawlings, 12 Sept 1824 (same), M. Donald MG, Matthew Donald Bm (AR)

- - - - - - - - - - - - -

BLACKWELL

TAXES (RHEA)
1819 (Capt. John Ramsey's Co.): James Blackwell 1 WP
1823 (Capt. Jackson's Co.): George W. Blackwell 1 WP
(Capt. McGill's Co.): Nathan Blackwell 1 WP
(Capt. Jackson's Co.): Strother Blackwell 1 WP
1830 RHEA CENSUS
Charles Blackwell 11000011 - 0131101 p. 353
James Blackwell 01211001 - 2100201 p. 362
1840 MEIGS CENSUS
Elizabeth Blackwell 001 - 002011 p. 247
Nathaniel Blackwell 2101001 - 013101 p. 247
William Blackwell 10001 - 00001 p. 247
1850 MEIGS CENSUS
Alfred Blackwell 27 (Farmer), Elizabeth 39, Heneretta 30, Sarah 22, Minerva 21 p. 812-759
Joab Blackwell 35 (Farmer), Leatha 31, Isaah M. 13, Isaac 7, Mary M. 4, Joshua RENTFRO 72 (Va) p. 801-680
William Blackwell 38 (Farmer), Eliza 29, Martha 10, Emaly 6, Alfred 4, James 1 p. 809-735
MARRIAGES (RHEA)
Anna Blackwell to William Blackwell q.v.
Ceclie Blackwell to Jacob Wilhelms q.v.
Darcus Blackwell to William Adams q.v.
George W. Blackwell to Nancy Bush, 19 Oct 1819 (same), Samuel Gamble Bm (A)
Minerva Blackwell to Joel Hannah q.v.
Strother Blackwell to Rebecca Marnes or Morris, 14 Sept 1820 (same), John Cozby JP, John C. Simpson Bm (AR) [1850 Henderson Census: Strother Blackwell 49, Rebecca 50, Daniel 22, Jane 15, Joseph 13, Daniel 11)
William Blackwell to Anna Blackwell, 29 Nov 1819, J. Fine JP, Charles Bradey Bm (A)
MARRIAGES (MEIGS)
William Blackwell to Eliza Dines, 29 Mar 1838, Isaac Baker JP
MISCELLANEOUS (RHEA)
George W. Blackwell: Bondsman for William Adams, 1831
James Blackwell: Bondsman for Wesley Hare, 1830
MISCELLANEOUS (MEIGS)
Alfred Blackwell: Private, Mexican War
Charles Blackwell: Private, Mexican War
" " Hiwassee District resident
George W. Blackwell: Cherokee Removal muster roll, 1836
Isaiah Blackwell: Cherokee Removal muster roll, 1836
James Blackwell: JP 1836
" " House used for elections in District 8
James M. Blackwell: Constable, District 8, 1836
" " " Cherokee Removal muster roll, 1836
Jeremiah M. Blackwell: Cherokee Removal muster roll
Joab Blackwell: Cherokee Removal muster roll, 1836
Joseph B. Blackwell: Cherokee Removal muster roll, 1836
Nathan Blackwell: Cherokee Removal muster roll, 1836
Peter Blackwell: Hiwassee District resident
William Blackwell: Hiwassee District resident

- - - - - - - - - - - - -

BLACKWOOD

1830 RHEA CENSUS
Nathan Blackwood 100001 - 31001 p. 362
William Blackwood 000101 - 0000001 p. 370
MARRIAGES (RHEA)
Mary Ann Blackwood to Alexander Mahan q.v.

- - - - - - - - - - - - -

BLADDEN

MISCELLANEOUS (MEIGS)
John Bladden: JP(?) 1843

BLAKE

1830 RHEA CENSUS
Howel Blake 0010001 - 0111 p. 368

BLAKELY / BLAKLEY / BLAKELEY

TAXES (RHEA)
1819 (Capt. W.S. Bradley's Dist.): James Blakely 1 WP
(Capt. John Ramsey's Co.): Thomas Blakely 1 WP
1823 (Capt. Smith's Co.): James Blakely 1 WP
1830 RHEA CENSUS
James Blakely 0000001 - 001001 p. 372
1840 MEIGS CENSUS
James Blakely 00000001 - 01000010001 p. 233
Samuel Blakely 001101 - 132011 p. 238
1850 MEIGS CENSUS
James Blakely 66 (NC)(Farmer), Dicy 58 (NC), Martha M. LAWSON 17 p. 751-308
MARRIAGES (RHEA)
Thomas Blakerly or Blackley to Annie Hiden, 16 Jan 1817, J. Fine JP (AR)
Thomas Blakley to Anny Hidun, 16 Jan 1819 (same), Geo Gillespie Bm (A)
William K. Blakiby or Blakely to Dorcus Hellums, 1 Mar 1821 (same), John Mitchell MG, William Hellums Bm (AR)
MARRIAGES (MEIGS)
Harriet Blakely to Phillip Blevins q.v.
MISCELLANEOUS (RHEA)
James Blakely: Bondsman for James Brandon, 1819
" " Bondsman for Hanson Philpot, 1829
" " Bondsman for James Lawson, 1831
" " Bondsman for Bartholomew Lawson, 1832
" " Bondsman for Lemuel Musick, 1835
Samuel Blakeley: Bondsman for John Casey, 1834

BLALOCK / BLAYLOCK

1840 MEIGS CENSUS
Elbert Blaylock 021001 - 212001 p. 245
John Blaylock 0000000001 - 0000000001 p. 243
1850 MEIGS CENSUS
Benjamin Blalock 59 (NC)(Farmer), Martha Ann 28 (SC), Catharine 81 (SC) p. 815-789
Elbert Blalock 57 (NC)(Farmer), Hannah 57 (NC), Fielding 24 (NC)(Farmer), Mary 21 (NC), Lucy 20 (NC), Samuel 17 (NC)(Farmer), Catharine 15 (NC), Jane 13 (NC), Sarah 11 (NC), Frankland 7, Matilda 5 p. 814-776
MARRIAGES (RHEA)
Millington Blaylock to Abby Moore, 21 Feb 1826 (same), Thomas Hall MG, John Moore Bm (AR)
MISCELLANEOUS (MEIGS)
John C. Blaylock: Pvt., Mexican War (died in service)

BLANE / BLAIN

1830 RHEA CENSUS
James H. Blane 00001 - 00001 p. 388
MARRIAGES (RHEA)
James H. Blain to Jane H. Gillespie, 8 Oct 1829 (same), John Henninger MG, Gideon B. Thompson Bm (AR) [Jane, dau of Geoand Ann Neilson Gillespie]

BLANKENSHIP

1830 RHEA CENSUS
Thos Blankenship 01130001 - 00000001 p. 369
Thos Blankenship 20001 - 00001 p. 369
1840 MEIGS CENSUS
Isham Blankenship 121001 - 111001 p. 224
Thomas Blankenship 121001 - 000001 p. 233
1850 MEIGS CENSUS
John W. Blankenship 58 (NC)(Hatter), Sarah 14 p. 751-310
Thomas Blankenship 45 (Va)(Hatter), Charlotte 44 (Ga), James 25 (Ediot), John 19 (Hatter), William W. 17, Wallis 13 p. 751-312
MARRIAGES (MEIGS)
Delpha Blankenship to William Allen q.v.
MISCELLANEOUS (RHEA and MEIGS)
Benj Blankenship: Bondsman for Clinton Norman, 1832
Thos Blankenship: Bondsman for James D. Howell, 1828
" " Private, Mexican War

BLANTON

1840 MEIGS CENSUS
John Blanton 120001 - 200001 p. 244
Thomas Blanton 00001 - 1001 p. 244
MARRIAGES (MEIGS)
Thomas Blanton to Mahalia Homes, 2 Mar 1839 (7 Mar), Wm Green MG [1850 Anderson Census: Thomas Blanton 32, Mahala 29, Mary J. 10, John S. 8, Sarah 6, Martha K. 3, Elmira 1]
MISCELLANEOUS (MEIGS)
John Blanton: JP(?) 1843

BLARE
(see also BLANE)

MARRIAGES (MEIGS)
Minerva Blare to Elisha Moore q.v.

BLEDSOE

MARRIAGES (RHEA)
Joel Bledsoe to Elizabeth Price, 26 July 1828 (27 July), D.M. Stockton JP, Wiley Murphy Bm (AR)
Joel K. Bledsoe to Juda Runnions, 20 or 29 Aug 1829 (same), Thomas Cox JP, John Lewis Bm (AR)

BLEVINS

TAXES (RHEA)
1823 (Capt. Smith's Co.): David Blevins 1 WP
1830 RHEA CENSUS
David Blevins 00000001 - 02010001 p. 375
H. T. Blevins 10001 - 00001 p. 376
Hardin Blevins 00211001 - 2120001 p. 374
Isaac Blevins 000001 - 000100001 p. 373
Jas or Jos Blevins 10011 - 02 p. 375
William Blevins 30001 - 10001 p. 374
1840 MEIGS CENSUS
Anny Blevins 121-0001001 p. 237
Hardin Blevins 100000001 - 110012001 p. 238
James Blevins 220011 - 00111 p. 235
John T. Blevins 00001 - 10002 p. 232
John W. Blevins 200001 - 030011 p. 238
Mosy Blevins 0001 - 00002 p. 234
Phillip Blevins 10001 - 00001 p. 238
Thomas V. Blevins 10001 - 00001 p. 234
William Blevins 121001 - 111001 p. 236
1850 MEIGS CENSUS
Ann Blevins 48, Rodney E. 21 (Farmer), Malissa F. 19, Samuel L. 18 (Farmer), Hugh V.T. 17, Racheal E. 12, Mary Ann 11, Sarah Jane 8, Mariah L. 6, Tennessee 4, Malissa 2 p. 769-443 [Ann, widow of Hugh T. Blevins]
Eliza Blevins 26, Ruth 7, James 5, Samuel 2 p. 750-305 [Eliza and her three children also are listed in household of her father, Hardin Blevins]
Elizabeth Blevins 30 (Va), Hardin 7, Judian 8, Moses 5 p. 752-316
Elizabeth Blevins 24 (Va), Judy Ann 11, Hardin 8, Moses L. 6 p. 750-303 [The previous two entries are for the same person; Elizabeth probably was widow of Moses Blevins]
Hardin Blevins 70 (Farmer), Elizabeth 66, Margaret 43, Catharine 25, Eliza 22, Sarah 14, Rutha 7, James 5, Samuel 4, Hardin BOUND 10 p. 766-424 [Hardin's wife was Elizbeth Vance]
John T. Blevins 39 (Farmer), Jane 33, Revenia 11, James B. 10, David P. 2, Bethenia K. 1, Sarah THOMAS 14, Sarah BLEVINS 73 (Pa) p. 759-371 [Sarah, widow of David Blevins, was dau of Hugh and Sarah Allison Torbett; Sarah Thomas was dau of Lucretia and Henson W. Thomas]
John W. Blevins 45 (Farmer), Elizabeth 39, Rutha Jane 19, Mary Ann 17, Sarah M. 15, James J. 13, David C. 11, Frances E. 9, Bartholomew K. 7, Edens M. 5 p. 766-423
Phillip Blevins 37 (Farmer), Harriet 31, James C. 10, Argile H. 8, Dicy 5, Margaret Jane 3, Thomas W. 1 p. 750-307
Ruth Blevins 42, Bershaba 21, Alfred 19 (Farmer), David 17 (Farmer), William 14, Hugh 12, Sarah 10, Malissa 6, James 2, Talbert ROCKHOLD 29 (Doctor) p. 748-289 [Ruth, widow of James Blevins]
Samuel Blevins 37 (Farmer), Sarah 37, Manda E. 17, Catharine 15, Allman 13, William 11, Tennessee 9, Margaret 7, Charles H. 5, Lucinda 3, Samuel H. 1 p. 766-425
Thomas Blevins 32 (Farmer), Levinia 30, Joseph P. 10, Licurgus R. 8, Cemintha 6, John W. 4, Phillip G. 2, Thomas C. 1 p. 750-304

MARRIAGES (RHEA)
Allen Blevins to Clarissa or Clarassey Owens, 21 Apr 1824 (22 Apr), Wm M. Smith JP, Solomon Neideffer Bm (AR) [1850 Bradley Census: Allen 64, Clarressa 45, Wm 26, Sorinda 22, Malinda 17, Mikel 14, Mariah 12, Thompson 6, Allen 6, Mary 3]
Hugh T. Blevins to Anna B. Looney, 3 Apr 1828 (5 Apr), Peach Taylor JP, Thomas Cox Bm (AR)
James Blevins to Ruth (Mary) Rockhold, 26 Dec 1827 (same), Peach Taylor JP, Samuel Igo Bm (AR)
John T. Blevins to Jane A. Darwin, 10 Nov 1838 (15 Nov), D.L. Godsey MG, Moses Blevins Bm (AR)
John W. Blevins to Elizabeth Guinn, 1 Nov 1830 (4 Nov), Peach Taylor JP, Benjamin F. Locke Bm (AR)
Lucretia Blevins to Henson W. Thomas q.v.
Mary Blevins to Peach Taylor q.v.
Moses Blevins to Nancy Taylor, 23 July 1834 (24 July), Peach Taylor JP, George Stokes Bm (AR)
Samuel Blevins to Sarah Blevins, 31 Dec 1832 (1 Jan 1833), Robert Cooley JP, George Stokes Bm (AR)
Sarah Blevins to Larkin M. Stokes q.v.
Sarah Blevins to Samuel Blevins q.v.
Susan Blevins to William S. Russell q.v.
MARRIAGES (MEIGS)
Anderson Blevins to Caroline Quiett, 30 Dec 1847 (7 Aug 1848), John T. Blevins JP (dates written as above in records)
Eleanor Blevins to Wilson C. Smith q.v.
Harrison Blevins to Nancy Blevins, 23 Nov 1848 (same), John W. Woods JP
Mahala Blevins to Abraham Knight q.v.
Moses Blevins to Elizabeth Thomas, 27 Aug 1839 (29 Aug), D.L. Godsey MG
Nancy Blevins to Harrison Blevins q.v.
Philip Blevins to Harriet Blakely, 10 Jan 1839 (same), D.L. Godsey MG
Thomas Blevins to Levina P. Gorley, 13 June 1839 (1 July), Daniel Cate JP
MISCELLANEOUS (RHEA)
Hugh T. Blevins: Bondsman for Jesse Combs, 1832
" " " Bondsman for Jesse McCarter, 1835
James Blevins: JP 1833-1834
John T. Blevins: Bondsman for Edward S. Stokes, 1833
Moses Blevins: Bondsman for Henson W. Thomas, 1834
" " Bondsman for John T. Blevins, 1838
William Blevins: Bondsman for John Roberts, 1830
MISCELLANEOUS (MEIGS)
Allen Blevins: Cherokee Removal muster roll, 1836
Harden Blevins: Hiwassee District, Lower Goodfield area
Hugh Blevins: Hiwassee District, Concord area
James Blevins JP 1836, 1841
James B. Blevins: Purchased Lot 42 in Decatur, 1836
John L. Blevins: Common School Commissioner, District 3, 1838
John T. Blevins: JP 1842-45, 1848-49
" " " Chairman of County Court, 1848-49
John V. Blevins: JP 1848
John W. Blevins: 2nd Lt., Cherokee Removal muster roll
Moses Blevins: Cherokee Removal muster roll, 1836
Phillip Blevins: Cherokee Removal muster roll, 1836
R. E. L. Blevins: Surety for Reece B. Cross, 1850
Rodney Blevins: Private, Mexican War
Samuel Blevins: 1st Sgt., Cherokee Removal muster roll
William Blevins: Purchased Lot 43 in Decatur, 1836

BLIZARD

MISCELLANEOUS (MEIGS)
A. Blizzard: First teacher at Decatur Academy

BLUMPIE

MISCELLANEOUS (RHEA)
William Blumpie: Bondsman for Josiah Birdsong, 1819

BLYTHE / BLITHE / BLYE

TAXES (RHEA)
1823 (Capt. Jackson's Co.): Daniel Blythe 1 WP
(Capt. Braselton's Co.): John Blithe 1 WP
1830 RHEA CENSUS
Mary Blythe 1001 - 1230001 p. 384
1840 RHEA CENSUS
Mary Blythe 0011 - 00130001
1850 RHEA CENSUS
Esther Blye 30, Mary 11, James M. 8, Rebecca 4 p. 567-201
Mary Blye 60 (NC), Sarah 26, Ellen 23, William 22 (Farmer), Rebecca 19 p. 567-202
1850 MEIGS CENSUS
Samuel M. Blythe 43 (Farmer), Mary 46 (Ky), George 24 (Ediot), James M. 20 (Farmer), Rebecca Jane 15, Susannah 12, Samuel 8 p. 801-683
William J. Blythe 22 (Farmer), Martha 30 p. 801-682
MARRIAGES (RHEA)
Betsey Blythe to Matthias Green q.v.
Elizabeth Blythe to Ira Gothard q.v.
Jerusha Blythe to James Roark q.v.
John Blythe to Polly Malony, 4 Nov 1809 (same), Edward Maloney Bm (A)
John R. Blythe to Jestin Cadle, 3 June 1829 (same), James Vaughn Bm (A)
Martha Blythe to Alexander Clingham q.v.
Mary Ann Blythe to Mumford Smith q.v.
Polly Blythe to Adam Derrick q.v.
Sally Blythe to Samuel Carr q.v.
William Blythe to Nancy Fields, 11 Oct 1809 (same), Samuel Mahan Bm (A) [Nancy, dau of Richard]
MARRIAGES (MEIGS)
William Blythe to Marthey Bayless, 12 Nov 1848 (same), S.G. Royster JP
MISCELLANEOUS (RHEA and MEIGS)
Elijah Blythe: Bondsman for Abner Hughes, 1834
" " Bondsman for Richard Fields, 1836
Samuel Blythe: JP(?), Meigs Co., 1843
William Blythe: Bondsman for Zeof Jackson, 1823
" " Lived south of Tennessee River
" " Operated Blythe's Ferry

BOBBETT

MARRIAGES (RHEA)
Polly Bobbett to Edmond Vaughn q.v.

BOGGESS / BAGGESS / BUGGESS

1840 MEIGS CENSUS
Abijah Boggess 1022111 - 111101 p. 240
1850 MEIGS CENSUS
Abijah F. Boggess 26 (Farmer) p. 802-687
Abijah Buggess 53 (Farmer), Susan 53 (NC), John B. 22 (Farmer), Isley H. 13, Susan 12, Texanna S. 7 p. 793-625
MARRIAGES (MEIGS)
Harriet C. Boggess to Robert R. Davis q.v.
John B. Boggess to Mary A. Lillard, 1 Aug 1850, J.M. Lillard Sur
M. E. Boggess to Thomas P. Stockton q.v.
Mary J. Boggess to David H. Sharp q.v.
Sarah Ann Boggess to John Sharpe q.v.
MISCELLANEOUS (RHEA and MEIGS)
A.F. Boggess: 1st Sgt., Mexican War
Abijah Boggess: Hiwassee District resident
" " Ensign, Cherokee Removal muster roll
" " Private, Mexican War
Simon M. Boggess: County Court Clerk, 1840-1841
" " " 3rd Sgt., Cherokee Removal muster roll

BOGGS

MARRIAGES (RHEA)
Vesty C. Boggs to Henry Latham q.v.

BOLEJACK

TAXES (RHEA)
1823 (Capt. Howard's Co.): Matthew Bolejack 1 WP

BOLEN / BOLIN / BOLING / BOWLAN / BOWLIN / BOWLING

TAXES (RHEA)
1823 (Capt. Brown's Co.): John Bowlin 1 WP
1830 RHEA CENSUS
Jeremiah Boling 0010101 - 12111 p. 368
Jno Boling 0001001 - 0001001 p. 374
John Boling 011011 - 002011 p. 379
1840 RHEA CENSUS
James P. Bolen 000001 - 00002
John Bolen 00011001 - 00011001
1840 MEIGS CENSUS
John Bowling 20001001 - 00001001 p. 232
1850 RHEA CENSUS
James F. Bolen 42 (SC)(Farmer), Elizabeth 27, Mary J. CATE 24 p. 620-543
John Bolen Unk (Va)(none), Meeky Unk (SC), Elizabeth 40 (SC), John P. 31 (SC)(Farmer) p. 619-540
Thomas M. Bolen 26 (Farmer), Nancy 25, Almira 9, Asbury 8, William 5, Hester 4, John 1 p. 616-513
1850 MEIGS CENSUS
David Bolin 40 (Farmer) p. 750-306
Henderson Bowlen 26 (Farmer), Sarah 22, William T. 6, Hannah 4, Joseph 3 p. 806-714

John Bowlen 67 (Va)(Farmer), Milly 65, David 37 (none), Sally 34 p. 767-427

MARRIAGES (RHEA)

Heathey Bolin to Jonathan Bandy q.v.

James F. Bolin to Elizabeth Cates, 13 Sept 1836 (15 Sept), Bryant R. McDonald JP, James Smith Bm (AR)

Jeremiah Bowling to Mary Gamble, 26 Aug 1828 (same), Thomas Cox JP, William S. Russell Bm (AR)

John Bowling to Sallie Whitney, 18 Oct 1818 (same), John Moore JP (R)

Mahala Bolen to John Roberts q.v.

Sarah Bolen to Gideon B. Mahan q.v.

Thomas M. Bolen or Bolin to Nancy Wicks or Weaks, 20 Jan 1841 (21 Jan), James Hooper JP, James Bolin Bm (AR)

MARRIAGES (MEIGS)

William Bolin to Polly M. Richards, 29 Oct 1848 (same), J.L. Aikman JP

MISCELLANEOUS (RHEA and MEIGS)

David Bolen: Cherokee Removal muster roll, 1836

James Bolin: Bondsman for Thomas M. Bolen, 1841

John Bolin: Bondsman for Jonathan Bandy, 1831

- - - - - - - - - - - - -

BOLES / BOWLS

1850 RHEA CENSUS

George Bowls 42 (Va)(Cobler?), Elizabeth 35 (Va), John 10 (Va), James 9 (Va), Daniel 8 (Va), David 6 (Va), Jesse 5 (Va), Samuel 4 (Va), William 6/12 (Va) p. 546-87

- - - - - - - - - - - - -

BOLINGER / BOWLINGER

1850 RHEA CENSUS

Andrew Bolinger 28 (Blacksmith), Sarah 27, William H. 5, Mary A. 2 p. 544-75

Frederick Bolinger 54 (Blacksmith), Mary 47, Henry H. 25 (Blacksmith), Bathena 24, Emily 22, Isaac H. 17 (Laborer), Lucinda 15, Hester A. 3, Rachel 10, Mary 6 p. 545-80

MARRIAGES (RHEA)

A.J. Bowlinger to Sarah Newport, 3 June 1841 (13 June), Asa Newport MG (R)

- - - - - - - - - - - - -

BOLLISON

MISCELLANEOUS (RHEA)

John Bollison: JP 1823

- - - - - - - - - - - - -

BOLT

1830 RHEA CENSUS

Adam C. Bolt 001000001 - 00100001 p. 369

- - - - - - - - - - - - -

BOLTON / BOULTON

TAXES (RHEA)

1819 (Capt. McGill's Co.): Robert Bolton 1 WP

1823 (Capt. Howard's Co.): Robert Bolton 1 WP

1830 RHEA CENSUS

Lewis Boulton 0121 - 0011001 p. 381

Robert Boulton 110101 - 00111001 p. 381

William Bolton 00001 - 00001 p. 394

1840 RHEA CENSUS

James Bolton (free colored) 1001 - 0101

Madison Bolton 0 - 00001 (101 - 1*)

William Bolton 0 - 00001 (101 - 1*)

(* free colored in household)

MARRIAGES (RHEA)

Eliza Ann Bolton to David Holt q.v.

Jesse Boulton to Betsy Pryor, 31 Jan 1837, Charles Smith Bm (A)

Martha Ann Boulton to Harry Roddy q.v.

Robert Boulton to Jane McNutt, 27 Aug 1817 (28 Aug), A. David JP, Thomas Harritt Bm (AR)

Robert Bolton to Anne Holt, 5 Sept 1822, A. David JP (AR)

- - - - - - - - - - - - -

BOND / BONDS

TAXES (RHEA)

1823 (Capt. Jackson's Co.):

Benjamin Bond 1 WP, 1 BP, 160a Agency Creek

MISCELLANEOUS (RHEA and MEIGS)

Benjamin Bonds: Hiwassee District resident

" " Bondsman for Isaac Mahan, 1823

- - - - - - - - - - - - -

BONHAM

1850 RHEA CENSUS

John Bonham 40 (Va)(Wagonmaker), Lucinda 34, Rachael E. 14, Orpha M. 12, Joseph M. 7, Milton G. 2 p. 585-327

MARRIAGES (RHEA)

Martha A Bonham or Borham to Walter A. Johnson q.v.

- - - - - - - - - - - - -

BONNER

MARRIAGES (MEIGS)

Thomas J. Bonner to Sarah Wammack, 5 Sept 1850, Moses Bonner Sur

MISCELLANEOUS (MEIGS)

Moses Bonner: Surety for Thomas J. Bonner, 1850

- - - - - - - - - - - - -

BORAM

MISCELLANEOUS (RHEA)

Ferguson Boram: Bondsman for Solomon Cox, 1823

- - - - - - - - - - - - -

BORDEN

MARRIAGES (RHEA)
David Borden to Mary Huff, 30 Mar 1833 (31 Mar), J.M. Callon JP, James Newland Bm (AR)

- - - - - - - - - - - - -

BOTTOM / BOTTOMS

1840 MEIGS CENSUS
Allen Bottom 012001 - 220001 p. 246
Thomas Bottom 000100001 - 00110001 p. 239
1850 MEIGS CENSUS
Thomas Bottom 72 (Va)(Millwright), Elizabeth 68 (Va), John O. 30 (Farmer) p. 794-638
MARRIAGES (RHEA)
Nancy Bottom to Joseph Allen q.v.
MARRIAGES (MEIGS)
Caroline C. Bottoms to J.R. Douglass q.v.
Sarah Bottom (Mrs.) to A.J. McCallen q.v.
MISCELLANEOUS (RHEA and MEIGS)
Charles Bottom: Bondsman for Joseph Allen, 1834
J. O. Bottom: Surety for J.R. Douglass, 1847
Peter Bottom: Bondsman for Hezekiah James, 1845

- - - - - - - - - - - - -

BOUCHER / BOCHER

1840 MEIGS CENSUS
William Boucher 02001 - 1110001 p. 224
1850 MEIGS CENSUS
Elisha Boucher 29 (Ky)(Farmer), Hester 25, Anna Jane 4, William 2 p. 716-25
Gadi Bocher 25 (Ky)(Farmer), Barbary Ann 24, William R. 6, Henry P. 5, Martha E. 1 p. 783-552
William Boucher 60 (NC)(Farmer), Anna 59, Nancy C. 23, Kiziah G. 19, Robert 18, John G. 16, Temperance 14 p. 715-24

- - - - - - - - - - - - -

BOUDEN

MARRIAGES (MEIGS)
Malinda Bouden to James Butler q.v.
MISCELLANEOUS (MEIGS)
John Bouden: JP(?) 1844

- - - - - - - - - - - - -

BOUND

1850 MEIGS CENSUS
Calvin Thorp Bound 19, Jas Leander 16: see John Atkinson
Hardin Bound 10: see Hardin Blevins
Zilpha Bound 15: see Thomas Coffee

- - - - - - - - - - - - -

BOWDRY

MARRIAGES (RHEA)
John Bowdry to Sally Whiting, 18 Oct 1815, William Lewis Bm (A)
John Bowdry to Sally Whitney, 18 Oct 1819 (same), John Moore JP (A)
[NOTE: This is one of several duplications in the Allen transcription)

- - - - - - - - - - - - -

BOWEN

MARRIAGES (RHEA)
Randel Bowen to Milla Becks, 31 Mar 1810 (same), Abraham Howard JP, James McCarty Bm (AR)

- - - - - - - - - - - - -

BOWER / BOWERS

MARRIAGES (RHEA)
James Bowers to Phoebe Kinman or Kinenon, 5 Jan 1819 (6 Jan), John Rice JP, Alexander Ferguson Bm (AR)
Rebecca Ann Bower to William Gibson q.v.
Samuel Bowers to Mary A. Underwood, 23 Feb 1842, R.N. Gillespie Bm (A) [1850 Roane Census: Samuel Bowers 30, Mary A. 27, Infant 2]
MARRIAGES (MEIGS)
Eliza J. Bower to Richard Grisham q.v.
Hiltha E. Bower to J.R. Cox q.v.
Martha M. Bower to Henry Johnston q.v.
MISCELLANEOUS (RHEA and MEIGS)
James Bower: JP(?) 1839
John Bowers: MG 1839,1840
William Bowers: MG 1839
" " Bondsman for William Whittenburg, 1839

- - - - - - - - - - - - -

BOWMAN / BOMAN

1830 RHEA CENSUS
Mary Boman 001011 - 022101 p. 365
1850 MEIGS CENSUS
James A Bowman 53 (NC)(Farmer), Mary Ann 20, Samuel H. 18 (Farmer), James L. 15 (Farmer), Kissiah 12, Elot M. 11, John F. 9, Tennessee M. 5 p. 734-170
MARRIAGES (RHEA)
Hannah Boman to Jesse Warren q.v.
John Bowman to Peggy Ann Noblett, 23 Dec 1835 (24 Dec), Matthew Hubbert JP, Thomas W. Noblett Bm (AR)
Samuel Bowman to Libby Smith, 14 May 1812 (same), John W. Wilkerson Bm (A)
MISCELLANEOUS (RHEA)
George Bowman: Land south of Tennessee River
Jno Bowman: PEMEC 1825
William Bowman: JP or MG 1840

- - - - - - - - - - - - -

BOX

1830 RHEA CENSUS
Samuel Box 4120001 - 10101 p. 375
1840 MEIGS CENSUS
Jackson F. Box 20001 - 00001 p. 241

MARRIAGES (RHEA)
Jackson F. Box to Elizabeth E. Baldwin, 10 Dec 1834, J.M. Collan [McCallon?] JP, William F. Dugan Bm (AR)

- - - - - - - - - - - -

BOXLEY / BOXLY

1840 MEIGS CENSUS
Burwell Boxly: 101001 - 0110001001 p. 244
1850 RHEA CENSUS
Burrell Boxley 51 (Va)(Farmer), Polly 39, John D. 10, Linville 7 p. 557-145
Malissa Boxley: see Sarah Rector
MARRIAGES (RHEA)
M. Boxley to W.R. Vicory q.v.

- - - - - - - - - - - -

BOYD

TAXES (RHEA)
1819 (Capt. W.S. Bradley's Dist.): John Boyd 2 lots
1850 RHEA CENSUS
Elizabeth A. Boyd 21, Joshua 18: see Catharine Mather
John Boyd 58 (Ga)(Wagonmaker), Clarissa 53 (NC), Samuel V. BROWN 23 (NC)(Wagonmaker), Elizabeth J. 16, John F. BOYD 20, Margaret V. DYAL 6 p. 539-44
MISCELLANEOUS (RHEA)
John Boyd: Resident of Town of Washington, 1816

- - - - - - - - - - - -

BOZE / BOAZ

TAXES (RHEA)
1823 (Capt. Wilson's Co.): Abednigo Boze 160a Sewee Cr.
MISCELLANEOUS (MEIGS)
Abednego Boaz: Hiwassee District resident

- - - - - - - - - - - -

BRACKET / BRACKETT

1840 MEIGS CENSUS
Amazaman Bracket 20001 - 00011 p. 226
1850 MEIGS CENSUS
Morgan Brackett 70 (NC)(Farmer), Elizabeth 60 (Va), Marion (m) 13, Rufus M. 11 p. 715-20
William Brackett 25, Eliza Jane 22 p. 715-18
MARRIAGES (MEIGS)
Morgan Bracket to Elizabeth Mayfield, 1 Nov 1841 (4 Nov), Absolem Foshee JP
William Bracket to Eliza J. Gilbreath, 21 Oct 1845 (22 Oct), John Seabourn JP
MISCELLANEOUS (MEIGS)
Joseph Bracket: JP(?) 1843
Richard Brackett: Cherokee Removal muster roll, 1836
Stephen Brackett: Private, Mexican War

- - - - - - - - - - - -

BRACKINS

1850 RHEA CENSUS
Alfred Brackins 30 (NC)(Farmer), Margaret 29, James G. 8, Susan A. 6, Sarah T. 4, Lucinda C. 1, John McCOY 26 (Farmer) p. 561-177
MARRIAGES (MEIGS)
Alfred Brckins to Margaret McCoy, 2 Jan 1841 (3 Jan), Wm Green MG

- - - - - - - - - - - -

BRADBURY

1850 RHEA CENSUS
James Bradbury 50 (Ga)(Carpenter), Polly 42 (SC), Sally 2 p. 629-609

- - - - - - - - - - - -

BRADFORD

1830 RHEA CENSUS
Richard Bradford 121001 - 11101 p. 366
MISCELLANEOUS (MEIGS)
Alexander B. Bradford: Hiwssee District resident
" " " *Knoxville Register*, Vol IX, No 422 (10 Sept 1824): Married on yesterday evening by the Rev. Thos H. Nelson, Maj. Alexander B. Bradford, Atty at law of the Western District, to Miss Darthula O. Miller, dau of Pleasant M. Miller Esq. of this vicinity.
James F. Bradford: Attorney, 1836
William B. Bradford: Hiwassee District, Lower Goodfield

- - - - - - - - - - - -

BRADLEY / BRADLY

TAXES (RHEA)
1819 (Capt. W.S. Bradley's Co.):
Bradley & Fulkerson 2 WP, 4 BP, ½a, 1 Town Lot
1823 (Capt. Brown's Co.):
Orlando Bradley 1 WP, 1 BP, 1 Town Lot
1850 RHEA CENSUS
Wm H. Bradley Unk (Va)(Farmer), Mary J. 22, Berryman G. 9, Thoms H. 6, John W. 2, Mary C. 1/12 p. 598-390
1850 MEIGS CENSUS
George W. Bradley 29 (Va)(Waggoner), Lucrecia 28, Trefonia (f) 20, James A. 5, Charles W. 3 p. 793-624
MARRIAGES (RHEA)
William H. Brady or Bradley to Mary Jane Mathis, 13 Apr 1840 (same), William H. Bell MG, Berryman C. Mather Bm (AR)
MARRIAGES (MEIGS)
Levi Bradly to Nancy Green, 22 Dec 1841 (23 Dec), A. Fooshee JP
MISCELLANEOUS (RHEA)
Charles Bradley: Signed petition to move Indian Agency
William Bradley: Bondsman for Audley P. Defrise, 1820
William L. Bradley: Bondsman for Washington John De-Witt, 1820

- - - - - - - - - - - -

BRADSHAW

1840 MEIGS CENSUS
Gamon Bradshaw 21001 - 01001 p. 234
MISCELLANEOUS (RHEA)
Samuel Bradshaw: Signed petition to move Indian Agency
MISCELLANEOUS (MEIGS)
Gannon Bradshaw: JP(?) 1841

- - - - - - - - - - - - -

BRADY / BRADEY

TAXES (RHEA)
1819 (Capt. John Ramsey's Co.): Charles Brady 150a
Jeremiah Brady 1 WP
1823 (Capt. McCall's Co.): Charles Brady 100a
Farley Brady 1 WP
1830 RHEA CENSUS
Aaron Brady 212001 - 10000100001 p. 362
Farlee Brady 12001 - 11002 p. 387
Frederick Brady 00001 - 000000001 p. 360
Merrel Brady 10001 - 1001 p. 390
1840 RHEA CENSUS
Farley Brady 020101 - 1301001
Merrel Brady 221001 - 01101
Wiley Brady 11001 - 00001001
1840 MEIGS CENSUS
Frederick Brady 0000001 - 0 p. 241
1850 RHEA CENSUS
Charles Brady 26 (Farmer), Mary L. 27, Farley 2, Micajah 8/12 p. 556-142
Farley Brady 52 (Farmer), Sarah 33, Smith 23 (farmer), Mahala 19, Patsy 16, Polly 14, Samuel 13, Elizabeth 10, Caroline 7, Owen 4, James K.P. 1, Mary RICHARDS 45 (Va), William SNELSON 47 (Stiller) p. 561-178
Merril Brady 43 (Farmer), Nancy 38, Farly 16 (Farmer), Pleasant 16 (Farmer), Reuben J. 14, Charles 12, William 10, Stephen 8, Samuel H. 5, Sarah A. 2, Hannah E. 2/12, James BRADY 22 (Farmer) p. 538-37
1850 MEIGS CENSUS
Jane Brady 33: see Harriet Butler
MARRIAGES (RHEA)
Charles Bradey to Polly Miller, 5 Sept 1821 (same), J. Fine JP, Frederick Bradey Bm (AR)
Charles Brady to Mary Limera Clack, 25 Jan 1847 (28 June), William Gwin JP or Bm (R) [dates written in records as above]
Elizabeth Brady to James Pharris q.v.
Farley Brady to Betsy Smith, 29 Dec 1822 (same), Thomas Price JP, George Henry Bm (AR)
Isaac Brady to Rebecca Goddy, 11 Nov 1835, William Fares Bm (R)
John Brady to Nancy Daniel, 21 Sept 1833 (24 Sept), Isaac Baker JP, Alexander Vines Bm (AR)
Mary Bradye to Dennis McClendon q.v.
Merral Brady to Nancy Munday, 20 Sept 1826 or 1825 (21 Sept), John Farmer MG, Samuel Cunningham Bm (AR)
Owen Brady to Nancy Butler, 29 May 1810, Charles Brady Bm (A)
Polly Brady to John Farris q.v.
Sally Bradey to John Burton q.v.
Wyly M. Brady to Elizabeth Cane or Case, 3 Aug 1839 (4 Aug), W.B. Gordon MG, John Gladden Bm (AR) [1850 VanBuren Census: Willie Brady 34, Elizabeth 38, William 10, Sarah Jane 8, Lavina 6, James CASE 15, Sarah COMB 80]
MISCELLANEOUS (RHEA and MEIGS)
Charles Brady: Bondsman for Owen Brady, 1810
" " Bondsman for Edmond Holt, 1819
" " Bondsman for William Blackwell, 1819
Farley Bradey: Bondsman for Samuel Cunningham, 1820
Frederick Bradey: Bondsman for Charles Bradey, 1831
Merrill Brady: Pvt., Mexican War (died during war)
R. L. Brady Jr.: Signed petition to move Indian Agency

- - - - - - - - - - - - -

BRAKEBILL

TAXES (RHEA)
1819 (Capt. Wm McCray's Co.): Henry Brakebill 1 WP
1823 (Capt. Howerton's Old Co.): Henry Brakebill 1 WP

- - - - - - - - - - - - -

BRAMLETT

1840 MEIGS CENSUS
Jesse Bramlet 00001-0001 p. 227
1850 RHEA CENSUS
Garlington Bramlett 32 (SC)(Farmer), Mary 33 (SC), Nancy A. 12 (SC), William E. 6 (SC), John M. 2 (SC), Thomas HOUSTON 15 (SC) p. 595-377

- - - - - - - - - - - - -

BRANDON

1830 RHEA CENSUS
Adam Brandon 0010001 - 10001 p. 357
Lewis Brandon 1010001 - 010201 p. 358
Philip Brandon 00001 - 10101 p. 358
1850 MEIGS CENSUS
Hiram Brandon 38 (Farmer), Louisa 38 (Va), William D. 22 (Va)(Farmer), Granville H. 8 (Farmer), Silas W. 16 (Farmer), Looney (f) 12, James P. 10, Martha Ann 3, Sarah Jane 2 p. 779-522 [H.B. Brandon married Louisa Waide on 1 Sept 1845 in McMinn Co]
Thomas Brandon 58 (NC)(Brickmason), Elinder 54 (NC), Nancy M. 22, Mary 20, James 18, Emily 14, Eliza 11, Columbus 9, Hudson 7 p. 715-21
MARRIAGES (RHEA)
James Brandon to Patience Lawson, 4 Jan 1819, James Blakeley Bm (A)
Malinda Brandon to Hiram Newkirk q.v.
Phillip Brandon to Elizabeth Childress, 15 Nov 1828 (16 Nov), Stephen Winton JP (AR)
MISCELLANEOUS (RHEA)
Hugh H. Brandon: Bondsman for Hiram Newkirk, 1831

- - - - - - - - - - - - -

BRANHAM

1850 MEIGS CENSUS
James Branham 33 (Farmer), Sally 35, William 17 (Farmer), John 15, Martha 3, Elizabeth 8 p. 768-436
MISCELLANEOUS (MEIGS)
Thomas Branham: JP(?) 1845

- - - - - - - - - - - - -

BRAZELTON / BRASELTON

TAXES (RHEA)
1819 (Capt. John Robinson's Co.): Isaac Brazelton 200a
1823 (Capt. Braselton's Co.): Shepherd Braselton 1 WP
MARRIAGES (RHEA)
Elizabeth Braselton to Adam Humbolt or Humbart q.v.
Sally Braselton to James Lawrence q.v.
MISCELLANEOUS (RHEA and MEIGS)
Isaac Brazelton: Bondsman for James Hall, 1836
J. Brazelton [Isaac?]: Hiwassee District, Sewee Cr. area
Stephen Brazelton: Bondsman for William Buster, 1820
" " Bondsman for Wiley Lewis, 1822

- - - - - - - - - - - - -

BREEDEN / BREEDING

TAXES (RHEA)
1819 (Capt. John Ramsey's Co.):
Byrum Breeding 1 WP, 1 BP, 205a
1823 (Capt. McCall's Co.):
Byrum Breeding 1 BP, 185a Piney River
1840 RHEA CENSUS
Beaty Breeden 210001 - 010001001
Stephen Breeden 10001 - 21001
1850 RHEA CENSUS
Baty Breeding 43 (Va)(Farmer), Lucinda 41, Adeline J. 19, James M. 16 (Farmer), Byron F. 14, William T. 1, Stephen A. 9, Margaret A. 3 p. 554-127
Stephen Breeding 39 (Farmer), Mary 38, Hannah J. 16, Sarah A. 14, Cyntha A. 12, Thomas J. 10, Susan M. 8, Mary D. 5, Lucinda M. 3, Abby E. 10/12, Sarah STACY 25, Pleasant BELL 14 p. 556-140
Thomas Breeding 45 (Va)(Farmer), Margaret 31 p. 556-139
MARRIAGES (RHEA)
Beaty Breeding to Lucinda Thompson, 9 June 1831, John Pardee MMEC, Stephen Breeding Bm (AR)
Bryant Breeding to Mariah Miller, 14 Nov 1834 (15 Nov), William Green JP, Baty Breeding Bm (AR) [1850 Overton Census: Bryant Breeding 42, Mariah 39, Susannah 14, Manerva 12, Margaret 10, Thomas 8, John 6, Susan 4, Evan 2, William 3/12]
Steven or Stephen Breeding to Polly Holloman, 23 May 1833 (10 June), John Pardee MMEC, Beaty Breeding Bm (AR)
MISCELLANEOUS (RHEA)
Beaty Breeding: Bondsman for Bryant Breeding, 1834
" " Bondsman for Stephen Breeding, 1833
Byrum Breeding: Bondsman for John Murphree, 1819
" " Bondsman for Landon Rector, 1822
" " Bondsman for George W. Black, 1823
Stephen Breeding: Bondsman for Beaty Breeding, 1831

- - - - - - - - - - - - -

BREEDWELL / BREDWELL / BRIDWELL / BIRDWELL

TAXES (RHEA)
1819 (Capt. McGill's Co.): George Birdwell 200a
1823 (Capt. Smith's Co.): George W. Bridwell 1 WP
1830 RHEA CENSUS
Augustine Bredwell 0120001 - 111101 p. 356
George Breedwell 21001 - 101001 p. 374
Hiram Breedwell 10001 - 22001 p. 386
John Birdwell 22010001 - 01110101 p. 353
Yoden Breedwell 101011 - 23101 p. 374
1840 MEIGS CENSUS
Julian Breedwell 01 - 012001 p. 238
1850 MEIGS CENSUS
John Breedwell 37 (Ky), Lorinda 36 (NC), Hannah 16, Eliza Ann 13, William 12, Jackson 11, George 9, Joseph 8, Nathan 6, Peter 1 p. 714-12 [John Bridwell or Breeden married Lurana Yoakley on 24 Feb 1833 in Roane Co]
Juda Breedwell 30, Elizabeth 17, Mary Ann 20, Nathan 18 (Farmer), Nancy 17 p. 766-420
Julian Breedwell (f) 57 p. 741-228
MARRIAGES (RHEA)
Aidin Braidwell or Bridwell to Juludian or Julindian Norman, 4 June 1825 (5 June), Thomas Cox JP, Elis Bridwell Bm (AR)
Lucinda Bridwell to William Hope [Houpt] q.v.
Rebecca Bridwell to Nathan Parksdale q.v.
MARRIAGES (MEIGS)
Casander Breedwell to David Jones q.v.
Margaret Breedwell to R. Smith q.v.
MISCELLANEOUS (RHEA and MEIGS)
Adam Breedwell: Land south of Tennessee River
Armsted Breedwell: Hiwassee District, Sewee Creek area [1850 Bradley Census: Armersted Breadwald 60, Elizabeth 57, Stanford 26, Elizabeth 19, Peter 14, Lucinda 12, Armanda 10]
Augustine Breedwell: Member, Goodfield Baptist Church of Christ, 1827
George Breedwell: Hiwassee District, Lower Goodfield area
John M. Breedwell: JP(?) 1843
Nancy Breedwell: Member, Goodfield Baptist Church etc.
Sanford Bridwell: Hiwassee District, Sewee Creek area
Washington Breedwell: Hiwassee District, Sewee Creek [1850 Monroe Census: Washington Breedwell 49 (Va), Ufama 49, William 27, Louisa 15, Robert 13, Elizabeth 10, Henry 7]

- - - - - - - - - - - - -

BREWER

1840 RHEA CENSUS
Ambrose Brewer 10001 - 0001
Elijah Brewer 00010001 - 0110001
Zabadee Brewer 0001 - 0001
1850 RHEA CENSUS
Elijah Brewer 56 (NC)(Farmer), Mary 58 (NC), Webby A. 23 p. 536-21
MARRIAGES (RHEA)
Dicy Brewer to Solomon Sively q.v.
Lewis Brewer to Elizabeth Danby, 12 Nov 1845 (13 Nov), Jesse Thompson JP, Joseph Windfield Bm (AR)

Lidia Brewer to James Hayes q.v.
Maloney Brewer to Alexander Smith q.v.
Mary Brewer to Pleasant Munday q.v.
Rebecca Brewer to Joseph Winfield q.v.
Sally Ann Brewer to Charles Adkins q.v.
Zebadee Brown or Brewer to Sarah Gipson, 6 Aug 1839 (no return), James Hayes Bm (AR)

MISCELLANEOUS (RHEA)
Nathan Brewer: Bondsman for Charles Adkins, 1830
Zebeedee Brewer: Bondsman for James M. Price, 1840

- - - - - - - - - - - - -

BREWSTER

1850 MEIGS CENSUS
Benjamin Brewster 27 (Farmer), Nancy 22, Mary F. 3, James T. 2, Malissa Jane 1 p. 769-441

- - - - - - - - - - - - -

BRICKER

MISCELLANEOUS (MEIGS)
David Bricker: JP(?) 1841

- - - - - - - - - - - - -

BRIDGES

MISCELLANEOUS (MEIGS)
Aaron Bridges: Cherokee Removal muster roll, 1836

- - - - - - - - - - - - -

BRIGGS

1830 RHEA CENSUS
Daniel Briggs 211001 - 110001 p. 359
James Briggs 10001 - 0001 p. 388
M. D. Briggs 11001 - 01001 p. 389

1850 MEIGS CENSUS
James D. Briggs 21 (Blacksmith), Mary Ann 23 p. 812-756
Nathan B. Briggs 50 (NC)(Blacksmith), Eliza 46 (Va), Polly Ann 27, Caroline S. 14, Jane 19, Daniel 16 (Farmer), Racheal 12, George C. 10, William M. 8 p. 811-755

MARRIAGES (RHEA)
James Briggs to Polly Kelly, 3 Jan 1829 (4 Jan), Daniel Briggs JP (A)

MARRIAGES (MEIGS)
James Briggs to Mary Fooshee, 10 Apr 1850, Harvey Green Sur

MISCELLANEOUS (RHEA and MEIGS)
Daniel Briggs: Hiwassee District, Moore's Chapel area
" " MG 1825-1835, 1838
N.B. Briggs: MG 1848

- - - - - - - - - - - - -

BRIGHTWELL / BRITEWELL

TAXES (RHEA)
1823 (Capt. Brown's Co.): Leonard Brightwell 1 WP

1830 RHEA CENSUS
Leonard Brightwell 121001 - 3111001 p. 368

1840 MEIGS CENSUS
Nancy Brightwell 1011 - 0210001 p. 228
Sally Brightwell 0 - 0001000001 p. 233
William W. Brightwell 10001 - 00001 p. 228

1850 MEIGS CENSUS
Elgin Brightwell 27 (Farmer), Lety B. 16, Telitha Jane 6 p. 732-154
Ganum Brightwell 26 (Farmer), Nancy 25, James 9, Lucinda 6 p. 755-341
Nancy Brightwell 55 (NC), Matilda 12, Jefferson 11 p. 747-275

MARRIAGES (RHEA)
Lucinda Britewell to William Hope q.v.

MARRIAGES (MEIGS)
Elgin Brightwell to Eliza Armstrong, 19 Aug 1843 (20 Aug), Jesse Martin JP
Elgin Brightwell to Mary Jane Houser, 24 Oct 1850, Gann Brightwell Sur
Ganium Brightwell to Nancy Walker, 29 Dec 1839 (same), B.F. McKenzie JP
Ganium Brightwell to Nancy Houser, 24 Sept 1850, J.W. Williams Sur
Milly Ann Brightwell to Ebenezer Harden q.v.

MISCELLANEOUS (RHEA)
Leonard Brightwell: Bondsman for Montford Frazier, 1825

MISCELLANEOUS (MEIGS)
Edward Brightwell: JP(?) 1840
Elgin Brightwell: 4th Sgt., Mexican War
Ganum Brightwell: Musician, Mexican War
Gann Brightwell: Surety for Elgin Brightwell, 1850

- - - - - - - - - - - - -

BRIMER

1840 RHEA CENSUS Wm Brimer 120001 - 001001

- - - - - - - - - - - - -

BRINDLES

MARRIAGES (RHEA)
Betsy Brindles to Levi Chancy q.v.

- - - - - - - - - - - - -

BRISENTINE

1840 RHEA CENSUS
Clem Brisentine 1121001-210001

- - - - - - - - - - - - -

BRITTIN / BRITON / BRITTIAN

1830 RHEA CENSUS
Thomas Briton 112001 - 2000001 p. 60

1840 RHEA CENSUS
Andrew Brittian 1101401 - 012101

1850 RHEA CENSUS
Andrew Brittin 54 (Va)(Farmer), Nancy 49 (SC), Andrew B. 19, John 13 p. 627-588

MARRIAGES (RHEA)
Catherine R. Brittin to Alfred Caldwell q.v.
Penelope Brittin to William Caldwell q.v.
Susan Britten to Peter Rolow q.v.

MISCELLANEOUS (MEIGS)
Nathaniel Britain: Hiwassee District, Lower Goodfield area

- - - - - - - - - - - - -

BROCK / BROCKE / BRACK

1830 RHEA CENSUS
Eli Brock 00101 - 2101 p. 358
1840 RHEA CENSUS
Madison Brack 00001 - 0001
MARRIAGES (RHEA)
Harriet T. Brock to William K. Alexander q.v.
Matilda C. Brock to William Clingan q.v.
William Brocke to Viney Walker, 18 Mar 1848 (same), Wm H. Bell MG (R)
MISCELLANEOUS (MEIGS)
John Brock: JP(?) 1845
William Brock: Private, Mexican War

- - - - - - - - - - - - -

BROGDON

MARRIAGES (RHEA)
Meredith Brogdon to Nancy Knight, 23 Sept 1823 (same), Thomas Cox JP, Lewis Knight Bm (AR)
Sarah Brogdon to John Fitzgerral q.v.

- - - - - - - - - - - - -

BROOKS / BROOK / BROKS / BROOX

TAXES (RHEA)
1808 (Joseph Brooks' List):
Joseph Brooks 1 WP, 168a Sale Creek
1819 (Capt. McCall's .): Mary Brooks 168a
1823 (Capt. Smith's Co.): Leonard Brooks 1 WP
(Capt. Jackson's Co.): Mary Brook 1 Town Lot
1830 RHEA CENSUS
Leonard Brooks 0000101 - 1222101 p. 374
1840 MEIGS CENSUS
Joel Brook 11001 - 11011 p. 235
John Broox 201101 - 210001 p. 236
Leonard Broox 01001001 - 001101001 p. 230
Tarlton Broox 00201001 - 00011101 p. 238
William Broox 00001 - 1101 p. 228
MARRIAGES (RHEA)
Elizbeth Brooks to Joshua Givins q.v.
Irena Brooks to Cawfield T. Tillery q.v.
Joel Brooks to Milly Keenum, 24 Oct 1831 (26 Oct), Daniel Briggs MG, Tavernor Runyon Bm (AR)
Polly Brook to William Hamie q.v.
Sally Brooks to John Ramsey q.v.
Sarah Brooks to James G. Moore q.v.
MARRIAGES (MEIGS)
A.J. Brooks to Mary Ann Warick, 9 Jan 1845 (12 Jan), T.B. McElwee JP
Belinda Broks to Hugh Tillery q.v.
John Brooks to Rebecca Hall, 30 May 1840 (31 May), John Seabourn JP
Letitia Brooks to Harvy McKenzie q.v.
Leonard Brooks to Margaret Kerr, 23 Dec 1841 (same), D.L. Godsey MG
William Brooks to Malinda McClanahan, 9 May 1838

MISCELLANEOUS (RHEA)
Joseph Brooks: JP 1808; Trustee 1808-1809
Leonard Brooks: Bondsman for John Ramsey, 1824
Moses Brook: Bondsman for William Hamie, 1835
R.W. Brooks: Signed petition to move Indian Agency
MISCELLANEOUS (MEIGS)
A.J. Brooks: JP(?) 1846
Leonard Brooks: Hiwassee District, Sewee Creek area
" " Deeded land for Decatur, 1836
" " Com. to construct Decatur Courthouse
" " Common School Com., District 2, 1838
Tarlton Brooks: Ocoee District

- - - - - - - - - - - - -

BROOKSHIRE

MARRIAGES (RHEA)
Elender Brookshire to Jacob Webb q.v.

- - - - - - - - - - - - -

BROWDER

1840 MEIGS CENSUS
James Browder 0110001 - 301101 p. 224
James Browder 100001 - 10001 p. 228
William Browder 1111101 - 1010001 p. 247
1850 MEIGS CENSUS
Louisa Browder 30, Mary 13, John 11, Nancy 5, William 3 p. 730-133
MARRIAGES (MEIGS)
Albert Browder to Gemima Matlock, 21 Dec 1846 (24 Dec), T.B. McElwee JP
James Browder to Louisa E. Childress, 19 Dec 1843
Louisa E. Browder to Jonathan Wood q.v.
MISCELLANEOUS (RHEA and MEIGS)
James Browder: War of 1812
" " Common School Com, District 1, 1838

- - - - - - - - - - - - -

BROWN

TAXES (RHEA)
1808 (John Henry's List): John Brown 1 WP, 100a
Thoms G. Brown 1 WP, 100a
1819 (Capt W.S. Bradley's Dist): Jacob Brown 1 WP, 1 TL
(Capt. McGill's Co.): John Brown 1 WP
1823 (Capt. Piper's Co.): Alexander Brown 1 WP
(Capt. Howard's Co.): Anthony Brown 1 WP, 50a
(Capt. Piper's Co.): Ezekiel Brown 1 WP
(Capt. Brown's Co.): Jacob Brown 1 WP, 2 TL
1830 RHEA CENSUS
Abner Brown 020001 - 000101 p. 364
D. W. Brown 000001 - 21001 p. 390
Isaac Brown 000000001 - 000000001 p. 360
Jacob Brown 31110001 - 010101 p. 383
Jeremiah Brown 111101 - 000001 p. 363
1840 RHEA CENSUS
Robert A. Brown 200001 - 00001
1840 MEIGS CENSUS
Abraham Brown 00001 - 20011 p. 241
Alexander Brown 0001101 - 0010101 p. 245
Elizabeth Brown 00111 - 0020001 p. 237
Jesse Brown 00001 - 10001 p. 246

Joseph Brown 1212001 - 1100001 p. 247
William Brown 0 - 000001 p. 245

1850 RHEA CENSUS

George W. Brown 27 (Farmer), Elizabeth 23, Artensa 1, Robert DOUGLASS 22 (SC)(Blacksmith) p. 635-658 [G.W. Brown married Elizabeth Harold on 28 July 1845 in McMinn Co.]
John Brown 37 (NC)(Farmer), Mary E. 38 (NC), Martha C. 15 (NC), William P. 13 (NC), Minerva 8 (NC), Peter A. 5 (NC), Elizabeth J. 2 (NC), John T. 2/12, Permelia MOORE Unk (Va)(black) p. 575-256
Lucy Brown 70 (Va): see Jack Durham
Samuel V. Brown 23, Elizabeth 16: see John Boyd

1850 MEIGS CENSUS

Alexander Brown 53 (Farmer), Mary 50 p. 817-794 [Alexander Brown married Polly Sharp on 19 Mar 1818 in Roane Co]
Edward H. Brown 40 (Va)(Farmer), Charlotte 36, Henry 17, Martha Ann 13, Sarah 12, Mitchell 8, Mary 6, James K.P. 3, Abee Jane 1 p. 716-30 [Edward H. Brown married Charlotte Taylor on 5 Aug 1831 in Roane Co.]
James Brown 61 (SC)(Farmer), Elizabeth 61 (SC), Hanah 21, Jackson 20 (Farmer), Joseph J. 5 p. 805-712 [James Brown married Betsy Hacker on 7 Feb 1819 in Roane Co]
Jesse Brown 32 (Farmer), Mary 30, Isaac 8, John 6, Newton 4, Elisha 1 p. 781-540
John K. Brown 30 (Merchant), Sarah E. 23, William A. 6, Mary C. 4, Seletha Jane 1, Adaline COLLINS 18 p. 817-796
Joseph Brown 55, Catherine 54, William M. 26 (Farmer), Thomas 24 (Farmer), Rebecca 22, James 20, Jeremiah 18, Nancy Jane 16, Joseph 14 p. 807-726
Ruth Brown 42 (Ky), McNail 22 (Farmer), Columbus 18 (Farmer), Mahala 16, Betsy Ann 13, Anna 9 p. 810-742
Thomas Brown 49 (Va)(Farmer), Nancy W. 52 (Va), William B. 21 (School Teacher), Robert H. 20 (Farmer), Henry G. 18 (Farmer), Thomas O. 16, Malinda A. 13 p. 718-42
William Brown 25, Betsy Ann 22, Benjamin J. 1 p. 817-795

MARRIAGES (RHEA)

Abraham Brown to Hetty Pharis, 24 Aug 1835 (30 Aug), William Green MG, Seabourn Johnson Bm (AR)
Ann Brown to James Paul q.v.
Anthony Brown Jr. to Sarah Cranmore, 15 May 1822 (same), John Cozby JP, George Gothard Bm (AR)
Esabella Brown to Sylus Shoat q.v.
G.W. Brown to Elizabeth Garwood, 11 May 1848 (same), R.M. Hickey MG (R)
Hannah Brown to Jackson Howerton q.v.
Isaac Brown to Sally Garrett, 27 May 1826, Elijah Runnals Bm (A)
Jane Brown to James Poteet q.v.
John Brown to Betsy Truett, 18 Nov 1809 (same), Azariah David Bm [probably 1850 Hamilton Census: John Brown 65, Elizabeth 60, William 35, Elizabeth CARR 25, Elizabeth BROWN 77, Jesse MUMFORD 70, Henry BARNES 20]
Mariah Brown to James Lay q.v.
Nancy Brown to Bright Johnson q.v.
Nancey Brown to John L. Thompson q.v.
Rebecca Brown to Abner Royal q.v.
Robert A. Brown to Mary J.R. Gillenwaters, 22 Oct 1836, R.N. Gillespie Bm (A)
Sarah Brown to Robert Douglas q.v.
Solomon Brown to Nancy Mayberry, 6 May 1823 (8 May), Wm Kennedy JP, Simon Jackson Bm (AR)

MARRIAGES (MEIGS)

Margaret S. Brown to B.F. Howell q.v.
Martha Brown to Leander Faris q.v.
Nancy E. Brown to S.W. Woods q.v.
Richard Brown to Luvena Lewis, 15 Dec 1848 (16 Dec), Robert Cooley JP
Suleta Brown to Peter Huff q.v.

MISCELLANEOUS (RHEA)

Abraham Brown: Bondsman for Hugh Harris, 1834
David Brown: Bondsman for William Bice, 1813
Isaac H. Brown: Bondsman for Thomas W. Noblett, 1827
Jacob Brown: Bondsman for William Gwinn, 1818
" " Bondsman for Walter B. Paine, 1822
" " Bondsman for David Leuty, 1825
John Brown: Bondsman for John Lauderdale, 1809
Thomas G. Brown: Ranger, 1808
William Brown: Solicitor, 1808

MISCELLANEOUS (MEIGS)

James Brown: Private, Mexican War
John Brown: MG 1838
" " Hiwassee District resident
John K. Brown: JP 1841-42, 1846-48
" " " Chairman of County Court, 1849
N. R. Brown: JP(?) 1844

BROYLES / BROLES / BROILES / BROILS

1830 RHEA CENSUS

Mathius Broles 0211101 - 2110001 p. 387
[NOTE: others have shown this entry as Nathan Broles, but I believe it to be Mathius. B.J.B.]

1840 RHEA CENSUS

Cornelius Broyles 0112001001 - 0012001 [son of Daniel]
Daniel Broyles age 80 [Revolutionry War Pensioner; son of Cyrus and Mary Wilhoit Broyles]
Mathias Broyles 10121001 - 010121001 [son of Ephraim and Grace McCain Broyles]
Thomas J. Broils 10001 - 1002 [son of Cornelius and Mary Farley Broyles]

1850 RHEA CENSUS

Cornelius Broyles 57 (Farmer), Mary 57 (Va), Mary H. 24, Onslow G.M. 22 (Farmer), Robert C. 17 (Farmer), Sarah M. DEARING 12 p. 598-390 [Cornelius and Mary Frley married in White Co. about 1814]
Daniel Broyles 46 (Farmer), Harriet N. 34, Isaac N. 5, Mary V. 3, Eliza T. 1, Polly THOMPSON 61 (NC), Thomas R. BROYLES 21 (Farmer) p. 564-322 [Daniel was son of Daniel Broyles]
Eglentine A. Broyles 21: see Wm Whittenburg
Joseph A. Broyles 28 (Blacksmith), Barbary A. 26, Franklin M. 4, Doctor G. 1 p. 600-411
Mary E. Broyles 26: see Samuel Whittenburg
Nile M. Broyles 31 (Farmer), Elenor C. 22, Mark W. 2 p. 556-137

Sanders D. Broyles 26 (Farmer), Delila 27, William T. 10/12, Samuel HOUSTON 10 p. 579-281

MARRIAGES (RHEA)

Daniel Broyles to Harriet Thompson, 10 Nov 1843 (A)

Eliza Broyles to William A. Ganaway q.v.

Ira D. Broyles to Mariah Hill, 31 Jan 1831 (3 Feb), John Pardee MMEC, Christopher Whittenburg Bm (AR) [Ira, son of Matthias and Barbara Lotspeich Broyles]

Jane Broyles to Quinn M. Hill q.v.

Joseph A. Broyles to Barbara Ann Thompson, 24 Feb 1843 (same), Jesse Rector JP (A)

Joseph D. Broyles or Bayles to Mary Casteel, 1 Feb 1838 (same), Wm B. Cozby JP, Freeland Casteel Bm (AR)

S. D. Broyles to Delila Compton, 8 Oct 1848 (same), J.P. Collins JP (A)

MARRIAGES (MEIGS)

Amos Broyles to Clemenza L. Wilson, 1 July 1845 (same), T.K. Munsey MG, Mark H. Wilson Bm [1850 Bradley Census: Amos Broyles 36, Clemenza 31, Elbert S. 4, Manry A.S. 2, Clemenza J. 1/12]

Nile M. Broyles to Elenor C. Wilson, 20 May 1845 (no return), William H. Stockton Bm
[Amos and Nile Broyles were sons of Mathias and Barbara Lotspeich Broyles; Clemenza, Elenor, and Mark H. were children of Wm C. and Elizabeth Stockton Wilson; Wm H. Stockton was brother of Elizabeth]

MISCELLANEOUS (RHEA)

Daniel Broyles:	JP 1845-50
" "	Revolutionary War pensioner, 1841 list
Ira D. Broyles:	Trustee, Sulphur Springs Presbyterian Meeting House, 1834
Matthias Broyles:	Trustee, Sulphur Springs Meeting House 1834; Methodist Church, 1841
Nathan S. Broyles:	Bondsman for Lincey McCary, 1837
" " "	Bondsman for Mark Stacy, 1839
" " "	Bondsman for James Carvey, 1840

\- - - - - - - - - - - -

BRUMLEY

1840 RHEA CENSUS

Lewis Brumley 010001 - 12102001

\- - - - - - - - - - - -

BRUMMET

MARRIAGES (RHEA)

George W. Brummet to Unity Ryon, 4 May 1835, V.H. Giles JP, Harris Ryan Bm

\- - - - - - - - - - - -

BRUSHIERS

MISCELLANEOUS (RHEA)

William Brushiers: Bondsman for William Tomison 1824

\- - - - - - - - - - - -

BRYAN

1850 MEIGS CENSUS

Joseph T. Bryan 31 (NC)(Merchant), Morgan 29 (NC) (Merchant), Robert 27 (NC)(Merchant), Samuel J. 18 (NC)(Merchant), Francis 7 (NC), Letis Ann 5 (NC) p. 796-652

\- - - - - - - - - - - -

BRYANT

1830 RHEA CENSUS

Wm Bryant 210000 - 11001 p. 365

MARRIAGES (RHEA)

James Bryant to Elizabeth Sexton, 9 July 1833 (same), A. David JP, William Gross Bm (AR)

John Bryant to Polly Mitchell, 29 Oct 1832 (same), John Farmer MG, John Gladden Bm (AR)

Stacy Bryant to William Talley q.v.

\- - - - - - - - - - - -

BRYSON / BRISON / BRUSON

TAXES (RHEA)

1819 (Capt. McGill's Co.):	Abraham Bryson 1 WP
	Hannah Bryson 200a
	Jacob Bryson 1 WP
1823 (Capt. Howard's Co.):	Abraham Bryson 1 WP
	Hannah Bryson 200a

1830 RHEA CENSUS

A. Bryson 101001 - 12201 p. 381

Hannah Bryson 0 - 0000000001 p. 381

1840 RHEA CENSUS

Abram Brison 00101001 - 0032001

1850 RHEA CENSUS

Abraham Bryson 58 (Ga)(Farmer), Sarah 56, Jane S. 30, Hannah 25, Thomas ANDERSON 32 (Farmer) p. 627-590

Andrew J. Bryson 34 (Farmer), Margaret J. 26, Sarah A. 6, John H. 4, Mary H. 3, James F. 5/12 p. 627-589

MARRIAGES (RHEA)

Abraham Bryson to Sally Day, 14 Oct 1812 (same), John Day Bm (AR)

Andrew J. Bryson to Margaret Witt, 27 Apr 1843 (same), Washington Morgan JP (A)

Caroline Bryson to Lafayette Norman q.v.

Jacob Bryson to Rachael or Rebecca Moore, 18 Dec 1820 (same), Isaac Benson Bm (AR)

Jane Bryson to Matthias Benson q.v.

Mary Bryson to John W. Foust q.v.

Nancy Bryson to B.F. Benson q.v.

Naomi Bryson to Isaac Benson q.v.

Sarah Bryson to John F. Walker q.v.

MISCELLANEOUS (RHEA)

Andrew J. Bryson: Bondsman for John W. Foust, 1839

John Bryson: Mexican War

\- - - - - - - - - - - -

BUCK

1830 RHEA CENSUS

Peggy Buck: 0021 - 0000001 p. 392

\- - - - - - - - - - - -

BUCKHANON / BUCHANNON

1840 MEIGS CENSUS
Mathew Buckhanon 000011 - 1001 p. 234
1850 MEIGS CENSUS
Joseph Buckhanon 25 (Farmer), Margaret 21, William R. 1 p. 815-785 [Joseph married Margaret Dolen on 13 Dec 1848 in McMinn Co.]
Mathew Buckhanon 40 (Va)(Merchant), Phebe 29, John S. 8, Jonah 5, Robert W.S. 1 p. 759-374
MARRIAGES (RHEA)
John Buchannon to Caty Areheart, 9 Nov 1822 (no return) (AR)
Polly Buchannon to Benjamin Putnam q.v.

- - - - - - - - - - - - -

BUCKNER

1840 MEIGS CENSUS
Barrow Buckner 0120001 - 0120001 p. 242
James Buckner 1100001 - 0000001 p. 233
Paschal Buckner 1200001 - 200001001 p. 233
MARRIAGES (MEIGS)
Elizabeth Buckner to Yance Norman q.v.
Katherine Buckner to Charles Williams q.v.
MISCELLANEOUS (MEIGS)
Burrow Buckner: Mexican War (discharged on surgeon's certificate)

- - - - - - - - - - - - -

BUFFINGTON

1850 RHEA CENSUS
William W. Buffington 17: see Thomas Russ

- - - - - - - - - - - - -

BULGER

MARRIAGES (RHEA)
Michael J. Bulger to Pamela Donald, 26 May 1828 (27 May), Wm M. Woods MG, Isaac Benson Bm (AR)

- - - - - - - - - - - - -

BULLARD / BULLERD

1830 RHEA CENSUS
Isaac Bullerd 1220001 - 010011 p. 370
MARRIAGES (RHEA)
Ann Bullard to Joseph Gamble q.v.
Peggy Bullard to Jesse Morris q.v.
MISCELLANEOUS (MEIGS)
Bower Bullard: Hiwassee District, Burkett Chapel area
Isaac Bullard: " " " " "

- - - - - - - - - - - - -

BULLER

TAXES (RHEA)
1823 (Capt. Jackson's Co.): Isaac Buller 1 WP
Joseph Buller 1 WP

- - - - - - - - - - - - -

BULLOCK

MARRIAGES (RHEA)
Peter H. Bullock to Jemima C. Morris, 5 Feb 1835, John Igou Bm (A)

- - - - - - - - - - - - -

BUNCH

MARRIAGES (RHEA)
Keziah Bunch to John Guthrey q.v.
MARRIAGES (MEIGS)
Charity Bunch to Francis M. Phariss q.v.
Nancy Bunch to Amos Hardin q.v.
Paul Bunch to Mahalda Goforth, 22 Dec 1849 (23 Dec), Andrew Johns MG
MISCELLANEOUS (MEIGS)
Martin Bunch: JP(?) 1843

- - - - - - - - - - - - -

BUNDREN

MARRIAGES (RHEA)
James Bundren to Sally Redwine, 29 Aug 1831 (3 Sept), James Whitten MG, Claiborn Bundren Bm (AR)
MISCELLANEOUS (RHEA)
Claiborn Bundren: Bondsman for James Bundren, 1831

- - - - - - - - - - - - -

BUNLINS

MARRIAGES (RHEA)
Turney Bunlins to Jane Genings [Jenings], 24 Dec 1812 (same), Wm Long JP (R)

- - - - - - - - - - - - -

BURCH

1840 MEIGS CENSUS
Henry L. Burch 2000001 - 11001 p. 235

- - - - - - - - - - - - -

BURCHUM / BURCHAM

1840 MEIGS CENSUS
Noah Burcham 121001 - 001011 p. 243
1850 MEIGS CENSUS
James Burchum 22 (Farmer), Catharine 20, Sarah 2, Jemima 1, Alfred THOMPSON 19 (Farmer) p. 780-524
Noah Burchum 42 (Farmer), Fatamy 40 (Va), Ross 18 (Farmer), Burrell B. 14, John 11, Elisha 8, Abijah 6, Henry 4, William R. 3, Littleton 1 p. 779-523
MARRIAGES (MEIGS)
James Burcham to Katharine Thompson, 3 Mar 1847 (4 Mar), T.B. McElwee JP
Sophia A. Burcham to John Cole q.v.

- - - - - - - - - - - - -

BURDIT

1840 RHEA CENSUS George Burdit 21001 - 1001

- - - - - - - - - - - - -

BURFORD

MISCELLANEOUS (RHEA)
John Burford: Bondsman for James Hannah, 1814

- - - - - - - - - - - - -

BURGESS

1850 MEIGS CENSUS
Edward T. Burgess 30 (Va)(Saddler), James M. 24 (NC) (Saddler) p. 753-328

- - - - - - - - - - - - -

BURK

MARRIAGES (RHEA)
Margaret Burk to Henry Morris q.v.
MISCELLANEOUS (MEIGS)
Andrew Burk: Hiwassee District, Burkett Chapel area

- - - - - - - - - - - - -

BURKET

1840 RHEA CENSUS
Isaac Burket 020001 - 21001 [1850 Hamilton Census: Isaac Burket 37, Nancy 38, Frederick 19, Eliza 17, George 15, Tennessee 13, Andrew 11, Malinda 7, Sarah 4]

- - - - - - - - - - - - -

BURKHART

MARRIAGES (RHEA)
Sally Burkhart to Paschal Simpson q.v.

- - - - - - - - - - - - -

BURNELL

MISCELLANEOUS (MEIGS)
Hezekiah Burnell: Hiwassee District resident

- - - - - - - - - - - - -

BURTZ

MARRIAGES (MEIGS)
James Burtz to Susanna Petitt, 15 July 1843 (same), William Johns JP

- - - - - - - - - - - - -

BURWICK / BARWICK

1850 RHEA CENSUS
John Burwick 20 (Shoemaker), Lyda 22, Mary E. 4/12 p. 635-655
Norris Burwick 55 (SC), Mary 44 (SC), Mary J. 26, Sarah A. 24, Elizabeth 18, William 15, Nancy 13, David H. 11, Penelope 8 p. 635-656
MARRIAGES (RHEA)
Catharine Barwick to John C. Gothard q.v.
John Burwick to Lidda Burwick, 8 Oct 1849 (same), S.E. Foust JP (R)

- - - - - - - - - - - - -

BUSH

MARRIAGES (RHEA)
John Bush to Hannah Howard, 9 Sept 1808 (10 Sept), Wm Long JP (R)
Nancy Bush to George W. Blackwell q.v.
MISCELLANEOUS (RHEA)
David Bush: Bondsman for Jacob Russell, 1814

- - - - - - - - - - - - -

BUSTER / BUSTARD

TAXES (RHEA)
1823 (Capt. Wilson's Co.): Michael W. Buster 1 WP, 160a
William Buster 1 WP
1830 RHEA CENSUS
M. W. Buster 020101 - 102001001 p. 364
Sarah Buster 0201 - 110111 p. 374
1840 MEIGS CENSUS
David Buster 02000001 - 0030101 p. 242
John Buster 21001 - 10001 p. 232
Samuel Buster 00001 - 00001 p. 242
Sarah Buster 0 - 00101001 p. 238
William Buster 10001 - 00001 p. 238
William Buster 00001 - 10001 p. 242
William Buster 00001 - 00001 p. 243
1850 MEIGS CENSUS
David Buster 62 (Va)(Farmer), Rebecca 61 (Va), Rosanna 20, Isaac 15, Jerry WEST 80 (NC) p. 786-575
Samuel Buster 30 (Va)(Farmer), Mary 28 (NC), Jane 10, Caroline 8, Lorinda 5, David 2 p. 787-582
William Buster 32 (Va)(Farmer), Bershaba 31, George W. 10, Sarah 9, Columbus 8, John B. 5, Stephen F. 5, Mary 3 p. 762-387
MARRIAGES (RHEA)
John Buster to Matilda Bedwell, 3 Apr 1833 (7 Apr), John Farmer MG, Hugh Pharris Bm (AR)
John Buster to Polly W. Eades [Edds], 17 Sept 1833 (same), Daniel Briggs MG, Berryman Aron Bm (AR)
Michael W. Bustard to Elizabeth Walker, 24 Oct 1812 (same), Charles Walker Bm (AR)
Nancy Buster to James W. English q.v.
Sarah Ann Buster to Andrew T. Chastain q.v.
William Buster to Isabella Hill, 13 July 1820 (same), Benjamin Edgemon MG, Shepherd Braselton Bm (AR)
MARRIAGES (MEIGS)
Jane Buster to Henry Looman q.v.
L. Buster (Miss) to Charles Franklin q.v.
Michael W. Buster to Elizabeth Wan, 24 Dec 1845 (25 Dec), Wm Green MG
Nancy Buster to Milton F. Jones q.v.
Samuel Buster to M.A. Royster, 15 Aug 1839 (18 Aug), Jacob Price JP
Sarah Buster to Cumberland Rector q.v.
Sarah Buster to William Lockmiller q.v.
William Buster to Nancy Price, 17 Jan 1839 (20 Jan) [no JP or MG]

William Buster to Matilda Guinn, 31 Dec 1846, Thomas V. Atchley JP

MISCELLANEOUS (RHEA)

David Buster: Bondsman for Moses Atchley, 1831
John Buster: Bondsman for James W. English, 1832
Mikel W. Buster: Bondsman for Wilson Kilgore, 1822

MISCELLANEOUS (MEIGS)

David Buster: JP(?) 1841
Francis Buster: Cherokee Removal muster roll, 1836
John Buster: Cherokee Removal muster roll, 1836
William Buster: Cherokee Removal muster roll, 1836

- - - - - - - - - - - -

BUSTON

TAXES (RHEA)

1819 (Capt. John Ramsey's Co.): Jesse Buston 1 WP

- - - - - - - - - - - -

BUT

MARRIAGES (RHEA)

Polly Ann But to John C. Davis q.v.

- - - - - - - - - - - -

BUTHER

1830 RHEA CENSUS

Caroline Buther 021 - 100001 p. 359

- - - - - - - - - - - -

BUTLER / BUTLAR

1830 RHEA CENSUS

William Butler 2210001 - 002001 p. 363

1840 MEIGS CENSUS

William Butlar 10220001 - 11001001 p. 247
Hampton Butler 0110001 - 211211 p. 247

1850 RHEA CENSUS

Mary Butler 70 (NC), Wade H. 19 (Farmer) p. 560-171
John Butler 17, William 15: see George W. Fullington

1850 MEIGS CENSUS

Harriet Butler 33, Amos B. 19 (Farmer), Mary 13, Henry 10, James T. 8, Lucinda C. 4, Jane BRADY 33 p. 796-654
Phebe Butler 32, Mernerva 15, Mary Ann 12, William J. 10, James W. 7, Asbury 4, Wade H. 0 p. 806-719

MARRIAGES (RHEA)

Elizabeth Butler to Larkin G. Gothard q.v.
Feby Butler to Thompson Hide q.v.
Hampton Butler to Sally Majors or Moyers, 23 Apr 1817 (same), J. Jine JP (AR)
James Butler to Polly Johnson, 17 Apr 1819 (same), John Cozby JP, James C. Reed Bm (AR)
Joshua Butler to Pattey Lucas, 22 Nov 1811 (24 Nov), James Edington Bm (A)
Molly Butler to William Smith q.v.
Nancy Butler to Owen Brady q.v.
Richard Butler to Isabella Mitchell, 21 Jan 1819, Micajah Howerton Bm (A)
Sally Butler to John Majors q.v.

MARRIAGES (MEIGS)

Agnes Butler to William B. Ford q.v.
Alsie Butler to John Alison q.v.
Elizabeth Butler to George Fullington q.v.
J.M. Butler to Hariet G. Johnson, 7 Apr 1845, A. Fooshee JP(?)
Jacob J. Butler to Matilda Gibson, 28 Nov 1849 (29 Nov), William Green MG
James Butler to Malinda Bouden, 29 May 1844 (same), Mark Refro JP
Mary J. Butler to John Powell q.v.
Sarah Jane Butler to James B. McCallon q.v.

MISCELLANEOUS (RHEA)

Hampton Butler: Bondsman for John Majors, 1817
James Butler: Revolutionary War Pensioner, 1835 list

MISCELLANEOUS (MEIGS)

J.M. Butler: JP 1848-49

- - - - - - - - - - - -

BUTTRAM / BUTRAM

1830 RHEA CENSUS

Elijah Butram 2210001 - 000001 p. 355
Heil Butram 210001 - 11 p. 354
Jacob Butram 00000001 - 00110001 p. 354
James Butram 111001 - 002001 p. 355
Larkin Butram 010001 - 21001 p. 354
Noah Butram 20001 - 01001 p. 354

1840 RHEA CENSUS

Elijah Buttram 20210001 - 02

1840 MEIGS CENSUS

John Butram 231101 - 0021001 p. 244

1850 RHEA CENSUS

Elijah Butram 60 (NC)(Farmer), Nancy A. 53 (NC), James C.M. 21 (Farmer), Catharine 18, Nancy 15, William 13, John S. 10 p. 608-489

1850 MEIGS CENSUS

Elza Butram 31 (Farmer), Susan 26, Mary Jane 11, Monterville (m) 4, Tennessee 1 p. 753-326
Elijah Butram 18, Michael F. 16, Francis A. 14, William D. 11: see Joseph G. Royster

MARRIAGES (RHEA)

Cornelius Butram to Catherine Waldrop, 1 Aug 1831 (2 Aug), Heil Butram JP, William L. Miller [Lockmiller?] Bm (AR)
Nancy Butram to Nicholas Keith q,v,
Polly Butram to Barton White q.v.

MARRIAGES (MEIGS)

Elzy Buttram to Susan Locke, 2 Sept 1847 (same), S.G. Swisher MG [Susan, dau of Robert and Nancy Moore Locke; Elzy, son of Elijah and Nancy Harmon Buttram]
Phebe Buttram to Joseph G. Royster q.v.
Pheriba Buttram to Hance Nelson q.v.

MISCELLANEOUS (RHEA)

Elzy Buttram: Bondsman for Nicholas Keith, 1844
Hiel Buttram: JP 1828-1833
Jacob Butram: Land south of Tennessee River
James Butram: Land south of Tennessee River
Larkin Butram: Land south of Tennessee River
Noah Butram: Land south of Tennessee River

MISCELLANEOUS (MEIGS)

Hiel Buttram: MG 1846-1847

- - - - - - - - - - - -

CADLE

MARRIAGES (RHEA)
Jestin Cadle to John R. Blythe q.v.

- - - - - - - - - - - - -

CAHILL / CAHIL

1830 RHEA CENSUS
Joseph Cahill 10001 - 00001001 p. 356
MARRIAGES (RHEA)
James Cahill to Rebecca Bedwell, 8 Feb 1827 (29 Feb), Daniel Briggs MG, Joseph Cahill Bm (AR)
Joseph Cahill to Polly Small, 19 Dec 1825 (20 Dec), Daniel Briggs MG, William Loughmiller Bm (AR)
MARRIAGES (MEIGS)
Mary Cahal to Edmund Henly q.v.
MISCELLANEOUS (RHEA)
Joseph Cahill: Bondsman for James Cahill, 1827

- - - - - - - - - - - - -

CAIN
(see also McCAIN)

1840 MEIGS CENSUS
Jacob Cain 02220001 - 2100001101 p. 239

- - - - - - - - - - - - -

CALDWELL

TAXES (RHEA)
1808 (James Campbell's List):
David Caldwell 1 WP, 1 BP, 200a Tenn Ri
1819 (Capt. W.S. Bradley's Dist.):
A.W. and C. Caldwell 2 WP, 3 Town Lots
1823 (Capt Brown's Co.): Adam W. Caldwell 1 WP, 4 TL
Alexander Caldwell 1 WP
Carson D. Caldwell 1 WP
David Caldwell 1 BP, 230a T Ri [part of 19,000a tract]
1830 RHEA CENSUS
Alex Caldwell 020001 - 1001 p. 378
David Caldwell 013200001 - 1001001 p. 377
1840 RHEA CENSUS
Alexander Caldwell 1102001 - 111001
David Caldwell 0001200001 - 00100001
1850 RHEA CENSUS
Audley P. Caldwell 28 (Farmer), Jonathan M. 29 (Farmer), Catharine 24, Henry E. 2/12 p. 605-469
MARRIAGES (RHEA)
A.P. Caldwell to C.J. Peters, 22 Sept 1849 (23 Sept), J.W. Thompson MG (R)
Alexander Caldwell to Lutitia Moore, 25 Jan 1821 (same), William Randolph, Elder [MG], Audley P. Defriese Bm (A)
Alfred Caldwell to Catherine J. or R. Brittin, 25 May 1842 (26 May), Benjamin Wallace MG, D.C. McMillin Bm (AR)
Jacob K. Caldwell to Eliza Jane Roddy, 25 Sept 1845 (same), T.K. Munsey MG (R)
James M. Caldwell to Mariah H. Whaley, 21 July 1847 (22 July), E.C. Childress MG (R)
Margaret A. Caldwell to James Mayo q.v.
Mary E. Caldwell to William G. Moleston q.v.
Nancy Caldwell to Audley P. Defriese q.v.
Rachel Caldwell to Robert W. McMillen q.v.
William A. Caldwell to Penelope D. Brittin, 14 Aug 1845 (AR)
William M.E. Cardwell or Caldwell to Elizabeth Ferguson, 25 Mar 1819 (26 Mar), Henry D.T. Roberts MG (AR)
MISCELLANEOUS (RHEA)
A.W. Caldwell: Signed petition to move Indian Agency
Adam W. Caldwell: Resident, Washington (Lot 38) 1812
Carson Caldwell: Signed petition to move Indian Agency
" " Trustee, 1823-1828; JP 1825-1835
" " Bondsman for Anson Dearmon, 1835
Daniel Caldwell: Signed petition to move Indian Agency
David P. Caldwell: Bm for Flemming H. Fulton, 1832
James H. Caldwell: Bondsman for Robert C. Johnson, 1834
James M. Caldwell: Private, Mexican War
Jonathan Caldwell: Private, Mexican War

- - - - - - - - - - - - -

CALIHEN

MISCELLANEOUS (RHEA)
Seymore Calihen: JP 1816

- - - - - - - - - - - - -

CALLOWAY

MARRIAGES (RHEA)
Joseph Calloway to Mary Wilson, 8 Sept 1834 (11 Sept), Robert Snead MG [Baptist], Coleman C. McReynolds Bm (AR) [Joseph, son of John F. and Sarah Hardin Calloway; Mary, dau of James and Nancy Blakey Stockton Wilson; Joseph and Mary moved to Missouri prior to 1850; he was a Baptist Minister]
MISCELLANEOUS (RHEA and MEIGS)
John Calloway: Hiwassee District resident
Thomas H. Calloway: Ocoee District resident

- - - - - - - - - - - - -

CALVIN / COLVIN

MARRIAGES (MEIGS)
Eli Corvin to Dinely Rogers, 11 July 1846 (same), Jesse Locke MG
Elizabeth Colvin to Joseph Gothard q.v.
Margaret Calvin to Jesse W. Dobbs q.v.
MISCELLANEOUS (MEIGS)
James Calvin: JP(?) 1845

- - - - - - - - - - - - -

CALLON / COLLAN
(see also McCALLEN / McCALLAM)

MISCELLANEOUS (RHEA)
J.M. Callon / Collan: JP 1833, 1834

- - - - - - - - - - - - -

CAMP

1830 RHEA CENSUS
William D. Camp 00000001 - 100001 p. 388
MARRIAGES (RHEA)
William Camp to Evaline Cowan, 21 Feb 1832 (23 Feb), John Courtney MG, Joseph Cowan Bm (AR)

- - - - - - - - - - - - -

CAMPBELL

TAXES (RHEA)
1808 (Jas Campbell's List): James Campbell 1 WP, 200a
1819 (Capt. W.S. Bradley's Dist):
Thomas J. Campbell 1 WP, 2 BP, 1a
(Capt. McGill's Co.): John Campbell 1 WP
1823 (Capt. Jackson's Co.):
David Campbell 1 WP, 83a mouth of Hiwassee Ri
1830 RHEA CENSUS
David Campbell 2000001 - 130001001 p. 368
Jno Campbell 0100001 - 010001 p. 369
Jno B. Campbell 010101 - 011001 p. 372
T. J. Campbell 120111 - 111011 p. 384
William Campbell 100001 - 20001 p. 374
1830 RHEA CENSUS
Isaac Campbell 3200001 - 0201
1850 RHEA CENSUS
Andrew Campbell 28 (Farmer), Sarah 25, William 7, Hyram 5, John 2, John SHIFLETT 22 (Farmer) p. 636-663
Esther Campbell 80 (Va)(black): see Newton Locke
Isaac Campbell 63 (Farmer), Darcus 40, Joseph 16 (Wagoner), Charles 5, Samuel 8 p. 543-67
John Campbell 34 (Mo)(Farmer), Elizabeth 33 (Unk), Mary J. 8, Joseph T. 5, Rebecca 4, Daniel P. 1 p. 617-517
William Campbell 29 (Farmer), Elizabeth 33, Martha 10, Harvey 9, Franklin 5, Norris H. 3, James H.R. 2, Nancy J. 6/12 p. 574-249 [William married Elizabeth Ballard on 14 Dec 1846 in McMinn Co]
1850 MEIGS CENSUS
James W. Campbell 33 (Doctor & Farmer), Margaritt J. 18, H.M. (m) 2 p. 722-70
John Campbell 31 (Farmer), Martha 20, Isabella E. 5, Julia 1 p. 722-69
MARRIAGES (RHEA)
Ann Eliza Campbell to Euclid Waterhouse q.v.
David Campbell to Susannah Pierce, 29 July 1830 (same), Robert Cooley JP and Bm (AR)
Dolly A. Campbell to Matthew W. McClellan q.v.
Elizabeth Campbell to William Lesly q.v.
Elizabeth O. Campbell to Carlisle Humphreys q.v.
Harriet A. Campbell to Carlisle Humphreys q.v.
Jane Campbell to William Walker q.v.
John Campbell to Polly Pearson, 9 May 1816 (same), John Pearson Bm (A)
Louisa P. Campbell to James W. Smith q.v.
Margaret P. Campbell to James Rodgers q.v.
Polly Campbell to Limon Matcile q.v.
MARRIAGES (MEIGS)
Andrew Campbell to Sarah Shiflett, 10 Nov 1840 (12 Nov), John Seaborn JP
James M. Campbell to Margaret J. Gamble, 13 Jan 1847 (21 Jan), H. Douglass MG
John B. Campbell to Caroline McClanhon, 21 Jan 1846 (same), Joseph McSpadin MG
MISCELLANEOUS (RHEA and MEIGS)
Anderson Campbell: Cherokee Removal muster roll, 1836
Campbell & Haynes: Early merchants in Washington
Cyrus Campbell: Bondsman for Allen H. McFall, 1839
David Campbell*: Judge; Attorney in Rhea County
" " Deeded land for County seat, Washington
" " Purchaded Lots 5 and 6 in Washington
" " Married Elizabeth Outlaw in 1779; children: Alexander O., Penelope S., Mary H., Elizabeth O., Thomas J., Dolly A., Margaret P., Harriet A., Letitia V., Caroline A., and Victor Moreau Campbell
" " Died in 1812; buried near Washington
David Campbell*: Bondsman for Robert Murphey, 1826
" " Bondsman for William Cannon, 1834
" " Owned property in Hiwassee District
James Campbell: Chairman of County Court, 1808
" " Commissioner for Town of Washington, 1812-13; purchased Lot 84 in town
" " Bondsman for David David, 1811
" " JP 1808, 1816
Thomas J. Campbell: Early member of Rhea County bar
" " " Signed petition to move Indian Agency
" " " Bondsman for Hopkins L. Turney, 1826
[*NOTE: two David Campbells resided in Rhea County; evidently no relation]

- - - - - - - - - - - - -

CAMREN / CAMERON / CAMERIN

1840 MEIGS CENSUS
James Camerin 010001 - 210001 p. 227
MARRIAGES (RHEA)
Elijah Cameron or Camren to Rebecca Staunton, 5 July 1823 (6 July), Thomas Price JP, John Huff Bm (AR)
MISCELLANEOUS (MEIGS)
James Cameron: Ocoee District

- - - - - - - - - - - - -

CANNON / CANON / KENNON

TAXES (RHEA)
1823 (Capt. Brown's Co.): Thomas M. Kennon 1 WP
MARRIAGES (RHEA)
Jane Cannon to Charles Stewart q.v.
William Cannon to Polly Thomas, 1 Dec 1834 (2 Dec), S.R. Russell MG, David Campbell Bm (AR)
MISCELLANEOUS (RHEA and MEIGS)
George R. Cannon: Ocoee District
James Canon: Signed petition to move Indian Agency

- - - - - - - - - - - - -

CANTRELL / CANTREL

1840 MEIGS CENSUS
William Cantrel 0200000001 - 200001 p. 239

MISCELLANEOUS (RHEA and MEIGS)
Nathan B. Cantrell: Cherokee Removal muster roll, 1836
Thomas Cantrell: Bondsman for James Clemons, 1816

- - - - - - - - - - - - -

CAPEMON

MISCELLANEOUS (MEIGS)
Leroy P. Capemon: JP(?) 1843

- - - - - - - - - - - - -

CARDIN

MARRIAGES (MEIGS)
Fanny Cardin to Samuel Sherrell q.v.

- - - - - - - - - - - - -

CARDWELL

MARRIAGES (RHEA)
Wm M.E. Cardwell or Caldwell to Elizabeth Ferguson, 25 Mar 1819 (26 Mar), Henry D.T. Roberts MG (AR)

- - - - - - - - - - - - -

CARIL
(see also CARROLL)

MARRIAGES (MEIGS)
Delisa Caril to Samuel H. Gourley q.v.

- - - - - - - - - - - - -

CARNAHAN / KARNAHAN

TAXES (RHEA)
1819 (Capt. John Lewis' Dist.): William Carnahan 1 WP
1823 (Capt. Lewis' Co.): Alexander E. Carnahan 1 WP
MARRIAGES (RHEA)
Elizabeth Karnahan to Daniel Chummy q.v.
James Carnahan to Prudence Smith, 9 Aug 1828 (same), James A. Darwin JP, Robert Goad Bm (AR)
Jane Carnahan to Frederick Thurman q.v.
MISCELLANEOUS (RHEA)
William Carnahan: Bondsman for Frederick Thurman, 1824
William Karnahan: Bondsman for David Chummy, 1815

- - - - - - - - - - - - -

CARNEY

TAXES (RHEA)
1823 (Capt. Brown's Co.): William Carney 1 WP

- - - - - - - - - - - - -

CARNS

1830 RHEA CENSUS
Josiah Carns 000011 - 1001 p. 364

- - - - - - - - - - - - -

CARPENTER

MISCELLANEOUS (RHEA)
Dan Carpenter: Deacon in MECS, 1849

- - - - - - - - - - - - -

CARR / KERR

TAXES (RHEA)
1819 (Capt. John Robinson's Co.): John Carr 1 WP
(Capt. McGill's Co.): Samuel Carr 1 WP
1823 (Capt. Wilson's Co.): Robert Kerr 1 WP
1830 RHEA CENSUS
Robert Kerr 101001 - 13001 p. 358
Thomas J. Carr 1001 - 10001 p. 359
Wm Kerr(?) 10001 - 10001 p. 369
1840 RHEA CENSUS
Alexander Carr 0001 - 0001
John Carr 00012 - 00000001
Thomas J. Carr 011001 - 11001
1840 MEIGS CENSUS
William Kerr 121001 - 101001 p. 228
1850 RHEA CENSUS
Amon or Amos Carr 28 (NC)(Farmer), Rebecca 28 (NC), Sarah J. 7, Nancy A. 5 p. 601-416
Daniel Carr 70 (NC)(Farmer), Catharine 65 (NC) p. 575-257
Joseph Carr 29 (NC)(Farmer), Mary A. 25 (NC), Nancy C. 3 p. 580-288
Thomas J. Kerr 45 (Farmer), Martha 46, Mary M. 21, Calloway 20 (Farmer), Sarah W. 18, Robert 17 (Farmer), Martha E. 6 p. 569-217
MARRIAGES (RHEA)
Alexander Carr to Mahala Ball, 25 Jan 1840 (no return), Henry M. Cunningham Bm
John Carr to Jane Land, 9 Apr 1829, George W. Clingham Bm (A) [possibly 1850 Dvidson Census: John 48, Jane 36, etc.]
Samuel Carr to Sally Blythe, 14 June 1810 (same), Abraham Howard JP, Henry Airheart Bm (AR)
Thomas J. Kerr to Martha Clack, 29 Aug 1826 (same), Daniel Briggs MG, Robert Kerr Bm (AR)
William Kerr to Patsey McCarroll, 4 Sept 1826, Robert Murphy Bm (A)
MARRIAGES (MEIGS)
Margaret Kerr to Leonard Brooks q.v.
MISCELLANEOUS (RHEA)
Joseph Carr: Bondsman for Martin Burns, 1816
Robert Kerr: Bondsman for Thomas J. Kerr, 1826
William Kerr: JP 1832
MISCELLANEOUS (MEIGS)
Ransom P. Kerr: Circuit Court Jury, 1836
William Kerr: County Court Clerk, 1836-1839
" " Purchased Lots 5,9,17,36,63 in Decatur
" " Purchased lot in Cottonport

- - - - - - - - - - - - -

CARROLL / CARRELL / CORRELL

1830 RHEA CENSUS
Cristan Carrell 10001 - 100001 p. 377
James Carroll 210111 - 011101 p. 356
Luke Carroll 01010101 - 00110001 p. 354

1840 MEIGS CENSUS
Christian Carell 031001 - 2010001 p. 237
1850 MEIGS CENSUS
Christian Carrell 46 (NC)(Farmer), Jane 50 (Va), John 20 (Farmer), Margaret 21, Alexander 19 (Farmer), William 7, Mary Ann 14, Ruth 12, Elizabeth 8 p. 769-438
James C. Carrell 19: see Susan Fine
Luke Carroll 78 (Va)(Farmer), Elizabeth 72 (NC) p. 785-567
MARRIAGES (RHEA)
Ann Carroll to Richmond Goddy q.v.
Christian Carrell or Corell to Jane Rice, 11 Jan 1827 (same), Peach Taylor JP, Valentine Hept [Houpt] Bm (AR)
Eliza Carrell to William Lockmiller q.v.
John Carroll to Milly Phillips, 16 Jan 1816, Robert Patterson Bm (R)
Patsey Carrell to Levi Stacy q.v.
Polly Carroll to George L. Miller [Lockmiller?] q.v.
MARRIAGES (MEIGS)
Delissa Caroll to Samuel H. Gourley q.v.
Margaret Mariah Carrell to Thomas Young q.v.
Nelly Correll to Dormen Kissur q.v.
MISCELLANEOUS (RHEA and MEIGS)
Alfred Carroll: Bondsman for Barton White, 1831
Christian Correll: Purchased land in Hiwassee District
George Carroll: Bondsman for Richmond Goddy, 1834
James Carroll: Bondsman for Elijah McPherson, 1826
" " Purchased land in Hiwassee District

- - - - - - - - - - - -

CARSON

1830 RHEA CENSUS
Thomas S. Carson 121001 - 10001 p. 353

- - - - - - - - - - - -

CARTER

TAXES (RHEA)
1819 (Capt. W.S. Bradley's Dist.):
Landon Carter heirs 1140a
1823 (Capt. Howard's Co.): James Carter 1 WP
1830 RHEA CENSUS
James Carter 222000001 - 0001001 p. 381
Thomas Carter 000001 - 23101 p. 364
William Carter 11001 - 101 p. 381
1840 RHEA CENSUS
Ruthey Carter 02101 - 001011
1850 RHEA CENSUS
John Carter 18 (Farmer): see Phillip Foust
MARRIAGES (RHEA)
Nancy Carter to George Gothard q.v.
Nathan Carter to Nancy McCoy, 24 Dec 1811 (same), Theophilus Johnson Bm (A)
Sally Carter to James McCoy q.v.
Sally Carter to William Johnson q.v.
Thomas Carter to Joahanna Hiden, 20 Mar 1818 (22 Mar), George Gillespie JP (R)
William Carter to Ruth McFarland, 1 June 1825 (same), A. Davis JP, Caswell Bean Bm (AR) [1850 Bradley Census: Ruth Carter 42, Charles 19, William 15, Elizbeth McFARLAND 76]
MARRIAGES (MEIGS)
James Carter to Emily Atkinson, 26 Sept 1843
MISCELLANEOUS (RHEA and MEIGS)
James Carter: Bondsman for William Johnson, 1816
" " 1st Bugler, Mexican War
Landon Carter: Bondsman for Ira Gothard, 1832
Thomas Carter: Purchased land in Hiwassee District
" " Bondsman for Joseph Rush, 1830
" " Bondsman for John Snelson, 1836

- - - - - - - - - - - -

CARTERRIGHT

MARRIAGES (RHEA)
Joseph C. Carterright to Nancy Davis, 20 Oct 1829, James Davis Bm (A)

- - - - - - - - - - - -

CARVEY / COVEY

MARRIAGES (RHEA)
James Covey to Sally Matthews, 15 Jan 1815, John McAllister Bm (A)
James Carvey to Vina Hill, 25 June 1840, Nathan S. Broyles Bm (AR)

- - - - - - - - - - - -

CARY / CAREY

MARRIAGES (RHEA)
Peggy Carey to Isaac Mahan q.v.
Rachel Cary to Wilson Nevins q.v.

- - - - - - - - - - - -

CASE

1830 RHEA CENSUS
John Case 11001 - 20001 p. 361
MARRIAGES (RHEA)
Elizabeth Case to Wyly M. Brady q.v.
MISCELLANEOUS (RHEA)
John Case: Bondsman for John Lawrence, 1833

- - - - - - - - - - - -

CASEY / CASY / CAISEY / CASSEY

TAXES (RHEA)
1823 (Capt. Piper's Co.): Abner Casey 1 WP, 160a
(Capt. Jackson's Co.): James Casey 160a
1830 RHEA CENSUS
Abner Casey 0310001 - 0011001 p. 357
E. Caisey 1111 - 1011 p. 371
Randolph Casey 0310001 - 200001 p. 391
1840 RHEA CENSUS
Randolph Casey 110310001 - 0110001
1840 MEIGS CENSUS
William Casey 22001 - 101001 p. 225
1850 RHEA CENSUS
Elizabeth Casy 65 (NC), Caroline 21, Newton 16 p. 583-317
Nancy Casey 21: see Robert Mitchell
Wesley Casy 26 (Farmer), Clerissa 25, John C. 2 p. 584-318

1850 MEIGS CENSUS
Wm Casey 46 (Farmer), John 20 (Farmer), Emeline 16, Isaac 12, Hester 8, Thomas 3 p. 723-80
MARRIAGES (RHEA)
Barbara Casey to Aron Maloney q.v.
Elizabeth Cassey to George Watson q.v.
Elizabeth Casey to Thomas W. Noblett q.v.
John Casey to Jane Akison, 18 Dec 1834, Samuel Blakely Bm (A)
Mary Casey to Braxton Edgemond q.v.
Nancy Casey to Benjamin McKenzie q.v.
Susannah Casey to Braxton C. Sams q.v.
Turner Casey or Caisey to Sally Clark, 22 or 29 July 1822 (same), Bird Deatherige JP (AR)
Wesley Casey to Clarissie Dudley, 30 Nov 1847 (same), Daniel Broyles JP (R)
MARRIAGES (MEIGS)
Mary C. Casey to Thomas E. Crossland q.v.
Nancy Ann Casey to Isaac McInturf q.v.
Wm Casey to Sarah A. Locke, ---? -- 1850, Thomas Miller Sur
MISCELLANEOUS (RHEA and MEIGS)
Abner Casey: Hiwassee District, Ten Mile Stand area
James Cassey: Bondsman for George Watson, 1835
James Casey: Hiwassee District, Burkett Chapel area
John Casey: Bondsman for William McDowell, 1835
John A. Casey: Bondsman for Braxton Edgemond, 1832
West M. Casey: Private, Mexican War
William Casey: Ocoee District

\- - - - - - - - - - - - -

CASH

1830 RHEA CENSUS
Bogan Cash 00001 - 01001 p. 357
James I. Cash 11001 - 100001 p. 357
James D. Cash 00100001 - 02001001 p. 354
1840 RHEA CENSUS
James I. Cash 111101 - 2110010001
1840 MEIGS CENSUS
Mary Cash 222 - 110021001 p. 246
Thomas Cash 111001 - 021001 p. 235
1850 RHEA CENSUS
Francis A. Cash 23, Eliza 25: see Mary West
James I. Cash 49 (Farmer), Elizabeth 39, Jane 21, James A. 18 (Farmer), Mary A. 17, Elizabeth R. 15, Harriet E. 10, Thompson H. 12, Sarah A. 6, Eliza J. 4, Jesse I. 1 p. 554-126
William W. Cash 27 (Farmer), Lucinda 24, Elizabeth J. 4, James I. 3 p. 575-258
1850 MEIGS CENSUS
Judy Cash 39 (Ky), Wiley 21 (Farmer), James 11, John 8, Elizabeth 6 p. 809-740
Sarah Cash 36 (Ky), Allen 18 (Farmer), Reuben 16 (Farmer), William 13, Abigal 12, Christopher 8 p. 810-741
MARRIAGES (RHEA)
Bryan [Boggan, according to Campbell 1940:123] Cash to Nancy Jones, 29 Oct 1828 (30 Oct), Stephen Martin JP (R)
F.A. [Francis A.] Cash to Eliza West, 20 Feb 1850 (21 Feb), J.A. Mitchell JP (R)
Leonard Cash to Cintha Litterall, 9 Sept 1834 (same), John Randles JP (R)
Thompson Cash to Amanda C. Smith, 30 Sept 1840 (same), A.D. Paul JP (R)
MARRIAGES (MEIGS)
Benjamin Cash to Louisa Rodes, 18 Mar 1846 (19 Mar), John Seabourn JP
John C. Cash to Adaline Moore, 4 Aug 1847 (same), Jesse Martin JP
MISCELLANEOUS (RHEA)
Bogan Cash: Living in McMinn County in 1850
James I. Cash: Trustee, Sulphur Springs Methodist Church, 1841
" " " Trustee, Mars Hill Academy, 1850
William W. Cash: Bondsman for Calvin M. Garrison, 1845
MISCELLANEOUS (MEIGS)
James I. Cash: Hiwassee District
" " " Com. to build Decatur Courthouse, 1836
" " " JP 1836

\- - - - - - - - - - - - -

CASKEY

MARRIAGES (MEIGS)
W.J. Caskey to Elizabeth Harper, 20 Feb 1849 (same), John Ford JP

\- - - - - - - - - - - - -

CASS

MARRIAGES (MEIGS)
Harriet Cass to James Adams q.v.

\- - - - - - - - - - - - -

CASTEEL / CASTELL

TAXES (RHEA)
1823 (Capt. Lewis' Co.): Andrew Casteel 1 WP
John Casteel 1 WP
1830 RHEA CENSUS
Andrew Casteel 11001 - 10001 p. 378
David Casteel 10001 - 00001 p. 378
Jno Casteel 01111001 - 0120101 p. 378
Joseph Casteel 10001 - 10001 p. 379
Morris Castell 001101 - 32201 p. 355
1840 RHEA CENSUS
Andrew Casteel 011101 - 22001
C.B. Casteel 100001 - 10001
John Casteel 011100001 - 00110001
John R. Casteel 00002 - 0001
Joseph Casteel 410001 - 21001
MARRIAGES (RHEA)
Andrew Casteel to Elizabeth Lisenby or Lasenby, 20 Jan 1829 (21 Jan), J. Fine JP, John Reecer Bm (AR)
David Casteel to Jane Sykes, 8 Feb 1828, John Wood Bm (A)
Elizabeth Casteel to Jacob C. Gwin q.v.
Freeland Casteel to Martha Cates, 24 Dec 1841* (same), James Hooper JP (AR)
[*Allen shows date as 1840]
Greenberry Casteel to July Clough, 23 Oct 1834, John Cozby JP, Andrew Casteel Bm (AR)
Jemima Casteel to William Simpson q.v.

John R. Casteel to Nancy Clough, 4 Dec 1839, Wm B. Cozby JP, Freeland Casteel Bm (AR)
Joseph Casteel to Nancy Bandy, 15 July 1828 (16 July), John Cozby JP, Andrew Casteel Bm (AR)
Margaret Casteel to David Bandy q.v.
Mary Castell to Joseph D. Bayles or Broyles q.v.
Nancy Casteel to Frederick Williams q.v.
Peggy Casteel to James Guffee q.v.

MISCELLANEOUS (RHEA)

Andrew Casteel: Bondsman for Joseph Casteel, 1828
" " Bondsman for Greenberry Casteel, 1834
Freeland Casteel: Bondsman for Joseph D. Bayles/Broyles, 1838
" " Bondsman for John R. Casteel, 1839
Greenberry Casteel: Bondsman for David Singleton, 1831
" " Bondsman for John S. Puckett, 1835
Samuel Casteel: Bondsman for James Griffie/Guffee, 1834

- - - - - - - - - - - - -

CATCHING / CATHING

MISCELLANEOUS (RHEA)

S. Cathing or Cathing: JP 1816

- - - - - - - - - - - - -

CATE / CATES

TAXES (RHEA)

1819 (Capt. Wm McCray's Co.): John Cates 1 WP
1823 (Capt. Howerton's Old Co.): John Cates 1 WP

1830 RHEA CENSUS

Clark Cate 20001 - 01001 p. 377
Daniel Cates 111101 - 10002 p. 352
James Cates 101001 - 202101 p. 352
Jno. Cate 00001 - 100001 p. 377
Robert Cate 0220101 - 200101 p. 364

1840 MEIGS CENSUS

Daniel Cate 2211101 - 101001 p. 236
Robert Cate 11110001 - 0110001 p. 237

1850 RHEA CENSUS

Hubbard Y. Cate 65 (Va)(Farmer), Lucinda 60, Joseph 21 (Va)(Farmer), Susan 20, Lucyana 18, John A. 15, Eliza 12 p. 616-514
Mary J. Cate 24: see James F. Bolen
Solomon Cate 22 (Farmer), Luisa 21, William 3, James 1, Sarah J. McCARROLL 7 p. 621-550

1850 MEIGS CENSUS

Alfred Cate 26 (Farmer), Nancy 28, John THOMAS 20, Daniel C. 5, Thomas H. 1 p. 778-513
Daniel Cate 53 (Farmer), Avy 47, Sally Ann 21, Elder 20, Noah 18, Mary Jane 16, Claborne R. 14, Samuel H. 12, James C. 10, George D. 5, Newton 4, Nancy L. 2 p. 777-507 [Daniel Cate and Eva Elder were married in Jefferson Co., Tenn., in 1817]
Joseph H. Cate 27 (Farmer), Tellithe 22, Daniel 4, Avy 2, Robert 1, John WHITEMAN 93 (Pauper) p. 819-811
William Cate 23 (Va)(Farmer), Vesta Jane 18, John M. 1 p. 736-190

MARRIAGES (RHEA)

Elizabeth Cates to James B. Bolin q.v.
Martha Cates to Freeland Casteel q.v.

MARRIAGES (MEIGS)

Alfred Cate to Nancy Thomas, 14 Aug 1845 (same), Ezekiel Ward Sr. MG
Elvina Cate to Demaseus Medley q.v.
Joseph H. Cate to Margaret Tillery, 1 Sept 1842 (same), Jesse Locke MG

MISCELLANEOUS (MEIGS)

Daniel and Eva Cate: Members Goodfield Baptist Church of Christ, 1827
Daniel Cate: Hiwassee District
" " Chairman of County Court 1838, 1845
" " JP 1836, 1838-39, 1842-43, 1845-47
William Cates: Private, Mexican War

- - - - - - - - - - - - -

CAWOOD / KAYWOOD / KEYWOOD

1840 MEIGS CENSUS

Willis Keywood 000312 - 10011 p. 233

1850 RHEA CENSUS

Rebecca Keywood 54 (Va), Stephen 25 (Farmer), Andrew J. 23 (Farmer), Jefferson C. 18 (School Teacher) p. 534-8

1850 MEIGS CENSUS

Thomas Kaywood 32 (Blacksmith), Charlotte 25, Sarah 23, Margaret 8, Mary E. 6, Mary FORD 40 (Ediot), Sarah SATTERFIELD 70 (N) p. 759-370

MARRIAGES (MEIGS)

Thomas Cawood to Ruth Ford, 22 Dec 1841 (23 Dec), B.F. McKenzie JP

MISCELLANEOUS (RHEA)

Stephen Cawood: Trustee, Mars Hill Academy, 1850

MISCELLANEOUS (MEIGS)

William Cawood: JP(?) 1840

- - - - - - - - - - - - -

CECILL

1840 MEIGS CENSUS

Thomas Cecill: 110001 - 11101 p. 242

- - - - - - - - - - - - -

CELLARS

MISCELLANEOUS (RHEA)

Mik Cellars: On 1826 Surveyor's list of residents south of Tennessee River

- - - - - - - - - - - - -

CERDS

TAXES (RHEA)

1823 (Capt. Piper's Co.): John A. Cerds 1 WP

- - - - - - - - - - - - -

CEROW

MARRIAGES (MEIGS)

Dausey Cerow to Lucinda Hail, 11 June 1840 (same), Prior Neil JP

- - - - - - - - - - - - -

CEVIN

MISCELLANEOUS (RHEA)
J. J. Cevin: MG 1846

- - - - - - - - - - - - -

CHAMBERLIN / CHAMBERLAIN

1850 RHEA CENSUS
Nathan Chamberlin 33 (Va)(Farmer), Polly 21, John M. 4, Rebecca 2, Minerva J. 1 p. 568-212
MARRIAGES (RHEA)
Isaac Chamberlin to Semerion Chambers, 28 July 1838 (30 July), Jacob Gear JP, Anderson Walker Bm (AR)
Nathan Chamberlain to Nancy or Mary Ann Minix, 18 Apr 1845 (24 Apr), Charles Cox JP, Anderson Walker Bm (AR)

- - - - - - - - - - - - -

CHAMBERS

1840 RHEA CENSUS
Geo. A. Chambers 010110001 - 1000101 [George married Mary Vaughn on 14 Mar 1835 in Roane Co.]
Kennedy Chambers 010001 - 11001
1840 MEIGS CENSUS
Betsy Ann Chambers 00001 - 0000001 p. 236
1850 RHEA CENSUS
John W. Chambers 46 (NC)(Shoemaker), Frances F. 26, Susannah H. 13, John R. 10, Charity M. 7, John FREEMAN 5 p. 611-429
MARRIAGES (RHEA)
John W. Chambers to Frankey Freeman, 27 May 1847, J.S. Evins JP (R)
Peggy Chambers to Walter R. Paine q.v.
Semarion Chambers to Isaac Chamberlin q.v.
MARRIAGES (MEIGS)
Daniel H. Chambers to Sarah Coffey, 14 Oct 1843 (same), Jesse Martin JP
MISCELLANEOUS (RHEA)
John Chambers: Bondsman for Joseph Adams, 1820
MISCELLANEOUS (MEIGS)
Abner Chambers: Surety for John L. Ellis, 1850

- - - - - - - - - - - - -

CHANDLER

1840 RHEA CENSUS
Stephen Chandler 110010001 - 11001
MISCELLANEOUS (RHEA)
Stephen Chandler: Private, Mexican War
Stephen H. Chandler: Bondsman for Thomas Davis, 1845

- - - - - - - - - - - - -

CHANEY / CHAINEY

1840 RHEA CENSUS
Charles Chaney 112001 - 123001
MARRIAGES (RHEA)
Levi Chaney to Betsy Brindles, 29 July 1819 (same), John Cozby JP, Lewis Roane Bm (AR)
Mary Chainey to John Moore q.v.
Polly Chaney to David David q.v.

- - - - - - - - - - - - -

CHAPIN

MARRIAGES (RHEA)
Elias J. Chapin to Margaret Ritchie or Richey, 21 Aug 1818 (23 Aug), A. David JP (AR)

- - - - - - - - - - - - -

CHAPMAN / CHATMAN

TAXES (RHEA)
1823 (Capt. Braselton's Co.): John Chapman WP
1830 RHEA CENSUS
Jeremiah Chapman 00001001 - 001001 p. 363
1840 MEIGS CENSUS
Jeremiah Chapman 000000001 - 00000001 p. 246
Sarah Chatman 0 - 0000001 p. 23
1850 RHEA CENSUS
Elizabeth Chapman 83 (NC): see Henry Eaton
John Chapman 40 (NC)(Shoemaker), Sarah 51 (NC), John 16 (Laborer), Mary A. 14 p. 569-219
1850 MEIGS CENSUS
Jeremiah Chapman 71 (Va)(Farmer), Elizabeth 51, William COLLINS 28 (Dentist) p. 811-750
MARRIAGES (RHEA)
John Chapman to Mary Knox, 2 Apr 1823 (6 Apr), John Robinson JP, Miller Francis Bm (AR)
Louisa Chatman to John Chastain q.v.
Mary Chapman to Nathan Harwood q.v.
Sarah Chapman to Edward E. Wassum q.v.
MARRIAGES (MEIGS)
Elizabeth Chapman to John Starnes q.v.
MISCELLANEOUS (RHEA and MEIGS)
Elizabeth Chapman: Member, Fellowship Baptist Church of Christ, 1829
Jeremiah Chapman: Immigrated from Ky. to Hiwassee Dist.
" " Donated land for Fellowship Church
J. Chapman: Circuit Court Jury, 1836 (Meigs Co.)

- - - - - - - - - - - - -

CHASE

MISCELLANEOUS (RHEA and MEIGS)
Dean W. Chase: Bondsman for Thomas Ganaway, 1845
Nelson H. Chase: Bondsman for Charles W. Ault, 1844
" " " 2nd Lt., Mexican War

- - - - - - - - - - - - -

CHASTAIN / CHASTEEN / CHASTINE / CHASTUN

TAXES (RHEA)
1823 (Capt. Wilson's Co.): Joseph Chastain 1 WP, 50a T Ri
1830 RHEA CENSUS
Joseph Chasteen 1210001 - 1000001 p. 364
Rial [Royal] Chasteen 212001 - 11001 p. 364

1840 RHEA CENSUS
B.A.Y. Chastine 10001 - 10001
Joseph Chastine 00120001 - 01100001
1840 MEIGS CENSUS
John Chastun 021001 - 00001 p. 246
1850 RHEA CENSUS
Jonathan Chastean 30 (Farmer), Jane 24 (NC), Eliza 6, William 4 p. 568-207
MARRIAGES (RHEA)
Andrew T. Chastain to Sarah Ann Buster, 16 Sept 1845 (18 Sept), A.D. Paul JP (AR)
John Chastain to Louisa Chatman, 21 Apr 1828 (29 Apr), Beal Gaither JP, Johnsey Parker Bm (AR)
Mahulda Chastain to Johnsey Parker q.v.
Mary Chastain to John Richmond q.v.
Nancy Chastain to Thomas Parker q.v.
Royal Chastain to Eleanor Hellems, 19 Oct 1836 (same), Spillsby Dyer JP, Dickson Jennings Bm (AR)
William Chastain to Polly Fry, 26 Nov 1831 (28 Nov), Thomas Hall MG, John Chastain Bm (AR)
William A. Chastain to Elizabeth White, 4 Aug 1836 (same), James McCanse JP, Gilbert Riggle Bm (AR)
MARRIAGES (MEIGS)
Jonathan E. Chastain to Jane L. Stone, 20 Aug 1843 (21 Aug), William Green MG
MISCELLANEOUS (RHEA and MEIGS)
John Chastain: Member, Fellowship Baptist Church of Christ, 1828-29
" " Bondsman for William Chastain, 1831
Joseph Chastain: Hiwassee District, Pinhook Ferry area
" " Bondsman for John S. Richmond, 1822
" " Member, Fellowship Church, 1828-29
" " MG 1841
Nancy Chastain: Member, Fellowship Church, 1828-29
William Chastain: Bondsman for Gilford Black, 1836
" " Cherokee Removal muster roll, 1836

\- - - - - - - - - - - - -

CHATTEN / CHATTIN / CHATTON

1830 RHEA CENSUS
Jesse Chattan 10001 - 00001 p. 377
Jno. Chatten 11010001 - 012101 p. 368
1840 MEIGS CENSUS
Jesse Chatten 020001 - 21001 p. 231
John Chatten 011200001 - 000110001 p. 231
George W. Chatten 00001 - 01001 p. 231
1850 RHEA CENSUS
Emily Chatten 10: see William B. Johnson
John D. Chattin 42 (Va)(Merchant), Susan 25, John C. 2, Mary J. 11 p. 613-445 [J.D. Chattin married Susan Cooke on 12 Apr 1847 in McMinn Co.]
1850 MEIGS CENSUS
Edward R. Chattin 23 (Farmer), Mary E. 18 (Va), Minerva C. 16 p. 735-172
John Chattin 73 (Va)(Farmer), Catherine 71 (Va), Jesse 45 (Va)(Farmer), Frederick 26 p. 735-174
MARRIAGES (RHEA)
Elizabeth Chattin to William W. Cowan q.v.
Jesse Chattin to Harriet Martin, 19 June 1828 (26 June), Samuel F. Gerrald [Fitzgerrald] MG, Thomas Cox Bm (AR)
Pamelia Chatten to William B. Cozby q.v.
Susan Chatten to Joseph Cowan q.v.
MARRIAGES (MEIGS)
Edward R. Chattin to Mary E. Todd, 3 Dec 1849 (5 Dec), A. C. Hunter MG
Martha G. Chattin to Alex H. Montgomery q.v.
Parthena W. Chattin to James Hoyl q.v.
MISCELLANEOUS (RHEA)
Chattin & Hoyle: Early merchants in Town of Washington
George W. Chatten: Bondsman for Joseph Cowan, 1836
MISCELLANEOUS (MEIGS)
Armster Chattin: Private, Mexican War
Edward R. Chattin: Mexican War (discharged on Surgeon's certificate)
George W. Chattin: 3rd Corp., Cherokee Removal muster roll, 1836
John Chattin: Common School Commissioner, Dist 2, 1838
John D. Chattin: Commissioner to lay off Meigs County into districts, 1836

\- - - - - - - - - - - - -

CHILDERS

1850 RHEA CENSUS
Edward C. Childers 50 (Farmer), Luisa 31, James 15, Bahathelon (f) 14, Lucy 12, Perry 10, Sarah 7, Mary 5, Alfred 2, John 2/12 p. 605-470
Malinda Childers 25, Mary E. 15, Minerva J. 10, Eliza E. 5 p. 607-487
MARRIAGES (RHEA)
Edmund P. Childers to Louisa Stewart, 2 Oct 1834 (same), John Henninger MG, John Whaley Bm (AR)
John Childers to Polly Clemm, 25 July 1811 (same), Theophilus Johnson Bm (A)
MISCELLANEOUS (RHEA)
Edward P. Childers: MG 1843-50

\- - - - - - - - - - - - -

CHILDRES / CHILDRESS

1850 MEIGS CENSUS
George Childres 34 (NC)(Farmer), Catharine 30 (NC), Mary Jane 1 p. 724-89
MARRIAGES (RHEA)
Elizabeth Childress to Phillip Brandon q.v.
MARRIAGES (MEIGS)
Louisa E. Childress to James Browder q.v.
William Childress to Sophia Taylor, 19 Sept 1841 (same), Peach Taylor JP [1850 Roane Census: Wm Childress 33, Sophia 25, James 8, Sarah L. 6, Martha A. 4, Mary 1]
William M. Childress to Hetty Ann Norman, 4 Nov 1841 (same), James Witton MG
MISCELLANEOUS (MEIGS)
Samuel L. Childress: Attorney, 1836
William Childress: JP(?) 1841

\- - - - - - - - - - - - -

CHILTON

TAXES (RHEA)
1819 (Capt. W.S. Bradley's Dist.):
Palatiah Chilton 1 WP, 600a
1830 RHEA CENSUS
Palatiah Chilton 001111 - 0121 p. 394
MISELLANEOUS (RHEA)
Asahel R. Chilton: Bondsman for William McElroy, 1831
" " " Bondsman for Anderson Jones, 1833
Palatiah Chilton: Bondsman for John Rawlings, 1812
Richard Chilton: Bondsman for Abraham Atchley, 1808

- - - - - - - - - - - -

CHRISMAN

1830 RHEA CENSUS
Charles Chrisman 00001 - 01001 p. 354
Isaac Chrisman 210001 - 10001 p. 354

- - - - - - - - - - - -

CHRISTIAN

1830 RHEA CENSUS
James Christian 00001 - 1001 p. 354
John Christian 10101 - 0 p. 363

- - - - - - - - - - - -

CHRISTOPHER

MARRIAGES (RHEA)
Garrett Christopher to Mary Ann Vines, 27 Jan 1831 (same), Isaac Roddy JP, Alexander Vines Bm (AR)
MISCELLANEOUS (RHEA)
Garrett Christopher: Bondsman for Alexander Vines, 1830

- - - - - - - - - - - -

CHUMLEY / CHUMMY
(see also CRUMLEY)

TAXES (RHEA)
1819 (Capt. John Lewis' Dist): Daniel Chumley 1 WP
1823 (Capt. Lewis' Co.): Daniel Chumley 1 WP
MARRIAGES (RHEA)
Daniel Chummy [Chumley] to Elizabeth Karnahan, 26 Jan 1813, William Karnahan Bm (R)
Elizabeth Chumley to Robert Goad q.v.

- - - - - - - - - - - -

CHURCHMAN

TAXES (RHEA)
1823 (Capt. Jackson's Co.): Joseph Churchman 1 WP

- - - - - - - - - - - -

CHURCHWELL

MARRIAGES (RHEA)
Eliza Churchwell to Allen Dalrimple q.v.

- - - - - - - - - - - -

CIBBLE

1850 RHEA CENSUS
William Cibble 24 (NC)(Farmer): see Thomas Largen

- - - - - - - - - - - -

CISLY

1830 RHEA CENSUS
Berron N. Cisly 00022001 -00100001 p. 389

- - - - - - - - - - - -

CLACK

TAXES (RHEA)
1823 (Capt. Wilson's Co.): Micajah C. Clack 1 WP
1830 RHEA CENSUS
John Clack 100001 - 10001 p. 385
M. Clack 120001 - 11001 p. 358
Raleigh Clack 11101001 - 2111001 p. 386
1840 RHEA CENSUS
Micajah Clack 2212001 - 011001
Rolly Clack 001111001 - 01111001
1850 RHEA CENSUS
Martha Clack 62, Missouri 44 (Farmer), Amy E. 28, Robert N. 24 (Farmer), Rebecca S. 22, Lemirah C. 20, Michael A. HALE 24 (Farmer) p. 569-214
Micajah Clack 51 (Ky)(Farmer), Margaret 53, Francis M. 26 (Farmer), Robert K. 25 (Farmer), Willie 23 (Farmer), Amy 21, John S. 19 (Farmer), Spencer 16 (Farmer), Micajah R. 14, William R. 1 p. 558-149
William M. Clack 33 (Farmer), Isabella G. 31, Martha A. 7, Missouri M. 6, Leander P. 4, John B. 2, Eliza J. 6/12 p. 568-205
MARRIAGES (RHEA)
John Clack to Prudence Rowden, 18 Dec 1828 (23 Dec), John Farmer MG, Robert N. Gillespie Bm (AR)
Mary Clack to William B. Miller q.v.
Mary Limere Clack to Charles Brady q.v.
Martha Clack to Thomas J. Kerr q.v.
William M. Clack to Isabella Wilson, 31 Aug 1841 (3 Sept), Jesse Thompson JP (R) [Isabella, dau of James M. and Anne Cozby Wilson]
MISCELLANEOUS (RHEA)
John Clack: Bondsman for William Hill, 1823
" " Bondsman for William Lewis, 1824
" " Bondsman for Nicholas C. Porter, 1825
Missoree Clack: Bondsman for Alexander Galbreath, 1828
" " Bondsman for William B. Miller, 1837
MISCELLANEOUS (MEIGS)
Alexander Clack: JP(?) 1842-43
John Clack: Hiwassee District
M. Clack: Hiwassee District

- - - - - - - - - - - -

CLABOUGH / CLAYBOUGH
(see also COLBOUGH)

MARRIAGES (RHEA)
Polly Clabough or Claybough to William Fuller q.v.

- - - - - - - - - - - -

CLARK / CLERK / CLEEK

TAXES (RHEA)
1808 (Joseph Brook's List): Thomas Clark 1 WP
1819 (Capt. W.S. Bradley's Dist.): Thomas N. Clark 600a

1830 RHEA CENSUS
Henry Clark 0000000001 - 10100101 p. 375
1840 MEIGS CENSUS
Alexander Clark 020001 - 0200001 p. 239
Cinthy Clark 0 - 0000010001 p. 234
George Clark 10001 - 00001001 p. 234
Jesse Clark 210001 - 020001 p. 240
Nancy Clark (free colored) 1-1201 p. 239
1850 RHEA CENSUS
Henry Cleek 41 (Farmer), Malinda 38, Henry 16 (Farmer), Rebecca 15, Thomas 13, Mary 12, Lilburn 7, Lucyann 5, Samuel 4, Margaret 2 p. 541-52
Adeline Clark 15 (mulatto), Alexander 9 (mulatto), Anderson 7 (mulatto): see John Whaley
1850 MEIGS CENSUS
Daniel M. Clark 27 (Farmer), Amaranda 18, Noble N. 0 p. 793-626
Elizabeth Clark 54 (NC) p. 763-392
Jesse Clark 84 (Va) p. 791-614

MARRIAGES (RHEA)
Anne Clark to James M. Sappington q.v.
John Clack or Clark to Rebecca Edgemon or Edgmon, 14 Oct 1835 (15 Oct), Stephen Winton JP, John Swafford Bm (AR)
Lucy Clark to David Lewis q.v.
Sally Clark to Moses Pittman q.v.
Sally Clark to Turner Caisey q.v.
William Clark to Elizabeth Holt, 17 Sept 1819 (same), Hezekiah Shelton Bm (A)
MARRIAGES (MEIGS)
Abraham Clark to Mary Ann Edgmon, 9 Nov 1840 (12 Nov), James Patterson JP
[1850 Roane Census: Abram H. Clark 33, Mary A. 36, James 9, Sarah J. 7, Nancy C. 4, Dely A. 2]
Ann Clark to Samuel McDaniel q.v.
Daniel M. Clark to Anney Mandy Molton, 17 Sept 1849 (20 Sept), Leander Wilson MG
John A. Clark to Drisanna Edgemon, 22 Nov 1843 (23 Nov), Richard Simpson MG

MISCELLANEOUS (MEIGS)
Abraham Clark: JP(?) 1842
Henry Clark: Revolutionary War Pensioner(?)
Jno. A. Clark: JP(?) 1840

\- - - - - - - - - - - -

CLAWSON

1850 RHEA CENSUS
Mariah Clawson 34 (black), James EDMONDS 21 (Apprentice) p. 608-496
MARRIAGES (RHEA)
Isabella T. Clawson to Franklin Locke q.v.
MISCELLANEOUS (MEIGS
John M. Clawson: Private, Mexican War

\- - - - - - - - - - - -

CLAY or WAY

1850 MEIGS CENSUS
James Clay or Way 38 (Va)(Farmer), Susanna 38, Andrew J. 18, Eliza Jane 16, Martha Ann 14, Judson 11 Nancy 9, William E. 7, Mary E. 5, Hesikiah 1 p. 755-346

\- - - - - - - - - - - -

CLAYTON

MARRIAGES (RHEA)
Eleanor Clayton to John Taylor q.v.

\- - - - - - - - - - - -

CLEMENT / CLEMENTS / CLEMONT

MARRIAGES (RHEA)
Frances Clemont to Jesse Sutton q.v.
Isaac Clement to Nancy Rigg, 1 Dec 1825, Jesse Sutton Bm (A)
William Clements to Louisa Black, 31 July 1835, Jesse Clements Bm (A)
MISCELLANEOUS (RHEA)
Jesse Clements: Bondsman for William Clements, 1835

\- - - - - - - - - - - -

CLEMENTSON

1850 MEIGS CENSUS
George M. Clementson [*] 25 (DC)(Doctor) p. 796-648 [*incorrectly spelled Clemison on census]

\- - - - - - - - - - - -

CLEMM

MARRIAGES (RHEA)
Polly Clemm to John Childers q.v.

\- - - - - - - - - - - -

CLEMONS / CLEMMONS

1840 MEIGS CENSUS
Cornelius Clemmons 002001 - 1110001 p. 237
MARRIAGES (RHEA)
James Clemons to Polly Black, 16 Apr 1816, Thomas Cantrell Bm (A)
MARRIAGES (MEIGS)
John Clemons to Susan Mavity, 8 July 1845 (same), B.F. McKenzie JP

\- - - - - - - - - - - -

CLENDENON

MISCELLANEOUS (MEIGS)
Robert W. Clendenon: Private, Mexican War

\- - - - - - - - - - - -

CLICK

1830 RHEA CENSUS
E. Click 012 - 100101 p. 377

1840 MEIGS CENSUS
Michael Click 20001 - 00001 p. 237
MARRIAGES (RHEA)
Rebecca Click to William Redmond q.v.
MARRIAGES (MEIGS)
G.W. Click to Mary Hughes, 4 Apr 1839 (same), John Taff JP
MISELLANEOUS (MEIGS)
George W. Click: JP(?) 1840

CLIFT

1830 RHEA CENSUS
Eliza Clift 011 - 1111201 p. 395

CLIFTON

1830 RHEA CENSUS
Baly Clifton 2130101 - 01200101 p. 383
1840 RHEA CENSUS
Bailey Clifton 00213002 - 00010001
Richmond Clifton 100001 - 21001
1850 RHEA CENSUS
Aldridge Clifton 30 (Farmer), Allis M. 24, Thomas B. 1 p. 572-236
Bailey Clifton 65 (NC)(Farmer), Elizabeth 35 (NC), Pincney BARTON 10 (NC), Alfred 11 (NC), Mary 11 (NC), Sarah 9 (NC), Martha 8 (NC), James 6 (NC), Pearson CLIFTON 2 (NC) p. 576-261
MARRIAGES (RHEA)
Aldridge Clifton to Alice M. Long, ---?--- (2 March 1848), T.J. Creede JP (R)
Bailey Clifton to Elizabeth Burton, 15 Apr 1848 (same), T.J. Creede JP (R)
Gilley Clifton to Thomas M. Pitmon q.v.
Jonah R. Clifton to Margaret Moore, 7 Aug 1846 (9 Aug), Charles Cox JP (R)
Martha Clifton to Woodson Page q.v.
Mary Clifton to Hiram Henry q.v.
Richard Clifton to Tabitha Armstrong, 5 Jan 1833 (21 Nov*), Daniel Walker JP, James Poe Bm (AR) [* dates were written thusly; the Nov date may only be when the papers of D. Walker were returned, although there was no notation to that effect as on other returns]
MARRIAGES (MEIGS)
John Clifton to E.R. Sadlers, 31 Dec 1843 (same), Daniel Cate JP

CLINE

TAXES (RHEA)
1819 (Capt. McGill's Co.): John Cline 1 WP
1850 RHEA CENSUS
Isaac P. Cline 23 (Carpenter), Polly A. 25, John W. 3/12 p. 545-79
MARRIAGES (RHEA)
Isaac Cline to Mary A. Newport, 30 May 1849 (same), Asa Newport MG (R)
John Cline to Nancy Vicory, 6 Dec 1812 (same), James Mea Bm (A)
Susanna Cline to George W. Morgan q.v.

CLINTON

MARRIAGES (RHEA)
Elizabeth Clinton to Henry Garrison q.v.
Polly Clinton to William Laycock q.v.

CLINGAN / CLINGON / CLINGHAN

1830 RHEA CENSUS
David Clingan 120001 - 200001 p. 379
1840 RHEA CENSUS
Edward Clingan 01101 - 10001
1850 RHEA CENSUS
William Clinghan 24 (Farmer), Caroline M. 25, Mary C. 3, Martha A. 2, Richard or Robert 1 p. 632-627
1850 MEIGS CENSUS
Elijah Clingon 22, Mary M. 21, William L. 1 p. 736-186
MARRIAGES (RHEA)
Alexander Clinghan to Martha Blythe, 30 Apr 1828 (1 May), Thos K. Clinghan MG, John Day Bm (AR) [1850 Bradley Census: Alexander Clingon 41, Martha 39, Elizabeth 20, Mary 19, William 17, Emaline 15, Martha 14, Judge H. 13, Adaline 11, Manerva 10, James 8, Alexander 6, Sila Ann 3, Edward 2, Infant 4/12]
David Clingan to Nancy Marbry or Marberry, 17 Dec 1822 (26 Dec), James McDonald JP, Benjamin Marberry Bm (AR)
Edward Clingan to Fanny Vines, 31 May 1833, John Day Bm (A)
Elijah Clingon to Malinda Starnis, 22 June 1848 (no return) (R)
James C. Clingham or Clingan to Jane Marbury, 9 Dec 1826 (10 Dec), James McDonald JP, Benjamin Marbury Bm (AR)
Jane E. Clingon to David Fox q.v.
Matilda Clingan to Jonathan Sullivan q.v.
William Clingan to Matilda C. Brock, 15 Jan 1846 (same), D. Ragsdale JP (R)
MISCELLANEOUS (RHEA and MEIGS)
Elijah Clingan: Private, Mexican War
George W. Clingham: Bondsman for John Carr, 1829
John Clingan: Bondsman for Hiram Raines, 1834
Thomas K. Clingham: MG 1828, 1835

CLOUD

1840 MEIGS CENSUS
Jeremiah Cloud 20210001 - 1100001 p. 236 [see 1850 Bradley County Census]
MISCELLANEOUS (MEIGS)
Jeremiah Cloud: Purchsed Lot 76 in Decatur, 1836

CLOUGH

MARRIAGES (RHEA)
Judy Clough to Greenberry Casteel q.v.
Martha Clough to John S. Puckett q.v.
Mary Clough to James Cobb q.v.
Nancy Clough to John R. Casteel q.v.
Patheny Clough to Joseph Bayless q.v.

\- - - - - - - - - - - - -

COBB / COBBS

TAXES (RHEA)
1823 (Capt. Brown's Co.): James L. Cobbs 1 WP
MARRIAGES (RHEA)
James Cobb to Mary Clough, 6 Feb 1834, John Crawford Bm (A)
William Cobb to Lucinda Howard, 28 Nov 1838, Azariah Barton Bm (A)
[1850 Hamilton Census: Wm W. Cobb 40, Loucinda 36, Elizabeth 15, Christopher 13]
MISCELLANEOUS (RHEA)
James Cobb: Bondsman for John Dozier, 1836

\- - - - - - - - - - - - -

COCKSON

1850 MEIGS CENSUS
Isaac Cockson 22 (Farmer), Martha 19, Sarah Jane 1 p. 733-160
MARRIAGES (MEIGS)
Isaac Cockson to Martha Moreland, ---?--- (15 Apr 1848), Jesse Locke MG

\- - - - - - - - - - - - -

COFER

1840 MEIGS CENSUS
Elizabeth Cofer 00001 - 020001 p. 240
1850 MEIGS CENSUS
James Cofer 56 (Farmer), Eliza 44 (Va), Martha 21, Sarah 20, Polly 19, Lewis 17, Nancy Ann 14, Margaret 9, Emely 4 p. 791-613 [James married Eliza Black on 10 June 1821 in Roane County]
James T. Cofer 37 (Va)(Blacksmith), Matilda 38, Charles G. 10, Abraham 7, George W. 3 p. 718-40
John Cofer 31 (NC)(Farmer), Nancy Jane 20, Emily C. 4, Mary Jane 2 p. 718-41
Joseph Cofer 30 (Va), Mary Ann 24, George W. 7, Betsy Jane 5, Lewis 3, Caswell 2, Juluan (f) 1 p. 718-39
MARRIAGES (MEIGS)
John Cofer to Nancy J. Shiflett, 30 July 1845 (same), John Seabourn JP
Joseph Cofer to Mary Ann Shiflet, 23 July 1842 (25 July), John Seaborn JP
MISCELLANEOUS (MEIGS)
Joseph Cofer: Ocoee District

\- - - - - - - - - - - - -

COKER

MARRIAGES (MEIGS)
Mahaly Ann Coker to Joseph Looney q.v.

\- - - - - - - - - - - - -

COFFEE / COFFY / COFFEY
(see also CROFT)

1830 RHEA CENSUS
Jno Coffy 202101 - 020101 p. 373
1840 MEIGS CENSUS
Robert Coffy 10002 - 10001 p. 234
Thomas Coffy 1031201 - 0001201 p. 235
1850 MEIGS CENSUS
Levin Coffy 30 (NC)(Farmer), Cialia 20, Thomas 4, Ruth 3, Sarah 1 p. 746-262
Thomas Coffee 57 (NC)(Farmer), Sarah 56 (NC), Celia 38 (NC), Francis M. 22 (Farmer), Edward J. 21 (Farmer), George N. 18 (Farmer), Joseph A. 14, Zilpha BOUND 13, Cealy STOKES 84 (Md) p. 768-431
William Coffee 30 (NC)(Farmer), Anna 26 p. 746-263
MARRIAGES (RHEA)
Jesse Coffee to Anne R. Hackett, 9 Sept 1817 (same), Matthew Donald MG, Benjamin C. Stout Bm (AR)
MARRIAGES (MEIGS)
Leven S. Coffey to Celia Perry, 24 Dec 1844 (same), D.L. Godsey MG
Michael W. Coffey to Anna Williams, 8 Apr 1842 (11 Apr), B.F. McKenzie JP
Sarah Coffey to Daniel H. Chambers q.v.
MISCELLANEOUS (MEIGS)
Irven S. Coffey: JP(?) 1846
Robert Coffey: JP(?) 1843
" " Cherokee Removal muster roll, 1836

\- - - - - - - - - - - - -

COLBOUGH
(see also CLABOUGH)

1850 MEIGS CENSUS
George Colbough 36 (Farmer), Elizabeth 32, John 12, Nathan 10, Henry 8, Robert E. 6, Mahala T. 1 p. 757-354
Henry Colbough 45 (Farmer), Mary 30, Samuel 15, Susannah 12, John 8, Charlotte 5, Minerva L. 1 p. 749-294
MARRIAGES (RHEA)
Betsy Colbough to Jacob Shults q.v.
MISCELLANEOUS (MEIGS)
George Colbough: Surety for John Hite, 1850

\- - - - - - - - - - - - -

COLE

TAXES (RHEA)
1823 (Capt. Piper's Co.): Adam Cole 1 WP
1830 RHEA CENSUS
Adam Cole 0101001 - 001101 p. 359
Thomas Cole 00001 - 201001 p. 352

1840 RHEA CENSUS
Adam Cole 00010001 - 0001001 p. 240
Harrington Cole 20001 - 00001 p. 242
Polly Cole 11 - 110101 p. 243
1850 MEIGS CENSUS
Adam Cole 62 (Va)(Farmer), Rebecca 57 p. 789-597
MARRIAGES (RHEA)
Harrington Cole to Mahaley Collins, 7 Mar 1836, Thomas J. Gillespie Bm (A)
James Cole to Margaret Bailey, 1 Mar 1824 (same), John Rice JP, Evan Evans Bm (A)
Nancy Cole to Robert Wann q.v.
MARRIAGES (MEIGS)
John Cole to Sophia A. Burcham, 18 June 1844 (20 June), D.L. Godsey MG
Lucinda Cole to Elijah Hutsell q.v.
MISCELLANEOUS (RHEA and MEIGS)
James Cole: Bondsman for Joshua Bailey, 1841
" " Hiwassee District, Sewee Creek area
John Cole: Bondsman for Braxton C. Sams, 1825

- - - - - - - - - - - - -

COLEMAN

1830 RHEA CENSUS
Absolom Coleman 2011001 - 2110001 p. 374
1850 RHEA CENSUS
William Coleman 17: see David M. Roddy
MARRIAGES (RHEA)
Chancy Coleman to George Kincannon q.v.
Rachel Coleman to William W. Hilton q.v.
MISCELLANEOUS (RHEA)
Absolem Coleman: First Clerk, Goodfield Baptist Church of Christ, 1837
Chana Coleman: Member, Goodfield Baptist C of C, 1837
Nancy Coleman: Member, Goodfield Baptist C of C, 1837
William Coleman: Bondsman for James H. Vernon, 1834
Wm Lillard Coleman: Bondsman for Thos Johnston, 1832

- - - - - - - - - - - - -

COLLIER

1850 MEIGS CENSUS
Wilson Collier 48 (NC)(Farmer), Cyntha 42 (SC), Cyntha L. 22 (SC), Malinda A. 16, Martha E. 10, Robert D. 4 p. 765-410
MARRIAGES (RHEA)
Mary W. Collier to William Fox q.v.

- - - - - - - - - - - - -

COLLINS / COLLENS / COLUNS

TAXES (RHEA)
1819 (Capt. John Lewis' Dist.): Henry Collins 1 WP, 460½a
(Capt. John Ramsey's Dist.): James Collins 100a
1823 (Capt. Jackson's Co.): Elijah Collins 1 WP, 1 BP
(Capt. Lewis' Co.): Henry Collins 1 WP, 456a
(Capt. Wilson's Co.): Jonathan Collins 1 WP
(Capt. Lewis' Co.): Lewis R. Collins 1 WP, 125a
(Capt. Jackson's Co.): William Collins 1 WP
1830 RHEA CENSUS
Henry Collins 0111101 - 1111001 p. 393
Jonathan Collins 01011 - 41001 p. 358
Joseph Coluns 110101 - 201111 p. 369
Lewis R. Collins 000001 - 100001 p. 393
William D. Collins 10101 - 022001 p. 364
1840 RHEA CENSUS
Henry Collins 00012001 - 00010001
Nancy Collins 122101 - 120101
1840 MEIGS CENSUS
John Collins 1001001 - 10101 p. 238
Joseph Collins 01110001 - 0111101 p. 283
William D. Collins 010001 - 0012001 p. 230
1850 RHEA CENSUS
Alfred Collins 22 (NC)(Farmer), Patsy A. 18 p. 574-248
Andrew J. Collins 28 (NC)(Farmer), Barbary A. 20 (NC), Mary J. 6, Elizabeth 4 p. 578-277
Henry Collins 28 (Farmer), Mary 26, Peyton 6, Julia 4, William P. 2 p. 588-355
James P. Collins 39 (Farmer), Susan H. 28, James J. 6, Henry C. 4, William G. 2 p. 594-367
Joshua Collins 25 (NC), Elizabeth 20 (NC), Cyntha A. 2, Thomas C. 3/12 p. 577-269
Kimbro Collins 22 (Farmer), Rebecca A. 20, John T. 3 p. 581-296
Nancy Collins 42 (NC), William C. 17 (Farmer), Malinda 15, Elizabeth 13, Bluford M. 11, Lenallen 7 (mulatto) p. 581-295
Pincney Collins 29 (NC)(Farmer), Charlotte 26 (NC), Edward L. 1, William H. 1/12 p. 574-251
William Collins 60 (NC)(Farmer), Mary 64 (NC), Eliza MOORE 26 (NC), William 9 (NC), Smith 7 (NC), Dotson 4 (NC), Madison EDMONDS 21 (Farmer) p. 574-247
1850 MEIGS CENSUS
Adaline Collins 6: see John K. Brown
Elizabeth Collins 60 (Va), Joseph 19 (Farmer), Elizabeth 8 p. 770-447
Enoch Collins 26 (NC)(Doctor), Elizabeth 17 p. 811-749
James E. Collins 33 (Farmer), Jane 33 (Va), Louisa C. 6, Elizabeth C. 4, Martha Jane 3, Emaline 1 p. 723-87
Jonathan M. Collins 21 (Ky)(Farmer), Caroline 21, Joseph G. 1 p. 785-568
Reuben C. Collins 23 (Farmer), Elizabeth 22 p. 740-217
William Collins 59 (Va)(Farmer), Elizabeth 55 p. 740-216
William Collins 28 (Dentist): see Jeremiah Chapman
MARRIAGES (RHEA)
Alfred Collins to Mahala E. Pierce, 28 Dec 1841* (31 Dec), Bryan R. McDonald JP
[NOTE: Allen shows year as 1840]
Alfred Collins to Datsia A. Snodgrass, 22 Aug 1849 (23 Aug), Daniel Broyles JP (R)
Celia Collins to Abraham Cox q.v.
Eliza M. Collins to Thomas C. Darwin q.v.
Henry C. Collins to Mary A. Darwin, 11 Mar 1844 (14 Mar), D. Ragsdale JP (R)
James P. Collins to Susan Darwin, 12 Jan 1842 (13 Jan), David Leuty JP (R)
Jane Collins to Robert Murphy q.v.
Jonathan Collins to Telutha or Lelitha Royster, 26 Aug 1834 (same), John Randles JP, Robert Wan Bm (AR) [1850 Bradley Census: Jonathan Collins 56, Leoth A. 30, Selia J. 14, John G. 11, Racheal 9, James J. 7, Caroline 4, Julia A. 2, Thomas J. COLLINS 26]
Joshua Collins to Betsy Mirah Essex, 11 Nov 1846 (12 Nov), Daniel Broyles JP (R)

Lydia Collins to Joshua Wann q.v.
Mahaley Collins to Harrington Cole q.v.
Margaret Collins to John Ferguson q.v.
Orthey Collins to Arthur L. Fulton q.v.
Pickney Collins to Charlotty King, 27 Jan 1848 (same), T.J. Creede JP (R)
Rachel E. Collins to Levi Ferguson q.v.
Sally Collins to Charles Woodward q.v.
Sarah Collins to George Minix q.v.
Sarah Collins to John Rodgers q.v.
William Collins to Ann Fergusson, 20 Dec 1850 (21 Dec), John O. Torbett JP (R)

MARRIAGES (MEIGS)
Angeline Collins to Richard Rice q.v.
Barbara Collins to Wm R. McMullen q.v.
Eleanor Collins to Horatio Leonard q.v.
Enoch Collins to Elizabeth Wasson, 28 July 1849 (9 Aug), Wm Green MG
James Collins to Jane Rigg, 13 Sept 1843 (14 Sept), B.F. McKenzie JP
Jane Collins to James A. Cowan q.v.
Jonathan M. Collins to Caroline Royster, 27 Jan 1849 (28 Jan), John Davis JP
Joseph Collins to Elender McDaniel, 6 Nov 1850, Wm Eaves Sur
Nancy Collins to Calvin R. Taff q.v.
Reubin C. Collins to Elizabeth C. Lock, 17 Aug 1849 (18 Aug), R.A. Giddens MG
William Collins to Eliza Jane Young, 15 Oct 1849 (same), J.M. Butler JP

MISCELLANEOUS (RHEA)
Henry Collins: Early merchant in Town of Washington
" " JP 1813, 1818, 1821, 1836-38
James P. Collins: JP 1848-49
" " " Bondsman for William O. Kent, 1839
Jonathan Collins: Bondsman for Joshua Wann, 1820
William Collins: Bondsman for Charles Woodward, 1821
" " Bondsman for Thomas Hunneycut, 1825
William D. Collins: Purchased Lot 36, Cottonport, 1834

MISCELLANEOUS (MEIGS)
James E. Collins: Cherokee Removal muster roll, 1836
" " " JP(?) 1840
Jonathan Collins: Hiwassee District, Sewee Creek area
" " Common School Com., Dist 4, 1838
" " Private, Mexican War

COLLISON / CALLISON / KELLISON

MARRIAGES (RHEA)
James Callison to Sarah Craig, 12 May 1818 (same), H. Collins JP, John Love Bm (AR)
Robert Kellison or Collison to Sidney Pharris or Cedney Farris, 28 Mar 1816, "I married the above" J. Fine JP, Reubin Philpot Bm (AR)

MISCELLANEOUS (RHEA)
John Collison: Bondsman for John Armstrong, 1818

COLVILLE

1850 RHEA CENSUS
John H. Colville 32 (Lawyer), Jannette B. 26, John S. 4, Gillespie W. 9/12 p. 612-412 [John married Jennette Lide on 6 July 1843 in McMinn Co.]
Warner E. Colville 32 (Farmer), Vesta 27, Richard W. 7, Young 4, Patrick C. 3 p. 568-204
[Warner married Vesta, dau of Richard Greene Waterhouse, in Warren County]

MARRIAGES (RHEA)
Luke Colville to Cinthia W. Hackett, 9 Jan 1815 (A)
Ruth Colville to Spencer Beavers q.v.

MISCELLANEOUS (RHEA)
George Colville: Town of Washington, Lots 82 and 88 [1850 McMinn Census: George Colville 82, Sarah WIER 46, J.C. WIER 35, Eliza RICHARDS 21]

COMBS

MARRIAGES (RHEA)
Jesse Combs to Priscella Maypes or Mapes, 8 or 18 May 1832 (same), Thomas Cox JP, Hugh T. Baldwin Bm (AR)

MISCELLANEOUS (RHEA)
Levi Combs: Hiwassee District
" " Elder, Concord Baptist Church of Christ, 1824

COMPTON / CUMPTON

TAXES (RHEA)
1823 (Capt. Lewis' Co.): William Cumpton 1 WP

1830 RHEA CENSUS
William Compton 1101001 - 0020101 p. 393
Zachariah Compton 010001 - 22101 p. 393

1840 RHEA CENSUS
William Compton 01111001 - 00002001
Zachariah Compton 1101001 - 112211

1850 RHEA CENSUS
John Compton 27 (Farmer), Elizabeth J. 22, Gregory P. 1 p. 576-262
William Compton 62 (Farmer), Susan 61, William 23 (Farmer), Alfred 17 (Farmer) p. 593-362
Zachariah Compton 60 (Farmer), Susan 48, Hetta 20, Mahala 18, Jeremiah 16 (Farmer), Gideon T. 14, Jane 10, Thomas 8, James T. 3 p. 576-263

MARRIAGES (RHEA)
Delila Compton to S.D. Broyles q.v.
John Compton to Elizabeth Ganaway, 12 July 1848 (13 July), Rufus M. Hickey MG (R)
Matilda Compton to Thomas I. Harwood q.v.
Rebecca Compton to Peter W. Miller q.v.
W.A. Compton to Wealthy Fergusson, 31 July 1850 (same), John O. Torbett JP (R)

MISCELLANEOUS (RHEA)
William Compton: Registerar of Deeds, 1848-1856

COMSON

MISCELLANEOUS (MEIGS)
James Comson: JP(?) 1841

- - - - - - - - - - - -

CONDUFF

1850 MEIGS CENSUS
Thomas Conduff 46 (Va)(Farmer), Mary 42 (Va), Isaac H. 20 (Va)(Farmer), Fanny Jane 18, Rhoda Ann 16, William R. 14, Mary E. 13, Catharine M. 11, James M. 10, Gabriel J. 8, Parthena 5, Milly C. 2, Isaac 70 (Va) p. 801-681

- - - - - - - - - - - -

CONLEY / CONLY / CONDLEY

TAXES (RHEA)
1819 (Capt. John Robinson's Co.): John Conley 7 BP, 300a
1830 RHEA CENSUS
Jno. Conley 000000001 - 0000000001 p. 292
1840 RHEA CENSUS
John Conly 00000000001 - 0
Silas Conly 00001 - 01
Thomas Conly 00001 - 00011
1850 RHEA CENSUS
Thomas Conley 31, Anna 26, Margaret J. 5, Arminda 3, Martha A. 3/12 p. 620-546
1850 MEIGS CENSUS
Hannah Conly 25, Michael A. 8, John W. 5, Mary E. 2 p. 749-291
MARRIAGES (RHEA)
Ann Condley to Jacob Moyers q.v.
Nancy J. Conley to Charles M.J. Welch q.v.
Silas Conley to Polly Ryan, 26 Feb 1829 (same), John McClure JP, Richard Conley Bm (AR)
Silas Conly or Condley to Sarah Covington, 15 Aug 1841 (17 Aug), Jas Hooper JP, Thos Condley Bm (AR)
MISCELLANEOUS (RHEA)
John Conly: Town of Washington (Lots 22,24), 1812
John Condley: JP 1827, 1830-40
Richard Conley: Bondsman for Silas Conley, 1829
Silas Conley: Bondsman for Thomas Condley, 1841
Thomas Condley, Bondsman for Silas Conley, 1841

- - - - - - - - - - - -

CONNER

1840 RHEA CENSUS
John Conner 00010001 - 0010001
1840 MEIGS CENSUS
Mordeci Conner (free colored) 55-100 yrs old
MARRIAGES (RHEA)
Eleanor Conner to Charles Woollard q.v.
Sarah Conner to Rufus Anderson q.v.

- - - - - - - - - - - -

COOK / COOKE

TAXES (RHEA)
1808 (John Henry's List): Jacob Cooke 1 WP
1819 (Capt. McGill's Co.): Jacob Cook 1 WP
1840 RHEA CENSUS
John Cook 131101 - 002001
Philip Cook 110001 - 00001
1850 RHEA CENSUS
Bromley Cook 18: see John L. Marsh
1850 MEIGS CENSUS
Eliza Jane Cook 23, Mary Jane 2, Martha 1 p. 791-612
MARRIAGES (RHEA)
J.N. Cook to Lethy [Aletha] Woodward or Underwood, 31 July 1845 (same), Samuel Frazier JP, O.B. Marsh Bm (AR)
Jacob Cooke to Nancy McRoberts, 11 Oct 1821 (same), A. David JP (AR)
John Cook to Jane Cox, 1 Aug 1833 (same), Joseph Mc-Corkle JP, Meredith Cox Bm (AR)
Nancy Cook to Samuel A. Erwin q.v.
Orinda Cook to John F. Marsh q.v.
MISCELLANEOUS (RHEA)
John Cook: Trustee, Sulphur Springs Meth. Church, 1841
" " Trustee, Rhea County, 1842-1844

- - - - - - - - - - - -

COOKSON

MARRIAGES (RHEA)
Joseph Cookson to Christina Vanagrift or Vandergrift, 24 Jan 1820 (25 Jan), Wm Randolph, Elder (AR)

- - - - - - - - - - - -

COOLEY / COOLY / COLEY / COOTLEY

TAXES (RHEA)
1823 (Capt. Smith's Co.): Robert Cooley 1 WP
1830 RHEA CENSUS
Robert Cooly 100001 - 22002 p. 373
1840 MEIGS CENSUS
Robert Cootley 0101001 - 1211001 p. 237
1850 MEIGS CENSUS
Robert Cooley 57 (Va)(Farmer), Mary 50 (Va), Sarah 27, Rebecca 24, Mary 20, John 18 (Farmer), Martha 16, Nancy 11, Wright 10, William 7, Mary Jane 2 p. 763-395
MARRIAGES (MEIGS)
Permely Cooley to John Hensley q.v.
Rebecca Coley to John Helton q.v.
MISCELLANEOUS (RHEA)
Robert Cooley: JP 1827-32
" " Bondsman for David Campbell, 1830
" " Bondsman for Joseph P. Stockton, 1831
MISCELLANEOUS (MEIGS)
Robert Cooley: Hiwassee District; JP 1848-49

- - - - - - - - - - - -

COOPER

TAXES (RHEA)
1819 (Capt. Wm McCray's Co.): Isham Cooper 1 WP
1830 RHEA CENSUS
Hiram Cooper 0101 - 20001 p. 388
Kennally Cooper 000001 - 311101 p. 384
Newsom Cooper 10000001 - 00001001 p. 392

1840 RHEA CENSUS
Cornelius Cooper 20001 - 00001
Newsom Cooper 001000001 - 000000001
1840 MEIGS CENSUS
Isaac Cooper 00001 - 00001 p. 229
1850 RHEA CENSUS
Isabella Cooper 56: see Jacob L. Wassum
MARRIAGES (RHEA)
Anderson Cooper to Melisa Pearce, 29 Aug 1849 (30 Aug), S.A. Wadland MG (R)
Benjamin Cooper to Nancy Jennings, 30 Apr 1834 (7 May), John Pardee MMEC, Randolph Cozby Bm (AR) [1850 Hamilton Census: Benjamin Cooper 38, Nancy 31, Sarah 12, Prira 8, Alexander 6, Anna 3, Martha 1]
Cinthia Cooper to William Thompson q.v.
Elbert E. Cooper to Nancy Wann, 5 Aug 1833 (8 Aug), Daniel Briggs MG, William Wann Bm (AR)
Margaret Cooper to Dickenson Jennings q.v.
Myram Cooper to John Ferguson q.v.
Richard Cooper to Phillis Davis, 8 Oct 1829 (same), Jesse Thompson JP, William Pollard Bm (AR)
Robert Cooper to Mary English, 2 Mar 1819, Micajah Howerton Bm (A)
Sally Cooper to Edward Kitchen q.v.
MISCELLANEOUS (RHEA)
Richard Cooper: Revolutionary War Pensioner, 1835 list; in 1829 (when they were married), Richard was 72 years old and his wife, Phillis, was 69
Robert Cooper: Bondsman for Edward Kitchen, 1820
MISCELLANEOUS (MEIGS)
E.E. Cooper: MG or JP 1839

\- - - - - - - - - - - -

COOTS / COATS

MARRIAGES (MEIGS)
Hiram Coots to Betsy Howerton, 22 Feb 1823 (2 Feb), Fred Fulkerson JP, Jeremiah Howerton Bm (AR)
William Coots or Coats to Polly Kale, 25 Jan 1835, V.H. Giles JP, Meredith Cox and Redden Harrods Bm (AR)

\- - - - - - - - - - - -

COPPICK / COPPECK

1830 RHEA CENSUS
Aaron Coppick 20001 - 00001
[1850 McMinn Census: Aaron Coppeck 48, Olly 41, Alfred 18, John 17, Margaret 12, George 10, Louisa 7, Harrison 6, Luke 4]

\- - - - - - - - - - - -

CORBET

MARRIAGES (RHEA)
Elisha Corbet to Mary Gann, 31 Dec 1817 (same), Jacob Davis Bm (A)

\- - - - - - - - - - - -

CORDER

1840 RHEA CENSUS
Enoch Corder 10001 - 10001
MARRIAGES (RHEA)
Betsey Corder to Frederick Prysock q.v.
Cynthia Corder to Isaac Goldsby q.v.
Cynthia Corder to Noah Williams q.v.

\- - - - - - - - - - - -

CORNELIUS

1830 RHEA CENSUS
Abner Cornelius 20001 - 10001 p. 55

\- - - - - - - - - - - -

CORNWALL

1840 MEIGS CENSUS
Hiram Cornwall 200001 - 110001 p. 227

\- - - - - - - - - - - -

CORVAN / CORVIN / CARVIN / CERVIN / CURVEN / CORVEL

1840 MEIGS CENSUS
Elizabeth Curven 11 - 012001001 p. 226
Thomas Corvel 0012201 - 0111001 p. 228
1850 MEIGS CENSUS
Duncan Corvin 33 (Va)(Farmer), Minerva 27, William 7, Thomas 6, Martha Ann 5, Nancy 3, Margaret 1 p. 737-198
Eli Corvin 23 (Va)(Farmer), Delilah 18, Charles M. 3, Malinda Jane 1 p. 76-181
Elizabeth Cervin 45 (SC), Anna 23 (SC), Mary 20 (SC), Hannah 18 (SC), Francis 12 p. 723-78
James Corvan 30 (Va)(Farmer), Sarah 25, Mary Jane 1 p. 736-183
Philo Corvin 32 (Va), Margaret 20, Plesent M. 4, Charles M. 1 p. 736-181
Thomas Corvan 58 (Va)(Farmer), Elizabeth 17 p. 736-185
MARRIAGES (RHEA)
William Corvin to Polly Ann Gullion, 17 Apr 1833, V.E. Giles JP, Harris Ryon Bm (AR)
MARRIAGES (MEIGS)
James Carvin to Sarah Martin, 21 Aug 1845 (25 Aug), Wm Johns JP
Nancy Carvin to Charles McCarrell q.v.
Philow Carvin to Peggy Teague, 7 Feb 1845 (10 Feb), Jesse Locke MG
MISCELLANEOUS (MEIGS)
James A. Carvan: JP(?) 1843
Philon Carvin: JP(?) 1843

\- - - - - - - - - - - -

COTTON

TAXES (RHEA)
1808 (John Henry's List): Robert Cotton, 2000a Richland Creek (Main and E. Ford)
1823 (Capt. Wilson's Co.): William Cotton 1 WP

\- - - - - - - - - - - -

COULSTON

1850 RHEA CENSUS
Sarah Coulston 52 (NC), Nathan 25 (Farmer), Nancy A. 23, John 20 (Farmer), Mary J. 4, Sarah E. 1 p. 587-396 [John Coulson married Sally Ketching on 17 Mar 1819 in Roane Co]

- - - - - - - - - - - - -

COULTER

TAXES (RHEA)
1819 (Capt. John Lewis' Dist.):
James Coulter 1 WP, 2 BP, 380a
Thomas Coulter 1 WP
1823 (Capt. Lewis' Co.): Alexander Coulter 1 WP
James Coulter 1 WP, 335a
1830 RHEA CENSUS
James Coulter 00012001 - 01114 p. 367
1840 RHEA CENSUS
James Coulter 00001 - 1001
1850 RHEA CENSUS
Eli Coulter 28 (Farmer), Lucinda 19 p. 594-372
Jane Coulter 46 (Va), Andrew 26 (Farmer), Patience 17, Mary A. 14, Charles 3 p. 601-419
1850 MEIGS CENSUS
Henry Coulter 34 (Farmer) p. 723-79
MARRIAGES (RHEA)
Ann Coulter to James B. Russell q.v.
Eli Coulter to Lucinda Pickard, 4 Jan 1849 (same), James P. Collins JP (R)
James Coulter to Matilda Coulter, 7 Apr 1849 (8 Apr), J.P. Collins JP (R)
Matilda Coulter to James Coulter q.v.
MISCELLANEOUS (RHEA)
Alexander Coulter: Bondsman for James Bean, 1821
" " Bondsman for Mansion Howard, 1824
" " Bondsman for James Holland, 1825
" " Bondsman for Robert Martin, 1826
Thomas Coulter: Bondsman for Joseph Alexander, 1818

- - - - - - - - - - - - -

COURTNEY

MISCELLANEOUS (RHEA)
John Courtney: MG 1832

- - - - - - - - - - - - -

COVINGTON

1840 RHEA CENSUS
John Covington 01001 - 21001
Richard Covington 21212001 - 10011101
1840 MEIGS CENSUS
William Covington 200001 - 02001 p. 231
1850 RHEA CENSUS
Andrew J. Covington 31 (Farmer), Rebecca 25, Richard 8, James M. 6, William J. 5, John 4, Lorenzo D. 2 p. 620-545
MARRIAGES (RHEA)
A.J. Covington to Rebecca Smith, 6 Dec 1841 (16 Dec), Bryan R. McDonald JP (R)
Anna Covington to Thomas Condley q.v.
Sarah Covington to Silas Condley q.v.

- - - - - - - - - - - - -

COWAN / COWEN

TAXES (RHEA)
1808 (Joseph Brooks' List):
James Cowan 1 WP, 170a W Fork Richland Creek
John Cowan WP
Joseph Cowan 1 WP, 100a W. Fork Richland Cr
1830 RHEA CENSUS
Jas or Jos Cowan 01101001 - 001101 p. 368
1840 MEIGS CENSUS
James Cowen 000100001 - 000010001 p. 230
1850 RHEA CENSUS
William Cowan 25 (Shoemaker), Harriet 24, Eliza J. 5/12, Ellen 5/12 p. 611-428
1850 MEIGS CENSUS
Elizabeth Cowan 70 (Pa) p. 740-215
James A.R. Cowan 28 (Farmer), Martha Jane 25, James R. 4, Elizabeth Ann 3, Martha E. 1 p. 740-214
James L. Cowan 29 (NC)(Farmer), Jane 26, Pauline E. 0 p. 743-244
John H. Cowan 33 (Farmer), Paulinia 30, Mary 10, James 8, William 6, Francis 2, Louisa 2 p. 740-222
Joseph Cowan 42, Susan 34 (Va), William D. 13, Mary E. 12, James 8, Partherenia F. 7, John C. 5, Robert A. 3, Martha E. 1 p. 745-254
MARRIAGES (RHEA)
Evaline Cowan to William Camp q.v.
Jane Cowan to William B. Russell q.v.
Joseph Cowan to Susan Chatten, 2 Mar 1836 (4 Mar), Eli Sutherland, Elder, George W. Chatten Bm (AR)
Peggy Cowan to William More q.v.
Polly Cowan to John L. McCarty q.v.
Polly Hanna Cowan to John Lauderdale q.v.
William Cowan to Isabela Cozby, 24 Oct 1839 (no return) (R) [1850 Bradley Census: Wm W. Cowin 50, Isabella 35, Sarah 10, Martha 8, William 6, Ellen 4, Eveline 2, W.W. McCLELLAND 25, Peter SLIGER 50]
William W. Cowan to Elizabeth Chattin, 6 May 1829, Abraham Cox Jr. Bm (A)
MARRIAGES (MEIGS)
James A. Cowan to Jane Collins, 24 July 1844 (25 July), W.S. Collins JP(?) [see also James McCOWAN]
MISCELLANEOUS (RHEA)
David Cowan: Bondsman for William Moon/Moore, 1822
James Cowan: On first Grand Jury, 1808
Joseph Cowan: Bondsman for William Camp, 1832
James Cowan: Postmaster at Cowansville, 1831
MISCELLANEOUS (MEIGS)
James Cowan: Commissioner to lay off Meigs County into Districts, 1836
" " Trustee, Dectur Academy, 1838-39
" " Hiwassee District and Ocoee District
Thomas Cowan: Ocoee District
William W. Cowan: Ocoee District

- - - - - - - - - - - - -

COWLY / COWLEY

1830 RHEA CENSUS
Isaac Cowly 01101001 - 0210001 p. 359
MISCELLANEOUS (MEIGS)
William C. Cowley: Cherokee Removal muster roll, 1836

- - - - - - - - - - - - -

COX

TAXES (RHEA)
1823 (Capt. Smith's Co.): Abraham Cox 160a Goodfield
Abraham Cox Jr. 1 WP
Meredith Cox 1 WP, 160a Goodfield
Thomas Cox 1 WP, 156a Tenn River
(Capt. Howard's Co.): Edmund Cox 1 WP
1830 RHEA CENSUS
Abraham Cox 20011 - 100010001 p. 373
Meredith Cox 1100001 - 1211101 p. 369
Samuel Cox 0000001 - 01000001 p. 373
Thomas Cox 0100211 - 012 p. 371
Thomas Cox 00001 - 0001 p. 373
1840 RHEA CENSUS
Charles Cox 0210001 - 200001
Elizabeth Cox 0001 - 00011001
William Cox 00001 - 0
1840 MEIGS CENSUS
Abraham Cox 1011001001 - 10210100001 p. 234
Luther B. Cox 01001 - 20010001 p. 234
Meredith Cox 00010001 - 00110101 p. 234
Samuel Cox 000000001 - 0001 p. 235
Thomas Cox 1000101 - 010001 p. 238
1850 RHEA CENSUS
Charles Cox 50 (Va)(Millwright), Rebecca 41, Elbert S. 22 (Wagoner), James H. 20 (Machinist), Madison 19 (Farmer), Malinda 16, Mary A. 13, Julia A. 11, Nancy A. 7 p. 603-421
Hardy Cox 15: see Andrew Lowe
Hardy Cox Unk (NC)(Farmer), Hardy 14, Ortha M. 12, Mary C. 10, William H.H. 8, Williamson G. 6, George W. 4 p. 556-141
1850 MEIGS CENSUS
Abraham Cox 50 (Md)(Farmer), Celia 44, Jane 15, Samuel M. 12, Sarah Ann 9, Summerfield 7, Abraham Cass 4, Samuel COX 74 (Md) p. 760-377
Jehue Cox 23 (Blacksmith), Maryann 25, Joseph A. 0 p. 759-368
Luther B. Cox 26 (Farmer), Talitha 25, Alexander 5, James L. 2, Marion 4 p. 732-149
Meredith Cox 61 (Farmer), Adaline 20 p. 732-151
Ruth Cox 31, Elizabeth 11 p. 732-150
Samuel Cox 74: see Abraham Cox
Thomas Cox 30 (Farmer), Mary 40, Meredith 3, Andrew J. 1 p. 759-373
Thomas Cox 43 (Blacksmith), Matilda 41, James 14 p. 775-493
MARRIAGES (RHEA)
Abraham Cox to Celia Collins, 29 Sept 1825 (same), Thomas Cox JP and Bm (AR)
Abraham Cox to Elizabeth Kelly, 24 Apr 1834 (same), John Henninger MG, John P. Long Bm (AR)
Elizabeth Cox to John Dudley q.v.
Jane Cox to Alexander Fletcher q.v.
Jane Cox to John Cook q.v.
Luther B. Cox to Malinda Lewis, 3 Mar 1835 (5 Mar), D.L. Godsey MG, Meredith Cox Bm (AR)
Rachel B. Cox to Samuel McDaniel q.v.
Sarah Cox to Cyrus Quiet q.v.
Solomon Cox to Nancy Knox, 3 May 1823 (4 May), Thomas Cox JP, Ferguson Boram Bm (AR)
Thomas Cox to Temperance McDaniel, 20 Dec 1815, Samuel McDaniel Bm (AR)
William Cox to Mary Rogers, 13 Nov 1835, William B. Gordon Bm (A)
MARRIAGES (MEIGS)
Emaline Cox to Ishmael A. Godsey q.v.
Gempy Cox to Master Long q.v.
Harriet Cox to Reece B. Cross q.v.
J.R. Cox to Hiltha E. Bower, 23 Oct 1843 (24 Oct), A. King MG
John Cox to Mary Ann Scott, 16 Feb 1848 (7 Aug), John V. Blevins JP
Nancy L. Cox to Wm Rayl q.v.
Rachel Cox to Jno Walker q.v.
Sarah E. Cox to Henry Martin q.v.
Thomas Cox to Mary Smith, 19 Mar 1847 (same), Jesse Martin JP
MISCELLANEOUS (RHEA)
Abraham Cox: Bondsman for James C. Greer, 1828
" " Bondsman for Anthony King, 1828
" " Bondsman for William S. Russell, 1828
" " Purchased land in Cottonport
Abraham Cox Jr.: Bondsman for William W. Cowan, 1829
Charles Cox: JP 1844-1847
" " Bondsman for Jacob L. Wasson, 1845
Meredith Cox: Bondsman for Cyrus Quiet, 1825
" " Bondsman for Jack Cook, 1833
" " Bondsman for William Coates, 1835
" " Bondsman for Luther B. Cox, 1835
Samuel Cox Sr.: War of 1812
Thomas Cox: JP 1821-1832
" " Bondsman for Samuel McDaniel, 1820
" " Bondsman for Abraham Cox, 1825
" " Bondsman for Sampson Prowell, 1827
" " Bondsman for Hugh T. Blevins, 1828
" " Bondsman for Jesse Chattin, 1828
" " Bondsman for John P. Hays, 1828
" " Bondsman for George W. Mullins, 1828
" " Bondsman for Thomas Lucas, 1832
William Cox: Bondsman for John Dudley, 1840
MISCELLANEOUS (MEIGS)
Abraham Cox: Cherokee Removal muster roll, 1836
" " Hiwassee District resident
Abraham Cox Jr.: Commissioner to lay off Meigs County into Districts, 1836
" " " JP(?) 1840, 1842
Luther B. Cox: JP(?) 1838-39
Meredith Cox: JP(?) 1843
Thomas Cox: Circuit Court Jury, 1836
" " Hiwassee District, Cottonport area

- - - - - - - - - - - - -

COXEY

MARRIAGES (MEIGS)
Matilda Coxey to William Stokes q.v.

- - - - - - - - - - - - -

COZBY / COSBY

TAXES (RHEA)
1819 (Capt. W.S. Bradley's Dist.):
James W. Cozby 1 WP, 1 BP, 250a
John Cozby 1 WP, 3 BP, 250a
(Capt. McGill's Co.): Robert Cozby 1 WP
1823 (Capt. Howard's Co.): James W. Cozby 250a
Robert Cozby 1 WP
(Capt. Brown's Co.): John Cozby 1 WP, 3 BP, 406a
1830 RHEA CENSUS
Jno Cozby 110101010001 - 202101 p. 378
1840 MEIGS CENSUS
John Cozby 101100001 - 02020001
William B. Cozby 000001 - 11001
MARRIAGES (RHEA)
Eliza Cozby to Lemuel Sugart q.v.
Isabela Cozby to William Cowan q.v.
Mary Ann Cozby to John D. Traynor q.v.

William B. Cozby to Parmelia S. Chatten, 29 July 1833 (30 July), Wm Smith JP, James W. Smith Bm (AR) [1850 Hamilton Census: W.B. Cozby 40, Pamelia 37, Mary 16, John 11, Elizabeth 8, James COZBY 60, Tennessee MUNCY 14]
MARRIAGES (MEIGS)
John W. Cozby to Angenire Lewis, 17 Dec 1850, J.F. Benson Sur
MISCELLANEOUS (RHEA)
John Cozby: JP 1817-34; Trustee, 1828-36, 1838-42
" " Bondsman for John L. McCarty, 1820
Randolph Cozby: Bondsman for Benjamin Cooper, 1834
Robert Cozby: Bondsman for John Greenwood, 1823
William B. Cozby: JP 1837, 1839
" " " Bondsman for Charles Revely, 1832

- - - - - - - - - - - - -

CRABTREE

1840 MEIGS CENSUS
William Crabtree 0011 - 10001 p. 224
1850 MEIGS CENSUS
Frances Crabtree 50 p. 803-697
Porter Crabtree 22 (Farmer), Huldah 25, Curtis 6, Susan 2, James 1 p. 819-815

- - - - - - - - - - - - -

CRAIG / CRAIGE

TAXES (RHEA)
1819 (Capt. John Lewis' Dist.): Alexander Craig 1 WP
(Capt. John Robinson's Co.): Samuel Craig 1 WP
1823 (Capt. Braselton's Co.): Samuel Craig 1 WP
MARRIAGES (RHEA)
Eliza J. Craig to James C. Ferguson q.v.
Elizabeth Craig to David Lawson q.v.
Jesse P. Craig to Elizabeth Daniel, 2 June 1834, John Craig Bm (A)
Patsey Craige to William H. Crawford q.v.
Sary Craig to James Collison q.v.
MISCELLANEOUS (RHEA)
John Craig: Bondsman for Jesse P. Craig, 1834

- - - - - - - - - - - - -

CRAIGHEAD

1850 MEIGS CENSUS
Mary Craighead 40, John N. 21 (Farmer), Mary Jane 19, Alexander B. 18 p. 722-74
MISCELLANEOUS (MEIGS)
John N. Craighead: Surety for Shadrack Williams, 1850

- - - - - - - - - - - - -

CRAMER

MARRIAGES (RHEA)
Mary Cramer to William Thompson q.v.

- - - - - - - - - - - - -

CRANFIELD

1850 MEIGS CENSUS
Isaac Cranfield 32 (NC)(Blacksmith), Mary 33 (NC), William P.H. 12, Martha A. 10, Nancy C. 6, Thomas L. 4, Joel C. 3, Mary M. 1 p. 754-333

- - - - - - - - - - - - -

CRANMORE

TAXES (RHEA)
1819 (Capt. McGill's Co.): James Cranmore 1 WP
Josiah Cranmore 100a
1825 (Capt. Howard's Co.): Mary Cranmore 70a
Sarah Cranmore 50a
1830 RHEA CENSUS
Mary Cranmore 010201 - 1101001 p. 381
Sarah Cranmore 21 - 00001 p. 380
1840 RHEA CENSUS
Mary Cranmore 00002 - 0001100
1850 RHEA CENSUS
Sarah Cranmore 81 (NC): see David Ragsdale
1850 MEIGS CENSUS
Wesley Cranmore 31 (Farmer), Nancy Ann 26, Mary C. 7, Sarah E. 6, James E. 5, William R. 4, Martha S. 1 p. 735-178
MARRIAGES (RHEA)
John W. Cranmore to Sarah Land, 8 Oct 1836, William S. Stiff Bm (A)
Josiah Cranmore to Catherine L. Land, 6 July 1838, Joshua S. Givin [or Gwin] Bm (A)
Sarah Cranmore to Anthony Brown Jr. q.v.

- - - - - - - - - - - - -

CRAVEN / CRAVENS

1840 RHEA CENSUS
Robert Cravens 100201 - 2100101
MARRIAGES (RHEA)
Robert Craven to Catherine Roddye, 29 Sept 1830 (7 Oct), Daniel Briggs MG, Wm T. Gillenwaters Bm (AR) [1850 Roane Census: Robert Cravens 45, C.E.W. 28, Nancy 18, Ann E. 16, Jane 13, Mary 11, Jesse R. 7, Luke LEA 27, James T. SHELBY 23, Martha J. 18]
MISCELLANEOUS (RHEA)
Robert Cravens: Trustee, Mars Hill Academy, 1850

- - - - - - - - - - - - -

CRAWFORD

1830 RHEA CENSUS
Jonathan Crawford 20201 - 00001 p. 354
William A. Crawford 0210201 - 01111011 p. 395
1840 RHEA CENSUS
John Crawford 320001001 - 00010101
1840 MEIGS CENSUS
James Crawford 10001 - 00001 p. 225
John Crawford 12010001 - 0200001 p. 224
Nancy Crawford 1 - 0000010001 p. 225
1850 RHEA CENSUS
John Crawford 40 (Farmer), Martha 40, James R. 16 (Farmer), Henry A. 14, Thomas H. 12, Mary A. 8, John T. 6, Sarah J. 3 p. 615-504
MARRIAGES (RHEA)
John Crawford to Martha Griffith, 16 Aug 1833 [John, son of Wm Ayers Crawford]
Malinda Crawford to John Glenn q.v.
Polly Ann Crawford to Joseph Day q.v.
Robert Crawford to Olivia Howard, 6 Mar 1833, Albert Howard Bm (A)
Rhoda Crawford to Lewis Pruitt [Privette] q.v.
Roda Crawford to Philip Parker q.v.
William H. Crawford to Patsey Craige, 11 Nov 1834 (same), Jesse Thompson JP (AR)
MARRIAGES (MEIGS)
Arvigine Crawford to David Lewis q.v.
Parthena Crawford to Joseph M. Parsons q.v.
MISCELLANEOUS (RHEA)
Andrew Crawford: Hiwassee District
John Crawford: Bondsman for James Cobb, 1834
" " Bondsman for Henry Black, 1835
" " Bondsman for John Goad, 1838
Robert Crawford: Bondsman for John McCrakin, 1831

\- - - - - - - - - - - -

CREAL

1830 RHEA CENSUS
William Creal: 02000 - 101001 p. 387

\- - - - - - - - - - - -

CREED / CREAD / CREEDE / COUDE

TAXES (RHEA)
1823 (Capt. Braselton's Co.): Thornton Creed 1 WP
1830 RHEA CENSUS
Thornton J. Creed 01<u>2</u>01 - 1100 p. 386 [the <u>2</u> may have been chanded to a 0]
1840 RHEA CENSUS
Thornton Creed 101001 - 121001
1850 RHEA CENSUS
Thornton J. Creed 49 (NC)(Farmer), Nancy P. 45 (Va), Arthur F. 26 (Farmer), Darthula E. 18, Sarah J. 13, Oswell J. 10, Tazwell P.J. 8, James T.G. 5 p. 569-218
MARRIAGES (RHEA)
Jestin Emaline Creed to Thomas Ault q.v.
Thornton Creed to Nancy Fulton or Fulte, 29 Aug 1822 (same), John Mitchell MG (AR)
Vesta A. Creede to John Price q.v.
D. A. Coude to John Jack q.v.

MISCELLANEOUS (RHEA)
Thornton J. Creed: JP 1843-44, 1847-50
" " " Bondsman for Rufus Harwood, 1843

\- - - - - - - - - - - -

CRES

MARRIAGES (RHEA)
Betsy Cres to Benjamin Armstrong q.v.

\- - - - - - - - - - - -

CREW / CREWS / CREWES

1830 RHEA CENSUS
Martin Crews 10001 - 0001 p. 389
Nancy Crews 11101 - 1101101 p. 389
1840 RHEA CENSUS
Mary Ann Crews 1 - 121001
Nancy Crews 0001 - 00011001
1850 RHEA CENSUS
Rufus M. Crews 31 (Farmer), Mira W. 24, John A. 4, Rufus J. 3, John A. 1, Vesta WASSON 19, Clark REESE 17 (Farmer) p. 540-47
Shiloh Crew 38 (Ky)(Farmer), Susan 39 (Va), Lyda A. 16, Elizabeth 15, Thomas M. 13, William M. 9, James L.B. 8 p. 548-97
1850 MEIGS CENSUS
James Crew 45 (NC)(Farmer), Nancy 55 (SC), Martha 15, Josiah H. 14, Lambert J. 8, Caroline 5 p. 739-211
MARRIAGES (RHEA)
Jane Crewes to P.M. Hollaway q.v.
Martha Cruese to Martin E. Paul q.v.
Rufus M. Crews or Cruese to Mira W. Wassum, 11 July* 1844 (18* Feb), Asa Newport MG (R) [*dates are as recorded; July probably should be January]
MARRIAGES (MEIGS)
Elizabeth Crew to H.P. Stockton, 25 July 1850, A.G. Godsey Sur

\- - - - - - - - - - - -

CRISP

MARRIAGES (MEIGS)
Elias Crisp to Mary Walding, 3 Sept 1838 (9 Sept), Prior Neil JP [probably 1850 Roane Census: Elias Crisp 34, Polly 29, Rutha C. 10, Martha T. 8, Susan E. 1, John CRISP 83, John R. 33, Ruth 73]

\- - - - - - - - - - - -

CRITTENDON

MISCELLANEOUS (MEIGS)
Jacob E. Crittendon: Cherokee Removal muster roll, 1836

\- - - - - - - - - - - -

CROFT
(see also COFFEE)

1830 RHEA CENSUS
Jesse Croft 00001 - 120001 p. 372

\- - - - - - - - - - - -

CROID

1830 RHEA CENSUS
William Croid 100011 - 220001 p. 356

- - - - - - - - - - - - -

CROSS

1840 MEIGS CENSUS
Zachariah Cross 00120001 - 0011 p. 235
1850 MEIGS CENSUS
Ann Cross 24: see A.W. Hodges
[Ann, dau of Zachariah and Sarah Hicks Cross]
MARRIAGES (MEIGS)
Artemizer Cross to William Arrants q.v.
[Artemisa, dau of Zachariah and Sarah]
Reece Cross to Harriet Cox, 10 Feb 1850, R.E.L. Blevins Sur
MISCELLANEOUS (MEIGS)
Absalom L. [Looney] Cross: 4th Cpl., Mexican War
Isaac [Grundy] Cross: Private, Mexican War
[A.L. and I.G., sons of Zachariah and Sarah]

- - - - - - - - - - - - -

CROSSLAND

MARRIAGES (MEIGS)
Thomas E. Crossland to Mary C. Casey, 4 July 1846 (9 July), E. Simpson MG

- - - - - - - - - - - - -

CROUCH

1840 RHEA CENSUS
Thomas Crouch 1010001 - 010101

- - - - - - - - - - - - -

CROW

TAXES (RHEA)
1823 (Capt. Lewis' Co.): Isaac Crow WP, 25a
1840 MEIGS CENSUS
Benjamin Crow 113001 - 211001 p. 246
Denison Crow 220001 - 00001 p. 244
Robert Crow 101001 - 120001001 p. 244
William Crow 0241001 - 100001 p. 244
1850 RHEA CENSUS
Benjamin Crow 48 (Farmer), Elizabeth 50 (Ky), John 23 (Farmer), James 21 (Farmer), Robert 19 (Farmer), Eliza 17, John J. 13, Elizabeth E. 11, Thomas J. 9, Sarah 6 p. 605-471
[Benjamin S. Crow married Betsy Sutton on 21 Aug 1823 in Roane Co., John Crow Sur.]
MARRIAGES (RHEA)
Catherine Crow to William Holland q.v.
Eliza Crow to William C. Edmonds q.v.
Elizabeth Crow to David Rhea q.v.
John P. Crow to Jane E. Hooper, 14 Nov 1850 (same), Edward P. Childers MG (R)
MISCELLANEOUS (RHEA and MEIGS)
James Crow: Hiwassee District, Sewee Creek area
John Crow: Hiwassee District, Sewee Creek area
William Crow: Bondsman for Reuben Phillips, 1835
" " Hiwassee District, Ten Mile Stand area
Wilson Crow: Cherokee Removal muster roll, 1836

- - - - - - - - - - - - -

CROZIER

MISCELLANEOUS (RHEA)
Hugh Crozier: Bondsman for Jeremiah Washam, 1824
" " Bondsman for William Rice, 1824
" " Bondsman for Alexander McPherson, 1825
Knoxville Register, Vol IX, No. 420 (27 Aug 1824): Married on Thursday evening, 12th inst. by the Rev. Wm Eagleton, Doctor Hugh Crozier of Washington, Rhea Co., to Miss Mary Oliver, dau of Douglas Oliver Esq., of Anderson Co.

- - - - - - - - - - - - -

CRUDINGTON / CUDGINGTON / CUDGENTON / CRUDJUNGTON

1840 MEIGS CENSUS
George Cudginton 10320001 - 0000100 p. 245
William Crudgington 10001 - 0001 p. 244
MARRIAGES (MEIGS)
William Crudjungton to Nancy Pharis, 13 May 1838 (same), Wm Green MG
MISCELLANEOUS (MEIGS)
Jno K. Cudgington: JP(?) 1840
William Cudgenton: JP(?) 1842
William Crudington: Cherokee Removal muster roll, 1836

- - - - - - - - - - - - -

CRUMBLISS / CRUMLESS

MARRIAGES (RHEA)
Hugh Crumbliss to July Ann Underwood, 14 Feb 1843, Calvin Underwood Bm (A)
[1850 Roane Census: Hugh Crumless 27, Julia A. 27, Martha C. 6, Sarah J. 5, Jonathan W. 2]

- - - - - - - - - - - - -

CRUMLEY
(see also CHUMLEY)

MARRIAGES (RHEA)
Narcissa Crumley to John Jennett q.v.
MISCELLANEOUS (RHEA and MEIGS)
Abner Crumley: Blacksmith, Mexican War
John Crumley: Private, Mexican War

- - - - - - - - - - - - -

CRUMPTON
(see also COMPTON / CUMPTON)

MARRIAGES (RHEA)
Henderson Crumpton to Ann Johnson, 4 Aug 1831 (same), James A. Darwin JP, Henry H. Miller Bm (AR)
Margaret Crumpton to George M. Snodgrass q.v.
Mary Crumpton to William Robertson q.v.
MISCELLANEOUS (RHEA)
William Crumpton: Bondsman for George Gross, 1835

- - - - - - - - - - - - -

CRUSON [CREESON?]

MARRIAGES (RHEA)
Elijah Cruson [Creeson] to Susan Price, 6 Sept 1841 (9 Sept), Asa Newport MG (R)

- - - - - - - - - - - - -

CRUTCHFIELD / CUTCHFIELD

TAXES (RHEA)
1823 (Capt. McCall's Co.): William Cutchfield 1 WP
MISCELLANEOUS (RHEA)
Thomas Crutchfield: Contractor for brick Courthouse, Town of Washington, 1833

- - - - - - - - - - - - -

CULBERSON

1830 RHEA CENSUS
John Culberson 000001 - 20001 p. 355

- - - - - - - - - - - - -

CUMMINGS

1850 MEIGS CENSUS
Adaline Cummings 17 or 77: see Stephen Taylor

- - - - - - - - - - - - -

CUNNINGHAM / CUNNYNGHAM

TAXES (RHEA)
1823 (Capt. Piper's Co.): Samuel Cunningham 1 WP
1830 RHEA CENSUS
Sarah Cunningham 32001 - 00001 p. 364
1840 MEIGS CENSUS
Abner Cunningham 01000 - 00001 p. 242
1850 RHEA CENSUS
James M. Cunningham 29 (Farmer), Louisa 29, Thomas 6, John W. 3, William V. 7/12 p. 599-400
Wylie H. Cunnyngham 38 (Farmer), Elvina 32, Thomas N. 9, Charlotte J. 7, Franklin L. 5, Robert C.M. 2 p. 571-233
1850 MEIGS CENSUS
Henry M. Cunningham 31 (Blacksmith), Martha Jane 26, Sarah F. 5, Mary L. 4, Cyntha E. 2, Cisley P. 1 p. 735-177
MARRIAGES (RHEA)
Fanny Cunningham to William Silvey Sr. q.v.
James M. Cunningham to Eliza Lewis, 4 Jan 1843, William Hutson Bell Bm (A)
Samuel Cunningham to Patsy Miller, 29 July 1820 (same), J. Fine JP, Farley Bradey Bm (AR)
Synthia A. Cunningham to Nathan Davis q.v.
Wylie H. Cunnyngham to Elvina Locke, 24 July 1837, Benjamin F. Locke Bm (A) [Wylie, son of Wm Henry and Magdaline Lewis Cunnyngham; Elvina, dau of John A. and Mary Jane Moore Locke]
MARRIAGES (MEIGS)
Martin Cunningham to Martha Sullivan, 25 Jan 1844, Ezekiel Sullivan JP or Bm
MISCELLANEOUS (RHEA)
Henry M. Cunningham: Bm for Alexander Carr, 1840
James W. Cunningham: Bondsman for Nathan Davis, 1841
O. F. Cunningham: MG 1845
Samuel Cunningham: Bondsman for Merral Brady, 1825
" " Bondsman for Henry Maner, 1827
W. H. Cunnyngham: JP 1850
MISCELLANEOUS (MEIGS)
Wylie Cunnyngham: Built store on Lot 26 in Decatur

- - - - - - - - - - - - -

CURRY

MARRIAGES (RHEA)
Fanny Curry to James McAlister q.v.

- - - - - - - - - - - - -

CURTON / CURTIN / CURTAIN / CURINGTON / CUNINGTON

TAXES (RHEA)
1823 (Capt. Wilson's Co.): Lewis Curton 1 WP
1830 RHEA CENSUS
George Curton 031101 - 01001 p. 363
Lewis Curton 1021001 - 0100101 p. 359
1840 MEIGS CENSUS
Catharine Curtin 0001 - 00010001 p. 242
Richard Curtin 022001 - 200001 p. 240
1850 MEIGS CENSUS
Catharine Curington 45, Magdaline 26, Isaac 24 (Farmer) p. 813-791
Easterly Curton 21, Edith B. 16 p. 725-101
Richard Cunington 44 (SC)(Blacksmith), Frances 40, Henry L. 19, Plesent S. 16, Seth 15, Mary M. 12, Martha R. 10, Jemima C. 8, Richard D. 6, Charles B. 4, Benjamin L. 2, William T. 1 ("Deaf & Dumb, Blind or more") p. 790-605
MARRIAGES (RHEA)
Levi Curtin to Polly Edington or Eddington, 1 Nov 1830 (same), D.M. Stockton JP, Luke Eddington Bm (AR)

- - - - - - - - - - - - -

CUSHING

1840 RHEA CENSUS
James Cushing 101001 - 120001001

- - - - - - - - - - - - -

DABNEY

1850 MEIGS CENSUS
James Dabney 25 (Ky)(Saddler), Hetty Ann 6 p. 753-329
MISCELLANEOUS (MEIGS)
John Dabney: Surety for James Revis, 1850

- - - - - - - - - - - - -

DAIL
(see also DYAL)

1830 RHEA CENSUS
Isaac Dail 000000001 - 000001 p. 367

- - - - - - - - - - - - -

DALRIMPLE / DALRYMPLE / DANRIMPLE

TAXES (RHEA)
1823 (Capt. Howard's Co.): William Danrimple 1 WP
MARRIAGES (RHEA)
Allen Dalrimple to Eliz Churchwell, 20 Aug 1823 (21 Aug), William Smith JP, Charles Witt Bm (R) [1850 Hamilton Census: Allen Dalrymple 46, Eliza 47, John A. HOOK 49, Mary L. 35, Elizabeth 11, Jas 8, Wm 5, Jane 2, Mary 6/12, Mary HORD 13]

- - - - - - - - - - - - -

DAME or DANET

MARRIAGES (RHEA)
Catharine Dame or Danet to Samuel M. Love q.v.

- - - - - - - - - - - - -

DANBY

1840 RHEA CENSUS
Hezekiah Danby 0010001 - 00111001
MARRIAGES (RHEA)
Alfred Danby to Polly Phillips, 25 Nov 1842, Calvin Morgan Bm (A)
Elizabeth Danby to Lewis Brewer q.v.
Margaret Danby to William McKiddy q.v.

- - - - - - - - - - - - -

DANE

1850 RHEA CENSUS
Eliza Dane 33 (SC), Milton 12, Preston 11, Andrew 9, William K.P. 6, David 5, Amanda C. 3 p. 628-603

- - - - - - - - - - - - -

DANIEL / DANIELS / DANNEL / DANNIL

TAXES (RHEA)
1819 (Capt. John Ramsey's Co.): John Daniel 1 WP
(Capt. Wm McCray's Co.): Peter Daniel 1 WP, 113½a
1823 (Capt. McCall's Co.): John Dannil 1 WP
Plummer Dannil 1 WP
1830 RHEA CENSUS
John Daniel 2000001 - 121201001 p. 362
Joseph Daniels 200001 - 10001 p. 391
Peter Daniel 101101 - 111101 p. 390
Plummer Daniel 10001 - 21001 p. 364
1840 MEIGS CENSUS
John Daniel 122000 - 0011101 p. 248
1850 RHEA CENSUS
William Daniel 18: see Levi Griffith
1850 MEIGS CENSUS
John Daniel 59 (NC)(Farmer), Sarah 56 (NC), Rebecca 25, Hiram 23, Eliza 21, Haskins 20 (Farmer), Alexander 16 (Farmer), John R. 16 (Farmer), James O. 14, Eliza C. 7 p. 908-736
MARRIAGES (RHEA)
Elizabeth Daniel to Jesse P. Craig q.v.
Elizabeth Daniel to John W. Denning q.v.
Nancy Daniel to John Brady q.v.
Solomon Dannel to Jane Ore, 10 July 1830 (same), Stephen Winton JP (AR)
MARRIAGES (MEIGS)
Acille A. Daniel to Jno Griffin q.v.
Lydia Daniel to Robert Renfrow q.v.
Mary Daniel to Thomas Roark q.v.
MISCELLANEOUS (MEIGS)
Jemima Daniel: Hiwassee District, Moore's Chapel area
Solomon Daniel: Cherokee Removal muster roll, 1836
William Daniel: JP(?) 1845

- - - - - - - - - - - - -

DANLEY / DANLY

1840 MEIGS CENSUS
Andrew Danly 110001 - 10001 p. 244
MARRIAGES (RHEA)
Rebecca Danley to William Gibson q.v.

- - - - - - - - - - - - -

DARWIN

TAXES (RHEA)
1823 (Capt. Lewis' Co.): James Darwin 1 WP, 300a
1830 RHEA CENSUS
James A. Darwin 1030011 - 221111 p. 393
1840 RHEA CENSUS
James A. Darwin 0011101 - 2122001
1850 RHEA CENSUS
James A. Darwin 53 (SC)(Farmer), Bethiah W. 52 (NC), Belinda 22, William P. 20 (Farmer), Anestatia 16, Tennessee 13, Victoria 11, Henry C. 7 p. 599-403 [Jas A. Darwin, 1798-1872, son of Wm and Jane Adams Darwin, and Bethiah White Clements, 1800-1873, were married in Jackson Co. on 4 Apr 1816; children in addition to those still at home in 1850 were Jane A., Susan H., Thomas C., Peyton C., Julia F., and Mary A.]
Thomas C. Darwin 33 (Farmer), Eliza E. 29, Orpha J. 6, Mary B. 4, Rebecca E. 3, Vesta A. 1, Andrew M. 29 (Farmer), John DERIAN 10 p. 583-312
MARRIAGES (RHEA)
Jane A. Darwin to John T. Blevins q.v.
Julia F. Darwin to Jacob Kelly q.v.
Mary A. Darwin to Henry C. Collins q.v.
Susan Darwin to James P. Collins q.v.
Thomas C. Darwin to Eliza M. Collins, 27 July 1842, Jas W. Gillespie Bm (A)
MISCELLANEOUS (RHEA)
James A. Darwin: JP 1825-1831

- - - - - - - - - - - - -

DAVENPORT

1830 RHEA CENSUS
Jeremiah Davenport 01220001 - 110101 p. 386
John Davenport 111001 - 031001 p. 387
MARRIAGES (RHEA)
William Davenport to Margaret Rhea, 10 July 1832 (17 July), J. Fine MG, Thomas Anderson Bm (AR)
Wilson Davenport to Eliza Riggle, 19 Oct 1837 (8 Nov), James McCanse JP, Gilbert Riggle Bm (AR)

- - - - - - - - - - - - -

DAVID

TAXES (RHEA)
1808 (John Henry's List):
Azariah David 350a E Fork Richland Creek
Jenkin David 1 WP
Owen David 1 WP
1819 (Capt. McGill's Co.): Azariah David 2 BP, 200a
Owen David 1 WP
1823 (Capt. Howard's Co.): Azariah David 2 BP 200a
1830 RHEA CENSUS
A. David 001000004 - 010000101 p. 382
Owen David 000000001 - 1 p. 382
1850 RHEA CENSUS
Jenkin David 85: see Harvey Roddy
Owen David 80 (SC), Magdalina 76 (Va), Nancy 32, John O. 16 (Farmer), William KELLY 45 (Well Digger) p. 624-574
MARRIAGES (RHEA)
David David to Polly Chaney, 23 Sept 1811 (same), James Campbell Bm (A)
[the Roane County records also contained the marriage of David David and Polly Chaney, but the date was 23 Sept 1810; bond and license missing]
Owen David to Magdaline Kelly, 7 Feb 1811 (same), Thomas Nolan Bm (AR)
MISCELLANEOUS (RHEA)
Azariah David: JP 1817, 1823-24, 1832-34
" " Bondsman for John Brown, 1809
" " Revolutionary War Pensioner, 1835 list

DAVIDSON / DAVISON

MARRIAGES (RHEA)
Edith Davison to Martin Burris q.v.
Frances Davison to Samuel Holloway q.v.
John Davidson to Elizabeth Walker, 8 Dec 1818, Randolph Smith Bm (AR)
Patsy Davidson to Joseph Barr q.v.
Patsy Davidson to Josiah Erp q.v.
MISCELLANEOUS (RHEA and MEIGS)
Jesse Davidson: Bondsman for Joseph Barr, 1811
" " Bondsman for Samuel Holloway, 1819
Thomas Davidson: Resident of Washington (Lot 55), 1814
William Davison: Bondsman for Nelson Battle, 1813
Wiley A. Davison: Private, Mexican War

DAVIS

TAXES (RHEA)
1808 (John Henry's List): Samuel Davis 1 WP
1819 (Capt. McGill's Co.): Jacob Davis 1 WP
1823 (Capt. Piper's Co.): Abraham Davis 40a
George Davis 40a
(Capt. Smith's Co.): Miles B. Davis 1 WP
(Capt. Brown's Co.): Robert H. Davis 1 WP
Thomas Davis 1 WP
1830 RHEA CENSUS
Abraham Davis 200001 - 00101 p. 361
Benjamin Davis 00111 - 1001301 p. 360
George Davis 01000001 - 122001 p. 389
Henry Davis 021001 - 010111 p. 395
J. P. Davis 00121001 - 01100101 p. 390
John Davis 01001 - 20101 p. 353
John Davis 0001 - 00001 p. 357
Miles B. Davis 11110001 - 0111001 p. 375
Nancy Davis 10001 - 0 p. 373
Rebecca Davis 1 - 00011 p. 390
Robert B. Davis 100011 - 00001 p. 361
Samuel Davis 0001 - 00001 p. 358
Thomas Davis 0001 - 00001 p. 358
Thomas Davis 2311001 - 101111 p. 378
1840 RHEA CENSUS
John Davis 121001 - 110001
John C. Davis 00001 - 00010001
Michael Davis 10001 - 00001
Rebecca Davis 011 - 00000101
Thomas Davis 02210001 - 0200011
1840 MEIGS CENSUS
Abraham Davis 0001001 - 0000001 p. 246
Edward Davis 121001 - 011001 p. 246
John Davis 000001 - 000010001 p. 239
John Davis 32001 - 11001 p. 240
Miles B. Davis 001101001 - 00010001 p. 229
Nancy F. Davis 0001 - 000001 p. 236
Phillip Davis 00101001 - 00010001 p. 240
Thomas P. Davis 00001000001 - 1220010001 p. 246
William Davis 20001 - 000001 p. 227
1850 RHEA CENSUS
John C. Davis 28 (Va)(Clerk) p. 627-596
Reuben Davis 21: see John S. Evans [Evens]
Thomas Davis 23 (Farmer), Emily 24, Elizbeth 1 p. 631-618
1850 MEIGS CENSUS
David Davis 46 (NC)(Blacksmith), Sarah 46, Nancy 23, Catherine 21, Jane 19, William 17 (Blacksmith), Isaac 15 (Blacksmith), Lewis J. 13, John 11, Mary 9, Rufus 7, Levina 5, Martha C. 3 p. 779-521 [David Davis married Sarah Snow in Feb 1828 in Roane County]
Edward W. Davis 45 (Farmer), Mary 45 (NC), Anna 21, Rebecca 20, Campbell 19 (Farmer), Samuel 16 (Farmer), Thomas H. 13, Carroll 9, Mary 7, Margaret 7, Harriet 5, George 2 p. 789-601 [Edward married Polly Underwood on 9 Dec 1824 in Roane County]
H. Davis 36 (Va)(Farmer), Minerva A. 31 (Va), Richard O. 11 (Va), Octavia L. 10 (Va), Sarah M. 9 (Va), Albert M. 7 (Va), Carthagna (f) 5 (Va), Benjamin F. 3, Alexander L. 1 p. 718-43
James Davis 23 (Farmer), Elizabeth Jane 20, Sarah C. 2, Infant (m) 0 p. 738-202
Jane Davis 60 (NC): see Martha Phillips
John Davis 38 (Farmer), Mary 40, William B. 18, Elizabeth L. 16, Plesent 16, Jackson A. 14, Catharine B. 14, William O. 12, John N. 13, Tennessee A. 9, Thomas 7, Eliza 5, Mary Jane 2 p. 784-562
John Davis 48 (SC)(Farmer), Eliza 49, Elizabeth 22, Sarah Jane 2 p. 764-403
John Davis 41 (Blacksmith), Deborah 64, John C. 38 (Farmer) p. 742-235
Nancy H. Davis 46 (Va), John H. 22 (Tailor) p. 773-475
Phillip L. Davis 38 (Farmer), Mary 38, Nancy Ann 9, Delilah 7, Joseph 5, Edward 3, Elizabeth Jane 1 p. 799-673

Rachael Davis 70 (Va): see Gabriel Medaris q.v.
Robert R. Davis 29 (Ky), Harriet 24, Susan 6, Abijah 4, Adaline 3, Zachery T. 1 p. 780-526
Thomas P. Davis 41 (Farmer), Cordelia 45, Sarah 17, Nancy Ann 15, Milly 12, Franklin B. 10, Patsy Jane 7, Elizabeth SUTTON 82 (NC), Marion HUTSON 18 (NC)(Farmer) p. 799-674
William Davis 31 (Va)(Farmer), Dicy 31 (Va), Betsy Jane 13, Isabella 11, Joseph H. 8, Mary 6, William 4, Jackson 2 p. 768-433
William Davis 26 (Farmer), Elizabeth 22, John 4, William 2 p. 765-411

MARRIAGES (RHEA)

Catherine Davis to Hiram Raines q.v.
Elizabeth Davis to Thomas O. George q.v.
Ganium Davis to Emaline Minicks, 30 Sept 1847 (same), Samuel Frazier JP (R)
James Davis to Elizabeth Eaves, 7 Aug 1847 (8 Aug), James Hooker JP (R)
John Davis to Lucinda Liles, 21 Apr 1841, E.E. Wasson JP, Wright Smith Bm (AR)
[1850 McMinn Census: John Davis 30, Lucinda 28, Elizabeth 8, Thomas 6, Martha 3, Elijah 1]
John C. Davis to Polly Ann But, 25 Dec 1850 (same), E. McKinney JP (R)
Martha Davis to William Philips q.v.
Martha Davis to John Lawrence q.v.
Mary Davis to Wilson Kilgore q.v.
Mary Davis to John W. Hughes q.v.
Michael Davis to Mary or Marial Riggle, 27 Sept 1838 (28 Sept), James McCanse JP, Gilbert Riggle Bm (AR)
Nancy Davis to Joseph C. Carterright q.v.
Nancy Davis to John George q.v.
Nathan Davis to Synthia M. Cunningham, 17 Sept 1841 (same), Wm H. Bell MG EPC, James M. Cunningham Bm (AR)
Peggy Davis to William Merriman q.v.
Phillis Davis to Richard Cooper q.v.
Pleasant Davis to Edna or Edney Bell, 17 Jan 1839 (same), Wm B. Cozby JP, John W. Walker Bm (AR)
[1850 Lincoln Census: Pleasant Davis 38, Edney 31, Martin C. 10, Louisa L.J. 8, Ira M.A. 6, Martha E.B. 5, John 2, Sisely A.E. 1]
Rebecca Davis to Garriett Garrison q.v.
Robert Davis to Polly Ann Inman, 24 Jan 1836, William T. Armstrong Bm (A)
Sally Davis to Nathaniel Gillom q.v.
Sally Davis to John S. Newton q.v.
Sarah Davis to James Elliott q.v.
Sarah Davis to Isaac Clandon q.v.
Sorena Davis to Squire Thompson q.v.
Thomas Davis to Elizabeth Stevens, 17 Dec 1845 (18 Dec), David Ragsdale JP, Stephen H. Chandler Bm (AR)
Zilpha Davis to Wright Smith q.v.

MARRIAGES (MEIGS)

Elizabeth Davis to Richardson Rhea q.v.
John Davis to Polly Adams, 19 Dec 1840, James Dyer Sur
John H. Davis to Margaret J. McAdoo, 11 Dec 1850, Franklin McCorkle Sur
Louisa Davis to Josiah Howser q.v.
Pheba Davis to John Gardner q.v.
Philip Davis to Mary McAdams, 24 Apr 1840 (26 Apr), William Green MG
Robert R. Davis to Harriet C. Boggess, 31 Oct 1843 (2 Nov), Robert Stockton JP
Samuel Davis to Phebe Harvey, 5 Nov 1842 (same), Robert Stockton JP
William Davis to Elizabeth Bennett, 10 Sept 1845, Thomas V. Atchley JP

MISCELLANEOUS (RHEA and MEIGS)

A. Davis: Hiwassee District
Alexander Davis: Bondsman for Isaac Clandon, 1834
" " Cherokee Removal muster roll, 1836
Edward Davis: Land south of the Tennessee River
Elbert Davis: Cherokee Removal muster roll, 1836
Ganium Davis: Private, Mexican War
Jacob Davis: Bondsman for William Gann, 1812
" " Bondsman for Elisha Corbet, 1817
James Davis: Bondsman for Joseph C. Carterright, 1829
John Davis: Cherokee Removal muster roll, 1836
" " JP 1849; Hiwassee District
" " Bondsman for Lewis Roark, 1821
" " Bondsman for John Atchley, 1825
" " Bondsman for Joel Hannah, 1831
" " Bondsman for Clayton Hoyal, 184
" " Bondsman for John Parker, 1834
" " Bondsman for Benjamin F. Jennings, 1842
John C. Davis: 2nd Sgt., Mexican War
Michael or Mitchell Davis: Cherokee Removal muster roll
Miles B. Davis: Private, Mexican War
Pleasant Davis: Bondsman for John George, 1838
Samuel Davis: Bondsman for James Mitchell, 1813
" " Bondsman for Joseph Dunham, 1814
Samuel G. Davis: Hiwassee District
Thomas Davis: Bondsman for David Richardson, 1821
Thomas P. Davis: JP(?) 1845
Wilbern Davis: JP(?) 1841

- - - - - - - - - - - - -

DAY

TAXES (RHEA)

1819 (Capt. Wm McCray's Co.): Hugh Day 1 WP
(Capt. John Lewis' Dist.): Jesse Day 1 WP, 150a
(Capt. W.S. Bradley's Dist.):
John Day 1 WP, 150a, 1 Town Lot
1823 (Capt. Brown's Co.): John Day 1 WP, 1 TL, 130½a E Fork Richland Creek (part of McClung's 809a)

1830 RHEA CENSUS

Jesse Day 00001001 - 00000001 p. 394
John Day 101101 - 1 p. 383

1840 RHEA CENSUS

John Day 0111001 - 001

1840 MEIGS CENSUS

Mary Day 0001 - 0023001 p. 228

1850 RHEA CENSUS

Addison C. Day 29 (Merchant), Hannah T. 28, Ann E. 2, Mary 1 p. 562-179
John Day 57 (Farmer), Rachael 33, Elbert S. 20 (Farmer), Emily H. 6, Tennessee N. 4, Hannah P. 2 p. 597-387

MARRIAGES (RHEA)

Emaline Day to Philemon K.W. Estell q.v.
Hetty Day to James Holland q.v.
Jesse Day to Elizabeth Lewis, 20 Jan 1825, D. Walker JP, D. Walker Bm (AR)

Jesse Day to Sarah Logan, 21 June 1827 (same), Matthew Hubbert JP, Robert N. Gillespie Bm (AR)
John Day to Jane Henry, 16 May 1816, J. Fine JP (AR)
John Day to Rachel Newman, 17 Jan 1843 (same), T.K. Munsey MG, James W. Gillespie Bm (AR)
Joseph Day to Polly Ann Crawford, 18 Oct 1832 (no return) (R)
Mary Jane Day to Thomas Muncy q.v.
Polly Day to Robert Martin q.v.
Sally Day to Abraham Bryson q.v.
Susanna Day to John Henry q.v.

MARRIAGES (MEIGS)

Katharine Day (Mrs.) to James P. Pierce q.v.
Lydia F. Day to Daniel R. Ramsey q.v.
Margaret Day to James Phillips q.v.
Mary Day to James Moore q.v.
Mary Day to James Pearce q.v.

MISCELLANEOUS (RHEA)

John Day: Bondsman for Abraham Bryson, 1812
" " Bondsman for Templin W. Ross, 1817
" " Bondsman for John Edmonson, 1818
" " Bondsman for John Woodward, 1818
" " Bondsman for Vandaman Anderson, 1821
" " Bondsman for Alexander Clingham, 1828
" " Bondsman for Edward Clingen, 1833
" " Resident of Town of Washington
William Day: Hiwssee District

\- - - - - - - - - - - - -

DAWSON

1850 MEIGS CENSUS

Josiah Dawson 35 (Farmer), Elizabeth 15, Jackson 11, Mary 8, Susan 6, Louisa 3 p. 805-708

\- - - - - - - - - - - - -

DEAN / DEANE

1850 RHEA CENSUS

Houston Dean 20: see Jesse P. Thompson
Mary Dean 42 (NC): see Francis Okelly
Nancy J. Dean 16: see Mary Presley
Thomas Dean 15: see Abraham Wright

MARRIAGES (RHEA)

Calvin Dean to Mary Wigington, 1 June 1845 (5 June), Sam Frazier JP (R)
Eliza Dean to John Warren q.v.

MARRIAGES (MEIGS)

P.J. Deane to Sarah C. Starnes, 24 Dec 1843 (same), B.F. McKenzie JP

\- - - - - - - - - - - - -

DEARMON / DEARMOND / DEARMAN / DEARMIN / DARMIN

TAXES (RHEA)

1823 (Capt. Smith's Co.): Anson Dearmin 1 WP

1830 RHEA CENSUS

Mary DeArman 00003 - 20000001 p. 376

1840 MEIGS CENSUS

John Darman 00001 - 0000100001 p. 237

1850 MEIGS CENSUS

John Dearmond 40 (Farmer) p. 770-448
William H. Dearmond 26 (Farmer), Susan 22, Thomas C. 2 p. 770-449

MARRIAGES (RHEA)

Anson Dearmon to Malinda Henry, 8 Nov 1836 (same), Carson Caldwell JP or Bm (R)
George W. Dearmon to Martha Long, 11 Dec 1832, Jeremiah Land Bm (A)
Polly Dearmon to John Parker q.v.

MARRIAGES (MEIGS)

Matilda J. Dearman to Thomas J. Eaves q.v.
William H. Dearmon to Susan Rice, 29 June 1847 (1 July), D.L. Godsey MG

MISCELLANEOUS (RHEA)

Anson Dearmon: Bondsman for Bright Johnson, 1830
" " Bondsman for Jas W. Thompson, 1832
" " Bondsman for Wilson Kilgore, 1835
" " Bondsman for John W. Denning, 1834

MISCELLANEOUS (MEIGS)

John Dearmond: Private, Mexican War

\- - - - - - - - - - - - -

DEARING / DEERING

TAXES (RHEA)

1823 (Capt. Jackson's Co.): Antalin L. Dearing 1 WP

1850 RHEA CENSUS

Sarah M. Dearing 17: see Cornelius Broyles

MARRIAGES (RHEA)

Thomas H. Deering to Elizabeth Reynolds, 30 Dec 1835 (31 Dec), Timothy Sullins MMEC, Jacob Kelly Bm (AR)

\- - - - - - - - - - - - -

DEATHERAGE / DETHERAGE / DETHRAGE

1840 MEIGS CENSUS

William Deatherage 110001 - 21001 p. 230

1850 RHEA CENSUS

James Deatherage 42 (Farmer), Susan 26, George 17, Sarah 16 p. 574-253

1850 MEIGS CENSUS

Abner Deatherage 46 (Farmer), Rebecca 44, Martha Ann 21, Catharine 18, William 15 (Deaf and Dumb), John 13, Mary E. 9, Eliza 7, Charles 4 p. 799-675
Samuel Detherage 23 (Farmer), Sarah A. 19 p. 797-659

MARRIAGES (MEIGS)

Samuel Deatherage to Sarah A. Read, 6 July 1850, R.C. Alford Sur
Sarah Dethrage to William Hawey q.v.

MISCELLANEOUS (RHEA and MEIGS)

Bird Deatherage: Elder, Concord Baptist Church, 1824
Harden Deatherage: Bm for Hezekiah McPherson, 1835
William Deatherage: JP(?) 1839

\- - - - - - - - - - - - -

DEEM

MISCELLANEOUS (MEIGS)

Patrick Deem: Teacher, District 1, 1842

\- - - - - - - - - - - - -

DEFRIECE / DEFRIESE / DEFRIESSE / FRIEZE

TAXES (RHEA)
1819 (Capt. W.S. Bradley's Dist.):
Hiram A. Defriese 1 WP, 1 TL
1823 (Capt. Brown's Co.): Audley P. Defriese 1 WP
1830 RHEA CENSUS
A.P. Defriece 110021 - 21101 p. 383
George Frieze 2010001 - 1020001 p. 375
1840 MEIGS CENSUS
Sarah Frieze 0102 - 0010001 p. 234
MARRIAGES
Audley P. Defrise to Nancy Caldwell, 7 Dec 1820 (same), John Rice JP, William Bradley Bm (AR) [1850 Bradley Census: Audley P. Defreese 44, Nancy L. 47, Thomas J. 26, Hiram A. 25, Anna J. 23, Jane E. 18, Mary 16, James A. 13, John M. 10, Henry C. 6, Theadore F. 6, Richard 4]
MISCELLANEOUS (RHEA)
Audley P. Defriesse: Bm for Alexander Caldwell, 1821
" " " Bondsman for Josiah Long, 1831
Hiram A. Defrese: Signed petition to move Indian Agency

- - - - - - - - - - - - -

DELOZIER

MARRIAGES (RHEA)
Betsy Delozier to Eli Marrs q.v.

- - - - - - - - - - - - -

DEMPSEY

MARRIAGES (MEIGS)
David C. Dempsey to Mary Ann Porter, 12 Sept 1842 (same), John Seabern JP
MISCELLANEOUS (MEIGS)
Charles Dempsey: Revolutionary War Pensioner(?)

- - - - - - - - - - - - -

DENNING / DENNON / DUNNING

1840 MEIGS CENSUS
John W. Dennon 11001 - 00001 p. 248
1850 MEIGS CENSUS
John Dunning 43 (Va)(Farmer), Abigal 42 (Va), Susan 17, Jane 16, Charles 11, Miles A. 10, Sarah R. 7, Andrew H. 4, Leanoris E. 3, Mary Ann 1 p. 717-35
MARRIAGES (RHEA)
John W. Denning to Elizabeth Daniel, 25 June 1834 (29 June), Isaac Baker JP, Anson Dearmon Bm (AR)

- - - - - - - - - - - - -

DENTON

1830 RHEA CENSUS
Uriah Denton 10001 - 000001 p. 369
1840 MEIGS CENSUS
Uriah Denton 111001 - 100001 p. 234
1850 MEIGS CENSUS
Uriah Denton 44 (Va)(Farmer), Mary Ann 46 (Md), Jeroe P. 22 (Farmer), John 20 (Farmer), Abraham 16, Mary Ann 13, Ellen B. 10, James 7, John 5, Elizabeth LEWIS 60 (Va) p. 754-339
MARRIAGES (RHEA)
Margaret Denton to William Harris q.v.
MISCELLANEOUS (MEIGS)
Garrow Denton: Surety for Thomas Purdy, 1850

- - - - - - - - - - - - -

DEORD

1840 RHEA CENSUS
Judy Deord 1211 - 1001001

- - - - - - - - - - - - -

DEREBURY

1850 RHEA CENSUS
Susannah Derebury 46 (NC), Charity 44 (NC): see Elihu McKinney

- - - - - - - - - - - - -

DERIAN

1850 RHEA CENSUS
John Derian 10: see Thomas C. Darwin

- - - - - - - - - - - - -

DEROSSETT / DEROUSET

1830 RHEA CENSUS
Margaret Derossett 0 - 0001101 p. 391
MARRIAGES (RHEA)
A. W. Derosset to Sallyan Whitmore, 7 Jan 1843, L.G. Hastler Bm (A)
Elizabeth C. Derosset to Joseph P. Holloway q.v.
George W. Derossett to Eliza Jane Hosler, 1 Oct 1836 (14 Oct or 7 Nov), James McCanse JP, John Poe Bm (AR)
Margaret Derouset to Johnson P. Leverett q.v.
Marvel Derossett to Myra Holloway, 14 Mar 1842 (A) [1850 Morgan Census: Marvel Derossett 26, Mariah 22, Pleasant 8, George 6, Sarah 5, Samuel 3, Richard 1]
Mary A. Derossett to Levi G. Hostler q.v.

- - - - - - - - - - - - -

DERRICK

MARRIAGES (RHEA)
Adam Derrick to Polly Blythe, 5 June 1809 (no return) (AR)
MARRIAGES (MEIGS)
Jesse C. Derrick to Jane F. Wier, 28 June 1838, B.F. McKenzie JP

- - - - - - - - - - - - -

DEWITT

MARRIAGES (RHEA)
Washington John DeWitt to Mary E. Bearden, 2 Apr 1820 (same), J. Beninger MG, Wm L. Bradley Bm (AR)

- - - - - - - - - - - - -

DEXTER

MARRIAGES (RHEA)
Martha Dexter to William Hoyle q.v.

- - - - - - - - - - - - -

DICKENS

TAXES (RHEA)
1819 (Capt. John Lewis' Dist.): John Dickens 1 WP

- - - - - - - - - - - - -

DICKEY

TAXES (RHEA)
1819 (Capt. W.S. Bradley's Dist): James Dickey 1 WP
Samuel Dickey 3 BP

1850 RHEA CENSUS
William Dickey 25 (Farmer), Elizabeth 23, William C. 5, Susan C. 2 p. 555-134

- - - - - - - - - - - - -

DILL

MISCELLANEOUS (RHEA) William Dill: MG 1827

- - - - - - - - - - - - -

DINES

MARRIAGES (MEIGS)
Eliza Dines to William Blackwell q.v.

- - - - - - - - - - - - -

DINNE

MISCELLANEOUS (RHEA and MEIGS)
Austin Dinne: Hiwassee District
Austin L. Dinne: Hiwassee District

- - - - - - - - - - - - -

DINSMORE

TAXES (RHEA)
1808 (Jonathan Fine's List): James Dinsmore 1 WP

- - - - - - - - - - - - -

DISMANY

1850 RHEA CENSUS
Dudley Dismany 46 (Va)(Farmer), Malinda 42, William 21 (Farmer), Matilda 17, John 15, James 19 (Farmer), Ann 12, Harvey 10, Ellen 8, Lucy A. 6, Robert 2, Silas 2/12, Martha A. ALTON or ALTUM 19, Nicholas PICKARD 8 p. 594-373

- - - - - - - - - - - - -

DIZNEY

1840 MEIGS CENSUS
Sollomon Dizney 120101 - 0011001 p. 238

- - - - - - - - - - - - -

DOAK / DOKE / DAKE / DACK

1830 RHEA CENSUS
John Doke 21110001 - 122001 p. 353
Keir Dack 0001 - 0001 p. 360

1840 MEIGS CENSUS
John Dake 040000001 - 0110001 p. 234

1850 MEIGS CENSUS
Rebecca Dake 55 (SC), Mahala 22, Phillip 20 (Farmer), Jonathan 18 (Farmer), Rebecca Ann 14, Asbury 12, Alexander 6 p. 784-559

MARRIAGES (RHEA)
Martha Dake to Samuel Underwood q.v.
Robert Doak to Rachel Pharis, 5 Dec 1833, William Moore Bm (A)

MARRIAGES (MEIGS)
Barbara Dake to Hes. Lucus q.v.

MISCELLANEOUS (RHEA and MEIGS)
John Dake: Member, Goodfield Baptist Church, 1827
" " House used for elections, District 4, 1836

- - - - - - - - - - - - -

DOBBS

1830 RHEA CENSUS
Caleb Dobbs 11201 - 300001 p. 370

1850 RHEA CENSUS
Martha R. Dobbs 22: see Francis O'Kelly q.v.

MARRIAGES (MEIGS)
Jesse W. Dobbs to Margaret Calvin, 31 Aug 1845 (3 Sept), Wm Johns JP

MISCELLANEOUS (MEIGS)
Egbert Dobbs: Cherokee Removal muster roll, 1836

- - - - - - - - - - - - -

DODSON / DOTSON / DOBSON

1840 RHEA CENSUS
Fountain Dodson 220001 - 01001

1850 RHEA CENSUS
Fountain Dotson 46 (NC)(Farmer), Mary 45, James S. 16 (Farmer), Littlebury J. 13, John 11, Eliza 9, Betsy 7, Abraham 5, Sarah 3 p. 570-223
[Fountain Dodson married Polly Parker on 27 July 1824 in Roane County]
Hannah M. Dotson 17: see Thomas Sims
James M. Dotson 24 (Farmer), Mary 24, William 4, Caroline 2, James 8/12 p. 617-522
Joel Dodson 27 (Day Laborer), Elizabeth A. 29, Martha J. 6, Sarah E. 4, William S. 2, James 7/12 p. 545-81
Nathaniel Dodson 27 (Farmer), Mary 29, James H. 6, Samuel W. 4, William 2, Joseph G. 2/12 p. 558-155
Samuel Dotson 50 (Farmer), Frances 46 (Va), Thomas 18 (Farmer), Nancy J. 17, Emeline 14, Eliza 12, Margaret 10, George W. 8, Caroline 6, Taylor 4 p. 559-161

Thomas Dodson 68 (Va)(Wagonmaker), Polly 63, James 22 (Farmer), Elizabeth McKEE 29 (Unk) p. 546-83
William S. Dotson 26 (Farmer), Jane 24, Adam 6, Catharine 4, William T. 2, Mary J. 1 p. 617-521
William Dotson 22 (Farmer), Judiah L. 22 p. 567-199
1850 MEIGS CENSUS
William J. Dodson 75 (SC), Anna 30 (SC)(Deaf and Dumb), Nancy 8, Lavina 54 (Va) p. 736-188
MARRIAGES (RHEA)
Dicey Dotson to Samuel Allen q.v.
Joel Dodson to Elizabeth Gillum, 11 May 1843 (same), J.P. Thompson JP (A)
Martha Dotson to Z. Key q.v.
Mary Dodson to William Fullington q.v.
Nancy Dotson to William G. Harwood q.v.
Nathan Dotson to Mary Smith, 10 Sept 1842 (no return) (R)
William Dotson to Juda L. Gear, 18 Dec 1849 (22 Dec), T.J. Creede JP (R)
MARRIAGES (MEIGS)
Abner Dotson to Susan Hembree, 28 July 1846 (same), Joseph Johnson JP
MISCELLANEOUS (RHEA)
Abner Dobson: Witness to Minutes of Commissioners, Town of Washington, 1814

- - - - - - - - - - - - -

DOLEN / DOLING

1830 RHEA CENSUS
John Dolen 1110001 - 11101 p. 355
1840 MEIGS CENSUS
John Dolen 21110001 - 011101 p. 229
MISCELLANEOUS (MEIGS)
John Doling: Hiwassee District, Moore's Chapel area

- - - - - - - - - - - - -

DOLLANO

MISCELLANEOUS (MEIGS)
William Dollano: Private, Mexican War

- - - - - - - - - - - - -

DONALD

TAXES (RHEA)
1819 (Capt. McGill's Co.): Matthew Donald 200a
1823 (Capt. Howard's Co.): Matthew Donald 195a
MARRIAGES (RHEA)
Pamela Donald to Michael J. Bulger q.v.
Peggy Donald to William Dunlap q.v.
MISCELLANEOUS (RHEA)
Matthew Donald: MG 1816-17, 1821, 1824
" " Bondsman for Isaac Mahan, 1812
" " Bondsman for Thomas Blackburn, 1824

- - - - - - - - - - - - -

DORAN

MISCELLANEOUS (RHEA)
John C. Doran: Bondsman for Cornelius Moyers, 1824

- - - - - - - - - - - - -

DORTON / DOUTEN / DOUBTEN / DOWTEN / DOWDEN

1830 RHEA CENSUS
Allen Dorton 3001 - 001011 p. 370
1850 MEIGS CENSUS
Andrew J. Dowden 22: see William Baldin [Baldwin]
MARRIAGES (RHEA)
Allen Doubten to Sarah Martin, 21 Oct 1831, Sebert Martin Bm (R) [1850 Hamilton Census: William Douten 25, Sarah 20, Sebron MARTIN 60]
Henry Dowten to Betsy Elizabeth Adams, 7 Mar 1834, William Adams Bm (A) [1850 Hamilton Census: Henry Douten 40, Elizabeth 45, William 15, Francis 13, Pussa 11, Calvin 11]

- - - - - - - - - - - - -

DOUTHAT

MISCELLANEOUS (MEIGS)
Isaac Douthat: Private, Mexican War

- - - - - - - - - - - - -

DOUGHTY / DAUGHTY / DOUGHTRY

1840 MEIGS CENSUS
James Doughty 1201101 - 110011 p. 227
1850 MEIGS CENSUS
James Doughty 68 (Va)(Farmer), Racheal 40, James 14, Ruthy C. 13, Thompson 10, Martha 7 p. 729-126
MARRIAGES (RHEA)
James Doughty to Rachel Rhea, 27 Oct 1834, V.H. Giles JP, Joseph G. Weaver Bm (AR)
Pleasant Doughtry to Martha J. Hutcherson, 30 Jan 1847 (31 Jan), E.F. Childress MG (R)
MARRIAGES (MEIGS)
Eleanor Daughty to William G. Martin q.v.
MISCELLANEOUS (RHEA and MEIGS)
James Doughty: Ocoee District
Pleasant Doughty: Private, Mexican War
" " JP(?) 1843-44

- - - - - - - - - - - - -

DOUGLAS / DOUGLASS

TAXES (RHEA)
1823 (Capt. Howard's Co.): William H. Douglas 1 WP
1840 RHEA CENSUS
Jesse Douglass 1100001 - 521001
1850 RHEA CENSUS
Edy Douglass 13: see Pleasant Snow
Robert Douglass 22: see George W. Brown
MARRIAGES (RHEA)
Robert Douglass to Sarah Brown, 14 Aug 1850 (15 Aug), C.A. Holland MG (R)
MARRIAGES (MEIGS)
J.R. Douglass to Caroline C. Bottoms, 9 Dec 1847, J.C. Bottom Bm [1850 Monroe Census: J.B. Douglas 27, Caroline 21]
MISCELLANEOUS (RHEA and MEIGS)
H. Douglass: MG 1842, 1846-48

- - - - - - - - - - - - -

DOWELL

MISCELLANEOUS (MEIGS)
Warren Dowell: Hiwassee District, Sewee Creek area

- - - - - - - - - - - - -

DOWLER

MISCELLANEOUS (RHEA)
Thomas Dowler: Bondsman for John Jacobs, 1811

- - - - - - - - - - - - -

DOZIER

MARRIAGES (RHEA)
John Dozier to Nancy McDaniel, 5 Jan 1836 (7 Jan), John Condley JP, James Cobb Bm (AR)

- - - - - - - - - - - - -

DRENNON / DRINEN

MARRIAGES (RHEA)
Thomas Drinen or Drennon to Mary Gravey or Gravely, 20 June 1816 (same), John Locke Bm (AR)

- - - - - - - - - - - - -

DUCKWORTH

1830 RHEA CENSUS
John Duckworth 1001 - 0001 p. 362
1830 MEIGS CENSUS
John Duckworth 40 (NC)(Farmer), Rebecca 40 p. 816-767
MARRIAGES (RHEA)
Hezekiah Duckworth to Elinda Ledfort, 6 Feb 1830 (same), Stephen Winton JP (AR) [1850 Coffee Census: Hezekiah Duckworth 37, Malinda 35, Elizabeth 18, William 16, Amos 13, George 12, Hezekiah 9, John 7, Charles 3, Evaline 1]
John Duckworth to Rebecca Snow, 3 Jan 1832 (5 Jan), Beal Gaither JP, Mark Massey Bm (AR)
MARRIAGES (MEIGS)
William Duckworth to Polly Hill, 7 Mar 1839 (same), Mark Renfrow JP

- - - - - - - - - - - - -

DUDDING

MARRIAGES (RHEA)
George Dudding to Sarah Fuill, 8 Mar 1850 (same), T.J. Creede JP (R)

- - - - - - - - - - - - -

DUDLEY

1840 RHEA CENSUS
John Dudley 100001 - 00001
Samuel G. Dudley 01211001 - 0110001
1850 RHEA CENSUS
Calvin G. Dudley 31 (Farmer), Caroline 29 (NC), Samuel 8, Benjamin 6, Martha J. 3, John C. 1 p. 553-123
Claborn J. Dudley 22, Elvira 23: see John Ferguson
Samuel Dudley 55 (Ga)(Farmer), Martha 62, Martha M. 18, Byrd 16 (Farmer) p. 583-315 [Samuel married Matty Sherald on 19 Aug 1806 in Roane Co.]
MARRIAGES (RHEA)
C. Dudley to Elvira Furguson, 1 Jan 1850 (3 Jan), John F. Torbett JP (R)
Calvin G. Dudley to Caroline Bingam or Bingham, 29 June 1841 (1 July), A.G. Wright JP, David M. Roddy Bm (AR)
Clarissie Dudley to Wesley Casey q.v.
John Dudley to Elizabeth Cox, 14 Jan 1840 (16 Jan), Wm B. Gordon MG, William Cox Bm (AR)
Sherrell Dudley to Sarah Thompson, 23 Jan 1837, George Preston JP, Darius Waterhouse Bm (AR)
Syrena Dudley to Moses C.R. Thompson q.v.

- - - - - - - - - - - - -

DUGAN or DUGEN

MARRIAGES (RHEA)
William F. Dugen or Dugan to Harriet Kenny or Kenney, 13 Aug 1834, J.M. Callon or J. McCallie JP (AR)
MISCELLANEOUS (RHEA and MEIGS)
William F. Dugan: Bondsman for Jackson F. Box, 1834
" " " Purchased Lot 60 in Decatur, 1836

- - - - - - - - - - - - -

DUNCAN / DUNCANS / DUNKIN / DINKINS

TAXES (RHEA)
1819 (Capt. John Robinson's Co.):
Jeremiah Dunkin 1 WP, 2 BP, 1 TL
1823 (Capt. Braselton's Co.):
Jeremiah Duncan heirs, 1 TL, 1000a Tenn River
1830 RHEA CENSUS
John Duncan 221001 - 01001 p. 365
1840 RHEA CENSUS
Hiram Duncan 010001 - 00001
1840 MEIGS CENSUS
John Duncans 110001 - 010001 p. 225
1850 RHEA CENSUS
Russel Dunkin 32 (Farmer), Luisa 26, London R. 9, Francis M. 8, Mary S. 6, Charles P. 4, John A. 3, Margaret E. 8/12 p. 589-356
MARRIAGES (RHEA)
Elizabeth Dunken to George W. Black q.v.
James I. Duncan to Elizabeth Robertson, 30 June 1835 (3 July), John Condley JP, Jas C. Ferguson Bm (AR)
James W. Duncan to Eliza Lee, 1 Dec 1832, William F. Seay Bm (A)
John Dinkins to Sally Thomas, 24 June 1819 (same), H. Collins JP, Hiram Webb Bm (AR)
Mary Duncan to Robert Simpson q.v.
Russel Duncan to Mary Louisa Rector, 4 Aug 1840 (same), A.D. Paul JP (AR)

- - - - - - - - - - - - -

DUNHAM

TAXES (RHEA)
1808 (John Henry's List): Joseph Dunham Sr. 3 BP
Joseph Dunham Jr. 1 WP, -?-a
1850 RHEA CENSUS
Jack Dunham 43 (Farmer), Sopha 47, Samuel 21 (Farmer), Lucinda 14, Joseph 9, Lucy BROWN 70 (Va) p. 632-632
MARRIAGES (RHEA)
Joseph Dunham to Charity Smith, 4 Jan 1814, Wm Long JP
Reubin Dunham to Rebecca Dunham, 23 Dec 1817 (same), Richard Dunham Bm (A)
[Rebecca, dau of Joseph Dunham Jr.]
MISCELLANEOUS (RHEA)
Joseph Dunham: First Grand Jury, Rhea County
Richard Dunham: Bondsman for Reubin Dunham, 1817

- - - - - - - - - - - - -

DUNLADY

MARRIAGES (RHEA)
Polly Dunlady to Robert Rilley q.v.

- - - - - - - - - - - - -

DUNLAP

1830 RHEA CENSUS
John Dunlap 11001 - 01001 p. 365
1840 RHEA CENSUS
John Dunlap 2020001 - 00011
1850 RHEA CENSUS
John Dunlap 50 (NC), Elizabeth 48, Jacob S. 25 (Farmer), John 23 (Farmer), William 16 (Farmer), James 14, Richard 10, Doctor A. 6 p. 539-41
MARRIAGES (RHEA)
John Dunlap to Elizabeth Wassum or Wasson, 25 June 1820 (29 June), J. Fine JP, John Garisson Bm (AR)
Polly Dunlap to Robert Beard q.v.
William Dunlap to Peggy Donald, 23 May 1810 (same), Wm Long JP (AR)

- - - - - - - - - - - - -

DUNLARY

1830 RHEA CENSUS
James Dunlary 10000001 - 00010001 p. 358

- - - - - - - - - - - - -

DUNN / DUN

1830 RHEA CENSUS
David Dunn 1202011 - 1100001 p. 376
Eliza Dunn 0121 - 001001 p. 376
1840 RHEA CENSUS
David Dunn 20011 - 01001
Elizabeth Dun 00111 - 1000001
1850 RHEA CENSUS
Elizabeth Dunn 50, Malinda GEARING 15 (NC)(mulatto) p. 602-682
MARRIAGES (RHEA)
James H. Dun to Martha Guis or Guerin, 3 Mar 1842 (same), Richard Waterhouse JP, L.M. Johnson Bm (AR)
Peggy Ann Dunn to Jesse McCarter q.v.
Rhoda Dunn to Allen Murphrie q.v.
William Dunn to Elizabeth Mariott or Merriott, 1 Aug 1814, John Murfree Bm (AR)
MISCELLANEOUS (RHEA)
James Dun: Bondsman for John Meriott, 1845

- - - - - - - - - - - - -

DURHAM

MARRIAGES (RHEA)
Dicy Durham to Robert Warren q.v.

- - - - - - - - - - - - -

DYAL

1850 RHEA CENSUS
Amanda Dyal 3: see David G. Scraggins
Frederick R. Dyal 7: see Moses C.R. Thompson
Margaret V. Dyal 6: see John Boyd
Rebecca A. Dyal 12: see Noah Fisher
Thomas Dyal Unk (NC)(Shoemaker), Martha 29, James 16, William 10 p. 593-363

- - - - - - - - - - - - -

DYER / DIER

TAXES (RHEA)
1819 (Capt. John Lewis' Dist.): Spilsby Dyer 1 WP, 180a
1823 (Capt. Piper's Co.): James Dyer 1 WP
(Capt. Lewis' Co.):
Spilsbee Dyer 1 WP, 160a Whites Creek
1830 RHEA CENSUS
Spills B. Dyer 0122001 - 1100001 p. 366
1840 RHEA CENSUS
John C. Dier 10001 - 10001
Robert H. Dier 112001 - 210001
Spills B. Dier 11002001 - 11010001
Stephen Dier 00001 - 0001
William Dier 021001 - 100001
1840 MEIGS CENSUS
Thomas Dyer 00000001 - 000000001 p. 226
1850 MEIGS CENSUS
Charity Dyer (f) 33 (NC), Martha Jane 8, Sarah E. 5, Harriet E. 3 p. 794-631
MARRIAGES (RHEA)
John C. Dyer to Rosanna Eller, 19 Nov 1834 (21 Nov), John Condley JP, Moses Eller Bm (AR)
Joseph Dyer to Armenta Parker, 10 Jan 1842 (A)
Leah Dyer to Moses Eller q.v.
Robert H. Dyer to Cairen Erwin, 25 Mar 1827, Jacob L. Wassum Bm (A)
Stephen H. Dyer to C.M. Elison, 4 Aug 1839 (same), Richard Waterhouse JP (R)
MARRIAGES (MEIGS)
Polly Dyer to Pleasant Gross q.v.
MISCELLANEOUS (RHEA and MEIGS)
John Dyer: Revolutionary War Pensioner
Joseph J. Dyer: Private, Mexican War

Spilsby Dyer: JP 1836-1841 [Rhea County]
" " Bondsman for Robert B. Harris, 1817
" " Bondsman for Woodson Tucker, 1820
" " Early resident of Town of Washington
" " Signed petition to move Indian Agency
Stephen H. Dyer: Private, Mexican War

- - - - - - - - - - - - -

DYKES

1830 RHEA CENSUS
David Dykes 1111 - 200001 p. 383

- - - - - - - - - - - - -

EAKEN— see AIKEN

- - - - - - - - - - - - -

EARLES

1840 RHEA CENSUS
Liles Earles 0001 - 00011
Robert Earles 00002 - 0001
MARRIAGES (RHEA)
Robert D. Earles to Eliza Whitmore, 29 June 1840 (30 June), Samuel Frazier JP, Henry Whittenburg Bm (AR) [1850 White Census: Robert B. Earles 30, Eliza 26, Margaret 9, Malinda 7]

- - - - - - - - - - - - -

EARLY

MISCELLANEOUS (RHEA)
Worsham Early: Signed petition to move Indian Agency

- - - - - - - - - - - - -

EARP / ERP

TAXES (RHEA)
1819 (Capt. John Lewis' Dist.): Josiah Erp 1 WP
1823 (Capt. Howerton's Old Co.): Josiah Earp 1 WP
MARRIAGES (RHEA)
Josiah Erp to Patsy Davidson, 26 Dec 1815, N. Hackworth Bm (A)

- - - - - - - - - - - - -

EASTERLY

MISCELLANEOUS (RHEA)
C. Easterly: MG 1828

- - - - - - - - - - - - -

EASTON

TAXES (RHEA)
1819 (Capt. W.S. Bradley's Dist.): James Easton heirs 3000a

- - - - - - - - - - - - -

EATON

1850 RHEA CENSUS
Henry Eaton 50 (Va)(Farmer), Rebecca 47 (NC), William S. 17 (Farmer), Adeline 15, Joshua 13, Elizabeth CHAPMAN 83 (NC) p. 568-211
Jesse Eaton 30 (Farmer), Susan 29 (Va), Virginia C. 7, Mary A. 5, Levi W. 2, Lucinda 2/12 p. 578-278
Josiah Eaton 21 (Farmer), Minerva 19, Mary O. 10/12 p. 570-221
1850 MEIGS CENSUS
John W. Eaton 51* (Farmer), Margaret 41, Thomas M.N. 15 (Farmer), Warren N. 13, George W.N. 10, Robert D.J.A. 7, Elizabeth B. 2 p. 737-193 [* age may be 37 instead of 51; numbers difficult to read]
MARRIAGES (RHEA)
Jesse Eaton to Susan Wyrick, 9 Nov 1842, Azariah Barton Bm (A)
Joseph Eaton to Manerva Minix, 5 Dec 1848 (same), Wm R. Rose MG (R)
Manda Jane Eaton to William Hains q.v.
Rebecca Eaton to John Edmonson q.v.
Susan Eaton to George Hail q.v.
MISCELLANEOUS (RHEA)
Jesse Eaton: Bondsman for S. Wyrick, 1831
" " Bondsman for William Readmon, 1839

- - - - - - - - - - - - -

EAVES / EVES

1830 RHEA CENSUS
Thomas Eaves 2111101 - 22101 p. 371
1840 MEIGS CENSUS
Thomas Eaves 00111001 - 0020001 p. 237
Violet Eaves 00001 - 00001 p. 237
1850 RHEA CENSUS
Mary Eves 5* (SC), Pleasant 21 (Farmer), Mary MARTIN Unk p. 607-482 [*Mary was born between 1790 and 1800, so age probably was 55]
1850 MEIGS CENSUS
Violet Eves 35 (SC)(Farmer), Mariah 32, Julian 7, Elizabeth 3 p. 769-440
MARRIAGES (RHEA)
Elizabeth Eaves to James Davis q.v.
Katherine Eaves to John Hunter q.v.
Lucy Eaves to Samuel F. Martin q.v.
Nancy Eaves to Edward S. Stokes q.v.
Nancy Eaves to Israel A. Vandike q.v.
P.L. [Pleasant L.] Eaves to Elizabeth Bean, 10 Oct 1850 (11 Oct), John Wyott JP (R) [Elizabeth, dau of Edmund and Lucretia Locke Bean]
Violet Eaves to Maria Leuty, 24 Feb 1836, John P. Long Bm (A) [Maria, dau of John and Susannah Sprowell Russell Leuty]
MARRIAGES (MEIGS)
Esther P. Eaves to Thomas Leuty q.v.
Thomas J. Eaves to Matilda J. Dearmon, 18 Dec 1841 (19 Dec), James Blevins JP
MISCELLANEOUS (RHEA and MEIGS)
Thomas Eaves: Bondsman for Levi Gerin, 1844
" " Circuit Court Jury, Meigs County, 1836
" " Commissioner to construct Decatur Court-house, 1836

Thomas Eaves: Common School Com., District 3, 1834
" " Hiwassee District, Cottonport area
Violet Eaves: Bondsman for Larkin M. Stokes, 1836
William Eaves: Ensign, Mexican War
" " Bondsman for Joseph Collins, 1850

EDDS / EADS / EIDES / ADDS

1840 MEIGS CENSUS
Gilbert E. Edds 1111001 - 0110001 p. 232
William B. Eides 0001 - 0001 p. 228
MARRIAGES (MEIGS)
Elizabeth A. Edds to Thomas E. Stanner q.v.
John Edds to Prudy Ann Peirce, 27 Mar 1845, M.C. Atchley MG, Philip Peirce Bm
Judy D. Edds to William Guine q.v.
Moses H. Edds to Sariah Peirce, 24 Sept 1849 (25 Sept), M.C. Atchley MG
Polly W. Eades [Edds] to John Buster q.v.
William P. Edds to Mira Knight, 23 Jan 1840, Edward Brightwell JP or Bm
MISCELLANEOUS (MEIGS)
John K. Edds: JP(?) 1843
Preston G. Eads: Resident of Cottonport
William P. Edds: JP(?) 1839

EDENS

MISCELLANEOUS (MEIGS)
Israel D. Edens: JP(?) 1841-1842

EDGEING / EDGING

1850 RHEA CENSUS
Eli Edging 19: see Mary West
Johnson Edgeing 52 (NC)(Farmer), Lyda 43 (Ga), Lewis H. 12 (Ala), Sarah B. 11 (Ala), George W. 10 (Ala), Adelaalis 7 (Ala), Sanora E. 4, William S.Y. 2 p. 601-417

EDGEMAN / EDGEMON / EDGMON / EDGMAN

1840 MEIGS CENSUS
Samuel Edgeman 1211001 - 001121 p. 239
1850 MEIGS CENSUS
Samuel Edgman 58 (Farmer), Jane 44 (Ky), Polly 21, Samuel 19 (Farmer), Simbel 17 (Farmer), James 13, Martha 6 p. 795-641 [Samuel Edgemon married Jane Allen on 30 July 1843 in McMinn County]
Thomas Edgman 27 (Farmer), Glatha 25, Sarah 7, Jeremiah 5, Elizabeth 4, Samuel 2 p. 798-672
MARRIAGES (RHEA)
Rebecca Edgmon to John Clack q.v.
MARRIAGES (MEIGS)
Drusanna Edgemon to John A. Clark q.v.
Mary Ann Edgmon to Abraham Clark q.v.
Nancy Edgemon to David Walker q.v.
MISCELLANEOUS (RHEA)
Benjamin Edgemon: MG 1819-1820

EDGEMOND

MARRIAGES (RHEA)
Braxton Edgemond to Mary Casey, 4 Apr 1832 (6 Apr), Stephen Winton JP, John A. Casey Bm (AR)

EDINGTON / EDDINGTON

1830 RHEA CENSUS
Ann Edington 0 - 0002101 p. 389
J. Edington 10001 - 00001 p. 389
James Edington 2011001 - 00101 p. 358
1850 RHEA CENSUS
Luke Eddington 20, Polly A. 19, Riley 17: see Austin Evans
1850 MEIGS CENSUS
Thomas Edington 74 (NY), Sally Ann 40 (Ga), Cynthia Ann 19, Mahala A. 18, James S. 15, William R. 12, Louisa A. 10, Aramete E. 8, Malinda 6 p. 791 - 611
MARRIAGES (RHEA)
Isaac Edington to Malinda M. Thompson, 12 Mar 1829, Squire L. Thompson Bm (A)
Joseph Edington to Elizabeth McAlester, 17 Apr 1811 (same), Charles Wright Bm (A)
Lucinda Eddington to John Looney q.v.
Malinda Edington to Austin Evans q.v.
Mary A. Eddington to William Rhea q.v.
Polly Eddington to Levi Curtain q.v.
MISCELLANEOUS (RHEA)
Hugh H. Edington: Bondsman for William Simpson, 1833
Isaac M. Eddington: Bondsman for Isham Reese, 1830
James Edington: Bondsman for Joshuaway Butler, 1811
Luke Eddington: Bondsman for Levi Curtain, 1830

EDMONDS / EDMOND / EDMONS / EDMUNDS

1840 RHEA CENSUS
Penelope Edmonds 0101 - 001101
1840 MEIGS CENSUS
Newton Edmond 00001 - 0001 p. 231
1850 RHEA CENSUS
James Edmonds 21: see Mariah Clawson
Madison Edmonds 21: see William Collins
Newton J. Edmonds 33 (Farmer), Unity H. 24, Saraseta S. 8, Martha A. 6, Philadelphia E. 2, Newton 4/12 p. 604-464
Penelope Edmonds 53 (NC), William C. 19 (Farmer), William A. KELLY 12 p. 607-480
MARRIAGES (RHEA)
Allen Edmonds to Elizabeth Kelly, 19 July 1844, John Moreland Bm (AR)
James Edmons to Elizabeth Minnas, 24 Dec 1850 (same), John Wyott JP (R)
Nancy Ann Edmunds to William N. Meriott q.v.

Newton J. Edmonds to Eunita H. Ryan, 11 July 1839 (same), Wm Bower MG, John Usery Bm (AR)
Rebecca Jane Edmonds to Bailey Minnick q.v.
William C. Edmonds to Eliza Crow, 12 Dec 1850 (same), S.R. Hackett JP (R)

MISCELLANEOUS (MEIGS)
Newton Edmonds: Cherokee Removal muster roll, 1836

- - - - - - - - - - - - -

EDMONSON / EDMONDSON / EDMONSTON

1840 RHEA CENSUS
Samuel Edmondson 100001 - 030101

1850 MEIGS CENSUS
Thomas Edmonson 35 (Farmer), Emaline 28, Euclid 8 p. 730-124

MARRIAGES (RHEA)
Barbary Edmonston to David Jacobs q.v.
John Edmonson to Rebecca Eaton, 9 Mar 1818 (same), Abraham Howard JP, John Day Bm (AR)
Thomas Edmondson to Polly Sams, 16 Sept 1826, John Edmondson Bm (A)

MISCELLANEOUS (RHEA)
John Edmondson: Bondsman for Hiram Burnett, 1822
" " Bondsman for Thos Edmondson, 1826

- - - - - - - - - - - - -

EDWARDS

TAXES (RHEA)
1808 (John Henry's List): Walter Edwards 1 WP
1819 (Capt. John Ramsey's Co.):
Walter Edwards 1 WP, 100a

1830 RHEA CENSUS
William Edwards 0110101 - 2212101 p. 385

MARRIAGES (MEIGS)
Adeline Edwards to Joseph Romines q.v.
Justice Edwards to Elizabeth Hufner, 27 Oct 1838 (28 Oct), John Taff JP

MISCELLANEOUS (RHEA)
Walter Edwards: Bondsman for Joseph King, 1811
" " Bondsman for Solomon Price, 1819
" " Bondsman for John Marshall, 1822
" " On first Grand Jury, 1808

- - - - - - - - - - - - -

ELDER

TAXES (RHEA)
1823 (Capt. Smith's Co.):
Robert Elder 1 WP, 1 BP, 160a Goodfield

1830 RHEA CENSUS
James Elder 10101 - 10001 p. 352
Robert Elder 10010011 - 1200001 p. 375

1840 MEIGS CENSUS
Robert Elder 00010011 - 00010001 p. 236

1850 MEIGS CENSUS
Robert Elder 70 (Va)(Farmer), Mary 40 (Va), William 17 (Farmer), Sarah Ann 15, Emaline 14, Mahala 7, Clarissa 5, Amanda 3, Martha 1 p. 768-432
William R. Elder 33 (NC)(Farmer), Malita 34 (NC), Susannah 15, Thomas 11, Martha E. 9, William H. 6, Milton L. 4, Malinda E. 3, Seripta E. 1 p. 762-386

MARRIAGES (RHEA)
James Elder to Sally Wommack, 25 Aug 1826 (same), Thomas Cox JP, Jacob Wommack Bm (AR)
John Elder to Mary Vernon, 30 Jan 1828 (6 Feb), Thomas Cox JP, Samuel Igou Bm (AR)
Nancy Elder to William Lillard q.v.
Robert Elder Jr. to Minerva Wright or Right, 4 Apr 1834 (6 Apr), James Wilson JP, William Lillard Bm (AR)
Robert Elder to Nancy Lucas, 20 Feb 1836, John M. Elder Bm (A)

MARRIAGES (MEIGS)
Mary Elder to James N. Newkirk q.v.
Sarah Elder to G.W. Houseley q.v.

MISCELLANEOUS (RHEA and MEIGS)
James Elder: Purchased Lot 44 in Decatur, 1836
John M. Elder: Bondsman for Robert Elder, 1836
Robert Elder: Member, Goodfield Baptist Church, 1827
" " Hiwassee District, Goodfield area
" " Purchased Lots 32,33,61 in Decatur, 1836
" " Trustee for Decatur Academy, 1838-39
" " Common School Commissioner, Dist 4, 1838

- - - - - - - - - - - - -

ELDRED

MARRIAGES (MEIGS)
William B. Eldred to Mary Keenum. 23 Oct 1844 (24 Oct), Ezekiel Ward MG

MISCELLNEOUS (MEIGS)
William Eldred: JP(?) 1844

- - - - - - - - - - - - -

ELDRIDGE / ELDRAGE

1840 MEIGS CENSUS
John Eldrage 00011 - 1001 p. 226

1850 MEIGS CENSUS
John B. Eldridge 38 (Farmer), Lorinda 31, Sarah Jane 14, Louisa 9, William 7, Charles 5, Leander 2 p. 725-95

MARRIAGES (RHEA)
John B. Eldridge to Lorenda Matlock, 8 Aug 1835, Thomas C. Jordan Bm (A) [Lorinda, dau of William and Sarah Dodson Matlock]

MISCELLANEOUS (RHEA)
John B. Eldridge: Ocoee District
Samson Eldridge: Bondsman for Jesse Morris, 1835

- - - - - - - - - - - - -

ELLER

1840 RHEA CENSUS
Catherine Eller 00011 - 00110001
George Eller 100001 -00001
Moses Eller 00001 - 20001

MARRIAGES (RHEA)
Joseph Ellis or Eller to Sally Evans or Evins, 2 Mar 1841, S. Dyer JP, Willis G. Evans Bm (AR)
[NOTE: this marriage was listed twice in the Rhea County records: #67 as Joseph Ellis and #90 as

Joseph Eller; Allen shows the name as Eller]
Moses Eller to Leah Dyer, 20 Aug 1836 (21 Aug), John Condley JP, Thomas Smith Bm (AR)
Rosannah Eller to John C. Dyer q.v.
MISCELLANEOUS (RHEA)
Moses Eller: Bondsman for John C. Dyer, 1834

- - - - - - - - - - - - -

ELLIN [ELKIN?]

MARRIAGES (MEIGS)
Larky Ellin [Elkin] to W.Y. Young q.v.

- - - - - - - - - - - - -

ELLIOT / ELLIOTT

MARRIAGES (RHEA)
James Elliott to Sarah Davis, 11 June 1814, Allen Asbell Bm (AR)
Jesse Elliot to Sally Frazier, 5 July 1810 (same), William Long JP, Abel Johnson Bm (AR)
MISCELLANEOUS (RHEA)
James Elliott: Early resident, Town of Washington
" " Security for John Moore, 1812

- - - - - - - - - - - - -

ELLIS

TAXES (RHEA)
1823 (Capt. Howard's Co.): Thomas Ellis 1 WP, 5a
1840 MEIGS CENSUS
John Ellis 10111 - 10001 p. 233
MARRIAGES (RHEA)
Betsy Ellis to James Knox q.v.
Dicey Ellis to James Wilson q.v.
Susanna Ellis to John Pearson q.v.
MARRIAGES (MEIGS)
Angeline Ellis to David Miller q.v.
John L. Ellis to Sarah F. Benson, 11 July 1850, Abner Chamber Sur
Katherine Ellis to William F. Gourley q.v.

- - - - - - - - - - - - -

ELLISON— see ALLISON

- - - - - - - - - - - - -

ELSEA / ELSEY / ELSAY

1840 RHEA CENSUS
Isaac Elsea 1111001 - 0012001
MARRIAGES (MEIGS)
Thomas Elsay to Elender A. Tillery, 16 Sept 1840 (17 Sept), D.L. Godsey MG
MISCELLANEOUS (RHEA)
John Elsey: 3rd Corp., Mexican War

- - - - - - - - - - - - -

EMBREE / EMBREY / EMERY– see HEMBREE

- - - - - - - - - - - - -

EMMETT / EMETT

1850 MEIGS CENSUS
Jacob Emett 64 (Farmer), Mary 58, Jacob 24 (Farmer), George 18 (Farmer), William 15, Bershaba 13 p. 758-363
John S. Emmett 35, Emaline 32, Jacob 13, Margaret Jane 10, Mary E. 6, Eliza L. 4, James E. 2, Elvire C. 1 p. 758-361

- - - - - - - - - - - - -

ENGLEDOW

MARRIAGES (RHEA)
John Engledow to Eliza Stoner, 2 June 1831, John Parker Bm (A)

- - - - - - - - - - - - -

ENGLISH

TAXES (RHEA)
1823 (Capt. Lewis' Co.): James English 1 WP
1830 RHEA CENSUS
Matthew English 00201101 - 00001001 p. 388
MARRIAGES (RHEA)
Elizabeth P. English to John C. Ferguson q.v.
James W. English to Nancy Buster, 23 July 1832 (26 July), D.L. Godsey JP, John Buster Bm (AR)
Mary English to Robert Cooper q.v.
MISCELLANEOUS (RHEA)
William G. English: Bondsman for John C. Ferguson, 1831
" " " Bondsman for Hugh L. Baldwin, 1832
" " " Bondsman for Arthur L. Fulton, 1835

- - - - - - - - - - - - -

EPERSON

1830 RHEA CENSUS
Jas or Jos Eperson 01101 - 320101 p. 372

- - - - - - - - - - - - -

ERWIN / ERVIN

TAXES (RHEA)
1819 (Capt. John Lewis' Dist.): Benjamin Erwin 113a
1823 (Capt. Lewis' Co.): Andrew Erwin 1 Town Lot
Benjamin Erwin Sr. 113a
Benjamin Erwin Jr. 1 WP
1830 RHEA CENSUS
Benjamin Erwin 100001 - 220001 p. 366
MARRIAGES (RHEA)
Benjamin Erwin to Anna Ferguson, 29 Mar 1824 (same), Fred Fulkerson JP, Levi Ferguson Bm (AR)
Benjamin Erwin to Dicey Jeffreys or Jeffers, 20 Nov 1834 (same), John Pardee MMEC, Andrew Wason Bm (AR) [1850 Jackson Census: Benjamin Erwin 54, Dicy 50, Polly A. 20, Lear E. 16, Andrew 14, Rosy 12, Amandy F. 10, Thomas 9]
Betsey Erwin to John Garrison q.v.
Cairen Erwin to Robert A. Dyer q.v.
Elizabeth Erwin to Jacob Garrison q.v.
Esther Erwin to Andrew Wasson q.v.

Samuel A. Erwin to Nancy Cook, 5 Aug 1818, Samuel --?-- Bm (A)
Sarah Ervin to Thomas Paul q.v.

MARRIAGES (MEIGS)

William Eawin or Erwin to Matilda T. Paine, 20 July 1848 (23 July), J.M. Butler JP

- - - - - - - - - - - - -

ESSEX / ESEX

1840 RHEA CENSUS

Isaac Essex 201001 - 120001
James Essex 000010001 - 00001001
William Essex 00001 - 20001

1850 RHEA CENSUS

Isaac Essex 44 (NC), Sarah 44 (NC), Catharine 17 (NC), William 15 (NC), Tempa C. 13 (Ky), Charles A. 9, Alfred S. 7, Henry H. 4 p. 577-268
James Essex 80 (Md), Elizabeth 67 (NC), Priscilla 33 (NC), Michael 27 (NC)(Farmer) p. 577-267
John Essex 35 (NC)(Farmer), Lueasa 30, Simpson 8, Albert 7, Lewis P. 3, Lovina 3/12 p. 577-266
William Essex 34 (NC)(Convict), Mary 35 (NC), Elizabeth 12, Priscilla 11, John 9, James 8, William 4, George W. 2 p. 580-291

MARRIAGES (RHEA)

Betsy Mirah Essex to Joshua Collins q.v.
John Esex to Louisa D. Ferguson, 17 Oct 1841 (22 Oct), Samuel Frazier JP (R)
William Esex to Mary Long, 4 Nov 1838 (5 Nov), Spillsby Dyer JP (R)

- - - - - - - - - - - - -

ESTELL

MARRIAGES (RHEA)

Philemon K.W. Estell to Emaline Day, 8 Jan 1828 (10 Jan), Stephen Winton JP, Richard Timberlake Bm (AR)

- - - - - - - - - - - - -

ESUMERY

MARRIAGES (RHEA)

Polly Esumery to Edmond Holt q.v.

- - - - - - - - - - - - -

EUBANKS

MARRIAGES (RHEA)

Sarah Banks or Eubanks to John Atchley q.v.

- - - - - - - - - - - - -

EVANS / EVENS / EVINS

TAXES (RHEA)

1819 (Capt. John Lewis' Dist.): Evin Evins 1 WP, 238a
Jonathan Evins 1 WP
(Capt McCall's Co.): Samuel A. Evin 1 WP
1823 (Capt. Lewis' Co.): Evan Evans 1 WP, 227a
(Capt. Howrd's Co.): Lemuel Evans 1 WP

1830 RHEA CENSUS

Andrew Evens 010120001 - 2212101 p. 385 [Andrew: b. 1 July 1763, d. 9 Apr 1839]
Willis Evans 200001 - 11001 p. 387 [Willis Evans married Rebecca Shaddrick on 12 Nov 1824 in Roane Co.]

1840 RHEA CENSUS

Austin Evans 01101 - 11011
John Evans 10002 - 10001
Willis Evans 0110001 - 222001

1850 RHEA CENSUS

Austin Evans 35, Malinda 40, Luke EDDINGTON 20 (Farmer), Polly A. 19, Riley 17 (Farmer), Emily EVENS 10, Moses 8, Squire 6, James S. 4, Austin 7/12 p. 540-45
Eliza Evans 29: see Hannah M. Frazier
Hiram Evans 32: see James Wilson
John S. Evans [Evens] 35 (Saddler), Elizabeth 35 (Ga), Hugh A. 11, Mary 9, Lucy 8, Sarah 5, Ann 3, Quintine 1, Mary EVANS 50, Christina 24, Angeline WROE 20, William S. HOGAN 40 (NC), Reuben DAVIS 21 (Deaf and Dumb) p. 611-431
Joseph S. Evans [Evens] 30 (Merchant), Sarah J. 27, James G. 3, Clementine 3/12 p. 611-430

1850 MEIGS CENSUS

Dorcus Evans (f) 65 (Va), Sarah 28 p. 768-437

MARRIAGES (RHEA)

Austin Evans to Malinda Edington, 6 Feb 1840, Benjamin D. Smith Bm (AR)
Eliza Evins to James M. Nelson q.v.
John S. Evens to Elizabeth Hampton, 1 or 2 Jan 1838 (4 Jan), E. Still JP, Bird Paine Bm (AR)
Joseph Evans to Betsey Vaughn, 29 Mar 1828 (30 Mar), John Henninger MG, James Agee Bm (AR)
Margaret Evans to William Smith q.v.
Mary Evans to Thomas C. Wroe q.v.
Sally Evins to Joseph Eller q.v.
Sarah Evans to George W. Smith q.v.

MISCELLANEOUS (RHEA)

Andrew Evans: Revolutionary War Pensioner, 1835 list
E. P. Evins: Bondsman for Bailey Minix or Minnick, 1844
Evan Evans: Bondsman for William Rogers, 1814
" " Bondsman for James Cole, 1824
" " Bondsman for Silas F. Barnes, 1825
John S. Evens: JP 1844-1848
" " " County Court Clerk, 1844-1852
" " " County Trustee, 1844-1852
" " " Bondsman for Anderson Jones, 1843
" " " Bondsman for Harry Roddy, 1838
Joseph Evens: Bondsman for Thomas Stokes, 1827
Willis G. Evans: Bondsman for Joseph Ellis, 1841

- - - - - - - - - - - - -

EVERETT / EVERAT

1830 RHEA CENSUS

William Everett 000001 - 00001 p. 381

1840 RHEA CENSUS

William Everat 00001 - 00001

1850 RHEA CENSUS

William D. Everett 34 (SC)(Hog Hunting), Nelly E. 40, Nancy WISEMAN 25, James EVERETT 8, John JONES 9 p. 639-681

MARRIAGES (RHEA)

Matilda Everett to Jesse Hudson q.v.
Simon Everett to Susana Hudson, 10 Mar 1820, John B. Hudson & John Birdsong Bm (A)

- - - - - - - - - - - - -

EVIT

MARRIAGES (RHEA)
Elizabeth Evit to C.M.K. Welch q.v.

- - - - - - - - - - - - -

EWING

1830 RHEA CENSUS
William Ewing 010000001 - 000100001 p. 392

- - - - - - - - - - - - -

FAIRBANKS / FARBANK / FURBANKS

1830 RHEA CENSUS
Jno Fairbanks 20201 - 310010001 p. 375
1840 MEIGS CENSUS
William Fairbanks 00001 - 00001 p. 231
MARRIAGES (RHEA)
David Fairbanks to Nancy Heart, 28 July 1832 (29 July), James McCorkle JP, Edward S. Stokes Bm (AR)
MARRIAGES (MEIGS)
Eleanor Fairbanks to William Hall q.v.
Emeretta Fairbanks to James Madison Robeson q.v.
M. Furbanks to Peggy Hart, 16 July 1839 (18 July), B.F. McKenzie JP
William Farbank to Sarah Ramsey, 26 Jan 1839 (27 Jan), Daniel Cate JP
MISCELLANEOUS (RHEA)
William Fairbanks: Bondsman for William Fuller, 1835
" " Bondsman for Joshua Givins, 1835

- - - - - - - - - - - - -

FALLS

1840 MEIGS CENSUS
William Falls 11000001 - 111001 p. 231
1850 MEIGS CENSUS
Mary Falls 45, Lorinda or Lavinda 2 p. 732-153
MARRIAGES (RHEA)
Esther Falls to Brinkley Hornsby q.v.
William Falls to Mary Moore, 21 Dec 1824 (23 Dec), Wm Gamble JP, Elisha Moore Bm (AR)
MARRIAGES (MEIGS)
Polly Ann Falls to Grimes Bankston q.v.

- - - - - - - - - - - - -

FAN

MARRIAGES (MEIGS)
Sarah Fan to T. J. Martin q.v.

- - - - - - - - - - - - -

FARLESS / FARLES / FARLIS

MARRIAGES (RHEA)
James Farles Jr. to Rebecca Townsby 18 Dec 1827 (19 Dec), Robert Cooley JP, James Farles Sr. Bm (AR) [1850 Rutherford Census: James R. Farless 45, Rebecca 40, Joseph M. 19, Nancy 17, Thomas 14, Sarah 10, John B. 8, Becky 4, Mary E. 2, Elisha 6, James W. 13]
Nancy Farlis to James C. Greer q.v.
MARRIAGES (MEIGS)
Martin Farless to Mary Bench, 31 Nov 1843 [1850 Rutherford Census: Martin Farless 22, Mary A. 24, James M. 2, William C. 5/12]
MISCELLANEOUS (RHEA)
James Farles Sr.: Bondsman for James Farles Jr., 1827

- - - - - - - - - - - - -

FARLEY

MARRIAGES (RHEA)
Sanford Farley to Sally Ragan, 5 Feb 1816 (11 Mar), S. Catching JP, Henry Myers Bm (AR)

- - - - - - - - - - - - -

FARMER

TAXES (RHEA)
1823 (Capt. Wilson's Co.): John Farmer (no other data)
1830 RHEA CENSUS
Fredk Farmer 20001 - 00101 p. 364
John Farmer 00121001 - 00110001 p. 364
John Farmer 0120101 - 3000021 p. 364
William Farmer 1001 - 20011 p. 352
1840 MEIGS CENSUS
Ames Farmer 2110001 - 201101 p. 225
Moses Farmer 200001 - 00001 p. 245
William Farmer 02111 - 0102001 p. 224
1850 RHEA CENSUS
Elijah Farmer 34 (Farmer), Mary M. 25, Hetta A. 7, James W. 5, John F. 2, Sarah J. MITCHELL 26, Maranda THOMPSON Unk (mulatto) p. 548-104
1850 MEIGS CENSUS
Aquilla Farmer 25 (SC)(Farmer), Mary 26, James 1 p. 725-94
Thomas S. Farmer 24 (Farmer), Ellen Jane 24, John M. 6, Newton R. 5, Mary A. 3, Sarah Jane 1, James MAJORS 23 (Farmer) p. 781-536
MARRIAGES (RHEA)
Eady Farmer to Josiah Keeran q.v.
Elizabeth Farmer to Prior Neal q.v.
Jeremiah Farmer to Eliza Bailey, 27 Dec 1832 (1 Jan 1833), Daniel Briggs MG, Moses Farmer Bm (AR)
John Farmer to Jane Ramy, 16 Feb 1845 (same), Jesse P. Thompson JP (R)
John M. Farmer to Jane Gibson, 16 Mar 1836, Andrew J. Farmer Bm (A)
Moses Farmer to Mahala Roddy, 3 Feb 1834 (13 Feb), John Farmer MG, Jesse Roddy Bm (AR)
MARRIAGES (MEIGS)
Aquilla Farmer to Mary T. Ford, 24 May 1845 (25 May), John Seabourn JP
Andrew Farmer to Susan Hague, 19 Sept 1828 (20 Sept), James Moore JP
Sarah Farmer to Hosea H. Williams q.v.
Thomas S. Farmer to Eleanor J. McCallon, 24 Jan 1842 (27 Jan), James M. Hoge JP
MISCELLANEOUS (RHEA)
Andrew J. Farmer: Bondsman for John M. Farmer, 1836
John Farmer: MG 1821-1835
" " Pastor, Fellowship Baptist Church, 1829
" " Elder, Concord Bapt. Church of Christ, 1824
Moses Farmer: Bondsman for Jeremiah Farmer, 1832

MISCELLANEOUS (MEIGS)

Elijah Farmer: Cherokee Removal muster roll, 1836
F. Farmer: On Circuit Court jury, 1836
Henry Farmer: Cherokee Removal muster roll, 1836
John Farmer: Hiwassee District
John H. Farmer: First physician in Decatur
" " " Built house on Lot 47 and store building on Lot 37 in Decatur
John K. Farmer: Postmaster at Decatur, 1836
" " " Trustee for Decatur Academy, 1838-39
Moses Farmer: JP 1842
William F. Farmer: Cherokee Removal muster roll, 1836

\- - - - - - - - - - - - -

FARNER

1850 RHEA CENSUS

Abraham Farner 50 (Farmer), Jane A. 25, Mary 23, Mahala 21, George 7, Polly A. 2 p. 557-144

\- - - - - - - - - - - - -

FARRAR / FARROW

1840 MEIGS CENSUS

Edward Farrar 211001 - 321001 p. 239

1850 MEIGS CENSUS

Edward Farrar 47 (NC)(Millwright), Elizabeth 47 (NC), Eliza Jane 21, Sarah E. 17, Bethena M. 16, Jackson R. 15, Lorinda E. 12, John T. 10, Lozedena D. (f) 8, Edward M. 5, Leander G. 2 p. 787-585

MARRIAGES (MEIGS)

Polly Farrow to William Moore q.v.

\- - - - - - - - - - - - -

FARRENSWORTH

TAXES (RHEA)

1823 (Capt. Brown's Co.): Samuel Farrensworth 1 WP

\- - - - - - - - - - - - -

FARRIS / FARIS / FARES

1850 MEIGS CENSUS

Stephen Farris 35, Anna 30, John L. 14, William 12, Hugh F. 8, Lucinda 5, Isaac G.L. 2 p. 713-7

MARRIAGES (RHEA)

Cedney Farris to Robert Collison q.v.
John Farris to Polly Brady, 30 Mar 1818 (2 Apr), J. Fine JP (AR)
Lethy Farris to Samuel Mantooth q.v.
Stephen Faris to Anna Norman, 28 Jan 1835, John Faris Bm (A)

MARRIAGES (MEIGS)

Leander Faris to Martha Brown, 11 July 1850, J.F. Farris Sur

MISCELLANEOUS (RHEA and MEIGS)

J. F. Farris: Surety for Leander Faris, 1830
John Fares: Bondsman for Stephen Faris, 1835
Robert Farris: Purchased Lots 53 & 55 in Decatur, 1836
William Fares: Bondsman for Isaac Brady, 1835

\- - - - - - - - - - - - -

FERGUSON / FERGASON / FURGUSON

TAXES (RHE)

1819 (Capt. John Lewis' Co.): Eli Ferguson 1 WP
Elias Ferguson 1 WP, 89a
John Ferguson 150a
Robert Ferguson 80a
(Capt. W.S. Bradley's Dist.):
Alexander Ferguson 1 WP, 2 BP, 500½a
1823 (Capt. Lewis' Co.): Eli Ferguson 1 WP
James & Robert Ferguson 1 WP, 104a
John Ferguson 1 WP
John Ferguson 150a
Moses Ferguson 115a
Robert Ferguson heirs 110a
Samuel Ferguson 1 WP, 181a
Samuel B. Ferguson 1 WP

1830 RHEA CENSUS

Abegail Ferguson 01 - 011001 p. 366
Eli Ferguson 110001 - 11001 p. 365
Elias Ferguson 10001 - 20001 p. 366
James Ferguson 0000010001 - 000000001 p. 366
John Fergason 210001 - 01001 p. 364
John Ferguson 001000001 - 001012001 p. 65
John Ferguson 00001 - 01001 p. 366
Leroy Ferguson 10001 - 00001 p. 366
Levi Ferguson 00001 - 10001 p. 365
Moses Ferguson 0000000001 - 0000220001 p. 366
Robert Ferguson 011001 - 01001 p. 366
Samuel Ferguson 200001 - 02201 p. 366
Tolifer Fergason 00001 - 0001 p. 360
William Ferguson 110001 - 20001 p. 366

1840 RHEA CENSUS

Abigail Furgison 00001 - 00000001
Eli Fergeson 1011001 - 120011
James Furgeson age 81, pensioner
James C. Furgeson 200001 - 1200101001
John Furgison 0211001 - 201001
Levi W. Furgeson 210001 - 020001
Robert Furgeson 00011001 - 1001001
Samuel Furgeson 10000100001 - 10001

1850 RHEA CENSUS

Abigail Ferguson 80 (NC), Robert 33 (Farmer) p. 579-282
James C. Ferguson 40 (Farmer), Tujah J. (f) 16, Ann 14, Hugh L.W. 12, John T. 10, Bithiah 9, Darius G. 7, Addison L. 5, Ruth GOAD 65 (SC) p. 588-353
John Ferguson 50 (NC)(Farmer), Margaret 48, Lewis C. 26 (Constable), Reuben 17 (Farmer), Letha 14, Eliza 11, William H.H. 9, Franklin S. 3, Claton J. DUDLEY 22 (Farmer), Elvira 23 p. 577-270
John M. Ferguson 23 (Farmer), Stacy M. 15 (NC) p. 623-567
Levi W. Ferguson 49 (NC)(Farmer), Elizabeth 47 (NC), Wealthy W. (f) 20, Samuel H. 17 (Farmer), Sarah A. 15, Milon M. 3, John H. 9 p. 581-298
Robert Ferguson 60 (NC)(Farmer), Sarah 27, Elizabeth 15, James C.J. 3, Sidnah F. 10/12 p. 581-297
Samuel B. Ferguson 57 (NC)(Farmer), Sarah B. 30, Mary A. 12, Perry N. 10, Enoch D. 6, Cyntha R. 3, James A. 1 p. 561-299

MARRIAGES (RHEA)

Aaron Ferguson to Catherine Beck, 25 Sept 1821, Richard G. Waterhouse Bm (A)

Ann Ferguson to William Collins q.v.
Anna Ferguson to Benjamin Erwin q.v.
Eli Ferguson to Margaret Kennedy, 10 May 1818 (11 May), H. Collins JP, Wm Kennedy Bm (AR)
Elias Ferguson to Betsy Hubbert, 5 Jan 1829 (same), James Swan JP, Martin Ferguson Bm (AR)
Elizabeth Ferguson to James E. Beck q.v.
Elizabeth Ferguson to Levi W. Ferguson q.v.
Elizabeth Ferguson to William M.E. Caldwell q.v.
Elvira Furguson to C. Dudley q.v.
James Ferguson to Sarah Wasson, 25 Apr 1836 (26 Apr), Matthew Hubbert JP, Joseph H. Inman Bm (AR)
James C. Ferguson to Eliza J. Craig, 29 Aug 1832 (30 Aug), Matthew Hubbert JP, Levi W. Ferguson Bm (AR)
Jane Ferguson to Henry Miller q.v.
Jane Ferguson to Joseph Hicks q.v.
Jirzah Ferguson to Edward Givens q.v.
John Ferguson to Margaret Collins, 24 May or July 1823 (same), William Kennedy JP, Cornelius Majors Bm (AR)
John Ferguson to Myram Cooper, 24 Dec 1828 (25 Dec), D.M. Stockton JP, Levi W. Ferguson Bm (AR)
John C. Ferguson to Elizabeth P. English, 3 Mar 1831, William G. English Bm (A)
John M. Ferguson to Stacy M. Allison, 22 June 1850 (same), S.F. Foust JP (R)
Leroy Ferguson to Myra Morris, 18 Jan 1827 (19 Jan), John Condley JP, Levi W. Ferguson Bm (AR)
Levi Ferguson to Rachel E. Collins, 15 Oct 1847 (25 Jan 1848), Samuel Frazier JP (R)
Levi W. Ferguson to Elizabeth Ferguson, 14 Nov 1829, Eli Ferguson Bm (A)
Louisa D. Ferguson to John Essex q.v.
Margaret Furgusson to James Mitchell q.v.
Margaret E. Furguson to William M. Thompson q.v.
Margaret Ferguson to Preston Knight q.v.
Martin Ferguson to Mary N. Kennedy, 20 Oct 1828 (same), Matthew Hubbert JP, Chase Piper Bm (AR)
Mary Ferguson to Thomas Jackson q.v.
Miriam Ferguson to Jacob L. Wasson q.v.
Narcissa Ferguson to John Bailey q.v.
Samuel Ferguson to Sarah B. Wassum, 19 Mar 1836 (20 Mar), John Condley JP, Joseph Ferguson Bm (AR)
Wealthy Fergusson to W.A. Compton q.v.
William Furguson or Ferguson to Margaret Henry, 28 Jan 1822 (31 Jan), John Mitchell JP or MG, Rezin Rawlings Bm (AR)

MARRIAGES (MEIGS)

Rufus Furguson to E.J. Barmon, 19 Nov 1849 (20 Nov), William Johns JP

MISCELLANEOUS (RHEA)

Alexander Ferguson: Purchased Lot 23 in Washington
" " JP 1817
" " Registerar of Deeds, 1808-1821
" " Bondsman for John Sapp, 1814
" " Bm for Matthew Hubbert, 1817
" " Bondsman for James Bowers, 1819
Eli Ferguson: Bondsman for Levi W. Ferguson, 1829
" " Bondsman for Henry Miller, 1832
Elias Ferguson: On first Grand Jury, 1808
" " Bondsman for Aaron Maloney, 1831
" " Bondsman for Jesse Warren, 1838
James Ferguson: Revolutionary War Pensioner, 1835 and 1841 lists
James C. Ferguson: Bondsman for William T. Gass, 1844
John C. Ferguson: Bondsman for James J. Duncan, 1835
John G. Ferguson: Bondsman for James E. Beck, 1823
L. C. Ferguson: Private, Mexican War
Levi Ferguson: Private, Mexican War
" " Bondsman for Benjamin Erwin, 1824
Levi W. Ferguson: Bondsman for Leroy Ferguson, 1827
" " " Bondsman for John Ferguson, 1828
" " " Bondsman for Jas C. Ferguson, 1832
" " " Bondsman for Alecy R. Houpt, 1842
Martin Ferguson: Bondsman for Elias Ferguson, 1829
Rawlings P. Ferguson: Signed petition to move Indian Agency
Russell Ferguson: Bondsman for Joshua Goad, 1829
William Ferguson: Bondsman for Mathias Green, 1832

- - - - - - - - - - - - -

FERRELL / FERREL

1830 RHEA CENSUS

Jas or Jos Ferrell 00010001 - 0000001 p. 377
Jno Ferrell 220001- 11001 p. 377

1850 RHEA CENSUS

William J. Ferrel 36 (NC)(Farmer), Mary A. 35, Luisa 14, Sarah A. 10, Eleanor W. 9, Andrew J. 7, Rufus H. 3, William J. 5 p. 619-538

1850 MEIGS CENSUS

Elizabeth Ferrell 40 (NC), Mary C. 25, Louisa 18, Theopalis L. 17 p. 790-606

MARRIAGES (RHEA)

William Ferrell to Mary A. McCarty or McLearty, 8 July 1835 (9 July), D.L. Godsey JP, Cedron Piles Bm (AR)

- - - - - - - - - - - - -

FIELDS

1830 RHEA CENSUS

Green Fields 001 - 1001 p. 355
Jediah Fields 00002 - 000001 p. 354

MARRIAGES (RHEA)

James Fields to Jeniva Nimton, 1 May 1835, Henry Smith Bm (A)
Richard Fields to Polly Wells, 27 Jan 1836, Elijah Blythe Bm (A)
Nancy Fields to William Blythe q.v.

MISCELLANEOUS (RHEA and MEIGS)

J. Fields: Elder, Concord Baptist Church of Christ, 1824
James Fields: Cherokee Removal muster roll, 1836

- - - - - - - - - - - - -

FIKE / FYKE

1830 RHEA CENSUS

Josiah Fyke 10001001 - 111101 p. 357

1850 MEIGS CENSUS

James E. Fike 25 (Farmer), Elizabeth 28, Polly Ann 4, Isabella 1, Elizabeth 1 p. 776-505

MARRIAGES (RHEA)

Anney Fike to Reuben Phillips q.v.

MARRIAGES (MEIGS)
Dilla Fike to Eli F. Mouncy q.v.
Elizabeth Fyke to Jehu or Elihu Phillips q.v.
James E. Fike to Elizabeth Fooshee, 7 Oct 1845 (9 Oct), John Huff Esq.

- - - - - - - - - - - - -

FINDLEY

MISCELLANEOUS (RHEA)
Samuel Findley: Bondsman for William Fox, 1825

- - - - - - - - - - - - -

FINE

TAXES (RHEA)
1808 (Jonathan Fine's List): Jonathan Fine 150a Piney Ri
1819 (Capt. J. Ramsey's Co.): Jonathan Fine 1 WP, 170a
1823 (Capt. Smith's Co.): Isaac Fine 1 WP
(Capt. McCall's Co.):
Jonathan Fine 1 WP, 167a, 1 stud horse (tax .75)
(Capt. Wilson's Co.): Peter Fine 1 WP
1830 RHEA CENSUS
Peter Fine 0001001 - 000001 p. 352
1840 MEIGS CENSUS
Peter Fine 0101001 - 00000001 p. 244
1850 MEIGS CENSUS
Susan Fine 56 (Va), James C. CARRELL 19 (bound) (Farmer) p. 778-516
MARRIAGES (RHEA)
Baldwin H. Fine to Eliza Fulkerson, 11 Jan 1827 (same), Jesse Thompson JP, Jesse Atwood Bm (AR)
Elizabeth Fine to Thomas Jones q.v.
MISCELLANEOUS (RHEA)
Baldwin Fine: Bondsman for William Lemons, 1826
John Fine: JP 1829, 1832
Jonathan Fine: Purchased Lot 49, Washington
" " Registerar of Deeds, 1827-1829
" " Trustee, 1809
M. John Fine: JP 1813-1820
Peter Fine: Bondsman for Benjamin Armstrong, 1828
" " Bondsman for Jeremiah Wiggenton, 1830
MISCELLANEOUS (MEIGS)
Jonathan Fine: Common School Com., District 2, 1838
Peter Fine: Hiwassee District, Sewee Creek area
" " Circuit Court Jury, 1836
" " Cherokee Removal muster roll, 1836

- - - - - - - - - - - - -

FISHER

1840 RHEA CENSUS
Hance H. Fisher 00001 - 00001
Noah Fisher 21222001 - 0101101
1850 RHEA CENSUS
Charles N. Fisher 22 (Farmer), Catharine 24 p. 594-371
Henderson Fisher 23 (NC)(Farmer), Rebecca A. 23, Henry T. 1 p. 586-336
Henry Fisher 32 (NC)(Farmer), Sarah 30, Asbury 6, Emsley 4, Elizabeth 2, Ann E. 1/12 p. 615-506
Noah Fisher 70 (Md)(Farmer), Darcus P. 58 (Md), William 24 (Wagonmaker), George W. 20 (Farmer), William B. 15, Noah 13, Rebecca A. DYAL 12 p. 594-370
MARRIAGES (RHEA)
Henderson Fisher to Rebecca A. Godbyhere, 13 Oct 1847 (14 Oct), Samuel Frazier JP (R)
Henry Fisher to Sarah Pusey, 12 Mar 1843, Miller Francis Bm (A)
Owen Fisher to Martha J. Starbuck, 13 Aug 1846 (14 Aug), Samuel Frazier JP (R) [1850 Bradley Census: Owen Fisher 39, Martha 39]

- - - - - - - - - - - - -

FISK

1830 RHEA CENSUS
William H. Fisk 0111001 - 0020101 p. 357

- - - - - - - - - - - - -

FITCH

1850 MEIGS CENSUS
Isaac Fitch 23 (Farmer), Rebecca Ann 18 ("married within year") p. 794-635
Isaac E. Fitch 45 (Farmer), Betsy Ann 27, Polly Ann 16, John 14, Milly 12, George 10, Rhoda 7, Sterling T. 3, Samuel D. 1 p. 794-634 [Isaac married Betsy Ann Talley on 20 Dec 1845 in Roane County]
John Fitch 25 (Va), Edy W. 23, James J. 4, Jacob T. 1 p. 793-632
John Fitch 45 (Farmer), Mary 55, Mary A.E. 20, Wiley 17, Samuel 15, Joseph 13, Thomas 11, George W. 9 p. 793-629
William Fitch 23 (Farmer), Elizabeth 23, John A. 2 p. 802-690
MARRIAGES (MEIGS)
Edy W. Fitch to John Fitch q.v.
James Fitch to Edy Tally, 13 Jan 1846, license obtained by Isaac Fitch
John Fitch to Edy W. Fitch, 9 Mar 1847 (same), Thomas Witten MG
Mary Ann Fitch to Andrew Eakin q.v.
William Fitch to Elizabeth J. Phillips, 4 Aug 1847 (same), Robert Stockton JP
MISCELLANEOUS (MEIGS)
Isaac Fitch: JP(?) 1846
John Fitch: Surety for Andrew Eakin, 1850

- - - - - - - - - - - - -

FITZER

MISCELLANEOUS (MEIGS)
James Fitzer: Hiwassee District, Moore's Chapel area

- - - - - - - - - - - - -

FITZGERALD / FITZGERRAL / FITZGERRALD / FITZJARALD / F. GERALD / F. GERRALD / F. JURIALD

1830 RHEA CENSUS
A. F. Gerald 1112001 - 011001 p. 369
Anderson F. Gerald 220001 - 001101 p. 368

Jno F. Gerald 300000001 - 01111 p. 371
Samuel F. Gerald 10010011 - 1111001 p. 371
1840 MEIGS CENSUS
Christopher B. Fitzjerald 00002 - 1001 p. 236
Samuel F. Juriald 001000001 - 01000001 p. 228
MARRIAGES (RHEA)
Abraham or Arabian F. Gerrold or Gerald to Sally H. Looney, 28 Dec 1832 (same), Robert Cooley JP, Robert Murphy Bm (AR)
Anna F. Gerald to Tipton G. Wood q.v.
Jesse Fitzgerrald to Duannah Mation, 29 Oct 1833, Martin Fitzgerald Bm (A)
John Fitzgerral to Sarah Brogdon, 14 Feb 1826 (16 Feb), Thomas Cox JP, Washington Weems Bm (A)
Peggy Gerald to Tavenor Masoner q.v.
MARRIAGES (MEIGS)
Amelia F. Gerrald to Francis D. Okelly q.v.
MISCELLANEOUS (RHEA)
Archibald Gerrald: MG 1828, 1832
Jesse Fitzgerald: Bondsman for David W. Knight, 1832
Martin Fitzgerald: Bondsman for Jesse Fitzgerald, 1833
Samuel F. Gerrald: MG 1828
Samuel Fitzgerald: First Pastor, Goodfield Baptist Church of Christ, 1827
MISCELLANEOUS (MEIGS)
Anderson Fitzgerald: Hiwassee Dist, Burkett Chapel area
Andrew Fitzgerald: Hiwassee District, Burkett Chapel area
Archibald Fitzgerald Jr.: House used for elections, Dist 2
John Fitzgerald: Hiwassee District
Milton D. Fitzgerald: Cherokee Removal muster roll, 1836
Nacy Fitzgerald: Cherokee Removal muster roll, 1836
Samuel Fitzgerald: Purchased land in Cottonport
William Fitzgerald: Hiwassee District, Cottonport area

\- - - - - - - - - - - -

FLEMMING / FLEMING

1830 RHEA CENSUS
D.H. Fleming 00001 - 11001 p. 381
1840 RHEA CENSUS
David H. Fleming 720001 - 110101
1850 RHEA CENSUS
Margaret J. Fleming 20, Wm B.L. 17, Samuel H. 15, Mary E. 13, James K.P. 11: see Daniel Hodges
1850 MEIGS CENSUS
Mary Fleming 59 (NC), James C. 24 (Farmer), Gilbert 14 p. 817-798
MARRIAGES (RHEA)
David H. Flemming to Nancy Lauderdale, 29 Oct 1828, William B. Lauderdale Bm (R)
Nancy Fleming to Daniel Hodges q.v.

\- - - - - - - - - - - -

FLETCHER / FLECHER

1840 RHEA CENSUS
James Flecher 101001 - 010001
1850 RHEA CENSUS
Alexander Fletcher 23 (Va)(Farmer), Jane 17, John F. 1/12 p. 548-100
James Fletcher Unk (Va)(Farmer), Mary Unk (Va), Minerva A. 20 (Va), Barton M. 14, Benjamin F. 10, Newton 6 p. 548-98
MARRIAGES (RHEA)
Alexander Fletcher to Jane Cox, 7 Aug 1849 (9 Aug), Daniel Broyles JP (R)

\- - - - - - - - - - - -

FLOYD / FLOID / FLOYAD

TAXES (RHEA)
1819 (Capt. Wm McCray's Co.): David Floyd 1 WP; William Floyd 150a
1850 RHEA CENSUS
James J. Floyd 23 (Farmer), Luisa J. 18, Sarah E. 10/12, Sarah J. RHEA 14 p. 558-151
William Floyd 27 (Tanner), Elizabeth 27, Anderson 20 (Apprentice Tanner), John H. 5/12 p. 540-49
1850 MEIGS CENSUS
Sarah Floyd 40 (NC), George 17 (Farmer), Peggy 15, Cazy (f) 14, Sally R. 13, Alfred R. 11 p. 808-730
MARRIAGES (RHEA)
Nimrod Floid to Mahala Keller, 8 June 1837 (9 June), A.D. Paul JP, Hiram Floid Bm (AR)
MARRIAGES (MEIGS)
Elizabeth Floyad to Squire Forde q.v.
James J. Floyd to Levisa J. Richards, 16 Sept 1848 (17 Sept), J.L. Aikman JP
MISCELLANEOUS (RHEA)
Hiram Floid: Bondsman for Nimrod Floid, 1837

\- - - - - - - - - - - -

FONDREN

1850 RHEA CENSUS
Anoneseeus Fondren 30 (NC) (Shoemaker), Sarah 30, George W. 6, Isaac 3, Nancy A. 1 p. 616-510

\- - - - - - - - - - - -

FONTENBERRY

1840 RHEA CENSUS
Henry Fontenberry 20001 - 10001

\- - - - - - - - - - - -

FOOSHEE / FOSHEE / FOASHEE

TAXES (RHEA)
1823 (Capt. McCall's Co.): John A. Foashee 1 WP [John A. Foshee married Malinda Cooper on 28 Oct 1819 in Roane County]
1830 RHEA CENSUS
John Foshee 000200001 - 10001001 p. 363
Sampson Foshee 012011 - 22001 p. 363
1840 MEIGS CENSUS
Absolum Foshee 0101201 - 0022001 p. 246
John Fooshee 0000000001 - 000000001 p. 246
1850 MEIGS CENSUS
Absolem Foshee 53 (SC)(Farmer), Mary 57 (NC), Jonas 31 (Farmer), Michael 28 (Farmer), Nancy 24, Evley 22, George 19 (Farmer), John MAPLES 18 (pauper) p. 812-760 [Absolem Fooshee married Polly Arnold on 28 Sept 1816 in Roane County]

John R. Foshee 33 (Farmer), Susan 26, Jonas 8, Betsy Ann 6, James P. 4, Joseph M. 2 p. 797-657 [John Fooshee married Susan Hinds on 26 Sept 1840 in Roane County; John, son of Absolem and Polly]

MARRIAGES (RHEA)

Catherine C. Foashee to Benjamin Hutson q.v.

MARRIAGES (MEIGS)

Elizabeth Foshee to James E. Fike q.v.
Mary Fooshee to James Briggs q.v.

MISCELLANEOUS (MEIGS)

Absalom Fooshee: Com. to erect Decatur Courthouse, 1836
" " Appointed to sell town lots, 1836
" " JP 1841, 1843
" " Chairman of County Court, 1842 & 1846
Michael Foushee: Mexican War (discharged on Surgeon's certificate)

FOOTE / FOUT / FOUTE

1840 RHEA CENSUS

John Foute 00011001 - 010111

1850 RHEA CENSUS

John Foote 66 (Va)(Farmer), Dolly 56 (Va), Nancy BEAN 17 (Va) p. 629-608

MARRIAGES (RHEA)

Jacob Foute (Allen's spelling) [see Joab Foust]
John Fout or Lante to Nancy Trantham, 5 Dec 1840 (6 Dec), Wm H. Bell MG, Jacob Fout Bm (AR) [NOTE: the Rhea records are clearly Fout, but Allen shows the last name as Lante]

FORBES

TAXES (RHEA)

1819 (Capt. W.S. Bradley's Dist.): Alexander Forbes 1 WP

MISCELLANEOUS (RHEA)

Alexander Forbes: Bondsman for Thomas Stafford, 1810
William Forbes: Bondsman for James Reese, 1824

FORD / FORDS / FORDE / FOARD

TAXES (RHEA)

1819 (Capt. John Ramsey's Co.): Edward Ford 1 WP

1830 RHEA CENSUS

Edmund Ford 201001 - 10001 p. 363
Edmund Ford 0000000001 - 220010001 p. 363
Stephen Ford 20001 - 20001 p. 363

1840 MEIGS CENSUS

Edmond Ford 0011001 - 0011000101 p. 247
Horatio Ford 011001 - 110001 p. 235
Mary Ford 01 - 011201 p. 247
Mary Ford 0001 - 00111101 p. 234
Stephen Ford 010001 - 222001 p. 246
Wesly Ford 012001 - 10001 p. 246
William L. Ford 12020001 - 2120001 p. 247

1850 RHEA CENSUS

John Ford 51 (Day Laborer), Ann 54 (Va) p. 566-191
John F. Ford 25 (Merchant) p. 540-48
William Fords 25 (Blacksmith), Elizabeth 24 p. 549-106

1850 MEIGS CENSUS

Edmond Ford 53 (SC)(Farmer), Phoebe 56 (NC), Jane 29 (NC), Stephen 21 (Farmer), James 18 (Farmer), Newton 9 p. 804-701 [Edmond Ford married Pheby Butler on 11 Feb 1826 in Roane County]
Horatio Ford 40 (Farmer), Elizabeth 40, Mordaci 21 (Farmer), James M. 19 (Farmer), Elender 15, Ruthe 12, Catharine Jane 8, Sarah E. 3 p. 751-321
John Ford 19 (Farmer), Elender 21, Elisha 19 (Farmer) p. 789-600
Mary Ford 40 (Ediot): see Thomas Kaywood
Polly Ford 50 (SC), Frances 26, Emaline 23, Mary Jane 6, Mernirva B. 1 p. 804-703
Sarah Ford 39 (Va), Edward 16 (Farmer) p. 789-595
Squire Ford 21 (Farmer), Elizabeth 20, Sarah F. 16, Sarah E. 1 p. 789-599
Stephen Ford 21 (Farmer), Winny 21, Sarah E. 1 p. 810-743 [Stephen married Wineford Elizabeth Greene on 22 Oct 1848 in Roane County]
William D. Ford 58 (NC)(Farmer), Eda 53 (NC), Rhoda 25 (NC), James 20 (Farmer), Malinda 18, Charlotte 13, Samuel 11 p. 804-702

MARRIAGES (RHEA)

Joseph Foard to Martha Mars, 18 Sept 1829, Henry Reese Bm (A)
Joseph Ford to Sarah Mathis, 28 May 1837 (same), James Montgomery JP, Warren West Bm (AR)
Polly Foard to Hanse Nelson q.v.
William Ford to Elizabeth Bingham, 24 Sept 1849 (4 Oct) (R)

MARRIAGES (MEIGS)

Eliza Ford to Thomas Renfrow q.v.
Elizabeth Ford to Nathan Pelfrey q.v.
Frederick T.C. Ford to Elizabeth Pearce, 16 Oct 1841
John Ford to Elenor Elison, 24 Oct 1849 (25 Oct), William L. Adams JP
Mahaley Fords to James Massey q.v.
Mary Ford to Josie Rowden q.v.
Mary T. Ford to Aquilla Farmer q.v.
Ruth Ford to Thomas Cawood q.v.
Sarah Ford to James M. Steen q.v.
Squire Ford to Elizabeth Floyad, 30 Sept 1848 (1 Oct), John Ford JP
William B. Ford to Agnes Butler, 10 Mar 1841 (same), Mark Rentfrow JP

MISCELLANEOUS (MEIGS)

Edmond Ford: Common School Com., District 8, 1838
Ezekiel Ford: Fifer, Cherokee Removal muster roll, 1836
John Ford: JP 1848-1849
Mordacai Ford: Private, Mexican War

FORESTER / FORRESTER

1850 MEIGS CENSUS

Miles Forester 38 (NC)(Farmer), Manda 40, Malvina 17, James 15, Lydia Ann 12, Ephraim H. 8, Caroline 6, Margaret 4, Mathew 1 p. 772-474

MARRIAGES (RHEA)

Hannah Forrester to James Lawson q.v.

FORREST

MISCELLANEOUS (MEIGS)
W. F. Forrest: MG 1844

- - - - - - - - - - - - -

FORTNER

1840 MEIGS CENSUS
William Fortner 000001 - 2001 p. 242

- - - - - - - - - - - - -

FOSTER

1830 RHEA CENSUS
Rachel Foster 111 - 0011001 p. 354
1850 RHEA CENSUS
Margaret Foster 29, Mary S. 12, Jarusa V. 9, Joseph G.S. 8, Rebecca E. 4, Leah T. 1, Sarah IVY 37 p. 637-672
MARRIAGES (RHEA)
William Foster or Fowler to Betsy Hillums or Hellum, 31 Jan 1821 (2 Feb), John Mitchell MG (AR)
MISCELLANEOUS (RHEA and MEIGS)
J. Foster: Elder, Concord Baptist Church of Christ, 1824
William Foster: JP(?) 1838

- - - - - - - - - - - - -

FOUST

1840 RHEA CENSUS
David Foust 0100001 - 20101
Jacob Foust 1101101 - 1111001
John W. Foust 00001 - 10001
Philip Foust 0100101 - 001001
William Foust 110001 - 211001
1850 RHEA CENSUS
Catharine Foust 14: see Robert W. Byce
David Foust 51 (Blacksmith), Nancy 38, John A. 18 (Farmer), Elizabeth A. 17, William J. 16 (Farmer), Juli A. 10, Phillip T. 8, Hester E. 6, James C. 3, Andrew J. 1 p. 559-158
Elizabeth Foust 12: see Robert P. Able
Jack Foust 45 (Blacksmith), Ann 43, Wm M. 21 (Farmer), Mary 19, John 17, Thomas J. 10, Napolean B. 10, Margaret A. 8, Elizabeth C. 6, Samuel O. 3, Rebecca J. 1, Flemming HILL 23 (Blacksmith) p. 634-649
Jacob Foust 54 (Wheelwright), Susannah 57, James 17 (Farmer), Susan S. 14, Edmund G. 11, Bryant McDONALD 18 (Va)(Farmer) p. 621-549
[Jacob married Susannah L. Edgeman in 1811]
John W. Foust 32 (Carpenter), Mary 32, Martha J. 11, George W. 7, Sarah A. 5 p. 633-636
Phillip Foust 77 (NC)(Blacksmith), Hannah S. 14: see Andrew J. McCuiston
Phillip Foust 50 (Farmer), Catharine 44, Albert N. ACRE 7, Rachael 6, John CARTER 18 (Farmer) p. 634-645
Phillip T. Foust 33 (Farmer), Nancy A. 25, Sarah E. 7, John M. 5, Mary C. 3, William M. 1/12, William T. 11, James LAUDERDALE 17 (Farmer), John LAUDERDALE 16 (Farmer) p. 629-605
[Phillip T. Foust married Nancy A. McPherson on 16 Dec 1841 in Roane County]
Samuel E. Foust 30 (Farmer), Luisa 26, Houston 5, Jane 4, Margaret C. 1 p. 633-640
William T. Foust 37 (Farmer), Lutitia 30, Sarah J. 8, Rebecca 6, Mary 4, Rufus M. 3, Andrew 1, John 18 (Farmer), Phillip 17 (Farmer) p. 567-203
MARRIAGES (RHEA)
David Foust to Nancy Jourden, 31 Dec 1838 (R)
Elizabeth Foust to James J. Kelly q.v.
Ester E. Foust to C.W. Abel q.v.
Evaline Foust to R.W. Bise q.v.
Joab Foust to Mary Ann Goard, 9 May 1840 (12 May), Wm H. Bell MGCPC (AR)
John W. Foust to Mary Bryson, 11 Apr 1839 (12 Apr), Berry D. Jones JP, Andrew J. Bryson Bm (AR)
Mary Foust to Washington Morgan q.v.
Samuel E. Foust to Syntha L. Greenwood, 19 Aug 1845 (same), E.P. Childress MG (R)
Sarah Foust to Calvin Morgan q.v.
Sarah A. Foust to William H. Hughs q.v.
William P. Foust to Leatitia Lowe, 23 Jan 1841 (no return) (R)
MISCELLANEOUS (RHEA)
John Foust: Bondsman for James J. Kelly, 1838
S. E. Foust: JP 1849-50

- - - - - - - - - - - - -

FOWLER

TAXES (RHEA)
1819 (Capt. McGill's Co.): John Fowler 1 WP, 1 BP
1823 (Capt. Smith's Co.): John Fowler 1 WP
1830 RHEA CENSUS
Wm Fowler 000001 - 22102 p. 366
1840 RHEA CENSUS
John Fowler 3311101 - 010100100001
John H. Fowler 00001 - 10001
1850 MEIGS CENSUS
J.H.W. Fowler 33 (NC)(Farmer), Mary 33 (NC), Jasper 8, Elijah W. 7, John M. 5, Julian T. 4, Francis 4, Samuel 3, Simeon S. 1 p. 724-88
[John H.W. Fowler married Mary Ann Cofer on 9 July 1840 in Roane County]
MARRIAGES (RHEA)
William Foster or Fowler to Betsy Hillums or Hellum, 31 Jan 1821 (2 Feb), John Mitchell MG (AR)
Jane Fowler to John Baker q.v.

- - - - - - - - - - - - -

FOX

1850 MEIGS CENSUS
Andrew Fox 37 (Farmer), Elizabeth 47, Margaret Ann 19, Minerva 15, Robert 13, Joseph 11, Julia A. 9, Thomas J. 5 p. 729-127
David Fox 22 (Farmer), Elizabeth 20, John 20, Mary Jane 60 p. 738-199
James Fox 25 (Farmer), Elizabeth 21, Sarah Jane 5, Lennard 1 p. 729-129
MARRIAGES (RHEA)
David Fox to Jane E. Clingan, 13 Mar 1850 (15 Mar), S.E. Gould JP (R)
William Fox to Mary M. Collier, 6 June 1825 (7 June), Thos Hall JP or MG, Samuel Findley Bm (AR)

MARRIAGES (MEIGS)
Andrew Fox to Narcissa Genett, 4 Feb 1846 (14 Feb), William Johns JP
James Fox to Elizabeth Ramsey, 19 Feb 1846 (same), William Johns JP
MISCELLANEOUS (MEIGS)
David Fox: JP(?) 1845
James Fox: JP(?) 1846

- - - - - - - - - - - - -

FRABY

1830 RHEA CENSUS
Nicholas Fraby 0010001 - 01011010001 p. 355

- - - - - - - - - - - - -

FRANCIS

TAXES (RHEA)
1808 (John Henry's List):
Joseph Francis 380a E Fork Richland Creek
Miller Francis 1 WP
1819 (Capt. John Robinson's Co.):
Miller Francis* 1 WP, 180a
[* written as Frances Miller on tax list]
(Capt. John Lewis' Dist.):
Woodson Francis 1 WP, 300a
1823 (Capt. Brown's Co.): Miller Francis 1 WP, 1 BP
(Capt. Lewis' Co.): Woodson Francis 2 BP, 300a
MARRIAGES (RHEA)
Barbara Francis to William Shilton q.v.
Eliza Francis to William Rice q.v.
James C. Francis to Amey Ingram, 20 Oct 1832 (same), John Henninger MMEC, Allen Kennedy Bm (AR)
Judy Francis to Ezekiel Henry q.v.
Lucinda Francis to Jeremiah Washam q.v.
Terese Francis to Hopkins L. or Jopkinsh Turney q.v.
MISCELLANEOUS (RHEA)
Miller Francis: married Hannah Henry on 26 Apr 1807 in Roane County, Ezekiel Henry, Surety
" " Sheriff 1808-1817
" " Purchased Lot 42, Town of Washington
" " Bondsman for Joseph Williams (builder of jail), 1826
" " Bondsman for Ezekiel Henry, 1810
" " Bondsman for James Henry, 1815
" " Bondsman for Bearfoot Armstrong, 1820
" " Bondsman for John Chapman, 1823
Woodson Francis: married Betsy Henry on 19 Apr 1804 in Roane County
" " Sheriff 1817-1827
" " Purchased Lot 1, Town of Washington
" " Bondsman for Joseph Watson, 1810
" " Bondsman for John Henry, 1816
" " Bondsman for James Gasque, 1826
" " Hiwassee District, Concord area

- - - - - - - - - - - - -

FRANCISCO

1840 MEIGS CENSUS
George Francisco 0211001001 - 210101 p. 225
[1 is John Francisco, 1765-1849]

1850 MEIGS CENSUS
George Francisco 51 (Farmer), Frances 49 (Va), William T. 24 (Farmer), George C. 17 (Farmer), James M. 16 (Farmer), Nancy A. 16, Martha L. 12, Lewis 10, Wiley B. 7 p. 720-52
John A. Francisco 29 (Farmer), Naomia 29 p. 720-53
MARRIAGES (MEIGS)
E.M. Francisco to Seth Atchley q.v.
Mary J. Francisco to Noah Aloon q.v.
Sarah A. Francisco to James H. Moon or Moore q.v.
MISCELLANEOUS (MEIGS)
George Francisco: Ocoee District
John Francisco: War of 1812 (Lt. in Capt. Ezekiel's Company from Kentucky)

- - - - - - - - - - - - -

FRANKLIN

1850 MEIGS CENSUS
Charles D. Franklin 29 (NC)(Farmer), Lucinda 28 (Va), David 11, Jonathan 8, Mary M. 6, Nancy L. 4, Beaty 1 p. 791-615
Jonathan Franklin 26 (NC)(Farmer), Sarah 21, Mary C. 4, Martha Jane 2, Cyntha 0 p. 764-404
[Jonathan F. Franklin married Sarah Collier on 6 July 1845 in McMinn County]
MARRIAGES (MEIGS)
Charles Franklin to L. Buster, 17 Aug 1839 (18 Aug), Prior Neil JP

- - - - - - - - - - - - -

FRANKS

MARRIAGES (MEIGS)
James Franks to Sariah Green, 7 Sept 1849 (20 Sept), Wm L. Adams JP

- - - - - - - - - - - - -

FRAYER

MISCELLANEOUS (MEIGS)
J. P. Fryer: MG 1844

- - - - - - - - - - - - -

FRAZIER
(see also FRABY)

TAXES (RHEA)
1819 (Capt. W.S. Bradley's Dist.):
Beriah Frazier 1 WP, 2 BP, 1 TL, 500a
(Capt. McCray's Co.): Caleb Frazier 1 WP
(Capt. John Lewis' Co.): Samuel Frazier 1 WP
1823 (Capt. Brown's Co.):
Beriah Frazier 1 WP, 500a Tenn River (part of 2000a NC Grant)
Samuel Frazier 1 WP, 60a S side Tenn Ri (in Hiwassee District)
1830 RHEA CENSUS
Beriah Frazier 010110001 - 1121101 p. 378
Samuel Frazier 100001 - 1 p. 365

1840 RHEA CENSUS
Beriah Frazier 010100001 - 00111101
Samuel Frazier 1200001 - 100001
Samuel Frazier 100001 - 001101
Samuel Frazier 1200001 - 100001
1850 RHEA CENSUS
Abner W. Frazier 29 (Farmer) p. 617-520 [son of Beriah]
Beriah Frazier 73 (NC)(Farmer), Barbary 61 (NC), Sarah J. LOVE 33 (NC), Mariah L. 26 (NC), Beriah 17 (Clerk), James A. SYKES 11 p. 617-519
[Beriah Frazier married Barbara Gibbs in Knox County on 1 May 1806]
Hannah M. Frazier 31, Minerva M. 5, Emily P. 1, Eliz EVANS 29 p. 618-526
[Nicholas G. Frazier married Hannah Minerva McKamy on 4 May 1841 in Roane County]
Ruth Frazier 39, Mary E. 20, Samuel 10 p. 608-490
[Ruth Clawson Frazier, widow of Samuel Frazier]
Samuel Frazier 51 (Farmer), Pacify T. 40, George W. 17 (Carrying Mail), Joseph G. 15, William R. 13, Almira A. 11, Amanda E. 9, Caroline M. 8, Nicholas T. 5, Samuel 2 p. 586-333
[Samuel, son of Beriah and Annie Reece Frazier, married Pacify T. Gibbs]
Wilson Frazier 7: see John Gunter
MARRIAGES (RHEA)
Ann Frazier to Valentine Allen q.v.
Barbara F. Frazier to John L. Ramsey q.v.
Emily Frazier to Hercelin Whaley q.v.
Jane Frazier to Lewis Roark q.v.
Mary Frazier to William Moore q.v.
Montford Frazier to Sally Simpson, 12 Jan 1825 (13 Jan), John Cozby JP, Leonard Brightwell Bm (AR)
Pauline Frazier to Richard R. Gist q.v.
Rebecca Frazier to Thomas A. Moore q.v.
Sally Frazier to Jesse Elliot q.v.
Samuel Frazier to Lucinda Ryon, 16 Nov 1825 (17 Nov), J. Henneger MG (R)
Sarah J. Frazier to Jacob H. Love q.v.
MISCELLANEOUS (RHEA)
Abner W. Frazier: 3rd Sgt., Mexican War, 1846-47
Beriah Frazier: Hiwassee District
Nicholas G. Frazier: Early member of Rhea County bar
" " " Organized company for service in Florida Indian War, 1835
" " " County Court Clerk, 1836-1840
" " " Bondsman for Eli Sykes, 1831
Sam Frazier: Trustee, Sulphur Springs Meth. Church, 1841
Samuel Frazier: Early member Rhea County bar
" " JP 1838-1848
" " Bondsman for Andrew Wassum, 1819
" " Bondsman for Abner Witt, 1824
Thomas Frazier: MG 1841

\- - - - - - - - - - - -

FREEMAN / FREEMON

TAXES (RHEA)
1819 (Capt. John Lewis' Dist.): Reuben Freemon 1 WP
1823 (Capt. Brown's Co.): Reuben Freeman 1 WP
1830 RHEA CENSUS
Reuben Freeman 1020001 - 0100001 p. 384
1850 RHEA CENSUS
John Freeman 5: see John W. Chambers
MARRIAGES (RHEA)
Frankey Freeman to John W. Chambers q.v.
Reubin Freemon to Polly Birdsong, 10 Dec 1815 (11 Dec), David Murphree JP, Thomas Johnson Bm (AR)
MISCELLANEOUS (RHEA)
Green Freeman: Private, Mexican War
Reuben Freeman: Purchased Lot 82, Town of Washington
" " Signed petition to move Indian Agency
" " Furnished materials for new jail, 1826
" " Bondsman for William Henry, 1818

\- - - - - - - - - - - -

FRENCH

TAXES (RHEA)
1819 (Capt. McGill's Co.): Wm French 1 WP, 1 BP, 580a
1823 (Capt. Howard's Co.): William French heirs 400a
1830 RHEA CENSUS
Eliza French 00111 - 10100001 p. 382
1840 RHEA CENSUS
Joseph H. French 211001 - 01000101
1850 RHEA CENSUS
Joseph H. French 42 (Farmer), Elizabeth 16, Byron 14, Timothy 12, John 10, Harrison 8, Elizbeth 73 (Va) p. 621-552
MARRIAGES (RHEA)
Joseph H. French to Nancy Benson, 18 May 1831, James B. Lauderdale Bm (A)
MISCELLANEOUS (RHEA)
J.H. [Joseph H.] French: Bm for Lemuel Shugart, 1840
Timothy F. French: Bondsman for George Samples, 1831
" " " Bondsman for Peter L. Pharis, 1835

\- - - - - - - - - - - -

FRISBY / FREISBY

1850 RHEA CENSUS
Delany Freisby Unk (Unk), Elizabeth Unk (Unk), William F. 4/12 p. 619-536
Joseph T. Frisby 30 (Shoemaker), Caroline 26, Eliza J. 12, Adeline 9, Nancy 6, Newton 2 p. 611-427

\- - - - - - - - - - - -

FRITWELL

1830 RHEA CENSUS
William Fritwell 000001 - 00001 p. 383

\- - - - - - - - - - - -

FROST

1850 MEIGS CENSUS
Nicholas Frost 23 (Farmer), Mary Ann 23 p. 723-83
MARRIAGES (MEIGS)
Lucinda Frost to Andrew J. Seabourn q.v.

\- - - - - - - - - - - -

FRY / FRIE / FREE

TAXES (RHEA)
1823 (Capt. Jackson's Co.): Samuel Fry 1 WP
1830 RHEA CENSUS
Jno Fry 1210001 - 1221 p. 367
Jonathan Fry 11001 - 2001 p. 367
P. Fry 3200000001 - 200001 p. 367
Samuel Fry 0100001 - 221111 p. 367
1840 MEIGS CENSUS
Jonathan Frie 111001 - 111101 p. 231
L. R. Frie 10001 - 100011001 p. 231
MARRIAGES (RHEA)
Jonathan Fry to Betsy Green, 31 Jan 1825 (3 Feb), Thomas Hall MG, David Singleton Bm (AR)
[1850 Hardin Census: Jonathan Frie 46, Elizabeth G. 45, William G. 17, Cosly K. 14, Jonathan W. 12, Martha L. 11, Isabella F. 7, Caledonia A. 4]
Lorenzy R. Frie to Cisley Lea, 13 Oct 1835 (15 Oct), Eli Sutherland MG, Samuel Frie Bm (AR)
[1850 Hardin Census: Lorenzo R. Frie 37, Casly 36, Mary J. 13, Henry J. 11, Cynthia A. 9, Nancy A. 7, Horace M. 4, Missouri C. 3, Louisa E. 11/12]
Margaret Free to Gilford Black q.v.
Polly Fry to William Chastain q.v.
MARRIAGES (MEIGS)
Malinda Frie to Henry Bare q.v.
MISCELLANEOUS (RHEA)
Jonathan Fry: Bondsman for Johnsey Parker, 1824
" " Bondsman for William McCormick, 1831
Samuel Frie: Bondsman for Lorenzy R. Frie, 1833
MISCELLANEOUS (MEIGS)
Alfred Frie: Cherokee Removal muster roll, 1836
John Frie: Cherokee Removal muster roll, 1836
Jonathan Fry: 2nd Sgt., Cherokee Removal muster roll
" " JP 1838
Lorenzo Frie: Cherokee Removal muster roll, 1836

- - - - - - - - - - - -

FUGET / FUGIT

1840 RHEA CENSUS
Zachariah Fuget 21100 - 111001
MARRIAGES (RHEA)
Julia Ann Fugit to Rufus Harwood q.v.

- - - - - - - - - - - -

FUILL

MARRIAGES (RHEA)
Sarah Fuill to George Dudding q.v.

- - - - - - - - - - - -

FULKERSON / FULKISON

TAXES (RHEA)
1819 (Capt. W.S. Bradley's Dist.):
Fulkerson & Bradley 2 WP, 4 BP, ½a, 1 Town Lot
MARRIAGES (RHEA)
Eliza Fulkerson to Baldwin H. Fine q.v.
MISCELLANEOUS (RHEA)
Frederick Fulkerson: Early merchant in Washington
" " JP 1822-1824
" " Signed petition to move Indian Agency

- - - - - - - - - - - -

FULLER

1840 MEIGS CENSUS
William Fuller 000001 - 11001 p. 244
MARRIAGES (RHEA)
William or Williamson Fuller to Polly Clabough, 22 Dec 1835 (26 Dec), John Farmer MG, William Fairbanks Bm (A)
MARRIAGES (MEIGS)
Nancy Fuller to Coffield Tillery q.v.

- - - - - - - - - - - -

FULLINGTON / FULLENTON / FULTINGTON

1830 RHEA CENSUS
John Fullington 10001 - 11001 p. 361
William Fullington 322001 - 0001001 p. 361
1840 RHEA CENSUS
William Fullenton 0212101 - 0001001
1850 RHEA CENSUS
George W. Fullington 33 (Farmer), Elizabeth 36, John BUTLER 17 (Farmer), William 15, Jane FULLINGTON 7, James T. 2 p. 559-160
William Fullington 60 (Va)(Farmer), Clarissa 60 (NC), John 18, Squire 16 p. 536-20
William Fullington 24 (Farmer), Mary 21, Charlotte J. 1 p. 560-167
MARRIAGES (RHEA)
Nancy Fullington to John M. Nelson q.v.
William Fullington to Mary Dodson, 31 June 1847 (same), James Smith JP (R)
MARRIAGES (MEIGS)
Elizabeth Fullington to Elias Shoat q.v.
George Fullington to Elizabeth Butler, 7 Aug 1838 (8 Aug), J. Baker JP

- - - - - - - - - - - -

FULTON

TAXES (RHEA)
1819 (Capt. Wm McCray's Co.): Arthur Fulton 1 WP, 300a
1823 (Capt. Howerton's Old Co.): Arthur Fulton 1 WP, 2 BP, 200a Vann's Spring Cr
(Capt. Jackson's Co.): David Fulton 1 WP
Thomas Fulton 1 WP
1830 RHEA CENSUS
Arthur Fulton 120111 - 1020001 p. 391
MARRIAGES (RHEA)
Arthur L. Fulton to Orthey Collins, 21 Sept 1835 (23 Sept), Matthew Hubbert JP, Wm G. English Bm (AR)
Darthula Fulton to Raleigh J. Fulton q.v.
Elizabeth Fulton to Anderson Smith q.v.
Flemming H. Fulton to Ann Stacy, 24 Dec 1831 (no return), Abraham G. Wright Bm (AR)

Flemming H. Fulton to Anna M. Stacy, 4 Feb 1832 (5 Feb), John Pardee MMEC, David P. Caldwell Bm (AR)
Lauretta Fulton to Asa Glascock q.v.
Nancy Fulton to Thornton Cread q.v.
Raleigh J. Fulton to Darthula Fulton, 26 Apr 1835 (same), James McCanse JP, Seabourn Johnson Bm (AR)
Uphama Fulton to James Williams q.v.

MISCELLANEOUS (RHEA)
Arthur Fulton: JP 1820, 1826
" " Bondsman for Isaac Glasscock, 1823
Fleming M. Fulton: Bondsman for Levy Stacy, 1833

\- - - - - - - - - - - - -

GADDY / GODDY / GODY

1830 RHEA CENSUS
Jeremiah Goddy 01021001 - 00120001 p. 355
William H. Goddy 00001 - 10001 p. 355

1840 MEIGS CENSUS
Jeremiah Gaddy 000100001 - 00011001 p. 226

1850 MEIGS CENSUS
Richard D. Gaddy 38 (NC)(Blacksmith), Ann 35, George W. 13, Alfred M. 11, Jackson C. 9, James W. 3 p. 785-566

MARRIAGES (RHEA)
Bethenl or Bethwell Goddy or Gaddy to Rebecca Pharris, 5 Oct 1827 (11 Oct), Daniel M. Stockton JP, Elisha Sharp Bm (AR)
Rebecca Gaddy to Isaac Brady q.v.
Richard Gaddy to Ann Carrell or Carroll, 4 Mar 1834 (5 Mar), James Willis MG, George Carroll Bm (AR)

MARRIAGES (MEIGS)
Mary Gody to Peter Thornberry q.v.

MISCELLANEOUS (RHEA)
Harmon Gaddy: Bondsman for David Rhea, 1835
" " Bondsman for Robert Hill, 1834

\- - - - - - - - - - - - -

GAGE

MISCELLANEOUS (RHEA)
George W. Gage: Bondsman for John Nash, 1836
" " " Bondsman for James Hayes, 1837

\- - - - - - - - - - - - -

GAITHER / GATHER

1830 RHEA CENSUS
Bean Gather 0210001 - 111101 p. 362
Sarah Gather 0111 - 00201 p. 362

MARRIAGES (RHEA)
Elenor Gaither to Richard G. McFall q.v.
Thomas Gaither to Eliza McCoy, 23 Dec 1833 (24 Dec), E.E. Wasson JP, Bassel Parker Bm (AR)
Wm Harrison Gaither to Elizabeth McFall, 13 Aug 1835 (same), Wm Green MG, Jesse H. McFall Bm (AR)

MISCELLANEOUS (RHEA and MEIGS)
Beal Gaither: JP 1827-28, 1830, 1832
" " Hiwassee District, Moore's Chapel area
Sarah Gaither: Member, Fellowship Baptist Ch., 1828-29

\- - - - - - - - - - - - -

GALBREATH / GILBREATH / GILBRETH

TAXES (RHEA)
1808 (Joseph Brooks' List): James Galbreath 200a Sale Cr
1819 (Capt. McGill's Co.): James Galbreath 200a
1823 (Capt. Howard's Co.): James Galbreath heirs 200a

1850 MEIGS CENSUS
Mary Gilbreth 40 p. 715-19

MARRIAGES (RHEA)
Alexander Galbreath to Jane C. Hill, 14 Aug 1828 (same), James Simms JP, Missoree Clack Bm (AR)

MARRIAGES (MEIGS)
Eliza J. Gilbreath to William Bracket q.v.

MISCELLANEOUS (RHEA)
Alexander H. Galbraith: Bm for Isaac S. Binyon, 1828
James Galbreath: On first Grand Jury, 1808

\- - - - - - - - - - - - -

GALLANT

1830 RHEA CENSUS
James Gallant 01300001 - 3010001 p. 356

\- - - - - - - - - - - - -

GALLAWAY / GALLOWAY

1830 RHEA CENSUS
William Galloway 110001 - 10001 p. 374

1840 MEIGS CENSUS
William Galloway 1111001 - 111001 p. 238

1850 MEIGS CENSUS
Annis Galloway to Walter L. Rothwell q.v.
Eliza M. Galloway to John M. Albert q.v.
Thomas Gallaway 21 (School Teacher), Mary C. 23 (Va) p. 775-496 [Thomas Galloway married Miss M.C. Rothwell on 7 Feb 1848 in McMinn County]
William Gallaway 52 (Va)(Farmer), Sophia 45, Abram 26, James 15, Sarah 11, Mary 8, John F. 5, John 18 p. 774-488

\- - - - - - - - - - - - -

GALLION / GALLEN

1830 RHEA CENSUS
Wm Gallen 102101 - 2122001 p. 367
William Gallion 0101001 - 111101 p. 352

\- - - - - - - - - - - - -

GALLOTT / GILLOTT
(see also GILLET)

MARRIAGES (RHEA)
Nancy Gillott or Gallott to Peter Airheart q.v.

\- - - - - - - - - - - - -

GAMBLE

TAXES (RHEA)
1808 (Joseph Brooks' List): Charles Gamble 1 WP
Robert Gamble 1 WP
1819 (Capt. McGill's Co.): Chas Gamble 1 WP, 2 BP, 250a
Robert Gamble 1 WP, 3 BP, 468a
1823 (Capt. Jackson's Co.): Charles Gamble 160a Hiwassee
Robert Gamble 1 WP, 3 BP, 160a Hiwassee
Samuel Gamble 1 WP, 1 BP, 130a Hiwassee
William Gamble 1 WP, 1 BP, 224½a TennR
1830 RHEA CENSUS
Jno Gamble 001110001 - 12100001 p. 370
Robert Gamble 0010101 - 0000101 p. 368
Robert Gamble 1001001 - 0001101 p. 368
Samuel Gamble 2000001 - 100011 p. 368
1840 MEIGS CENSUS
Francis Gamble 0011001 - 1210001 p. 228
John Gamble 0000100001 - 001020001 p. 226
John W. Gamble 100001 - 10101 p. 226
Samuel Gamble 10200001 - 120001 p. 226
1850 MEIGS CENSUS
Charles Gamble 34 (Farmer), Martha E. 1 p. 740-221
John Gamble 43 (Farmer), Frances 36, Charles P. 13, Sarah E. 10, Mary Ann 8, Louisa E. 6, Margaret E. 5, Robert L. 2, Nancy M. -- [blank, probably 0] p. 731-142
John Gamble 82 (Va)(Farmer), Margaret Ann 39, Elizbeth 32 p. 744-251 [John married Betsy Evins on 12 July 1803 in Roane County]
Samuel Gamble 67 (Farmer), Matilda 47, William A. 22 (Farmer), Charles R. 20 (Farmer), Margaret J. 18, Charity A. 16, Robert L. 13, Mary A.B. 11, John C. 9, Samuel H. 7 p. 727-106
MARRIAGES (RHEA)
Joseph Gamble to Ann Bullard, 25 Mar 1835, John C. Lewis Bm (A)
Mary Gamble to Jeremiah Bowling q.v.
Mary M. Gamble to Alfred N. Patterson q.v.
Nancy Gamble to Howel Whitmore q.v.
Nancy Ann Gamble to Samuel R. Russell q.v.
Robert Gamble to Polly Anderson, 20 May 1823 (same), Thomas Cox JP, David Leuty Bm (AR)
Robert Gamble to Betsy Jones, 7 Nov 1832 (8 Nov), William Smith JP, Anderson Jones Bm
[1850 Hamilton Census: Robert L. Gamble 37, Elizabeth 45, Adelea 5]
Samuel Gamble to Matilda Riggs, 18 Aug 1823 (same), James C. Mitchell Bm (A)
MARRIAGES (MEIGS)
Charity A. Gamble to Joseph N. Witt q.v.
Charles Gamble to Nancy A. Reed, 17 Feb 1847 (18 Feb), Jesse Locke MG
Margaret J. Gamble to James M. Campbell q.v.
MISCELLANEOUS (RHEA)
John W. Gamble: Bondsman for Howel Whitman, 1830
Robert Gamble: Early resident of Town of Washington
Samuel Gamble: Bondsman for George W. Blackwell, 1819
William Gamble: JP 1823-1825
MISCELLANEOUS (MEIGS)
Charles Gamble: War of 1812
" " Cherokee Removal muster roll, 1836
Francis Gamble: Purchased land in Ocoee District
John Gamble: Hiwassee District, Burkett Chapel area
John W. Gamble: Cherokee Removal muster roll, 1836
" " " Constable, District 1, 1838
" " " Surety for Masoner Gross, 1850
Joseph B. Gamble: Cherokee Removal muster roll, 1836
Robert Gamble: Hiwassee District
Samuel Gamble: On Circuit Court jury, 1836
" " House used for elections, District 1
" " Common School Com., District 1, 1838
" " Hiwassee District
William Gamble: Hiwassee District

GANN / GAN

MARRIAGES (RHEA)
Jane Gann to John Simmons q.v.
Jenna Gann to Joshua Gann q.v.
John Garr or Gann to Jane Auston or Austin, 4 June 1823 (5 June), William Gamble JP or MG, Zeof Jackson Bm (AR)
Joshua Gann to Jenna Gann, 1 Sept 1813, Jacob Gann Bm (A)
Leah Gann to William Gann q.v.
Lindsey Garr or Gan to Thomas M. Penny q.v.
Mary Gann to Elisha Corbet q.v.
Thomas Gann to Polly McArster, 10 June 1818, John Myers Bm (A)
William Gann to Lean Gann, 18 Mar 1812 (same), Jacob Davis Bm (A)
MISCELLANEOUS (RHEA)
Jacob Gann: Bondsman for Joshua Gann, 1813

GANNAWAY / GANAWAY / GONERWAY

1850 RHEA CENSUS
John F. Gonerway 29 (Va)(Farmer), Elizabeth 30, Martha S. 5, Margaret J. 4, Robeson G. 3, Matilda V. 6/12 p. 593-366
William Gonerway 53 (Farmer), Margaret A. 54, Rhoda R. 30 (Va), Thomas C. 18 (Farmer), Edmund N. 16 (Farmer), Mary B. 14 p. 593-365
William R. Gonerway 28 (Va)(Farmer), Eliza J. 28, Leonadas J. 2 p. 593-365
MARRIAGES (RHEA)
Elizabeth Ganaway to John Compton q.v.
Thomas Ganaway to Rebecca Johnson, 18 or 24 Feb 1845, William Nail JP, Dean W. Chase Bm (AR)
William A. Ganaway to Eliza Broyles, 18 Aug 1848 (same), J.R. Billings JP (R)
MISCELLANEOUS (RHEA)
William Ganaway: MG 1849

GANTT

TAXES (RHEA)
1819 (Capt. W.S. Bradley's Dist.):
R. & Edward Gantt heirs 1500a

GARDNER / GARDINER

1850 MEIGS CENSUS
John Gardner 65 (Va), Phoebe 50 (SC) p. 801-678
MARRIAGES (MEIGS)
John Gardner to Phoebe Davis, 17 June 1849 (same), J.L. Aikman JP
MISCELLANEOUS (RHEA)
John Gardiner: Purchased Lot 20 in Town of Washington

- - - - - - - - - - - - -

GAREN / GEREM / GERREN / GURIN / GUERRIN / GOOEN / GOINE

TAXES (RHEA)
1819 (Capt. W.S. Bradley's Dist.): Simeon Geren 1 WP
1830 RHEA CENSUS
I.W. Gerren 0200001 - 011001 p. 378
1840 RHEA CENSUS
Isaac W. Gurin 02010001 - 1102001
1840 MEIGS CENSUS
Elizabeth Gooen 0011 - 0000001 p. 230
[see also Elizabeth GIRET]
MARRIAGES (RHEA)
Isaac W. Garen to Jinsey Richardson, 12 or 15 Mar 1830 (17 Mar), John Cozby JP, Samuel R. Hackett Bm (AR)
Jane Guin or Gerin to John Meriott q.v.
Levi Garen to Betsy Petet, 26 Dec 1832 (same), John McClure JP, Samuel R. Hackett Bm (AR)
Levi Goine or Gerin to Mary Lambert, 29 June 1844 (15 July), James Hooper JP, Thomas Eaves Bm (AR)
Martha Guin or Guerin to James H. Dun q.v.
Susan Guerin to James Meriott q.v.
MARRIAGES (MEIGS)
Abagail Guron to Jacob Rray (Bray or Rhea) q.v.
MISCELLANEOUS (RHEA)
J.C. Gerin: Bondsman for H.M. Smith q.v.
Levi Goren: Bondsman for Charles Johnson, 1835
Simeon Garen: Bm for Spencer Beavers or Benson, 1819
" " Bondsman for Jesse Matthews, 1820

- - - - - - - - - - - - -

GARGLE

TAXES (RHEA)
1808 (James Campbell's List): Caleb Gargle 1 WP

- - - - - - - - - - - - -

GARNER

1830 RHEA CENSUS
Alfred Garner 100001 - 101 p. 367
1850 MEIGS CENSUS
Riley Garner 27 (Farmer), Elizabeth 21, James M. 3, Rebecca 2, Nancy Jane 1 p. 747-277
MARRIAGES (RHEA)
Cyntha Garner to Zorable Tanksly q.v.
John C. Garner to Eliza J. Majors, 12 Nov 1850 (same), Asa Newport MG (R)
Ruth Garner to William Rogers q.v.

- - - - - - - - - - - - -

GARNIGAN

1840 MEIGS CENSUS
William Garnigan 1000001 - 01001 p. 225

- - - - - - - - - - - - -

GARRETT

TAXES (RHEA)
1823 (Capt. Howard's Co.): Elijah Garrett 1 WP
MARRIAGES (RHEA)
Sally Garrett to Isaac Brown q.v.

- - - - - - - - - - - - -

GARRISON

TAXES (RHEA)
1823 (Capt. Howerton's Old Co.): Joseph Garrison 1 WP
1830 RHEA CENSUS
Isaac Garrison 10001 - 00001 p. 391
Jacob Garrison 010001 - 10001 p. 389
John Garrison 10001 - 1200002001 p. 389
John Garrison 10001 - 11001 p. 390
Joseph Garrison 10001 - 12001 p. 367
1840 RHEA CENSUS
Alfred Garrison 220001 - 010001
Garrett Garrison 000000001 - 00001
Henry Garrison 210001 - 000001
Jacob Garrison 0001001 - 000101
John Garrison 00100001 - 00010101
John Garrison Jr. 111001 - 21201
Joseph Garrison 01000001 - 002001
1850 RHEA CENSUS
Garrett Garrison 73 (NC)(Farmer), Rebecca 69 (NC) p. 549-109
Jacob Garrison 20 (Farmer), Elizabeth C. 25 p. 582-304
Jacob Garrison 53 (NC)(Farmer), Calvin M. 28 (Farmer), Eliza M. 26, Melville L. 4, Myra A. 2, Nancy F. 6/12, Richard L. 24 (NC)(School Teacher), Elizabeth J. GEARING 11, Rebecca A. GEARING 11 p. 541-54
John Garrison 47 (NC)(Farmer), Elizabeth 47 (NC), Margaret 24, James 21 (Farmer), Garrett 17 (Farmer), Elizabeth 14, Moses 13, Lucinda 12, Jane 10, Emeline 8, Andrew J. 5 p. 539-40
Joseph Garrison 57 (NC)(Farmer), Mary 47 (Va) p. 581-301
MARRIAGES (RHEA)
Barbary Ann Garrison to Calvin R. McFalls q.v.
Cassa Garrison to Elijah Wasson q.v.
Calvin M. Garrison to Eliza Mitchell, 19 Feb 1845 (same), Jesse P. Thompson JP, Wm W. Cash Bm (AR)
Garriett Garrison to Rebecca Davis, 29 May 1841 (1 June), Asa Newport MG (R)
[the above marriage was listed twice, identically, in the Rhea County records, #73 and #93]
Henry Garrison to Elizabeth Clinton, 2 May 1834, John F. Paul Bm (A)
Hannah Garrison to Shadrack Hase or House q.v.
Isaac Garrison to Almira Haynes, 10 Nov 1828, Richard Waterhouse Bm (A)
Jacob Garrison to Nancy Waterhouse, 1 Aug 1820 (11 Aug), J. Fine JP (R)

Jacob Garrison to Elizabeth Erwin, 8 Apr 1850 (9 Apr), Daniel Broyles JP (R)
John Garrison to Betsy Erwin, 23 Apr 1824 (same), Fred Fulkerson JP, Joseph Garrison Bm (AR)
Myra Garrison to Allen H. McFalls q.v.
MISCELLANEOUS (RHEA)
Jacob Garrison: Bondsman for Aron Rhea, 1822
John Garrison: Bondsman for John Dunlap, 1820
Joseph Garrison: Bm for John Guerin or Garrison, 1824

- - - - - - - - - - - - -

GARWOOD / GORWOOD

1840 RHEA CENSUS
Samuel Gorwood 1210001 - 2220001
MARRIAGES (RHEA)
Elizabeth Garwood to G.W. Brown q.v.
Sarah Garwood to William F. Ragsdale q.v.

- - - - - - - - - - - - -

GASS / GUESS

1850 RHEA CENSUS
William T. Gass 30 (Farmer), Ann 35 or 45 [numbers not clear], Elijah KELLEY 57 (Farmer) p. 588-354 [William, son of Andrew and Mary P. Collins Gass; grandson of Samuel Gass of Jefferson County]
MARRIAGES (RHEA)
William T. Gass to Ann Moyers, 25 July 1844 (same), Samuel Frazier JP, James C. Ferguson Bm (AR) [Ann was widow of Jacob Moyers and dau of Rev. John Condley]
MARRIAGES (MEIGS)
Fisha Guess to Masoner Gross q.v.
Mary Guess to Francis Gross q.v.
MISCELLANEOUS (MEIGS)
James Gass: Bondsman for William Moore, 1848

- - - - - - - - - - - - -

GASKEY

MARRIAGES (RHEA)
Margaret Gaskey to Isaac Lakins q.v.

- - - - - - - - - - - - -

GASQUE

1830 RHEA CENSUS
James Gasque 20001 - 00001 p. 393
MARRIAGES (RHEA)
James Gasque to Susan Ollivet or Oliver, 6 Jan 1826 (same), James Darwin JP, Woodson Francis Bm (AR)

- - - - - - - - - - - - -

GASTON or GASTINE

MARRIAGES (RHEA)
John Gastine or Gaston to Mary Ann McCame or McCanse, 24 Dec 1841* (same), Thomas Frazier MG (AR)
[*Allen shows the year as 1840]
[1850 McMinn Census: John Gaston 35, Mary Ann 28, Joseph 8, Elizabeth 4, John W. 1]

GATES

TAXES (RHEA)
1823 (Capt. Wilson's Co.): George Gates 1 WP

- - - - - - - - - - - - -

GEAR

1840 RHEA CENSUS
Jacob Gear 0110001 - 3122101
1850 RHEA CENSUS
Elizabeth Gear 52, Caroline H. 27, Edwin R. 16 (Farmer), Eliza A. 15, Harriet S.A. 13, Zilpha A. 11, Emily S. 8 p. 573-245
MARRIAGES (RHEA)
Ellen E. Gear to George J. Stults q.v.
Jane Gear to Jeremiah Mapes q.v.
Juda L. Gear to William Dotson q.v.
Mary Gear to Isaac Seymore q.v.
Nancy Gear or Lear to William Owens q.v.
Rachel Gear to W.W. Price q.v.
MISCELLANEOUS (RHEA)
Jacob Gear: JP 1837-1841

- - - - - - - - - - - - -

GEARING

1850 RHEA CENSUS
David Gearing 74 (NJ)(Farmer), Polly 56 (Va), Susan A. 12 (NC) p. 606-474
Elizabeth J. Gearing 11, Rebecca A. 11: see Jacob Garrison
John Gearing 38 (NC)(Farmer), Agness 33 (NC), Marion 13 (NC), Mary A. 8 (NC) p. 605-473
Malinda Gearing 15: see Elizabeth Dunn

- - - - - - - - - - - - -

GENETT

MARRIAGES (MEIGS)
Narcissa Genett to Andrew Fox q.v.

- - - - - - - - - - - - -

GENOE / GENOW / GINNO / GENO / JANOE

1830 RHEA CENSUS
Patsy Janoe 31 - 000001 p. 353
Permelia Janoe 1 - 10001 p. 353
1850 MEIGS CENSUS
David Gino 27 (Carpenter) p. 772-468
James Genoe 25 (Carpenter), Emaline 24, David 6, William R. 4, Hezekiah 3, Calvin 1 p. 765-413
[James Ginow married Emeline Robeson on 4 Aug 1844 in McMinn County]
Martha Ginno 55 (SC), Mary Ann 22 p. 765-412
MARRIAGES (RHEA)
May Genoe to John Atchley q.v.
Pamelia Geno to Clayton Hoyal q.v.
Patsy Genoe to Robert B. Harris q.v.
MARRIAGES (MEIGS)
Franklin Genow to Catharine Moore, 2 Aug 1848 (3 Aug), J.L. Aikman JP
Louisa Jane Genno to James W. More q.v.

MISCELLANEOUS (MEIGS)
David Geno: Surety for Amedia Rice, 1850

- - - - - - - - - - - - -

GENTRY

TAXES (RHEA)
1823 (Capt. Jackson's Co.): Allen Gentry 1 WP
Cain Gentry 1 WP
Mrs. ---- Gentry 1 BP

1830 RHEA CENSUS
Robert Gentry 000011 - 1001 p. 379

MARRIAGES (RHEA)
Allen Gentry to Sarah Fine, 6 July 1825 (14 July), Thomas Cox JP, Jesse Sutton Bm (AR)
[1850 Bledsoe Census: Allen Gentry 59, Sarah 48, Zelzy A. 24, Any L. 20, Sarah E. 17, Eliza L. 14, Joshua C. 12, James K. 9, Francis M. 5]
Cain Gentry to Patsy Philpot, 14 Jan 1823 (16 Jan), Thomas Cox JP, Joseph McDaniel Bm (AR)
John Gentrey or Gentry to Elizabeth Hays, 13 Dec 1824 (same), Jas McDonald JP, George Lea Bm (AR)

MISCELLANEOUS (RHEA)
Allen Gentry: Bondsman for Jesse Sutton, 1825
David Gentry: Bondsman for William Rodgers, 1813

- - - - - - - - - - - - -

GEORGE

1830 RHEA CENSUS
David George 210001 - 01001 p. 379
Thomas George 102101 - 1110001 p. 378
W. H. George 00001 - 0001 p. 378

1840 RHEA CENSUS
John George 10002 - 00001
Thomas George 00100001 - 00110001

1840 MEIGS CENSUS
Retten H. George 000001 - 010001 p. 230

1850 RHEA CENSUS
Jacob George 35 (Farmer), Sally A. 30, William 6, James 4, Barbary 2 p. 615-507
John George 39 (SC)(Farmer), William 11, Levesta 10 p. 618-529
Thomas George 62 (SC), Barbary 64 (SC), Mary 24, Mahala 22, James 21 (Farmer) p. 618-528
Thomas O. George 30 ("None"), Darcus 25, Mahala 6, Thomas J. 4, Elizabeth 3, Jacob 1 p. 618-530

1850 MEIGS CENSUS
Brittan H. George 40 (NC)(Farmer), Isabella 40 (NC), Sarah 15, Thomas M. 10 p. 752-319
John George 20 (Farmer), Mary 9 p. 747-271
Sarah George 40 (SC), Martha 12, Mary 11, Sarah 10, Gahida (m) 8, Phillip 4 p. 807-722

MARRIAGES (RHEA)
Jacob George to Sarah Ann Ryan, 14 Aug 1840 (16 Aug), James Hooper JP, Thomas Knight Bm (AR)
John George to Nancy Davis, 16 Jan 1838 (18 Jan), Wm B. Cozby JP, Pleasant Davis Bm (AR)
Polly George to James Smith q.v.
Retten H. George to Ibby Moore, 11 June 1829, John Cozby JP, David Singleton Bm (AR)
Thomas C. George to Elizabeth Davis, 2 Oct 1840 (4 Oct), James Hooper JP, John W. Hewes Bm (AR)

MARRIAGES (MEIGS)
John C. George to Mary Wammack, 31 Aug 1850, Ezekiel Atkinson Sur [McMinn County MB D: 31 contained the following record: John C. George to Mary Womack, 28 Aug 1850]

- - - - - - - - - - - - -

GERL

MARRIAGES (MEIGS)
Irene Gerl to James H. Ward q.v.

- - - - - - - - - - - - -

GIBBS

1850 RHEA CENSUS
Sarah Gibbs 28, John 7: see Daniel McFall

MARRIAGES (RHEA)
Keziah Gibbs to Asahel Jackson q.v.
Polly Gibbs to Pleasant Manor q.v.
Sarah Gibbs to Jonathan B. Sullivan q.v.

MISCELLANEOUS (RHEA)
John Gibbs: Bondsman for Asahel Jackson, 1832

- - - - - - - - - - - - -

GIBSON / GIPSON

TAXES (RHEA)
1808 (James Campbell's List): Jacob Gibson 1 WP
1819 (Capt. Robinson's Co.): Randolph Gibson 1 WP, 1 BP
1823 (Capt. Piper's Co.): Hiram Gibson 1 WP
Randolph Gibson 1 BP, 171½a, 1 stud horse (tax: $5.00)

1830 RHEA CENSUS
Allen Gibson 00001 - 000001 p. 357
David Gibson 111001 - 101001 p. 370
G. W. Gibson 1101 - 01002 p. 391
Hiram Gibson 010001 - 110001 p. 359
James Gibson 10001 - 10001 p. 359
Randolph Gibson 001110001 - 00100001 p. 363
William Gibson 10003 - 0001 p. 390

1840 RHEA CENSUS
Jacob Gibson 10001 - 10001
William Gibson 01002001 - 0000101

1840 MEIGS CENSUS
Jane Gipson 00002 - 000000001 p. 246
Hiram Gipson 0001001 - 112101 p. 244

1850 RHEA CENSUS
William Gipson 32 (Farmer), Rebecca 28, Alfred 5, Mary A. 4, Judy 2, William S. 7/12 p. 544-71
William Gipson 67 (Va) (Farmer), Sarah 67 (Va), John HUDDLESTON 16 (NC) (Farmer), Elizabeth PRICE 9, William L. PRICE 6 p. 536-26

1850 MEIGS CENSUS
Alfred Gibson 32 (Ky)(Farmer), Sarah 27, John 6, Isaac 5, Elizabeth Jane 3, Randolph 0 p. 813-768
Hiram Gibson 51 (Ky), Mary 50, Mahala 18, Lorinda 13, James 10, Thomas 5 p. 780-528
Jacob Gibson 35 (Ky)(Farmer), Mary Ann 31, Isaac 18 (Farmer), Samuel 15 (Farmer), John 13, James 11, George W. 9, Doctor F. 7, Mary 4 p. 812-761
Randolph Gibson 43, Sarah 26, James 6, Charles 5, Farley 3, Smith 2, Elizabeth 0 p. 812-757

MARRIAGES (RHEA)
George W. Gibson to Esther Atchley, 14 Sept 1827 (same), William Dill MG, Thomas Atchley Bm (AR)
Hiram Gibson to Mary Stockton, 9 Nov 1819, Daniel Walker JP, Randolph Gibson Bm (AR)
Jacob Gibson to Mary Ann McCaleb, 12 Jan 1836, Randolph Gibson Bm (A)
James Gibson to Matilda McCoy, 19 Oct 1826 (22 Oct), James Helton JP, William Gibson Bm (AR)
Jane Gibson to John M. Farmer q.v.
Judith Gibson to James M. Price q.v.
Matilda Gibson to Robert Rhea q.v.
Pleasant Gibson to Mary Lea, 30 Sept 1823 (same), James Kelly Bm (A)
Sarah Gipson to Zabadee Brewer q.v.
William Gibson to Rebecca Ann Bower, 18 Apr 1828 (24 Apr), Daniel Briggs MG, Andrew Jack Bm (AR)
William Gibson to Rebecca Danby or Danley, 6 Mar 1844 (7 Mar), Asa Newport MG (R)
MARRIAGES (MEIGS)
Alford Gibson to Sarah Baker, 11 Mar 1842 (13 Mar), William Green MG
Elizabeth Gibson to William Wan q.v.
Matilda Gibson to Jacob J. Butler q.v.
Nancy Jane Gibson to Archibald McCaleb q.v.
William E. Gibson to Elizabeth C. Hague, 11 Sept 1842 (same), Moses Farmer JP
MISCELLANEOUS (RHEA)
Randolph Gibson: Bondsman for Hiram Gibson, 1819
" " Bondsman for Benjamin Hutson, 1828
" " Bondsman for Jacob Gibson, 1836
William Gibson: Bondsman for James Gibson, 1826
MISCELLANEOUS (MEIGS)
Hiram Gibson: Hiwassee District, Moore's Chapel area
" " Cherokee Removal muster roll, 1836
Jane Gibson: Member, Fellowship Baptist Church, 1828-29
Randolph Gibson: Donated land for Fellowship Baptist Church of Christ, 1829
" " Cherokee Removal muster roll, 1836

- - - - - - - - - - - - -

GILBERT

1840 RHEA CENSUS
Archibald Gilbert 00003 - 10001 [Archibald married Sally Allen on 19 May 1831 in Roane County]
1850 MEIGS CENSUS
E. D. Gilbert 22 (Pa)(Doctor) p. 772-473
MISCELLANEOUS (MEIGS)
E. D. Gilbert: Bondsman for Richard Binyon, 1850
John Gilbert: Cherokee Removal muster roll, 1836
Peter Gilbert: Cherokee Removal muster roll, 1836

- - - - - - - - - - - - -

GILCHRIST

MISCELLANEOUS (MEIGS)
Malcolm Gilchrist: Hiwassee District resident

- - - - - - - - - - - - -

GILES / JILES

1830 RHEA CENSUS
Vaden H. Giles 210001 - 31211 p. 372
1840 MEIGS CENSUS
Thomas Giles 000011 - 100001 p. 225
MARRIAGES (RHEA)
Vaden H. Giles to Sarah Phillamon, 30 Sept 1834 (9 Sept) [as written, but probably should be 9 Oct], John Cozby JP, John G. Phillamon Bm (AR)
MISCELLANEOUS (RHEA)
Vaden H. Giles: JP 1833-1835
" " " Bondsman for Henry Martin, 1833
" " " Bondsman for John Phillamon, 1839
MISCELLANEOUS (MEIGS)
Joseph Jiles: JP(?) 1842

- - - - - - - - - - - - -

GILLENWATERS

TAXES (RHEA)
1819 (Capt. John Ramsey's Co.): Wm T. Gillenwaters 1 WP
1823 (Capt. Howerton's Old Co.):
W.T. Gillenwaters 1 WP, 1 BP, 360a Camp Cr
1830 RHEA CENSUS
W.T. Gillenwatters 01131 - 010001 p. 390
1840 RHEA CENSUS
Wm T. Gillenwater 00010001 - 0001001
MARRIAGES (RHEA)
Mary J.R. Gillenwaters to Robert A. Brown q.v.
William T. Gillenwaters to Elizabeth Roddy, 17 Feb 1819, J. Fine JP, George Preston Bm (AR)
MISCELLANEOUS (RHEA)
Wm T. Gillenwaters: Bondsman for James Johnson, 1816
" " " Bondsman for Robert Craven, 1830
" " " Bondsman for Richard Wallard, 1835

- - - - - - - - - - - - -

GILLESPIE

TAXES (RHEA)
1819 (Capt. John Ramsey's Co.): Geo Gillespie 6 BP, 1000a
1823 (Capt. McCall's Co.):
George Gillespie 8 BP, 1519a Tenn River
1830 RHEA CENSUS
George Gillespie 023220001 - 0000001 p. 383
R. N. Gillespie 00001 - 0001 p. 383
1840 RHEA CENSUS
George Gillespie 0002110001 - 000000001
Robert N. Gillespie 00001 - 20001
1850 RHEA CENSUS
David E. Gillespie 27 (Farmer) p. 560-163
George L. Gillespie 14, William S.L. 12: see James F. Ladd
James W. Gillespie 29 (Physician) p. 612-433
Robert N. Gillespie 43 (Merchant), Hannah 36, Adelade 14, Adelia 11, Ann 8, Thomas 6, Robert 4, James 1 p. 611-425
Thomas J. Gillespie 45 (Farmer), William ALLEN 19 (Farmer) p. 560-162
MARRIAGES (RHEA)
Jane H. Gillespie to James H. Blain q.v.
Robert N. Gillespie to Hannah Leuty, 13 May 1830 (same), F. Pope MG (R)

Sidney Ann Gillespie to James F. Ladd q.v.
Sovina Gillespie to William Pierce q.v.
William N. Gillespie to Sidney Ann Leuty, 3 Apr 1834 (same), Benjamin Wallace MG, John P. Long Bm (AR) [Wm N. and Robert N., sons of Col. George and Ann Neilson Gillespie; Sidna Ann and Hannah Leuty, daus of William S. and Mary Roddye Leuty]

MISCELLANEOUS (RHEA)

Charles K. Gillespie: Signed petition to move Indian Agency
" " " Bondsman for John A. Hooks, 1835
David E. Gillespie: Private, Mexican War
George Gillespie: Signed petition to move Indian Agency
" " JP 1818
" " Bondsman for Thomas Blakey, 1819
James H. Gillespie: Private, Mexican War
James W. Gillespie: Bondsman for David Bell, 1842
" " " Bondsman for Thomas C. Darwin, 1842
" " " Bondsman for John Day, 1843
" " " 1st Lt., Mexican War
" " " Trustee, Mars Hill Academy, 1850
Robert N. Gillespie: Early merchant in Washington
" " " Bondsman for John Chack, 1828
" " " Bondsman for Richard R. Gist, 1830
" " " Bondsman for Richard G. McFall, 1834
" " " Bondsman for Robert A. Brown, 1836
" " " Bondsman for Alexander Smith, 1836
" " " Bondsman for Isaac Benson, 1838
" " " Bondsman for Samuel Bowers, 1842
Thomas J. Gillespie: Bondsman for William Monday. 1831
" " " Bondsman for John P. Long, 1834
" " " Bondsman for Harrington Cole, 1836
" " " Bondsman for William McKiddy, 1841

- - - - - - - - - - - - -

GILLET

1840 RHEA CENSUS

Bice Gillet 2300001 - 000011

- - - - - - - - - - - - -

GILLIAM / GILLEM / GILLUM / GILLIAN / GILLHAND

TAXES (RHEA)

1819 (Capt. W.S. Bradley's Dist): John Gilliam 1 WP
1823 (Capt. Howerton's Old Co.): Nathaniel Gillem 1 WP

1830 RHEA CENSUS

Nat Gillhand 2201010001 - 01001001 p. 388

1840 RHEA CENSUS

Nathaniel Gillam 0222001 - 2101001

1850 RHEA CENSUS

Nathaniel Gullum 59 (Tanner), Sarah S. 49, James D. 25 (Farmer), Major C. 19 (Farmer), Richard A. 17 (Farmer), Mary E. 15, Nancy J. 13, Sarah R. 11, Letha M. 8, Jesse P. 4 p. 549-110

MARRIAGES (RHEA)

Elizabeth Gillum to Joel Dotson q.v.
George M. Gilliam to M.A. Mitchell, no date, no return, but between 4 Nov and 14 Nov 1850 in records (R)
John W. Gilliam or Gillum to Elizabeth Long, 23 July 1845 (24 July), Asa Newport MG, James D. Gillum Bm (AR)
Nathaniel Gillom to Sally Davis, 26 Sept 1822, Edward Stuart Bm (A)
William Gillian to Jane Gorden or Gooden, no date, no return, probably 1848 (R)

MISCELLANEOUS (RHEA)

James D. Gillum: Bondsman for John W. Gilliam, 1845

- - - - - - - - - - - - -

GIRET / GUIST
(see also GAREN)

1830 RHEA CENSUS

Elizabeth Giret or Guist: 00001 - 00010001 p. 375
[NOTE: last name has been written over; only thing certain is that it is a short name beginning with a G]

- - - - - - - - - - - - -

GIST

1830 RHEA CENSUS

Richard Gist 00001 - 00001 p. 383

MARRIAGES (RHEA)

Richard R. Gist to Pauline Frazier, 20 Apr 1830 (same), John Bennington MG, R.N. Gillespie Bm (AR)

- - - - - - - - - - - - -

GIVENS / GIVINS / GIBBINS / GIBBONS

TAXES (RHEA)

1823 (Capt. Jackson's Co.):
William Given 1 BP, 160a Agency Creek

1850 MEIGS CENSUS

Nicholas Gibbins 23 (Farmer), Rebecca 23, Louisa 1, Martha GIBBONS 21 p. 743-238
[Martha, sister of Nichols]
William Gibbons 50 (Farmer) p. 736-184

MARRIAGES (RHEA)

Ann Givin to James W. Thompson q.v.
Edward Givins to Jirsah Ferguson, 7 Dec 1815, Edward Goad Bm (A)
Joshua Givins [possibly Gwin] to Elizabeth Brooks, 6 Feb 1835, William Fairbanks Bm (A)
Nancy Givin to Hezekiah Lucus q.v.
Nancy Givens to William Richerson q.v.

MARRIAGES (MEIGS)

Nicholas Gibson [Nicholas Gibbs Givens] to Rebecca Locke, 18 Aug 1848 (20 Aug), J.M. Miller MG [Rebecca, dau of Robert and Nancy Moore Locke]

MISCELLANEOUS (RHEA and MEIGS)

Joshua S. Givin: Bondsman for Josiah Cranmore, 1838
Mark Givens: Hiwassee District, Ten Mile Stand area
Nicholas G. Givens: Private, Mexican War
" " " Surety for Samuel Woody, 1850
William Givens: Hiwassee District, Burkett Chapel area

- - - - - - - - - - - - -

GLADDEN

1840 RHEA CENSUS

John Gladden 201001 - 11001

MISCELLANEOUS (RHEA)
John Gladden: Bondsman for John Bryant, 1832
" " Bondsman for Wyly M. Brady, 1839

- - - - - - - - - - - - -

GLANDON

MARRIAGES (RHEA)
Isaac Glandon to Sarah Davis, 6 Apr 1834 (8 Apr), J. McCallon JP, Alexander Davis Bm (AR)

- - - - - - - - - - - - -

GLASCOCK / GLASSCOCK

1830 RHEA CENSUS
Acy Glasscock 10001 - 10001 p. 390
MARRIAGES (RHEA)
Isaac or Asa Glascock to Loretta or Lauretta Fulton, 18 Sept 1823 (same), Fred Fulkerson JP, Arthur Fulton Bm (AR)

- - - - - - - - - - - - -

GLAZE

MARRIAGES (RHEA)
Henry Glaze to Maryann Stuart, 21 Feb 1839, James M. Hale Bm (A)

- - - - - - - - - - - - -

GLENN / GLINN

1830 RHEA CENSUS
Joseph Glinn 0000001 - 00000001 p. 364
Robert Glinn 230001 - 101001 p. 364
MARRIAGES (RHEA)
John Glenn to Malinda Crawford, 3 July 1832 (same), John McClure JP (R)
Malinda Glenn to David Singleton q.v.
MISCELLANEOUS (RHEA)
John Glenn: Bondsman for William Walls, 1834

- - - - - - - - - - - - -

GOAD / GOOD / GOURD / GOARD

TAXES (RHEA)
1819 (Capt. John Lewis' Dist): Edward Goad 1 WP
Robert Goad 1 WP
Thomas Goad 1 WP
William Goad 160a
1823 (Capt. Lewis' Co.): Edward Good WP
Robert God 1 WP
Thomas G. Goad 1 WP
William Goad 160a
1830 RHEA CENSUS
Joshua Goad 10001 - 0001 p. 393
Mary Goad 0 - 000001011 p. 393
Robert Goad 001001 - 000001 p. 393
Ruthy Gourd 0001001 - 0 p. 371
Thos Goad 11122001 - 1100101 p. 394
1840 RHEA CENSUS
Joshua Gourd 220001 - 00001
Mary Gourd 0 - 00000011001
Thomas G. Gourd 00100001 - 01010001
1850 RHEA CENSUS
Joshua Good 45 (Farmer), Sarah 38, William 19 (Farmer), Charles 16 (Farmer), James P. 15, George 11, Sarah A. 5 p. 569-213
Ruth Goad 65 (SC): see James C. Ferguson
Ruth Goad 66 (SC), Sarah 70 (SC): see James Purser
1850 MEIGS CENSUS
Jacob Good 36 (Farmer), Jane 36, David A. 14, William H. 12, Thomas C. 10, Robert 8, Abraham 6, Sarah 4, Martha 3, James 1 p. 720-54
MARRIAGES (RHEA)
Agnes Good to Joseph Watson q.v.
Joshua Goad to Sarah Barnett, 20 Jan 1829 (same), Matthew Hubbert JP, Russell Ferguson Bm (AR)
John Goad to Anna Silvey, 23 June 1838 (24 June), Henry Griffett JP, John Crawford Bm (AR)
Luke Goad to Martha Minick, 23 July 1838 (28 July), H. Colling JP (AR)
Mary Ann Goard to Jacob Foute q.v.
Nelly Goad to Michael Runnels q.v.
Peggy Good to Simeon Jackson q.v.
Robert Goad to Elizabeth Chumley, 17 Jan 1826, Daniel Walker JP, Edward Goad Bm (AR)
MISCELLANEOUS (RHEA)
Edward Goad: Bondsman for Simeon Jackson, 1811
" " Bondsman for Edward Givins, 1815
" " Bondsman for Robert Goad, 1826
" " Bondsman for Phillip Parker, 1834
John Goad: Bondsman for William Silva Sr., 1839
Joshua Goad: Bondsman for Thomas Jackson, 1832
Robert Goad: Bondsman for James Carnahan, 1828
Thomas Goad: Bondsman for James Pincer, 1812

- - - - - - - - - - - - -

GODBY

MARRIAGES (RHEA)
Sally Godby to Pleasant Ripley q.v.
Zannah Godby to Robert Elison q.v.

- - - - - - - - - - - - -

GODBYHERE / GODBEHERE / GODSBEHERE

1830 RHEA CENSUS
Thomas Godbyhere 11100001 - 1100001 p. 367
1840 RHEA CENSUS
Thomas Godbehere 011110001 - 00110001
1850 RHEA CENSUS
Sabella Godsbehere 63 (NC), Richard D. 25 (Farmer) p. 586-335
Thomas Godsbehere 29 (Farmer), Mary A. 21, William S. 2, Mary A. 3/12 p. 586-337
MARRIAGES (RHEA)
Rebecca A. Godbyhere to Henderson Fisher q.v.
Richard Godbyhere to Martha J. Rose, 10 Aug 1850 (13 Aug), S. Roberts MG (R)
Thomas Godbehere to Isabella Taylor, 15 June 1818 (same), Wm Kennedy JP (AR)
William Godbyhere to Nancy W. Holland, 3 Feb 1841 (4 Feb), William Stuart MG (R)

- - - - - - - - - - - - -

GODDARD

MARRIAGES (MEIGS)
Hugh Goddard to Martha W. Winton, 16 Nov 1847 (same), James Sewell MG

- - - - - - - - - - - - -

GODSEY

TAXES (RHEA)
1823 (Capt. Smith's Co.): Burley Godsey 1 WP
1830 RHEA CENSUS
Drury L. Godsey 100001 - 10001 p. 373
Mary Godsey 012 - 0100101 p. 376
1840 MEIGS CENSUS
Drury L. Godsey 0110001 - 210001 p. 235
Mary Godsey 00012 - 000101 p. 232
1850 MEIGS CENSUS
Drury L. Godsey 55 (NC)(Farmer), Sarah 43, Abraham C. 25 (Doctor), Elizabeth 20, Margaret 18, Riley F. 16, Ellen 11, Samuel 8, Matilda 5, William 1 p. 754-337
Ismeal A. Godsey 33 (Farmer), Emaline 20, Elizabeth C. 16, Thomas 1 p. 775-494
Mary Godsey 49, James L. 25 (Farmer), Anas V. 22, Mary Jane 18 p. 775-498
Stephen J. Godsey 43 (Va)(Farmer), Mary 43, Sarah E. 14, John P.H. 12, Julett F. 9, Nancy Ann 7, William C. 6, James A. 2 p. 735-173
[Stephen J. Godsey and Mary Gibbons were married in Hawkins County about 1835]
William A. Godsey 31 (Farmer), Juda 28, George W. 9, Sarah E. 4, Mary Ann 1, Casandra M. THOMAS 30 p. 771-456
MARRIAGES (MEIGS)
Ishmeal A. Godsey to Emaline Cox, 15 June 1847 (same), D.L. Godsey MG
Sarah Ann Godsey to Thomas Hunter q.v.
Wm Godsey to Julia Thomas, 18 Dec 1840 (21 Dec), Drury L. Godsey MG
MISCELLANEOUS (RHEA and MEIGS)
A. G. Godsey: Surety for H.P. Stockton, 1850
Drury L. Godsey: MG 1828-40 (Rhea), 1838-48 (Meigs)
" " " Meigs County Court Clerk, 1841-48
Ishmael Godsey: Cherokee Removal muster roll, 1836
William A. Godsey: 2nd Corp., Mexican War

- - - - - - - - - - - - -

GOFF

1830 RHEA CENSUS
Ambrose Goff 00001 - 0001 p. 373
William Goff 001 - 00001 p. 379
MARRIAGES (RHEA)
Ambrose Goff to Elizabeth P. Lewis, 27 Aug 1828 (29 Aug), D.L. Godsey JP [MG], Ira Hill Bm (AR)
Elizabeth Goff to Oliver Massey q.v.
Isham Goff to Sareaner McBride, 21 Jan 1831, James Smith Bm (A)

- - - - - - - - - - - - -

GOFORTH

1850 MEIGS CENSUS
Samuel Goforth 24 (Farmer), Columbus 17 (Farmer) p. 732-146
MARRIAGES (MEIGS)
Mahala Goforth to Paul Bunch q.v.

- - - - - - - - - - - - -

GOLDSBY / GOLDBY / GOOLSBY

TAXES (RHEA)
1823 (Capt. Brown's Co.): Charles Goldsby 1 WP
1830 RHEA CENSUS
Charles Goldsby 0120001 - 00010001 p. 378
1840 RHEA CENSUS
Charles P. Goldby 10001 - 00002
MARRIAGES (RHEA)
Isaac Goldsby to Cynthia Corder, 4 May 1835, Fredrick Prisock Bm (A)
Isaac A. Godsby or Goolsby to Luvana Skillen or Skillern, 1 May 1833 (5 May), John Cozby JP, Isaac A. Goolsby Bm (AR)
Polly Goldsby to Washington Woody q.v.

- - - - - - - - - - - - -

GOLDWIN / GOLDEN / GOALDEN

1830 RHEA CENSUS
William Goldwin 200001 - 111001 p. 356
1840 MEIGS CENSUS
William Golden 1002001 - 0221101 p. 240
MARRIAGES (MEIGS)
Elizabeth Goalden to William Phariss q.v.

- - - - - - - - - - - - -

GOODWIN

1830 RHEA CENSUS
Sarah Goodwin 0112 - 0101011 p. 368
MARRIAGES (RHEA)
Elizabeth Goodwin to Robert Bell q.v.
MISCELLANEOUS (RHEA)
William Goodwin: Bondsman for John Moore, 1825

- - - - - - - - - - - - -

GORDON / GORDEN

1830 RHEA CENSUS
William Gorden 00001 - 21001 p. 390
1840 RHEA CENSUS
William B. Gorden 00100001 - 002001
MARRIAGES (RHEA)
Eliza Gordon to Washington Atchley q.v.
Jane Gorden or Gooden to William Gillian q.v.
John Gordon to Mary Seabolt, 29 June 1812 (same), Philip Taylor Bm (A)
Mary Ann Gordon to James F. Ritchie q.v.
William Gorden or Gordon to Margaret Rogers, 24 Nov 1824 (25 Nov), F.E. Fulkerson JP, James Rogers Bm (AR) [1850 Overton Census: William B. Gordon 49, Margaret 46, Elliner 24]

MISCELLANEOUS (RHEA)
William B. Gordon: MG 1839-40
" " " Bondsman for William Cox, 1835

- - - - - - - - - - - - -

GORLEY / GORELY / GOURLY / GOURLEY

1840 MEIGS CENSUS
John Gourly 1011001 - 022001 p. 238
1850 MEIGS CENSUS
John Gorely 50 (Farmer), Jane 46, Eliza Jane 20, John D. 12, Amentha 8 p. 765-416
MARRIAGES (MEIGS)
Clarissa Gourley to John Leaver q.v.
Levina P. Gorley to Thomas Blevins q.v.
Mary Ann Gourley to Simon McGinnis q.v.
Samuel Gorley to Emily J.L. Melton, 25 June 1839 (30 June), Daniel Cate JP
Samuel H. Gourley to Delisa Caroll, 16 July 1844 (same), J.R. Frayer MG
Sarah F. Gourley to Benjamin F. Benson q.v.
William P. Gourley to Katherine Ellis, 14 Mar 1843 [no other data]
MISCELLANEOUS (MEIGS)
John Gourley: JP 1842

- - - - - - - - - - - - -

GORMAN

MARRIAGES (RHEA)
Desdamony Gorman to Jacob Prillamon q.v.

- - - - - - - - - - - - -

GOSSAGE

TAXES (RHEA)
1823 (Capt. Piper's Co.): John Gossage 1 WP
William Gossage 1 WP
MARRIAGES (RHEA)
William Gossage to Polly Ledford or Leadford, 12 July 1823 (13 July) (AR)

- - - - - - - - - - - - -

GOTHARD / GOTHERD / GOTHERT

TAXES (RHEA)
1819 (Capt. McGill's Co.): George Gotherd 1 WP
1823 (Capt. Howrd's Co.): George Gothard 1 WP
James Gothard 1 WP
1830 RHEA CENSUS
Allen Gothard 2000001 - 01131 p. 381
George Gothard 20001 - 02001 p. 380
James Gothard 20001 - 20001 p. 380
1840 RHEA CENSUS
Allen Gothard 10200001 - 1100101
George Gothard 00301001 - 120001
1850 RHEA CENSUS
Ann Gothard 13: see Lewis Morgan
Allen Gothard 56 (SC), Mariah 48 (SC), Joseph 23, Elias 21, Lucinda 16 p. 634-648
Emeline Gothard 33 (SC), Peter 15, Ann 13, Amanda 12, Josiah A. 6, Rufus S. 4, Zachary T. 2 p. 634-646
George Gothard 55 (SC)(Farmer), Nancy 49, Jane C. 22, William B. 20 (Farmer), Susan E. 16 p. 635-654
John C. Gothard 31 (Shoemaker), Catharine 28, Larkin G. 3, John T. 1 p. 635-653
MARRIAGES (RHEA)
Angeline Gotherd to John Moore q.v.
Ann Gothart to John Lea q.v.
Betsy Gothard to Lewis Morgan q.v.
George Gothard to Nancy Carter, 12 May 1818, Isaac Benson Bm (A)
Ira Gothard to Elizabeth Blythe, 21 Mar 1832, Landon Carter Bm (A)
James Gothard to Susanna Lea, 8 Dec 1821 (no return) (AR) [1850 Hamilton Census: James Gothard 45, Susan 42, Mary 28, Ira 21, John 18, Mahala 16, Lewis 13, Nancy 11, Isabel 9, Arabel 7, Margaret 6, Ibba 2]
John C. Gothard to Catherine Birwick or Barwick, 9 Oct 1844 (no return), Lewis Morgan Jr. Bm (AR)
Joseph Gothard to Elizabeth Calvin, 7 June 1850 (same), S.C. Foust JP (R)
Larkin Gothard to Louisa Taylor, 28 July 1830, James C. Airhart Bm (A) [Louisa, dau of Robert and Catharine Sevier Taylor][1850 Hamilton Census: Larkin Gothard 43, Louisa 40, Mary 18, Nancy 10, Henry 5, Elizabeth 3]
Larkin G. Gothard to Elizabeth Butler, 26 Oct 1848 (28 Dec), Washington Morgan JP (R) [1850 Hamilton Census: Larkin Gothard 23, Hulda 20]
Oma Gothart to Archibald McKissick q.v.
MISCELLANEOUS (RHEA and MEIGS)
Elias Gothard: Private, Mexican War
George Gothard: Bondsman for James Steen, 1820
" " Bondsman for Anthony Brown, 1822
Larkin G. Gothard: Private, Mexican War
William Gothard: Bondsman for John Gutherie, 1831

- - - - - - - - - - - - -

GOUGE

TAXES (RHEA)
1808 (John Henry's List): James Gouge 1 WP
James Goue Sr. 300a E Fk Richland Cr
(Jonthan Fine's List): John Gouge 300a Piney River
(John Henry's List): Josiah Gouge 2 WP, 180a
Martin Gouge 1 WP
MARRIAGES (RHEA)
Dorothy Gouge to John Poe q.v.
Polly Gouge to John Morrow q.v.
MISCELLANEOUS (RHEA)
Josiah Gouge: Bondsman for John Poe, 1812
James Gouge Sr.: On first Grand Jury, 1808

- - - - - - - - - - - - -

GOULD

MISCELLANEOUS (RHEA)
S. E. Gould: JP 1850

- - - - - - - - - - - - -

GOWING

MARRIAGES (RHEA)
Jane Gowing to Finney Rawlins q.v.

- - - - - - - - - - - - -

GRAGG

1830 RHEA CENSUS
Abner Gragg 102001 - 122001 p. 356

- - - - - - - - - - - - -

GRAHAM

MARRIAGES (RHEA)
Abraham Graham to E.C. Seymore, 8 July 1847 (18 July), Charles Cox JP (R)
MISCELLANEOUS (RHEA)
John Graham: Bondsman for John Purdon 1809
William Graham: Bondsman for Thomas Jones, 1835

- - - - - - - - - - - - -

GRANT

MISCELLANEOUS (MEIGS)
William Grant: Ocoee District

- - - - - - - - - - - - -

GRANTEM

MARRIAGES (RHEA)
Mary Ann Grantem to Alexander Vines q.v.

- - - - - - - - - - - - -

GRAVELY

MARRIAGES (RHEA)
Mary Gravely to Thomas Drennon q.v.
Richard Gravely to Elizabeth Harwood, 11 Nov 1812 (no return), Philip Taylor Bm (AR)

- - - - - - - - - - - - -

GRAVES

1840 MEIGS CENSUS
Union Graves 0101 - 00001 p. 229
MISCELLANEOUS (MEIGS)
S. Graves: JP(?) 1842
W. C. Graves: MG MEC 1847

- - - - - - - - - - - - -

GRAY

TAXES (RHEA)
1823 (Capt. Howard's Co.): Edward Gary 200a
1830 RHEA CENSUS
Edmund Gray 000030001 - 00001001 p. 380
1840 RHEA CENSUS
John Gray 200001 - 000001
Stephen Gray 000001 - 0000020001
1850 RHEA CENSUS
John Gray 48 (Farmer), Malinda 45, Edward 14, Abraham 12, William 10, Benjamin 8, Jane 6, Stephen 2, Nancy WALLACE 76 (NC) p. 637-668
Stephen Gray 42 (Farmer), Nancy 52, Ann 50 p. 630-612
MARRIAGES (MEIGS)
Nancy Gray to John Hatfield q.v.
William J. Gray to Lydia Burton, 23 May 1838 (same), James Patterson Esq.
MISCELLANEOUS (RHEA)
William K. Gray: Bondsman for Edmund Worley, 1833

- - - - - - - - - - - - -

GREEN / GREENE

1830 RHEA CENSUS
Brincle Green 00121 - 0010101 p. 357
J. S. Green 200001 - 02201 p. 379
James R. Green 0010001 - 311101 p. 355
Jno Green 00001 - 30001 p. 368
Robert Green 1000101 - 200001 p. 390
William Greene 11100100001 - 21001 p. 358
1840 RHEA CENSUS
James R. Green 00010001 - 0310101
Joshua S. Green 2120001 - 012201
Robert Green 00100001 - 0111001
1840 MEIGS CENSUS
Hannah Green 0 - 1000010001 p. 242
William Green 2111101 - 012101 p. 246
1850 RHEA CENSUS
James B. Green 9, William B. 7: see James D. McFall
Joshua S. Green 52 (Carpenter), Ann 48, Sarah 25, George 23 (Farmer), Jane 23, Nancy 20, Thomas 19 (Farmer), James 15, Alexander 12, Robert 7, Harvey ALEXANDER 18 (Farmer) p. 636-660
William A. Green 25 (Carpenter), Lyda 17, Susan J. McPHERSON 15 p. 636-661
1850 MEIGS CENSUS
Daniel Green 50 (NC)(Wheelwright), Jane 18, Richard F. 14, James K. 12, Thomas H.H. 10 p. 813-771
Hannah Green 49 (NC), Emily V. 18, Marion (m) 2 p. 802-688
Jacob Green 29 (Shoemaker), Susan 37, Winny 16, Cassandra 6, Manda 4 p. 800-672 [Jacob married Susannah Crisp on 26 Oct 1842 in McMinn Co]
John Green 31 (Va)(Farmer), Mahala 21, Henry C. 5, Manda 2 p. 800-681 [John married Mahala Bledsoe on 11 Mar 1843 in McMinn County]
Nancy Green 53 (Va) Jackson 16 (Farmer), Daniel 14, James 12, Elizabeth 11, Samuel 9, Virginia C. 1 p. 795-646
Rotan Green 20 (Farmer), Rebecca 18, Thomas 1 p. 797-665
Thomas Green 25 (Farmer), Susan 23, James 1 p. 800-675 [Thomas married Susan Foister on 20 Dec 1849 in Roane County]
William Green 57 (Va)(Farmer), Ruth 49 (Ky), Henry 26, Martin 24, Caroline 19, William H. 18, Elizabeth 16, Daniel 14, Farly 12, Thomas B. 10, Robert B. 7 p. 811-751 [William married Ruth Westmoreland on 30 Mar 1820 in Roane County]

MARRIAGES (RHEA)
Betsy Greene to John Lea q.v.
Betsy Green to Jonathan Fry q.v.
Betsey Greene to John Bird q.v.
Elizabeth Green to John Thompson q.v.
Joshua S. Green to Anne Alexander, 10 Jan 1821 (11 Jan) A. David JP, John Witt Bm (AR) [Joshua, son of George and Judith Spillman Green]
Juda Greene to William Morgan q.v.
Matthias Green to Betsy Blythe, 8 May 1832 (same), Oliver C. Miller MG, Wm Ferguson Bm (AR)
Sutton Green to Elizabeth Bird, 24 June 1829, George W. Miller Bm (A)
W.A. Green to L.C. McFerson, 20 Sept 1849 (no return) (R) [William A., son of Joshua and Annie Alexander Green]
MARRIAGES (MEIGS)
John S. Green to Pheby Newkirk, 19 Sept 1842 (20 Sept), Jesse Locke MG
Lurena Green to A.H. McCall q.v.
Nancy Green to Levy Bradley q.v.
Sariah Green to James Franks q.v.
Sarah Jane Green to William Johnson q.v.
MISCELLANEOUS (RHEA)
Joshua Green: Bondsman for John H. Alexander, 1827
William Green: JP 1834-36, 1843
MISCELLANEOUS (MEIGS)
Harvey Green: Surety for James Briggs, 1850
William Green: MG 1839-49

- - - - - - - - - - - -

GREENLER

1850 RHEA CENSUS
Margaret Greenler 50, Elizabeth 15, Arthur McKEE 46 (Va) p. 536-35

- - - - - - - - - - - -

GREENWAY

MISCELLANEOUS (RHEA)
Richard Greenway: Named on Surveyor General's list for residents south of the Tenn River

- - - - - - - - - - - -

GREENWOOD

MARRIAGES (RHEA)
John Greenwood to Nancy Lauderdale, 25 Dec 1823 (28 Dec), M. Donald MG, Robert Cozby Bm (AR)
Syntha L. Greenwood to Samuel E. Foust q.v.

- - - - - - - - - - - -

GREER / GREAR

1840 RHEA CENSUS
John Grear 110001000001 - 20101
William Greer 11001 - 011001
MARRIAGES (RHEA)
James C. Greer to Nancy Farlis, 15 Mar 1828 (same), Robert Cooley JP, Abraham Cox Bm (AR)

- - - - - - - - - - - -

GREGG

MISCELLANEOUS (MEIGS)
James Gregg: Hiwassee District, Lower Goodfield area

- - - - - - - - - - - -

GREGORY

1840 MEIGS CENSUS
David Gregory 00001 - 200010001 p. 227
George Gregory 200001 - 10001 p. 227
Richard Gregory 1100001 - 1121101 p. 227
Sally Gregory 0 - 0000100001 p. 227
1850 MEIGS CENSUS
David Gregory 40 (Farmer), Elizabeth 31, Mary Jane 13, Cynthia A. 11, George 9, James 7, Sally 5, William 3, Wesley H. 1 p. 720-59
George Gregory 45 (SC)(Farmer), Dianna 38, Sarah J. 15, Thomas 13, John 11, David 9, Hiram 7, James 5, Catharine 3 p. 721-60
MARRIAGES (MEIGS)
Elizabeth E. Gregory to William Maberry q.v.
Green C.M. Gregory to Katherine Hill, 9 Jan 1846 (21 Jan), Ezekiel Ward MG [1850 McMinn Census: Green C. Gregory 23, Catharine 30, Matilda 3, William 1]
Miss ---- Gregory to Sterling Shelton q.v.
MISCELLANEOUS (MEIGS)
David Gregory: Ocoee District
George Gregory: Ocoee District
Green Gregory: Surety for Wilson Baker 1850

- - - - - - - - - - - -

GRICE

1850 MEIGS CENSUS
James M. Grice 39 (NC)(Farmer), Nancy 26 (Va), William M. 7, Thomas J. 4, Elijah T. 2 p. 747-274
MARRIAGES (MEIGS)
James Grice to Nancy Mavity, 6 July 1842 (8 July), Wm Johns JP

- - - - - - - - - - - -

GRIFFIN / GRIFFEN

TAXES (RHEA)
1823 (Capt. Piper's Co.): Thomas Griffen 1 WP
1840 MEIGS CENSUS
Samuel Griffin 0001 - 1001 p. 239
MARRIAGES (MEIGS)
Anderson Griffin to Iseller Ann Griffin, 23 July 1842 (24 July), Thomas V. Atchley JP
Jno Griffin to Acilla A. Daniel, 17 Mar 1840
William Griffin to Elizabeth Harvy, 8 Sept 1843 (9 Sept), R. Stockton JP

- - - - - - - - - - - -

GRIFFITH / GRIFFET

1830 RHEA CENSUS
James Griffith 00001 -101 p. 360
Jane Griffith 00001 - 0000101 p. 395
1840 RHEA CENSUS
Henry Griffith 120001 - 10101
1840 MEIGS CENSUS
James Griffith 010001 - 00101 p. 240
1850 RHEA CENSUS
Henry Griffith 46 (Physician), Catharine 39, Jane 14, Henry C. 12, Azariah 10 p. 636-662
Levi Griffith 72 (Va)(Farmer), Jane 66 (Va), William DANIEL 18 (Farmer) p. 615-505
[Levi married Jane Shelton in 1801]
1850 MEIGS CENSUS
James Griffith 43 (Farmer), Mary 34, Gideon 16 (Farmer), Eliza Ann 14, James 10, Thomas 6, Rebecca 4, John 1 p. 801-677
MARRIAGES (RHEA)
Edward Griffitt or Griffet to Barbary Hays, 23 Feb 1824 (26 Feb), Fred K. Fulkerson JP, Nathaniel Hays Bm (AR) [1850 Monroe Census: Edward Griffith 40, Barbary 40, John 25]
Henry Griffith to Catherine Bell, 24 Apr 1832 (same), Oliver C. Miller MG, John Parker Bm (AR)
James Griffith or Griffett to Mary Raglin, 18 Dec 1828 (same), Stephen Winton JP (A) [Mary, dau of Gideon and Artemisa Wilson Ragland]
Leta Griffith to John Witt q.v.
MARRIAGES (MEIGS)
Salin Griffith to John L. Baldwin q.v.
MISCELLANEOUS (RHEA)
Henry Griffith: JP 1838-39
" " Bondsman for John Witt, 1827
MISCELLANEOUS (MEIGS)
James Griffith: Purchased Lots 62,78 in Decatur, 1836

GRIGSBY

TAXES (RHEA)
1823 (Capt. Piper's Co.): Samuel Grigsby 1 WP
1850 MEIGS CENSUS
Benjamin F. Grigsby 30 (Farmer), Washington L. 21 (Farmer), Mary Jane 12, Eli 8, Samuel 5, Elik 7, Nancy R. 3, James A. 1 p. 787-581
Samuel Grigsby 60 (Va), Martha 53, Cyrus 18, Mary Jane 23, Rhoda 21, Martha 16, Almira T. 14, Julia 12 p. 786-580 [Samuel H. Grigsby married Polly Lindsey on 4 Dec 1815 in Roane County]
MARRIAGES (RHEA)
Charles Grigsby to Delphia Witt, 21 Jan 1832 (26 Jan), Oliver C. Miller MG, Thos W. Munsey Bm (AR)
MARRIAGES (MEIGS)
Nancy R. Grigsby to Thomas C. Jordan q.v.

GRIMMETT

MARRIAGES (RHEA)
Abraham Grimmett to Sally Wear, 2 Jan 1818, Hugh Berry Bm (R)

GRIMSLEY / GIMSLEY

1840 RHEA CENSUS
John Grimsley 220001 - 0100010001
1850 RHEA CENSUS
John Grimsley 41 (Farmer), Eleanor C. 40, James P. 19 (Farmer), Joseph S. 17 (Farmer), George K. 15, William 12, John M. 8, Eliza E. 3, Nancy E. 1, Kezziah GRIMSLEY 92 (Va) p. 554-125
Joseph Gimsley 38 (Carpenter), Mahala C. 23, John H. 13, Mark K. 12, Sarah J. 10, William S. 8, Margaret E. 6, Minerva A.F. 2, Emily A. 1/12 p. 553-121 [Joseph Grimsley married Mahaley Catharine Hale on 5 Nov 1846 in Roane County]

GRISHAM / GRESHAM / GRISSUM

1840 MEIGS CENSUS
James Grisham 011001 - 31001 p. 225
Jesse Grisham 021001 - 310001 p. 225
Richard Grisham 00220001 - 120010101 p. 225
1850 MEIGS CENSUS
Ervin Grisham 19 (Farmer), Mary Jane 23 ("married within year") p. 719-50
Jesse Grisham 45 (Farmer), Levina 43, James M. 21, John N. 14, Lucinda Jane 16, Peggy C. 12, Ruth E. 10, Mary A. 9, William C. 8, Levina 6, Jesse M. 4, Harriet M. 3, Sarah E. 1 p. 719-51
William Grisham 27 (Farmer), Mary Ann 22, Minerva Jane 4, Malinda E. 2 p. 717-33
MARRIAGES (MEIGS)
Calloway Gresham to Rebecca S. Thompson, 16 Aug 1845 (17 Aug), Jesse Gresham JP
Peggy Grissum to Carter Young q.v.
Richard Grisham to Eliza J. Bower, 2 Sept 1844 (3 Sept), Jesse Grisham JP
[1850 Bradley Census: Richard Grissum 28, Eliza 22, Elizabeth 5, Nancy 2, Benjamin 1]
MISCELLANEOUS (MEIGS)
Jesse Grisham: JP 1844-49
" " Surety for W.J. Young, 1850
Lyre Grisham: Teacher, District 1, 1842
Richard Grisham: JP(?) 1840
William Grisham: JP(?) 1845

GROSS

TAXES (RHEA)
1823 (Capt. Brown's Co.): Jacob Gross 1 WP
1830 RHEA CENSUS
George Gross 00012001 - 01000001 p. 385
Jacob Gross 320001 - 0001 p. 370
1840 MEIGS CENSUS
Jacob Gross 1220001 - 2000001 p. 227
William Gross 202001 - 010001 p. 228
1850 MEIGS CENSUS
George Gross 26 (Farmer), Manda 21, James 5, Jane 3, Mary L. 2, William E. 1 p. 734-165
Jacob Gross 56 (Farmer), Mary 47, Jacob 21 (Farmer), Mason 19 (Farmer), Margaret 16, Catharine 13, Alexander R. 10, Mary L. 2 p. 726-107

MARRIAGES (RHEA)

George Gross to Lucinda Johnson, 20 Nov 1835 (same), Matthew Hubbert JP, William Crumpton Bm (AR)

Jacob Gross to Polly McClanahan, 20 Aug 1820 (same), William Locke Bm (A)

William Gross to Mahala Sexton, 3 Dec 1833 (5 Dec), F. David JP (R)

MARRIAGES (MEIGS)

Francis Gross to Mary Guess, 20 Jan 1848 (same), Jesse Locke MG [1850 Hamilton Census: Francis Gross 25, Mary 22, James 2]

George Gross to Sarah Armstrong, 19 Aug 1843 (20 Aug), Jesse Martin JP

John Gross to Eliza Jane Bear, 27 Feb 1844 (28 Feb), John Seabourn JP

Masoner Gross to Fisha Gess, 26 Dec 1850, John W. Gamble Sur

Pleasant Gross to Polly Dyer, 12 Nov 1845 (13 Nov), Jesse Locke MG [1850 Hamilton Census: Pleasant Gross 23, Mary 22, John 2, Louisa 1]

MISCELLANEOUS (RHEA)

William Gross: Bondsman for Solomon Henry 1832
" " Bondsman for James Bryant, 1833
" " Bondsman for John Bennett, 1834

\- - - - - - - - - - - -

GRUBB / GRUBBS / GRUB

1830 RHEA CENSUS

Eldridge Grub 00001 - 2100001 p. 372

1840 MEIGS CENSUS

Abner Grubb 010001 - 10101 p. 230

Edward Grubbs 12001 - 20001101 p. 229

1850 MEIGS CENSUS

Eldred Grubb 40 (Va)(Farmer), Nancy 37 (SC), William C. 18, Alfred G. 16, James M. 14, Frances V. 12, Julian 10, Nancy P. 8, Andrew J. 6, Jasper N. 2 p. 743-240

MARRIAGES (RHEA)

Ambler Grubbs to Rebecca M. Carroll or McCarroll, 4 Dec 1828 (same), Archibald Gerald [Fitzgerald] MG, Josiah Houser Bm (AR)

Eldred Grubb to Nancy McKenzie, 12 Oct 1831 (same), Robert Cooley JP, Josiah Howser Bm (AR)

MISCELLANEOUS (MEIGS)

Eldridge Grubb: Lived in District 2

William C. Grubb: Mexican War (discharged on Surgeon's certificate)

\- - - - - - - - - - - -

GUFFEE / GUFFY / GUFEY

TAXES (RHEA)

1823 (Capt. Howard's Co.): James Guffee 1 WP

1840 MEIGS CENSUS

Ephraim Guffy 200001 - 021001 p. 224

MARRIAGES (RHEA)

James Griffie or Guffee to Peggy Casteel, 26 Mar 1834 (no return), Samuel Casteel Bm (AR)

Nancy Guffey to William Thomason q.v.

Reway Guffee to John Walker q.v.

Sally Gufffy to John Marshall q.v.

MARRIAGES (MEIGS)

Jacob Gufey to Elizabeth Lauder, 4 June 1840 (same), James Patterson JP

\- - - - - - - - - - - -

GULLION

MARRIAGES (RHEA)

Polly Ann Gullion to William Corvin q.v.

\- - - - - - - - - - - -

GUN

1840 MEIGS CENSUS

James Gun or Geen 10001 - 001001 p. 238

\- - - - - - - - - - - -

GUNTER / GUNTHER

1830 RHEA CENSUS

Jno Gunther 10001 - 01001 p. 384

1850 RHEA CENSUS

John Gunter 50 (NC)(Farmer), Tempa 50, Elizabeth 28, Adeline 19, Seth 16 (Farmer), Emeline 14, William 11, Wilson FRAZIER 7 p. 607-481

1850 MEIGS CENSUS

Lewis Gunter 23 (Farmer), Mary Ann 26, George A. 8, Andrew J. 5 p. 770-453

\- - - - - - - - - - - -

GUTHRIE / GUTHREY

MARRIAGES (RHEA)

John Guthrie or Guthrey to Keziah Bunch, 24 June 1831 (25 June), Wm Smith JP, Wm Gothard Bm (AR)

Nancy Guthrie or Guttery to Wm Tomison / Thompson q.v.

\- - - - - - - - - - - -

GWIN / GWINN / GWYNN / GUINN / GUINE

TAXES (RHEA)

1823 (Capt. Wilson's Co.): Almond Gwin 1 WP
Bartholomew Gwin 1 WP

1830 RHEA CENSUS

Absolom Gwynn 210001 - 20101 p. 374

Almon Gwynn 230101 - 102001001 p. 374

1840 RHEA CENSUS

William Gwinn 0000001 - 0000001

1840 MEIGS CENSUS

Absolom Guinn 1112001 - 112011 p. 243

Barthollomew Guinn 00001001 - 00211001 p. 238

Joshua Guinn 10001 - 20001 p. 238

1850 MEIGS CENSUS

Abner Gwin 25 (Farmer), Malinda Jane 22, Andrew J. 1 p. 784-56

Absalom Gwin 57 (Va)(Farmer), Kissiah 50, John 16 (Distiller), Rachael 14, George 12, Elizabeth 10, Kissiah 6 p. 776-500

Almon Gwin 32 (Blacksmith), Nancy S.A. 30, Jesse N. 8, George C. 1 p. 774-485

Joshua Gwin 36 (Farmer), Elizabeth 36, John 14, Mary 12, Susannah 11, Lennard B. 10, Joel F. 8, Andrew 6, Sarah L. 4, Bartholomew 2, Thomas J. 1 p. 741-225

Sarah Gwin 62 (Va), Mary Ann 2, Nancy J. 22 p. 772-466

MARRIAGES (RHEA)

Elizabeth Gwinn to John W. Blevins q.v.

Jacob C. Guin to Elizabeth Casteel, 18 June 1840 (same), R. Waterhouse JP (R)

Jane Guin or Gerin to John Meriott q.v.

Joshua Gwin or Givens to Elizabeth Brooks, 6 Feb 1835, William Fairbanks Bm (A)

Martha Guin or Guerin to James H. Dun q.v.

William Gwin to Margaret Woodard or Woodward, 5 May 1818 (same), H. Collins JP, Jacob Brown Bm (AR)

MARRIAGES (MEIGS)

Abner Guinn to Malindy Jane Smith, 11 Apr 1850, James Smith Sur

Malinda H. Guinn to William J. Abel q.v.

Martha L. Guinn to Calvin C. Robeson q.v.

Matilda Guinn to William Buster q.v.

Sarah Guinn to James Smith q.v.

William Guine to Judy D. Edds, 30 Dec 1847 (same), Nathaniel Barnett MG

MISCELLANEOUS (RHEA)

Jacob Gwin: JP 1840

Joshua Gwin: Bondsman for Josiah Cranmore, 1838

William Gwin: Bondsman for Henry Reece, 1828

" " Carpenter on new jail in Washington, 1827

MISCELLANEOUS (RHEA)

Abner Guinn: Surety for James Smith, 1850

" " Mexican War (discharged on Surgeon's certificate)

Almond Guinn: Hiwassee District, Sewee Creek area

Bartholomew Guin: Hiwassee District, Sewee Creek area

" " Purchased Lots 73,79,80,83,84 in Decatur, 1836

- - - - - - - - - - - - -

HACKER / HACKLER

1840 MEIGS CENSUS

Alfred Hackler 10001 - 10001 p. 225

1850 MEIGS CENSUS

Julius Hackler 36 (Farmer), Susan 24, Isaac J. 6, Joseph C. 3 p. 804-705

Thomas Hackler 42, Jane 39, Manda 18, Harriet 17, John 15, William 14, Mary 10, Malissa 8, Rebecca 5, James 2 p. 783-550

MARRIAGES (MEIGS)

Crisley Hackler to Mary Ann Roark, 6 Oct 1840

Julius Hackler to Susan Emery, 15 Nov 1844 (same), Mark Renfrow JP

MISCELLANEOUS (MEIGS)

Charles [Crisley] Hackler: Cherokee Removal muster roll

Henry Hackler: Cherokee Removal muster roll, 1836

- - - - - - - - - - - - -

HACKETT

1830 RHEA CENSUS

Samuel R. Hacket 000111 - 000010001 p. 384

1840 RHEA CENSUS

Samuel R. Hackett 110000 - 20001

1850 RHEA CENSUS

Samuel R. Hackett 51 (Farmer), Ann 87 (Pa), Harriet H. 46, Wright S. 16 (Farmer), John P. 15, Margaret A. 10 p. 609-587

MARRIAGES (RHEA)

Anne R. Hackett to Jesse Coffee q.v.

Cinthia W. Hackett to Lusk Colville q.v.

Elizabeth Hackett to Richard G. Waterhouse q.v.

Margaret Hackett to Allen Kennedy q.v.

Mary Hackett to James More q.v.

Samuel R. Hackett to Mary Ann Smith, 24 Jan 1833 (same), James Wilson JP, John Hoyal Bm (AR)

MISCELLANEOUS (RHEA)

Betsy Hackett: Lot in "Southern Liberties" of Washington

Cynthia W. Hackett: Lot in "Southern Liberties"

Samuel R. Hackett: Bondsman for Orville Paine, 1828

" " " Bondsman for Isaac W. Geren, 1830

" " " Bondsman for Wright Smith, 1831

" " " Bondsman for Levi Garen, 1832

" " " Bm for Benjamin Suddath, 1832

" " " Bondsman for Joseph Winfield, 1834

" " " Bm for Thomas V. Atchley, 1836

" " " JP 1844-1850

" " " Sheriff 1836-1840

William P. Hackett: Bondsman for Allen Kennedy, 1818

- - - - - - - - - - - - -

HACKLEM

MISCELLANEOUS (RHEA)

John Hacklem: On Surveyor's list for land south of Tenn Ri

- - - - - - - - - - - - -

HACKWORTH

TAXES (RHEA)

1808 (Jonathan Fine's List):

Nichodemus Hackworth 1 WP, 100a Piney Ri

1819 (Capt. W.S. Bradley's Dist.): Henry Hackworth 1 WP

1823 (Capt. Smith's Co.): John Hackworth 1 WP

Henry Hackworth 1 WP

1830 RHEA CENSUS

Rebecca Hackworth 0 - 220001 p. 373

MISCELLANEOUS (RHEA and MEIGS)

Henry Hackworth: Hiwassee District, Lower Goodfield

John Hackworth: On Surveyor's list, land south of Tenn Ri

N. Hackworth: Bondsman for Joseph Erp, 1813

- - - - - - - - - - - - -

HALE / HALES / HAIL

TAXES (RHEA)
1819 (Capt. W.S. Bradley's Dist.):
----- Hale [or Hall] 1 WP, 1 BP, 1 Town Lot
1823 (Capt. Wilson's Co.): George Hale 1 WP
(Capt. Howerton's Co.): Hezekiah Hale 1 WP
1830 RHEA CENSUS
Abednego Hale 00211001 - 00011001 p. 360
George Hale 12001 - 101001 p. 386
1840 RHEA CENSUS
Abednego Hale 000010001 - 00001
A. G. Hale 00002 - 0001
George Hale 2013001 - 0011001
Hezekiah Hale 01010001 - 2112001
James M. Hale 00002 - 00001
1850 RHEA CENSUS
Claudius Hale 29 (Farmer), Delila 30, George W. 6, Harriet P. 3 p. 566-195
George Hale 51 (Farmer), Susan 22, William 18 (Farmer), John 14, Wyly M. 12, George H. 10, Margaret E. 5, James 1 p. 567-196
Hezekiah Hale 60 (Farmer), Roseana 50, Polly 29, John 25, Eliza J. 17, Abednego 15, Bethena 13, Ann E. 11, Margaret D. 18 [may be an 8, as 1 is very dim] p. 553-118
James M. Hale 34 (Farmer), Mary 30 (Va), Houston M. 8, Phebe A. 7, John G. 5, James J. 4, Myra J. 2, Mary E. 2/12 p. 619-535
Jefferson Hale 30 (Unk)(Farmer), Elizabeth 26, Jane 2 p. 617-516
Michael A. Hale 24: see Martha Clack
Nancy J. Hale 16: see James Mayo
Polly Hale 30: see Samuel Stuart
1850 MEIGS CENSUS
George W. Hales 33 (Tailor), Mary Ann 25 (Va), Hazy S. 25, Elizabeth 7, Lea 6, David 2, John 1 p. 773-481
MARRIAGES (RHEA)
A.G. Hale to H.E.J. Beard, 12 Jan 1839 (10 Jan)[sic], B.R. McDonald JP (R)
Elizabeth A. Hail to Samuel Stewart q.v.
George Hail to Susan Eaton, 5 Nov 1847 (same), T.J. Creede JP (R)
George W. Haley or Hale to Lucinda Henderson, 21 July 1818 (21 June)[sic], Abraham Howard JP (AR)
J.M. Hale to Mary McDonald, 18 Jan 1840 (21 Jan), Wm Bowman JP(?) (R)
Jane Hale to H. Mahaffy q.v.
Mahala Hale to James Spence q.v.
Thomas J. Hail to Elizabeth Spence, 8 July 1847 (same), James Hooker JP (R)
MARRIAGES (MEIGS)
Claudius Hail to Delila Ledford, 26 Nov 1843 (same), John Huff Esq.
George Hail to Mary A. Woods, 18 Dec 1845 (same), Drury L. Godsey MG
M.P. Hail to Sarah Baldwin, 7 Aug 1844
MISCELLANEOUS (RHEA)
George Hale: Bondsman for Josiah Keenam, 1827
George W. Hale: Bondsman for John D. Jones, 1816
James Hail: Bondsman for James Majors, 1819
James M. Hale: Bondsman for Henry Glaze, 1839
William F. Hail: Private, Mexican War

\- - - - - - - - - - - - -

HALEY / HALLEY

MARRIAGES (RHEA)
Allen Haley to Lydia or Liddey Roddy, 20 Apr 1827 (3 May), Jesse Thompson JP (AR) [Allen, son of John C. and Elizabeth Matlock Haley; in 1850, Allen, 46 yrs old, was living in McMinn Co with his second wife, Elizabeth Rice Haley]
Eliza B. Haley to Edmund Bean q.v.
MISCELLANEOUS (RHEA)
Mark Halley: Bondsman for Wilson Nevins, 1815

\- - - - - - - - - - - - -

HALL

TAXES (RHEA)
1819 (Capt. W.S. Bradley's Dist.):
---- Hale or Hall 1 WP, 1 BP, 1 Town Lot
1840 MEIGS CENSUS
Elijah Hall 10001 - 110001 p. 233
John Hall 121010001 - 000101 p. 226
1850 MEIGS CENSUS
John Hall 69 (Va)(Farmer), Delilah 48 (Va), Jesse F. 18 (Farmer), Joseph M. 17 (Farmer), William H. 13, Martha D. 9, Andrew J. 7 p. 721-63
MARRIAGES (RHEA)
Elijah M. Hall to Mary Phillips, 26 May 1834 (22 Sept), V.H. Giles JP, Thomas Hall Bm (AR)
James Hall to Mary Rockholt, 14 Oct 1826 (30 Oct), Thomas Cox JP, Isaac Braselton Bm (AR)
Jane Hall to William Johnson q.v.
Joseph Hall to Catharine Matlock, 31 May 1825 (2 June), Thomas Hall MG, John Mahan Bm (AR)
Polly Hall to John Jackson q.v.
William Hall to Isabella Moon or Moore, 14 Nov 1821 (18 Nov), John Cozby JP, John Moore Bm (AR)
MARRIAGES (MEIGS)
Rebecca Hall to John Brooks q.v.
William Hall to Eleanor Fairbanks, 22 Sept 1847 (same), D.L. Godsey MG
[1850 Bledsoe Census: William Hall 23, Eleanor 21, Tennessee 9/12, John FAIRBANKS 48]
MISCELLANEOUS (RHEA and MEIGS)
John Hall: Ocoee District
Robert Hall: MG 1828
Roswell Hall: Bondsman for Charles A. Taylor, 1816
" " Signed petition to move Indian Agency
Thomas Hall: MG 1825, 1831
" " Bondsman for Elijah M. Hall, 1834
" " Hiwassee District

\- - - - - - - - - - - - -

HAMIE

MARRIAGES (RHEA)
William Hamie to Polly Brook, 18 July 1835 (23 July), Thomas C. Clingham or Clingan MG, Moses Brook Bm (AR)

\- - - - - - - - - - - - -

HAMILTON / HAMBLETON

TAXES (RHEA)
1808 (James Campbell's List): James Hamilton 1 WP
1819 (Capt. John Lewis' Dist.): Thomas Hamilton 1 WP
1823 (Capt. Braselton's Co.): Thomas Hamilton 1 WP
1830 RHEA CENSUS
Thomas Hamilton 000020001 - 10021001 p. 386
1840 RHEA CENSUS
Thomas Hamilton 11000000001 - 01110001
1840 MEIGS CENSUS
Robert Hambleton 020021 - 20012 p. 236
1850 MEIGS CENSUS
Rebecca Hamilton 37 (Va), Albert 15, Margaret 13, Martha Jane 11, Mary Ann 9, Narcissa 7, Samuel H. 4, James H. 2 p. 772-467 [widow of Robert]
MARRIAGES (RHEA)
John H. Hamilton to Keziah Applegate, 29 May 1826 (3 June), Jesse Thompson JP, Samuel Applegate Bm (AR)
Thomas Hamilton to Polly Kirksey, 27 Apr 1818 (30 Apr), Matthew Donald MG, John Robinson Bm (AR)
MISCELLANEOUS (RHEA and MEIGS)
James Hamilton: Hiwassee District, Ten Mile Stand area
R.M. Hamilton: Registerar, Meigs County, 1840-44
Thomas Hamilton: Hiwassee District, Pinhook Ferry area
" " 1835 and 1841 list of Revolutionary War Pensioners (80 years old in 1830)

\- - - - - - - - - - - - -

HAMINTREE

MARRIAGES (RHEA)
Lucinda Hamintree to Henry Black q.v.

\- - - - - - - - - - - - -

HAMMONS / HAMMOND

1850 RHEA CENSUS
Elcany Hammons 26 (Unk)(Farmer), Mary 26 (NC), Martha E. 5, John E. 2, Campbell 1 p. 542-57
Milton Hammons 25 (Farmer), Martha A. 20 (NC), William S. 3, Margaret F. 2, Absalum E. 3/12 p. 537-33
MARRIAGES (RHEA)
Jeremiah Hammond to Milly Robinson, 25 Sept 1813 (same), William Long JP and Bm (AR)
Milton Hammons to Martha Ann Harris, 22 Sept 1845 (24 Sept), B.W. Holloway JP (R)
MISCELLANEOUS (RHEA)
Jeremiah Hammons: Bondsman for Lewis James, 1813
" " Bondsman for Eli Marrs, 1813

\- - - - - - - - - - - - -

HAMPTON

MARRIAGES (RHEA)
John Hampton to Rachel Walker, 24 Dec 1833 (25 Dec), Jesse Thompson JP, Jesse Roddy Bm (AR)
[1850 Bradley Census: John Hampton 37, Racheal 38, Robert 12, Mary 11, Wade 10, John W. 8, Nancy 7, Deniza 6, Racheal 5, James H. 4, Infant 1]
MISCELLANEOUS (MEIGS)
Wade L. Hampton: Lived at Cottonport

\- - - - - - - - - - - - -

HANCOCK

MARRIAGES (MEIGS)
James Hancock to Lavina Renoe, 9 Oct 1838 (same), Jacob Price JP

\- - - - - - - - - - - - -

HANDY
(see also HARDY)

MISCELLANEOUS (RHEA)
John Handy: Bondsman for Jonathan Barnes, 185

\- - - - - - - - - - - - -

HANES / HAINES / HAYNES
(see also HINDS / HINES)

TAXES (RHEA)
1819 (Capt. Wm McCray's Co.): Henry Haynes 1 WP
1823 (Capt. Howerton's Co.):
Henry Haynes 1 WP, 58½a foot Walden's Ridge
1830 RHEA CENSUS
Ira Haines 110001 - 1000001 p. 373
Jeremiah Haines 0100011 - 0022002 p. 365
Samuel Harue or Hanes 300001 - 01111001 p. 357
Thomas Haines 01001001 - 011001 p. 395
Thomas Haines 310000001 - 220001 p. 364
1840 MEIGS CENSUS
Ira Hanes 0011001 - 0010001 p. 232
1850 MEIGS CENSUS
Ira Hanes 51 (Mass)(Farmer), Rebecca 54 (SC), Joseph T. 26 (SC)(Farmer), Malinda 24 (SC), John W. 22 p. 748-286
MARRIAGES (RHEA)
Almira Haynes to Isaac Garrison q.v.
Margaret Haines to Henry Hines q.v.
Richard Haynes to Catherine Majors, 28 Feb 1829 (1 Mar), Jesse Thompson JP, John R. Paul Bm (AR)
William Hains to Mandy Jane Eaton, 3 July 1843 (6 July), William Green MG (A)
MISCELLANEOUS (MEIGS)
Ira Haynes: Cherokee Removal muster roll, 1836
" " Hiwassee District, Lower Goodfield area

\- - - - - - - - - - - - -

HANEY / HAINY

1850 MEIGS CENSUS
Haywood Haney 45 (Farmer), Mahala 53, Margaret 17, Mary 15, Martha 12, John 10 p. 773-477
Isaac V. Haney 31 (SC)(Farmer), Mary 25 (SC), Malinda Jane 6, John T. 5, William W. 4, Mary E. 1 p. 747-273
James Haney 33 (SC)(Farmer), Sarah Ann 23 (NC), Andrew J. 2 p. 747-272
MARRIAGES (MEIGS)
Betsy Hainy to James Morgan q.v.
James Haney to Sarah Ann Rector, 27 May 1847 (same), B.F. McKenzie JP

\- - - - - - - - - - - - -

HANKINS

1840 RHEA CENSUS
Ann Hankins 0 - 0000000001
MARRIAGES (RHEA)
Rebecca Hankins to Francis Monday q.v.

- - - - - - - - - - - - -

HANKS

1850 RHEA CENSUS
David Hanks 30 (Farmer), Elizabeth 18 p. 560-168
[David Hanks married Elizabeth Mathis on 20 Feb 1844 in Roane County]
MISCELLANEOUS (RHEA)
William Hanks: Bondsman for Eli Renno, 1821

- - - - - - - - - - - - -

HANNA / HANNAH / HANNER / HANNASS

TAXES (RHEA)
1819 (Capt. J. Ramsey's Co.): James Hanna Jr. 1 WP, 30a
James Hanna Sr. 1 WP
Joshua Hanna 1 WP
Robert Hanna [marked through]
(Capt. McGill's Co.) : John Hanna 1 WP
1823 (Capt. Braselton's Co.): Joshua Hannah 1 WP
1830 RHEA CENSUS
Avra Hannah 00101 - 000201 p. 359
1840 MEIGS CENSUS
Avery Hannass 0110001 - 0001001 p. 224
James Hannah 00000001 - 01000001 p. 247
1850 MEIGS CENSUS
Avery Hannah 55 (NC)(Farmer), Matilda 40, Patsy 47, James 21 (Farmer), Nathaniel 20 (Farmer), Violet 17, Calvin M. 17 (Farmer), Silas 16, Jesse 14 p. 713-1
MARRIAGES (RHEA)
Betsey Hannah to Abenego Rowden q.v.
David Hanna to Rebecca Atchley, 25 Feb 1820, Young Hanna Bm (A)
James Hannah to Cary Ledbetter, 10 Jan 1814, John Burford Bm (A)
Joel Hannah to Minerva Blackwell, 4 Jan 1831 (6 Jan), Daniel M. Stockton JP, John Davis Bm (AR)
William Hannah to Polly Myers, 3 Mar 1826 (same), Thomas Cox JP, William Myers Bm (AR)
MARRIAGES (MEIGS)
Avery Hannah to Matilda Witt, 3 Jan 1842 (1 Feb), John Seabern JP
MISCELLANEOUS (RHEA and MEIGS)
Avara Hannah: Bondsman for Nathaniel W. Wilson, 1827
" " Bondsman for William Rodgers, 1831
Avery Hannah: Hiwassee District, Pinhook Ferry area
" " On Circuit Court jury, 1836
David Hanna: Bondsman for Absalem Barnes, 1819
David Hannah: Hiwassee District, Sewee Creek area
James Hannah: Bondsman for Abenigo Rowden, 1815
" " Bondsman for Solomon Hensen, 1815
Young Hannah: Bondsman for David Hanna, 1820

- - - - - - - - - - - - -

HANSE

MISCELLANEOUS (RHEA)
James Hanse: Bondsman for John Alexander, 1810

- - - - - - - - - - - - -

HARDIN / HARDEN

TAXES (RHEA)
1823 (Capt. Lewis' Co.): Francis Hardin 1 WP
Francis Hardin 1 WP
(Capt. Brown's Co.): Solomon Hardin 1 WP
1840 MEIGS CENSUS
Joseph Hardin 100001 - 130001 p. 228
1850 RHEA CENSUS
Josiah Harden 26 (Unk), Polly 30, James 7, Elizabeth 5, Seten or Latin 3 p. 602-683
MARRIAGES (RHEA)
Isham S.E. Hardin to Rebecca Lester, 6 Apr 1816 (7 Apr), Daniel Walker JP, Samuel Reid Bm (AR)
Visey Hardin to William Parmer q.v.
MARRIAGES (MEIGS)
Amos Hardin to Nancy Bunch, 18 Jan 1841
[1850 Bradley Census: Amos Hardin 30, Nancy 25, Jinsy 6, Eli 4, Emily 1]
Solomon Harden to Mary Ann Prewitt, 12 June 1845
[1850 Bradley Census: Solomon Hardin 24, Mary 22, Elizabeth 5]
MISCELLANEOUS (RHEA)
Benjamin Harden: Bondsman for Samuel Underwood, 1835

- - - - - - - - - - - - -

HARDY
(see also HANDY)

MARRIAGES (MEIGS)
Samuel Hardy to Margaret Houpt, 2 Oct 1850, Calvin Rice Surety

- - - - - - - - - - - - -

HARE / HAIR / HAIRE

1840 MEIGS CENSUS
John R. Hare 0110001 - 0100001 p. 232
William Hare 221001 - 200001001 p. 245
1850 MEIGS CENSUS
Caleb G. Hare 30 (Wagonmaker), Eliza E. 23, Harriet Jane 13, Christopher C. 12, Elizabeth Ann 9, Andrew J. 6, Lucinda C. 5, Sarah M. 3, Archibald M. 0 p. 815-793 [Caleb G. Hair married Ella Elizabeth Foster on 8 Jan 1848 in McMinn County]
MARRIAGES (RHEA)
Wesley Hare to Jane Rhea, 23 Mar 1830 (25 Mar), Beal Gaither JP, James Blackwell Bm (AR)
MARRIAGES (MEIGS)
William Hair to Annes Ray, 27 Jan 1840
MISCELLANEOUS (MEIGS)
William Haire: Common School Commissioner, District 5

- - - - - - - - - - - - -

HARMON

TAXES (RHEA)
1819 (Capt. McGill's Co.): Philip Harmon 108a
(Capt. Wm McCray's Co.): William Harmon 130a
1823 (Capt. Howard's Co.): Philip Harmon 100a
(Capt. Piper's Co.): Richard Harmon 1 WP
William Harmon 1 WP, 80a
1830 RHEA CENSUS
Richard Harmon 00001 - 1001 p. 357
William Harmon 000020001 - 00012001 p. 357
MISCELLANEOUS (RHEA and MEIGS)
W. Harmon: Elder, Concord Baptist Church, 1824
William Harmon: Hiwassee District

- - - - - - - - - - - - -

HARNER

1830 RHEA CENSUS
James Harner 0031 - 1100001 p. 353
1850 RHEA CENSUS
Abagail Harner 17: see S.T. Whittenburg
Adam Harner 50 (Unk)(Carpenter), Rachel 19, William 13, Susan M. 6, Louisa 3, Malissa 1 p. 546-88
[Adam married Mary Hines on 20 Apr 1826 and Rachel Cates on 6 Mar 1848; both in Roane Co]

- - - - - - - - - - - - -

HARNETT / HARRITT / HOWITT

MARRIAGES (RHEA)
Thomas Harnett or Howitt to Nancy James or Jones, 5 Aug 1817 (same), A. David JP, Jackson Howerton Bm (AR)
MISCELLANEOUS (RHEA)
Thomas Harritt: Bondsman for Robert Boulton, 1817

- - - - - - - - - - - - -

HARP

TAXES (RHEA)
1823 (Capt. Smith's Co.): Thomas Harp 1 WP
1830 RHEA CENSUS
Joseph Harp 00000001 - 0001001 p. 369
Thomas M. Harp 110001 - 0 p. 371
1840 MEIGS CENSUS
Joseph Harp 10001 - 10001 p. 228
MARRIAGES (RHEA)
Joshua Harp to Minerva Thornhill, 2 Aug 1834, Mark Powers Bm (A)
Mary Harp to Mark Powers q.v.
MISCELLANEOUS (RHEA and MEIGS)
Joshua Harp: Bondsman for Mark Powers, 1834
Thomas M. Harp: Bondsman for James Stewart, 1831
Thomas Harp: Hiwassee District, Valley Road

- - - - - - - - - - - - -

HARPER

MARRIAGES (MEIGS)
Elizabeth Harper to W.J. Caskey q.v.

- - - - - - - - - - - - -

HARRIS

TAXES (RHEA)
1819 (Capt. McGill's Co.): Abijah Harris 1 WP
1830 RHEA CENSUS
A. Harris 000110001 - 0212101 p. 377
Cornelius Harris 100001 - 20001 p. 387
Harrison Harris 00001 - 00001 p. 388
Henry Harris or Hanes 220001 - 01211 p. 390
Thomas Harris 102020001 - 00001001 p. 388
1840 RHEA CENSUS
Nancy Harris 0111 - 211001
Neoma Harris 0 - 00001001
1850 RHEA CENSUS
Dawson Harris Unk (NC), Tempa 47 (NC), Magillra 20 (NC)(Waggoner), Luvisa 19 (NC), Benjamin 16 (Farmer), Charles W. 14, Margaret C. 11, James F. 1 p. 542-64
Elizabeth Harris 60 (NC), Cynderella 21 (NC) p. 538-34
Lorenzo D. Harris 31 (NC)(Farmer), Lucinda 25, Mary E. 5, Emily 2, Harriet J. 2/12 p. 536-25
Sarah J. Harris or Hays 14: see James Hays
Thomas Harris 38 (Va)(Farmer), Elizabeth 32, William J.H. 12, Rhoda C. 10, Joseph B. 7, Mary A. 5, Robert T. 2 p. 537-28
W.O.T. Harris 35, Celia 26, David 11, Henry H.M. 8, Peter F. 6, Mary A. 4, Adelhide 1 p. 538-36
MARRIAGES (RHEA)
Alford Harris to Sally Newport, 9 Dec 1821 (same), Jesse Thompson JP (AR)
Elizabeth Harris to William James q.v.
Hugh Harris to Peggy Sears, 23 Dec 1834 (24 or 25 Dec), James Willis MG, Abraham Brown Bm (AR)
Martha Ann Harris to Milton Hammons q.v.
Robert B. Harris to Patsy Genoe, 10 July 1817 (same), S.B. Dyer Bm (A)
Thomas Harris to Elizabeth Hayes, 4 Sept 1835, James Hayes Bm (A)
William Harris to Margaret Denton, 7 June 1816 (same), J. Fine JP, Michel Stoner Bm (AR)

- - - - - - - - - - - - -

HARRISON

1840 RHEA CENSUS
David Harrison 3010001 - 11001
1840 MEIGS CENSUS
Abner Harrison 111011 - 220101 p. 231
1850 RHEA CENSUS
John Harrison 16: see Bailey Minick
John Harrison 22 (Farmer), Elizabeth 37 (NC), Addison L. 6, Richard R. 3, Salina F. 6/12 p. 549-108
Luisa N. Harrison 34 p. 613-452

- - - - - - - - - - - - -

HARROD / HARRID / HERRID

(see also HOWARD)
1830 RHEA CENSUS
Redden Harrod 01101 - 2101 p. 367
MARRIAGES (MEIGS)
Elizabeth Harrid to John Ashburn q.v.
Sarah Herrid to Franklin Peirce q.v.

- - - - - - - - - - - - -

HART / HEART

TAXES (RHEA)
1823 (Capt. Smith's Co.): Samuel Heart 1 WP
1830 RHEA CENSUS
Samuel Hart 11001 - 110101 p. 372
1840 RHEA CENSUS
Absolom Hart 20001 - 10011
Adam Hart 01122001 - 00000001
David Hart 00001 - 00001
MARRIAGES (RHEA)
David Hart to Rebecca Wheeler, 6 Apr 1839 (8 Apr), Samuel Frazier JP, William Lea Bm (AR)
Nancy Heart to David Fairbanks q.v.
MARRIAGES (MEIGS)
Lewis Hart to Elizabeth Loony, 14 Oct 1841 (same), James Moore JP
Peggy Hart to M. Furbanks q.v.

- - - - - - - - - - - - -

HARTLEY

1850 RHEA CENSUS
Margaret Hartley 39, William F. 8 p. 575-259

- - - - - - - - - - - - -

HARVER
(see also HARNER)

TAXES (RHEA)
1808 (John Henry's List): James Harver 1 WP

- - - - - - - - - - - - -

HARVERSON / HARVISON

1840 MEIGS CENSUS
William Harvison 1210001 - 031101 p. 231
1850 MEIGS CENSUS
Nancy Harverson 49 (NC), Mary 22 (NC), Harriet 20 (NC), Martha 18, William 16, Elizabeth 16, Benjamin F. 14, James A. 12, John 8 p. 733-157
Rufus Harverson 23 (NC)(Farmer), Nancy Jane 23 (NC) p. 733-158
MISCELLANEOUS (MEIGS)
Rufus Harvison: Private, Mexican War

- - - - - - - - - - - - -

HARVEY / HARVY

1840 MEIGS CENSUS
Phebe Harvy 111 - 0002101 p. 241
1850 RHEA CENSUS
John Harvey 25 (Farmer), Nancy 24, Sampson 4, Eli M. 2 p. 636-659
William Harvey 18: see Elihu McKenney
1850 MEIGS CENSUS
John F. Harvy 40 (NC)(Farmer), Neomia 30 (NC), Francis Marrion (m) 11 (NC), James W. 9 (Ga), William A. 7 (Ga), Rhoda C. 4, Margaret E. 2 p. 714-17
Thomas Harvey 35 (NY)(Tailor), Martha Ann 45 (Va), Jessee 28, Susan 18, Henry 14 p. 781-533
William Harvy 23 (Farmer), Sarah 26, Levina p. 800-673
MARRIAGES (RHEA)
Jamima H. Harvy to Alexander Underwood q.v.
Mary Ann Harvy to Reuben Nickson q.v.
MARRIAGES (MEIGS)
Elizabeth Harvey to William Griffin q.v.
Phoebe Harvey to Samuel Davis q.v.
Vina Harvey to Calvin Mantooth q.v.
William Harvey or Hawey to Sarah Dethrage, 15 July 1848 (same), John K. Brown JP
MISCELLANEOUS (RHEA)
Allen Harvy: Bondsman for Alexander Underwood, 1831

- - - - - - - - - - - - -

HARWELL

MISCELLANEOUS (MEIGS)
S.B. Harwell: T.E. 1849

- - - - - - - - - - - - -

HARWOOD / HARDWOOD

TAXES (RHEA)
1823 (Capt. Piper's Co.): Nathan Harwood 1 WP, 30a
1830 RHEA CENSUS
Joseph Hardwood 000040001 - 02021001 p. 382
Mals Harwood 11001 - 10001 p. 383
Randolph Hardwood 10001 - 11001 p. 382
1840 RHEA CENSUS
Burwell Harwood 00001 - 00001
Malichi Harwood 110101 - 210001
Martha Harwood 000001 - 000120001
Mary Harwood 1111 - 011001
1850 RHEA CENSUS
Jesse Harwood 47 (NC)(Farmer), Mary 24, Luisa T. 1, Benjamin D. SMITH 6 p. 568-208
Martha Harwood 75 (SC): see Hezekiah Robison
Mary Harwood 45, Riley 19 (Farmer), Sarah 16, Eli 14 p. 565-192
Rufus M. Harwood 25 (Farmer), Juli A. Unk, William 5, John 4, Claborn 1 p. 567-200
Ruth Harwood Unk: see William F. Smith
Thomas J. Harwood 23 (Farmer), Matilda 22 p. 566-193
MARRIAGES (RHEA)
Burwell M. Harwood to Ann Rigle, 27 June 1838 (same), James McCanse JP, James M. Harwood Bm (AR)
Delila Harwood to Hiram Henry q.v.
Edy Harwood to Michael S. Jones q.v.
Eliza Harwood to David Robinson q.v.
Elizabeth Harwood to Richard Gravely q.v.
Elizabeth Harwood to Hezekiah Roberson q.v.
Fanny Harwood to Lorenzo D. Rush q.v.
Harriet Harwood to William E. Robinson q.v.
Jesse Harwood to Mary Smith, 2 Nov 1847 (7 Nov), Charles Cox JP (R)
Nancy Harwood to Ryal Burton q.v.
Nancy Harwood to John Miller q.v.
Nathan Harwood to Mary Chapman, 3 Aug or 22 Nov 1824 (no return), John Rice Bm (AR)
Nathan Harwood to Polly Jackson, 6 June 1826 (8 June), John Robinson JP, John Love Bm (AR)
Polly Harwood to Thomas Piper q.v.
Randolph Harwood to Polly Barnett, 24 Feb 1825 (same), John Robinson JP, David Leuty Bm (AR)

Rhoda Harwood to Samuel Quinton q.v.
Rufus Harwood to Julia Ann Fugit, 6 Dec 1843 (14 Dec), T.J. Creede Bm (A)
Thomas I. Harwood to Matilda Compton, 20 Sept 1849 (same), W.E. Colville JP (R)
William Harwood to Malinda Jones, 25 July 1822 (28 July), John Robinson JP, John Miller Bm (AR)
William G. Harwood to Nancy Dotson, 31 Dec 1849 (same), John Wytt JP (R)
MISCELLANEOUS (RHEA and MEIGS)
Elias Harwood: Cherokee Removal muster roll, 1836-37
James M. Harwood: Bm for Burwell M. Harwood, 1838
Jesse Harwood: Bondsman for Jesse Webb, 1842
Nathan Harwood: Bondsman for William Merriman, 1827
" " Hiwassee District, Pinhook Ferry area
William Harwood: Private, Mexican War

- - - - - - - - - - - -

HASKINS

MARRIAGES (RHEA)
Hulda Haskins to John Taylor q.v.

- - - - - - - - - - - -

HASLER / HASSLER / HOSTLER / HOSLER / HORSLER

1840 RHEA CENSUS
Levi G. Hosler 00001 - 10001
William Horsler 10001 - 30001
1850 RHEA CENSUS
Adam Hasler 62 (Pa)(Miller), Sophia 51, Harriet 17, Sidney 17 (Farmer), Lyda 13 p. 603-422
George W. Hasler 11: see Elias Morgan
Michael Hassler 25 (Farmer), Sarah A.C. 16, Eleanor C. 4/12, Mary A. RAGLE 43 p. 608-488
MARRIAGES (RHEA)
Eliza Jane Hosler to George W. Derossett q.v.
Levi G. Hostler to Mary A. Derossett, 2 Nov 1837 (7 Mar 1837)[sic], James McCanse JP (AR)
Mariah H. Hosler to Harrison Barnett q.v.
MARRIAGES (MEIGS)
William R. Hassler to Malinda Simpson, 1 Jan 1836 (same), Edward E. Wasson JP, John Hickey Bm (AR)
MISCELLANEOUS (RHEA)
L.G. Hasler: Bondsman for A.W. Derossett, 1843
Michael T. Hosler: Private, Mexican War

- - - - - - - - - - - -

HASLERIG / HAZELRIGG

TAXES (RHEA)
1819 (Capt. W.S. Bradley's Dist.): Richard Haslerig 4 BP
1823 (Capt. Brown's Co.): Richard Haslerig 3 BP, 300a Tenn R (part of 2300a tract)
1830 RHEA CENSUS
Thomas J. Hazelrigg 1001 - 00010001 p. 384
MARRIAGES (RHEA)
Jane C. Hazelrigg to Benjamin C. Stout q.v.
MISCELLANEOUS (RHEA)
Richard Haslerig: Security for Thompson G. McMayo, 1826
" " Married Mary Shaun in Va (four children: Thos J., Conley, Jane Conn, and Nancy)
Thomas J. Haslerig: Married Delilah Coulter, dau of Alexander and Margaret (McReynolds) Coulter; one son, Thomas Richard Alexander Haslerig

- - - - - - - - - - - -

HASSLETT / HAYSLETT

MARRIAGES (RHEA)
Matthew S. Hasslett to Esther Johnson, 4 Apr 1820 (same), Jesse Thompson JP, James Higgins Bm (AR)
MARRIAGES (MEIGS)
Florence Hayslett to Anderson Hunter q.v.

- - - - - - - - - - - -

HATFIELD

1840 MEIGS CENSUS
John Hatfield 00001 - 1001 p. 224
Joseph Hatfield 0030001 - 120211 p. 224
MARRIAGES (MEIGS)
John Hatfield to Nancy Gray, 24 Oct 1838
Katherine Hatfield to Thomas J. Hicks q.v.
MISCELLANEOUS (MEIGS)
John Hattfield: Cherokee Removal muster roll, 1837

- - - - - - - - - - - -

HAVEN

1840 RHEA CENSUS
John Haven 011001 - 0

- - - - - - - - - - - -

HAWK / HAWKS

1840 MEIGS CENSUS
Alfred Hawks 10004 - 00001 p. 230
MISCELLANEOUS (MEIGS)
M.C. Hawks: MG 1845

- - - - - - - - - - - -

HAWKINS

MARRIAGES (RHEA)
Harriet Hawkins to Pleasant M. Holloway q.v.

- - - - - - - - - - - -

HAWS

1830 RHEA CENSUS
Richard Haws 00001 - 10001 p. 392
1840 RHEA CENSUS
Thomas Haws 000100001 - 1001101
1850 RHEA CENSUS
Thomas Haws 71 (Pa)(Farmer), Jane 55, John W. 26 (Farmer), Leopatra 10 p. 599-401

- - - - - - - - - - - -

HAYS / HAYES
(see also MAYS / MAYES)

TAXES (RHEA)
1823 (Capt. McCall's Co.): Nathaniel Hays 2 BP
1830 RHEA CENSUS
Jno P. Hays 100001 - 000001 p. 369
1840 RHEA CENSUS
James Hayes 00000001 - 01100001
James H. Hayes 10001 - 1001
John Hayes 1022001 - 111001
1850 RHEA CENSUS
James Hays 65 (Va)(Farmer), Rhoda 64 (Va), Sarah J. HARRIS 14 p. 536-27
James H. Hays 30, Lyda 29 (NC), John 12, Mary S. 10, Luisa 9, Pleasant 6, Rebecca 3, Joana 1 p. 536-24
Shadrack Hays 28 (Farmer), Hannah 22 p. 581-300
1850 MEIGS CENSUS
John P. Hays 58 (Ga)(Farmer), Anna 58 (Ga), Joel 19 (Farmer), Sarah Ann 16, Jackson 21 p. 755-342
MARRIAGES (RHEA)
Barbary Hays to Edward Griffet q.v.
Elizabeth Hays to John Gentry q.v.
Elizabeth Hayes to Thomas Harris q.v.
James Hayes to Lidia Brewer, 3 Nov 1837 (6 Nov), George Preston JP, G.W. Gage Bm (AR)
John P. Hays to Ann Rice, 11 Apr 1828 (13 Apr), Samuel F. Gerald [Fitzgerald] MG, Thomas Cox Bm (AR)
MISCELLANEOUS (RHEA and MEIGS)
James Hayes: Bondsman for Thomas Harris, 1835
" " Bondsman for Zebadee Brown, 1839
John P. Hayes: Lived in Cottonport
Nathaniel Hays: Bondsman for Edward Griffitt, 1824

\- - - - - - - - - - - -

HELMS / HELLAMS / HELLUMS

1830 RHEA CENSUS
John Hellams 10001 - 200001 p. 357
1840 MEIGS CENSUS
Elizabeth Helms 111 - 011101 p. 241
MARRIAGES (RHEA)
Betsy Hellums to William Fowler q.v.
Dorcus Hellums to William K. Blakely q.v.
Eleanor Hellems to Royal Chastain q.v.
John Helms or Hellense to Betsy Newkirk, 29 Dec 1824 (30 Dec), John Farmer MG, Uriah Newkirk Bm (AR)
Tharsey Helms to Thomas Hunnycut q.v.
MISCELLANOUS (RHEA)
Jacob Helms: On Surveyor's list of land south of Tenn Ri
Jesse Helms: On Surveyor's list of land south of Tenn Ri
William Hellums: Bondsman for William K. Blakely, 1821

\- - - - - - - - - - - -

HELTON / HILTON

1830 RHEA CENSUS
Jas or Jos Hilton or Helton 10001 - 10001 p. 394
1840 MEIGS CENSUS
James Helton 120101 - 001000101 p. 225
1850 MEIGS CENSUS
John Helton 18 (Farmer), Rebecca 16 p. 766-418
MARRIAGES (RHEA)
William W. Hilton to Rachel Coleman, 3 Jan 1831 (4 Jan), Peach Taylor JP, William Lillard Bm (AR)
MARRIAGES (MEIGS)
Eliza Emeline Helton to John Young q.v.
John Helton to Rebecca Coley, 12 June 1850, William Howard Sur

\- - - - - - - - - - - -

HEMBREE / HEMBRO / EMBREE / EMBREY / EMERY

1830 RHEA CENSUS
Benjamin Emery 421001 - 011101 p. 363
1840 RHEA CENSUS
Abraham Hembre 00001 - 00001
Andrew Hembree 01001 - 10001
Andrew Hembree Sr. 211120001 - 02111001
1840 MEIGS CENSUS
James Emery 02210001 - 1100001 p. 247
1850 RHEA CENSUS
Abraham Embree 37 (Farmer), Rhoda 35, James M. 8, Sarah J. 5 (Idiot) p. 560-169
[Abraham Hembree or Emery married Rhoda Mallacote on 2 Jan 1836 in Roane County]
Andrew Emery 38 (Farmer), Elizabeth 36, James 5, Nancy A. 11, Louisa J. 9, Fanny D. 7, Lucyana 4, Harriet 1 p. 559-159
1850 MEIGS CENSUS
James Hembro 61 (Farmer), Nancy 45 (SC), John 22 (Farmer), William 18 (Farmer), Manuel 17 (Farmer), Benjamin 15, Nancy 12 p. 807-721
MARRIAGES (RHEA)
Catey Embrey to James McCarter q.v.
MARRIAGES (MEIGS)
Susan Emery to Julius Hacker q.v.
Susan Hembree to Abner Dotson q.v.

\- - - - - - - - - - - -

HENDERSON

TAXES (RHEA)
1823 (Capt. Howard's Co.): Allen Henderson 1 WP
(Capt. Braselton's Co.): John Henderson 1 WP
1830 RHEA CENSUS
Martha Henderson 1 - 0000111 p. 381
1840 RHEA CENSUS
William Henderson 10001 - 10001
MARRIAGES (RHEA)
Delila Henderson to William Walton q.v.
Lucinda Henderson to George W. Hale q.v.
William Henderson to Florina Ryan, 8 June 1837 or 1839 [listed twice by Allen], William B. Cozby JP, James Henderson Bm (A)
[1850 Bledsoe Census: William Henderson 54, Florina 36, John 10, Elizabeth A. 8, Edwina 7, Martha J. 5, Thomas F. 4, Samuel 1]
William Henderson to Elizabeth Sanders, 13 Feb 1841 (14 Feb), S. Dyer JP (R)
MISCELLANEOUS (RHEA)
Allen Henderson: Bondsman for Samuel Sullivan, 1823
James Henderson: Bondsman for William Henderson, 1839

\- - - - - - - - - - - -

HENLEY / HENLY

1830 RHEA CENSUS
William C. Henley 001001 - 22101 p. 368
MARRIAGES (MEIGS)
Edmund Henly to Mary Cahal [no date given, but on page with 1840]

- - - - - - - - - - - - -

HENNES

MARRIAGES (RHEA)
Polly Hennes to Willie McCarver q.v.

- - - - - - - - - - - - -

HENNIGER / HENEGAR

1830 RHEA CENSUS
Jno Henniger 1100001 - 112001 p. 377
MISCELLANEOUS (RHEA)
John Henniger [Henegar]: MG MEC 1820-1834

- - - - - - - - - - - - -

HENRY

TAXES (RHEA)
1808 (John Henry's List): Ezekiel Henry 770a
Squire John Henry 1 WP, 1 BP
1819 (Capt. John Lewis' Dist.): John Henry 1 WP, 210a
1823 (Capt. Brown's Co.): George Henry Jr. WP
Thomas Henry 1 WP
(Capt. Lewis' Co.): James Henry 1 WP
James Henry 1 WP
William Henry WP
1830 RHEA CENSUS
George Henry Jr. 00101 - 00001 p. 385
George Henry Sr. 0000200001 - 00020001 p. 385
Henry Henry 00001 - 20001 p. 385
Nancy Henry 0 - 000101001 p. 395
Thomas Henry 010001 - 20101 p. 385
1840 RHEA CENSUS
Elizabeth Henry 0101 - 0011001
Henry Henry 120001 - 102001
Hiram Henry 2000001 - 10001
John Henry 02011001 - 2021101
Solomon Henry 11001 - 210001
1850 RHEA CENSUS
Andrew J. Henry 7: see Margaret Barnett
Elizabeth Henry 45, Luvina 33, Calvin 25 (Farmer), Rua A. 18, Thomas 16 (Farmer) p. 572-234
George Henry 47 (Farmer) p. 572-239
Hyram Henry 46 (Farmer), Delila 40 (SC), Franklin 13, Amanda C. 13, Snelson 11, Addison 9, James M. 8, Martha 5, George 2 p. 573-246
Solomon Henry 39 (Farmer), Mary 29, Malissa 17, William R. 15, Lucinda S. 13, Cyrus W. 11, Reuben M. 10, Joel L. 5, Elizabeth 3, Addison S. 2, Hardy PACE 72 (NC)(Hatter) p. 572-240

MARRIAGES (RHEA)
Calvin Henry to Isabella Kenedy, 4 Nov 1850 (same), W.H. Cunnyngham JP (R)
Elizabeth Henry to Jesse Webb q.v.
Elizabeth Henry to John Overstreet q.v.
Ezekiel Henry to Judy Francis, 19 Jan 1810, Miller Francis Bm (A)
George Henry to Ruanna Manley, 26 May 1821, James E. Kennon Bm (A)
Henry Henry to Jane Montgomery, 30 Oct 1825 (same), John Rice JP, William Locke Bm (AR)
Hiram Henry to Delila Harwood, 21 Feb 1833 (same), Daniel Walker JP, Joseph Thornton Bm (AR)
Hiram Henry to Mary Clifton, 8 June 1841 (same), Jacob Gear JP, John Jones Bm (AR)
James Henry to Ann McCoy, 15 Dec 1815, Miller Francis Bm (A)
Jane Henry to John Day q.v.
John Henry to Elizabeth Williams, 10 Oct 1816, Woodson Francis Bm (A)
John Henry to Susannah Day, 5 Dec 1816 (same), Abraham Howard JP, Edmond Bean Bm (R) [probably 1850 White Census: John Henry 62, Susannah 59]
Malinda Henry to Anson Dearmon q.v.
Margaret Henry to George Mayberry q.v.
Margaret Henry to William Ferguson q.v.
Matilda Henry to George Barnett q.v.
Nancy Henry to John McCrakin q.v.
Polly Henry to Joseph Thornton q.v.
Solomon Henry to Catharin A. Smith, 21 Nov 1832 (same), Daniel Walker JP, William Gross B, (AR) [Solomon, son of George Henry]
Solomon Henry to Mary Long, 6 Dec 1843 (7 Dec), T.J. Creede JP (A)
Susan Henry to Wyly Lewis q.v.
Susan Henry to Samuel Minnick q.v.
William Henry Jr. to Betsy Lauderdale, 10 June 1813 (same), Ezekiel Henry Bm (A)
William Henry to Nancy McCanless, 10 June 1818 (11 June), Matthew Donald MG, Reuben Freeman Bm (R)

MISCELLANEOUS (RHEA)
Ezekiel Henry: Bondsman for William Henry, 1813
George Henry: Bondsman for Farley Brady, 1822
James Henry: Bondsman for John Monroe or Morrow, 1818
John Henry: JP 1808
Solomon Henry: Bondsman for Mumford Smith, 1841
" " Bondsman for George Barnett, 1841
" " Bondsman for Samuel Minnick, 1841
William Henry: On first Grand Jury, 1808
" " Home used for temporary County seat, 1808-1812

- - - - - - - - - - - - -

HENSLEY

1830 RHEA CENSUS
Terry H. Hensley 002201 - 0000101 p. 382
MARRIAGES (MEIGS)
John Hensley to Permely Cooley, 22 July 1849 (same), Robert Cooley JP [1850 Bledsoe Census: John Hensley 30, Permelia 1]

- - - - - - - - - - - - -

HENSON

MARRIAGES (RHEA)
Edward Henson to Mariah Houpt, 30 Mar 1830 (same) Joseph McCorkle JP, Samuel Bass Bm (AR)
Polly Henson to Elijah Self q.v.
Solomon Henson to Rebecca Self, 18 Dec 1815 (20 Dec), David Murphree JP, James Hannah Bm (AR)
MARRIAGES (MEIGS)
John Henson to Elizabeth Slaughter, 18 Aug 1838 (21 Aug), Benjamin McKenzie JP
MISCELLANEOUS (RHEA)
Solomon Henson: Bondsman for William Self, 1812
" " Bondsman for Martin Shultz, 1815

- - - - - - - - - - - - -

HERD

1850 MEIGS CENSUS
Sarah Herd 56 (Va), Frances 7 (Ga) p. 793-623

- - - - - - - - - - - - -

HICKEY

MARRIAGES (RHEA)
John Hickey to Sally Silvey, 26 July 1832 (same), F. or A. Davis JP, John Barnet Bm (AR)
MISCELLANEOUS (RHEA)
John Hickey: Bondsman for Willim R. Hassler, 1836
Rufus M. Hickey: MG 1848

- - - - - - - - - - - - -

HICKLEN

MISCELLANEOUS (MEIGS)
Barnett Hicklen: Hiwassee District, Burkett Chapel area

- - - - - - - - - - - - -

HICKMAN

1830 RHEA CENSUS
Henry Hickman 10001 - 31001 p. 369
Samuel Hickman 002000001 - 00010001 p. 356
1840 RHEA CENSUS
Elias Hickman 1112001 - 0010001
1840 MEIGS CENSUS
Barbary Hickman 011 - 0110001 p. 234
1850 RHEA CENSUS
Alexander Hickman 27 (Farmer), Ann E. 9 p. 632-628
Elias Hickman 59 (Md)(Farmer), Margaret 54, John 20 (Farmer), William 16 (Farmer), David 13, William S. McKINLEY 25 (School Teacher) p. 630-614
Henry Hickman 26 (Farmer), Lawira or Laura E. 21 p. 632-629
MARRIAGES (RHEA)
Mary Hickman to Samuel O. Woods q.v.
MISCELLANEOUS (MEIGS)
Austin Hickman: Cherokee Removal muster roll, 1837
John Hickman: Private, Mexican War

- - - - - - - - - - - - -

HICKS / HIX

TAXES (RHEA)
1819 (Capt. Wm McCray's Co.): William Hicks 1 WP
1840 RHEA CENSUS
Joseph Hicks 001001 - 000110001
1840 MEIGS CENSUS
Leroy J. Hicks 00001 - 0001 p. 224
1850 RHEA CENSUS
Leroy Hicks 50 (Va)(Farmer), Jane 35, Newton C. 9, John T. 4, Mary 2 p. 600-406
1850 MEIGS CENSUS
John Hix 30 (Farmer), Susannah 29, Reuben 8, Catherine 7, George 5, Kissiah 4, Margaret 2, John 1 p. 758-364
MARRIAGES (RHEA)
Dianah Hicks to Benjamin Ward q.v.
Joseph Hicks to Jane Ferguson, 19 Dec 1839 (same), James Montgomery JP, Micajah Howerton Bm (AR)
Samuel Hix or Hicks to Nancy Ward, 10 Nov 1824 (same), Thomas Price JP, Duke Ward Bm (AR)
MARRIAGES (MEIGS)
Albert Hix to Jan Man, 19 Apr 1845, Jesse Locke MG
Thomas J. Hicks to Katherine Hatfield, 22 Nov 1845 (same), J. Seaburn JP
MISCELLANEOUS (RHEA and MEIGS)
James Hicks: Bondsman for Daniel McPhail, 1828
John P. Hicks: JP(?) 1845
Joseph Hicks: Bondsman for John Orr, 1839

- - - - - - - - - - - - -

HICKSON [HIXSON?]

MARRIAGES (RHEA)
Reuben Hickson to Mary Ann Harvy, 1 Nov 1845 (3 Nov), D. Ragsdale JP, James Stewart Bm (AR)

- - - - - - - - - - - - -

HIDE

MARRIAGES (RHEA)
Thompson Hide to Febey Butler 10 May 1817, Martin Randolph Bm (A)

- - - - - - - - - - - - -

HIDEN / HIDON

TAXES (RHEA)
1819 (Capt. John Ramsey's Co.): David Hiden 1 WP
(Capt. W.S. Bradley's Dist.): David Hiden 1 Town Lot
MARRIAGES (RHEA)
Anny Hiden or Hidon to Thomas Blackley [Blakely] q.v.
David Hiden to Polly Mallason or Mallan, 15 May 1816, J. Fine JP, Thomas Lucus Bm (AR)
Joahanna Hiden to Thomas Carter q.v.

- - - - - - - - - - - - - -

HIGDON

1850 MEIGS CENSUS
E.L. Higdon 30 (NC)(Merchant), Emily Jane 26, William 15, James C. 10 p. 751-313
[Eleazer L. Higdon, born 5 June 1818 in Burke Co., NC, married Emily Jane Wear about 1835. Her age probably is incorrect on the census]

- - - - - - - - - - - - -

HIGGINS

TAXES (RHEA)
1808 (Jonathan Fine's List): Burrel Higgins 1 WP
Joel Higgins 1 WP

MARRIAGES (RHEA)
Daniel Higgins to Peggy Riddle, 7 Jan 1824 (no return), Jeremiah Riddle Bm (AR)
Josiah Higgins to Mary Baker, 26 Feb 1829, Daniel Higgins Bm (A)

MISCELLANEOUS (RHEA)
Daniel Higgins: Bondsman for Josiah Higgins, 1829
James Higgins: Bondsman for Matthew S. Hasslett, 1820

- - - - - - - - - - - - -

HILBURN / HILBORNE / HILLBORN

TAXES (RHEA)
1823 (Capt. Wilson's Co.): John Hillburn 1 WP
Samuel Hillburn 1 WP

1830 RHEA CENSUS
Allen Hilborn 1000001 - 000001 p. 386
John Hillborn 21001 - 1000100001 p. 386
Sarah Hilborne 01 - 101001 p. 364

MARRIAGES (RHEA)
Allen Hilburn to Patsy Vincent, 3 July 1824 (4 July), John Garner or Farmer JP, John Hilburn Bm (AR)
Dempsey or Dimsey Hillborne or Hilburn to Linsey or Junsey Able, 8 Apr 1823 (same), John Robinson JP (AR)
John Hilburn to Nancy Vincent, 1 Sept 1824 (2 Sept), John Farmer JP, Hamilton Vincent Bm (AR)

MISCELLANEOUS (RHEA)
Allen Hilburn/Hilbourn: Bondsman for Silas Sevely, 1827
" " Bondsman for Moses Pittman, 1829
John Hilburn: Bondsman for Allen Hilburn, 1824

- - - - - - - - - - - - -

HILL

TAXES (RHEA)
1819 (Capt. John Robinson's Co.):
John Hill 1 WP, 1 BP, 550a
1823 (Capt. Braselton's Co.): William Hill 1 WP

1830 RHEA CENSUS
Hiram Hill 20001 - 01001 p. 390
John Hill 01212001 - 02110001 p. 386
Nathan N. Hill 00001 - 110001 p. 365
Sarah Hill 011 - 0011101 p. 353
William Hill 21001 - 00001 p. 386

1840 RHEA CENSUS
Hiram Hill 1020001 - 0101

1840 MEIGS CENSUS
Susannah Hill 1 - 3110201 p. 245

1850 RHEA CENSUS
Fleming Hill 23 (Blacksmith): see Jack Foust
Jane Hill 38, William 23 (Carpenter), Alexander 20, Rebecca 17, Arthur S. 13, Sarah J. 10, Thomas G. 7, Francis 4, John HOUSE 30 (Va)(Carpenter), Levena 25, Martha J. 9/12 p. 537-30

1850 MEIGS CENSUS
Susannah Hill 43, Celia 23, Mary 27, William J. 9 p. 782-547

MARRIAGES (RHEA)
Elizabeth Hill to Francis Monday q.v.
Isabell Hill to William Buster q.v.
Jane C. Hill to Alex Galbreath q.v.
Jesse A. Hill to Jane G. Jenkins, 7 July 1842 (same), Richard Waterhouse JP (A)
Lucinda Hill to James H. Stewart q.v.
Mariah Hill to Ira D. Broyles q.v.
Mary Ann Hill to D. Whittenburg q.v.
Matilda Hill to John Myers q.v.
Nancy Hill to Isaac S. Binyon q.v.
Polly Hill to Jeremiah Tindal q.v.
Quinn M. Hill to Jane Broyles, 11 Mar 1844 (no return) (A)
Robert Hill to Peggy Rhea, 20 Mar 1834, Harmon Gaddy Bm (A)
Sally Hill to Wyle Murphrie q.v.
Vina Hill to James Carvey q.v.
Vina Hill to John House q.v.
William Hill to Jerusha Stuart, 27 Oct 1820 (same), John Whaley Bm (A)
William Hill to Nancy Worley, 16 Apr 1823 (same), John Cozby JP, John Clack Bm (AR)

MARRIAGES (MEIGS)
Eleanor E. Huie or Hill to William F. Pierce q.v.
Katherine Hill to G.C.M. Gregory q.v.
Polly Hill to William Duckworth q.v.
Rebecca Hill to William Smith q.v.

MISCELLANEOUS (RHEA)
G.M. Hill: Bondsman for John D. Traynor, 1834
Hiram Hill: Bondsman for Francis Monday 1823
Ira Hill: Bondsman for Ambrose Goff, 1828
John W. Hill: Bondsman for John R. Barnett, 1827

- - - - - - - - - - - - -

HINDS / HINES
(see also HANES / HAINES / HAYNES)

1830 RHEA CENSUS
Nat Hinds 021001 - 201001 p. 385

MARRIAGES (RHEA)
Elizabeth Hines to Alexander Walker q.v.
Henry Hines to Margaret Haines, 3 Aug 1849 (no return) (R)
Rutha Hinds to E.W. Martin q.v.
Simon Hinds to Judith Miller, 2 Apr 1811 (same), Joel Long Bm (A)

MISCELLANEOUS (RHEA)
Hazlet Hines: Bondsman for Caleb Bedwell, 1828

- - - - - - - - - - - - -

HINKLE

MARRIAGES (RHEA)
Rebecca Hinkle to John Poe q.v.

- - - - - - - - - - - - -

HITE / HIGHT / HAITE

1850 RHEA CENSUS
Barbary Hight: see William Thompson
MARRIAGES (RHEA)
Catherine Hite to Moses Thompson q.v.
MISCELLANEOUS (RHEA)
Hezekiah Haite: Bondsman for Moses Thompson, 1824

- - - - - - - - - - - - -

HOBBS

1840 MEIGS CENSUS
Richard Hobbs ??? - 1000??
[lower portion of page 225 missing]
1850 MEIGS CENSUS
Richard Hobbs 75 (Va), Nancy 63 (Va) p. 726-103
MARRIAGES (MEIGS)
James Hobbs to Mary Thornberry, 20 Mar 1839 (4 Apr), John Seaburn JP

- - - - - - - - - - - - -

HODGE / HODGES

1830 RHEA CENSUS
William Hodge 11001 - 20001 p. 354
1840 RHEA CENSUS
William Hodge 112001 - 120001
1840 MEIGS CENSUS
Henry Hodge 00001 - 1001 p. 238
1850 RHEA CENSUS
Daniel Hodges 26 (Saddler) Nancy 45, Wm B.L. FLEMMING 17 (Farmer), Samuel H. 15, Mary E. 13, James K.P. 11, Margaret J. 20, Howel HODGES 24 (Saddler) p. 622-557
John Hodges 15, Abraham 13, William 9: see John Jolly
Jane Hodges 17: see C. Whitehouse Abel
William Hodges 16 (Farmer): see Robert P. Able
1850 MEIGS CENSUS
A.W. Hodges 35 (Doctor), Evaline 23, Ann CROSS 24, Olivia HODGES 2, Elizabeth P. 1 p. 772-469
MARRIAGES (RHEA)
Daniel Hodges to Nancy Fleming, 12 Jan 1850 (13 Jan), Benjamin Wallace MG (R)
Ambrose W. Hodge to Eveline McCorkle, 6 Oct 1847 (7 Oct), D.L. Godsey MG
[Ambrose, son of Francis and Priscilla King Hodge of Sullivan County; Eveline, dau of Joseph and Elizabeth Allison McCorkle]
Henry J. Hodge to M. Philpot, 12 Oct 1838 (same), B.F. McKenzie JP
MISCELLANEOUS (MEIGS)
Thomas Hodges: Bondsman for William Shoemaker, 1834

- - - - - - - - - - - - -

HODSDEN

MARRIAGES (RHEA)
Robert H. Hodsen or Hodsden to Elizabeth Hooks, 29 Aug 1832 (same), B. Wallace MG, Thomas McCallie Bm (AR)
MISCELLANEOUS (RHEA)
Robert H. Hodsden: Bondsman for Robert M. Hooks, 1831

- - - - - - - - - - - - -

HOGAN / HAGAN

1850 RHEA CENSUS
William S. Hogan 40: see John S. Evans
MARRIAGES (RHEA)
Robert Hogan or Hagan to Letus or Lettes Kirkpatrick, 20 Dec 1824, Thomas Price JP, George Washington Rector Bm (AR)

- - - - - - - - - - - - -

HOGGART [HAGGARD?]

MISCELLANEOUS (RHEA)
Noah Hoggart: MG 1847 [a Noah Haggard was living in McMinn County in 1850]

- - - - - - - - - - - - -

HOGUE / HAGUE / HOGG

1840 MEIGS CENSUS
James M. Hague 021111 - 200101 p. 242
John Hague 101000001 - 1010001 p. 245
MARRIAGES (RHEA)
Berry Hogg to Dicey Howerton, 3 Sept 1821 (4 Sept), H. Collins JP, J. Walton Bm (R)
Jane Hogg to Henry Maner q.v.
Polly Ann Hoy or Hog to Jesse Huddleston q.v.
MARRIAGES (MEIGS)
Elizabeth C. Hague to William E. Gibson q.v.
Sarah J. Hague to Daniel Wan q.v.
Susan Hague to Andrew Farmer q.v.
MISCELLANEOUS (RHEA and MEIGS)
James M. Hague: JP 1841-42
Samuel Hogue: Bondsman for Isaac N. Swan, 1836

- - - - - - - - - - - - -

HOLCOMB

1850 MEIGS CENSUS
David D. Holcomb 27 (NC)(Farmer), Letha Ann 26, Andrew J. 6, John W. 4, Sarah F. 3, James T. 1 p. 817-799
Elizabeth Holcomb 42 (Va) p. 817-800
[NOTE: the number 800 was entered twice on consecutive lines: first, next to Elizabeth's name (no last name) and next to the following household of James S. Paul. Since the last name always was written on the first individual in each new household, it is most likely that Elizabeth was living in the household of David Holcomb]

- - - - - - - - - - - - -

HOLDAWAY

MISCELLANEOUS (MEIGS)
Hamilton Holdaway: Private, Mexican War

- - - - - - - - - - - - -

HOLLADAY

MISCELLANEOUS (RHEA)
Daniel Holladay: Bondsman for William Poynor, 1821

- - - - - - - - - - - - -

HOLLAND

TAXES (RHEA)
1819 (Capt. John Lewis' Dist.): Isaac Holland 1 BP, 50a
Samuel Holland 1 WP, 1 BP
(Capt. W.S. Bradley's Dist.): John Holland 1 WP, 40a
1823 (Capt. Smith's Co.): Daniel Holland 1 WP
(Capt. Brown's Co.): John Holland 1 WP, 42a Tenn R
1830 RHEA CENSUS
Allen Holland 0301 - 110001 p. 384
John Holland 010011001 - 0011101 p. 392
1840 RHEA CENSUS
Allen Holland 001201 - 321001
Daniel Holland 0110001 - 2102
John Holland 000101001 - 001110001
John E. Holland 10001 - 00001
1850 RHEA CENSUS
Allen Holland 47 (Ga)(Farmer), Mary 50, William T. 27 (Farmer), Luisa J. 21, Patsey M.T. 18, Sarah S. 15, Nancy E. 13, Pamelia C. 11, James K.P. 5, Catharine 25, Jackson THURMAN 23 (SC)(Farmer) p. 606-475
John Holland 29 (Farmer), Elizabeth 24, James F. 3, Amanda A. 1 p. 606-476
Thomas R. Holland 44 (Ga)(Farmer), Sarah S. 38, Martha A. 5, Anagina C. 3, Hannah J. 1 p. 583-332
MARRIAGES (RHEA)
Allen Holland to Polly Merriott, 20 Apr 1819 (same), Wm Randolph, Elder, John Holland Bm (AR)
Caty Holland to Joseph Johnson q.v.
Daniel Holland to Elizabeth Smith, 14 May 1841 (16 May), Samuel Frazier JP, William Holland Bm (AR)
Emely B. Holland to William W. Pile q.v.
James Holland to Hetty Day, 23 or 31 Dec 1825 (1 Jan 1826), Wm Smith JP, Alexander Coulter Bm (AR)
John M. Holland to Elizabeth Snodgrass, 10 Aug 1847 (same), W.W. Rose MG (R)
Martha M. Holland to Jackson Thurman q.v.
Nancy W. Holland to William Godbyhere q.v.
Nancy W. Holland to J.A. Snodgrass q.v.
Patience Holland to J.S. Thompson q.v.
Polly Ann Holland to Thomas Godbyhere q.v.
William Holland to Catharine Crow, 22 Aug 1850 (23 Aug), E.P. Childers MG (R)
William J. Holland to Caroline Wasson, 27 Sept 1843, John Holland Bm (A)
MISCELLANEOUS (RHEA)
Allen Holland: Bondsman for William W. Pile, 1842
" " Private, Mexican War
C. A. Holland: MG 1850
John Holland: Bondsman for Allen Holland, 1819
John Holland: Bondsman for William J. Holland, 1843
Thomas R. Holland: Bondsman for Alvin Hornsby, 1838
" " " Bondsman for John A. Wasson, 1839
William Holland: Bondsman for Daniel Holland, 1841
" " Private, Mexican War

- - - - - - - - - - - - -

HOLLINS

1850 RHEA CENSUS
William C. Hollins 29 (Va)(Clerk), Juli A. 24, Lucilla 6, James 4, William 2, Theodore 2/12 p. 627-597

- - - - - - - - - - - - -

HOLLOWAY / HOLLAWAY

TAXES (RHEA)
1819 (Capt. John Ramsey's Co.):
Bramillion Holloway 1 WP, 150a
1823 (Capt. Howerton's Co.):
Bermilion Holloway 150a Piney River
1830 RHEA CENSUS
Bermetta Hollaway 002210001 - 00000001 p. 392
James Holloway 1001 - 00001 p. 391
Jesse Holloway 120001 - 1001 p. 368
McGee Holloway 01001 - 10001 p. 392
Samuel Holloway 12001 - 020001 p. 366
William Holloway 31001 - 01001 p. 390
1840 RHEA CENSUS
Burmillian Holloway 0000000001 - 0
Burton W. Holloway 210001 - 010001
James Holloway 121001 - 110001
Joseph P. Holloway 20001 - 11001
Major Holloway 031001 - 320001
Samuel Holloway 3202001 - 0021101
1850 RHEA CENSUS
James Holloway 48 (NC)(Farmer), Elvira 46, Blackstone 20 (Farmer), John M. 19 (Farmer), Richard 17 (Farmer), Mary 15, Samuel H. 13, Ann 11, Jane 9, William D. 5, Milo 3, Harriet 9/12 p. 533-1
John Holloway 24 (Laborer), Margaret 21, Reuben 4, Isaac 1 p. 543-68
Joseph P. Holloway 39 (NC)(Blacksmith), Elizabeth C. 35, Mary J. 16, Nancy E. 14, Berry F. 10, Eliza A. 7, Minerva A. 5, Lovena 3, unnamed 6/12 p. 583-314
Major Holloway 46 (NC)(Farmer), Phebe F. 43, Richard W. 25, Sarah L. 23, Lucinda J. 20, Isaac W. 19, William T. 17, James S. 15, Phebe C. 14, Delila D. 12, Abagail E. 10, Major B. 8, Thomas H. 6, Robert G. 4 p. 535-13
Pleasant Holloway 25 (Farmer), Harriet 31 (Va), Sarah 5, Mary E. 2, Emily 1/12 p. 547-95
Samuel Hollaway 51 (NC)(Farmer), Frances 51 (NC), Eliza A. 28, Emeline 22, John 20 (Farmer), Joseph 17 (Farmer), Andrew J. 14, George W. 14, Samuel H. 11 p. 583-313
Sterling Hollaway 32 (Farmer), Emily 19 p. 547-94
MARRIAGES (RHEA)
Burton W. Holloway to Malinda Wasson, 19 Apr 1831 (26 Apr), James Swan JP (R)
Delila Holloway to William Lemons q.v.
James Holloway to Elvira Miller, 5 Nov 1828, Burton W. Holloway Bm (A)

Joseph P. Holloway to Elizabeth C. Derossett, 5 Oct 1833, Major Holloway Bm (A)
Myra Holloway to Mareel Derossett q.v.
P.M. Holloway to Jane Crews, 24 Feb 1843 (26 Feb), James Holloway Bm (AR)
Pleasant M. Holloway to Harriet Hawkins, 2 Mar 1845 (same), E.E. Wasson JP (AR)
Samuel Holloway to Frances Davison, 23 Dec 1819, J. Fine JP, J. Davison Bm (AR)
Sterling Holaway to Emily Rector, 22 Oct 1849 (24 Oct), Snelson Roberts MG (R)
Thomas Holloway to Anne Worman, 21 Nov 1835, Joseph Worman Bm (A)

MISCELLANEOUS (RHEA)

Burton W. Holloway: Bondsman for James Holloway, 1828
" " " Bm for Dennis McClendon, 1845
Benjamin W. Holloway: Hiwassee District, Lower Goodfield area
J. P. Holloway: Bondsman for Daniel Lemons, 1842
James Holloway: Bondsman for Elijah Runnels, 1823
" " Bondsman for Thomas Majors, 1826
" " Bondsman for M. D. Thompson, 1840
" " Bondsman for P. M. Holloway, 1843
Major Holloway: Bondsman for Joseph P. Holloway, 1833

\- - - - - - - - - - - - -

HOLMES / HOMES

MARRIAGES (RHEA)

Winney Holmes to Thomas Bicknell q.v.

MARRIAGES (MEIGS)

Isah Homes to Rachel Sharp, 12 June 1846 (same), Thomas V. Atchley JP
[1850 Marion Census: Isah Homes 26, Rachell 20, Elizabeth 4, Mary 2, Emily ROBBERTS 19]
Mahala Homes to Thomas Blanton q.v.
Mary Holmes to Charles Prater q.v.

MISCELLANEOUS (MEIGS)

John Homes: Hiwassee District, Ten Mile Stand area

\- - - - - - - - - - - - -

HOLOMAN / HOLMAN / HOLLOMAN / HALAMAN

1830 RHEA CENSUS

Pleasant Holoman 0002 - 2002 p. 387

1840 MEIGS CENSUS

Binton Holman 00001 - 00011 p. 236
Plessant Hollomon 020101 - 202001 p. 246

1850 MEIGS CENSUS

Burton Holman 38 (NC)(Merchant), Sarah 38, Lafayette 18, Samuel W. 16, Newton 14, James 12, Levander M. (m) 6, Infant (m) 1, Lodemia (f) -- [blank] p. 730-131
Plesent Holomon 47 (Farmer), Susannah 41, John 18 (Farmer), Owen 16, Polly Jane 14, Nancy A. 12, Jeremiah 10, Texas (f) 6, Elizabeth 3, Plesant 1 p. 817-801

MARRIAGES (RHEA)

Polly Holloman to Stephen Breeding q.v.

MARRIAGES (MEIGS)

Burton Holman to Sarah Hutchinson, 24 Dec 1844 (3 Jan 1845), Jesse Locke MG
Hannah Holloman to John M. Alford q.v.

MISCELLANEOUS (MEIGS)

Pleasant Holaman: Constable, District 5, 1836
Pleasant Holloman: Representative to General Assembly (House), 1849-1851

\- - - - - - - - - - - - -

HOLT

1840 RHEA CENSUS

David Holt 10001 - 10001

MARRIAGES (RHEA)

Anne Holt to Robert Bolton q.v.
David Holt to Eliza Ann Bolton, 8 June 1835, Abner Witt Bm (A)
Edmond Holt to Polly Emmery or Esumery, 11 July 1819 (same), John Fine JP, Charles Bradey Bm (AR)
Elephus Holt to Elizabeth E. Adams, 22 Dec 1846 (28 Dec), E.P. Childress MG (R)
Eliphius Holt to Martha Benson, 26 Dec 1831, Robert Bell Bm (A)
Elizabeth Holt to William Clark q.v.
Jane Holt to Charles Witt q.v.

\- - - - - - - - - - - - -

HOOD

TAXES (RHEA)

1819 (Capt. McGill's Co.): Robert Hood 1 WP
1823 (Capt. Howard's Co.): Robert Hood 1 WP, 100a

1830 RHEA CENSUS

Robert Hood 21012001 - 102001 p. 381

MISCELLANEOUS (RHEA)

John B. Hood: Established *The Valley Freeman* at Washington in 1825

\- - - - - - - - - - - - -

HOOKE / HOOKS

MARRIAGES (RHEA)

Elizabeth Hooke to Robert H. Hodsden q.v.
John A. Hooks to Mary L. Long, 18 Aug 1835 (same), Benjamin Wallace JP, Charles K. Gillespie Bm (AR)
Robert M. Hooks to Mary K. Rawlings, 22 Mar 1831 (same), Fielding Pope MG, Robert H. Hodsden Bm (AR)

MISCELLANEOUS (RHEA)

John A. Hooke: Early member of Rhea County bar
Robert M. Hooke: Early member of Rhea County bar

\- - - - - - - - - - - - -

HOOPER

1840 RHEA CENSUS

James Hooper 101001 - 211001

1850 RHEA CENSUS

James Hooper 46 (NC)(Farmer), Luisa 43 (NC), John 22 (Farmer), Jane E. 20, Mary A. 18, Caroline 16, Elvira 12, James P. 10, Martha 8, William 5, Eveline 3 p. 604-466

MARRIAGES (RHEA)

Jane E. Hooper to John P. Crow q.v.

MISCELLANEOUS (RHEA)
James Hooper or Hoover: JP 1840-1847

- - - - - - - - - - - - -

HOOVER

1840 RHEA CENSUS
Frederick Hoover 10220001 - 3001101
MARRIAGES (RHEA)
Ann Hoover to Carroll Johnston q.v.
MISCELLANEOUS (RHEA)
Frederick Hoover: Bondsman for Frederick Prysock, 1834
" " Bondsman for Charles H. Royster, 1834

- - - - - - - - - - - - -

HOPKINS

TAXES (RHEA)
1823 (Capt. Brown's Co.) Thomas Hopkins 5 Town Lots
MARRIAGES (RHEA)
Polly Hopkins (Mrs) to Henry Tuttle q.v.
MISCELLANEOUS (RHEA)
Robert Hopkins: Lot 43, Town of Washington, 1812

- - - - - - - - - - - - -

HORN

1850 MEIGS CENSUS
H. W. Horn 43 (SC)(School Teacher), Mary 36 (SC), Joseph C. 8 (SC), Sarah Ann 10 (SC), Samuel L. 6, John W. 2 p. 727-112

- - - - - - - - - - - - -

HORNER

1850 RHEA CENSUS
Doctor W. Horner Unk (Unk)(Blacksmith), Vicey Unk (Unk), Margaret Unk, Nancy A. 3, Lucretia 1, William THOMPSON 18 (SC)(Apprentice Blacksmith) p. 617-524
George W. Horner 21 (Farmer), Elizabeth 19, Margaret E.J. 1/12 p. 617-518

- - - - - - - - - - - - -

HORNSBY

TAXES (RHEA)
1823 (Capt. Braselton's Co.): Brenkley Hornsby 1 WP
(Capt. Brown's Co.): William Hornsby 141a
1830 RHEA CENSUS
B. Hornsby 10002 - 00001 [2 written over 1 or vice versa]
Winny Hornsby 0011 - 0211101 p. 366
1840 RHEA CENSUS
Alvin Hornsby 00001 - 20011
Brenkly Hornsby 211001 - 020101
1850 RHEA CENSUS
Dealthea E. Hornsby 34, Mary A. 10, Winny T. 8, Sarah W. 7, William W. 5 (Ill), Dealthea E. 3 (Ky) p. 565-184
MARRIAGES (RHEA)
Alvin Hornsby to Delthia or Dealtha Wilson, 12 Aug 1836 (same), James McCanse JP, Thomas R. Holland Bm (AR)
[Dealtha, dau of James M. and Anne Cozby Wilson; Alvin, son of William and Winning Hornsby]
Brinkley Hornsby to Ester or Esther Falls, 12 Jan 1828 (13 Jan), Matthew Hubbard JP, Richard Waterhouse Bm (AR)
Elizabeth Hornsby to John Paul q.v.
MISCELLANEOUS (RHEA and MEIGS)
Brinkley Hornsby: Hiwassee District, Pinhook Ferry area
" " House used for elections in District 5
" " Sold lots in Peakland (Pinhook Landing)

- - - - - - - - - - - - -

HORTON

1840 MEIGS CENSUS
Robert Horton 000001 - 000001 p. 226
MARRIAGES (RHEA)
Archibald Horton to Ellen or Eleanor Newman, 18 Mar 1812 (no return), Jesse Horton Bm (AR)
Patsy Horton to Jacob Shultz q.v.
MISCELLANEOUS (RHEA)
Jesse Horton: Bondsman for Archibald Horton, 1812

- - - - - - - - - - - - -

HOSLIN

MARRIAGES (RHEA)
Catherine Hoslin to Hiram Richenson q.v.

- - - - - - - - - - - - -

HOUNSHELL

1830 RHEA CENSUS
David Hounshell 001211 - 000001 p. 360
1840 MEIGS CENSUS
David Hounshell 001011 - 000101 p. 241
MARRIAGES (MEIGS)
M. H. Hounshell to L. L. Wear q.v.
Nancy A. Hounshell to Jonathan Wood q.v.
William Hounshell to Harriet J. Peters, 13 Feb 1849 (14 Feb), Snelson Roberts MG
MISCELLANEOUS (MEIGS)
David Hounshell: Hiwassee District
" " Lots 8,18,20,23,25,49 in Decatur, 1836
" " Commissioner to lay off Decatur Courthouse and to sell town lots, 1836
" " On Circuit Court jury, 1836
" " Common School Com., District 7, 1838
William Hounshell: Private, Mexican War

- - - - - - - - - - - - -

HOUPT / HOPE

1830 RHEA CENSUS
Volotine Houpt 12001001 - 111101 p. 393
William Hope 200001 - 00001 p. 394
1840 RHEA CENSUS
Valentine Houpt 0101000001 - 0010001

1850 RHEA CENSUS
Margaret Houpt 27: see John Taff
Mary Houpt 53 (Va), Sarah 26, Adeline 22, Benjamin F. 17 (Farmer), John A. 4 p. 578-280
Valentine Houpt 85: see Berryman G. Mather
MARRIAGES (RHEA)
Alcy R. Houpt to Sarah Perigin, 27 July 1842, James W. Vernon and Levi W. Ferguson Bm (A)
Jane Houpt to John Taff q.v.
Mariah Houpt to Edward Henson q.v.
William Hope to Lucinda Britewell, 24 Aug 1825 (same), John Rice JP, Orville Paine Bm (AR)
MARRIAGES (MEIGS)
Margaret Houpt to Samuel Hardy q.v.
MISCELLANEOUS (RHEA)
Valentine Houpt: Bondsman for Christian Carrell, 1827
" " Revolutionary War Pensioner(?)
Vollentine Houpt: Hiwassee District

HOUSE / HAUSE / HASE

1850 RHEA CENSUS
John House 30, Levena 25, Martha J. 9/12: see Jane Hill
MARRIAGES (RHEA)
Harriet Hause to John W. Thompson q.v.
John House to Vina Hill, 6 Nov 1848 (same), W. R. S. Thompson JP (R)
Polly House to Hollingsworth Vandever q.v.
Shadrick Hase (Hose) to Hannah Garrison, 2 July 1849 (5 July), Daniel Broyles JP (R)
MISCELLANEOUS (RHEA)
Adam House: Bondsman for Hollingsworth Vandever, 1810

HOUSER / HOWSER

1830 RHEA CENSUS
James Howser 110001 - 011001 p. 371
Josiah Howser 100001 - 30001 p. 372
1840 MEIGS CENSUS
James Houser 0111001 - 0201001 p. 229
Josiah Houser 2201001 - 003001 p. 232
1850 MEIGS CENSUS
Ebenezer Houser 25 (Farmer), Milly Ann 25, Sarah Ann 4, Betsy Jane 2, Joseph JENKINS 25 (NC)(Farmer) p. 755-344
James Houser 57 (Va)(Farmer), Mary 53 (Va), Mary Ann 25, James A. 22 (Doctor), John M. 20 (Farmer), Elizabeth Jane 18, Minerva E. 14 p. 742-234
Josiah Houser 56 (Va)(Millwright), Malinda 43 (Va), Mary Jane 23, Betsy Ann 22, Jessee 15 (Farmer), Milton 14, Henry 11, Virginia 8, Caroline 6, James K.P. 5, Eliza 3 p. 755-340
Josiah Houser Jr. 28 (Va)(Farmer), Louisa 28, James L. 8, Dorian (f) 6, Deborah Jane 4, Thomas B. 2 p. 742-233
MARRIAGES (MEIGS)
Ebenezer Houser to Milly Ann Brightwell, 28 June 1845 (29 June), B.F. McKenzie JP
Frances Houser to William A. Reynolds q.v.
Josiah Howser to Louisa Davis, 26 Nov 1840 (same), B.F. McKenzie JP
Mary Jane Houser to Elgin Brightwell q.v.
Nancy Houser to Ganium Brightwell q.v.
MISCELLANEOUS (RHEA and MEIGS)
James Houser: Hiwassee District
" " House used to hold elections, 1836
" " On Circuit Court jury, 1836
John Houser: Private, Mexican War
Josiah Houser: Bondsman for Ambler Grubbs, 1828
" " Bondsman for Eldrid Grubb, 1831
" " Purchased Lot 66 in Decatur, 1836
" " Cherokee Removal muster roll, 1836

HOUSLEY / HOUSELEY

MARRIAGES (MEIGS)
G.W. Houseley to Sarah Elder, 9 May 1839 (same), John Taff JP [1850 Hamilton Census: George W. Housley 33, Sarah 31, Robert 10, William 8, Mary 7, Elizabeth 5, James 2, William RAY 16, William BEELING 16]

HOUSTON

1850 RHEA CENSUS
Daniel Houston 28 (NC)(Farmer), Sally 27, Joseph H. 8, John H. 7, Louisa E. 3, Margaret D. 1, Margaret HOUSTON 52 (Scotland) p. 614-459
Samuel Houston 10: see Sanders D. Broyles
Thomas Houston 15: see Garlington Bramlett
MISCELLANEOUS (RHEA)
Sam Houston: Bondsman for Benjmin C. Stout, 1818

HOWARD

TAXES (RHEA)
1808 (John Henry's List): Abraham Howard 1 WP
John Howard 1 WP
1819 (Capt. McGill's Co.): Abraham Howard 1 WP, 362a
1823 (Capt. Howard's Co.): Samuel Howard 1 WP, 234½a
William Howard 1 WP, 204½a
1830 RHEA CENSUS
Eliza Howard 1111 - 0010201 p. 395
Samuel Howard 000101 - 112001 p. 395
William Howard 221101 - 01001 p. 395
1840 RHEA CENSUS
Albert Howard 00001 - 20101
1850 RHEA CENSUS
Abraham Howard 70 (Pa)(Hammerman), Kizziah 28, William 13, Martha 2 p. 582-310 [William married Kizziah Thrailkill on 15 Apr 1838 in Roane Co]
Allison Howard 46 (Blacksmith), Margaret 45, Robert T 23 (Farmer), Penelope 26, Ruth C. 15, Thomas J. 5, William A. 1 p. 534-13
John Howard 24 (Blacksmith), Sophia 24, Ruth J. 2, John VANPELT 67 (Va)(School Teacher) p. 585-328
1850 MEIGS CENSUS
William Howard 29 (Farmer), Elizabeth Jane 24, Martha Ann 6, James E. 4, George W. 1 p. 766-419

MARRIAGES (RHEA)
Allison Howard to Margaret Parks, 23 June 1821 (26 June), John Rice JP (AR)
Hannah Howard to John Bush q.v.
Logan Howard to Mariena Howard, 9 Aug 1832 (same), W.H. Bell MG (R)
Lucinda Howard to William Cobb q.v.
Mansion Howard to Mariah Parks, 20 Jan 1824 (same), A. David JP, Alexander Coulter Bm (AR)
Marienia Howard to Logan Howard q.v.
Olivia Howard to Robert Crawford q.v.
Robert T. Howard to Penelopy Majors, 18 Apr 1844 (same), Asa Newport MG (R)
[Robert, son of Allison and Margaret]
MISCELLANEOUS (RHEA and MEIGS)
Abraham Howard: JP 1808-1819
Albert Howard: Bondsman for Robert Crawford, 1831
William Howard: Surety for John Helton, 1850

- - - - - - - - - - - - -

HOWE

MARRIAGES (RHEA)
Mary Howe or Polly Hall to David D. Stockton q.v.

- - - - - - - - - - - - -

HOWELL / HAWELL / HOWEL

1830 RHEA CENSUS
John Hawell 100001 - 1001 p. 353
1840 RHEA CENSUS
John Howel 121011 - 101001
MARRIAGES (RHEA)
James B. Howell to Betsey Jones, 29 Jan 1828 (same), Peach Taylor JP, Thomas Blankinship Bm (AR)
MARRIAGES (MEIGS)
B.F. Howell to Margaret S. Brown, 3 Apr 1841 (4 Apr), Stephen Winton JP
MISCELLANEOUS (RHEA)
Thomas Howell: Bondsman for Jeremiah Howerton, 1817

- - - - - - - - - - - - -

HOWERTON / HOOVERTON

TAXES (RHEA)
1808 (John Henry's List): Jackson Howerton 1 WP
1819 (John Lewis' Dist.): Edward Howerton 1 WP
Grief Howerton 358a
Jackson Howerton 1 WP
Micajah Howerton 1 WP
(Capt. Wm McCray's Co.): Jeremiah Howerton 1 WP
John Howerton 175a
1823 (Capt. Lewis' Co.): Edmond Howerton 1 WP
Grief Howerton 350a
Jackson Howerton 1 WP
Micajah Howerton 1 WP
1830 RHEA CENSUS
Ed Hooverton 100101 - 120221001 p. 391
[2 is blurred; may have been erased]
Jeremiah Howerton 022001 - 200201 p. 391
Jackson Hooverton 2211001 - 002001 p. 391
Micajah Hooverton 001001 - 0001 p. 391
1840 RHEA CENSUS
Micajah Howerton 0010001 - 000001
1850 RHEA CENSUS
Micajah Howerton 46 (Va)(Farmer), Jane 46 p. 599-404
[Micajah Howerton married Jane Brown on 19 Aug 1819 in Roane County]

MARRIAGES (RHEA)
Betsey Howerton to Hiram Coots q.v.
Dicey Howerton to Berry Hogg q.v.
Edmund Howerton to Polly Oliver, 3 Jan 1822, Henry Collins JP (AR)
Jackson Howerton to Hannah Brown, 3 Oct 1812, Grief Howerton Bm (A)
Jeremiah Howerton to Lucy Johnson, 3 Jan 1817 (same), A. Ferguson JP, Thomas Howell Bm (R)
Lucy Howerton to Johnson Williams q.v.
Polly Howerton to John Purdon q.v.
MARRIAGES (MEIGS)
Jonathan D. Howerton to Louiza J. Ledbetter, 23 July 1847 (same), Leroy Looney JP

MISCELLANEOUS (RHEA)
Grief Howerton: Bondsman for Jackson Howerton, 1812
Jackson Howerton: Bondsman for Johnson Williams, 1810
" " Bondsman for Thomas Harnett, 1817
Jeremiah Howerton: Bondsman for Wm Singleton, 1819
" " Bondsman for Hiram Coots, 1823
Micajah Howerton: Bondsman for Richard Butler, 1819
" " Bondsman for Robert Cooper, 1819
" " Bondsman for Joseph Hicks, 1839

- - - - - - - - - - - -

HOYAL / HOYLE / HOIL

1840 RHEA CENSUS
Clayton Hoyle 00101 - 03001 p. 245
William Hoyle 10001 - 10011 p. 227
1850 RHEA CENSUS
John Hoyle 50 (Va)(Physician), Rebecca A. 30, Virginia 8, Barbary C. 4 p. 612-437
1850 MEIGS CENSUS
Claton Hoyl 33 (Farmer), Permelia 40 (SC), Catharine 19, Mary 17, Sarah 4 p. 818-807
Jane Hoyl 22, Mary 1 p. 783-556
MARRIAGES (RHEA)
Clayton Hoyal to Pamelia Genoe or Genno, 1 Apr 1834 (3 Apr), James Wilson JP, John Davis Bm (AR)
Mary Ann Hoyal to John Porter q.v.
MARRIAGES (MEIGS)
Jonas Hoyl to Parthena W. Chatten, 30 Sept 1845 (9 Oct), M.C. Hawk MG
Wm Hoyle to Martha Dexter, 6 Nov 1838, John Brown MG
MISCELLANEOUS (RHEA and MEIGS)
Clayton Hoyle: Private, Mexican War
James Hoil: Ocoee District
Jacob Hoyal: Private, Mexican War
John Hoyal: Bondsman for Samuel R. Hackett, 1833
" " Bondsman for James H. Stewart, 1835
" " Bondsman for Larkin F. Thompson, 1836
" " Bondsman for John Gaston, 1840

- - - - - - - - - - -

HOYT

MARRIAGES (RHEA)
Catherine Ann Hoyt to William O. Kent q.v.

- - - - - - - - - - - - -

HUBBERT / HUBBERD / HUBBARD

TAXES (RHEA)
1819 (Capt. J. Lewis' Dist.): Matthew Hubbert 1 WP 200a
1823 (Capt. Lewis' Co.): Matthew Hubbard 1 WP, 200a
MARRIAGES (RHEA)
Betsy Hubbard to Elias Ferguson q.v.
Jane Hubbert to Laben B. Rowden q.v.
Matthew Hubbert to Polly Woodward, 17 Feb 1817, Alexander Ferguson Bm (A)
MISCELLANEOUS (RHEA and MEIGS)
Aden Hubbard: Hiwassee District
Matthew Hubbert: JP 1827-29, 1831-36 (Rhea)
William Hubbard: Hiwassee District

- - - - - - - - - - - - -

HUCKABAY

1830 RHEA CENSUS
Arthur Huckabay 0000001 - 01001 p. 364

- - - - - - - - - - - - -

HUDDLESTON / HUDELSTON

TAXES (RHEA)
1819 (Capt. J. Lewis' Dist.): Thomas Huddleston 1 WP, 80a
1850 RHEA CENSUS
John Huddleston 16: see William Gipson
MARRIAGES (RHEA)
Catherine Huddleston to John Birdsong q.v.
Jesse Huddleston to Polly Ann Hoy or Hog, 6 Feb 1840 (7 Feb), Wm B. Gordon MG, David Able Bm (AR)
Nancy Huddleston to Josiah Birdsong q.v.
Sedney Hudleston to David Able q.v.
Thomas Hudelston to Maryann Martin, 8 Apr 1839 (9 Apr), Wm B. Gordon JP/MG, David N. Roddy Bm (AR)
MISCELLANEOUS (RHEA and MEIGS)
Jesse Huddleston: Bondsman for William Lowry, 1839
Wm A. Huddleston: JP(?) 1842 [Meigs Co]

- - - - - - - - - - - - -

HUDSON / HUTSON

TAXES (RHEA)
1823 (Capt. Wilson's Co.): David Hutson 1 WP, 50a TennR
(Capt. Brown's Co.): John Hudson 3 BP, 219a T Ri
1830 RHEA CENSUS
Benjamin Hudson 00001 - 100001 p. 363
David Hudson 1210001 - 100201 p. 363
Jesse Hudson 0012101 - 0000001 p. 361
Jesse A. Hudson 0001 - 1001 p. 355
John B. Hutson 02010001 - 10101001 p. 355
1840 RHEA CENSUS
Benjamin Hudson 031001 - 101001
1840 MEIGS CENSUS
Andrew Hutson 00001 - 0 p. 234
Clinton Hudson 002001 - 230001 p. 228
1850 MEIGS CENSUS
Benjamin Hutson 41 (NC)(Farmer), Jane 37 (Ky), Ramsey M. 20 (Farmer), John J. 15 (Farmer), David N. 15 (Farmer), Nancy Ann 11, Edward 10, Elizabeth 10, George W. 8, Delilah 4, Lorinda 1 p. 812-758
Marion Hutson 18: see Thomas P. Davis
MARRIAGES (RHEA)
Benjamin Hutson to Catharine C. Foashee, 9 Sept 1828 (16 Sept), Beal Gaither JP, Randolph Gibson Bm (AR)
Jesse Hudson to Matilda Everett, 10 Mar 1820 (same), John B. Hudson Bm (A)
Susana Hudson to Simpson Everett q.v.
Susannah Hudson to Benjamin G. Parker q.v.
William Hutson to Elizabeth Ryon, 15 Dec 1835 (16 Dec), William Green MG, Benjamin Hutson Bm (AR)
MARRIAGES (MEIGS)
Benjamin Hutson to Jane Wan, 4 Sept 1848 (5 Sept), William Green MG
Mary Hutson to Grover M. Benson q.v.
Nancy Hutson to Wilie O. Martin q.v.
MISCELLANEOUS (RHEA and MEIGS)
Benjamin Hutson: Bondsman for William Hutson, 1835
John Hutson: Bondsman for Peach Taylor, 1824
John B. Hudson: Bondsman for Jesse Hudson, 1820
" " " Hiwassee District

- - - - - - - - - - - - -

HUEY

TAXES (RHEA)
1823 (Capt. Piper's Co.): Lazarus Huey 1 WP

- - - - - - - - - - - - -

HUFF

TAXES (RHEA)
1823 (Capt. Wilson's Co.): John Huff 1 WP
(Capt. Howerton's Co.): John Huff 1 WP
1830 RHEA CENSUS
John Huff 0130001 - 100101 p. 364
Susan Huff 101012 - 110101 p. 365
1840 MEIGS CENSUS
John Huff 00032001 - 0010001 p. 245
Urial S. Huff 00001 - 10001 p. 245
1850 MEIGS CENSUS
B.F. Huff 30 (Mo)(Farmer), Nancy 30, Elizabeth C. 6, Elmira Jane 4, John T. 1 p. 815-787
John Huff 61, Nancy 55 (Va) p. 815-786
Louisa Huff 32, Malinda C. 10, Nancy Jane 8, John F. 7, Isaac M. 6, William E. 5 p. 815-784
MARRIAGES (RHEA)
Mary Huff to David Borden q.v.
MARRIAGES (MEIGS)
B.F. Huff to Nancy Wassen, 20 Dec 1842 (same), John Farmer MG
Leonard Huff to Frankey Sears, 19 Nov 1845 (20 Nov), William Green MG
Mary J. Huff to James S. Lillard q.v.

Peter Huff to Soleta Brown, 25 Nov 1841 "this license was returned to my office May 1, 1847 and recorded" C.C. Robeson, Clerk

MISCELLANEOUS (RHEA and MEIGS)

John Huff: Chairman of County Court, 1847
" " Bondsman for Elijah Cameron, 1823
" " Hiwassee District, Pinhook Ferry area
Peter Huff: Cherokee Removal muster roll, 1836

HUFNER

MARRIAGES (MEIGS)

Elizabeth Hufner to Justice Edwards q.v.

HUGHES / HUGHS / HUGH / HEWS

TAXES (RHEA)

1819 (Capt. W.S. Bradley's Dist.): Ezekiel Hughes 1 WP
1823 (Capt. Brown's Co.): Abraham Hughes 1 WP
(Capt. Howard's Co.): John Hughes 200a
Thomas Hughes 1 WP

1830 RHEA CENSUS

Caswell Hughs 02001 - 20001 p. 374
John Hughes 000110001 - 00000001 p. 380
Nancy Hughs 012 - 01100001 p. 379
Thomas Hughs 11001 - 20001 p. 380

1840 RHEA CENSUS

Jno W. Hugh 22001 - 11001

1840 MEIGS CENSUS

Caswell Hews 0010001 - 00001 p. 232
George Hews 021101 - 200001 p. 226
John Hews 1102001 - 1310101 p. 234
Rice Hews 00001 - 00001 p. 234

1850 RHEA CENSUS

Abner Hughs 35 (Farmer), Mary 38, John 14, Mary 12, Priscilla 10, Luisa J. 9, Elizabeth 7, Nancy 6, Thomas J. 1 p. 636-665

John Hughs 45 (Farmer), Elizbeth 46 (Ky), Elizabeth M. 18, Emaline 16, Sarah A. 14, Luisa J. 10, Jerusa E. 8, John C. 4, Orlinda C. 4, Lucinda H. 1 p. 631-625

John W. Hugh 38 (NC)(Farmer), Mary 39 (SC), McHenry 18 (Farmer), Rufus C. 17 (Farmer), Martha 15, Jackson 12, Thomas P. 10, Elizabeth 9, John 7, Mary M. 5, James P. 3, Eliza R. 3/12 p. 619-541

Josiah Hughs 37 (Hammerman), Patsey Unk (Va), Nancy A. 18, William J. 14, Samuel G. 2, Sarah C. 1, Martha C. 1/12 p. 544-72

William Hughs 22 (Farmer), Sarah A. 21, Elizabeth C. 1 p. 632-626

1850 MEIGS CENSUS

Caswell Hughes 53 (Va), Paulina 34, Jack S 18 (Farmer), Martha Jane 10, Eliza Ann 10, Mahala C. 6, Matilda 4, Roena 2 p. 756-349

MARRIAGES (RHEA)

Abraham Hughes to Mary Lea, 24 Nov 1821 (same), J. Cozby JP, George Weeks Bm (AR)

Abraham Hughes to Easter Reacer, 16 July 1828 (no return), William Hughes Bm (AR)
[1850 Macon Census: Abram Hughes 49, Easter 39, John 21, Margaret 18, Barbara 16, Nancy 12, James 10, Ezekiel 8, Abram 5, Mary Ann 3]

Abner Hughes to Mary Olinger, 5 Apr 1834 (6 Apr), Benjamin Posey MG, Elijah Blythe Bm (AR)

James Hughes to Jane Stockton, 23 Oct 1825 (24 Oct), Daniel Briggs MG, William Wann Bm (AR)

Jefferson Hughes to Leney Percy, 29 Aug 1848 (30 Aug), Washington Morgan JP (R)

John Hughs to Mary Parker, 1 Feb 1827 (2 Feb), Thomas Hall MG, Stephen Hughs Bm (AR)

John W. Hughes to Mary Davis, 2 Feb 1830 (5 Feb), John Cozby JP, David Singleton Bm (AR)

Louisa Hughes to William A. Burns q.v.
Mary Ann Hughes to William R. Presly q.v.
Nancy Hughes to Joseph Alexander q.v.
Rebecca Hughes to Thomas Romines q.v.
Selah Hughes to Elijah Rowden q.v.

William H. Hughs to Sarah A. Foust, 16 Sept 1848 (17 Sept), John O. Torbett JP (R)

MARRIAGES (MEIGS)

Mary Hughs to G.W. Click q.v.

Rice Hughes to Martha E. Taff, 2 Jan 1840 (same), J.W. Oakes JP

MISCELLANEOUS (RHEA and MEIGS)

Abraham Hughs: Bondsman for George Weeks, 1821
Caty Hughes: Hiwassee District, Lower Goodfield
John Hughs: Hiwassee District
John W. Hewes: Bondsman for Thomas O. George, 1840
Stephen Hughes: Bondsman for John Hughs, 1827
William Hughs: Bondsman for Abraham Hughs, 1828
" " Bondsman for Jacob Wells, 1833
" " Cherokee Removal muster roll, 1836

HUGHSON

TAXES (RHEA)

1819 (Capt. John Lewis' Dist.): James Hughson 1 WP

HUMBART / HUMBOLT / HUMBURD / HUMBERT / HAMBERT

TAXES (RHEA)

1823 (Capt. Piper's Co.): William Humburd 1 WP

1830 RHEA CENSUS

Jaden Humbert 100001 - 1001 p. 361
Samuel Humbert 220001 - 11001 p. 362
William Hambert 110001 - 01101 p. 360

MARRIAGES (RHEA)

Adam Humbolt or Humbart to Elizabeth Brazelton, 11 Dec 1827 (same), Daniel M. Stockton JP and Bm (AR)

HUMPHREY / HUMPHRY / HUMPHRYS

TAXES (RHEA)

1819 (Capt. McGill's Co.): Hester Humphrys 1 WP
1823 (Capt. Smith's Co.): John Humphrey 1 WP

1830 RHEA CENSUS

David Humpry 1011 - 2222001 p. 395

1850 MEIGS CENSUS

Thomas Humphrey 30 (Va)(Farmer), Elizabeth 24, William 2, Sarah 1 p. 717-36

MARRIAGES (RHEA)

Carlisle Humphreys to Elizabeth O. Campbell, 9 May 1814, Wm D. Wilson Bm (A)

Carlisle Humphreys to Harriet A. Campbell, 4 Mar 1816, M. Donald MG, Asahel Rawlings Bm (AR)

MISCELLANEOUS (RHEA)

Carlisle Humphreys: Signed petition to move Indian Agency
" " Lot 16, Town of Washington, 1812

- - - - - - - - - - - - -

HUNNYCUT

MARRIAGES (RHEA)

Thomas Hunnycut to Tharsey Helm, 24 Mar 1825, William Collins Bm (A)

- - - - - - - - - - - - -

HUNTER

1830 RHEA CENSUS

Joshua Hunter 00000000001 - 0000000001 p. 376
Thomas Hunter 01111001 - 0111201 p. 376
William Hunter 110001 - 1001 p. 368

1840 MEIGS CENSUS

Joshua Hunter 00001 - 01 p. 237
Samuel Hunter 0112101 - 0110101 p. 236
Thomas Hunter 000130001 - 00121 p. 237
William Hunter 2311001 - 000001 p. 224

1850 MEIGS CENSUS

Andrew Hunter 27 (Farmer), Angaline 22, Mary Ann 1, Hugh McKINLEY 33 (Farmer) p. 769-444 [Angaline and Hugh, children of John and Susanna Locke McKinley]

John Hunter 33 (Farmer), Ruena 22, Plesant 7 p. 771-461

Samuel Hunter 55 (NC)(Farmer), Catharine 57 (Va), Sarah Ann 18, Samuel 15 p. 723-82

Sarah Hunter 42, Margaret 36, Elizabeth 27, Martha 22, George W. SMITH 10 p. 770-445
[Sarah, Margaret, Elizabeth, and Martha, daus of Thomas Hunter who died in 1849]

William Hunter 52 (Va)(Farmer), Minerva 47 (NC), William 23 (Farmer), Robert 18 (Farmer), Eli 16 (Farmer), John 14, Jasper 12, Joseph 10, Sarah Jane 6 p. 724-91

William H. Hunter 34 (Farmer), Catharine E. 24, William O. 4, Thomas M. 3, Robert A. 1 p. 723-81

MARRIAGES (RHEA)

George Hunter to Margaret Small, 23 Apr 1811 (same), James Kelly Bm (AR)

John Hunter to Katherine Eaves, 26 Jan 1843, Thomas Leuty Bm (A)

Joshua Hunter to Louisa Locke, 13 Nov 1833 (14 Nov), John Henninger MGMEC (R)
[Joshua, son of Thomas Hunter; Louisa, dau of Robert and Nancy Moore Locke. Joshua and Louisa had one dau, Almira. In 1850, Joshua was living in Hamilton County with his second wife, Susan Gardenhire Hunter]

Fanney Hunter to Sampson Prowell q.v.

Mariah Hunter to John W. Smith q.v.
[Mariah, dau of Thomas Hunter]

Peggy Hunter to Green Powell q.v.

MARRIAGES (MEIGS)

Anderson Hunter to Florence Hayslett, 7 Nov 1843 (8 Nov), John Seabourn JP

Andrew Hunter to Angeline McKinley, 1 Aug 1848 (same), William Arrants JP

Dorcas A. Hunter to W. C. Hutchison q.v.

Harriet M. Hunter to Thomas Miller q.v.

John Hunter to Roena Moore, 25 Dec 1849 (same), William Arrants JP

John P. Hunter to Mary T. Johnson, 4 Jan 1842

Thomas Hunter to Sarah Ann Godsey, 19 Nov 1842 (20 Nov), Peach Taylor JP

William H. Hunter to Catherine E. Johnson, 14 June 1842 (same), H. Douglass MG

MISCELLANEOUS (RHEA)

Jacob Hunter: Bondsman for Henry Nave, 1809
" " Living in Town of Washington in 1813
William Hunter: Bondsman for Martin Rigg, 1825

MISCELLANEOUS (MEIGS)

A.C. Hunter: MG 1849-50
J. Hunter: Hiwassee District
John Hunter: 3rd Corp., Cherokee Removal muster roll
John P. Hunter: Pvt., Cherokee Removal muster roll, 1836
T. Hunter: JP 1849
Thomas Hunter: Hiwassee District, Concord area
" " On Circuit Court jury, 1836
" " Will dated 1849 mentions children: Joshua, John, Thomas, Andrew, Mariah (Smith), Sarah, Margaret, Elizabeth, and Martha
William M. Hunter: Cherokee Removal muster roll, 1837

- - - - - - - - - - - - -

HURST

1840 RHEA CENSUS

Eli Hurst 01001 - 30001

MISCELLANEOUS (MEIGS)

Elijah Hurst: Hiwassee District

- - - - - - - - - - - - -

HURT

MISCELLANEOUS (RHEA)

John Hurt: On Surveyor's list of land south of Tenn River
Joseph Hurt: On Surveyor's list of land south of Tenn River

- - - - - - - - - - - - -

HUTCHESON / HUTCHERSON / HUTCHINSON

1840 RHEA CENSUS

Alfred Hutchinson 101121 - 12011
Margaret Hutchinson 12121 - 0201001

1840 MEIGS CENSUS

Charles Hutcheson 220011 - 00101 p. 228
Isaac Hutcheson 00001 - 00001 p. 235

1850 RHEA CENSUS

Alfred Hutcheson 42 (Farmer), Matilda 38, William N. 21 (Farmer), Arvagena F. 15, Darius C. 12, Luvena 11, Cyrus 9, Rebecca T. 7, George N. 5, Samantha 3, George MILLICAN 22 (Farmer) p. 631-622

Isaac S. Hutcheson 24 (Farmer), Ruth 21, Charles A. 3/12, John WEST 15 p. 636-666
1850 MEIGS CENSUS
William Hutcherson 29 (Merchant) p. 740-57
MARRIAGES (RHEA)
Martha J. Hutcherson to Pleasant Doughtry q.v.
MARRIAGES (MEIGS)
Isaac Hutchinson to Mary Stokes, 29 Jan 1840
Mary A. Hutcherson to Robert E. Schoolfield q.v.
Sarah Hutchinson to Burton Holman q.v.
W.C. Hutchison to Dorcas A. Hunter, 20 Oct 1850, M.A. Wood Sur
MISCELLANEOUS (RHEA and MEIGS)
Alfred Hutchinson: Bondsman for Peter Ryan, 1844
" " Ocoee District
Charles Hutcheson: Ocoee District

\- - - - - - - - - - - -

HUTSELL

1850 MEIGS CENSUS
Samuel Hutsell 38 (Va)(Brickmason), Mary 30 (Ireland), Hester V. 8, Lydia Ann 7, Mary E. 6, William W. 5, John A. 4, Charles L. 2, Samuel S. 1 p. 789-596 [Samuel married Mary Gibbony on 12 Aug 1839 in Ashe Co., NC; Samuel, son of John and Christina Hounshell Hutsell; Mary born in County Tyrone, Ireland, 2 Feb 1820, the dau of William and Jane Gibbony]
MARRIAGES (MEIGS)
Elijah Hutsell to Lucinda Cole, 1 Nov 1841 (2 Nov), James M. Hague JP
[1850 McMinn Census: Elijah Hutsell 44, Lucinda 31, James 7, Ellen 6, Martha 4, Taylor 3, Infant 1]

\- - - - - - - - - - - -

IGOU

1830 RHEA CENSUS
Jno Igou 30001 - 02011 p. 372
Saml Igou 000011 - 110001 p. 375
MARRIAGES (RHEA)
Ruth Igou to William Wheeler q.v.
MISCELLANEOUS (RHEA and MEIGS)
John Igou: Hiwassee District, Lower Goodfield area
" " Bondsman for Peter H. Bullock, 1835
Samuel Igou: Bondsman for James Blevins, 1827
" " Bondsman for John Elder, 1828
" " Hiwassee District, Cottonport area

\- - - - - - - - - - - -

INGLE

1830 RHEA CENSUS
William Ingle 0120001 - 0110001 p. 375
1840 MEIGS CENSUS
John Ingle 00021001 - 00010001 p. 237
William Ingle 00012001 - 00020001 p. 237
1850 RHEA CENSUS
Jefferson Ingle 38 (Farmer), Mahala 37, John 16, Juli A. 15, Eliza J. 13, Barbery E. 12, William 10, James G. 5 p. 549-107
1850 MEIGS CENSUS
John Ingle 63 (Farmer), Betsey 55, William 34 (Farmer), Adam 29 (Farmer), Michael 24 (Farmer) p. 771-462
William Ingle 63 (Md)(Farmer), Rebecca 65 (Va), Jacob 26, Elizabeth 23 p. 749-297
MARRIAGES (MEIGS)
John Ingle Sr. to Marthena Moore, 20 Dec 1843, John T. Blevins JP
Polly Ingle to Emanuel Rhinehart q.v.
MISCELLANEOUS (RHEA and MEIGS)
Adam Ingle: Cherokee Removal muster roll, 1837
John Ingle: War of 1812
" " Died during Mexican War, 1846-47
William Ingle: Mexican War
" " Bondsman for James M. Sappington, 1826
" " Hiwassee District, Concord area

\- - - - - - - - - - - -

INGRAM

MARRIAGES (RHEA)
Amey Ingram to James C. Francis q.v.
MARRIAGES (MEIGS)
Hiram Ingram: Purchased Lot 24 in Decatur, 1836

\- - - - - - - - - - - -

INLAND

1830 RHEA CENSUS
Lewis Inland 0000001 - 22001 p. 380

\- - - - - - - - - - - -

INMAN

1840 MEIGS CENSUS
William Inman 00001 - 00001 p. 240
MARRIAGES (RHEA)
Polly Ann Inman to Robert Davis q.v.
MARRIAGES (MEIGS)
Lurenna Inman to Andrew Stuart q.v.
MISCELLANEOUS (RHEA and MEIGS)
Argyl Inman: Cherokee Removal muster roll, 1837
J. W. Inman: Early merchant in Town of Washington
Joseph H. Inman: Bondsman for James Ferguson, 1836

\- - - - - - - - - - - -

IRELAND

TAXES (RHEA)
1823 (Capt. Piper's Co.): William Ireland 1 WP

\- - - - - - - - - - - -

ISH

TAXES (RHEA)
1819 (Capt. Bradley's Dist.): Alexander Ish 1 Town Lot
MISCELLANEOUS (RHEA)
Alexander Ish: Lot 21, Town of Washington, 1812
[1850 Blount Census: Alex Ish 60, Elizabeth 46, Amos 20, Nancy 15, Hester 12, Wm 10, Benjamin 9, Josephus 6, Lucy WEST 60]

\- - - - - - - - - - - -

ISHAM / ISUM / ISAM

1850 MEIGS CENSUS
Bolen Isum 41 (Farmer), Elizabeth 35, Lavena 17, Henry 14, William 12, Frankland 10, Juda 6, Jasper 3, Noah 1 p. 736-347
Judy Isam 65 (Va), Jonathan 23 (Farmer), Angaline S. 14, Charles S. 10 p. 756-350
MARRIAGES (RHEA)
Rebecca Isom to Jefferson B. Love q.v.
MARRIAGES (MEIGS)
Jonathan Isom to Susan Stanley, 23 Dec 1850, J.W. Williams Sur
MISCELLANEOUS (MEIGS)
James Isham: Hiwassee District, Pinhook Ferry area

- - - - - - - - - - - - -

ISLEY / ISELY

1840 MEIGS CENSUS
George Isley 0121001 - 113001 p. 244
MARRIAGES (MEIGS)
Nancy Isley to Nichodemus Ward q.v.
1850 MEIGS CENSUS
George Isely 50 (Farmer), Nancy 44, Martin R. 22 (Farmer), Nancy 20, John 18 (Farmer), Mary 16, James 15 (Farmer), Barbary 14, Louisa 6 p. 781-530
MISCELLANEOUS (MEIGS)
George Isley: Musician, Mexican War

- - - - - - - - - - - - -

IVES

1840 RHEA CENSUS
Thomas Ives 10001 - 1001
William Ives 001200001 - 2100001
1850 RHEA CENSUS
John Ives 25 (NC), Aby 33, Sampson 4, William 3, John STORY 12, Mary KELLY 84 (Va) p. 607-486
Thomas Ives 36 (Farmer), Polly 30, Elizabeth A. 15, Henry D. 12, James M. 10, Luisa J. 8, Julia A. 6, Thomas N. 5, Zachary T. 2, George W. 8/12 p. 604-464 [Thomas Ives married Polly McNite on 9 Jan 1831; also married Mary Silvey on 8 Oct 1835; both in Roane County]
William Ives 74 (Va)(Farmer), Elizabeth 58 (Va), Martin 28 (Farmer), George 23 (Farmer), Caroline 21 p. 598-391

- - - - - - - - - - - - -

IVY

1850 RHEA CENSUS
Sarah Ivy 37: see Margaret Foster

- - - - - - - - - - - - -

JACK

TAXES (RHEA)
1819 (Capt. McGill's Co.): John Jack 1 WP, 202a
(Capt. Bradley's Dist.): Thomas Jack 1 WP
1823 (Capt. Howard's Co.): John Jack 1 WP, 202a
1830 RHEA CENSUS
Jeremiah Jack 10001 - 01001 p. 394
John Jack 011 - 002001 p. 394
1840 RHEA CENSUS
John Jack 000200001 - 00001001
1850 RHEA CENSUS
John Jack 26 (Farmer), Mary 69 (Pa), Michael KELLY 15 p. 626-583
Thomas Jack 30 (Farmer), Sarah 30, Mary 4, Andrew T. 3, James A. 2 p. 624-576
MARRIAGES (RHEA)
Eliza Jack to Nicholas Keith q.v.
Isabella Jack to Hazard Bean q.v.
John Jack to D.A. Caude [Creede], 9 Oct 1850 (11 Oct), John H. Thompson MG (R)
Margaret H. Jack to John Prillamon q.v.
Thomas Jack to Polly Shoun, 3 Sept 1818, Matthew Donald MG, Rezin Rawlings Bm (AR)
Thomas P. Jack to Sarah Pearce, no dates [1844-1845] (R)
MISCELLANEOUS (RHEA)
Andrew Jack: Bondsman for Hazard Bean, 1828
" " Bondsman for William Gibson, 1828
Anderson Jack: Bondsman for Thomas J. Alexander, 1828
Thomas Jack: Signed petition to move Indian Agency
" " Bought lot in "Southern Liberties" of Town of Washington

- - - - - - - - - - - - -

JACKSON

TAXES (RHEA)
1819 (Capt. John Lewis' Co.): Simeon Jackson 1 WP
1823 (Capt. Jackson's Co.): Jacob Jackson 1 WP
(Capt. Lewis' Co.): Simeon Jackson 1 WP
1830 RHEA CENSUS
Reuben Jackson 00112001 - 001000001 p. 379
Simeon Jackson 0012001 - 00000001 p. 393
William Jackson 1101101 - 12111011 p. 393
1840 MEIGS CENSUS
Daniel Jackson 0000000001 - 0000000001 p. 231
MARRIAGES (RHEA)
Asahel Jackson to Keziah Gibbs, 24 Jan 1832 (27 Jan), William Smith JP, John Gibbs Bm (AR)
Fanny Jackson to Spencer Benson q.v.
John Jackson to Polly Hall, 26 Aug 1831 (27 Aug), Stephen Winton JP (AR)
Nancy Jackson to William Lea q.v.
Polly Jackson to Nathan Harwood q.v.
Simeon Jackson to Peggy Good, 2 Mar 1811, Robert Good Bm (A)
Susanna Jackson to Hamlen Vinsen q.v.
Thomas Jackson to Mary Ferguson, 19 Apr 1832, Joshua Goad Bm (A)
Yeof or Zeof Jackson to Susan Saunders, 15 or 16 Apr 1823 (17 Apr), Wm Gamble JP, Wm Blythe Bm (AR)
Zerimah W. Jackson to John H. Alexander q.v.
MISCELLANEOUS (RHEA and MEIGS)
Amelia Jackson: Hiwassee District, Moore's Chapel area
Jefferson Jackson: Bondsman for James P. Rector, 1839
Simon Jackson Bondsman for Solomon Brown, 1823
Zeof Jackson: Bondsman for John Gann [Garr], 1823

- - - - - - - - - - - - -

JACOBS

1830 RHEA CENSUS
David Jacobs 00001 - 00000101 p. 379
Jacob Jacobs 100000011 - 1000101 p. 378
MARRIAGES (RHEA)
David Jacobs to Barbary Edmondston, 3 Nov 1828 (6 Nov), John Cozby JP (AR)
Jincey Jacobs to Davis Richardson q.v.
John Jacobs to Jane Battles, 22 Jan 1811 (same), Thomas Dowler Bm (A)

- - - - - - - - - - - - -

JAMES

TAXES (RHEA)
1823 (Capt. Howerton's Co.): William James 1 WP
1850 MEIGS CENSUS
John James 36 (Coppersmith), Olivia 32, Eliza Jane 10, Richard P. 8, Penelope 6, Charles 5, Olivia 3, Elizabeth 1 p. 751-309
MARRIAGES (RHEA)
Hizakiah or Hezekiah James to Margaret Ann Taylor, 24 Sept 1845 (same), John S. Evens JP, Peter Bottom Bm (AR)
Lewis James to Fanny Robinson or Robertson, 13 Jan 1813 (14 Jan), Henry Collins JP, Jeremiah Hammon Bm (AR) This record was listed twice by Allen; the second entry is as follows:
Lewis James to Fanny Robertson, 8 Apr 1823 (same), John Robertson Bm (A)
Nancy James or Jones to Thomas Howitt [Harnett] q.v.
Patsy James to Elisha Parker q.v.
William James to Elizabeth Harris, 20 Jan 1821 (21 Jan), A. David JP, Hezekiah Shelton Bm (AR)

- - - - - - - - - - - - -

JAMESON

MARRIAGES (MEIGS)
Milton E. Jameson to Mary Vaughn, 15 Dec 1846 (same), John Huff Esq.

- - - - - - - - - - - - -

JAQUISH / JAQUESS / JACQUISH

1840 RHEA CENSUS
Isaac Jacquish 221001 - 2001
Gabriel Jaquish 000001 - 1001
[Gabriel Jaquiss or Jakewick married Levice Yandle on 7 Apr 1829 in Roane County]
MARRIAGES (RHEA)
Malcome M. Jaquish to Elizabeth Jane Lewis, 11 Dec 1850 (14 Dec), Asa Newport JP [MG] (R)
Peter M. Jaquess to Mary Sutton, 26 Apr 1834, James C. Baldwin Bm (A)

- - - - - - - - - - - - -

JEFFERS

MARRIAGES (RHEA)
Dicey Jeffers to Benjamin Erwin q.v.
Polly Jeffers to Henry Reece q.v.

- - - - - - - - - - - - -

JENKINS / KINKINS

TAXES (RHEA)
1808 (John Henry's List): William Jenkins 1 WP, 1 BP
1819 (Capt. Bradley's Dist.): William Jinkins 1 WP, 1 BP
1823 (Capt. Brown's Co.): William Jenkins 1 BP
1830 RHEA CENSUS
Edward Jenkins 1211001 - 011001 p. 376
1850 MEIGS CENSUS
James Jenkins 30 (NC)(Farmer), Sarah 36 (NC), John 21 (NC)(Farmer) p. 755-343
Joseph Jenkins 23 (NC)(Farmer): see Ebenezer Houser
MARRIAGES (RHEA)
Catherine A. Jenkins to Philip Parker q.v.
Cinthia Jenkins to John Acre q.v.
Elizabeth E. Jenkins to Thomas Pile q.v.
Jane C. Jenkins to Jesse A. Hill q.v.
MARRIAGES (MEIGS)
John Jinkins to Mary Whaley, 24 Sept 1850, Joe Jenkins Sur
William R. Jenkins to E.E. Woods, 24 Feb 1842 (same), James M. Hague --(?)
MISCELLANEOUS (MEIGS)
Edward Jenkins: Hiwassee District, Lower Goodfield area
Joseph Jenkins: Surety for John Jinkins, 1850

- - - - - - - - - - - - -

JENNETT

MARRIAGES (RHEA)
John Jennett to Narcissa Crumley, 2 Jan 1834 (same), A. David JP, William Gross Bm (AR)

- - - - - - - - - - - - -

JENNINGS / JENINGS / GENINGS

1840 RHEA CENSUS
Dickerson Jenings 11001 - 1101
John Jenings 0000001 - 10001
MARRIAGES (RHEA)
Benjamin F. Jennings to Mary D. Black, 21 Jan 1842 (26 Jan), Samuel Frazier JP, John Davis Bm (AR)
Dickenson Jennings to Margarett Cooper, 14 Apr 1834 (same), John Pardee MMEC, Andrew Owens Bm (AR)
Jane Genings to Turney Burlins q.v.
Nancy Jennings to Benjamin Cooper q.v.
Sally Jennings to J.A. McFalls q.v.
Sorrena Jennings to Jonas Likinse q.v.
MISCELLANEOUS (RHEA)
Dickson Jennings: Bondsman for Royal Chastain, 1836

- - - - - - - - - - - - -

JESTER

1840 MEIGS CENSUS
Jacob Jester 0100401 - 02001 p. 231
John Jester 000211 - 00100001 p. 231
MISCELLANEOUS (RHEA)
Jacob Jester: Bondsman for Robert White, 1835
MISCELLANEOUS (MEIGS)
Jacob Jester: Circuit Court jury, 1836
" " Cherokee Removal muster roll, 1836

- - - - - - - - - - - - -

JEWELL

1830 RHEA CENSUS
William Jervel or Jewel 1111001 - 110001 p. 380
1840 RHEA CENSUS
John Jewell 10001 - 21001
1850 RHEA CENSUS
John Jewell 39 (Ga)(Farmer), Jane 30, Elizabeth 16, Mary C. 14, William 12, Susan 10, James 8, John H. 6, Audley A. 4, Nancy J. 2, George H. 2/12 p. 624-572
MARRIAGES (RHEA)
John Jewell to Jane Lea, 4 Feb 1822, James Pickett Bm (A)

- - - - - - - - - - - - -

JOELAND

1830 RHEA CENSUS
William Joeland 200011 - 211001 p. 363

- - - - - - - - - - - - -

JOHNS

TAXES (RHEA)
1823 (Capt. Brown's Co.): Thomas Johns 1 WP
William Johns 1 WP
1830 RHEA CENSUS
Henry Johns 100011 - 20001 p. 367
John Johns 30001 - 0101001 p. 372
1850 MEIGS CENSUS
David Johns 10001 - 23001 p. 230
Henry Johns 210001 - 202001 p. 230
William Johns 20031001 - 2120001 p. 230
1850 MEIGS CENSUS
David Johns 39 (Farmer), Nancy 41, Jane 17, Elizabeth 16, Mary 14, Nancy A. 12, Margaret 9, John 9, William 6, Lucy C. 3 p. 738-200
Jesse Johns 30 (Farmer), Hannah 23, Martha Jane 4, William J. 2 p. 733-159
William Johns 62 (Va)(Farmer), Nancy 47, James 26 (Farmer), John 24 (Farmer), Thomas 23, Elizabeth Ann 21, James F. 3, Mary C. 17, William R. 15, Nancy 13, Marion J. (m) 11, Caroline 10 p. 738-205
MARRIAGES (RHEA)
David Johns to Nancy Sykes, 17 May 1831 (same), S.R. Russell MG, Eli Sykes Bm (AR)
Henry Johns to Elizabeth Sykes, 25 Jan 1825 (27 Jan), John Cozby JP, William Johns Bm (AR)
MARRIAGES (MEIGS)
Henson T. Johns to Mary Atchley, no date, but on page from 1850, William Whiteside Sur
Jesse Johns to H.R. Morelon, 14 Mar 1845 (17 Mar), B.F. McKenzie JP
MISCELLANEOUS (RHEA and MEIGS)
Andrew Johns: MG 1849
Henry P. Johns: Died during Mexican War
Thomas Johns: Hiwassee District, Cottonport area
" " Bondsman for John Lea, 1822
William Johns: JP 1842-1849
" " Bondsman for Henry Johns, 1825

- - - - - - - - - - - - -

JOHNSON / JOHNSTON

TAXES (RHEA)
1808 (Joseph Brooks' List): John Johnson 1 WP
1819 (Capt. Bradley's List): Thomas Johnson 1 WP, ½a
(Capt. McGill's Co.): Joseph Johnson 100a
Theophilus Johnson 1 WP
William Johnson 1 WP
(Capt. Ramsey's Co.): William Johnson 1 WP, 100a
1823 (Capt. Howard's Co.): Collier Johnson 1 WP
(Capt. Howerton's Co.): Hiram Johnson 1 WP
(Capt. McCall's C.): William Johnson 100a Tenn Ri
1830 RHEA CENSUS
Asil Johnson 0110001 - 01110001 p. 395
Bright Johnson 00001 - 0001 p. 384
Caswell Johnson 10111 - 01001 p. 395
David Johnson 00001 - 0001 p. 359
Henry Johnston 100001 - 00001 p. 355
John Johnston 120001 - 10001 p. 364
John L. Johnson 00001 - 31001 p. 363
Joseph Johnson 01001 - 21001 p. 366
Mark Johnson 0112001 - 2121001 p. 359
Sarah Johnson 101 - 11101 p. 380
William Johnson 00001 - 00001 p. 386
William Johnson 0210001 - 00101001 p. 387
William Johnson 00000001 - 00000001 p. 384
1840 RHEA CENSUS
Asabel Johnson 000100001 - 01
Benjamin Johnson 1201001 - 021201
Christina Johnson 00001 - 000011011
John Johnson 00001 - 20001
Thomas Johnson 000011 - 10001
Thomas C. Johnson 10001 - 01001
William Johnson 100031001 - 0
William Johnson Sr. 000001 - 00000001
William L. Johnson 10001 - 0001
1840 MEIGS CENSUS
David Johnson 101001 - 00001 p. 240
Elious Johnson 00120001 - 11001 p. 228
James Johnson 1003001 - 201201 p. 228
John Johnson 0112001 - 220001 p. 246
Madison B. Johnson 10101 - 01001 p. 225
Thomas Johnson 100001 - 10001 p. 241
William Johnson 000100001 - 00100001 p. 226
1850 RHEA CENSUS
Hiram Johnson 23 (Farmer), Lyda 23 (NC), Elizabeth 2 p. 569-216
John Johnson 20 (Farmer), James 27 (Farmer), Salissa T. 22, Elizabeth 22, Gideon T. 1, Ann J. 2/12 p. 561-174

Thomas C. Johnson 34 (Farmer), Mary A. 34, John F. 11, Nancy J. 9, Asabel 7, Isabella M. 5, William 5/12 p. 627-598

William B. Johnson 27 (Farmer), Martha G. 29 (Va), Catharine C. 1, John ACRE 47 (SC)(Farmer), John LAUDERDALE 14, Emily CHATTIN 10 p. 625-578

William S. Johnson 33 (Farmer), Sarah 35 (SC), Mary J. 14, Nancy A. 13, James W. 12, Quin W. 7 (Deaf and Dumb), Cyrus J. 1 p. 533-5

1850 MEIGS CENSUS

Benjamin Johnston 51 (NC)(Farmer), Martha 35, Malinda 20, Wesley 10, Martha Jane 6 p. 728-124

C.T. Johnson 33 (Va)(Saddler), Virginia 8 (Va) p. 720-56

John Johnson 52 (Farmer), Mary 42, Elizabeth 22, John 21 (Farmer), Susannah 18, Sarah 17, Prudence 14, Mahala 13, Richard F. 9, Humphrey S.V. 6, A.O.P NICHOLASON 4, Naoma E. 1 p. 816-764

Joseph J. Johnson 30 (Farmer), Mary 23, William 2, Martha J. 1 p. 722-67

Malinda Johnson 34, Elizabeth Jane 8, Martha Ann 5, James H. 3, Thomas M. 1 p. 744-247

Richard M. Johnson 30 (Carpenter), Jane 25, Henry 6, Robert 4 p. 721-65

William Johnson 26 (Farmer), Sarah Jane 23, William G. 0 p. 811-752

MARRIAGES (RHEA)

Andrew Johnson to Jane Wallace, 14 Dec 1835, Nathan Pelphray Bm (A)

Ann Johnson to Henderson Crumpton q.v.

Anne Johnson to James McMillan q.v.

Annie Johnson to Lewis Tiner q.v.

Betsy Johnson to Thomas Lucas q.v.

Bright Johnson to Nancy Brown, 27 Feb 1830 (28 Feb), C. Caldwell JP, Anson Dearmon Bm (AR)

Carroll Johnston to Ann Hoover, 28 Nov 1834, John Cozby JP, Calvin Johnston Bm (AR)

Charles Johnson to Eliza Pettit, 25 May 1835, V.H. Giles JP, Levi Geren Bm (AR)

Chenea Johnson to Henry Smith q.v.

Elizabeth Johnson to John Johnson q.v.

Esther Johnson to Matthew S. Hasslett q.v.

Ett N. or Elliot Johnson to Lenticia or Lucretia Qualls, 14 May 1839 (15 May), Benjamin F. Jones JP, Berry Qualls Bm (AR)

Isabella Johnson to William K. Alexander q.v.

Isabella Johnson to William Kelly q.v.

James Johnson to Elizabeth Philpot, 3 Oct 1816 (same), Jonathan Fine JP, Wm T. Gillenwaters Bm (AR)

James Johnston to Mary Thompson, 20 Nov 1841 (28 Dec) (R) [James, son of William and Sarah Forbush Johnson]

James Johnson to Nancy Piper, 3 Sept 1833 (same), John Randles JP (R)

James Johnson to Suesy(?) P. Thompson, 19 Dec 1846 (20 Dec), A.D. Paul JP (R)

Jane Johnson to James Lauderdale q.v.

Jane Johnson to Thomas Simcox q.v.

John Johnston to Ann Burton, 16 Apr 1822 (17 Apr), Jonathan Fine JP (AR)

John Johnston to Polly McFalls, 20 Dec 1830 (same), B. Gaither JP (AR)

John Johnson to Elizabeth Johnson, 6 Apr 1836 (7 Apr), Timothy Sullins MMEC, Thomas C. Johnson Bm (AR)

Joseph Johnson to Caty Holland, 14 Oct 1822 (15 Oct), Wm Randolph MG, Joseph W. McMillen Bm (AR)

Lucinda Johnson to George Gross q.v.

Lucy Johnson to Jeremiah Howerton q.v.

Margaret Johnson to William Murphy q.v.

Martha J. Johnson to Anderson Jones q.v.

Mary Johnson to Andrew McFarland q.v.

Mary Johnson to John H. Singleton q.v.

Mary A. Johnson to Thomas C. Johnson q.v.

Polly Johnson to James Butler q.v.

Polly Johnson to John McDonald q.v.

Rebecca Johnson to Thomas Clemmons q.v.

Rebecca Johnson to Thomas Gannaway q.v.

Richard M. Johnson to Mary Roberson or Robinson, 19 Mar 1840 (same), Jacob Gear JP (AR)

Robert C. Johnson to Eliza Peppers, 3 Mar 1834 (same), Carson Caldwell JP, James H. Caldwell Bm (AR)

Seibby Johnson to Presley Rector q.v.

Serena A. Johnson to Alexander McPherson q.v.

Thomas Johnson to Rachel P. Seay, 25 Aug 1832 (26 Aug), Matthias Shaffer JP, William Lillard Coleman Bm (R)

Thomas C. Johnson to Mary A. Johnson, 1 Jan 1838 (2 Jan), B.F. Jones JP (A) [Thomas, son of Asahel and Nancy Howard Johnson]

Walter A. Johnson to Martha A. Bonham, 22 Feb 1840 (22 Feb), Samuel Frazier JP, Aaron Suthard Bm (AR)

West Walter Johnson to A. Thompson, 23 Oct 1837, William Johnson Bm (A)

William Johnson to Sally Carter, 7 Oct 1816, James Carter Bm (A)

William Johnson to Jane Hill, 20 Apr 1837 (23 Apr), William Cozby JP (AR)

William L. Johnson to Sally McCary, 26 Aug 1834 (same), Matthew Hubbert JP (R)

MARRIAGES (MEIGS)

Catherine E. Johnson to William H. Hunter q.v.

Ewell Johnson to Susan Rowden, 22 Dec 1846 (23 Dec), Joseph Johnson JP

Frederick M. Johnson to Jane Small, 10 Feb 1847, "Executed in due time" Thomas V. Atchley JP

Harriet G. Johnson to J. M. Butler q.v.

Henry Johnston to Martha M. Bower, 19 Sept 1839, John Bower MG

James Johnson to Hannah Bear, 8 July 1844 (same), John Seabourn JP

Mary T. Johnson to John P. Hunter q.v.

Madison B. Johnson to M. Kincannon, 10 Oct 1838 (13 Oct), Wilford Rucker JP

William Johnson to Harriet J. Wadkin, 1 July 1844 (5 July), John Seaborn JP

William Johnson to Sarah Jane Green, 18 Oct 1848 (19 Oct), John K. Brown JP

MISCELLANEOUS (RHEA)

Abel Johnson: Bondsman for Jesse Elliott, 1810

Benjamin Johnson: Bondsman for Thomas Piper, 1819

Calvin Johnson: Bondsman for Carroll Johnston, 1834

" " Bondsman for Thomas Clemmins, 1834

John Johnson: Bondsman for James McCoy, 1820

John Johnson: Bondsman for Robert Rhea, 1828
" " Bondsman for B. F. Benson, 1842
Joseph Johnson: On first Grand Jury, 1808
L.M. Johnson: Bondsman for James H. Dun, 1842
Martin Johnson: Bondsman for Oliver Massey, 1836
Robert Johnson: Bondsman for Johnson P. Loverett, 1833
Seabourn Johnson: Bondsman for Henry Smith, 1833
" " Bondsman for Raleigh J. Fulton, 1835
" " Bondsman for Abraham Brown, 1835
Theophilus Johnson: Bondsman for Nathan Carter, 1811
" " Bondsman for John Childers, 1811
" " Bondsman for Nathan Neely, 1812
Thomas Johnson: Bondsman for Reubin Freeman, 1815
" " Bondsman for Nicholas Starnes, 1816
Thomas C. Johnson: Bondsman for John Johnson, 1836
W. Johnson: Signed petition to move Indian Agency
West W. Johnson: Bondsman for Thomas J. Simcox, 1840
William Johnson: Rhea County Trustee 1823
" " Bondsman for Preston Knight, 1827
" " Bondsman for William Murphy, 1832
" " Bm for West Walter Johnson, 1837
" " Born 1766 in Va.; died about 1842; wife, Sarah Forbish (1769-1845)

MISCELLANEOUS (MEIGS)

Caswell Johnson: Privte, Mexican War
James Johnson: JP(?) 1841
James M. Johnson: JP(?) 1838
John Johnson: Hiwassee District, Fooshee & Hardwick Islands area
Joseph Johnson: JP 1846
Mark Johnson: Hiwassee District, Moore's Chapel area
Marshel Johnson: Private, Mexican War
Samuel Johnson: Purchsed Lots 19,27,28 in Decatur, 1836
W. C. Johnson: Surety for Jonathan Wood, 1850
William Johnson: Private, Mexican War
William D. Johnson: JP(?) 1845
William H. Johnson: JP(?) 1844

- - - - - - - - - - - - -

JOLLY / JOLLEY

1840 MEIGS CENSUS

Hiram Jolly 0110001 - 211001 p. 244

1850 RHEA CENSUS

John Jolly 41 (Farmer), Lyda 44, Franklin 11, Nancy J. 9, Sarah 7, Caroline 5, Pleasant H. 3, John HODGES 15, Abrham 13, William 9 p. 570-226
[John Jolly married Lydia Hodge on 5 Nov 1849 in Roane County]

1850 MEIGS CENSUS

Hiram Jolly 51 (NC)(Farmer), Jane 46 (NC), Lucinda 22, Joel 19, Lety STEWART 20 ("married within year, alone"), Mahala 17, Rebecca C. 15, Margaret Jane 12 p. 778-518
William Jolly 21 (Farmer), Mary 20 p. 779-520

MARRIAGES (MEIGS)

Joseph Jolley to Susanna Knight, 9 Mar 1842 (11 Mar), James Knight JP or MG
Lucinda Jolley to Wilson Baker q.v.
William Jolly to Polly Ward, 4 Aug 1849 (same), Daniel Carpenter MMECS

- - - - - - - - - - - - -

JONES

TAXES (RHEA)

1823 (Capt. Howard's Co.): Benjamin Jones 2 BP, 464a
Benjmin F. Jones 1 WP, 113a
John Jones 1 WP
(Capt. Piper's Co.): Michael S. Jones 1 WP, 37a
(Capt. Wilson's Co.): Richard Jones 1 BP, 80a

1830 RHEA CENSUS

Benjamin Jones 00001 - 00002 p. 380
Frank Jones 110001 - 110001 p. 381
James B. Jones 00001 - 00101 p. 359
Oliver Jones 021 - 011001 p. 369
William Jones 00110001 - 000100001 p. 357

1840 RHEA CENSUS

Anderson Jones 1000110001 - 11001
Benjamin F. Jones 1011001 - 021001
Edward Jones 10001 - 10011

1840 MEIGS CENSUS

Christopher Jones 00010001 - 122001 p. 238
James Jones 10001 - 00001 p. 244
Oliver Jones 0001 - 0000001 p. 230

1850 RHEA CENSUS

Anderson Jones 41 (Mo)(Farmer), Martha 30, Sarah 15. Benjamin 13, Myra 11, Christina 6, Mary C. 3, Isabella 9/12 p. 633-642
Edward E. Jones 43 (Farmer), Nancy 33, James M. 12, Letha M. 11, Isaac R. 7, Henry C. 5, Pryor S. 1, Hugh L.W. 1 p. 567-198
James O. Jones 28 (Md)(Housejoiner), Mary A. 26 (Md), William 19 (Md), Elizabeth C. 7 (Md), Oliver 1 (Md) p. 607-484
John Jones 9: see William D. Everett
Margaret Jones 35, Mary 13, Margaret 9 p. 622-559

1850 MEIGS CENSUS

Anderson Jones 32 (Ky)(Farmer), Frances 32, Thomas 12, Mahala 11, Elizabeth 8, William 5, James 4, Jane 2, Abindergo (m) 1 p. 804-700
David Jones 25, Cassaann 23, William J. 6, Mary E. 3 p. 766-422
Drury Jones 60 (Ga), Susanna 24, Thomas J. 5, Andrew J. 3, Nancy Jane 2, William L. 1 p. 717-34
Lydia Jones 63 (NC), Calvin 24 (Farmer), Stewart 22 (Farmer), Sally 21, Nancy 19, Thomas W. 16 (Farmer) p. 813-769 [William Jones married Lydia Moon on 7 Sept 1826 in Roane County, Thomas Stockton JP, Jonas Moon Sur]
William Jones 28 (Farmer), Sarah Jane 25, Thomas L. 5, Dicy Jane 3, John M. 4 p. 741-226

MARRIAGES (RHEA)

Anderson Jones to Martha Shelton, 21 Oct 1833 (22 Oct), William Smith JP, Asahel R. Chilton Bm (AR)
Anderson Jones to Martha J. Johnson, 16 Aug 1843, Joseph S. Evens Bm (A)
Benjamin F. Jones to Jane Lauderdale, 8 Jan 1821 (14 Jan), Matthew Donald MG, James Kelly Bm (AR)
Betsey Jones to James B. Howell q.v.
Betsy Jones to Robert Gamble q.v.
Elizabeth Jones to Clinton Norman q.v.
Esther Jones to James Acree q.v.
John D. Jones to Betsy White, 23 May 1816 (24 May), Jonathan Fine JP, George W. Hale Bm (AR)
Kitty Jones to James McDonald q.v.

Lucinda Jones to William Monday q.v.
Mlindy Jones to Willim Harwood q.v.
Michael S. Jones to Edy Harwood, 20 Dec 1815 (same), Robert Walker Bm (AR)
Nancy Jones to Byron Cash q.v.
Sally Jones to Wyly Moyers q.v.
Samuel Jones to Eleanor Matheny, 20 Nov 1812 (same), William Lester and Job Lewis Bm (A)
Thomas Jones to Elizabeth Fine, 8 Oct 1835, William Graham Bm (A)

MARRIAGES (MEIGS)

David Jones to Casander Breedwell, 25 Dec 1843 (28 Dec), D.L. Godsey MG, John M. Breedwell Bm
Dicey Ann Jones to Alex Tharp q.v.
Huldah Jones to Joseph Stuart q.v.
M. Jones to William McCarroll Jr. q.v.
Martha M. Jones to Benjamin F. McKenzie q.v.
Milton F. Jones to Nancy Buster, 4 Feb 1843
Samuel Jones to Dicy Ann Owen, 22 May 1846, "Executed and returned in time" Thomas V. Atchley JP
William Jones to Sarah J. White, 25 Nov 1844 (same), B.F. McKenzie JP

MISCELLANEOUS (RHEA and MEIGS)

Anderson Jones: Bondsman for Robert L. Gamble, 1832
Benjamin (Berry) F. Jones: JP 1838-39
Henry Jones: Bondsman for George Bennett, 1824
" " Bondsman for Joshua Richards, 1825
John Jones: Bondsman for James Kelly, 1817
" " Bondsman for James McDonald, 1820
" " Bondsman for Hiram Henry, 1841
John D. Jones: Lot 59, Town of Washington, 1813
Michael S. Jones: Bm for Royal Barton [Burton], 1818
Thomas S. Jones: Bm for Thomas P. Robits [Roberts], 1819
Wm Jones: Bugler, Cherokee Removal muster roll, 1836

\- - - - - - - - - - - -

JORDAN / JOURDEN

1850 MEIGS CENSUS

Thomas C. Jordan 19 (Farmer), Nancy R. 29, Martha E. 5, Jane 3, Thomas 1 p. 803-699

MARRIAGES (RHEA)

Nancy Jourden to David Foust q.v.

MARRIAGES (MEIGS)

Thomas C. Jordan to Nancy R. Grigsby, 11 Apr 1844 (same), Thomas V. Atchley JP

MISCELLANEOUS (RHEA and MEIGS)

Robert Jordan: Bondsman for William Phillips, 1826
Robert H. Jordan: Purchased Lots 1 & 14 in Decatur, 1836
Thomas C. Jordan: Bondsman for John B. Eldridge, 185
" " " Bondsman for Henry Latham, 1835
" " " Cherokee Removal muster roll; 1st Corp in 1836; Ensign in 1837

\- - - - - - - - - - - -

KALE

MARRIAGES (RHEA)

Polly Kale to William Coats q.v.

\- - - - - - - - - - - -

KARSEY

1850 RHEA CENSUS

Riley Karsey 51 (SC)(Farmer), Rhean 55 (NC), Rachael NEWTON 27 (SC)("married within year"), John KARSEY 23 (Farmer), Sarah 20 p. 534-9

\- - - - - - - - - - - -

KEELAND

1840 RHEA CENSUS

William Keeland 00001 - 10001

\- - - - - - - - - - - -

KEELER

MISCELLANEOUS (MEIGS)

Joseph Keeler: Mexican War (discharged on Surgeon's Certificate)

\- - - - - - - - - - - -

KEEN

1830 RHEA CENSUS

William Keen [or Kerr] 10001 - 10001 p. 369

\- - - - - - - - - - - -

KEENUM / KEENON / KEENAM / KEYNUM

TAXES (RHEA)

1819 (Capt. Wm McCray's Co.): Thomas M. Kennon 1 WP

1830 RHEA CENSUS

George Keenum 0101001 - 1220001 p. 374

1840 MEIGS CENSUS

George Keenam 00000001 - 00120001 p. 235

1850 MEIGS CENSUS

George Keynum 61 (Va)(Farmer), Elizabeth 65 (Va) p. 768-434

MARRIAGES (RHEA)

Milly Keenum to Joel Brooks q.v.

MARRIAGES (MEIGS)

Delpha Keenon to Samuel Wallen q.v.
Mary Keenum to William B. Eldred q.v.
Susan Kednum* to G.W. McKenzie
[* Allen shows last name as Keenum]

MISCELLANEOUS (RHEA and MEIGS)

James E. Kennon: Bondsman for George Henry, 1821
Barry Keenum: Cherokee Removal muster roll, 1837

\- - - - - - - - - - - -

KEERAN

MARRIAGES (RHEA)

Josiah Keonam or Keeran to Eady Farmer, 19 Feb 1827 (20 Feb), Daniel Briggs MG, George Hale Bm (AR)

MISCELLANEOUS (RHEA)

Josiah Keeran: Bondsman for David Lions, 1827
" " Bondsman for Prior Neil, 1829

\- - - - - - - - - - - -

KEETON

MARRIAGES (MEIGS)
Artimissa M. Keeton to John Royster q.v.
MISCELLANEOUS (RHEA and MEIGS)
James Keeton: Land south of Tennessee River
William Keeton: Hiwassee District

- - - - - - - - - - - -

KEITH / KIETH / KEETH

1840 RHEA CENSUS
Nicholas Keeth 20001 -10001
1850 RHEA CENSUS
Nicholas Keith 41 (Wool Carder), Eliza 35, Martha 15, Timothy S. 13, John H. 11, Jane 9, Mary J. 5, Margaret M. 3, Nealy M. 2, William T. 7/12 p. 579-283
MARRIAGES (RHEA)
Nicholas Keith to Nancy Buttram, 23 Dec 1833 (25 Dec), Heil Buttram JP, Wm H. Neeley Bm (AR)
Nicholas Keith to Eliza Jack, 9 May 1844, Elzy Buttram Bm (A)

- - - - - - - - - - - -

KELLER

TAXES (RHEA)
1823 (Capt. Howerton's Co.): Peter Keller 1 WP
MARRIAGES (RHEA)
Mahala Keller to Nimrod Floid q.v.

- - - - - - - - - - - -

KELLY / KELLEY

TAXES (RHEA)
1808 (Jas Campbell's List): Thomas Kelly 1 WP, 100a TR
1819 (Capt. Bradley's Dist.): James Kelly 1 Town Lot
Thomas Kelly 1 WP, 1 BP, 250a
(Capt. McCray's Co.): Josh Kelly* 1 WP
[*written as Kelly Josh]
William Kelly 1 WP, 450a
1823 (Capt. Smith's Co.): James Kelly 1 WP, 55a Tenn Ri
Robert Kelly 1 WP
(Capt. Howerton's Co.): Joshua Kelly 1 WP
John Kelly 1 WP
William Kelly 1 WP, 450a Whites Cr
1830 RHEA CENSUS
Elijah Kelly 010001 - 111 p. 366
Jos Kelly 0000001 - 11201 p. 377
Thomas Kelly 0011201 - 00021001 p. 382
William Kelly 10001 - 10001 p. 370
William Kelly 2120001 - 021011 p. 388
1840 RHEA CENSUS
James Kelly Jr. 00001 - 10001
James Kelly Sr. 01000001 - 1111101
William Kelly 200101 - 011001
1840 MEIGS CENSUS
James Kelly 010001 - 21001 p. 245
1850 RHEA CENSUS
Anderson Kelly 15: see Phillip T. Rawlings
Elijah Kelley 57: see William T. Gass
Jacob Kelly 38 (Farmer), Julia F. 27, Mary C. 7, Bethiah W. 3, Thomas 11/12 p. 612-436
James J. Kelly 32 (Va)(Farmer), Elizabeth 33 (Va), Mary J. 11 (Va), John W. 10 (Va), Malissa 8 (Va), James 6 (Va), Sarah T. 5 (Va), William 4 (Va), Virginia 1 (Va) p. 629-606
Mary Kelly 84 (Va): see John Ives
Michael Kelly 15: see John Jack
William Kelly 46: see Owen David
William A. Kelly 12: see Penelope Edmonds
1850 MEIGS CENSUS
Tyri Kelly 30 (Farmer), Delilah 32, Polly Ann 9, Louisa E. 8, Susannah C. 7, James 6, Elizabeth 2, Martha 0 p. 807-720 [Terry Kelly married Delily Emmerson on 4 Jan 1839 in McMinn County]
MARRIAGES (RHEA)
Elizabeth Kelly to Allen Edmonds q.v.
Elizabeth Kelly to Abraham Cox q.v.
Jacob Kelly to Julia F. Darwin, 23 June 1842 (same) (R)
James Kelly to Sarah Lauderdale, 27 Nov 1817, John Jones Bm (A)
James J. Kelly to Elizabeth Foust, 16 Feb 1838 (18 Feb), Elijah Still JP, John Foust Bm (AR)
Magdaline Kelly to Owen David q.v.
Polly Kelly to James Briggs q.v.
William Kelly to Isabella Johnson, 4 Aug 1831, George C. Airheart Bm (A)
MARRIAGES (MEIGS)
John Kelly to Lorinda Taylor, 15 Oct 1840 (same), J.W. Oakes JP
Lourinda Kelley to Augustine Lillard q.v.
MISCELLANEOUS (RHEA)
Jacob Kelly: Bondsman for Thomas H. Dearing, 1835
James Kelly: Bondsman for George Hunter, 1811
" " Bondsman for Benjamin F. Jones, 1821
" " Bondsman for Pleasant Gibson, 1823
John Kelly: Bondsman for William Martin, 1841
Thomas Kelly: Bondsman for Joseph Barkley, 1810
" " Bondsman for Martin Murphree, 1816
" " Bondsman for William Pierce, 1819
" " Bondsman for James Taylor, 1821
MISCELLANEOUS (MEIGS)
Elisha Kelly: Cherokee Removal muster roll, 1837
James Kelly: Common School Commissioner, District 5
" " Hiwassee District, Cottonport area
Samuel Kelly: Cherokee Removal muster roll, 1836-37
Thomas Kelly: Hiwassee District, Cottonport-Concord area

- - - - - - - - - - - -

KENNEDY / KENNADY / KENNIDY / KENNALLY

TAXES (RHEA)
1808 (John Henry's List): Daniel Kennedy 1 WP, 100a
Jacob Kennerdy 1 WP
1819 (Capt. Lewis Dist.): G. Washington Kennedy 1 BP
William Kennedy 1 WP, 181a
1823 (Capt. Piper's Co.): John Kennedy 1 WP, 80a
(Capt. Lewis Co.): William Kennedy 1 WP, 171a
1830 RHEA CENSUS
Allen Kennedy 01053 - 221001 p. 384
Gilbert Kennedy 212101 - 01110001 p. 370
William Kennally 0020101 - 2001201 p. 392

1850 RHEA CENSUS
Isabella Kennedy 36, Margaret A.E. 31, Daniel T. 29 (Farmer), Susannah M. 24, George M.J. SMITH 17 (Farmer), Salina J. SMITH 15, Elizabeth M.T. KENNEDY 8, James C. 3, Malinda E. 5 p. 573-242

MARRIAGES (RHEA)
Allen Kennedy to Margaret Hackett, 26 May 1818 (same), Matthew Donald MG, Wm P. Hackett Bm (AR) [1850 Hamilton Census: Allen Kennedy 52, Margaret 50, William 29, Marcus 15, John 11, Daniel 9, Ann 7; living in a Hotel]
Daniel R. Kennedy to Marjora Woodward, 20 Nov 1825 (same), James A. Darwin JP, John McClure Bm (AR) [1850 Blount Census: Daniel R. Kennedy 43, Margt 38, Thomas J. 22, Nancy J. 16, William M. 13]
Isabella Kenedy to Calvin Henry q.v.
Margaret Kennedy to Eli Ferguson q.v.
Maria Kennedy to Levi Worthington q.v.
Mary N. Kennedy to Martin Ferguson q.v.
Polly Ann Kennedy to Rezin Rawlings q.v.

MARRIAGES (MEIGS)
Barbara Keneda(?) to Isaac Widows q.v.
Moses Kennidy to Emily Wilson, 1 Nov 1841 (7 Nov), Mark Renfrow JP [Emily, dau of William C. and Elizabeth Stockton Wilson]

MISCELLANEOUS (RHEA)
Allen Kennedy: Bondsman for Isaac Binyon, 1831
" " Bondsman for Joseph McDaniel, 1821
" " Bondsman for Jonathan B. Sullivan, 1831
" " Bondsman for James C. Francis, 1832
G. W. Kennedy: Bm for Fredinburgh Thompson, 1822
Gilbert Kennedy: Bondsman for Jas Aikens [Eaken], 1828
J. Kennedy: Elder, Concord Baptist Church of Christ, 1824
William Kennedy: Bondsman for Richard Wilhelm, 1809
" " Bondsman for Jacob Kinchlow, 1814
" " Bondsman for Eli Ferguson, 1819
" " Bondsman for Levi Worthington, 1833
" " JP 1818-19; on first Grand Jury

- - - - - - - - - - - - -

KENNEY

MARRIAGES (RHEA)
Harriet Kenney to William F. Dugan q.v.

- - - - - - - - - - - - -

KENT

MARRIAGES (RHEA)
William O. Kent to Catherine Ann Hoyt, 23 Feb 1839 (25 Feb), H. Collins JP, James P. Collins Bm (AR)

- - - - - - - - - - - - -

KERNS

TAXES (RHEA)
1823 (Capt. Wilson's Co.): Jehu Kerns 1 WP

- - - - - - - - - - - - -

KERTON

1830 RHEA CENSUS
Joseph Kerton 12210001 - 0101101 p. 366

- - - - - - - - - - - - -

KEY / KEYS '

1840 MEIGS CENSUS
Elizabeth Key 0003 - 021001 p. 240

MARRIAGES (RHEA)
Z. Key to Martha Dotson, 19 Jan 1850 (same), Asa Newport MG (R) [Zachariah Key 26, Martha 26, living in Roane County in 1850]

MARRIAGES (MEIGS)
William Key to Catharine McClure, 18 Apr 1849 (25 Apr), J.M. Butler JP
[1850 Roane Census: Wm Key 25, Catharine 15]

MISCELLANEOUS (MEIGS)
Alexander D. Keys: Attorney 1846
[see 1850 McMinn County census]

- - - - - - - - - - - - -

KEYTON / KEETON

1830 RHEA CENSUS
Allen Keyton 00000001 - 0000001 p. 355
Burton Keyton 2000101 - 02001 p. 354
James Keeton 120011 - 11201 p. 356
Littleton Keyton 10101 - 2001 p. 355
William Keyton 1010001 - 11001 p. 355

- - - - - - - - - - - - -

KILGORE / KILLGORE

TAXES (RHEA)
1823 (Capt. Wilson's Co.): Wilson Kilgore 1 WP

1830 RHEA CENSUS
Wilson Kilgore 01001 - 00001 p. 385

1840 RHEA CENSUS
Wilson Kilgore 000101 - 300001

1850 RHEA CENSUS
Wilson Kilgore 48 (Farmer), Mary 38, Nancy A. 12, Mary E. 9, Harriet 7, Sarah 4 p. 599-398

MARRIAGES (RHEA)
Wilson Kilgore to Patsy Walker, 30 Oct 1822 (31 Oct), Thomas Price JP, Mikel W. Buster Bm (AR)
Wilson Kilgore to Mary Davis, 24 Oct 1835 (26 Oct), V.H. Giles JP, Anson Dearmon Bm (AR)

MISCELLANEOUS (RHEA)
Wilson Kilgore: Bondsman for Alexander Wasson, 1835

- - - - - - - - - - - - -

KILLINGSWORTH

TAXES)RHEA)
1823 (Capt. Brown's Co.): Stephen Killingsworth 1 WP
[Stephen married Nancy Hart on 18 Dec 1821 in Roane Co]

- - - - - - - - - - - - -

KILLOUGH / KELLOUGH / KELOUGH

TAXES (RHEA)
1819 (Capt. John Lewis' Dist.): Joseph Killough 1 WP
1823 (Capt. Lewis' Co.): Joseph Kelough 1 WP
MARRIAGES (RHEA)
Mariah Killough to Pleasant Rhea q.v.
Orleana Kellough to James T. Nanny q.v.
Peggy Killough to John Still q.v.
Pulaski Killough to Sarah Martin, 18 Oct 1849 (same), John Wyott JP (R)
MISCELLANEOUS (MEIGS)
Robert Killough: Private, Mexican War
William B. Killough: 2nd Corp., Mexican War

- - - - - - - - - - - -

KIMBREE

MISCELLANEOUS (RHEA)
Merriman Kimbree: Bondsman for James Varnell, 1824

- - - - - - - - - - - -

KIMBRELL

1830 RHEA CENSUS
Benjamin Kimbrell 011002 - 20130001 p. 364 [Benjamin A. Kimbrell married Catharine Luttrell on 9 Jan 1827 in Roane County]
MARRIAGES (RHEA)
Matilda Kimbrell to William Arnold q.v.
Mary Kimbrell to Thomas Mitchell q.v.
Robert Kimbrell to Betsy Williams, 8 Oct 1828 (same), Jesse Thompson JP, John McDonough Bm (AR)
MISCELLANEOUS (RHEA)
Berryman Kimbrel: Bm for Zorobable Tanksly, 1828
John Kimbrell: Bondsman for William Arnold, 1832
" " Bondsman for Thoms Mitchell, 1833

- - - - - - - - - - - -

KINCANON / KINCANNON

1830 RHEA CENSUS
Andrew Kincannon 121011 - 10101 p. 352
George Kincannon 000010001 - 00010001 p. 352
George Kincannon 10001 - 0001 p. 374
1840 MEIGS CENSUS
Andrew Kincannon 022101 - 0200001 p. 229
1850 MEIGS CENSUS
Elizabeth Kincanon 55, Craton Jane 16 p. 744-246
George Kincannon 21 (Farmer), Mary Jane 19 p. 713-8
Thomas J. Kincanon 26 (Farmer), Charlotte 30, Mary E. 5, Tennessee 3, Andrew W. 1 p. 743-245
MARRIAGES (RHEA)
George Kincannon to Caney or Chancy Coleman, 3 Nov 1828 (4 Nov), Peach Taylor JP, James Lillard Bm (AR)
MARRIAGES (MEIGS)
George Kincannon to Mary J. Barnhart, 6 July 1847, John Seaborn JP
M. Kincannon to Madison B. Johnson q.v.
Thomas H. Kincannon to Charlotte J. Miller, 29 June 1844

MISCELLANEOUS (RHEA and MEIGS)
A. Kincannon: Commissioner to lay off Decatur Courthouse, 1836
" " Meigs County Registerar, 1836-1840
Andrew Kincannon: Bondsman for Joshua Atchley, 1825
" " Hiwassee District and Ocoee District
Ann and Elizabeth Kincannon: Members, Goodfield Baptist Church of Christ, 1837

- - - - - - - - - - - -

KINCHLOW

MARRIAGES (RHEA)
Jacob Kinchlow to Kiziah Poe, 15 Mar 1814, Wm Kennedy Bm (A) [1850 McMinn Census: Kessiah Kinchlow 60, Elmyra 32, Paulina 25, William 20]

- - - - - - - - - - - -

KINDRICK

TAXES (RHEA)
1819 (Capt. J. Lewis' Dist.): Drury Kindrick 1 WP, 1 BP
(Capt. W.S. Bradley's Dist.): Jas Kindrick 5 BP, 2 TL

- - - - - - - - - - - -

KING

TAXES (RHEA)
1819 (Capt. John Ramsey's Co.): Thomas King 1 WP
1830 RHEA CENSUS
Amos King 1001 - 00001 p. 371
Anthony King 000001 - 1000101 p. 371
Samuel King 00001 - 1000101 p. 360
1840 MEIGS CENSUS
Ames King 021001 - 000001 p. 233
John King 1110101 - 2110001 p. 224
1850 MEIGS CENSUS
John King 53 (Va)(Farmer), Eliza 53 (NC), Nancy M. 26 (NC), Alfred M. 18 (NC), Susannah Jane 14, Marann 12 p. 716-28
Joshua King 23 (NC)(Farmer), Elizabeth 26 (NC) p. 716-29
Martha Jane King 27, Mary E. 6, Nancy E. 4, James A. 2, Craton E. 4 p. 774-487
MARRIAGES (RHEA)
Amos King to Temperance McDaniel, 29 Dec 1827 (same), Thomas Cox JP, William Russell Bm (AR)
Anthony King to Malinda Turley, 17 Jan 1828 (same), Thomas Cox JP, Abraham Cox Bm (AR)
Charlotte King to Pinkney Collins q.v.
Joseph King to Genny Long, 14 Nov 1811
Rhoda King to James Riddle q.v.
Sarah King to Allen Gentry q.v.
MARRIAGES (MEIGS)
Aaron King to Martha J. Lillard, 21 Apr 1842 (same), Peach Taylor JP
Ara King to Joseph Stuart q.v.
Nancy M. King to Shadrack Williams q.v.
MISCELLANEOUS (MEIGS)
Aaron King: JP(?) 1840-46
Alfred King: MG 1849
Elcana King: Cherokee Removal muster roll, 1836

- - - - - - - - - - - -

KINNON / KINENON
(see also CANNON}

MARRIAGES (RHEA)
Phoebe Kinenon to James Bowers q.v.
Polly Kinnon to George Washington Acre q.v.

- - - - - - - - - - - - -

KIRBY / KERBY

1840 RHEA CENSUS
Wesley Kirby 1000001 - 10001
1850 RHEA CENSUS
Houston Kerby 14, Thomas J. 17: see Dralow Rozier

- - - - - - - - - - - - -

KIRKLIN

MARRIAGES (RHEA)
E. Kirklin to Nancy Stockton, 28 Mar 1849 (29 Mar), N.C. Long JP (R) [1850 Bledsoe Census: Elisha Kirklen 18, Nancy 17; Nancy, dau of William H. and Charlotte Rector Stockton]

- - - - - - - - - - - - -

KIRKPATRICK

MARRIAGES (RHEA)
Lettes Kirkpatrick to Robert Hagan q.v.

- - - - - - - - - - - - -

KIRKSEY

TAXES (RHEA)
1823 (Capt. Braselton's Co.): William Kirksey 1 WP
MARRIAGES (RHEA)
Polly Kirksey to Thomas Hamilton q.v.
Rebecca Kirksey to Eli Renowe q.v.

- - - - - - - - - - - - -

KISSUR

MARRIAGES (MEIGS)
Dormen Kissur to Nelly Correll, 26 Sept 1849 (same), William Arrants JP

- - - - - - - - - - - - -

KITCHEN / RITCHEN

1850 MEIGS CENSUS
John Kitchen 71 (Va)(Farmer), Catharine 47, James 19 (Farmer), Baxter 16 (Farmer), Rebecca Ann 14, Susannah 11, Hanson 8 p. 786-574
MARRIAGES (RHEA)
Edward Ritchen or Kitchen to Sally Cooper, 5 Sept 1820 (same), Jesse Thompson JP, Robert Cooper Bm (AR)

- - - - - - - - - - - - -

KNIGHT / NIGHT / NITE

TAXES (RHEA)
1819 (Capt. John Ramsey's Co.): John Knight Sr. 63a
1823 (Capt. Braselton's Co.):
John Knight 1 WP, 130a Wolf Creek
(Capt. Smith's Co.):
Lewis Knight 1 WP, 160a Goodield
1830 RHEA CENSUS
Edward Knight 20201 - 000001 p. 352
Jacob Knight 000001 - 000101 p. 352
Jno Knight 000001 - 2001 p. 371
Jno Knight 10001 - 0001 p. 394
Levi Knight 00001 - 100001 p. 361
Lewis Knight 320001 - 010001 p. 373
Preston Knight 20001 - 00001 p. 361
Thomas Knight 00001 - 2001 p. 352
1840 RHEA CENSUS
John Knight 210001 - 120001
Thomas Knight 10001 - 00101
[1 was erased; not clear whether 1 or 0]
1840 MEIGS CENSUS
Jacob Night 00000001 - 0011 p. 226
James Knight 00001 - 10001 p. 243
John Knight 0000001 - 00000001 p. 229
Levi H. Knight 032001 - 0010030011 p. 241
Lewis Knight 1212101 - 100101 p. 234
1850 RHEA CENSUS
Andrew Knight 29 (Farmer), Naoma 20, John 1 p. 618-531
Emeline Knight 8: see Oliver Seal
John Knight 49, Jane 48, Nancy A. 16, John H. 13, Emeline 12, Asbury 10, Franklin 8, Mary 6, Andrew 1 p. 639-680
Thomas Knight 34 (NC)(Farmer), Philadelphia 34, James 14, Tennessee 8, Luisa J. 7, Thomas 5, Richard G. 4, Stephen 2, John SYLVESTER 7 p. 615-508
Thomas Knight 63 (NC)(Hatter), Martha 20, John 18, Richard 14, Rhoda C. 8, Sarah 6 p. 617-515
1850 MEIGS CENSUS
Levi H. Knight 45 (NC)(Farmer), Margaret 45, Harriet Jane 22, James 20 (Farmer), John 18 (Farmer), Isaac 16 (Farmer), Newton 13, Jesse 10, Margaret 10, George W. LOCKE 52 p. 796-655
MARRIAGES (RHEA)
David W. Knight to Rachel Underwood, 2 Aug 1832 (same), Archibald F. Gerald [Fitzgerald] MG, Jesse Fitzgerld Bm (AR)
John Knight to Polly Owens, 7 Feb 1818, William Randolph, Elder (AR)
John Knight to Jane Stewart, 7 Aug 1829 (9 Aug), James A. Darwin JP, William Tindle Bm (AR)
Levi H. Knight to Margaret Thompson, 14 Aug 1826 (15 Aug), Stephen Winton JP, Hiram Mahaffy Bm (AR)
Lewis Knight to Rebecca Wassum, 28 July 1819 (same), Elisha Knox Bm (A)
Nancy Knight to Meredith Brogdon q.v.
Preston Knight to Margaret Ferguson, 17 Mar 1827 (18 Mar), Matthew Hubbard JP, William Johnson Bm (AR)
Tennessee Knight to John Spence q.v.
Thomas Knight to Delphia Ryon, 26 Jan 1839, Stephen Spence Bm (AR)

MARRIAGES (MEIGS)
Abraham Knight to Mahala Blevins, 20 July 1844 (21 July), D.L. Godsey MG
Elizabeth Knight to Madison Massengill q.v.
Jacob Knight to Nancy Mitchell, 22 Apr 1841 (same), John Seabern JP
John Nite to Nancy Nite, 21 Apr 1850, George Colbaugh Sur [probably 1850 Hamilton Census: John Knight 27, Nancy 26]
Julian Knight to William Lewman q.v.
Mira Knight to William P. Edds q.v.
Nancy Nite to John Nite q.v.
Susanna Knight to Joseph Jolley q.v.
MISCELLANEOUS (RHEA)
John Knight: Bondsman for Jonathan Owens, 1819
Lewis Knight: Bondsman for Meredith Brogdon, 1823
Thomas Knight: Bondsman for Jacob George, 1840
MISCELLANEOUS (MEIGS)
James Knight: JP(?) 1839-42
John Knight: Mexican War
" " Hiwassee District, Burkett Chapel area
Levi H. Knight: Cherokee Removal muster roll, 1836
Lewis Knight: Hiwassee District
Lewis A. Knight: Private, Mexican War

- - - - - - - - - - - - -

KNOX

TAXES (RHEA)
1819 (Capt. John Ramsey's Co.): David Knox 1 WP
(Capt. John Robinson's Co.): James Knox 1 WP
William Knox 1 WP
1823 (Capt. Smith's Co.): James Knox 1 WP
William Knox 1 WP
1850 MEIGS CENSUS
William Knox 29 (Farmer), Margaret 36, Nancy E. 8, Samuel D. 5, Jesse M. 2 p. 818-808
MARRIAGES (RHEA)
Betsy Knox to Jonathan Owens q.v.
James Knox to Betsy Ellis, 17 Apr 1817, William Lewis Bm, "Returned to the Clerks Office with the papers of D. Walker, Esq." (AR)
Mary Knox to John Chapman q.v.
Nancy Knox to Solomon Cox q.v.
William Knox to Cintha or Senthy Wood, 6 Jan 1817 (no return) (AR)
MARRIAGES (MEIGS)
William Knox to Margaret Roark, 24 Feb 1843, Robert Williams Bm
MISCELLANEOUS (RHEA)
Elisha Knox: Bondsman for Lewis Knight, 1819

- - - - - - - - - - - - -

LACEY / LACY

TAXES (RHEA)
1823 (Capt. Piper's Co.): Joseph Lacy 1 WP
MARRIAGES (RHEA)
Andrew Lacey to Catherine Riley, 21 Oct 1814 (same), Samuel B. Mitchell Bm (A) [1850 Knox Census: Catherine 70, John A. 25, Abigal 28, Mary A. 24]
MISCELLANEOUS (RHEA)
Joseph Lacey: Bondsman for Thomas York, 1811

- - - - - - - - - - - - -

LACKEY / LACKY

1840 RHEA CENSUS
Hugh Lacky 01011001 - 0002001 p. 354
Robert Lacky 20001 - 00001 p. 354
MARRIAGES (RHEA)
Margaret Lackey to Leroy Bedwell q.v.
MISCELLANEOUS (MEIGS)
Isham Lackey: Hiwassee District, Euchee area

- - - - - - - - - - - - -

LADD / LAD

1840 MEIGS CENSUS
Enoch C. Lad 10001 - 0001 p. 246
1850 RHEA CENSUS
James F. Ladd 30 (Farmer), Sidnah A. 30, Thomas F. 2, George L. GILLESPIE 14, William S.L. 12 p. 597-388
1850 MEIGS CENSUS
Andrew Ladd 54 (Va)(Farmer), Mary 48 (Va), Virginia 16 (Va), Andrew 13 (Va), William 11 (Va), Victoria 9 (Va) p. 731-137
Enoch Ladd 32 (SC)(Farmer), Angaline 28 (Ireland), William 9, Isabella 6, Emaline 4, John 1 p. 807-725
George R. Ladd 34 (Va)(Farmer), Sarah 21 (Va), William 18 (Va)(Farmer), John 10 (Va), Milly 4 (Va) p. 731-138
MARRIAGES (RHEA)
James F. Ladd to Sidney Ann Gillespie, 15 Oct 1846 (16 Oct), W.H. Bell MG (R)
[Sidna Ann, widow of William N. Gillespie; dau of William S. and Mary Roddye Leuty]
MARRIAGES (MEIGS)
Enoch Ladd to Angelina McCall, 4 Mar 1839 (14 Mar), James T. Stockton JP
MISCELLANEOUS (MEIGS)
Enoch Ladd: Private, Mexican War

- - - - - - - - - - - - -

LAFERTY

MISCELLANEOUS (MEIGS)
William L. Laftery: JP(?) 1846

- - - - - - - - - - - - -

LAKINS / LIKINS / LIKINSE

MARRIAGES (RHEA)
Elizabeth Likins to Mark Stacy q.v.
Isaac Lakins to Margaret Gaskey, 11 May 1842 (12 May), W.C.W. --?-- (A)
Jonas Likinse to Surrena Jennings, 12 Oct 1836 (13 Oct), James McCanse JP, Wyatt Silcox Bm (R)
Lerena Ann Likins to Wyatt Silcox q.v.

- - - - - - - - - - - - -

LAMBERT

MARRIAGES (RHEA)
Mary Lambert to Levi Gerin q.v.

- - - - - - - - - - - - -

LANCRY

MARRIAGES (RHEA)
Clarinda Lancry to Thomas E. Stewart q.v.

- - - - - - - - - - - - -

LAND

TAXES (RHEA)
1823 (Capt. Howard's Co.): Francis Land 40a
1830 RHEA CENSUS
Franklin Land 20000000001 - 130001 p. 381
1840 RHEA CENSUS
Sarah Land 00101 - 1021001
MARRIAGES (RHEA)
Catherine L. Land to Josiah Cranmore q.v.
Jane Land to John Carr q.v.
Sarah Louisa Land to John W. Cranmore q.v.
Susan E. Land to Edmund Worley q.v.

- - - - - - - - - - - - -

LANE

1840 MEIGS CENSUS
Elias Lane 11001 - 10001 p. 224
John Lane 000121 - 121101 p. 244
1850 RHEA CENSUS
Thomas Lane 20 (Farmer): see Anthony Robison
1850 MEIGS CENSUS
Elias Lane 35 (Farmer), Mahala 32, James 14, John 12, Elizabeth 10, Sarah 7, Maranda 5, Leander W.D. 1 p. 725-96 [Elias married Mahala Bowers on 17 Feb 1835 in Roane County]
MARRIAGES (RHEA)
Mary Jane Lane to William D. Mandy or Munday q.v.
MARRIAGES (MEIGS)
Rachel C. Lane to William D. Michael q.v.
MISCELLANEOUS (MEIGS)
Nathaniel Lane: Private, Mexican War
P. W. Lane: Ocoee District

- - - - - - - - - - - - -

LANGLYWITH

1830 RHEA CENSUS
Burgess Langlywith 0001 - 10001 p. 377

- - - - - - - - - - - - -

LANKFORD / LANGFORD

1850 RHEA CENSUS
Robert Lankford 24 (Brickmason), Mary A. 24, William 7, Samuel 5, Sarah J. 2, Robert 2/12 p. 613-453 [Robert Langford married Mary Hughs on 26 July 1843 in McMinn County]
MARRIAGES (MEIGS)
Polly Ann Langford to Samuel Price q.v.
MISCELLANEOUS (MEIGS)
Henry Lankford: Mexican War (discharged)
William Lankford: Private, Mexican War

- - - - - - - - - - - - -

LARGEN / LARGAN

1850 RHEA CENSUS
Elijah Largen 35 (NC)(Farmer), Catharine 29 (NC), Margaret 11, Emeline 8, Rebecca 6, William A. 6, Thomas 4, Washington 2, William ACRE 20 (Farmer) p. 626-585
McCamy Largan or McCassay Sasgen [writing unclear] 20 (NC), Eliza A. 22 (NC), Lucinda 4, Susan A. 3, Margry A. 8/12 p. 615-502
Thomas Largen 25 (NC)(Farmer), Rebecca 30 (NC), Elija B. 3 (NC), William CIBBLE 24 (NC)(Farmer) p. 626-584

- - - - - - - - - - - - -

LARUR

MISCELLANEOUS (MEIGS)
William Larur: Hiwassee District

- - - - - - - - - - - - -

LASENBY / LISENBY / LISENDY

TAXES (RHEA)
1823 (Capt. Lewis' Co.): John Lisenby 1 WP
William Lisenby 1 WP
1830 RHEA CENSUS
William S. Lisendy 120001 - 202001 p. 387
MARRIAGES (RHEA)
Elizabeth Lasenby to Andrew Casteel q.v.

- - - - - - - - - - - - -

LASLEY / LESLY / LASATLY

1830 RHEA CENSUS
Jno Lasatly 012001 - 01000001 p. 376
MARRIAGES (RHEA)
Barbara Lasley to Abraham T. White q.v.
William Lesly to Elizabeth Campbell, 15 June 1847 (no return) (R) [1850 Roane Census: William Lesly 19, Elizabeth 22, Darena 1]

- - - - - - - - - - - - -

LASSEYTON

TAXES (RHEA)
1823 (Capt. Howard's Co.): Jonathan Lasseyton 1 WP

- - - - - - - - - - - - -

LATHAM

1850 MEIGS CENSUS
Silas G. Latham 43 (Va)(Coopersmith) p. 813-774

MARRIAGES (RHEA)
Henry Latham to Vesta C. Boggs, 19 Mar 1835, Thomas C. Jordan Bm (A) [1850 McMinn Census: Henry 39, Vesty 33, Abigail 13, Amanda 12, Thomas 10, Martha 9, Calvin 7, Susan 5, John 3, Vesty C. 1]

- - - - - - - - - - - - -

LAUDER / LOUDER / LOWDER

1830 RHEA CENSUS
Nathaniel Louder 12101 - 01001 p. 356
1840 MEIGS CENSUS
Nathaniel Lowder 011211 - 010101 p. 240 [1850 McMinn Census: Nat Lowder 50, Margaret 50, etc.]
MARRIAGES (MEIGS)
Elizabeth Lauder to Jacob Gufey q.v.
MISCELLANEOUS (MEIGS)
George K. Lauder: JP(?) 1842
Nathaniel Lauder: Cherokee Removal muster roll, 1837
Wesley O. Lowder: Cherokee Removal muster roll, 1837 [Wesley married Caroline Walker on 26 Mar 1842 in Roane County]

- - - - - - - - - - - - -

LAUDERDALE / LEATHERDALE

TAXES (RHEA)
1808 (John Henry's List):
James Leatherdale 1 WP, 136a, Richland Creek
1819 (Capt. McGill's Co.): James Lauderdale heirs 228a
1823 (Capt. Howard's Co.): Nancy Lauderdale 128a
1830 RHEA CENSUS
James Lauderdale 10001 - 10001 p. 395
Nancy Lauderdale 00101 - 0001001 p. 381
1850 RHEA CENSUS
James Lauderdale 17, John 16: see Philip T. Foust
John Lauderdale 14: see William B. Johnson
Nancy Lauderdale Unk (Va) p. 622-556
MARRIAGES (RHEA)
Betsy Lauderdale to William Henry Jr. q.v.
Cinthy Lauderdale to Charles Revely q.v.
James Lauderdale to Jane Johnson, 17 Jan 1827 (18 Jan), William Smith JP, Hazard Bean Bm (AR)
Jane Lauderdale to Benjamin F. Jones q.v.
John Lauderdale to Polly Hanna Cowan, 20 Oct 1809 (26 Oct), Abraham Howard JP, John Brown Bm (AR)
Mary Lauderdale to William Rogers q.v.
Nancy Lauderdale to David N. Flemming q.v.
Nancy Lauderdale to John Greenwood q.v.
Sarah Lauderdale to James Kelly q.v.
MISCELLANEOUS (RHEA)
James D. Lauderdale: Bm for Joseph H. French, 1831
William B. Lauderdale: Bm for David N. Flemming, 1828

- - - - - - - - - - - - -

LAVENDER

MARRIAGES (RHEA)
Polly L. Lavender to John Robinson q.v.

- - - - - - - - - - - - -

LAWRENCE / LARRANCE / LARENCE / LORRANCE

1830 RHEA CENSUS
Mary Larence 101 - 0001101 p. 360
1840 MEIGS CENSUS
John Lorrance 11001 - 10002 p. 240
Nancy Larrence 0 - 210021 p. 241
1850 MEIGS CENSUS
Elizabeth Lawrence 60 (NC), Wily 20 (NC), Norva 16, Harriet 14, Caroline 12 p. 803-696
MARRIAGES (RHEA)
James Lawrence to Sally Brazelton, 13 Dec 1824 (same), Thomas Price JP, David Leuty Bm (AR)
John Lawrence to Martha Davis, 12 Sept 1833 (13 Sept), William I. Newbern JP, John Case Bm (AR)

- - - - - - - - - - - - -

LAWSON / LASON / LASSON

TAXES (RHEA)
1823 (Capt. Lewis' Co.): Richard Lasson 1 WP
1830 RHEA CENSUS
Barklay Lawson 11001 - 0011010001 p. 373
1840 RHEA CENSUS
Clem Lawson 112101 - 20001
1840 MEIGS CENSUS
Clark Lawson 01101 - 00101 p. 233
John Lawson 0112000001 - 000200001 p. 230
Sally Lawson 0011 - 10012001 p. 235
William Lawson 221001 - 10001 p. 243
1850 MEIGS CENSUS
Catharine Lawson 27, Mary E. 7, James M. 13, Eliza 1 p. 750-307 [NOTE: the next household, Phillip Blevins, also was number 307]
Judah Lawson (f) 44 (NC), Louisa 21 (NC), Polly 17, Green (m) 15, Martha C. 13, James 7, John 5, Franklin 3, Lafayett 4 p. 715-22
Martha M. Lawson 17: see James Blakely
Nancy Lawson 29 (Va), Caroline E. 5 p. 797-684
Newton Lawson 22 (Farmer), Mary 20, Benjamin 1 p. 734-168
Sarah Lawson 73 (Va), Mary 22 p. 749-293
Susan Lawson 40, Sidney Ann 15, Frankland 6, Gilbert 4 p. 752-317
William Lawson 45 (NC)(Farmer), Jesse 17 (Farmer), John 16 (Farmer), Alfred 14, Eliza Jane 12, Pryor N. 8, Houston 7, James F. 5, Sarah C. 3, David 1, Elizabeth 40 (NC) p. 811-754
Zadack Lawson 20 (NC)(Farmer), Margarett 27 (NC), Henry C. 8, John 4 p. 715-23
MARRIAGES (RHEA)
Bartholomew Lawson to Lavicy Viccorry or Vicory, 26 July 1832 (same), Thomas Cox JP, James Blakely Bm (AR)
David Lawson to Elizabeth Craig, 20 Feb 1828 (same), Matthew Hubbert JP, John Logan Bm (AR)
James Lawson to Hannah Forrister or Forrester, 25 Aug 1831 (same), Thos Cox JP, Jas Blakely Bm (AR)
Jane Lawson to Lemuel Musick q.v.
Levicey Lawson to Vincent Oden q.v.
Nancy Lawson to Marlin Manis q.v.

Patience Lawson to James Brandon q.v.
Polly Lawson to Jacob Manice q.v.
MARRIAGES (MEIGS)
Allen Lawson to Dicy Lawson, 24 Mar 1838 (25 Mar), D.L. Godsey MG
Anna Lawson to Thomas Stapleton q.v.
Bartly Lawson to Nancy Yonas, 29 Jan 1847, D.L. Godsey JP
Catharine Lason to Joseph Manis q.v.
Dicy Lawson to Allen Lawson q.v.
Edmond Lawson to Margaret Lawson, 5 Aug 1850, Rufus Perry Sur
Isom Lawson to Katherine Lauson, 21 July 1842 (24 July), Robert Stockton JP
Jane Lawson to Blackburn O'Neal q.v.
Katherine Lauson to Isom Lawson q.v.
Margaret Lawson to Edmond Lawson q.v.
Martin Lawson to Polly Pettit, 22 Nov 1844 (same), Jesse Locke MG
Newton Lawson to Mary Ann Armstrong, 9 Dec 1848, John M. Lillard DC
Samuel Lasson to Sarah Lasson, 10 Apr 1843 (11 Apr), William Johns JP
Sarah Lasson to Samuel Lasson q.v.
Thomas J. Lawson to Nancy Munsey, 4 Sept 1844 (same), John T. Blevins JP, Arthur Lawson Bm
Tiry Lawson to Charlotte McCorkle, 18 July 1848 (7 Aug), John T. Blevins JP

\- - - - - - - - - - - -

LAYCOCK

MARRIAGES (RHEA)
William Laycock to Polly Clinton, 1 Feb 1834, Jesse Majors Bm (A)

\- - - - - - - - - - - -

LAYMON / LAYMAN
(see also LEMMON)

TAXES (RHEA)
1819 (Capt. McGill's Co.): Thomas Laymon Jr. 1 WP
Thomas Laymon Sr. 1 WP
1830 RHEA CENSUS
William Layman 01001 - 10001 p. 391
MARRIAGES (RHEA)
Nathaniel Layman to June McFall, 23 June 1842, B.W. Smith Bm (A)

\- - - - - - - - - - - -

LEA / LEE

TAXES (RHEA)
1819 (Capt. McGill's Co.): James Lea 1 WP
1823 (Capt. Jackson's Co.): George Lea 1 WP
John Lea 1 BP, 300a Tenn Ri
William Lea 1 WP
(Capt. Smith's Co.) Jacob Lee 1 WP
Jesse Lee 1 WP
Stephen Lee 1 WP
1830 RHEA CENSUS
Edward Lea 010001 - 200001 p. 361
George Lea 0021001 - 2 p. 367
James Lea 00010001 - 0010001 p. 380
John Lea 010000001 - 00110001 p. 379
Jno Lea 03221001 - 0101 p. 367
Miller Lea 11001 - 22001 p. 392
William Lee 122001 - 0010111 p. 368
William Lea 20001 - 00101 p. 392
1840 RHEA CENSUS
James Lee 000000001 - 001100001
John Lee 20001 - 01001
William Lee 202001 - 120001
1850 RHEA CENSUS
James Lea 75 (NC)(Farmer), Mary 72 (NC), Elizabeth 25, Nancy 23 p. 622-560
MARRIAGES (RHEA)
Cisley Lea to Lorenzy R. Frie q.v.
Eliza Lee to James W. Duncan q.v.
Jane Lea to John Jewell q.v.
John Lea to Betsy Greene, 18 Feb 1822 (same), Thomas Johns Bm (A)
John Lea to Ann Gothart, 27 Feb 1832 (28 Feb), William Smith JP (AR) [1850 Hamilton Census: John Lea 37, Ann 30, Louiza 16, Albert 13, Joseph 10, Emoline 9, James 4, Tennessee 1]
Mary Lea to Abraham Hughes q.v.
Mary Lea to Pleasant Gibson q.v.
Susan Lea to Jesse Roddy q.v.
Susanna Lea to James Gothard q.v.
William Lea to Nancy Johnson, 1 Dec 1831 (same), James McDonald JP, John H. Alexander Bm (AR)
William W. Lea to Caroline C. Smith, 27 Feb 1840 (same), Samuel Frazier JP, Joseph B. Peters Bm (AR)
MISCELLANEOUS (RHEA)
George Lea: Bondsman for John Ganfray, 1825
James Lea: Bondsman for John Cline, 1812
John Lea: Sheriff, 1827-1829
Shelby Lea: Private, Mexican War
William Lea: Bondsman for David Hart, 1839
MISCELLANEOUS (MEIGS)
John Lee: Hiwassee District, Armstrong Ferry area
William Lea: JP 1836-1838

\- - - - - - - - - - - -

LEACH / LEECH

TAXES (RHEA)
1808 (Joseph Brooks' List): George Leech 1 WP
MARRIAGES (RHEA)
Betsy Leach to Solomon Price q.v.

\- - - - - - - - - - - -

LEAGINS

MARRIAGES (RHEA)
Polly Leagins to John Taylor q.v.

\- - - - - - - - - - - -

LEAR

MARRIAGES (RHEA)
Nancy Lear to William Owens q.v.

\- - - - - - - - - - - -

LEAVER / LEAVERIS

TAXES (RHEA)
1819 (Capt. John Ramsey's Co.): Joseph Leaveris 1 WP
MARRIAGES (MEIGS)
John Leaver to Clarissa Gourley, 11 Apr 1846, Isaac Leaveris Bm(?)

- - - - - - - - - - - - -

LEBES / LEEBER / LIDER

1830 RHEA CENSUS
Philip Lebes 112001 - 001001 p. 356
MISCELLANEOUS (RHEA)
Philip Lider or Leeber: MG 1831

- - - - - - - - - - - - -

LEDBETTER / LEDBEATOR

MARRIAGES (RHEA)
Eliza Ledbetter to Doctor Pharis q.v.
Louisa L. Ledbetter to Jonathan D. Howerton q.v.
MARRIAGES (MEIGS)
Caty Ledbetter to James Hannah q.v.
Polly Ledbeator to Joseph Barkley q.v.

- - - - - - - - - - - - -

LEDFORD / LEDFORT / LEADFORD

MARRIAGES (RHEA)
Elinda Ledfort to Hezekiah Duckworth q.v.
Polly Leadford to William Gossage q.v.
MARRIAGES (MEIGS)
Delila Ledford to Claudius Hail q.v.

- - - - - - - - - - - - -

LEMONS / LEMMON / LEMMONS / LEEMAN / LAMON / LIMONS

TAXES (RHEA)
1808 (Joseph Brooks' List): Jacob Lemmons 1 WP
1819 (Capt. Wm McCray's Co.): Levi Lemmons 1 WP
1823 (Capt. Howerton's Co.): Levi Lemons 1 WP
William Lemons 1 WP
1840 RHEA CENSUS
John Lemmon 00001 - 22001
William Lemmon 0100001 - 110001
1840 MEIGS CENSUS
Zedock Leeman 1010201 - 021201 p. 224
1850 RHEA CENSUS
Allen Lemmons 36 (Va)(Farmer), Polly 35 (Va), William 17, John W. 14, Darthula 14, Margaret J. 6, Charles 1, James F. 2/12 p. 544-74
John Lemmons 48 (Cooper), Sarah 30, Delila 16, Mary 15, Sarah 13, Lucinda 11, Lorinda J. 9, John M. 7, Amy 5, George W. 3, James M. 2/12 p. 535-17
Thomas Lemmons 77 (Va)(Farmer), Betsy 54, Joseph 18, Angeline 16, Jane 13 p. 535-18
William Lemmons 52 (Farmer), Amy 35, Reuben 17 (Farmer), Sarah 15, Mary J. 13, Elizabeth 11, William 8, Richard 6, Samuel 4, Addison 2 p. 539-43
MARRIAGES (RHEA)
Daniel Lemons to Huldah Seay, 10 Feb 1842, J.P. Holloway Bm (A)
John Lemmons to Sally Reese, 24 Dec 1832, Joseph Reese Bm (A)
Thomas Simons or Limons to Elizabeth Love, 21 Mar 1813, William McAllister Bm (A)
Thomas Lemmons to Pollyann Rhea, 15 Sept 1846 (same), Daniel Broyles JP (R)
William Lemons to Delila Holloway, 21 Sept 1826, Baldwin Fine Bm (A)
William Lemon or Lamond Jr. to Any or Anny Reese, 11 Apr 1829 (12 Apr), James Swan JP, William Lamon Sr. Bm (AR)
MISCELLANEOUS (RHEA)
Matthew Limon: Bondsman for Robert Simpson, 1833

- - - - - - - - - - - - -

LEONARD / LENNARD

1840 MEIGS CENSUS
Obadiah Leonard 21001 - 00001 p. 225
Sarah Leonard 00121 - 0000001 p. 225
1850 MEIGS CENSUS
Horatio Lennard 30 (Farmer), Elender 27, Sarah C. 5, Mary 3, Angaline 1 p. 740-212
MARRIAGES (RHEA)
Mary Lenard to Thomas Young q.v.
MARRIAGES (MEIGS)
Horatio Leonard to Eleanor Collins, 31 July 1844 (4 Aug), Jesse Locke MG, W.S. Miller Sur
T.J. Leonard to Sarah Porter, 21 Dec 1850, Thos Miller Sur

- - - - - - - - - - - - -

LESSARD

1840 MEIGS CENSUS
Ezekiel Lessard 0001000001 - 001 p. 224

- - - - - - - - - - - - -

LESTER

MARRIAGES (RHEA)
Rebecca Lester to Isham S.E. Hardin q.v.
MISCELLANEOUS (RHEA)
William Lester: Bondsman for Samuel Jones, 1812
" " Indicted by first Grand Jury

- - - - - - - - - - - - -

LEUTY / LUTY

TAXES (RHEA)
1819 (Capt. W.S. Bradley's Dist.):
William S. Leuty 1 WP, 1 BP, 10½a, 2 Town Lots
1823 (Capt. Smith's Co.): John Luty 1 WP
(Capt. Brown's Co.): David Leuty 1 WP, 2 Town Lots
Wm S. Leuty 1 WP, 2 BP, 2 TL, 10a adjoining town; 150a mouth of Clear Creek
1830 RHEA CENSUS
David Leuty 110052 - 002011 p. 383
Mary Leuty 21 - 011011 p. 383 [widow of William S.]

1840 RHEA CENSUS
David Leuty 0010412 - 1101101
Mary Leuty 0111 - 0000001
1840 MEIGS CENSUS
Thomas Lootty [Leuty] 00001 - 00001 p. 237
1850 RHEA CENSUS
David Leuty 55 (Va)(Landlord), Elizabeth 51, Mary LEUIN 66 (Va), Myra WATERHOUSE 14, John G. STUART 27 (Lawyer) p. 614-491 [David, half-brother of Wm S., was son of Thomas and Elizabeth Hess Leuty; Elizabeth, David's second wife, was dau of Charles and Mary Sutton Lewen; Myra Waterhouse was granddaughter of Mary Lewen; John Stuart was not related, but a resident of the tavern]
Mary Leuty 54, Stanton W. 28 (Farmer), Burton 24 (Farmer) p. 576-264 [Mary, widow of Wm S.; dau of James and Lydia Russell Roddye of Jefferson Co.; Wm S., son of Thomas and Hannah Stanton Leuty; Wm and Mary married on 10 Apr 1813]
1850 MEIGS CENSUS
Thomas Luty 38 (Constable), Easter 25 (SC), Catharine 8, William 7, Thomas 5, Racheal 3, Mariah 1 p. 771- 465 [Thomas, son of John and Rosa Sprowell Russell Leuty; Easter, dau of Thomas Eaves; John Leuty was brother of David]
MARRIAGES (RHEA)
David Leuty to Elizabeth McClure, 24 Oct 1825 (25 Oct), Carson Caldwell JP, Jacob Brown Bm (AR)
Elizabeth Leuty to Joseph Rose q.v.
Elizabeth H. Leuty to George W. Selvidge q.v.
Hannah Leuty to Robert N. Gillespie q.v.
Maria Leuty to Violet Eaves q.v.
Nancy H. Leuty to Thomas J. Locke q.v.
S.W. [Stanton W.] to H.O. [Harriet O.] McDonald, 20 Nov 1850 (same), Snelson Roberts MG (R)
Sidney Ann Leuty to William N. Gillespie q.v.
MARRIAGES (MEIGS)
Thomas Leuty to Esther P. Eaves, 10 Jan 1839
MISCELLANEOUS (RHEA)
David Leuty: Bondsman for James Lawrence, 1824
" " Bondsman for Randolph Harwood, 1825
" " Bondsman for Alexander Rice, 1825
" " Bondsman for Robert Gamble, 1823
" " Supplied material for new jail, 1827; JP 1842
Thomas Leuty: Bondsman for John Hunter, 1843
William S. Leuty: Bondsman for James Roark, 1825
" " " Purchsed Lot 25, Town of Washington
" " " Commissioner, 1826-28
" " " Board of Commissioners to supervise construction of new jail, 1825
" " " Early merchant in Town of Washington
MISCELLANEOUS (MEIGS)
John Leuty: Hiwassee District, Concord area
Thomas Leuty: Constable; JP(?) 1838-48

\- - - - - - - - - - - -

LEVERETT / LOUVETT / LOVERETTE

1830 RHEA CENSUS
Joseph Louvett 11111 - 111021 p. 392
MARRIAGES (RHEA)
Eliza Loverette to Marrow Maddox q.v.
Johnson P. Loverett to Margaret Derossett or Derouset, 19 Feb 1833 (same), John Pardee MMEC, Robert Johnson Bm (AR)

\- - - - - - - - - - - -

LEVI

MISCELLANEOUS (RHEA)
William Levi: Signed petition to move Indian Agency

\- - - - - - - - - - - -

LEWALLEN

MARRIAGES (RHEA)
Henry Lewallen to Vicey Lewallen, 17 Aug 1826 (same), Thomas Cox JP, William Lewallen Bm (AR)

\- - - - - - - - - - - -

LEWEN / LEWIN

1850 RHEA CENSUS
Mary Lewin 66 (Va) [widow of Charles]: see David Leuty
1850 MEIGS CENSUS
Claressa Lewen or Leuven 18, Francis A.N. 3 p. 766-417

\- - - - - - - - - - - -

LEWIS / LOIS

TAXES (RHEA)
1819 (Capt. John Lewis' Co.): John Lewis 1 WP, 200a
(Capt. John Robinson's Co.):
George N. Lewis 1 WP, 174a
Isaac Lewis 1 WP
John Lewis 1 WP
William Lewis Jr. 1 WP
William Lewis Sr. 1 WP, 100a
(Capt. W.S. Bradley's Dist.): Wm T. Lewis heirs 301a
1823 (Capt. Lewis' Co.): John Lewis 1 WP, 200a
(Capt. Braselton's Co.): James Lewis 1 WP
Isaac Lewis 1 WP, 200a Clear Cr
William Lewis 1 WP
1830 RHEA CENSUS
David Lewis 10101 - 20001 p. 373
Elizabeth Lewis 01 - 20000001 p. 372
Margaret Lewis 011 - 0010001 p. 376
Wiley Lewis 00002 - 11001 p. 395
William Lewis Jr. 00001 - 01001 p. 383
William Lewis 01001001 - 200010001 p. 383
1840 RHEA CENSUS
Thomas D. Lewis 00001 - 00001001
Wiley Lewis 010101 - 212001
1840 MEIGS CENSUS
Charles Lewis 10001 - 10001 p. 236
David Lewis 00001 - 0111 p. 224
Joshua Lewis 10001 - 00001 p. 240
Lewallen Lewis 001101 - 101001 p. 242
1850 RHEA CENSUS
Charles Lewis 55 (Ga)(Coleier), Mary 60 (NC), Harriet N. 20, Elizabeth J. 17, Martin V.B. 15 p. 553-119

1850 MEIGS CENSUS

David Lewis 42 (Farmer), Eliza Jane 28, Ephraim B. 18, Margaret H. 7, Jonathan W. 4, Sarah T. 1 p. 724-92

Elizabeth Lewis 60 (Va): see Uriah Denton

Wiley Lewis 48, Susannah 51, James 30 (Farmer), Susan A. 23, Angaline M. 20, John T. 16 (Farmer), Sally A. 14, Hannah E. 11, Mary B. 8 p. 720-55

MARRIAGES (RHEA)

Charles W. Lewis to Polly Tillery, 15 Feb 1833 (25 Feb), D.L. Godsey MG, Tavenor Runnyon Bm (AR)

David Lewis to Lucy Clark, 29 Nov 1823 (4 Dec), Thomas Cox JP, John Barnett Bm (AR)

Eliza Lewis to James M. Cunningham q.v.

Elizabeth Lewis to Jesse Day q.v.

Elizabeth J. Lewis to James E. Roddy q.v.

Elizabeth Jane Lewis to Malcome M. Jaquish q.v.

Elizabeth P. Lewis to Ambrose Goff q.v.

Isaac Lewis was listed by Allen, but the last name was Mahan in Courthouse records [see Isaac Mahan]

Jesse Lewis to Catherine Moore, 5 May 1809 (same), James Lewis and William Seymore Bm (A)

Lorinda Lewis to John Runyon q.v.

Malinda Lewis to Luther B. Cox q.v.

Mary Lewis to Bearfoot Armstrong q.v.

Sally Lewis to Thomas Shafer q.v.

Sarah Lewis to William Seymore q.v.

Scotty Lewis to James Skillern q.v.

Thomas Lois to Margaret Wheeler, 20 Oct 1817, William Bearman Bm (A)

William Lewis to Margaret McLaughlin or McLaughlan, 1 Feb 1816 (same), Daniel Walker JP, Hugh Berry and William Lewis Bm (AR)

William Lewis Sr. to Milissent or Millissant Rowden, 3 Feb 1824 (same), D. Walker JP, John Clack Bm (AR)

Wiley or Wylie Lewis to Susan Henry, 25 July 1822 (same), Shepherd Brazelton Bm (AR)

MARRIAGES (MEIGS)

Angenire Lewis to John W. Cozby q.v.

David Lewis to Arvijine Crawford, 4 Jan 1840 (8 Jan), J. Seabern JP

Jane Lewis to James Mays q.v.

Jesse A. Lewis to Mary Locke, 3 Sept 1849 (5 Sept), Alfred King MG [see 1850 Carroll County Census]

Joshua Lewis to Martha Shelton, 2 Mar 1839 (3 Mar), Prior Neal JP, Thomas P. Stockton Bm
[1850 Roane Census:Joshua Lewis 35, Martha 36, James J. 12, Nancy R. 7, John A. 5, Lydia C. 2]

Luvena Lewis to Richard Brown q.v.

Polly Lewis to William Marshall q.v.

Sophia Lewis to Jeremiah Miller q.v.

MISCELLANEOUS (RHEA)

Amos Lewis: Security for James C. Mitchell, contractor
" " Purchased Lot 11, Town of Washington

C.W. Lewis: Revolutionary War Pensioner(?)

Charles W. Lewis: Bondsman for William P. Tillary, 1835

George Lewis: Security for James C. Mitchell, contractor

George W. Lewis: Signed petition to move Indian Agency

James Lewis: Bondsman for Jesse Lewis, 1809

Jesse Lewis: Bondsman for William Seymore, 1810
" " Purchased Lot 11, Town of Washington

Job Lewis: Bondsman for Samuel Jones, 1812

John Lewis: Bondsman for Joel K. Bledsoe, 1829
" " Security for James C. Mitchell, contractor

John C. Lewis: Bondsman for Joseph Gamble, 1835

Levi Lewis: Security for James C. Mitchell, contractor

William Lewis: Bondsman for John Bowdry, 1815
" " Bondsman for William Lewis, 1816
" " Bondsman for James Knox, 1817
" " Bondsman for Elijah C. Rice, 1833
" " Security for James C. Mitchell, contractor

Willie Lewis: Sheriff, 1848-1850

MISCELLANEOUS (MEIGS)

David Lewis: Cherokee Removal muster roll, 1837

Lapsley Lewis: Cherokee Removal muster roll, 1836

Lapsley I. Lewis: 2nd Sgt., Cherokee Removal, 1837

LEYONA

MISCELLANEOUS (RHEA)

Robert Leyona: Bondsman for Wilson Putnam, 1830

LILLARD

1830 RHEA CENSUS

Jas Lillard 210111 - 20001 p. 374

Jno Lillard 122001 - 200001 p. 373

William Lillard 100001 - 1001 p. 352

1840 MEIGS CENSUS

James Lillard 0221321 - 210101 p. 236

John Lillard 02331001 - 1020001 p. 232

William Lillard 1110001 - 111001 p. 236

1850 MEIGS CENSUS

Asbury Lillard 21 (Farmer), Eliza 20 p. 758-365

James Lillard 54 (Va)(Farmer), Mary 45, John M. 23, Newton J. 18, Mary A. 16 ("married within year, alone"), Elvina L. 14, Texanna (f) 13 p. 774-486

John Lillard 60 (Va)(Farmer), Cynthia Ann 20, Frances 15, Mary 12 p. 771-464

McMinn Lillard 24 (School Teacher), Sarah Jane 23, Mary 15, Mary Ann 5, Cyntha 3, John 1 p. 813-773

Miles V. Lillard 21 (Tanner), Elmira J. 22, John J. 3, Infant (m) 0, Nathan VAUGHN 21 (Tanner) p. 815-788

William Lillard 54 (Farmer), Nancy 41, James E. 20 (Farmer), Sarah C. 18, Francis 12, John M. 8, William L. 3 p. 777-506

William W. Lillrd 33 (Farmer), Lucretia 35, Sarah* 15, Hugh* 13, Minerva 9, Amanda 7, John W. 4, Susan 1 p. 759-366
[*last name should have been THOMAS; children of Lucretia and Henson W. Thomas]

MARRIAGES (RHEA)

Jeremiah Lillard to Jemimah Thompson, 21 Mar 1836, Wm M. Rogers Bm (A) [1850 Polk Census: Jeremiah Lillard 54, Jemimah 45, Wm 11, Caroline 15, Mary A. 13, John 9, James 6, Jeremiah D. 4, Augustine 2, Augustine LILLARD 45]

Nancy Lillard to James Taylor q.v.

William Lillard to Nancy Elder, 27 Dec 1820, Augustine Lillard Bm (A)

William Lillard to Nancy Elder, 27 Dec 1826 (28 Dec), Peach Taylor JP (AR) [The record for William and Nancy appeared twice in the Allen transcription as shown, but only once in the Courthouse record; the latter probably is correct]

MARRIAGES (MEIGS)
Asbury S. Lillard to Elisha McCorkle, 20 Sept 1849 (1 Oct), John T. Blevins JP
Augustine Lillard to Louinda Kelley, 10 Oct 1850, J.E. Lillard Sur
James Lillard Sr. to Mary J. Huff, 17 Oct 1847 (same), Jno K. Brown JP
John Lillard to Mary Ann McCortney, 8 May 1844 (9 May), D.L. Godsey MG
Martha J. Lillard to Aaron King q.v.
Mary A. Lillard to John B. Boggess q.v.
R.M. Lillard to Sarah J. McCortney, 8 May 1844 (9 May), D.L. Godsey MG
William W. Lillard to Lucretia Thomas, 22 Oct 1845 (same), Peach Taylor JP [Lucretia, dau of David and Sarah Torbett Blevins; widow of Henson W. Thomas]
MISCELLANEOUS (RHEA)
Augustine Lillard: Bondsman for William Lillard, 1820
James Lillard: Bondsman for George Kincannon, 1823
William Lillard: Bondsman for Andrew Anderson, 1826
" " Bondsman for William W. Hilton, 1831
" " Bondsman for Robert Elder Jr., 1834
MISCELLANEOUS (MEIGS)
Asbury S. Lillard: 2nd Sgt., Mexican War
James Lillard: War of 1812 (may have been a Capt. in Col. William Lillard's 2nd E. Tenn Volunteers 1813-1814 from Cooke County]
" " House used to hold elections, District 4
" " Ranger 1836; owned a Tavern
" " Deeded land for Decatur; purchased Lot 64
" " Trustee, Decatur Academy, 1838-1839
" " Deacon, Goodfield Baptist Church, 1827
James M. Lillard: Cherokee Removal muster roll, 1836
John Lillard: Purchased Lot 5, Cottonport
" " House used to hold elections, District 3
John (Jack) Lillard: Hiwassee District, Lower Goodfield
John M. Lillard: Private, Mexican War
" " " Circuit Court Clerk, 1849-53
" " " Surety for John B. Boggess, 1850
J.E. Lillard: Surety for Augustine Lillard, 1850
Newton J. Lillard: Private, Mexican War
Polly Lillard: Member, Goodfield Baptist Church, 1827
Thomas Lillard: Private, Mexican War
William Lillard: Trustee 1840-1854
" " Com. to lay off Decatur Courthouse
William C. Lillard: 1st Lt., Mexican War
William W. Lillard: Cherokee Removal muster roll, 1837

\- - - - - - - - - - - - -

LINDSEY / LINDSAY

TAXES (RHEA)
1808 (John Henry's List): John Lindsey 1 WP, 126a
MISCELLANEOUS (MEIGS)
George W. Lindsay: Hiwassee District, Ten Mile Stand area

\- - - - - - - - - - - - -

LIPFORD

1850 MEIGS CENSUS
Emanuel Lipford 40 (NC), Matilda 30 (NC), William A. 5 p. 713-9

\- - - - - - - - - - - - -

LISLE / LISLES / LILES

1840 MEIGS CENSUS
Joseph Liles 111101 - 020001 p. 241
MARRIAGES (RHEA)
Lucinda Liles to John Davis q.v.
MISCELLANEOUS (RHEA and MEIGS)
Joseph Lisles: JP(?) 1842
Samuel Lisle: MG 1834

\- - - - - - - - - - - - -

LITTLE

1830 RHEA CENSUS
Thomas Little 00101001 - 01001001 p. 376
1840 MEIGS CENSUS
Thomas Little 000001001 - 000001001 p. 237
MARRIAGES (RHEA)
Jemima Little to Samuel Montgomery q.v.
Milly Little to James Pincer q.v.
MARRIAGES (MEIGS)
Sarah Little to John W. Smith q.v.
MISCELLANEOUS (RHEA and MEIGS)
Henry Little: Bondsman for Nicholas Neal, 1818
Thomas Little: Hiwassee District, Concord area

\- - - - - - - - - - - - -

LOCKE / LOCK

TAXES (RHEA)
1808 (James Campbell's List): John Locke 1 WP
1819 (Capt. W.S. Bradley's Dist.):
John Locke 1 WP, 335a, 3 Town Lots
Robert Locke 1 WP, 50a
William Locke 2 WP
1823 (Capt. Brown's Co.):
John Locke 1 WP, 286a Tenn R., 3 T L
Ralph B. Locke 1 WP
Robert Locke 1 WP, 150a Spring Creek
" " 212a Hiwassee District
William Locke 1 WP, 109a Tenn River
1830 RHEA CENSUS
John Locke 0001011 - 0001001 p. 384
Robert Locke 032101 - 111201 p. 366
William Locke 1100101 - 0 p. 384
1840 RHEA CENSUS
John Locke Jr. 0022 - 001112
John Locke Sr. 000010001 - 0000001001
1840 MEIGS CENSUS
George W. Lock 000001 - 0 p. 237
1850 RHEA CENSUS
Addison Locke 32 (Physician), Eliza 28, Susan 6, James L. 4, Byron 1, Ralph B. 53 (School Teacher), Adeline 32 (Insane) p. 582-311
[Addison and Adeline, children of Robert and Nancy Moore Locke; Ralph B. and Robert, sons of Thomas and Susanna Henry Locke]
Franklin Locke 38 (Lawyer), Isabella T. 33 p. 608-495
[Franklin, son of John and Mary J. Moore Locke]
James H. Locke 34 (Farmer), Phebe A. 27, Olinda J. 8, Mary E. 6, Leah A. 3, Josephine 9/12 p. 607-433
[James, son of Robert and Nancy]

Newton Locke 37 (Farmer), Esther CAMPBELL 80 (Va) (black) p. 608-493
[Newton, son of John and Mary J.]

1850 MEIGS CENSUS

Benjamin F. Locke 40 (Merchant), Mary 30, Harriet Jane 9, Sarah C. 7, Victor M. 5, Susan A. 3 p. 796-649 [Benjamin, youngest son of Thomas and Susanna Henry Locke]

George W. Locke 52 [son of Thomas and Susanna]: see Levi H. Knight

Jesse Lock 57 (Va)(Farmer), Agnes 55 (SC), Jonathan N. 19 (SC)(Farmer), Benjamin F. 14 p. 727-117

Joseph Lock 54 (NC)(Farmer), Mary 55 (NC), Sarah Ann 27 (NC), Nancy M. 20 (NC), Martha 15 (NC), Jonathan 14 p. 727-113

Josiah Lock 22 (SC)(Farmer) p. 727-111

Leneas Lock 30 (Farmer) p. 770-452
[son of Robert and Nancy Moore Locke]

Rhoda Lock 36 (SC), William C. 22 (SC)(Farmer), Mary Ann 18 (SC), Amanda 14 (SC), Martha G. 12 (SC), Adaline 10 (SC), Emaly 8 (SC), Jane 6 (SC), John 4 (SC) p. 731-143

Thomas J. Locke 26 (Farmer), Nancy H. 27, David L. 4, Robert 2 p. 770-454
[Thomas J., son of Robert and Nancy; Nancy H., dau of David and Margaret Woodson Leuty]

MARRIAGES (RHEA)

Addison Locke to Louisa Barton, 28 Apr 1843, Newton Locke Bm (A)

Elvina Locke to Wylie H. Cunnynham q.v.

Elvira Locke to Orville Paine q.v.

Franklin Locke to Isabella T. Clawson, 3 Dec 1840 (same), Benjamin Wallace MG (R)

James H. Locke to Phoebe A. Smith, 25 Aug 1841 (no return) (R)

John A. Locke to Mary Jane Moore, 17 Sept 1808 (no return) (R) [John and Mary had four children: Elvina, Elvira, Franklin, and Newton]

Lucretia Locke to Edmund Bean q.v.

Louisa (Elmira) Locke to Joshua Hunter q.v.

Robert Locke to Nancy Moore, 18 Oct 1808, John Locke Bm (A) [Robert and Nancy had 11 children: Minerva, John, Elmira, James Harvey, Addison, Adaline, Lineus, Pliny, Rebecca, Thomas Jefferson, and Susan]

Thomas J. Locke to Nancy H. Leuty, 19 Nov 1844 (20 Dec), Samuel A. Miller MG (R)

MARRIAGES (MEIGS)

B.F. [Benjamin Franklin] Locke to Mary Sharp, 19 Nov 1840 (same), D.L. Godsey MG
[Mary, dau of Elisha and Eleanor Huff Sharp]

Elizabeth C. Lock to Reubin C. Collins q.v.

James H. Locke to Matilda Rogers, 20 June 1846 (same), William Johns JP

Mary Locke to Jesse A. Lewis q.v.

Rebecca Locke to Nicholas G. Givens q.v.

Sarah A. Locke to William Casey q.v.

Susan Locke to Elzy Buttram q.v.

MISCELLANEOUS (RHEA)

Addison Locke (Dr.): Trustee, Mars Hill Academy, 1850

Benjamin F. Locke: Bondsman for John W. Blevins, 1830
" " " Bondsman for John W. Smith, 1831
" " " Bm for Wylie H. Cunnyngham, 1837

Franklin Locke: Circuit Court Clerk, 1835-36

Franklin Locke: Member of Rhea County Bar and Judge
" " Witnessed minutes of Commissioners (Town of Washington), 1830

George Locke: War of 1812 (Pvt., Capt. Wm Henderson's Company, 1814-15)

Jesse Locke: Minister 1847, 1849

James H. Locke: JP 1848

John Locke: Bondsman for Robert Locke, 1808
" " Bondsman for Thomas Drinen, 1816
" " Circuit Court Clerk, 1821-1835
" " Signed petition to move Indian Agency
" " Commissioner, Town of Washington, 1812
" " Commission to build new jail, 1826; Clerk & Treasurer of Commission, 1828
" " On first Grand Jury

John Locke Jr.: Private, Mexican War

Linneas Locke: Private, Mexican War

Newton Locke: Bondsman for Addison Locke, 1843

Ralph B. Locke: Bondsman for Robert Wallace, 1819
" " " Bm for Samuel Montgomery, 1826
" " " Bondsman for Joseph McDonald, 1843
" " " Mathematics Prof., Tennessee Academy
" " " Witness, minutes of Commissioners, 1828

Robert Locke: Signed petition to move Indian Agency

William Locke: Bondsman for Jacob Gross, 1820
" " Bondsman for Joseph Thornton, 1823
" " Bondsman for Henry Henry, 1825

MISCELLANEOUS (MEIGS)

Albert G. Locke: Private, Mexican War

Benjamin F. Locke: Common School Com., District 4, 1838
" " " Circuit Court Clerk, 1840-1844
" " " Purchased Lot 41 in Decatur for residence and store building
" " " Trustee for Decatur Academy, 1840
" " " Commissioner to lay off Decatur, 1836

Jesse Locke: Minister 1841-42, 1844-49

John Locke: Surveyor to lay off lots in Decatur, 1836
" " Hiwassee District, Concord area

Newton Locke: Private, Mexican War

Robert Locke: Hiwassee District, Concord area

William Locke: Hiwassee District, Concord area

\- - - - - - - - - - - - -

LOCKENS

1840 RHEA CENSUS

Jonas Lockens 10001 - 10001

\- - - - - - - - - - - - -

LOCKMILLER / LOUGHMILLER / L. MILLER

TAXES (RHEA)

1823 (Capt. Wilson's Co.): Will Lockmiller 1 WP

1830 RHEA CENSUS

George L. Miller 00001 - 0001 p. 355

John L. Miller 2010001 - 0121001 p. 355

William L. Miller 200001 - 10101 p. 355

1840 MEIGS CENSUS

George L. Miller 110001 - 12001 p. 239

John Lockmiller 00201001 - 00022001 p. 242

Samuel L. Miller 20001 - 10001 p. 238

1850 MEIGS CENSUS
George Lock Miller 44(Farmer), Mary 40, Eliza Jane 20, Elizabeth 18, James 17, Emeline 14, Harrison 10, Nancy Ann 8, John 5, Hodge 1 p. 775-499
John Lockmiller 65 (Va)(Farmer), Mary 64 (Va), Harriet 28 p. 786-578
Luke Lockmiller 24 (Brickmason), Jane C. 24 p. 791-609
Samuel Lockmiller 30 (Farmer), Agnes 28, Benjamin F. 13, Permelia Jane 12, John 10, Mary Ann 9, Harriet 6, Jacob 3 p. 739-208
William Lockmiller 23 (Farmer), Sarah 22, Isaac 3, James 2 p. 786-577
MARRIAGES (RHEA)
George L. Miller to Polly Carroll, 8 Mar 1830 (31 Mar), D. M. Stockton JP, John Lundigan Bm (AR)
Jane N. L. Miller to Pleasant L. Wilhelms q.v.
Samuel L. Miller to Aggy Ragsdale, 29 Sept 1835, Pleasant L. Wilhelms Bm (A)
Tinsy Lockmiller to George Bennett q.v.
William Lockmiller to Eliza Carroll, 24 Nov 1826 (30 Nov), John Farmer MG, George Bennett Bm (R)
MARRIAGES (MEIGS)
Matilda L. Miller to Nathan Qualls q.v.
Nancy L. Miller to George W. Qualls q.v.
William Lockmiller to Sarah Buster, 10 Sept 1846 (13 Sept), Ezekiel Ward MG
MISCELLANEOUS (RHEA and MEIGS)
George Lockmiller: House used for elections, District 4
Isaac L. Miller: Hiwassee District
William Loughmiller: Bondsman for Joseph Cahill, 1825

\- - - - - - - - - - - -

LODER / LODEN

MARRIAGES (RHEA)
Benjamin Loder or Loden to Margaret H. Long, 29 Dec 1836 (10 Jan 1837), A.G. Wright MG, Blount Morris Bm (AR)
[1850 Bledsoe Census: Benjamin Loden 42, Margaret 41, Susannah 12, James 11, Nicholas 9, Joel 7, John 6, William 4, Benjamin 1, Susannah 74]

\- - - - - - - - - - - -

LOGAN

TAXES (RHEA)
1819 (John Lewis' Dist.): Samuel Logan 1 WP, 250a
1823 (Capt. Lewis' Co.): Samuel Logan 1 WP, 330a
1830 RHEA CENSUS
Samuel Logan 0111001 - 10001001001 p. 392
1850 RHEA CENSUS
Anthony Logan 30 (Va)(Farmer), Lucinda 31, John H. 8, George L. 6, James A. 5, Samuel W. 3, Thomas A. 1, Barbary ROBESON Unk (Va) p. 584-325
MARRIAGES (RHEA)
Jane Logan to William Woodward q.v.
John Logan to Obedience L. Rowden, 31 Dec 1828 (same), Peach Taylor JP, Samuel E. Rowden Bm (AR)
Sarah Logan to Jesse Day q.v.
MISCELLANEOUS (RHEA)
John Logan: Bondsman for Warren West, 1827
" " Bondsman for David Lawson, 1828

\- - - - - - - - - - - -

LONDAGAN / LONDIGAN / LONAGAN

TAXES (RHEA)
1823 (Capt. Wilson's Co.): John Londigan 1 WP
1840 MEIGS CENSUS
John Lonagan 10110001 - 1111001 p. 243
MARRIAGES (MEIGS)
Mary Londagan to George Mitchell q.v.
William Londagan to Margaret Mitchell, 1 Oct 1846 (same), T.B. McElwee JP
MISCELLANEOUS (RHEA)
John Londigan: Bm for George L. Miller [Lockmiller], 1830

\- - - - - - - - - - - -

LONG

TAXES (RHEA)
1808 (Jonathan Fine's List): William Long 1 BP, -?-a
1819 (Capt. W.S. Bradley's Dist.): William Long 1 WP, 1 BP, 50a
1823 (Capt. Brown's Co.): William Long 1 WP, 1 BP, 1 TL
1830 RHEA CENSUS
Benjamin Long 00011 - 22001 p. 376
Jerry Long 12101 - 310001 p. 375
Jno Long 100001 - 0000101 p. 376
William Long Sr. 0011001 - 00012001 p. 376
William Long 300001 - 010001 p. 376
William Long 00001001 - 011001 p. 384
1840 RHEA CENSUS
Joel Long 001202001 - 01122001
1840 MEIGS CENSUS
William Long 1230001 - 0002001 p. 237
1850 RHEA CENSUS
Elizabeth Long 63 (Va), Ann 35, Lenard 22 (Farmer), Susan 19 p. 542-62
1850 MEIGS CENSUS
Martin Long 23 (Farmer), Tempy 25 p. 771-460
Mary Long 63 (NC), Caroline 25, Henry 21, William 15 (Farmer), Peyton 12 p. 770-450
MARRIAGES (RHEA)
Alice M. Long to Aldridge Clifton q.v.
Elizabeth Long to John W. Gillum q.v.
Genny Long to Joseph King q.v.
Jane Long to David Majors q.v.
John P. Long to Eliza Smith, 6 Nov 1834 (same), Benjamin Wallace MG, Thomas J. Gillespie Bm (AR)
[1850 Hamilton Census: John P. Long 42, Eliza 37, William P. 12, Elizabeth J. 8, James C. 5, John P. 3, Miloe 6/12, Robert SMITH 32, William SMITH 25]
Josiah Long to Rebecca Long, 24 Feb 1831, Audley P. Defriese Bm (A)
Margaret H. Long to Benjamin Loden q.v.
Martha Long to George W. Dearmon q.v.
Mary Long to William Essex q.v.
Mary Long to Solomon Henry q.v.
Mary L. Long to John A. Hooke q.v.
Nicholas H. Long to Margaret J. Paul, 3 Nov 1843 (5 Nov), Jesse P. Thompson JP (AR) [1850 Roane Census: Nicholas H. Long 33, Margaret J. 26, Mary J. 5, Zachary T. 3, Amanda C. 8/12]
Rebecca Long to Josiah Long q.v.

MARRIAGES (MEIGS)
James Long to Ruth E. Masoner, 28 July 1842 (same), David Cate JP
Master [Martin?] Long to Gempy [Tempy?] Cox, 18 Oct 1849, John T. Blevins JP
MISCELLANEOUS (RHEA)
Benjamin T. Long: Bondsman for Thos W. Stewart, 1832
Jeremiah Long: Bondsman for George W. Dearmon, 1832
Joel Long: Bondsman for Simeon Hinds, 1811
John P. Long: Bondsman for Henry McCary, 1834
" " " Bondsman for Jesse McFall, 1834
" " " Bondsman for Wm N. Gillespie, 1834
" " " Bondsman for James W. Smith, 1834
" " " Bondsman for Abraham Cox, 1834
" " " Bondsman for Violet Eaves, 1836
" " " Early merchant, Town of Washington
" " " Salesman in McCallie store
Martin Long: Mexican War
N. C. Long: JP 1849
William Long: Bondsman for Jeremiah Hammond, 1813
" " Bondsman for Lewis Thornberry, 1835
" " JP 1808-1814
" " Early resident, Town of Washington
" " Signed petition to move Indian Agency
MISCELLANEOUS (MEIGS)
Aaron Long: Circuit Court Clerk, 1844-1849
Henry Long: Private, Mexican War
Henry H. Long: Mexicn War (discharged on Surgeon's Certificate)
Franklin Long: Mexican War
James H. Long: JP(?) 1843
John Long: JP(?) 1844
Masten Long: Mexican War
Samuel H. Long: Mexican War

\- - - - - - - - - - - -

LOOMAN

MARRIAGES (MEIGS)
Henry Looman to Jane Bruster, 3 Nov 1846 (3 Dec), Jesse Locke MG

\- - - - - - - - - - - -

LOONEY / LOONY

TAXES (RHEA)
1823 (Capt. Smith's Co.): Samuel Looney 1 WP, 1 BP
1830 RHEA CENSUS
Samuel Looney 00000001 - 00202001 p. 373
Moses Looney 222001 - 110101 p. 388
1840 MEIGS CENSUS
Joseph Loony 0000100001 - 000010001 p. 247
Joseph Loony Jr. 01001 - 11001 p. 247
Leroy Loony 0211 - 101001 p. 247
Lewallen Loony 10001 - 0100101 p. 247
Samuel Loony 000000001 - 000001001 p. 235
1850 MEIGS CENSUS
Leroy Looney 47 (Wagonmaker), Leanna 44 (Va), William 17 (Farmer), Sarah Jane 12, Isaac J. 7 p. 808-731
Samuel Looney 72 (Farmer), Sarah 72 (Va) p. 750-300
MARRIAGES (RHEA)
Anna B. Looney to Hugh T. Blevins q.v.
Jane Looney to Isaac Baker q.v.
John Looney to Lucinda Eddington, 17 Mar 1830, Absolom Thompson Bm (A)
Margaret Looney to Archibald Taylor q.v.
Sally Looney to Thomas York q.v.
Sally H. Looney to Arabian or Abraham F. Gerrald [Fitzgerald] q.v.
MARRIAGES (MEIGS)
Elizabeth Loony to Lewis Hart q.v.
Joseph Looney to Mahaly Ann Coker, 15 May 1838 (16 May), James Patterson Esq.
[1850 Roane Census: Joseph Looney 35, Mahaly 34, James B. 14, Sally A. 11, Mary E. 9, Margaret J. 7, Nancy C. 4, Milly A. 1]
Polly Looney to John Wommack q.v.
MISCELLANEOUS (MEIGS)
Leroy Looney: JP 1841, 1845-47, 1849
" " Bondsman for Joshua Renfroe, 1850
" " Bondsman for Samuel Baker, 1850
Samuel Looney: Hiwassee District, Concord area

\- - - - - - - - - - - -

LOOPER

1830 RHEA CENSUS
Allen Looper 20001 - 11001 p. 396

\- - - - - - - - - - - -

LOVE

TAXES (RHEA)
1808 (John Henry's List): Robert Love 1 WP
1819 (Capt. W.S. Bradley's Dist.):
John Love 1 WP, 3 BP, ½a, 4 Town Lots
Joseph Love 600a
William Love 1 Town Lot
(Capt. John Lewis' Dist.): Robert Love 1 WP, 441a
1823 (Capt. Lewis' Co.): Robert Love 1 WP, 200a
(Capt. Brown's Co.): John Love 1 WP, 3 BP, 3 TL, ½a Southern Liberties
Joseph Love 1 WP, 6 BP, 640a TennRi
Robert Love 1 WP, 441a Richland Cr
1830 RHEA CENSUS
Edmond Love 000000001 - 0001001 p. 356
Jefferson Love 10001 - 00001 p. 377
Joseph Love 00112001 - 0021001 p. 384
1840 RHEA CENSUS
Jacob H. Love 100011 - 000010001
1850 RHEA CENSUS
Sarah J. Love 38 (NC), Mariah L. 26 (NC), Beriah 17 (Clerk): see Beriah Frazier
MARRIAGES (RHEA)
Elizabeth Love to Thomas Simons q.v.
Jacob H. Love to Sarah J. Frazier, 27 Nov 1837 (30 Nov), Benjamin Wallace MG (A)
Jefferson B. Love to Rebecca Isom, 30 Oct 1827 (same), William Woods MG, James P. Miller Bm (AR)
John Love to Mary Wassum, 3 Sept 1836 (4 Sept), John Condly JP, Thomas Smith Bm (AR)
Margaret Love to Hezekiel Shelton q.v.
Rebecca Love to Isaac N. Swan q.v.

Samuel M. Love to Catharine Dame (or Danet), 12 Oct 1844 (same), Samuel R. Hackett JP (R)
[NOTE: this marriage was listed twice in the Courthouse records, #119 and #127, the only difference being the spelling of the bride's last name]
Sarah K. Love to R.J. Meigs q.v.
MISCELLANEOUS (RHEA)
Edmund Love: Revolutionary War Pensioner, 1835 list
John Love: Bondsman for James Rodgers, 1813
" " Bondsman for James Callison, 1818
" " Bondsman for John Robinson, 1826
" " Purchased Lots 3,4,25,27,28,33,34 Washinton
" " Hotel keeper, Town of Washington
Joseph Love: Chairman, Board of Commissioners, 1826-28
Robert Love: Purchased Lot 4, Town of Washington
William Love: Purchased Lot 39, Town of Washington

- - - - - - - - - - - - -

LOVEING

1840 MEIGS CENSUS
Jane Loveing 011011 - 0000001 p. 246

- - - - - - - - - - - - -

LOW / LOWE

1840 RHEA CENSUS
Andrew Lowe 1010101 - 1202201
1850 RHEA CENSUS
Andrew Lowe 56 (Farmer), Jane 52 (Va), Kizziah 25, William W. 22 (Farmer), Jane T. 20, Mary P. 17, Malinda 14, James A. 12, Samuel H. DICKEY 24 (Farmer), Hardy COX 15 p. 565-188
1850 MEIGS CENSUS
Micajah Low 26 (Farmer), Mary Ann 24, Martha T. 4, John A. 2 p. 759-367
MARRIAGES (RHEA)
Elizabeth Low to A.W. McAlpin q.v.
Leatitia Lowe to William P. Foust q.v.
MARRIAGES (MEIGS)
Cage [Micajah] Low to Mary Ann Price, 3 July 1845 (same), John T. Blevins JP, Thomas Leuty Bm
MISCELLANEOUS (RHEA)
Andrew Lowe: Trustee, Sulphur Springs Methodist Church, 1841

- - - - - - - - - - - - -

LOWMAN

MARRIAGES (MEIGS)
William Lowman to Julian Knight, 26 June 1840 (5 July), John Seabourn JP, James Knight Bm

- - - - - - - - - - - - -

LOWRY / LOWERY

1830 RHEA CENSUS
Adam Lowry 1001 - 00001 p. 394
Ellenor Lowery 0 - 100000001 p. 375
William Lowry 212002 - 010001 p. 377
1840 RHEA CENSUS
Charles Lowery 00000001 - 0000001
William T. Lowery 10001 - 00001
1850 RHEA CENSUS
Henry Lowry 70 (Cooper), Sally 34, Polly 12, Susana 10, Fanny 7, Sarah 6, Mary A. 4, Elizabeth 2/12 p. 544-70 [birth places unknown except for Elizabeth, who was born in Tennessee]
Ishner Lowry 40 (Ga)(Farmer), Cyntha A. 34 (Ky), George W. 17 (Farmer), Hannah J. 14, William C. 12, Luisa A. 9, Joseph A. 7, Sarah C. 5, Margaret M. 3 p. 574-254
William Lowry 36 (Ga)(Hammerman), Elizabeth 30, George M. 9, Margaret D. 7, Mary J. 6, Nancy C. 4, Mary QUALLS 22 p. 545-76
MARRIAGES (RHEA)
William Lowry or Lowrey to Elizabeth Bean, 17 July 1839 (18 July), W.B. Gordon JP, Jesse Huddleston Bm (AR)
MISCELLANEOUS (RHEA)
William Lowry: Bondsman for Josiah Smith, 1826

- - - - - - - - - - - - -

LOY / LAY

1830 RHEA CENSUS
Richard Loy or Lay 00001 - 20001 p. 395
1840 RHEA CENSUS
Yancy Loy 00001 - 21001
1850 RHEA CENSUS
Yancy Loy 33 (NC)(Farmer), Sarah 40 (NC), Elizabeth 15 (NC), Sarah M. 13 (NC), Mary J. 11, George W. 8, Priscilla 6 p. 580-290
MARRIAGES (RHEA)
James Lay to Mariah Brown, 5 June 1830 (same), James A. Darwin JP, Leven Stokes Bm (AR)

- - - - - - - - - - - - -

LUCAS / LUCUS

TAXES (RHEA)
1819 (Capt. John Ramsey's Co.): Thomas Lucas 1 WP
1830 RHEA CENSUS
Thomas Lucus 00111 - 0000101 p. 375
1840 MEIGS CENSUS
Hezakeah Lucus 00001 - 0001 p. 234
MARRIAGES (RHEA)
Hezekiah Lucus to Nancy Givins, 15 July 1833 (16 July), Joseph McCorkle JP, Larkin M. Stokes Bm (AR)
Nancy Lucas to Robert Elder q.v.
Pattey Lucas to Joshaway Butler q.v.
Thomas Lucas to Betsy Johnson, 6 Nov 1813, Presley Burton (A)
Thomas Lucus to Narcissa Wammack, 24 Mar 1832 (25 Mar), Joseph McCorkle JP, Thomas Cox Bm (AR)
MARRIAGES (MEIGS)
Hos. Lucus to Barbara Dake, 28 Nov 1839 (same), D.L. Godsey MG, L.M. Stokes Bm
MISCELLANEOUS (RHEA and MEIGS)
Hezekiah Lucus: Cherokee Removal muster roll, 1837
Thomas Lucas: Bondsman for David Hiden, 1816
Thomas Lucus: Hiwassee District

- - - - - - - - - - - - -

LUNSFORD / LUMFORD

1850 MEIGS CENSUS
Eliza Lunsford 25, William R. 3, Rebecca 1 p. 728-121
Henry Lunsford 26 (Farmer), Rebecca 26 p. 728-122
MARRIAGES (MEIGS)
Henry A. Lumford to Rebecca Meyers, 14 Feb 1846 (19 Feb), Jesse Locke MG, Robert Simpson Bm
Wiley G. Lunsford to Eliza Myers, 11 Feb 1847 (same), Jesse Locke MG

- - - - - - - - - - - - -

LUST [LUSK?]

1830 RHEA CENSUS
Joseph Lust 020101 - 011001 p. 373

- - - - - - - - - - - - -

LUTTRELL / LITTERALL

TAXES (RHEA)
1808 (Joseph Brooks' List): Mason Luttrell 1 WP [married Elizabeth Eldridge on 24 Jan 1810 in Roane Co]
1840 MEIGS CENSUS
Caswell D. Luttrell 12013 - 100001 p. 226
James Luttrell 20001 - 010001 p. 231
MARRIAGES (RHEA)
Cintha Litterall to Lemond Cash q.v.
Susan Litterall to John Yeates q.v.
MISCELLANEOUS (RHEA)
Caswell D. Luttrell: Ocoee District
William Litterall: Bondsman for John Yeates, 1829

- - - - - - - - - - - - -

LYON / LYONS / LIONS

1830 RHEA CENSUS
David Lyons 20001 - 21002 p. 392
MARRIAGES (RHEA)
David Lions to Polly Putnam, 27 Jan 1827 (1 Feb), James Wilson JP, Josiah Keeran Bm (AR)
MISCELLANEOUS (RHEA)
William Lyon: On first Grand Jury

- - - - - - - - - - - - -

McADAMS

1840 MEIGS CENSUS
Joseph McAdams 0101001 - 112001 p. 239
1850 MEIGS CENSUS
Delilah McAdams 55 (NC), George 18 (Farmer), Deborah 16, Margaret 14, Alexander 11, Melvina A. 20 p. 795-645
James McAdams 23 (Blacksmith), Mary 23, George W. 20 (Blacksmith), John G. 6, Sarah 4, Mary Jane 2, Nelson R. 1 p. 798-670
MARRIAGES (MEIGS)
James McAdams to Mary Neil, 11 July 1843 (same), Robert Stockton JP, Calvin Mantooth Bm
Mary McAdams to Philip Davis q.v.
Melisina McAdams to William Alexander q.v.
Telitha McAdams to John Wood q.v.

- - - - - - - - - - - - -

McADOO / McADOE

1840 MEIGS CENSUS
Samuel McAdoe 10000001 - 120001 p. 238
1850 MEIGS CENSUS
Nancy McAdoo 49 (NC), Margaret Jane 19, Judith T. 16, Elias P. 14, Prudence E. 12, Mary M. 10, Nancy E. 8 p. 775-495
MARRIAGES (MEIGS)
Margaret J. McAdoo to John H. Davis q.v.

- - - - - - - - - - - - -

McALLEN

1840 MEIGS CENSUS
John McAllen 1111001 - 0121001 p. 241
1850 MEIGS CENSUS
James B. McAllen 22 (Farmer), Sarah Jane 20, Cyntha B. 9, Andrew J. 1 p. 795-647*
John McAllen 63 (NC)(Farmer), Emily W. 20, Eliza 18, John J. 16 (Farmer), Newton H. 14 p. 795-647* [NOTE: both households were numbered 647]
Sarah McAllen 28, John P. 6, Eliza T. 5, Thomas 4, Morgan L. 1 p. 794-637
MISCELLANEOUS (MEIGS)
John McAllen: Purchased Lots 21,22,31,35,59 in Decatur

- - - - - - - - - - - - -

McALLISTER / McALESTER

MARRIAGES (RHEA)
Elizabeth McAlester to Joseph Edington q.v.
MISCELLANEOUS (RHEA)
John McAllister: Bondsman for James Covey, 1815
William McAlister: Bondsman for Thomas Simons, 1813

- - - - - - - - - - - - -

McALPIN / McALPHIN

TAXES (RHEA)
1823 (Capt. Brown's Co.): Robert McAlpin 1 WP
1850 RHEA CENSUS
Alexander McAlpin 28 (Farmer), Elizabeth 28, Sarah 30, John 20 (Farmer), George 17 (Farmer), Eliza J. 14, Christiana J. 5, Margaret 3 p. 555-135
David J. McAlpin 32 (Farmer), Eliza J. 32, William 11, Sarah E. 9, Joshua A. 7, John W. 5, Rebecca E. 5, Samuel N. 2 p. 547-92
John McAlpin 55 (Farmer), Temperance M. 30, Robert F. 2/12 p. 565-186
MARRIAGES (RHEA)
A.W. McAlpin to Elizabeth Low, 15 July 1844 (18 July), Jesse P. Thompson JP (R)
MARRIAGES (MEIGS)
John E. McAlpin to Temperance M. Robeson, 17 June 1849 (19 June), William Green MG
MISCELLANEOUS (RHEA)
Robert McAlpin (Rev.): Principal of Tennessee Academy

- - - - - - - - - - - - -

McAMMES

1830 RHEA CENSUS
John McAmmes 010001 - 201001 p. 365

- - - - - - - - - - - - -

McANALLY / McHANRALLY

1850 MEIGS CENSUS
John McAnally 32 (Farmer), Angaline 30 p. 723-86
MARRIAGES (RHEA)
Mary McAnally or McHanrally to William Miller q.v.

- - - - - - - - - - - - -

McANS

TAXES (RHEA)
1808 (Joseph Brooks' List): Robert McAns 200a Sale Ck

- - - - - - - - - - - - -

McARSTER

MARRIAGES (RHEA)
Polly McArster to Thomas Gass q.v.

- - - - - - - - - - - - -

McARTHUR

TAXES (RHEA)
1819 (Capt. Wm McCray's Co.): Joseph McArthur 1 WP
William McArthur 1 WP

- - - - - - - - - - - - -

McBRIDE

1830 RHEA CENSUS
David McBride 0001000011 - 0 p. 380
William McBride 00001 - 00011 p. 380
MARRIAGES (RHEA)
Sereaner McBride to Isham Goff q.v.

- - - - - - - - - - - - -

McBRYAN

MISCELLANEOUS (MEIGS)
Polly McBryan: Hiwassee District, Sewee Creek area

- - - - - - - - - - - - -

McCAIN

1840 MEIGS CENSUS
Elizabeth McCain 0 - 000001 p. 236
1850 MEIGS CENSUS
Elizabeth McCain 38 (Va) p. 781-532

- - - - - - - - - - - - -

McCALEB

TAXES (RHEA)
1808 (Jonathan Fine's List): William McCaleb 1 WP
1840 RHEA CENSUS
Andrew McCaleb 00001001 - 0022001
1850 RHEA CENSUS
Andrew McCaleb 61 (Farmer), Ann 57 (Va), Lucinda 24, Elizabeth 19 p. 560-164
Archibald McCaleb 30 (Farmer), Nancy J. 23 p. 559-156
MARRIAGES (RHEA)
Harriet McCaleb to James W. Vernon q.v.
Jane McCaleb to John A. Murphey q.v.
Mary Ann McCaleb to Jacob Gibson q.v.
MARRIAGES (MEIGS)
Archibald McCaleb to Nancey Jane Gibson, 30 Oct 1848 (3 Nov), William Green MG
[Archibald, son of Andrew; Nancy, dau of Hiram and Mary Stockton Gibson]

- - - - - - - - - - - - -

McCALL

TAXES (RHEA)
1819 (Capt. John Ramsey's Co.): Alexander McCall 1000a
Joseph McCall 1 WP
1830 RHEA CENSUS
Alexander McCall 110001 - 010001 p. 362
1840 RHEA CENSUS
Thomas McCall [McCallie?] 1100001 - 100001
1840 MEIGS CENSUS
Alexander McCall 1020001 - 10001 p. 248
1850 MEIGS CENSUS
Alexnder H. McCall 64 (Ireland)(Farmer), Sarena 36, Margaret 11, Charles A. 10, William 9, Mary 8, Harriet 7, Sarah 5, Martha 4, Enoch C.L. 1 p. 809-738
MARRIAGES (MEIGS)
A.H. McCall to Serena Green, 4 Sept 1841 (5 Sept), James Moore JP, William Wan Bm
Angelina McCall to Enoch Ladd q.v.
MISCELLANEOUS (MEIGS)
A.H. McCall: Common School Commissioner, Dist 8, 1838
John J. McCall: Mexican War

- - - - - - - - - - - - -

McCALLEN / McCALLAM / McCALLON / McCOLLON

1830 RHEA CENSUS
John McCallen 1100101 - 22101 p. 360
MARRIAGES (RHEA)
Alley McCallam to Hiram Miller q.v.
MARRIAGES (MEIGS)
A.J. McCallen to Mrs. Sarah Bottom, 10 Oct 1843 (12 Oct), William L. Adams JP
Eleanor J. McCallon to Thomas S. Farmer q.v.
James B. McCallon to Sarah Jane Butler, 26 Sept 1848 (28 Sept), Wm L. Adams JP, John M. Lillard Bm
Mary E. McCollon to Elijah Turner q.v.
Netty Ann McCollon to Newton Peak q.v.
MISCELLANEOUS (RHEA and MEIGS)
Andrew McCallon: Cherokee Removal muster roll, 1836
John McCallon: 1st Lt., Cherokee Removal muster roll
" " Trustee for Decatur Academy, 1838-39
J. McCallen: JP 1834 (Rhea Co.)
Thomas McCallon: JP(?) 1845

- - - - - - - - - - - - -

McCALLIE

1840 RHEA CENSUS
Thomas McCall [McCallie?] 1100001 - 100001
[Thomas married Mary Hooke]
MISCELLANEOUS (RHEA)
Thomas McCallie: Bondsman for George W. Rice, 1827
" " Bm for Gideon B. Thompson, 1830
" " Bondsman for Robert H. Hudson, 1832
" " Early merchant in Washington [moved to Chattanooga in 1841]
" " Purchased land in Ocoee District

- - - - - - - - - - - -

McCANDLESS / McCANLESS / McANDLESS

TAXES (RHEA)
1819 (Capt. W.S. Bradley's Co.): John McCandless 64a
Richard A. McCandless 1 WP
1823 (Capt. Brown's Co.): Richard A. McAndless 1 WP
John McAndles 40a Tenn River
MARRIAGES (RHEA)
Margaret McCandless to Jacob Reynolds q.v.
Nancy McCanless to William Henry q.v.
MISCELLANEOUS (RHEA)
Richard A. McCandless: Bm for Jacob Reynolds, 1821

- - - - - - - - - - - -

McCANSE

TAXES (RHEA)
1819 (Capt. John Ramsey's Co.): James McCanse 1 WP
1823 (Capt. Braselton's Co.):
James McCanse 1 WP, 1 BP, 389a Piney River
1830 RHEA CENSUS
James McCanse 03220001 - 10100101 p. 387
1840 RHEA CENSUS
James McCanse 00020001 - 1210001
MARRIAGES (RHEA)
Mary Ann McCanse to John Gaston q.v.
MISCELLANEOUS (RHEA)
James McCanse: JP 1835-1838

- - - - - - - - - - - -

McCARROLL / McCARRELL

1830 RHEA CENSUS
Jas or Jos McCarrell 00100001 - 0011001 p. 369
John McCarrell 00110001 - 0020001 p. 365
John McCarroll 01110001 - 00200001 p. 395
1840 MEIGS CENSUS
Simon McCarroll 11010001 - 1020001 p. 228
William McCarroll 00001 - 10001 p. 228
1850 RHEA CENSUS
Charles McCarroll 23 (Farmer), Nancy 27 (Va), Eli 5, Sarah E. 3, James F. 5/12 p. 633-635
Sarah J. McCarroll 7: see Solomon Cate
Simon McCarroll 66 (NC)(Farmer), Sarah 56 (Ky), James 18, Harvey L. 15, Sarah J. 9, William V. 8 p. 632-633
William McCarroll 31 (Farmer), Margaret 20 p. 633-634
MARRIAGES (RHEA)
Patsey McCarroll to William Kerr q.v.
Rebecca McCarroll to Ambler Grubb q.v.
MARRIAGES (MEIGS)
Charles McCarroll to Eliza Pettitt, 5 Feb 1842 (6 Feb), John Seabern JP
Charles McCarrell to Nancy Carvin, 26 July 1843 (same), William Johns JP, Philon Carvin Bm
William McCarroll Jr. to M. Jones, 13 July 1839 (16 July), B.F. McKenzie JP, Wm M. McCarroll Sr. Bm

- - - - - - - - - - - -

McCARTER

1830 RHEA CENSUS
William McCarter 23200001 - 001001 p. 365
1840 RHEA CENSUS
Jesse McCarter 00001 - 30001
1850 RHEA CENSUS
Able McCarter 23, Meredith 24: see James Stuart
William R. McCarter 26 (Unk)(Farmer), Martha 21, Sarah J. 6/12 p. 601-418
MARRIAGES (RHEA)
Able McCarter to Emaline Stewart, 22 Nov 1849 (same), S.E. Foust JP (R)
Betsy McCarter to Nathan Ware q.v.
James McCarter to Cathy Emrey or Embrey, 26 Sept 1821 (same), John Fine JP, Nathaniel Moore Bm (AR) [1850 Bledsoe Census: James McCarter 50, Catharine 48, Mary A. 33, Elizabeth J. 19, Mira 17, George 15, Rebecca 13, John W. 11, Maston H. 9, James C. 7, Catharine 6, Benjamin F. 4]
Jesse McCarter to Peggy Ann Dunn, 6 May 1835 (7 May), D.L. Godsey JP, Hugh T. Blevins Bm (AR)

- - - - - - - - - - - -

McCARTNEY / McCORTNEY

1840 MEIGS CENSUS
Jane McCartney 0021 - 012001 p. 229
MARRIAGES (MEIGS)
Mary Ann McCortney to John Lillard q.v.
Sarah J. McCortney to R.M. Lillard q.v.
MISCELLANEOUS (MEIGS)
Hanson R. McCartney: 2nd Lt., Mexican War

- - - - - - - - - - - -

McCARTY

TAXES (RHEA)
1819 (Capt. John Ramsey's Co.): Timothy McCarty 1 WP
William McCarty 1 WP
1823 (Capt. Piper's Co.): Benjamin McCarty 1 WP, 225a
Thomas McCarty 1 WP
William McCarty 1 WP
1830 RHEA CENSUS
Benjamin McCarty 0001001 - 121001 p. 361
Thomas McCarty 12101 - 101001 p. 361
William McCarty 100001 - 311001 p. 361

MARRIAGES (RHEA)
John L. McCarty to Polly Cowan, 27 Sept 1820 (same), John Cozby JP and Bm (AR)
[1850 McMinn Census: John L. McCarty 66, Polly 47, James E. 25, John 16, William 10, Joseph 7]
Thomas McCarty to Polly Baker, 25 Feb 1817 (29 Feb), John Fine JP, Timothy McCarty Bm (AR)
MARRIAGES (MEIGS)
Timothy H. McCarty to Mary J. Manson, 16 Mar 1846 (10 Mar), H. Douglass MG, Stephen H. Miller Bm [1850 Bradley Census: Timothy McCarty 28, Jane 21, Robert 3, Sarah 2, E.H. Morrison 19]
MISCELLANEOUS (RHEA and MEIGS)
Benjamin McCarty: Hiwassee District
James McCarty: Bondsman for Randel Bowen, 1810
John L. McCarty: Ocoee District
Timothy McCarty: Bondsman for Thomas McCarty, 1817
Thomas McCarty: Hiwassee District

\- - - - - - - - - - - - -

McCARVER

1830 RHEA CENSUS
Archibald McCarver 10101001 - 1201001 p. 382
MARRIAGES (RHEA)
Willis McCarver to Polly Kennes, 2 Oct 1830, Isham McCarver Bm, "Returned with papers of D. Walker, Esq." (AR)
MISCELLANEOUS (RHEA and MEIGS)
Isham McCarver: Bondsman for William McCarver, 1830
William McCarver: Private, Mexican War

\- - - - - - - - - - - - -

McCARY / McCROY

1830 RHEA CENSUS
Sarah(?) McCary 00001 - 00001 p. 387
1840 RHEA CENSUS
Henry McCroy 002001 - 10001 [ink blob]
Linsey McCary 00001 - 00010001
1850 RHEA CENSUS
Lindsey McCary 34 (SC)(Cabnetmaker), Polly A. 24, John T. 8, Joseph B. 6, Agness A. 5, unnamed 10/12 p. 584-319
1850 MEIGS CENSUS
Henry McCroy 50 (NC)(Miller), Lively 30 (Va), Rosa M. 12, Thomas J. 10, Anderson M. 8, Jessee C. 7 p. 746-269
MARRIAGES (RHEA)
Henry McCary to Jane Thompson, 9 June 1834 (12 June), Matthew Hubbert JP, John P. Long Bm (AR)
Linsey McCary to Mary A. Peters, 8 Nov 1837, Azariah Barton JP, N.S. Broyles Bm (AR)
Nancy McCary to Jesse Tyson q.v.
Sally McCary to William L. Johnson q.v.
MISCELLANEOUS (RHEA)
Henry McCary: Bondsman for Edward E. Wasson, 1832

\- - - - - - - - - - - - -

McCLANAHAN / McCLENNEHAN / McCLENNIHAN

1830 RHEA CENSUS
Jno McClanahan 00001001 - 01020001 p. 370
Jno McClanahan 10001 - 00010001 p. 370
Mason McClannahan 0001 - 0001 p. 370
1840 MEIGS CENSUS
John McClennihan 011001 - 210001 p. 231
Mason McClennehan 032011 - 100001 p. 227
1850 MEIGS CENSUS
Mason McClanahan 45, Malinda 40, Jehu 20, John 18, Nancy Jane 16, James 13, Hiram 11, William A. 9, Mason 7, Miles B. 5, Lacy (m) 1 p. 726-110
Jehu McClanahan 33 (Farmer), Catharine 25, Simon 9 p. 726-109
John McClanahan 44 (Farmer), Mernerva 42, Alexander M. 20 (Farmer), Catharine 18, Nancy 16, Martha Jane 14, Thomas 10, Elender 7, Lucinda 3 p. 761-381
MARRIAGES (RHEA)
Darkie McClanahan to George W. Mullins q.v.
John McClanahan to Miranda Rice, 15 Feb 1829, Alexander Rice Bm (A)
Nancy McClenahan to Joel Sharp q.v.
Peggy McClanahan to Moses Price q.v.
Polly McClanahan to Jacob Gross q.v.
MARRIAGES (MEIGS)
Caroline McClanhon to John B. Campbell q.v.
Malinda McClanahon to Gilliam Brooks q.v.
Stephen J. McClennahon to Mila Ramsey, 2 May 1844 (15 May), William Jones JP, P. Daughty Sur

\- - - - - - - - - - - - -

McCLARON

MARRIAGES (MEIGS)
Sarah Ann McClaron to C.M.K. Welch q.v.

\- - - - - - - - - - - - -

McCLELAND

1840 RHEA CENSUS
Rebecca McCleland 0 - 000001001

\- - - - - - - - - - - - -

McCLELLAN

MARRIAGES (RHEA)
Matthew W. McClellan to Dolly A. Campbell, 27 Sept 1814, Alexander Outlaw Bm (A)

\- - - - - - - - - - - - -

McCLENDON

1840 RHEA CENSUS
John McClendon 121101 - 21100001
1850 RHEA CENSUS
Dennis McClendon 25 (Farmer), Polly 21, Nancy J. 4, Rebecca A. 1 p. 556-138

John McClendon 51 (NC)(Farmer), Nancy 49 (NC), Elizabeth 23 (NC), Willis 21 (NC)(Farmer), Charity 20 (NC), Edmund 18 (Farmer), Mary 17, Sanders 15, Isaac 12, Malinda 10, Nancy 8, Charlotte 6 p. 538-39

MARRIAGES (RHEA)

Dennis McClendon to Mary Bradye [dates are confused: Allen shows 19 June 1845 and 3 July for date of solemnization; the Courthouse record shows 5 June 1845 for both; Allen also shows only B.W. Holloway as Bm; Courthouse record shows S. Frazier JP, B.W. Holloway Bm] (AR)

- - - - - - - - - - - - -

McCLUNG

TAXES (RHEA)

1819 (Capt. McGill's Co.): Charles McClung 3560a

MISCELLANEOUS (RHEA)

Charles McClung: Hiwassee District, Garrison Bluff area

- - - - - - - - - - - - -

McCLURE

TAXES (RHEA)

1823 (Capt. Brown's Co.): John McClure 1 WP, 274a

1830 RHEA CENSUS

Moses McClure 200101 - 21011 p. 374
Jno McClure 11310001 - 110001 p. 377
Robert McClure 000001 - 00010001 p. 377

MARRIAGES (RHEA)

Elizabeth McClure to David Leuty q.v.
Joseph McClure to Nancy Youniss [Yonniss or Younip], 7 July 1850 (9 July), Asa Newport MG (R)

MARRIAGES (MEIGS)

Catharine McClure to William Key q.v.
Elizabeth V. McClure to Thomas R. Rogers q.v.
Polly McClure to Stephen Matlock q.v.

MISCELLANEOUS (RHEA)

John McClure: JP 1826-1834
" " Bondsman for Daniel R. Kennedy, 1825
Joshua McClure: JP 1827

MISCELLANEOUS (MEIGS)

Thomas B. McClure: JP 1836, 1843-44, 1846
" " " [McClower]: Cherokee Removal muster roll, 1826
Thomas McClure: Chairman of County Court, 1846

- - - - - - - - - - - - -

McCONNEY

1850 RHEA CENSUS

Jane McConney 44 (Va), Mary J. 23 (Va) p. 620-547

- - - - - - - - - - - - -

McCORD

MISCELLANEOUS (MEIGS)

Joseph McCord: Hiwassee District, Lower Goodfield

- - - - - - - - - - - - -

McCORKLE / McCORCLE / McKORKLE

1830 RHEA CENSUS

Joseph McCorcle 200011 - 10001 p. 372

1840 MEIGS CENSUS

Joseph McCorkle 0120001 - 111001 p. 236

1850 MEIGS CENSUS

Christina McCorkle 52, Minerva 24, Clarissa 22, Lucinda 19 p. 756-352
George C. McCorkle 38 (Farmer), Susannah 39, Franklin H. 9, Catharine L. 7, Joseph 3 p. 756-351
Joseph McKorkle 58 (Merchant), Elizabeth 46, Avander T. 21 (Merchant), Franklin 19 (Merchant), Tennessee 15, Evina 11, Sarah 9, Lafayette 7 p. 774-489

MARRIAGES (MEIGS)

Charlotte McCorkle to Tiry Lawson q.v.
Elisha McCorkle to Asbery S. Lillard q.v.
Eveline McCorkle to Ambrose W. Hodge q.v.

MISCELLANEOUS (RHEA)

Joseph McCorkle: JP 1828-1834
Robert E. McCorkle: Mexican War (died in service)

MISCELLANEOUS (MEIGS)

Franklin McCorkle: Surety for John H. Davis, 1850
Joseph McCorkle: Circuit Court Clerk, 1836-1840
" " Purchased Lots 29,30 in Decatur; erected store and residence
" " Trustee for Decatur Academy, 1838-39
Lilburn McCorkle: 3rd Sgt., Mexican War

- - - - - - - - - - - - -

McCORMICK / McCORMACK

MARRIAGES (RHEA)

William McCormick to Sally Thompson, 15 Mar 1831 (same), Thomas Hall MG, Jonathan Fry Bm (AR)

MISCELLANEOUS (RHEA and MEIGS)

Robt T. McCormack: Cherokee Removal muster roll, 1836
William McCormack: Cherokee Removal muster roll, 1836
Wm F. McCormick: Bondsman for Robt E. Singleton, 1833

- - - - - - - - - - - - -

McCOWAN / McCOWEN / McKEOWN / McKEON / McKOWAN

(see also COWAN)

1840 MEIGS CENSUS

James McKowen 00211001 - 000111 p. 228

1850 MEIGS CENSUS

James McCowen 68 (Ireland)(Farmer), Cordelia 58 (NC), William 22 (NC)(Farmer), John 24 (NC)(Farmer) p. 743-243

MARRIAGES (RHEA)

Thomas D. McKeown to Polly Ann Mahan, 12 Oct 1834 (1 Jan 1835 according to Courthouse record), Vaden H. Giles JP, Hanson Philpot Bm (AR)

MARRIAGES (MEIGS)

Isaac McKeown to Matilda Reynolds, 30 Nov 1842 (1 Dec), D.L. Godsey MG, Israel S. Edens Sur
James A. McCowan to Jane Collins, 24 July 1844 (25 July), W.S. Collins Sur
Manervy J. McKeon to Felix Barnhart q.v.
Nancy McKown to Henry C. Vanzant q.v.

- - - - - - - - - - - - -

McCOY / McKOY / MACOY

TAXES (RHEA)
1819 (Capt. John Ramsey's Co.): James McCoy 1 WP
John McCoy 150a
1823 (Capt. McCall's Co.): James McCoy 1 WP
John McCoy 150a Piney River
1830 RHEA CENSUS
James McCoy 210001 - 11001 p. 387
John McCoy 00110001 - 0002001 p. 363
Wyley McCoy 10001 - 0001 p. 364
1840 MEIGS CENSUS
Sarah McKoy 0111 - 011101 p. 246
1850 RHEA CENSUS
John McCoy 26: see Alfred Brackins
Sarah McCoy 49, Ann S. 25, James W. 20 (Farmer), Sarah 18, Jackson 4 p. 561-175
MARRIAGES (RHEA)
Ann McCoy to James Henry q.v.
Elizabeth Macoy to Samuel Snelson q.v.
Eliza McCoy to Thomas Gaither q.v.
James McCoy to Sally Carter, 2 Aug 1820, John Johnson Bm (A)
James Macay or McCoy to Sally Carter, 21 or 24 Aug 1820 (same), J. Fine JP (AR)
[Allen shows the last name as McCoy in both listings, but the Courthouse record shows it as Macay]
Matilda McCoy to James Gibson q.v.
Nancy McCoy to Nathan Carter q.v.
Wylie or Wiley McCoy to Harriet Parker, 13 Mar 1829 (15 Mar), Beal Gaither JP (AR)
MARRIAGES (MEIGS)
Margaret McCoy to Alfred Brackins q.v.
MISCELLANEOUS (RHEA)
Josiah McCoy: Trustee, Sulphur Springs Presbyterian Meeting House, 1834

- - - - - - - - - - - - -

McCRACKEN / McCRAKIN

1830 RHEA CENSUS
Robert McCracken 2111001 - 111101 p. 378
MARRIAGES (RHEA)
John McCrakin to Nancy Henry, 2 July 1831, Robert Crawford Bm (A)

- - - - - - - - - - - - -

McCRAY

TAXES (RHEA)
1819 (Capt. Wm McCray's Co.):
William McCray 1 WP, 131a

- - - - - - - - - - - - -

McCUISTON

1850 RHEA CENSUS
Andrew J. McCuiston 33 (Farmer), Hannah S. 39, Phillip T. 9, Christopher C. 8, David H. 5, Mary J. 3, James H. 3/12, Hannah S. FOUST 14, Phillip FOUST 77 (NC)(Blacksmith) p. 560-72 [Andrew married Hannah Foust on 23 Aug 1838 in Roane County]

- - - - - - - - - - - - -

McCULLY
(see also McCALLIE)

1850 RHEA CENSUS
Jonathan McCully 50 (Va)(Miller), Elizabeth 47, Eliza 26, Peter 20 (Farmer), Sarah 19, Rutha 18, Margaret 17, Catharine 16, Luvina 14, Elizabeth 13, Mary 10, Minerva 9, Emeline 7, Nancy 3 p. 579-286

- - - - - - - - - - - - -

McDANIEL / McDANEL / McDANNEL

TAXES (RHEA)
1819 (Capt. Wm McCray's Co.): James McDaniel 1 WP
1823 (Capt. Smith's Co.): John McDaniel 2 BP, 573a T Ri
Joseph McDaniel 1 WP
Samuel McDaniel 1 WP, 3 BP
1830 RHEA CENSUS
Charles McDannel 10001 - 100002 p. 372
Jno McDanel 000001 - 0000100001 p. 372
Joseph McDaniel 000011 - 000001 p. 372
Samuel McDannel 01000101 - 32001 p. 372
1840 MEIGS CENSUS
John McDanil 0000000000001 - 0000101 p. 235
Samuel McDaniel 10011001 - 114201 (also a free colored male 25-26 years old) p. 234
1850 MEIGS CENSUS
Anney McDaniel 45 (NC), Abram C. 6 p. 763-391
James McDaniel 27 (Farmer), Sarah 25 (Blind), Mary J. 21, Louisa 19, Elender 15, John E. 14, Elenoria 13 p. 760-376
MARRIAGES (RHEA)
Flora McDaniel to William Armstrong q.v.
John McDaniel to Sally Stout, 3 Apr 1828 (same), James A. Darwin JP, John Underwood Bm (AR)
Joseph McDaniel to Patsey McDaniel, 3 Mar 1821 (4 Mar), Thomas Cox JP, Allen Kennedy Bm (AR)
Nancy McDaniel to John Dozier q.v.
Patsey McDaniel to Joseph McDaniel q.v.
Samuel McDaniel to Rachael B. Cox, 2 Dec 1820 (same), "I Solomonized the Rights of Matrimony" John Rice JP, Thomas Cox Bm (AR)
Temperance McDaniel to Amos King q.v.
Temperance McDaniel to Thomas Cox q.v.
MARRIAGES (MEIGS)
Elender McDaniel to Joseph Collins q.v.
John M. McDaniel to Elinder Quiett, 4 Dec 1850, A.J. Quiett Sur
Martha McDaniel to Jesse Martin q.v.
Samuel McDaniel to Ann Clark, 25 Feb 1840 (same), John Taff JP, A. Cox Sur
MISCELLANEOUS (RHEA)
Joseph McDaniel: MG 1831
" " Bondsman for Cain Gentry, 1823
Samuel McDaniel: Bondsman for Thomas Cox, 1815
" " Bondsman for John Martin, 1821
MISCELLANEOUS (MEIGS)
James McDaniel: Hiwassee District
John McDaniel: Hiwassee District, Cottonport area
Joseph McDaniel: Hiwassee District
Samuel McDaniel: Hiwassee District
" " House used to hold elections, Dist 3
" " On Circuit Court jury, 1836

Samuel McDaniel: Trustee for Decatur Academy, 1838-39
W. McDaniel: Hiwassee District

McDONALD

TAXES (RHEA)
1823 (Capt. Howard's Co.):
James McDonald 1 WP, 1 BP, 1529a
William & Bryan McDonald 280a
1830 RHEA CENSUS
Bryant McDonald* 1000102 - 2001 p. 367
James McDonald* 1100001 - 120011 p. 379
William McDonald* 010001 - 20001 p. 379
[* sons of Edward and Elizabeth Foster McDonald]
1840 RHEA CENSUS
B.R. McDonald 1110001 - 111001
Bryant McDonald 12110001 - 001
Joseph McDonald 000001 - 0
William McDonald 10001001 - 111001
1850 RHEA CENSUS
Bryant McDonald 18 (Va)(Farmer): see Jacob Foust
Bryant McDonald 53 (Va)(Farmer), Elizabeth 44 (Va), Lewis F. 23, Harriet O. 20, Charles T. 18, Mary E. 15, Virginia T. 12, Joseph F. 9, George A. 5, Sidnah C. 3 p. 624-573
Joseph McDonald 24 (Va)(Farmer) p. 633-637
William McDonald 50 (Va)(Farmer), Nancy 46 (Va), Rowland F. 24 (Farmer), Lavena 21, Caroline 19, Ellen 13, Milton 11 p. 622-558 [William married his first cousin, Nancy McDonald]
MARRIAGES (RHEA)
Harriet O. McDonald to S.W. Leuty q.v.
James McDonald to Kitty Jones, 7 Apr 1820, John Jones Bm (AR)
John McDonald to Polly Johnson, 12 or 24 Feb 1812 (26 or 24 Feb), Wm Long JP, George Sherrill Bm (AR)
Mary McDonald to J. M. Hall q.v.
Rebecca McDonald to Isaac Benson q.v.
MISCELLANEOUS (RHEA and MEIGS)
Bryant McDonald: Hiwassee District
Bryan R. McDonald: JP 1836-1841
James McDonald: JP 1822-1828
William McDonald: Hiwassee District

McDONEY

1840 MEIGS CENSUS
Jane McDoney(?) 0 - 000101

McDONOUGH

MARRIGES (RHEA)
John McDonough to Margaret Armstrong, 24 Dec 1821 (25 Dec), John Rice JP, Jonathan Rogers Bm (AR)
MISCELLANEOUS (RHEA)
John McDonough: Bondsman for Robert Kimbrell, 1828

McDOWELL / McDOWEL

1840 MEIGS CENSUS
Elizabeth McDowel 0001 - 01100001 p. 226
Isaac McDowel 0310001 - 00001 p. 226
Samuel McDowel 00002 - 0001 p. 226
1850 MEIGS CENSUS
Isaac McDowell 49 (NC)(Farmer), Joseph C. 21, John B. 18, William W. 14, Mary Jane 9, Isaac 5 p. 725-98
Nancy McDowel 73 (SC) p. 722-76
MARRIAGES (RHEA)
William McDowell to Malinda Riddle, 15 Oct 1835, John Casey Bm (A)
MARRIAGES (MEIGS)
Daniel McDowell to Sarah Simpson, 16 June 1838, Wilford Rucker JP
Isaac McDowell to Sariah Whitson, 31 Dec 1849 (1 Jan 1850), A.C. Hunter MG, John Seabourn Sur
James W. McDowell to Nancy Baldwin, 20 Dec 1850, W.M. Benson Sur
Rebecca McDowell to Emanuel Parsons q.v.
MISCELLANEOUS (MEIGS)
James McDowell: Surety 1843

McDUFFEE

1850 MEIGS CENSUS
Mahala McDuffee 30 (Ky), Joseph N. 8 (Ala), William 5 (Ala) p. 717-37

McDUNNER / McDUSMER

MARRIAGES (RHEA)
James McDunner or McDusmer to Catharine Morgan, 12 Jan 1847 (no return) (R)

McELROY

MARRIAGES (RHEA)
William McElroy to Missouri VanDike, 5 Jan 1831 (6 Jan), Thomas Cox JP, A.R. Chilton Bm (AR)
MISCELLANEOUS (RHEA)
William McElroy: Bondsman for Israel A. VanDyke, 1831

McELWEE

TAXES (RHEA)
1808 (Jonathan Fine's List):
John McElwee 1 WP, 100a Piney River[John married Betsy True or Trice, 25 Dec 1805 in Roane Co]
1840 MEIGS CENSUS
Thomas B. McElwee 10004 - 00001 p. 240
1850 MEIGS CENSUS
Thomas B. McElwee 34 (Manufacturer), Martha 29, William M. 10, James M. 8, Franklin B. 7, Rutha Jane 5, Mary Ann 3, Charles L. 1 p. 792-617 [Thomas, son of James and Nancy Johnson McElwee; Martha, dau of William and Sarah Dodson Matlock]

McENTIRE [McINTIRE?]

TAXES (RHEA)
1819 (Capt. Ramsey's Co.): Archibald McEntire 1 WP

- - - - - - - - - - - - -

McEWING / McUEN

1830 RHEA CENSUS
William McUen 111001 - 000101 p. 370
1840 MEIGS CENSUS
Robert McEwing 32000001 - 01201 p. 231

- - - - - - - - - - - - -

McFADDEN

TAXES (RHEA)
1819 (Capt. W.S. Bradley's Dist): David McFadden 1 WP

- - - - - - - - - - - - -

McFALL / McFALLS / McPHAIL

1830 RHEA CENSUS
John McFalls 001001 - 12000101 p. 387
(the 1 may have been erased)
1840 RHEA CENSUS
Allen McFalls 00001 - 0001
Daniel McFall 00120001 - 1200001
1850 RHEA CENSUS
Allen H. McFall 29 (Farmer), Myra 27, Luisa J. 9, Mary A. 7, Samantha E. 6, Wade H. 1/12 p. 582-303
Calvin R. McFall 22 (NC)(Farmer), Barbary A. 24, Myra C. 1 p. 578-279
Daniel McFalls 61 (NC)(Farmer), Mary 50 (NC), Francis 20, Sarah GIBBS 28, John GIBBS 7 p. 578-275
Henry McFall 28 (SC)(Farmer), Mariah 29, Juli A. 7, Vesta J. 5, Sarah C. 3, Hulda E. 1 p. 578-273
James D. McFall 60 (NC)(Farmer), Frances 60 (NC), Matilda 18, James B. GREEN 9, William B. GREEN 7 p. 582-307
MARRIAGES (RHEA)
Allen H. McFall to Myra Garrison, 7 Mar 1839 (8 Mar), S. Dyer JP, Cyrus Campbell Bm (AR)
Arthur McFalls to Sally Jennings, 30 Jan 1843 (same), E.E. Wasson JP (A)
Calvin R. McFalls to Barbary Ann Garrison, 27 Dec 1845 (28 Dec), Daniel Broyles JP (AR)
Daniel McPhail to Patsy Sims or Sams, 15 Sept 1828 (16 Sept), Heil Buttram JP, James Hicks Bm (AR)
Elizabeth McFall to William Harrison Gaither q.v.
Frances McFalls to John Thompson q.v.
Jesse H. McFall to Jane Richmond, 15 Sept 1834 (16 Sept), Daniel Briggs MG, John P. Long Bm (AR)
June McFall to Nathaniel Layman q.v.
Martha McFalls to William Thurman q.v.
Polly McFall to John Johnston q.v.
Richard G. McFall to Eleanor Gaither, 13 Oct 1834 (14 Oct), Wm Green JP, Robert N. Gillespie Bm (AR)
MISCELLANEOUS (RHEA)
Jesse H. McFall: Bondsman for Wm Harrison Gaither, 1835

- - - - - - - - - - - - -

McFARLAND / McFARLIN

1830 RHEA CENSUS
Elias McFarland 0001 - 0111001 p. 381
1850 RHEA CENSUS
Elizabeth McFarland 25: see James J. Able
MARRIAGES (RHEA)
Andrew McFarland to Mary Johnson, 27 Nov 1839 (no return), John Silkirk Bm (R)
Margaret McFarlin to Nathaniel Rowden q.v.
Nancy McFarland to John Silcock q.v.
Ruth McFarland to William Carter q.v.

- - - - - - - - - - - - -

McGEE / McGHEE / MAGE / MAGHEE

TAXES (RHEA)
1819 (Capt. W.S. Bradley's Dist.): George Maghee 1 WP
1823 (Capt. Lewis' Co.): Daniel McGhee 1 WP
(Capt. Brown's Co.): George Mage 1 WP
MISCELLANEOUS (MEIGS)
A.J. McGee: MG 1838

- - - - - - - - - - - - -

McGILL / MAGILL

TAXES (RHEA)
1808 (James Campbell's List):
William Magill 1 WP, 200a Sale Creek
1819 (Capt. McGill's Co.): John McGill 1 WP
William McGill 1 WP, 2 BP, 200a
1840 MEIGS CENSUS
Elizabeth McGill 020101 - 0110001 p. 247
MISCELLANEOUS (RHEA)
John McGill: Bondsman for John Riddle, 1824

- - - - - - - - - - - - -

McGINNIS / McGINNES

1840 MEIGS CENSUS
Simon McGinnis 00011 - 1001001 p. 238
1850 MEIGS CENSUS
R.H. McGinnes 24 (Merchant) p. 819-819
Simon McGinnis 31 (Farmer), Mary Ann 26, Caroline 9, Sarah Jane 8, William F. 5, Cordelia E. 3, John 1 p. 802-686
William C. McGinnis 27 (Farmer), Martha 54 (NC)(Insane) p. 795-640
MARRIAGES (MEIGS)
Simon McGinnis to Mary Ann Gourley, 8 Nov 1838 (same), Daniel Cate JP
MISCELLANEOUS (MEIGS)
Simon McGinnis: Constable 1847
" " 1st Corp., Cherokee Removal muster roll, 1837
William C. McGinnis: Private, Mexican War

- - - - - - - - - - - - -

McGUFFA

MARRIAGES (RHEA)
Ester McGuffa to Woodson Tucker q.v.

- - - - - - - - - - - - -

McGUIRE

1850 RHEA CENSUS
Elijah McGuire 27 (Farmer), Eliza 29, Sarah 5, Rebecca J. 3, Toliver L. 6/12, John M. SEXTON 2 p. 621-554

- - - - - - - - - - - - -

McHENRY

1840 MEIGS CENSUS
Robert McHenry 1020001 - 321001 p. 242
MISCELLANEOUS (MEIGS)
Robert McHenry: Lived in District 6 [Robert married Patsey Highen on 4 Apr 1824 in Roane County]

- - - - - - - - - - - - -

McINTURF / McINTUFF

1850 MEIGS CENSUS
Isaac McIntuff 27 (Farmer), Nancy Ann 22 p. 722-71
MARRIAGES (MEIGS)
Isaac McInturf to Nancy Ann Casey, 17 Dec 1846 (22 Dec), John Seaborn JP, D.L. Godsey Sur
MISCELLANEOUS (MEIGS)
Meradith McInturf: JP(?) 1845

- - - - - - - - - - - - -

McKAMEE / McCAME / McCAMEY

MARRIAGES (RHEA)
Mary A. McCame to John Gastine q.v.
MISCELLANEOUS (RHEA and MEIGS)
E. McKamee: JP 1850
John M. McCamey: Private, Mexican War

- - - - - - - - - - - - -

McKEDDY / McKIDDY / McKEEDY

TAXES (RHEA)
1823 (Capt. Howerton's Co.):
Thomas McKeedy 150a Whites Creek
1840 RHEA CENSUS
William McKeedy 00000100001 - 0000000001
MARRIAGES (RHEA)
William McKiddy to Margaret Danby, 2 Nov 1841, Thomas J. Gillespie Bm (A)
MISCELLANEOUS (RHEA)
Thomas McKiddy: Revolutionary War Pensioner, 1835 and 1841 lists

- - - - - - - - - - - - -

McKEE

1850 RHEA CENSUS
Arthur McKee 46: see Margaret Greenler
Elizabeth McKee 29: see Thomas Dodson

- - - - - - - - - - - - -

McKENZIE / McKINZIE / McKINSEY

TAXES (RHEA)
1823 (Capt. Smith's Co,):
Benjamin McKenzie 3 BP, 160a Agency Creek
(Capt. Jackson's Co.):
Benjamin McKenzie 2 BP, 160a Agency Creek
1830 RHEA CENSUS
Benjamin McKenzie 121020001 - 0002001 p. 369
1840 MEIGS CENSUS
Benjamin McKinsey 0002000001 - 000000001 p. 233
Benjamin F. McKinsey 231001 - 10001 p. 229
Reuben McKinsey 00011 - 1 p. 229
1850 MEIGS CENSUS
Benjamin McKinzie 82 (Va)(Farmer), Thomas E. 4, Margaret 1, Alfred 26 p. 751-322
Benjamin F. McKinsey 45 (Farmer), Martha 30, Jeremiah 18 (Farmer), Elias G. 14, Malinda 12, George M. 10, Menirva M. 10 p. 743-239
George W. McKinzie 32 (SC)(Farmer), Susan 24, Andrew J. 5, Alfred B. 4, Frances 1 p. 763-394
Harvy McKinzie 29 (Farmer), Julia 21, Mary F. 8, LaFayette 5, Susan 3 p. 753-323
Reuben McKenzie 40 (SC)(Farmer) p. 763-393
MARRIAGES (RHEA)
Benjamin McKenzie to Kaney Casey, 12 Sept 1830 (same), Thomas Cox JP, Henry Askin Bm (AR)
Julia Ann McKenzie to James H. Vernon q.v.
Nancy McKenzie to Eldrid Grubb q.v.
MARRIAGES (MEIGS)
Benjmin F. McKenzie to Marthy M. Jones, 9 Sept 1847, James Pierce MG
G. W. McKenzie to Susan Kedman, 5 Feb 1844 (same), M. Shaver MG [George, son of Benjamin McKenzie; born 7 Feb 1818 in Cherokee Nation, now Forsythe County, Georgia]
Harvy McKenzie to Letitia Brooks, 3 Feb 1841 (4 Feb), J.W. Oakes JP
Harvey McKenzie to July Ann Pierce, 17 Oct 1849 (18 Oct), M.C. Atchley JP or MG, J. Seaburn Sur
MISCELLANEOUS (MEIGS)
Alfred McKenzie: Private, Mexican War
Benjamin McKenzie: Hiwassee District; JP 1836
" " Common School Com., Dist 3, 1838
Benjamin F. McKenzie: JP 1838-49
" " " Private, Mexican War
" " " Common School Com., Dist 2, 1838
George McKenzie: Capt., Mexican War
James W. McKenzie: Mexican War (discharged on Surgeon's Certificate)
Jeremiah McKenzie: Private, Mexican War
Reuben McKenzie: Hiwassee District, Burkett Chapel area
" " Deputy Sheriff 1836
" " Commissioner to lay off Decatur, 1836

- - - - - - - - - - - - -

McKINLEY / McKINLY / McKINDLEY / McKENLY

TAXES (RHEA)
1823 (Capt. Smith's Co.): John McKindley 1 WP
1830 RHEA CENSUS
John McKinly 0110001 - 110001 p. 375

1840 MEIGS CENSUS
Ann McKenly 0 - 0000000001 p. 238
John McKenly 1211001 - 001101 p. 238
1850 RHEA CENSUS
Wm L. McKinley 25 (School Teacher): see Elias Hickman
1850 MEIGS CENSUS
Hugh McKinly 33: see Andrew Hunter
John McKinly 55 (Va)(Farmer), Menerva 30, Louisa 25, Thomas 18 (Farmer), Francis M. 14, Robert [Bean] 9 p. 771-458
MARRIAGES (MEIGS)
Angeline McKinley to Andrew Hunter q.v.
John McKinley to Manerva Bean, 15 Dec 1849 (16 Dec), T. Hunter JP [John's first wife was Susanna, dau of Thomas and Susanna Locke Henry; she died about 1845; six children: Hugh H., William L., Louisa, Angeline, Thomas A., and Francis M.]

\- - - - - - - - - - - - -

McKINNA

MISCELLANEOUS (RHEA)
E. M. McKinna: JP 1848-1850

\- - - - - - - - - - - - -

McKINNEY / McKINEY

1840 RHEA CENSUS
Elihu McKiney 000001 - 300011
1850 RHEA CENSUS
Elihu McKinney 40 (NC)(Hammerman), Kissiah 47 (NC), Nancy 14 (NC), Eliza 12, Malissa 10, William H. 9, Mary M. 7, Webster 5, Susannah DEREBURY 46 (NC), Charity DEREBURY 44 (NC), William HARVEY 18 (Farmer) p. 622-564

\- - - - - - - - - - - - -

McKISSICK

MARRIGES (RHEA)
Archibald McKissick to Oma Gothart, 27 Dec 1834, Peter Pharis Bm (A)

\- - - - - - - - - - - - -

McKNIGHT

MISCELLANEOUS (MEIGS)
B. F. McKnight: JP 1844

\- - - - - - - - - - - - -

McLAUGHLAN

MARRIAGES (RHEA)
Margaret McLaughlan to William Lewis q.v.

\- - - - - - - - - - - - -

McLEARTY

MARRIAGES (RHEA)
Mary A. McLearty to William Ferrill q.v.

\- - - - - - - - - - - - -

McLINN

1850 MEIGS CENSUS
William C. McLinn 31 (Merchant), Nancy Ann 31, Josephine E. 10, Mary E. 8, William A. 5, Granville 3, Infant (m) 0 p. 792-618

\- - - - - - - - - - - - -

McMARTY

TAXES (RHEA)
1819 (Capt. John Ramsey's Co.): Thomas McMarty 1 WP

\- - - - - - - - - - - - -

McMAYO

MISCELLANEOUS (RHEA)
Thompson George McMayo: Furnished timber for new jail, 1826

\- - - - - - - - - - - - -

McMEANS

MISCELLANEOUS (RHEA)
Isaac S. McMeans: Early merchant in Town of Washington

\- - - - - - - - - - - - -

McMEANY

MISCELLANEOUS (RHEA)
J.R. McMeany: Early resident of Town of Washington

\- - - - - - - - - - - - -

McMILLIAN / McMILLEN / McMILLON

TAXES (RHEA)
1829 (Capt. W.S. Bradley's Co.):
Robert W. McMillon 1 WP, 1 BP, 200a
1840 MEIGS CENSUS
John McMillon 001100001 - 0021001 p. 233
1850 MEIGS CENSUS
Dillard McMillian 27 (NC)(Farmer), Hetty 29, Catharine 9, Polly 7, Harrison 5, Louisa 3, Allison W. 2, Henderson 1 p. 760-375
MARRIAGES (RHEA)
James McMillan to Anne Johnson, 21 Mar 1811 (same), Abraham Howard JP (A)
Robert W. McMillen to Rachel Caldwell, 11 Feb 1819 (same), John Fine JP, John Rice Bm (AR)
MARRIAGES (MEIGS)
Dillard L. McMillon to Netty Ann Norman, 4 Nov 1841 (same), D.L. Godsey MG, William Inman Sur
MISCELLANEOUS (RHEA)
D.C. McMillin: Bondsman for Alfred Caldwell, 1842
James McMillan: Early resident of Town of Washington
Joseph McMillan: Bondsman for Jacob Plowman, 1822
" " Bondsman for Joseph Johnson, 1822

\- - - - - - - - - - - - -

McMULLEN

1850 MEIGS CENSUS
John McMullen 65 (Va)(Farmer), Martha 23, John Henry 3, James F. 1 p. 754-334
MARRIAGES (MEIGS)
Lavina McMullen to R.J.D.W. Allen q.v.
Martha McMullen to Leander Melton q.v.
William R. McMullen to Barbara Collins, 22 Feb 1842 (same), John Taff JP

- - - - - - - - - - - - -

McNABB

MISCELLANEOUS (RHEA)
Thomas McNabb: Bondsman for Elijah Rowden, 1820

- - - - - - - - - - - - -

McNUTT / McNATT

1830 RHEA CENSUS
Thomas McNutt 120101 - 001101 p. 394
1840 MEIGS CENSUS
James McNutt 00001 - 0001 p. 227
William McNatt 1000001 - 1120010001 p. 227
1850 RHEA CENSUS
John A. McNutt 37 (School Teacher), Sarah 29 (Va), Jane A. 7, Benjamin 6, Susan C. 4, Jeremiah 2 p. 607-485 [John A. McNutt married Sarah Stone on 28 Oct 1841 in McMinn County]
MARRIAGES (RHEA)
Fanny McNutt to G.W. Black q.v.
Jane McNutt to Robert Boulton q.v.
MARRIAGES (MEIGS)
James McNutt to Eliz Sutherland, 8 Oct 1839, John Bowers MG, James P. Sutherland Bm
Mary McNutt to Thomas Rhea q.v.
MISCELLANEOUS (MEIGS)
William McNutt: Ocee District
" " Common School Com., District 1, 1838

- - - - - - - - - - - - -

McPHERSON / McFERSON

TAXES (RHEA)
1819 (Capt. John Ramsey's Co.): Barton McPherson 141a
1823 (Capt. Piper's Co.): Barton McPherson 1 WP, 2 BP, 1 Stud Horse (tax, $3.00)
1830 RHEA CENSUS
Daniel McPherson 20001 - 1001000001 p. 355
1840 MEIGS CENSUS
Charles McPherson 00001 - 0001 p. 241
Hezekiah McPherson 200001 - 00001 p. 241
1850 RHEA CENSUS
Hezekiah McPherson 40 (Farmer), Malinda 35, Hardin 12 (Mo), James M. 10, Parthena 7, Barton 5, Mahala 4, William 2, Elizabeth 2/12 p. 557-146
Susan J. McPherson 15: see William A. Green
MARRIAGES (RHEA)
Alexander McPherson to Serena A. Johnson, 21 Apr 1825 (same), John Henninger MG, Hugh Crozier Bm (AR)
Elijah McPherson to Sarah Small, 9 Oct 1826 (same), Daniel Briggs MG, James Carroll Bm (AR)
Hezekiah McPherson to Malinda Rector, 11 Nov 1835 (14 Nov), William Green MG, Harden Deatherage Bm (AR)
L. C. McFerson to W. A. Green q.v.
MISCELLANEOUS (MEIGS)
D. McPherson: Hiwassee District, Moore's Chapel area

- - - - - - - - - - - - -

McREYNOLDS / McRENNELS

1840 MEIGS CENSUS
Coleman C. McReynolds 01001 - 10001 p. 244
MARRIAGES (RHEA)
Sarah McRennels to Nathaniel Watson q.v.
MISCELLANEOUS (RHEA and MEIGS)
Coleman C. McReynolds: Bm for Joseph Calloway, 1834
" " " Cherokee Removal muster roll
" " " Commissioner to lay off County into Civil Districts, 1836
" " " Common School Commissioner, District 6, 1838

- - - - - - - - - - - - -

McROBERTS

TAXES (RHEA)
1823 (Capt. Piper's Co.): John McRoberts 1 WP
MARRIAGES (MEIGS)
Nancy McRoberts to Jacob Cook q.v.
MISCELLANEOUS (RHEA)
David McRoberts: Revolutionary War Pensioner, 1835 list

- - - - - - - - - - - - -

McSPADIN

MISCELLANEOUS (MEIGS)
Joseph McSpadin: MG 1846

- - - - - - - - - - - - -

McVAY

MARRIAGES (MEIGS)
Henry McVay to Lively Taylor, 11 Apr 1846 (same), Daniel Cate JP, John Young Sur

- - - - - - - - - - - - -

McVINTON

MARRIAGES (MEIGS)
Rodey McVinton to William Ray [Rhea] q.v.

- - - - - - - - - - - - -

MABRY [MABERRY?]

1850 MEIGS CENSUS
William Mabry 80 (NC)(Farmer), Nancy 28 (NC) p. 782-542

William Mabry 30 (NC)(Farmer), Elender C. 30, James L. 6, Thomas J. 4, George C. 2, Mary E. 1 p. 782-543 [William Maberry married Ellender Cofer on 3 Feb 1848 "at the house of Geo. Cofer" in Roane Co.]

- - - - - - - - - - - - -

MADDOX

TAXES (RHEA)

1823 (Capt. Braselton's Co.): Morrow Maddox 1 WP

MARRIAGES (RHEA)

Marrow Maddox to Eliza Loverett, 9 Mar 1819 (same), John Fine JP (AR)

- - - - - - - - - - - - -

MAGERAS

MARRIAGES (RHEA)

Elizabeth Mageras to John Thomas q.v.

- - - - - - - - - - - - -

MAHAFFY

1840 RHEA CENSUS

Susan Mahaffy 0001 - 0110101

1850 RHEA CENSUS

Susan Mahaffy 57, Hiram 28 (Farmer), Jane 31, Thomas N. 2, Susan E. 10/12 p. 555-133

MARRIAGES (RHEA)

Elizabeth Mahaffy to Bartley Atkins q.v.

H. Mahaffy to Jane Hale, 25 Aug 1846 (3 Sept), J.W. Swicher MG (R)

Hiram Mahaffy to Susannah Thompson, 12 Oct 1809, Richard Philpot Bm (A)

Margaret Mahaffy to Russell Walker q.v.

MISCELLANEOUS (RHEA)

Hiram Mahaffy: Bondsman for Levi H. Knight, 1826

- - - - - - - - - - - - -

MAHAN / MAHIN / MAHON

TAXES (RHEA)

1819 (Capt. McGill's Co.): Isaac Mahan 1 WP, 30a
John Mahan 1 WP
1823 (Capt. Jackson's Co.): Alexander Mahan 1 WP
David Mahan 1 WP
Isaac Mahan 1 WP
(Capt. Howard's Co.): John Mahan 1 WP

1830 RHEA CENSUS

Alex Mahan 11001 - 21001 p. 370
Brazeal Mahan 0100001 - 200001 p. 370
David Mahan 1010001 - 121001 p. 370
Isaac Mahan 20021 - 12100101 p. 370
John Mahan 011101 - 110001 p. 381

1850 MEIGS CENSUS

Harrison Mahin or Malone 29 (Farmer), Louisa 25, Betsy Jane 5, Emily D. 3, Nancy Ann 1 p. 770-455

MARRIAGES (RHEA)

Alexander Mahan to Mary Ann Blackwood, 30 Nov 1821 (2 Dec), Thomas Cox JP, John Mahan Bm (AR) [1850 Hamilton Census: Alexander Mahan 51, Mary 50, Elizabeth 21, Orina 20, Elkenah 19, Nathaniel 18, Tabitha 14, Houston 13, Athalinda 11]

Elizabeth Mahan to Hanson Philpot q.v.

Gideon B. Mahan to Sarah Bolen, 21 July1838 (22 July), Henry Griffitt JP (AR)

Isaac Mahan to Peggy Carey, 4 Mar 1812 (same), Matthew Donald Bm (A)

Isaac Mahan to Charlotte Owens, 26 May 1823 (same), Thomas Cox JP, Benjamin Bonds Bm (AR) [NOTE: Allen lists the groom as Isaac Lewis]

James A. Mahan to Susan Rice, 27 Oct 1835, Wm Rice Bm

Polly Ann Mahan to Thomas D. McKeown q.v.

MARRIAGES (MEIGS)

Elizabeth Mahon to Philip Pierce q.v.

MISCELLANEOUS (RHEA and MEIGS)

Isaac Mahon: Hiwassee District, Burkett's Chapel area
John Mahan: Bondsman for Alexander Mahan, 1821
" " Bondsman for Joseph Hall, 1825
Samuel Mahan: Bondsman for William Blythe, 1809

- - - - - - - - - - - - -

MAJORS / MAGORS

TAXES (RHEA)

1819 (Capt. Wm McCray's Co.): Absolom Majors 1 WP, 1 Stud Horse (tax, $1.00)
James Majors 1 WP
Peter Majors 1 WP, 117a
1823 (Capt. Howerton's Co.): Abner Majors 1 WP
Peter Majors 123a Camp Ck
William Majors 1 WP

1830 RHEA CENSUS

Abnor Majors 001000001001 - 001001001 p. 391
Jesse(?) Majors 001 - 00001 p. 391
Peter Majors 00200001 - 01211001 p. 390
Thomas Magors 11011 - 20001 p. 391

1840 RHEA CENSUS

Abner Majors 000010001 - 000100001
Larkin Majors 130001 - 200001
Peter Majors 010120001 - 0001301
Thomas Majors 111001 - 111001

1850 RHEA CENSUS

Elias Majors 19 (Farmer), Martha 20, William T. 4/12 p. 542-59

James Majors 32 (Farmer), Jane 34 p. 550-115

Larkin Majors 47 (Farmer), Elizabeth 50, John 17 (Farmer), Francis 15, Margaret 13, Mary 10, James 8, George 4 p. 542-60

Mariah Majors 35: see Abraham G. Wright

Pleasant Majors 40 (Farmer), Rachael 23 p. 550-113

William Majors 51 (Farmer), Mary 52, James W. 21 (Ga) (Farmer), William J. 18 (Farmer), Augustus A. 14, Martha M. 12 p. 534-12

1850 MEIGS COUNTY

James Majors 23 (Farmer): see Thomas S. Farmer

MARRIAGES (RHEA)

Artimes Majors to Larkin F. Thompson q.v.

Betsy Majors to Elijah Runnels q.v.

Catherine Majors to Richard Haynes q.v.

Dardant Majors to Andrew Owens q.v.

David Majors to Jane Long, 29 Aug 1848 (same), Jesse P. Thompson JP (R) [1850 Roane Census: David Majors 22, Martha J. 30, Elizabeth 2, Larkin 3/12]

Elias Majors to Martha L. Rogers, 2 Aug 1848 (same), Asa Newport MG (R)

Eliza I. Majors to John C. Garner q.v.
Emaline Majors to John Orr q.v.
James Majors to Jane Upton, 22 Dec 1819, Jas Nail Bm (A)
James Majors to Jane Thompson, 8 Apr 1847 (no return) (R)
Jesse Majors to Rachel Thompson, 27 Feb 1830 (18 Mar), James Swan JP, Moses W. Thompton Bm (AR)
John Majors to Sally Butler, 10 Feb 1817, "I married John and Sallie" J. Fine JP, Hampton Butler Bm (AR)
Penelopy Majors to Robert T. Howard q.v.
Sally Majors to Hampton Butler q.v.
Sidney Majors to James Moore q.v.
Thomas Majors to Matilda Runnels, 8 Mar 1826 (9 Mar), Arthur Fulton JP, James Holloway Bm (AR)

MISCELLANEOUS (RHEA and MEIGS)

Cornelius Majors: Bondsman for John Ferguson, 1823
" " Bondsman for Wylie Moyers, 1832
Jesse Majors: Bondsman for William Laycock, 1834
John Majors: Hiwassee District
Peter Majors: Bondsman for James Moore, 1824

- - - - - - - - - - - - -

MAKEN

1840 MEIGS CENSUS

Jane Maken 0001 - 012111 p. 230

- - - - - - - - - - - - -

MALCOTE / MALICOAT

1840 RHEA CENSUS

Simeon Malcote 0001 - 0001

MARRIAGES (RHEA)

Simon Malcote to Polly Campbell, 2 Dec 1839 (no return) (R) [1850 Campbell Census: Simeon Malicoat 33, Sarah 20, Phillip 21]

- - - - - - - - - - - - -

MALLAN

MARRIAGES (RHEA)

Polly Mallan to David Hiden q.v.

- - - - - - - - - - - - -

MALONE / MALONEY

TAXES (RHEA)

1819 (Capt. W.S. Bradley's Dist.): Edward Maloney 1 WP
1823 (Capt. Brown's Co.): Edward Maloney 1 Town Lot

1830 RHEA CENSUS

David Malone 00101001 - 00121001 p. 389

1840 RHEA CENSUS

David Maloney 00010001 - 00003001

1850 RHEA CENSUS

David Maloney 71 (NC)(Farmer), Jane C. 71 (NC), Mary A. 38, Sarah 36, David 30 (Farmer) p. 588-348 [David married Ginney Christianbury on 26 Jan 1805 in Roane County]

1850 MEIGS CENSUS

Billy Malone 66 (Farmer), Nancy 56, Mahersa (f) 28, Julian 26, F.M.C. 24 (Farmer) p. 758-360
Jane Malone 49, Margaret A. 22 (Ediot), Anna 21, Easter E. 19 p. 745-255
Harrison Mahin or Malone— see under Mahan

MARRIAGES (RHEA)

Aron Maloney to Barbara Casey, 20 Oct 1831 (same), Matthew Hubbert JP, Elias Ferguson Bm (AR)
Elenor Maloney to George W. Snodgrass q.v.
Margaret Maloney to William W. Rose q.v.
Polly Maloney to John Blythe q.v.

MARRIAGES (MEIGS)

Wallace Malone to Mrs. Louisa Moore, 2 Nov 1843 (same), John T. Blevins JP, William Maynor Sur

MISCELLANEOUS (RHEA)

David Malony: Purchased Lot 81, Town of Washington
Edward Maloney: Bondsman for John Blythe, 1809

- - - - - - - - - - - - -

MANER / MANNER / MANES / MAYNOR

(see also MASONER)

TAXES (RHEA)

1819 (Capt McGill's Co.): George Manes 1 WP
1823 (Capt. Howard's Co.): George Maynes 1 WP, 200a

MARRIAGES (RHEA)

Henry Maner to Jane Hogg, 11 June 1827, Samuel Cunningham Bm (A)
Larkin Manes to Nelly Sample, 18 Dec 1833, Pleasant Manes Bm (A)
Pleasant Manner or Maner to Polly Gibbs, 22 Feb 1832 (23 Feb), William Smith JP, John Parker Bm (AR)

MARRIAGES (RHEA)

Stephen Maner to Rebecca Faress [Pharris], 21 May 1840 (same), John Taff JP, Uriah Maner Bm
William Maynor to Mary Moore, 30 Dec 1841 (same), Drury Godsey MG, Gannon Bradshaw Sur

MISCELLANEOUS (RHEA and MEIGS)

Pleasant Manes: Bondsman for Larkin Manes, 1833
Uriah Maner: Bondsman for Stephen Maner, 1840
William Maynor: JP{?) 1843

- - - - - - - - - - - - -

MANIFEE

TAXES (RHEA)

1808 (Jonathan Fine's List): John Manifee 640a

- - - - - - - - - - - - -

MAINARD / MANERD / MAYNERD

1850 MEIGS CENSUS

William Maynerd 35 (Farmer), Mary C. 26, James F. 11, Martha E. 8, Stephen M. 6, Talitha R. 3, Mary E. 1 p. 758-362

MARRIAGES (RHEA)

Edy Maynerd to Curtis Richards q.v.
Rachel Mainard to Edmond Tredway q.v.

MARRIAGES (MEIGS)

Susan Manerd to Harvey Roark q.v.

MISCELLANEOUS (RHEA and MEIGS)

George Maynard: Hiwassee District, Moore's Chapel area
James Mainard: Bondsman for Edmund Tredway, 1822

- - - - - - - - - - - - -

MANIS / MANICE

1830 RHEA CENSUS
George Manis 0133101 - 1210101 [2 not clear]
MARRIAGES (RHEA)
Jacob Manice to Polly Lawson, 22 July 1809 (no return), R. Rawlings Bm (AR)
Malin Manis or Mulin Morris [Allen's spelling] to Nancy Lawson, 2 Feb 1839 (same), Richard Waterhouse JP, James Sebral Bm (AR)
MARRIAGES (MEIGS)
Joseph Manis to Catharine Lason [Lawson?], 5 Feb 1840, Newton Locke Sur

\- - - - - - - - - - - - -

MANLEY

TAXES (RHEA)
1823 (Capt. Brown's Co.): Fleming Manley 1 WP
Richard Manley 2 BP, 1 Stud Horse (tax, $4.00)
1830 RHEA CENSUS
Joshua Manley 00000001 - 000000001 p. 388
MARRIAGES (RHEA)
Nancy Manley to William Walker q.v.
Richard Manly or Manley to Elizabeth Ann Stuts, 8 Oct 1822 (same), Thomas Cozby or Cox JP, Bruten Peters Bm (AR)
Ruanna Manley to George Henry q.v.
MISCELLANEOUS (RHEA)
Fleming Manley: Bondsman for James Piper, 1821

\- - - - - - - - - - - - -

MANSON

MARRIAGES (MEIGS)
Mary J. Manson to Timothy H. McCarty q.v.

\- - - - - - - - - - - - -

MANTOOTH / MONTOOTH / MANTEITH

TAXES (RHEA)
1823 (Capt. Piper's Co.): Samuel Mantooth 1 WP
1830 RHEA CENSUS
Robert Manteith 011201 - 321001 p. 383
Samuel Mantooth 111001 - 10001 p. 358
1840 MEIGS CENSUS
Samuel Mantooth 1111101 - 1010001 p. 240
MARRIAGES (RHEA)
Samuel Mantooth to Lethy Farris, 1 Apr 1819 (same), John Fine JP (AR) [1850 Polk Census: Samuel Mantooth 51, Leth 49, Thomas 21, Hugh 17, Houston 14, Elizabeth 10, Sarah 6]
MARRIAGES (MEIGS)
Calvin Montooth to Vina Harvey, 7 Sept 1844, William Griffin JP or Sur [1850 Polk Census: Calvin Mantooth 28, Viney 28, Sarah E. 5, Hugh L. 2, Margaret 2/12]
MISCELLANEOUS (MEIGS)
Samuel Montooth: Hiwassee District, Moore's Chapel area

\- - - - - - - - - - - - -

MAPES

1830 RHEA CENSUS
J.W. Mapes 12001 - 111 p. 376
1840 MEIGS CENSUS
Priscilla Mapes 0121 - 001101 p. 245
1850 MEIGS CENSUS
Joseph Mapes 23, Sarah Jane 20, Elizabeth C. 1 p. 782-548
MARRIAGES (RHEA)
Jeremiah Mapes to Jane Gear, no dates, probably 1848 (R)
Priscilla Mapes to Jesse Combs q.v.
MARRIAGES (MEIGS)
Joseph Mapes to Minerva Price, 29 July 1846 (same), E. Ward MG
Mary Mapes to Thomas J. Price q.v.
Pricey Mapes to James T. Price q.v.
Sariah Mapes to William Watson q.v.
MISCELLANEOUS (RHEA)
Joseph C. Mapes: Bondsman for W.W. Price, 1845

\- - - - - - - - - - - - -

MAPLES

1850 MEIGS CENSUS
Elizabeth Maples 29, Sarah F. 1 p. 802-691
John Maples 18: see Absolem Foshee
MARRIAGES (MEIGS)
W.S. Maples to Elizabeth Elison, 6 Sept 1849 (same), J.L. Aikman JP

\- - - - - - - - - - - - -

MARIOTT / MARIAT / MARRIOTT / MERRITT

TAXES (RHEA)
1808 (James Campbell's List):
John Merritt 1 WP, 1 BP, 300a Tenn Ri
1819 (Capt. W.S. Bradley's Dist.): John Merriott heirs 200a
Mary Merriott 2 BP
1823 (Capt. Brown's Co.): John T. Merriot 1 WP
1850 RHEA CENSUS
William N. Merriott 43 (Farmer), Nancy A. 26, Matilda 17, William N. 7, John A. 5, James G. 2, Mary J. 8/12 p. 603-463
1850 MEIGS CENSUS
Archibald Mariat 22 (Farmer), Sarah 20 p. 813-772 [Archibald married Sarah Lawson on 15 Aug 1850 in McMinn County]
MARRIAGES (RHEA)
Elizabeth Merriott to William Dunn q.v.
James Merriott to Susan Guerin, 21 Dec 1843, William N. Meriott Bm (A)
John Meriott to Jane Guin or Gerin, 22 Jan 1845 (23 Jan), S.R. Hackett JP, James Dun Bm (AR)
John Thompson Merriott to Cinthia Taylor, 11 Nov 1819 (same), William Randolph MG (AR) [John, son of John and Mary Thompson Merriott; Cinthia, dau of Robert and Catherine Sevier Taylor]
Mary Ann Merriott to William W. Pile q.v.
Polly Merriott to Allen Holland q.v.
William N. Meriott to Nancy Ann Edmunds, 3 Feb 1845 (same), S.R. Hackett JP, James Meriott Bm (A)

MISCELLANEOUS (RHEA and MEIGS)
Archibald Meriot: Private, Mexican War
James Meriott: Bondsman for Wm N. Meriott, 1845
John Marriot/Merriot: Hiwassee District, Concord area
Wm N. Mariott: Bondsman for James Meritt, 1843
" " " Private, Mexican War

- - - - - - - - - - - - -

MARLAN

MISCELLANEOUS (RHEA)
Jonathan Marlan: Bondsman for Elijah Self, 1812
" " Bondsman for Jacob Weir, 1813

- - - - - - - - - - - - -

MARLER / MARLOW

1840 RHEA CENSUS
Nathaniel Marlow 000001 - 00001
1850 RHEA CENSUS
Nichademus Marlow 26 (Farmer), Elizabeth J. 18, Francis M. 1, Mary C. MONTGOMERY 11 p. 636-554
MARRIAGES (RHEA)
N. Marler to Elizabeth J. Montgomery, 18 Sept 1848 (19 Sept), E. Ward MG (R)
Nathaniel Marlow to Martha Yates, 5 July 1842, William D. Averett Bm (A)
[1850 White Census: Nathaniel Marlow 44, Martha 37, Asa M. 11, Thomas 9, George W. 7, Henry N. 6, Martha 4, Larkin Y. 3, Nathaniel 4/12]
Rubin or Reuben Marlow to Susan Ward, 13 Dec 1824, Thomas Price JP, Benjamin Ward Bm (AR)
Thomas Malony or Marlow to Betsy Ward, 3 Nov 1824, "I have executed the within" Thomas Price JP, Andrew Walker Bm (AR)
MISCELLANEOUS (MEIGS)
George Marlow: Hiwassee District, Sewee Creek area

- - - - - - - - - - - - -

MARR / MARRS

TAXES (RHEA)
1819 (Capt. Wm McCray's Co.): Benjamin Marrs 1 WP
MARRIAGES (RHEA)
Aron Marr to Betsy Reece or Reese, 1 Apr 1824 (same), Fred K. Fulkerson JP, Jesse Read Bm (AR)
Eli Marrs to Betsy Delozier, 4 Nov 1813 (same), Jeremiah Hammons Bm (A)
Joseph Marr to Vinney Rhea, 23 Aug 1820 (24 Aug), Arthur Fulton JP (AR)
Jane Marr or Wan to Thomas C. Thomas q.v.
Martha Marrs to Joseph Foard q.v.
Nathan Marr to Betsy M. Carter or McCarter, 7 or 3 Feb 1820 (same), J. Fine JP (AR)
Polly Mars(?) to Robert White q.v.

- - - - - - - - - - - - -

MARSH / MARCH

1830 RHEA CENSUS
Alfred March 40001 - 000101 p. 356
1840 RHEA CENSUS
Alfred Marsh 0131001 - 2100101
1850 RHEA CENSUS
Alfred Marsh 51 (NC)(Farmer), Celia 51 (NC), Onslow G. 24 (Farmer), Franklin 22 (School Teacher), Thomas 20 (Farmer), Aderian 18 (Farmer), Susannah 16, Jane 14, Emeline 12 p. 585-331
John L. Marsh 25 (Farmer), Orinda 22, Gravenor S. 4, Edward W.M. 2, Alfred F. 2/12, Bromley COOK 18 (Farmer) p. 550-116
MARRIAGES (RHEA)
John L. Marsh to Orinda Cook, 23 Dec 1844 (same), William H. Bell MGCPC (R)
MISCELLANEOUS (RHEA)
Alfred Marsh: Trustee, Mars Hill Academy, 1850
O. B. Marsh: Bondsman for J.N. Cook, 1845

- - - - - - - - - - - - -

MARSHALL / MARSHEL

1840 MEIGS CENSUS
Ruth Marshel 021 - 001001 p. 242
1850 MEIGS CENSUS
Ezekiel Marshall 25 (Farmer), Betsy Ann 24, Catharine 6, John 4, William 1 p. 788-590
John Marshall 54, Sarah 54, John L. 23, Mary Ann 16, Milly Jane 14: see Calvin R. Toffe
Ruth Marshall 54, David M. 22 (Farmer), Obid F. 18, William 16 p. 787-586
William Marshall 22 (Farmer), Sarah 33, John W. 3, Benjamin F. 1 p. 773-478
MARRIAGES (RHEA)
John Marshall to Sally Guffy, 6 July 1822 (7 July), John Farmer MG, Walter Edwards Bm (AR)
MARRIAGES (MEIGS)
Ezekiel Marshall to Elizabeth Ann Owens, 6 Apr 1844, Luke Peak Sur
William Marshall to Polly Lewis, 20 Oct 1846 (same), D.L. Godsey MG
MISCELLANEOUS (RHEA and MEIGS)
John Marshel: Bondsman for John Walker, 1822
Thomas Marshall: Hiwassee District, Sewee Creek area
William Marshall: Hiwassee District, Sewee Creek area

- - - - - - - - - - - - -

MARSHBURN

1830 RHEA CENSUS
Levi Marshburn 000001 - 20010001 p. 388

- - - - - - - - - - - - -

MARSLIN

MISCELLANEOUS (MEIGS)
John B. Marslin: Hiwassee District, Sewee Creek area

- - - - - - - - - - - - -

MARTIN

TAXES (RHEA)
1808 (James Campbell's List): John Martin (for Andrew & James Russell) 400a
1819 (Capt. McGill's Co.): Joseph Martin 1 WP, 100a
Patrick Martin 1 WP, 110a
1823 (Capt. Smith's Co.):
Jesse Martin 1 WP, 3 BP, 219a Tenn R
John Martin 1 WP
(Capt. Howard's Co.): Joseph Martin 1 WP, 60a
Patrick Martin 1 WP, 110a

1830 RHEA CENSUS
Jesse Martin 3112001 - 010001 p. 372
Jno Martin 0200011 - 1101 p. 372
Jno Martin 1111000001 - 0000000001 p. 371
Joseph Martin 011001 - 2111 p. 380
Johnston Martin 100001 - 011001001 p. 355
Patrick Martin 100001 - 202201 p. 380
Robert Martin 000001 - 11001 p. 371
Robert Martin 0100001 - 0010111 p. 368
Samuel Martin 201 - 0001 p. 371
William Martin 0000001 - 00010001 p. 371
------ Martin 211001 - 210001 p. 364

1840 RHEA CENSUS
Catherine Martin 0101 - 0110001
James Martin 110001 - 11001
Samuel Martin 101001 - 20001
Samuel Martin 212101 - 011001
Sarah Martin 0 - 0000100001

1840 MEIGS CENSUS
Alfred Martin 10001 - 10001 p. 243
Jane Martin 11222 - 01001001 p. 233
John Martin 0001000001 - 0000001 p. 229
Surret Martin 00000001 - 00000001 p. 230
Wesly Martin 10001 - 01001001 p. 243

1850 RHEA CENSUS
Catharine Martin 54, William A. 25 (Farmer), Mary E. 23, Martha E. 20, Isaac A. 17 (Farmer) p. 630-613
Mary Martin Unk: see Mary Eaves
Nancy Martin 45, Nancy A. 17, Susan 15, Gilbert 13, John 12, Thomas 11, Eliza J. 7, Elbert 4 p. 570-225
William Martin 32 (Ga)(Farmer), Mary A. 27, Melissa 8, George 6, Barbery C. 3, Gillum 3/12 p. 632-630

1850 MEIGS CENSUS
Bob Martin 59 (Va)(black)(Doctor) p. 726-104
Eliza Martin 34, Samuel F. 6, Hugh L. 3, James S. 15, Thomas B. 8 p. 732-148
Jane Martin 61 (Va), Josiah 22 (Farmer), Luke P. 20 (Farmer), John 18 (Farmer), James S. 15, James 24 p. 732-152
Jesse Martin 30 (Farmer), Martha Jane 25, Racheal 8, Maza P. 6, John H. 4, Samuel B. 2 p. 750-302
Wesley Martin 37 (NC)(Blacksmith), Rachael 35 (Va), John W. 14, Martha E. 11, Nancy Ann 8, William J. 5, Mary 2 p. 792-621
Willie O. Martin 33 (Va)(Farmer), Ellen 30, Jane 16 p. 732-147
Zachariah Martin 36 (Merchant), Margaret Ann 34, Mary Jane 17, James M. 11, Marcellus 9, Mary C. 5, Louisa Ann 4, Benjamin F. 2, Harrison W. 1, Ruth R. (blank, probably 0) p. 729-130

MARRIAGES (RHEA)
E.W. Martin to Rutha Hinds, 19 June 1841 (no return) (R)
Harriet Martin to Jesse Chattin q.v.
Henry Martin to Polly Prilliman or Prillamon, 18 Oct 1833, V.H. Giles JP/Bm (AR)
Jane Martin to John Moore q.v.
John Martin to Martha Slover, 3 Aug 1821 (5 Aug), Thomas Cox JP, Samuel McDaniel Bm (AR)
Joseph Martin to Anne Moore, 16 Nov 1819 (same), Benjamin Edgemon MG (AR)
M. E. Martin to S. Wyrick q.v.
Maryann Martin to Thomas Hudleston q.v.
Nancy Martin to Silas Sevely q.v.
Robert Martin to Nancy Massengale, 27 Aug 1822 (no return), George Weeks Bm (AR)
Robert Martin to Polly Day, 16 Nov 1826, Alexander Coulter Bm (A)
Samuel F. Martin to Lucy Eaves, 13 Oct 1827 (14 Oct), Thomas Cox JP, Isaac Roddye Bm (AR)
Sarah Martin to Allen Doubten q.v.
Sarah Martin to Pulaska Killough q.v.
William Martin to Mary Ann Presley, 17 July 1841 (no return), John Kelly Bm (AR)

MARRIAGES (MEIGS)
Henry Martin to Sarah E. Cox, 23 Nov 1840 (same), John Taff JP
Jesse Martin to Martha McDaniel, 9 June 1841 (same), John Taff JP
Owen Martin to Sarah Starns, 6 Jan 1844 (same), Jesse Martin JP
Sarah Martin to James Carvin q.v.
T.J. Martin to Sarah Fan, 11 May 1844 (same), D.L. Godsey MG
Willie O. Martin to Eleanor Doughty, 15 Nov 1843 (16 Nov), B.F. McKenzie JP
Willie O. Martin to Nancy Hutson, 30 Jan 1844 (same), Wm Johns JP

MISCELLANEOUS (RHEA)
Silbert Martin: Bondsman for Allen Doubten, 1830
Stephen Martin: JP 1828

MISCELLANEOUS (MEIGS)
James Martin: Private, Mexican War
Jesse Martin: Hiwassee District, Cottonport area
" " JP 1843-1844, 1847
" " Chairman of County Court, 1846
John Martin: Ocoee District
John W. Martin: Private, Mexican War
Samuel F. Martin: 4th Sgt., Mexican War (died in service)
Sebert Martin: JP(?) 1844
T.J. Martin: JP(?) 1844
Thomas Martin: Private, Mexican War
W.O. Martin: JP(?) 1840

- - - - - - - - - - - - -

MASON / MASONER / MASENER
(see also MANER / MANNER)

TAXES (RHEA)
1823 (Capt. Smith's Co.): Isaac Masoner 1 WP, 1 Stud Horse (tax, $3.00)
Tavender Masoner 1 WP

1830 RHEA CENSUS
Jno Masoner 000001001 - 0100010001 p. 373
Isaac Mason 000001 - 1001 p. 371
1840 RHEA CENSUS
Martha Mason 0 - 20002001
1840 MEIGS CENSUS
Isaac Masoner 1100001 - 121001 p. 229
Tabner Masoner 010001 - 00101 p. 228
Russel Mason 100001 - 110101 p. 234
1850 RHEA CENSUS
Mary Mason 70 (NC), Ruth 34 (NC), Saloma 16 p. 589-358
Pleasant Masener 35 (Farmer), Mary 38, Ann E. 9, Martha J. 11, Sarah S. 3, Mary 1/12 p. 599-399
1850 MEIGS CENSUS
Dicy Mason 53, Louisa C. 14, Lucinda E. 17, John H. 12 p. 745-256
Isaac Masoner 53 (Farmer), Mahala 41, Sally Ann 18, John T. 16, James M. 13, Margaret M. 11, George W. 10, Mahala A. 7, Vilina T. 3 p. 743-242
MARRIAGES (RHEA)
Isaac Masener to Mahala Templeton, 14 Feb 1828 (same), Archibald F. Gerald [Fitzgerald] MG, Edward Templeton Bm (AR)
Tavenor Masoner to Peggy Gerral or Gerald [probably Fitzgerald], 13 Dec 1832 (14 Dec), Archibald F. Gerrold [Fitzgerld] MG
MARRIAGES (MEIGS)
Elizabeth A. Masoner to Calvin B. Atkinson q.v.
Ruth E. Masoner to James Long q.v.
MISCELLANEOUS (MEIGS)
Isaac Masoner: Hiwassee District, Burkett Chapel area
John Masoner: Hiwassee District, Shiloh-Goodfield area
Tavener Masoner: Hiwassee District, Burkett Chapel area

- - - - - - - - - - - - -

MASSENGILL / MASSINGELL

1830 RHEA CENSUS
James Massengill 122001 - 201001 p. 352
1850 MEIGS CENSUS
James Massingell 33 (Farmer), Elizabeth 31, Sarah 12, Ezekal 9, Penelope 8, James 6, Margaret 4, Tennessee 1 p. 778-517
MARRIAGES (RHEA)
Nancy Massengale to Robert Martin q.v.
MARRIAGES (MEIGS)
Madison Massengill to Elizabeth Knight, 29 Aug 1839 (30 Aug), Pryor Neil JP, James Knight Bm

- - - - - - - - - - - - -

MASSY / MASSEY / MASSEE

TAXES (RHEA)
1823 (Capt. McCall's Co.): John Massee 1 WP
1830 RHEA CENSUS
Abel Massey 221001 - 10001 p. 369
James Massey 00000001 - 321001 p. 360
Mark Massy 010101001 - 001100001
1840 RHEA CENSUS
Mark Massy 0010000001 - 000000001 p. 247
Mark Massy Jr. 103001 - 000101 p. 247
Oliver Massy 0001 - 10001 p. 242
1850 RHEA CENSUS
Elizabeth Massey 80 (NC) p. 790-602
James Massy 22 (Farmer), Mahala 21, Mary E. 3, Wesley A. 1 p. 809-737
Mark Massy 45 (NC)(Farmer), Jane 52 (Va), Emily 25, Hugh 21 (Farmer), John 14 p. 809-739
MARRIAGES (RHEA)
Eliza Mssey to Nathniel Watson q.v.
Oliver Massey to Elizabeth Goff, 16 Mar 1836, Martin Johnson Bm (A)
Ruthy Massey to Richard Nelson q.v.
MARRIAGES (MEIGS)
James Massey to Mahaley Forde, 18 Sept 1846 (same), Joseph Johnson JP
MISCELLANEOUS (RHEA)
John Massey: Bondsman for John M. Nelson, 1823
" " Bondsman for Richard Nelson, 1833
" " Bondsman for Nathaniel Watson, 1833
Mark Massey: Bondsman for John Duckworth, 1832
MISCELLANEOUS (MEIGS)
Able Massee: Circuit Court jury, 1836
Mark Massey: Cherokee Removal muster roll, 1836

- - - - - - - - - - - - -

MASTISON

MISCELLANEOUS (MEIGS)
Aaron W. Mastison: Mexican War

- - - - - - - - - - - - -

MATHENY / MATHENA

TAXES (RHEA)
1823 (Capt. Smith's Co.): Luke Mathena 1 WP
MARRIAGES (RHEA)
Eleanor Matheny to Samuel Jones q.v.

- - - - - - - - - - - - -

MATHERLY

1850 MEIGS CENSUS
John Matherly 31 (NC)(Farmer), Emaline 31 (NC), James W. 9, Henry F. 7, Nancy E. 5, William T. 2 p. 737-194

- - - - - - - - - - - - -

MATHEWS / MATTHEWS

TAXES (RHEA)
1823 (Capt. Jackson's Co.): Jesse Matthews 1 WP
1830 RHEA CENSUS
Berry G. Mathews 11001 - 11001 p. 366
Jesse Mathews 010001 - 2100001 p. 369
MARRIAGES (RHEA)
Jesse Matthews to Eleanor Sharp, 5 Feb 1820 (6 Feb), Wm Randolph MG, Simeon Geren Bm (AR)
Sally Matthews to James Covey q.v.
MARRIAGES (MEIGS)
Jefferson Matthews to Margaret D. Bean, 13 Jan 1844 (25 Jan), William Johns JP
G.W. Mathews to Mary E. Watkins, 23 July 1842

MISCELLANEOUS (MEIGS)
Jefferson Matthews: JP(?) 1842
Jesse Matthews: Cherokee Removal muster roll
" " Hiwassee Dist., Concord-Burkett Chapel area

- - - - - - - - - - - - -

MATHIS / MATHES / MATHER

1840 RHEA CENSUS
Benjamin G. Mathis 131011 - 0010001
James Mathis 00100001 - 211
James Mathis 020001 - 200001
Penelope Mathis 0 - 00010001
1840 MEIGS CENSUS
Horton Mathes 00001 - 10001 p. 226
Jesse Mathis 11000001 - 212001 p. 229
1850 RHEA CENSUS
Berryman G. Mather 46 (NC)(Farmer), Catharine 46 (NC), William 12, Margaret 10, Valentine HOUPT 85 (NC) p. 602-685
Catharine Mathis 39 (NC), Elizabeth A. BOYD 21, Joshua 18, Margaret D. MATHES 1 p. 600-412
Hiram Mathes 60 (NC)(Grindstone Cutter), Elizabeth 45 (NC), Suhaney 21 (Insane), Arthur L. 18 (Farmer), Rachael 16, Stephen 14, Ruth J. 12, Nancy A. 10, Avis A. (f) 7 p. 537-31
James Mathis 60 (Va)(Potter), Nancy 22, Pleasant N. 20 (Farmer), Lusetta 14, Louisiann 12 p. 595-374
James Mathis 25 (Farmer), Caroline L. 21, Wealthy A. 1 p. 588-350
1850 MEIGS CENSUS
Darcus Mathis (f) 42, Elender M. 25, Nancy Jane 16, Cullen (m) 14, Narcissa 12, Obediah 10 p. 726-108
James J. Mathes 40 (Va)(Farmer), Sarah R. 42, Rufus 18 (Farmer), Hardin 16, Angaline 14, Mary Ann 12, Amanda 8, Luke 5, Raphel (m) 3 p. 816-763
Thomas J. Mathes 26 (Merchant), Margaret D. 28, Penny Ann 21, Elender 18, Franklin 6, Jesse L. 4, Mary E. 4, Sarah E. 2 p. 745-258
MARRIAGES (RHEA)
James Mathis to Caroline Stults, 4 Mar 1848 (5 Mar), Jesse Rector JP (R)
Mary Jane Mathis to William H. Bradley q.v.
Sarah Mathis to Joseph Ford q.v.
MARRIAGES (MEIGS)
L.J. Mathes to Elias L. Weir q.v.
MISCELLANEOUS (RHEA and MEIGS)
Berryman G. Mather: Bm for Wm H. Brady/Bradley, 1840
James Mathis: Private, Mexican War

- - - - - - - - - - - - -

MATIAN

MARRIAGES (RHEA)
Diannah Matian to Jesse Fitzgerrald q.v.

- - - - - - - - - - - - -

MATLOCK / MEDLOCK

TAXES (RHEA)
1823 (Capt. Piper's Co.): Charles Medlock 300a
1830 RHEA CENSUS
William Matlock 110101 - 0111011 p. 356
1840 MEIGS CENSUS
Thomas Matlock 12210001 - 101001 p. 244
1850 RHEA CENSUS
John C. Matlock 62 (Day Laborer), Sarah 58 p. 545-82
MARRIAGES (RHEA)
Catharine Matlock to Joseph Hill q.v.
Lorinda Matlock to John B. Eldridge q.v.
MARRIAGES (MEIGS)
Jemima Matlock to Albert Browder q.v.
Stephen Matlock to Polly McClure, 12 July 1847, Thomas V. Atchley JP
MISCELLANEOUS (MEIGS)
Charles Matlock: Hiwassee District, Ten Mile Stand area [b. 1782, d. 1838 unmarried; brother of William, Henry, and John]
William Matlock: Hiwassee District, Ten Mile area; gristmill operator
" " On Circuit Court jury, 1836
" " Common School Com., District 7, 1838
" " Trustee, Decatur Academy, 1838-39 [b. 1795, d. 1844; son of John and Sarah McPherson Matlock of Grainger Co.; married Sarah, dau of Rev. Jesse and Ruth Dodson Dodson on 23 Dec 1817]

- - - - - - - - - - - - -

MAVITY / MAVERTY

1840 MEIGS CENSUS
Jesse Mavity 0110001 - 011111 p. 229
1850 MEIGS CENSUS
Jesse Maverty 59 (Va)(Farmer), Susannah 48 (Va), Andrew J. 16 p. 746-264
MARRIAGES (MEIGS)
Jane Mavity to Noah Perry q.v.
Mary Ann Mavity to Francis M. Sewell q.v.
Nancy Mavity to James Grice q.v.
Susannah Mavity to John Clemons q.v.
MISCELLANEOUS (MEIGS)
Jesse Mavity: JP(?) 1845

- - - - - - - - - - - - -

MAXFIELD

TAXES (RHEA)
1823 (Capt. Piper's Co.): Benjamin Maxfield 1 WP, 160a

- - - - - - - - - - - - -

MAYBERRY / MABERRY / MABARY / MARBURY / MARBERRY

1840 MEIGS CENSUS
John Maberry 021001 - 200001 p. 244
William Maberry 0001100001 - 000030001 p. 245
MARRIAGES (RHEA)
George Mayberry to Margaret Henry, 11 Apr 1816 (same), John Fine JP, James Berry Bm (AR)
Jane Marbury to James C. Clingan q.v.
Nancy Mayberry to Solomon Brown q.v.
Nancy Marberry to David Clingan q.v.
MARRIAGES (MEIGS)
Elizabeth Maberry to Samuel Snow q.v.
Martha Maberry to James Robinson q.v.

William Maberry to Elizabeth B. Gregory, 28 May 1842 (29 May), James M. Hague MG or JP
William Mabary to Drucilla Phillips, 15 Feb 1843, Thomas Atchley JP
MISCELLANEOUS (RHEA and MEIGS)
Benjamin Marberry: Bondsman for David Clingin, 1822
" " Bm for James C. Clingham, 1826
George Mayberry: Lot 55, Town of Washington
Thomas Maberry: JP(?) 1843
William Mayberry: JP(?) 1842

- - - - - - - - - - - - -

MAYFIELD

MARRIAGES (RHEA)
Stephen Mayfield to Sarah Whitehead, 15 Dec 1826 (same), James A. Darwin JP, George Ransom Bm (AR)
MARRIAGES (MEIGS)
Elizabeth Mayfield to Morgan Bracket q.v.

- - - - - - - - - - - - -

MAYO

1850 RHEA CENSUS
James Mayo 40 (Saddler), Margaret 35, Adeline 16, Mary 14, Eliza 12, George 8, Ellen 6, Catharine C. 2, Nancy J. HALE 16 p. 604-468
MARRIAGES (RHEA)
James Mayo to Margaret A. Caldwell, 4 Sept 1833 (same), B. Wallace MG (R)
MISCELLANEOUS (RHEA)
James Mayo: Bondsman for James Wilson, 1832

- - - - - - - - - - - - -

MAYS / MAY / MAYES
(see also HAYS / HAYES)

MARRIAGES (RHEA)
Nelly May to William Rodgers q.v.
MARRIAGES (MEIGS)
James Mays to Jane Lewis, 11 July 1842 (12 July), John T. Blevins JP
MISCELLANEOUS (RHEA and MEIGS)
Asa May: Bondsman for William Shelton, 1816
David Mayes: Cherokee Removal muster roll, 1836
James Mayes: Mexican War (discharged on Surgeon's Cer.)

- - - - - - - - - - - - -

MEADOWS

1830 RHEA CENSUS
David Meadows 22001 - 10001 p. 365
David Meadows 130001 - 100001 p. 367

- - - - - - - - - - - - -

MEDARIS

1850 MEIGS CENSUS
Gabriel Medaris 45 (Va)(Farmer), Rebecca 44 (NC), Racheal A. 20, Oliver 19 (Farmer), Alfred 18 (Farmer), William 13, Hiram or Herman 12, Harriet 10, Almira Jane 9, Levina 6, Martha 5, Mary 3, John J. 1, Racheal DAVIS 70 (Va) p. 803-698
MARRIAGES (MEIGS)
Nancy Caroline Meadaris to John Baker q.v.

- - - - - - - - - - - - -

MEDLEY

MARRIAGES (MEIGS)
Demaseus Medley to Elvina Cate, 19 Mar 1845 (20 Mar), Jesse Locke MG

- - - - - - - - - - - - -

MEE

TAXES (RHEA)
1823 (Capt. Piper's Co.): John Mee 1 WP
Joseph Mee 1 BP, 160a
1830 RHEA CENSUS
Joseph Mee 00212001 - 00011001 p. 360
1840 MEIGS CENSUS
Andrew Mee 00001 - 00001 p. 241
William Mee 112200001 - 0101001 p. 241
1850 MEIGS CENSUS
Anderson Mee 30 (Farmer), Mary 36, John 7, James K. 4, William R. 2 p. 804-704
MISCELLANEOUS (RHEA)
Joseph Mee: Surveyor's list of land S of Tennessee River

- - - - - - - - - - - - -

MEEKS

1850 RHEA CENSUS
William J. Meeks 74 (NC)(Slaymaker), Esther 54 (NC), Clerissa 14, Reuben 13 p. 536-19

- - - - - - - - - - - - -

MEIGS

MARRIAGES (RHEA)
Emily S. Meigs to John Walker Jr. q.v.
R.J. Meigs to Sarah K. Love, 1 Nov 1825 (same), Matthew Donald MG (AR)
[1850 Davidson Census: R.J. Meigs 49, Sarah K. 46, James L. 23, Return J. 20, John 15, Josiah 10, Fielding 6, Amanda J. LOVE 31]
MISCELLANEOUS (RHEA)
R.J. Meigs Jr.: Bondsman for John Walker Jr., 1824

- - - - - - - - - - - - -

MELTON / MILTON

1840 MEIGS CENSUS
James Milton 00121001 - 0011001 p. 232
John W. Milton 00001 - 10001 p. 235
1850 MEIGS CENSUS
Leander M. Melton 20, Martha 20, John 3, James 1 p. 754-336
Martin Milton 35 (Farmer), Minerva 26, Wiley 12, Robert 10, Sally 8, George 7, Nancy 5, Elizabeth 3 p. 749-292
Nancy Melton: see Nancy SHELTON
Robert Melton 27 (Va)(Blacksmith), Nancy Ann 9, William 7, James 5, John 3 p. 757-358

MARRIAGES (MEIGS)
Elizabeth O. Melton to Thomas Purdy q.v.
Emily J.L. Melton to Samuel Gorley q.v.
James F. Melton to Jane C. Allen, 21 Dec 1843 (same), Drury L. Godsey MG, John N. Melton Bm or Sur
Leander Melton to Martha McMullen, 15 Aug 1847 (same), D.L. Godsey MG
Nancy Melton to William Rockhold q.v.
Sarah Melton to John Vaughn q.v.

- - - - - - - - - - - - -

MERCHANT

1830 RHEA CENSUS
William S. Merchant 0002101 - 000101 p. 382
MISCELLANEOUS (MEIGS)
William S. Merchant: Hiwassee District, Pinhook Ferry area

- - - - - - - - - - - - -

MERRIMAN / MERIMAN

TAXES (RHEA)
1823 (Capt. Wilson's Co.): Jeremiah Meriman 1 WP
1830 RHEA CENSUS
William Merriman 0002000001 - 000000001 p. 386
MARRIAGES (RHEA)
William Merriman to Peggy Davis, 19 Sept 1827, Nathan Harwood Bm (A)

- - - - - - - - - - - - -

MERSON

1830 RHEA CENSUS
A. P. Merson 1001 - 01 p. 368

- - - - - - - - - - - - -

MICHAEL / MICHEL / MICLES

1840 MEIGS CENSUS
Joseph Michel 211101 - 111001 p. 244
1850 MEIGS CENSUS
William Micles 23 (Farmer), Racheal 25, Mary E. 3, Nancy 2 p. 728-123
MARRIAGES (MEIGS)
A.B. Michals to Nancy Singleton, 8 Jan 1846 (same), Jesse Locke MG [1850 McMinn Census: Abraham Micheals 28, Nancy 21, John H. 8/12]
William D. Michael to Rachel C. Lane, 2 Dec 1844, N.R. Brown and William Miller [no indication of MG, JP, or Bm]
MISCELLANEOUS (MEIGS)
A. B. Michael: JP(?) 1845

- - - - - - - - - - - - -

MILDHAM

MARRIAGES (RHEA)
Sally Mildham to Dempsey Sullivan q.v.

- - - - - - - - - - - - -

MILESHAM

MARRIAGES (RHEA)
Polly Milesham to Jonathan Williams q.v.

- - - - - - - - - - - - -

MILLED

TAXES (RHEA)
1819 (Capt. Bradley's Dist.): Adam Milled 1 WP, 1½a

- - - - - - - - - - - - -

MILLER

TAXES (RHEA)
1819 (Capt. J. Robinson's Co.): Francis Miller* 1 WP, 180a [*probably should be Miller Francis]
(Capt. John Ramsey's Co,): Hiram Miller 1 WP
John Miller 1 WP
1823 (Capt. Smith's Co.): Abraham Miller 1 WP
(Capt. Piper's Co.): Hiram Miller 1 WP
(Capt. Brown's Co.): Jacob Miller 32a
(Capt. Lewis' Co.): John Miller 1 WP
(Capt. Wilson's Co.): John Miller 1 WP
William Miller 1 WP, 1 BP, 1 Stud Horse (tax, $3.00), 160a
1830 RHEA CENSUS
Abraham Miller 01102 - 000011 p. 383
Abraham Miller 1200001 - 112001 p. 395
Eliza Miller 0001 - 0001001 p. 384
George L. Miller* 00001 - 0001 p. 355
Hyram Miller 132001 - 010101 p. 356
J. M. Miller 00001 - 0001 p. 358
J. P. Miller 20002 - 02001 p. 384
John Miller 020001 - 221001 p. 364
John Miller 0021101 - 1202001 p. 384
John Miller 2213001 - 1010001 p. 365
John L. Miller* 2010001 - 0121001 p. 355
Oliver Miller 00001 - 0001 p. 384
Robert Miller 01120001 - 1022001 p. 388
William Miller 11112001 - 1100001 p. 358
William L. Miller* 200001 - 10101 p. 355
1840 RHEA CENSUS
Henry H. Miller 10001001 - 21001
J. L. Miller* 00001 - 0001
John Miller 12110001 - 1121001
Peter W. Miller 10101 - 10001
Pleasant Miller 000001 - 21001
Robert Miller 000110001 - 0011001
Thomas Miller 00001 - 00001
1840 MEIGS CENSUS
George L. Miller* 110001 - 12001 p. 239
Rally Miller 00001 - 10001 p. 239
Samuel L. Miller* 20001 - 10001 p. 238
William Miller 001100001 - 00101001 p. 230
[* probably Lockmiller]
1850 RHEA CENSUS
Henry H. Miller 39 (Farmer), Martha A. 14, John T. 12, Elizabeth L. 10, Eliza 8, Joseph E. 5, Pocahontas 3, Jane 1, Narcissa BAILEY 54 p. 580-292
Peter W. Miller 35 (Farmer), Rebecca 33, Martha 12, William C. 10, Susan M. 9, John H. 7, Wright S. 6, James L. 4, Delila A. 3, Zachary T. 1 p. 577-271

Robin Miller 73 (NC)(Wheelwright), Margaret Unk (Pa), Arcady 21 p. 558-153
Thomas Miller --*, Emeline --*, Jane --*, Arcada (f) --*, Mose --*, Hannah --*, Peggy A. 3, Thomas 2, Amanda 4/12 p. 558-150 [* ages unknown]
William R. Miller 26 (Farmer), Mary 23, John L. 4, Thomas 2, Robbin 9/12 p. 558-152

1850 MEIGS CENSUS

Hiram Miller 70 (NC)(Farmer), Ally 60 (Ky), Nancy 22, Martha Jane 19, Pheraba 15, James 12 p. 747-279
Jeremiah Miller 28 (SC), Margaret 26, Isaac 6, Milly 3 p. 819-816
Mary Miller 66 (Va), Thomas 22, Minerva T. 24, Mark H. 16 p. 713-2
Plesant M. Miller 31 (Tanner), Margaret 30, Thomas 5, Sarah Ann 3, Lety E. 1, Micheal THORP 10 p. 778-512
Plesant M. Miller 45 (Farmer), Mahala 35, Nancy 17, Angalina 12, John B. 15 p. 753-330
Thomas Miller 24, Harriet M. 16, John N. 15 p. 713-3
W.S. Miller 28 (Farmer), Elizabeth 23, Levina 1 p. 727-115
Wesly Miller 24 (Farmer), Nancy Ann 24 ("married within year") p. 816-762

MARRIAGES (RHEA)

Anna Miller to John Bell q.v.
Darthula O. Miller to Alexander B. Bradford q.v.
Elvira Miller to James Holloway q.v.
Elvira Miller to Hughlett W. Smith q.v.
George L. Miller: see LOCKMILLER
Henry Miller to Jane Ferguson, 24 or 26 Oct 1832 (24 or 28 Oct), Matthew Hubbert JP, Eli Ferguson Bm (AR)
Hiram Miller to Alley McCallon, 23 Feb 1825, John Miller Bm (A)
James Miller to Pailee or Phereby Poe, 18 Dec 1817 (same), John Cozby JP (AR)
Jane N.L. Miller: see LOCKMILLER
John Miller to Nancy Harwood, 21 Oct 1819 (no return), Hiram Miller Bm (AR)
John Miller to Sarah Adkins, 5 July 1837 (6 July), A.D. Paul JP, Elijah Bell Bm (AR)
Judith Miller to Simeon Hinds q.v.
Lavina Miller to Nicholas C. Porter q.v.
Malinda Miller to Elijah Bell q.v.
Mariah Miller to Bryant Breeding q.v.
Mary Miller to Joseph Rice q.v.
Mary Miller to James H. Parker q.v.
Matilda Miller to Sheley Munday q.v.
Melica Miller to John Snelson q.v.
Oliver Miller to Rebecca Bell, 26 June 1828, Gideon B. Thompson Bm (A)
Patsy Miller to Samuel Cunningham q.v.
Peter W. Miller to Rebecca Compton, 23 Nov 1836 (24 Nov), H. Collins JP, Robert Mitchell Bm (AR)
Pleasant M. Miller to Mahalia Rector, 8 Aug 1829 (25 Aug), James Wilson JP, Wm S. Russell Bm (AR)
Polly Miller to Charles Brady q.v.
Samuel L. Miller: see LOCKMILLER
Sarah Miller to Nathaniel W. Wilson q.v.
Sarah P. Miller to B.F. Thompson q.v.
Viney Miller to Resin Rawlings q.v.
William Miller to Mary McAnally, 25 Sept 1845 (same), A.D. Paul JP (R)
William B. Miller to Mary Clack, 31 Dec 1836 (3 Jan 1837), Jacob Gear JP, Missouri Clack Bm (AR)

MARRIAGES (MEIGS)

Charlotte J. Miller to Thomas H. Kincannon q.v.
David Miller to Angeline Elis, 23 Dec 1845 (same), D.L. Godsey MG, Jackson Miller Bm [1850 McMinn Census: David 23, Angeline 26, Wm 5, Samuel 2]
Henry M. Miller to Sarah M. Peirce, 15 Aug 1849 (16 Aug), B.F. McKenzie JP
Jeremiah Miller to Sophia Lewis, 2 Sept 1840 (12 Sept), James W. Oakes JP
Mary Miller to James Revis q.v.
Nancy L. Miller [Lockmiller?] to George W. Qualls q.v.
Matilda L. Miller [Lockmiller?] to Nathan Qualls Jr. q.v.
P. Miller to M. Stuart, 9 Nov 1843 (same), D.L. Godsey MG
Thomas Miller to Harriet M. Hunter, 26 Sept 1849 (4 Oct), J.M. Miller MG
Wright S. Miller to Elizabeth A. Russell, 12 Aug 1847 (same), John Seabourn JP

MISCELLANEOUS (RHEA)

Aaron Miller: Bondsman for James Riddle, 1833
Abraham Miller: Trustee 1836-38
" " Bondsman for Joseph Bayless, 1828
Henry H. Miller: Bondsman for Henderson Compton, 1831
Hiram Miller: Bondsman for John Miller, 1819
James C. Miller: Bm for Wm Robinson/Robertson, 1844
James P. Miller: Bondsman for Jefferson B. Love, 1827
" " " Bondsman for Paschal Simpson, 1826
John Miller: Bondsman for William Harwood, 1822
" " Bondsman for Hiram Miller, 1825
Oliver C. Miller: MG 1832
P. W. Miller: Bondsman for William C. Murry, 1839
Rolley C. Miller: Bondsman for Gilbert Riggle, 1837
Samuel Miller: Bondsman for Pleasant L. Wilhelms, 1835
Samuel A. Miller: MG 1844
Wm B. Miller: Bondsman for Jackson S. Thompson, 1835
Wm L. Miller [Lockmiller?]: Bondsman for Cornelius Butram, 1831

MISCELLANEOUS (MEIGS)

E. J. Miller: Hiwassee District, Lower Goodfield area
Jackson Miller: JP(?) 1845
Jacob Miller Hiwassee District
Jeremiah Miller: Private, Mexican War
John Miller: Cherokee Removal muster roll, 1836
" " Hiwassee District, Pinhook Ferry area
John M. Miller: MG 1848-49
" " " Cherokee Removal muster roll, 1837
Mark M. Miller: 1st Sgt., Cherokee Removal muster roll, 1836
Stephen H. Miller: JP(?) 1846
Thomas Miller: Surety for T.J. Leonard, 1850
" " Surety for William Casey, 1850
W. S. Miller: JP(?) 1844
Willer Miller: Hiwassee District, Moore's Chapel area
William Miller: Hiwassee District
Zachariah Miller or Miles: Cherokee Removal muster roll, 1836

\- - - - - - - - - - - - -

MILLICAN / MILLIGAN

1850 RHEA CENSUS

Elizabeth Millican 16: see John Wyatt
George Millican 22: see Alfred Hutcheson

Harvy Millican 46 (Chairmaker), Permelia 42 (Va), Franklin 21 (Farmer), Calvin 20 (Farmer), Riley 18 (Farmer), Elizabeth 16, Mary 14, Martha 12, Margaret 9, James 6, John T. 4, Robert N. 3 p. 595-375

1850 MEIGS CENSUS

James Milligan 50 (Farmer), Margaret 55 (NC), Deborah 18, Alexander 16 (Farmer) p. 810-745

MISCELLANEOUS (MEIGS)

Franklin Millican: Mexican War

Harvey Millican: Mexican War

- - - - - - - - - - - - -

MILLS / MILES

(see also MITTS)

MARRIAGES (RHEA)

Elizabeth Mills to John Armstrong q.v.

MISCELLANEOUS (MEIGS)

John Miles: Cherokee Removal muster roll, 1836

- - - - - - - - - - - - -

MILOWAY / MILLOWAY

1850 MEIGS CENSUS

John T. Miloway 46 (NC)(Farmer), Polly 42 (NC), Betsy Ann 20 (NC), Martin 17 (NC), John C. 16 (NC), Mary C. 14 (NC), Rebecca Jane 12 (NC), James M. 10 (NC), Eliza 2 p. 716-26

MISCELLANEOUS (MEIGS)

John T. Milloway: Ocoee District

- - - - - - - - - - - - -

MIMS

MISCELLANEOUS (RHEA)

Robert Mims: On first Grand Jury

- - - - - - - - - - - - -

MINICK / MINNICK / MINICKS / MINIX

TAXES (RHEA)

1823 (Capt. Braselton's Co.): Peter Minick 1 WP

Samuel Minnick 1 WP, 75a Yellow Cr

1830 RHEA CENSUS

Peter Minnick 1120001 - 1201 p. 385

Samuel Minnick 2220001 - 211 p. 386

1850 RHEA CENSUS

Bailey Minick 25 (NC)(Farmer), Rebecca J. 20, Sarah E. 3, Mary A. 1, John HARRISON 16 p. 608-492

George Minick 23 (Farmer), Sarah 29 (NC), William 1, unnamed twins 1/12 p. 608-498

Henry Minick 27 (Farmer), Elizabeth 24, William H. 4, John M. 2, Martha E. 1/12, Sarah A. 22 p. 565-183

Peter Minick 34 (Farmer), Rachael 38, Mary J. 7, Eliza A. 5, William M. 20 (Farmer), Mathias WILLIAMS 61 (Va)(Carpenter) p. 571-232

MARRIAGES (RHEA)

Bailey Minix or Minnick to Rebecca Jane Edmons or Edmonds, 16 Sept 1844 (18 Sept), Charles Cox JP, E.P. Evins Bm (AR)

Emeline Minicks to Gainum Davis q.v.

George Minix to Sarah Collins, 23 Feb 1848 (same), T.J. Creede JP (R)

Henry Minix to Elizabeth Williams, 23 Dec 1844 (same), Charles Cox JP (R)

Henry Minick to Elizabeth Williams, 2 June 1845, David P. Seymore Bm (A)

[the above two records were thusly entered by Allen and the Courthouse record]

Manervia Minix to Joseph Eaton q.v.

Martha Mineck to Luke Goad q.v.

Mary Ann Minix to Nathan Chamberlain q.v.

Peter Minnick or Minich to Syntha or Cynthia Armstrong, 23 July 1823 (24 July), John Robinson JP, Samuel Minich Bm (AR)

Peter Minick or Minnick to Rachel Williams, 9 Feb 1836 (same), Matthew Hubbert JP, Harrison Barnett Bm (AR)

Samuel Minnick to Susan Henry, 6 Feb 1843, Solomon Henry Bm (A)

MISCELLANEOUS (RHEA)

Peter Minach: Bondsman for Harrison Barnett, 1841

Samuel Minick: Bondsman for Peter Minnick, 1823

- - - - - - - - - - - - -

MINNAS

MARRIAGES (RHEA)

Elizabeth Minnas to James Edmons q.v.

- - - - - - - - - - - - -

MINTON

TAXES (RHEA)

1823 (Capt. Piper's Co.): Johnson Minton 1 WP

MISCELLANEOUS (RHEA)

J. Minton: Elder, Concord Baptist Church of Christ, 1824

- - - - - - - - - - - - -

MITCHELL

TAXES (RHEA)

1819 (Capt. J. Lewis' Dist.): James C. Mitchell 1 WP, 168a

(Capt. Bradley's Dist.): Jas C. Mitchell 1 WP, 1 BP, 4 Town Lots, 118a

Mitchell & Rice 2 Town Lots

Samuel B. Mitchell 1 WP

1823 (Capt. Howerton's Co.):

Charles Mitchell 1 WP, 200a Muddy Cr

Thomas Mitchell 1 WP

(Capt. Lewis' Co.): James C. Mitchell 1 WP, 168a

(Capt. Brown's Co.): James C. Mitchell 1 WP, 3 lots

1830 RHEA CENSUS

Charles Mitchell 001002 - 111001 p. 391

David Mitchell 01001 - 00001 p. 364

James Mitchell 2120101 - 32101 p. 352

James C. Mitchell 2211001001 - 202010101 p. 392

John Mitchell 2010101 - 0210001 p. 364

Joseph Mitchell 01101 - 2001 p. 352

1840 RHEA CENSUS

Charles Mitchell 21001001 - 0011101

Robert Mitchell 010321 - 200002001

1840 MEIGS CENSUS

James Mitchell 00010001 - 0011101 p. 236

1850 RHEA CENSUS

Francinah Mitchell 57, Minerva A. 20, William G.F. 15, John C.H. 14 p. 553-122
[Charles Mitchell married Francine Perriman on 16 Feb 1814 in Roane County]

James A. Mitchell 31 (Farmer), Mary A. 27, Eliza J.P. 5, Isaac H. 3, Charles G. 1 p. 615-503

James Mitchell 60 (NC)(Colier), Margaret 49, Minerva FERGUSON 20, Elizabeth 18, Vesta J. 15, Robert 12, Samantha E. 10 p. 623-569

James M. Mitchell 25 (Farmer), Sarah M. 19, Jesse P. 5, Louisa J. 2, Richard 1/12, Mariah 22 p. 593-361

Robert Mitchell 49 (Farmer), Ann 42, Margaret J. 13, Susan A. 11, Esther J. 9, Sarah J. 6, Bunavista 3, Esther WOODWARD 85 (Va), Nancy 45, Nancy CASEY 21 p. 601-420

Sarah J. Mitchell 26: see Elijah Farmer

MARRIAGES (RHEA)

Catherine Mitchell to Jeremiah Wiggenton q.v.

Eliza Mitchell to Calvin M. Garrison q.v.

Emeline Mitchell to William S. Wiles q.v.

Isabella Mitchell to Richard Butler q.v.

James Mitchell to Catherine Woodward, 29 Apr 1813 (same), Samuel Davis Bm (A)

James Mitchell to Margarett Furgusson, 16 Sept 1848 (17 Sept), J.O. Torbett JP (R)

M. A. Mitchell to George M. Gilliam q.v.

Masterson Mitchell to Sarah Jane Wright, 19 or 29 Feb 1845 (19 Feb or 3 Mar), Asa Newport MG (AR)

Polly Mitchell to John Bryant q.v.

Robert Mitchell to Ann Woodward, 15 Feb 1837 (16 Feb), H. Collins JP, Jesse Warren Bm (AR)

Thomas Mitchell to Mary Kimbrell, 6 July 1833 (12 July), John Farmer MG, John Kimbrell Bm (AR)

MARRIAGES (MEIGS)

David Mitchell to Katherine Smith, 6 Apr 1846, "Executed and returned in due time" Thomas V. Atchley JP, Miles Atchley Bm [1850 Roane Census: David Mitchell 23, Catharine 22, James 4, Martha 2]

Elizabeth Mitchell to Metes Alcley [Atchley?] q.v.

George Mitchell to Mary Landagan, 18 Nov 1846, "Executed as commanded" Thomas V. Atchley JP, D.L. Godsey Bm

John Mitchell to Margaret Smith, 15 Oct 1846 (same), T.V. Atchley JP [1850 Roane Census: John Mitchell 21, Margaret 19, Sarah 6/12]

Margaret Mitchell to William Londagan q.v.

Nancy Mitchell to Jacob Knight q.v.

MISCELLANEOUS (RHEA)

Charles Mitchell: MG MEC 1840

James Mitchell: Came from Staunton, Auusta Co., Va., via Sevier Co., Tenn
" " Hiwassee District

James A. Mitchell: JP 1850

James C. Mitchell: Bondsman for Samuel Gamble, 1823
" " " Bondsman for John Person, 1817
" " " Signed petition to move Indian Agency
" " " Lots 17,21,40,86,87 in Washington
" " " Early member of Rhea County bar
" " " Built first Courthouse in Washington

J.C. Mitchell: Signed petition to move Indian Agency

John Mitchell: MG 1821

Robert Mitchell: Bondsman for William Woodward, 1822
" " Bondsman for James Woodward, 1829

Robert Mitchell: Bondsman for Peter W. Miller, 1836

S. K. Mitchell: Signed petition to move Indian Agency

Samuel B. Mitchell: Bondsman for Andrew Lacy, 1814

- - - - - - - - - - - - -

MITES

TAXES (RHEA)

1808 (Jonathan Fine's List): John Mites 1 WP

- - - - - - - - - - - - -

MITTS

1840 MEIGS CENSUS

Thomas Mitts 310001 - 210001 p. 227

1850 MEIGS CENSUS

Thomas Mitts 38 (Farmer), Sarah Jane 29, Martin 20 (Farmer), Elender 18, Joseph C. 16, Jonathan 14, Adeline 12, Elizabeth 10, Cynthia 8, Jacob 9, Nancy Ann 5, Thomas 4, William 1 p. 730-136

- - - - - - - - - - - - -

MIZER

1840 MEIGS CENSUS

Hartwell Mizer 00001 - 11001 p. 242

John Mizer 010001 - 13001 p. 244

Michael Mizer 1120001 - 11101 p. 242

- - - - - - - - - - - - -

MOLESTON

MARRIAGES (RHEA)

William G. Moleston to Mary E. Caldwell, ---?--- (4 Aug 1845), T.K. Munsey MG (R)
[1850 Hamilton Census: William G. Molleston 38, William RUTHAGE 24]

- - - - - - - - - - - - -

MOLTON / MOULTON

1830 RHEA CENSUS

Noble Molton 00001 - 00001 p. 357

1840 MEIGS CENSUS

Noble N. Moulton 21001 - 020001 p. 239

1850 RHEA CENSUS

Thomas Moulton 54 (NC)(Farmer), Mary 40, Caroline 16, Wesley 14, Francis 10, James 5 p. 571-231

1850 MEIGS CENSUS

Noble N. Molton 44 (Farmer), Mary 45, Incy 17, John 15 (Farmer), Newton11 p. 794-636

MARRIAGES (MEIGS)

Anney Mandy Molton to Daniel M. Clerk q.v.

- - - - - - - - - - - - -

MONDAY / MUNDAY

1830 RHEA CENSUS

Arthur Monday 00111001 - 01100001 p. 390 [looks like a 1 with ink smeared]

Frank Monday 20002 - 011 p. 352

1840 RHEA CENSUS
Arthur Monday 0010000001 - 000100001
Shell Monday 00001 - 11001
William Monday 0100001 - 20001
1840 MEIGS CENSUS
Francis Monday 112001 - 000001 p. 246
1850 RHEA CENSUS
Francis Monday 46 (Blacksmith), Elizabeth 40, James 24 (Blacksmith), Calvin 19, John 12, Sarah 6, Abraham 4, Rebecca 4, Orison 4/12 p. 537-29
Pleasant Monday 21 (Farmer), Mary 17 p. 536-22
William Monday 54 (NC)(Farmer), Lucinda 34 [possibly 54], Shelby Y. 17 (Farmer), America 14, Esther 10, Maleia 8, Henry 3, Rebecca 1 p. 558-154
MARRIAGES (RHEA)
Francis Monday to Rebecca Hawkins or Hankins, 22 Oct 1822 (same), John Rice JP, Saml Stark Bm (AR)
Francis Monday to Elizabeth Hill, 28 Dec 1823 (1 July 1824)[sic], James McDonald JP, Hiram Hill Bm (AR)
Nancy Monday to Merral Brady q.v.
Pleasant Monday to Mary Brewer, 10 Oct 1849 (11 Oct), A.G. Wright JP (R)
Sheley Munday to Matilda Miller, 22 Jan 1834 (23 Jan), John Pardee MMEC, William Snelson Bm (AR) [1850 Roane Census: Shelby Monday 33, Matilda 33, Rebecca 12, Elizabeth 6, Susan 4, Mary 2, Stephen Mathes 16]
Viney Monday to Hiram Burnett q.v.
William Monday to Lucinda Jones, 13 July 1831, Thos J. Gillespie Bm (A)
William D. Mundy* to Mary Jane Lane, 23 June 1844 (25 June), J.P. Thompson JP (R)
[*or Denardy, last name difficult to read]

\- - - - - - - - - - - -

MONTGOMERY

TAXES (RHEA)
1819 (Capt. Bradley's Dist.): James Montgomery 1 WP, 87a
1823 (Capt. Brown's Co.):
James Montgomery 1 WP, 1 BP, 87a
1830 RHEA CENSUS
J. T. Montgomery 10001 - 00101 p. 384
James Montgomery 21120001 - 00103001 p. 382
Samuel Montgomery 00001 - 02001 p. 382
1840 RHEA CENSUS
Harvy Montgomery 10001 - 10001
James Montgomery Sr. 002120001 - 000113001
James Montgomery Jr. 121001 - 21001
Samuel Montgomery 120001 - 12201
1850 RHEA CENSUS
James Montgomery 42 (Va)(Shoemaker), Christinah 40 Pleasant 22 (Farmer), Howard 16, George 14, Martha 13, Mary 11, James 9, Margaret 7, Malinda 5 p. 629-610
Mary C. Montgomery 11: see Nichademus Marlow
Robert C. Montgomery 34 (Farmer), Sarah 51, Mary 43 p. 603-423
1850 MEIGS CENSUS
William Montgomery 47 (Farmer), Susanna 40, Mary Jane 12, Rebecca 90 (Pa) p. 803-695
MARRIAGES (RHEA)
Dorcus Montgomery to William Murphy q.v.
Elizabeth Montgomery to James Woodward q.v.
Elizabeth J. Montgomery to N. Marler q.v.
H.H. Montgomery to E.M. Russell, 12 Oct 1849 (14 Oct), J.O. Collins JP (R)
Harvey Montgomery to Nancy Ann Smith, 22 Oct 1834 (24 Oct), John Condley JP, Harrison Barnett Bm (AR)
Jane Montgomery to Henry Henry q.v.
Peggy Montgomery to William Barnett q.v.
Samuel Montgomery to Jemima Little, 30 Mar 1826 (same), John Robinson JP, Ralph B. Locke Bm (AR)
MARRIAGES (MEIGS)
Alex H. Montgomery to Martha G. Chattin, 24 July 1843, A. Witt Bm
MISCELLANEOUS (RHEA)
James Montgomery: JP 1837-1839
" " Bondsman for Robert Moore, 1812
Robt C. Montgomery: Bondsman for Wm L. Murphy, 1845

\- - - - - - - - - - - -

MOODY

1830 RHEA CENSUS
Thomas Moody 20201 - 201001 p. 354
MISCELLANEOUS (RHEA)
John Moody: On Surveyor's list of land S of Tenn River
Samuel Moody: On Surveyor's list, land S of Tenn River
Thomas Moody: On Surveyor's list, land S of Tenn River

\- - - - - - - - - - - -

MOORE / MORE

TAXES (RHEA)
1808 (Jonathan Fine's List): Agnes Moore 1 WP [Piney Ri]
1819 (Capt. W.S. Bradley's Dist.): John Moore Sr. 100a
John Moore Jo. 1 WP
Thoms Moore 1 BP
1823 (Capt. Brown's Co.): Elisha Moore 1 WP
(Capt. Jackson's Co.): Elisha Moore 1 WP
John Moore 1 WP
Thomas Moore 1 BP
William Moore 1 WP
(Capt. McCall's Co.): James Moore 1 WP, 43a Piney R
(Capt. Howard's Co.): James Moore 1 WP
(Capt. Smith's Co.):
James Moore 1 BP, 160a Goodfield
Kenzie Moore 1 WP
Richard Moore 1 WP
Stephen Moore 1 WP
1830 RHEA CENSUS
Abegail Moore 0112 - 0020001 p. 378
James Moore 101001 - 001101 p. 364
James Moore 02000000001 - 1001 p. 375
Jas or Jos Moore 200001 - 100010001 p. 389
James A. Moore 00001 - 10001 p. 352
Jno Moore 1001 - 0000001 p. 368
Jno Moore 11001 - 012010001 p. 371
Rebecca Moore 0 - 000001001 p. 384 [widow of John]
Richard Moore 02001 - 21211 p. 372
Robert Moore 20011 - 100001 p. 378
Stephen Moore 011001 - 22001 p. 373
William Moore 1110001 - 00211001 p. 368

William Moore 211001 - 20001 p. 374
William Moore 20001 - 10001 p. 385
William Moore 00000001 - 00010001 p. 386

1840 RHEA CENSUS

James Moore 2110001 - 001001
Nimrod Moore 110001 - 110001
William Moore 00000001 - 000000001

1840 MEIGS CENSUS

Abigal Moore 00012 - 0000101 p. 232
Anny Moore 0 - 0000000001 p. 227
Bethena Moore 0 - 0012001 p. 232
Caleb Moore 20001 - 00001 p. 242
Daniel Moore 0100001 - 0021001 p. 227
David Moore 10001 - 00001 p. 234
Elisha Moore 10001 - 00001 p. 231
Greenbury Moore 10001 - 00001 p. 232
James Moore 0111101 - 0110001 p. 245
John Moore 111001 - 111001 p. 227
Jones Moore 2 - 0001001 p. 229
Robert Moore 010001 - 001101 p. 230
William Moore 22110001 - 0020001 p. 232
William Moore 231001 - 001001 p. 237

1850 RHEA CENSUS

Elisha Moore 28 (Farmer), Milbery 25 p. 633-639
Eliza Moore 26, Wm 9, Smith 7, Dodson 4: see Wm Collins
Jefferson Moore 35, Catherine 35, John BITTIX 22, Mary J. 18 p. 631-621
John Moore 24 (NC), Angeline 27, Margaret N. 10, Caroline 5 p. 634-647
Nimrod Moore 57 [possibly 37](Va)(Farmer), Kezziah 44 (Ga), Eliza A. 22, Drucilla J. 17, Jerry C. 15, Sarah 7 p. 573-243 [Nimrod Moore married Cassa Davis on 26 Aug 1826 in McMinn County]
Permelia Moore Unk (Va)(black): see John Brown
Samuel Moore 53 (Va)(Farmer), Elizabeth 50 (NC), Nancy 21 (NC), Sarah 20 (NC), Moses 18 (NC)(Farmer), Fanny 16 (NC), Susan 14 (NC), Malinda 11 (NC), Catherine 8 (NC), Marion 5 (NC) p. 570-227

1850 MEIGS CENSUS

Abegail Moore 70 (NC), William 35 (Farmer), Thomas 34 (Farmer), Anna 31, Isaac 20, Jane F. 14, Elizabeth 13, Sarah E. 9 p. 738-204
Alexander Moore 39 (Va)(Farmer) p. 747-278
Caleb Moore 41 (NC)(Farmer), Levina 39, William 18 (Farmer), James 14, Thomas 11, Ruth 7, Joseph 6, Paralee 5, Jackson 2 p. 789-598
Chaney Moore 29 (Farmer), Mary Ann 26 (NC), Martha Jane 15 p. 748-285
Elisha Moore 39 (Farmer), Lydia M. 19, John R.F. 12, James D. 3 p. 733-162
James Moore 25 (Farmer), Mary 23 (NC), Harriet J. 4, Mary E. 2, William D. 1 p. 748-284
James Moore 50 (SC)(Farmer), Polly 57 (NC), Isaac 19 (Farmer), Michael 16 p. 814-781
James W. Moore 22 (Farmer), Eliza 24, James C. 3, Sarah 1 p. 814-782
John Moore 45 (Farmer), Nancy Ann 24, Emaline 19, John 18, Robert 15, Sarah 12, David 10, William 8 p. 737-195
Lewis Moore 29 (Farmer), Sarah 26, Nancy C. 4, Elizabeth C. 3 p. 736-187
Robert Moore 42 (Farmer), Nancy 45 (Va), William 16, Robert 13, Aaron 8 p. 740-218

MARRIAGES (RHEA)

Abby Moore to Millington Blaylock q.v.
Anne Moore to Joseph Martin q.v.
Catherine Moore to Jesse Lewis q.v.
Catherine Moore to James H. Owens q.v.
Elisha Moore to Judy Ryon, 9 Aug 1824 (12 or 24 Aug), John Henninger MG, Charles Ryon Bm (AR)
Ibby Moore to Retten W. George q.v.
Isabella Moore to William Hall q.v.
James Moore to Mary Hackett, 2 Dec 1812, Jacob Riggle Bm (A)
James Moore to Sidney Moyers or Majors, 29 Dec 1824 (same), F.K. Fulkerson JP, Peter Majors Bm (AR)
James G. Moore to Sarah Brooks, 16 Dec 1822 (no return) (AR)
Jane Moore to John Locke q.v.
John Moore to Mary Chainey, 3 Aug 1842, David Robinson Bm (A)
John Moore to Angeline Gothard, 1 Apr 1848 (9 Apr), Washington Morgan JP (R)
John Moore to Jane Martin, 19 Feb 1824 (19 Feb or 6 June), John Cozby JP, William Moore Bm (AR)
John Moore to Elizabeth Nelson, 26 May 1825 (same), Thomas Hall MG, William Goodwin Bm (AR)
Joshua Moore or Moon to Cinthia Williams, 22 June 1824 (same), Thomas Cox JP, Stephen Moore Bm (AR)
Lentitia Moore to Alex Caldwell q.v.
Margaret Moore to Jonah R. Clifton q.v.
Martha Moore or Moon to Joseph P. Stockton q.v.
Martha C. Moore to John M. Neil q.v.
Mary Moore to William Falls q.v.
Mary Ann Moore to William Shoemaker q.v.
Mary H. Moore to John B. Beddix q.v.
Nancy Moore to Robert Locke q.v.
Rebecca Moore to Jacob Bryson q.v.
Robert Moore to Sarah Birdsong, 11 June 1812 (same), James Montgomery Bm (AR)
Robert Moore to Nancy Billingsley, 21 Jan 1825 (no return), William Thompson Bm (AR)
Thomas A. Moore to Rebecca Frazier, 10 Mar 1828 (same), C. Easterly MG, Alex Moore Bm (AR)
William Moon or Moore to Peggy Cowan, 25 Sept 1822 (same), David Cowan Bm (AR)
William Moore to Mary Frazier, 8 Sept 1841 (no return) (A)

MARRIAGES (MEIGS)

Adaline Moore to John G. Cash q.v.
Catharine Moore to Franklin Genow q.v.
David A. Moore to Lucinda Nideffer, 11 Jan 1840, L.J. Lewis JP(?)
Elisha Moore to Minerva Blare, 27 Dec 1847 (2 Jan 1848), William Johns JP
Elisha Moore to Milbery Sulivan, 3 Oct 1848 (5 Oct), William Johns JP
Elvira More to Abner Myers q.v.
F.M. Moore to Martha Reins, 6 Oct 1840 (same), B.F. McKenzie Esq.
James Moore to Mary Day, 27 Mar 1845 (same), M. C. Atchley MG
James H. Moon or Moore to Sarah H. Francisco, 15 Aug 1841, James H. Vernon JP(?)
James W. Moore to Louisa Jane Geno, 30 Oct 1846, "Executed as commanded" Thomas V. Atchley JP
Louisa Moore (Mrs.) to Wallace Malone q.v.
Marthena Moore to John Ingle Sr. q.v.

Mary Moore to William Maynor q.v.
Mary Ann Moore to John J. O'Neal q.v.
Nancey Moore to James F. Richardson q.v.
Pheaby Moore to John W. Smith q.v.
Roena Moore to John Hunter q.v.
Thomas Moore to Nancy Williams, 23 Jan 1841 (24 Jan), Prior Neal JP
William Moore to Polly Farrow, 29 Apr 1843, George W. Hall JP or Bm
William Moore to Eliza Selph, ------ (12 Sept 1848), James Gass Bm

MISCELLANEOUS (RHEA)

Alexander Moore: Bondsman for Thomas A. Moore, 1828
Elisha Moore: Bondsman for William Falls, 1824
John Moore: Bondsman for Lewis Morgan, 1815
" " Bondsman for William Hall, 1821
" " Bondsman for William Thompson, 1825
" " Bondsman for William Blaylock, 1826
" " Builder of first jail in Washington, 1812
" " Purchased Lot 43 in Town of Washington
" " JP 1818-1819, 1823
Kensey Moore: Bondsman for Benjamin Allen, 1823
Nathaniel Moore: Bondsman for James McCarter, 1821
Stephen Moore: Bm for Joshua Moore or Moon, 1824
" " Bondsman for David Bennett, 1832
Thomas Moore: Revolutionary War pensioner, 1835 list
William Moore: Bondsman for John Moore, 1824
" " Bondsman for Robert Doak, 1833

MISCELLANEOUS (MEIGS)

Alexander Moore: Private, Mexican War
Caleb Moore: Representative, General Assembly (House), 1847-49
Chain Moore: Private, Mexican War; JP(?) 1844
Daniel Moore: Ocoee District
James Moore: On Circuit Court jury, 1836
" " Common School Com., District 5, 1838
" " Chairman of County Court, 1839-40
" " JP 1838, 1841-42
" " Revolutionary War pensioner(?)
" " Hiwassee District, Lower Goodfield area
Jones Moor: Elder, Concord Baptist Church, 1824
Lukey Moore: JP(?) 1848
Richard Moore: Hiwassee District
Silas Moore: JP(?) 1844
Stephen Moore: Hiwassee District, Lower Goodfield area
William Moore: Hiwassee District, Lower Goodfield area

- - - - - - - - - - - - -

MOREHEAD

1840 RHEA CENSUS

James T. Morehead 00001 - 10001 [1 written over 2 or vice versa]

- - - - - - - - - - - - -

MORELAND / MOORELAND

1830 RHEA CENSUS

Thomas Moreland 321001 - 010001 p. 372

1840 MEIGS CENSUS

John Moreland 20001 - 0011 p. 231

1850 MEIGS CENSUS

Berry Mooreland 29 (Farmer), Orlenia 26, Polly A. 19, Martha E. 8, Thomas 7, Mary Jane 5, Louisa C. 3, John 1 p. 737-197

MARRIAGES (MEIGS)

H.R. Moreland to Jesse Johns q.v.
Martha Moreland to Isaac Cockson q.v.

MISCELLANEOUS (RHEA and MEIGS)

John Moreland: Bondsman for Allen Edmonds, 1844
Micajah Moreland: Mexican War
Micajah D. Moreland: 2nd Lt., Mexican War
Thomas Moreland: Member, Goodfield Baptist Church of Christ, 1827

- - - - - - - - - - - - -

MORGAN

TAXES (RHEA)

1819 (Capt. McGill's Co.): John Morgan 1 WP
Lewis Morgan 1 WP, 70a
1823 (Capt. Howard's Co.): John Morgan 1 WP, 1 BP
Lewis Morgan 1 WP, 113a
Washington Morgan 1 WP, 40a
Willis Morgan 1 WP

1830 RHEA CENSUS

Lethby Morgan 101 - 1000101 p. 382
Lewis Morgan 1320011 - 11011 p. 382
Washington Morgan 21001 - 011001 p. 382

1840 RHEA CENSUS

John Morgan 10001 - 00001
Letty Morgan 00101 - 0000201
Lewis Morgan 2122301 - 0011001
Washington Morgan 2310101 - 01020001
William Morgan 100001 - 110001

1850 RHEA CENSUS

Allison Morgan 23: see C. Whitehouse Able
Calvin Morgan 29 (Wagonmaker), Sarah L. 21 p. 635-652
Charles Morgan 32 (Wagonmaker), Emeretta 28, Henry S. 8, Franklin R. 7, William M. 5, unnamed 2, Rufus W. 5/12, Mary BENSON 12, Margaret BENSON 10 p. 634-650
Elias Morgan 31 (Wagonmaker), Elizabeth 25 (NC), William B. 6, John D. 3, George W. HASSLER 11, Asbury ACRE 16 (Farmer) p. 622-562
Lewis Morgan 57 (SC)(Wagonmaker), Elizabeth 47 (SC), Rufus 18 (Farmer), Gideon 14, Clementine ACRE 14, Henry MORGAN 12 p. 622-561
Lewis Morgan 30 (Blacksmith), Elizabeth 23, Samantha 2, Parthena 6/12, Ann GOTHARD 13 p. 638-678
Martin Morgan 29 (Tanner), Mary 21, Elizabeth 5/12 p. 635-651
Washington Morgan 36 (Farmer), Mary 19 p. 624-575
Washington Morgan 49 (SC)(Blacksmith), Susannah 55 (NC), Mary A. 28, David 24 (Farmer), John 22 (Blacksmith Apprentice), Susannah 20, Francis M. 17 (Farmer), George 15, William 13 p. 638-677
William Morgan 28 (Ga), Emily 35 (SC), Micajah 4 p. 582-309
William Morgan 30 (Farmer), Judy M. 27, Mary A. 8, Calvin A. 5, Albert A. 2 p. 635-657

MARRIAGES (RHEA)
Calvin Morgan to Sarah Foust, 16 Jan 1850 (same), E. McKamee JP (R)
Catherine Morgan to James McDusmer [McDunner] q.v.
Charles Morgan to Ameritta Riddle, 23 Apr 1840 (no return), Barkley S. Benson Bm (AR)
Elias H. Morgan to Tomese J. Pickett, 24 Dec 1842, Washington Morgan Jr. Bm (AR)
George W. Morgan to Susanna Cline, 7 May 1818 (same), John Morgan Bm (A)
John Morgan to Sarah A. Pearce, 24 Dec 1849 (same), John Wyott JP (R)
Lewis Morgan to Betsey Gothard, 17 Apr 1815, John Moore Bm (A)
Martin Morgan to Mary Morgan, 18 Apr 1849 (same), S.E. Foust JP (R)
Mary Morgan to Martin Morgan q.v.
Washington Morgan to Mary House, 17 Oct 1849 (same), Snelson Roberts MG (R)
William Morgan to Juda Greene, 20 Jan 1841 (21 Jan), Washington Morgan JP (R)
William Morgan to E. A. Rosen, 27 Feb 1850 (28 Feb), Daniel Broyles JP (R)
MARRIAGES (MEIGS)
James Morgan to Betsy Hainy, 1 Feb 1847 (2 Feb), M. Atchley MG or JP
MISCELLANEOUS (RHEA)
Calvin Morgan: Bondsman for Alfred Danby, 1842
Charles Morgan: Bondsman for James I. Alexander, 1838
John Morgan: Bondsman for George W. Morgan, 1818
Lewis Morgan: Bondsman for Dempsey Sullivan, 1825
" " Bondsman for William K. Alexander, 1841
Lewis Morgan Jr.: Bondsman for John C. Gothard, 1844
Washington Morgan: JP 1841-44, 1848
Washington Morgan Jr.: Bm for Elias H. Morgan, 1842

- - - - - - - - - - - - -

MORRIS
(see also MANIS / MANICE)

TAXES (RHEA)
1808 (Jonathan Fine's List): Richard Morris 1 WP
1819 (Capt. John Lewis' Dist.): William Morris 1 WP
1823 (Capt. Lewis' Co.): William Morris 1 WP
1830 RHEA CENSUS
Jourdan Morris 2220001 - 10101 p. 373
1840 RHEA CENSUS
Blount Morris 200001 - 10001
1850 RHEA CENSUS
Isaac Morris 38 (Day Laborer), Ann 40 (Unk), John 21 (Day Laborer), Luvisa 18, George 15, Minerva 10, Ephraim 8, Albert 5, Zachary T. 3, Dicey 6/12 p. 540-46
MARRIAGES (RHEA)
Henry Morris to Margaret Burk, 24 Jan 1811 (same), Abraham Howard JP, William Barnett Bm (AR)
Jemima C. Morris to Peter H. Bullock q.v.
Jesse Morris to Peggy Bullard, 28 Dec 1835, Simon Eldridge Bm (A)
Myra Morris to Mercy Ferguson q.v.
Rebecca Morris to Strother Blackwell q.v.
MISCELLANEOUS (RHEA and MEIGS)
Blount Morris: Bondsman for Benjamin Loder, 1837
Dickson Morris: JP or Bm 1845 (Meigs Co)
John [Jorden?] Morris: Hiwassee District, Lower Goodfield
Jordan Morris: Surveyor's List of land S of Tenn River
Joseph Morris: Ocoee District

- - - - - - - - - - - - -

MORRISON

1850 RHEA CENSUS
James F. Morrison 28 (Farmer), Catharine A. 35 (Va), Hannah E. 6, Hugh M. 2, John R. 8/12 p. 588-347
1850 MEIGS CENSUS
Joseph Morrison 26 (Farmer), Catharine 25, William 21 (Va)(Farmer) p. 721-61

- - - - - - - - - - - - -

MORROW

TAXES (RHEA)
1819 (Capt. McGill's Co.): John Morrow 1 WP
MARRIAGES (RHEA)
John Morrow to Polly Gouge, 19 Dec 1818 (same), Abraham Howard JP, James Henry Bm (AR)

- - - - - - - - - - - - -

MOSELEY

TAXES (RHEA)
1819 (Capt. John Ramsey's Co.) Joshua Moseley 1 WP
1840 RHEA CENSUS
Joshua Mosely 0000000001 - 0000000001

- - - - - - - - - - - - -

MOSIER

MISCELLANEOUS (MEIGS)
Lewis H. Mosier: Private, Mexican War

- - - - - - - - - - - - -

MOSS / MOSSES

1850 MEIGS CENSUS
Joseph Moss 53 (SC)(Farmer), Elizabeth 45, John 20 (Farmer), Aspac (f) 15, William F. 12, Martha M. 10, Caroline 6, James M. 4, Thomas 3 p. 805-713 [Joseph married Betsy Ellis in 1822 in Roane Co.]
MISCELLANEOUS (MEIGS)
Joseph Mosses: JP(?) 1841

- - - - - - - - - - - - -

MOYERS / MEYERS / MYERS / MYRES

TAXES (RHEA)
1823 (Capt. Lewis' Co.): Ann Moyers 7 BP, 700a
(Capt. Brown's Co.): Cornelius Moyers 1 WP
(Capt. Wilson's Co.): John Meyers 1 WP
1830 RHEA CENSUS
Cornelius Moyers 10002 - 200011 p. 371
George Myers 00011 - 20002 p. 354
John Moyers 10021001 - 02011 p. 367

1840 MEIGS CENSUS
Christopher Myers 121001 - 103001 p. 230
John Moyers 11010001 - 100001 p. 242
Lasly Myres 210001 - 11011 p. 229
William Moyers 10001 - 11001 p. 243

1850 MEIGS CENSUS
Abner Myers 17 (Farmer), Helen A. 25, Nancy Jane 1 p. 740-219
Christopher Myers 60 (Va)(Farmer), Lydia 58 (Va), Hiram 21 (Farmer), George 17, Henderson 14, Nancy 12 p. 728-120
Lesly Myers 43 (Farmer), Indianna 38, George B. 18, Lydia Ann 15, William R. 13, Mary E. 12, Plesant 9, James 8, Racheal E. 6, Christopher 3, Eliza N. 2, Noah E. 1 p. 728-119
Nancy Myres 49, Polly 25, Lesly 13, Jackson 11, Racheal C. 10 p. 738-203
William Myres 60 (NC)(Farmer), Lones 55 (Va), Robert 29 (NC)(Convict), Jackson 20 (Va)(Farmer), William 16 (Farmer), Julian 14 p. 741-230

MARRIAGES (RHEA)
Ann Moyers to William T. Gass q.v.
Cinthia Myers to Riley Smith q.v.
Cornelius Moyers to Myra or Altimira Payne, 24 Feb 1824 (26 Feb), John Rice JP, John C. Doran Bm (AR)
Elizabeth Moyers to William Rutherford q.v.
Henry Myers to Agabis or Aggebis Ragan, 5 Feb 1816 (6 Feb), Seymore Calihen JP, Sanford Turley Bm (AR)
Jacob Moyers to Ann Condley, 24 Dec 1822 (1 Jan 1823), John Rice JP (AR)
John Myers to Matilda Hill, 11 Apr 1831 (12 Apr), Daniel Briggs MG, Jeremiah Tindle Bm (AR)
Permealy Moyers to Benjamin Roberts q.v.
Polly Myers to Thomas J. Alexander q.v.
Polly Myers to William Hannah q.v.
William Meyers to Nancy Rowdon, 3 Aug 1831, Daniel Stockton Bm (A)
Wylie or Wyly Moyers to Sally Jones, 16 Aug 1832 (same), John Henninger MG, Cornelius Meyers Bm (AR) [1850 Knox Census: Wiley M. Myers 40, Sarah 30, Ann E.C. 14, Jacob M. 12, Mathias H. 10, Mary J. 7, Sarah P. 6, Cassandra S. 2]

MARRIAGES (MEIGS)
Abner Myers to Elvira More, 30 Dec 1849 (31 Dec), William Johns JP
Eleanor Moyars to Robert Simpson q.v.
Eliza Myons or Myers to Wiley G. Lunsford q.v.
Rebecca Moyers to Henry A. Lunsford q.v.
Rutha Moyers to Davis Singleton q.v.
William Myers to Lones Reed, 17 Dec 1847 (18 Dec), B.F. McKenzie JP

MISCELLANEOUS (RHEA)
Henry Myers: Bondsman for Sanford Farley, 1816
John Myers: Bondsman for Thomas Gann, 1818
" " Bondsman for John Simons, 1820
" " Hiwassee District
William Myers: Bondsman for William Hannah, 1826
" " Bondsman for Riley Smith, 1826

- - - - - - - - - - - - -

MULLER

1850 MEIGS CENSUS
William R. Muller 26 (Farmer), Reuben A. 25 (Farmer), Joseph L. 20 (Farmer), Rebecca E. 22, Elizabeth 18, Charles 16 (Farmer) p. 755-345

- - - - - - - - - - - - -

MULLINS / MULLONS / MULLEN

1830 RHEA CENSUS
Eliza Mullins 11 - 1020001 p. 392
Joseph Mullins 00001 - 0001 p. 365
1840 MEIGS CENSUS
Richard Mullons 21001 - 00001 p. 243
MARRIAGES (RHEA)
George W. Mullins to Darkie McClenahan, 11 Sept 1828, Thomas Cox Bm (A)
Joseph Mullins to Ann Anderson, 25 Apr 1830 (same), Matthew Hubbert JP (AR)
MISCELLANEOUS (RHEA and MEIGS)
George W. Mullen: Bondsman for Sutton Green, 1829
James Mullins: Private, Mexican War

- - - - - - - - - - - - -

MULVANEY

1850 RHEA CENSUS
Elizabeth Mulvaney 54, Loretta SMITH 18, Sarah C. SMITH 6/12 p. 618-532

- - - - - - - - - - - - -

MUNGER

1850 MEIGS CENSUS
Henry Munger 24 (Farmer), Lydia 25, Wright 2 p. 732-145

- - - - - - - - - - - - -

MUNSEY / MONSEY / MUNCY / MONSY / MOUNCY

1830 RHEA CENSUS
Hiram Monsy 10001 - 11001 p. 364
1840 RHEA CENSUS
Thomas W. Muncy 020001 - 10001
1840 MEIGS CENSUS
Hiram Monsy 101001 - 121101 p. 240
1850 RHEA CENSUS
Margaret Munsey 45, Richard 18 (Farmer), Nathaniel 16 (Farmer), Harriet 12, Henry C. 10, James J. 7 p. 630-615
1850 MEIGS CENSUS
Eli F. Munsey 21 (Farmer), Delilah 24, Susannah 23 p. 786-573
Hiram Munsey 53 (Va)(Farmer), Cindarilla 46 (Va), Susannah 23, Darcus (f) 17, Gilbert F. 15, Levina 13, Harriet 12, Mary F. 7 p. 797-663
MARRIAGES (RHEA)
Thomas K. Monsey or Muncy to Mary Jane Day, 21 Oct 1845 (same), O.F. Cunningham MG, W.F. Ragsdale Bm (AR)

MARRIAGES (MEIGS)
Eli F. Mouncy to Dilla Fike, 28 Nov 1848 (30 Nov), John Ford JP
Nancy Munsey to Thomas J. Lawson q.v.
MISCELLANEOUS (RHEA and MEIGS)
Thomas K. Monsey: MG 1843-48 (Rhea), 1845 (Meigs)
Thomas W. Munsey: Bondsman for Charles Witt, 1831
" " " Bondsman for Charles Grigsby, 1832
- - - - - - - - - - - - -

MURPHY / MURPHEY / MURPHIE / MURPHREE / MURFREE / MURPEE

TAXES (RHEA)
1819 (Capt J. Robinson's Co.): Allen Murphree 1 WP
John Murphree 1 WP
Wyly Murphree 1 WP
(Capt. Bradley's Dist.): H. & E. Murphey 1 WP, 76a
Samuel Murphey 1 WP, 1 TL, 150a
1823 (Capt. Wilson's Co.): Cadar Murfree 1 WP
Willie Murfree 1 WP
(Capt. Jackson's Co.): Hugh Murphey 1 WP
James Murphey 1 WP
1830 RHEA CENSUS
Dennis C. Murphy 011 - 00011 p. 353
James Murphy 21001 - 10011 p. 379
John Murphy 00000001 - 00000001 p. 380
Robert Murphy 01001 - 30001 p. 362
Wm Murfree or Murpee 0011000001 - 00010001 p. 385
1840 MEIGS CENSUS
Robert Murphy 310101 - 002101 p. 248
1850 RHEA CENSUS
John B. Murphy 55 (NC)(Blacksmith), Lucy R. 51, Nancy E. 18, Malinda E. 16, Martha E. 14 p. 613-448
1850 MEIGS CENSUS
Robert Murphy 49 (Va)(Farmer), Sarah 44, Sonna 25, Elizabeth 23, Mary Ann 21, William J. 19 (Farmer), James F. 16 (Farmer), Robert W. 14, Edward W. 10, Prudence J. 7, George M.D. 5, Sarah Ann 5 p. 810-746
MARRIAGES (RHEA)
Allen Murphie to Rhoda Dunn, 22 Jan 1812 (no return) (AR)
Cader or Cedar Murphrie to Ruth Atchley, 21 Aug 1819, "Returned to office with papers of D. Walker, Esq." Isaac Price Bm (AR)
John Murphrie to Tilda Walker, 19 Oct or 17 Nov 1819 (same), J. Fine JP, Byrium Breeding Bm (AR)
John A. Murphey to Jane McCaleb, 27 Nov 1847 (9 Dec), Thomas Witten MG (R)
Martin Murphree to Leah Walker, 11 Sept 1816 (12 Sept), James Campbell JP, Thomas Kelly Bm (AR)
Pamelia I. Murphy to Charles W. Peterson q.v.
Polly Murphrie to Absolem Barnes q.v.
Ransom Murphree to Mary Walker, 12 Mar 1816 (no return), James Reid Bm (AR)
Robert Murphey or Murphy to Jane Collins, 9 Oct 1826 (same), Thos Cox JP, David Campbell Bm (AR)
William Murphy to Margaret Johnson, 24 Feb 1832 (26 Feb), George Preston JP, Wm Johnson Bm (AR)
William L. Murphy to Dorcess L. Montgomery, 3 Feb or 30 Jan 1845 (same), Samuel R. Hackett or Charles Cox JP, Robert C. Montgomery Bm (AR)
Wylie or Wyley Murphrie to Sally Hill, 24 Feb 1820 (no return) (AR)
MISCELLANEOUS (RHEA)
Cadar Murphree: Bondsman for Jacob Price, 1820
Daniel (David) Murphree: JP 1814-16
David Murphree: Com., Town of Washington, 1812-13
Dennis C. Murphy: Bondsman for Jacob Wilhelms, 1833
Elijah Murphree: Bondsman for Harrison Barnet, 1835
John Murfree: Bondsman for William Dodd, 1814
Richard S. Murphy: Bondsman for Cofield T. Tillery, 1830
Robert Murphy: Bondsman for William Kerr, 1826
" " Bondsman for Abraham F. Gerrold, 1832
" " Hiwassee District, Moore's Chapel area
Samuel Murphey: Lot 59, Town of Washington
Wiley Murphy: Bondsman for Joel Bledsoe, 1828
Willie (William?) Murphey: Hiwassee District
- - - - - - - - - - - - -

MURRY / MURRAY

1840 RHEA CENSUS
William C. Murry 10001 - 0001
MARRIAGES (RHEA)
Thomas W. Murray to Nancy A. Noblett, 19 Sept 1833 (same), B. Wallace MG, Thos W. Noblet Bm (AR)
William C. Murry to Jane Nelson or Nilsson, 5 Jan 1839 (6 Jan), S. Dyer JP, P.W. Miller Bm (AR)
MISCELLANEOUS (MEIGS)
Archibald Murray: Mexican War (died in service)
Mary Murray: Purchsed Lot 16 in Decatur, 1836
- - - - - - - - - - - - -

MUSICK / MUSIC

1840 MEIGS CENSUS
Samuel Music 200001 - 000001 p. 233
MARRIAGES (RHEA)
Lemuel Musick to Jane Lawson, 12 Mar 1835 (same), D.L. Godsey MG, James Blakley Bm (AR)
- - - - - - - - - - - - -

MYRUM

MARRIAGES (RHEA)
Nancy Myrum to Thomas Stafford q.v.
- - - - - - - - - - - - -

NANNY

1850 RHEA CENSUS
James T. Nanny 33 (Blacksmith), Orlina 34, Richard 8, Mary 3, Ruhanny 1 p. 598-394
Nicholas Nanny 59 (NC)(Farmer), Mary 58 (NC), John 21 (Farmer) p. 598-393
MARRIAGES (RHEA)
T.J. or James T. Nanny to Orlina Killough, 31 Aug 1845 (same), John S. Evens JP, C.W. Peterson Bm (AR)
- - - - - - - - - - - - -

NARIMORE / NARRIMORE

MARRIAGES (RHEA)
Nancy Narrimore to Howard Swafford q.v.
Nelson M. Narimore to Dolly Smith, 17 Dec 1833 (same), John McClure JP, Andrew Igou Bm (AR)

- - - - - - - - - - - - -

NASH

1840 RHEA CENSUS
John Nash 10001 - 20001
1850 RHEA CENSUS
James Nash 24 (Apprentice Tanner): see James J. Able
John Nash 46 (Va)(Farmer), Betsy 42, John M. 21 (Farmer), Mary 18, Rachael 16, Margaret 13, William H. 9, Henry C. 5, Thomas J. 3 p. 625-579
William Nash 30 (Ky)(Farmer), Susannah 34 (Va), Elizabeth 36 (Va), Sarah 36 (Va), Sarah 50 (Va), Elizabeth 75 (Va) p. 637-670
MARRIAGES (RHEA)
Elizabeth Nash to Warren Rhea q.v.
John Nash to Nancy Bean, 26 Dec 1836 (29 Dec), A.G. Wright JP, George W. Gage Bm (AR)

- - - - - - - - - - - - -

NAVE

MARRIAGES (RHEA)
Henry Nave to Susanna Ross, 9 Sept 1809, Jacob Hunter Bm (A)

- - - - - - - - - - - - -

NEAL / NEIL / NEEL / NAIL

TAXES (RHEA)
1819 (Capt. Wm McCray's Co.): James Neal 1 WP, 72½a
1830 RHEA CENSUS
James Nail 2110001 - 111201 p. 390
1840 MEIGS CENSUS
John Neil 20001 - 00001 p. 232
Prior Neil 011001 - 12001 p. 243
1850 MEIGS CENSUS
Delilah Neal 40, Joseph 5: see Ury Neaves
John M. Neal 36 (Farmer), Martha C. 30, James C. 12, William M. 10, Bathena Ann 8, John H. 6, Peter W. 1 p. 771-459
John R. Neil 33 (Farmer), Alender Jane 20, Eglantine 2, Tennessee 1 p. 768-435
Pryor Neil 41 (Farmer), Elizabeth 36, Lea 20, John 18, Mary Jane 14, Louisa 12, Mahala 9, Thomas B. 7, William R. 5, James K.P. 2, Jeremiah F. 1 p. 780-525
MARRIAGES (RHEA)
John M. Neil to Martha C. Moore, 10 Feb 1835, Peter A. Neil Bm (A)
Nicholas Neal to Sally Vaughn, 11 Aug 1818, Henry Little Bm (A)
Peter Neil to Susan Runions or Runyon, 7 Oct 1835 (8 Oct), D.L. Godsey JP, Robert B. Suthard Bm (AR) [1850 Hamilton Census: Peter A. Neil 38, Susanna 32, John 14, William 12, Nancy 11, Minrel 8, Isaac 6, Moranda 4, Emoline 2, Ann RUNYANS 9]
Prior Neil to Elizabeth Farmer, 2 Jan 1829, Josiah Keeran Bm (A)
MARRIAGES (MEIGS)
James Neil to Judy Louisa Reed, 8 Aug 1848 (10 Aug), J.M. Butler JP
Mary Neil to James McAdams q.v.
MISCELLANEOUS (RHEA and MEIGS)
John M. Neil: Cherokee Removal muster roll, 1837
Nicholas Nail: Bondsman for Abner Royal, 1815
Peter A. Neil: Bondsman for John M. Neil, 1835
Pryor Neil: JP 1838-42
William Nail: JP or MG 1845 (Rhea Co)

- - - - - - - - - - - - -

NEASE

1840 RHEA CENSUS
Joseph Nease 01000001 - 00001001

- - - - - - - - - - - - -

NEAVES / NEAVE / NEIVES / NEEVES

TAXES (RHEA)
1823 (Capt. Smith's Co.): John Neeves 1 WP
1840 MEIGS CENSUS
John Neave 0000001 - 00000010001 p. 232
1850 MEIGS CENSUS
Ury Neaves 55, Delilah NEAL 40, Joseph 5 p. 748-288
MISCELLANEOUS (RHEA and MEIGS)
John Neaves: Bondsman for Tavenor Masoner, 1832
" " Hiwassee District, Moore's Chapel area

- - - - - - - - - - - - -

NEELY / NEELEY

MARRIAGES (RHEA)
Nathan Neely to Syntha Williams, 24 Jan 1812 (same), T. Johnson Bm (A)
MISCELLANEOUS (RHEA)
Robert Neeley: Bondsman for John Overstreet, 1810
William M. Neeley: Bondsman for Nicholas Keith, 1833

- - - - - - - - - - - - -

NEIDEFFER / NIDEFFER / NEIGHDEFFER

TAXES (RHEA)
1823 (Capt. Smith's Co.): Solomon Neighdeffer 1 WP
1830 RHEA CENSUS
Solomon Nideffer 220101 - 101001 p. 372
1840 MEIGS CENSUS
Solomon Nideffer 0111101 - 01100010001 p. 233
MARRIAGES (MEIGS)
Lucinda Nideffer to David A. Moore q.v.
MISCELLANEOUS (RHEA and MEIGS)
Isaac Neideffer: Cherokee Removal muster roll, 1837
Jacob Neideffer: Cherokee Removal muster roll, 1837
Solomon Neideffer: Bondsman for Allen Blevins, 1824
" " Hiwassee Dist., Lower Goodfield area

- - - - - - - - - - - - -

NELSON

TAXES (RHEA)
1819 (Capt. Robinson's Co.): James N. Nelson 1 WP, 75a
1823 (Capt. Wilson's Co.): Zachariah Nelson 1 WP
1830 RHEA CENSUS
Adam Nelson 00001 - 10001 p. 361
Hansel Nelson 00101001 - 00000001 p. 361
Henry Nelson 2001 - 10001 p. 361
James Nelson* or Snelson* 000030001 - 000010001 p. 387 [*one name written over the other]
John Nelson 200001 - 0401 p. 388
John Nelson 0000000001 - 000000001 p. 388
William Nelson 00003 - 101001 p. 388
1840 RHEA CENSUS
James Nelson 001000001 - 00000001
1840 MEIGS CENSUS
David Nelson 10001 - 10001 p. 231
Hans Nelson 2000100001 - 000100001 p. 247
Richard Nelson 11001 - 00001 p. 242
1850 MEIGS CENSUS
Hanse Nelson 39 (Farmer)(Deaf & Dumb), Henry 14, Adam 12, William 10, Hannah 8, Delilah 76 p. 803-694
John Nelson 35 (Farmer), Nancy 33, Francis M. 14, George W. 8, Hugh H. 6 p. 803-693
Richard Nelson 41 (SC)(Farmer), Ruth 35 (NC), Mary 16, William 14, Mahala 10, James 7, Elizabeth 5, Mary D. 2 p. 790-603
MARRIAGES (RHEA)
Elizabeth Nelson to John Moore q.v.
Elizabeth Nelson to J.A. Wasson q.v.
Hanse Nelson to Polly Foard, 14 Jan 1835 (15 Jan), Isaac Baker JP, John Nelson Bm (AR)
James M. Nelson (or Wilson) to Elizabeth Evens or Evins, 21 Mar 1822 (same), John Mitchell JP, Joseph Williams Bm (AR)
Jane Nelson or Nilsson to William C. Murry q.v.
John M. Nelson to Nancy Fullington, 16 Aug 1833 (29 Aug), Isaac Baker JP, John Massey Bm (AR)
Richard Nelson to Ruth Massey, 15 Apr 1833 (16 Apr), Isaac Baker JP, John Massey Bm (AR)
Sally Nelson to William Thompson q.v.
Viney Nelson to James Varnell q.v.
Zachariah Nelson to Sarah Walker, 1 Jan 1824 (same), D. Walker JP, John Varnell Bm (AR)
MARRIAGES (MEIGS)
Hance Nelson to Pheriby Buttram, 7 Jan 1847, "The within not celebrated" D.L. Godsey MG, S. McGinnis, Constable
MISCELLANEOUS (RHEA and MEIGS)
David Nelson: Hiwassee District, east of Hiwassee River
Henry Nelson: Hiwasse District, Euchee area
James Nelson: JP 1826 (Rhea Co)
John Nelson: Bondsman for Hanse Nelson, 1835
John R. Nelson: Hiwassee District, Euchee area
W. Hance Nelson: Hiwassee District, Euchee area
Zachariah Nelson: Bondsman for William Walker, 1825

\- - - - - - - - - - - -

NETHERLAND

MISCELLANEOUS (MEIGS)
George W. Netherland: Hiwassee District

\- - - - - - - - - - - -

NEVINS

MARRIAGES (RHEA)
Wilson Nevins to Rachel Cary, 16 Apr 1815, Mark Halley Bm (A)

\- - - - - - - - - - - -

NEWBERN

MISCELLANEOUS (RHEA)
William I. Newbern: JP 1833

\- - - - - - - - - - - -

NEWBERRY / NEWBURY

TAXES (RHEA)
1823 (Capt. Smith's Co.): Thomas Newberry 1 WP
1840 MEIGS CENSUS
Jesse Newbury 10001 - 10001 p. 233

\- - - - - - - - - - - -

NEWKIRK / NEWKERK

1830 RHEA CENSUS
Henry Newkirk 00111001 - 0000001 p. 356
Uriah Newkirk 01001 - 10001 p. 357
1840 MEIGS CENSUS
James Newkirk 1100001 - 112001 p. 239
John Newkirk 10001 - 10001 p. 241
Uriah Newkirk 000101 - 010101 p. 242
MARRIAGES (RHEA)
Betsy Newkirk to John Helms q.v.
Hiram Newkirk to Malinda Brandon, 12 Mar 1831 (same), Philip Lider or Leeber MG, Hugh M. Brandon Bm (AR)
Polly Newkirk to Caleb Bedwell q.v.
MARRIAGES (MEIGS)
James N. Newkirk to Mary Elder, 27 Nov 1842 (same), Thos V. Atchley JP, J.K. Brown Bm(?)
Pheby Newkirk to John S. Green q.v.
MISCELLANEOUS (RHEA and MEIGS)
Henry Newkirk: Surveyor's list of land south of Tenn River
James W. Newkirk: JP(?) 1842 (Meigs Co)
Uriah Newkirk: Constable, District 7, Meigs Co
" " Bm for John Helms [Hellense], 1824

\- - - - - - - - - - - -

NEWLAND

MISCELLANEOUS (RHEA)
James Newland: Bondsman for David Borden, 1833

\- - - - - - - - - - - -

NEWMAN

1840 MEIGS CENSUS
Aremedon Newman 10001 - 0001 p. 236
Joshua Newman 00110001 - 0001101 o, 236
Nimrod Newman 00001 - 11001 p. 237
1850 MEIGS CENSUS
Ceala Newman (f) 37, Mary Ann 28 p. 785-571

MARRIAGES (RHEA)
Betsy Newman to Daniel Barr q.v.
Eleanor Newman to Archibald Horton q.v.
Rachel Newman to John Day q.v.
MISCELLANEOUS (RHEA)
Nathaniel Newman: Bondsman for Daniel Barr, 1812

- - - - - - - - - - - -

NEWPORT

1850 RHEA CENSUS
Asa Newport 47 (Blacksmith), Elizabeth 47, John 22 (Blacksmith), Ezekiel 20 (Farmer), Elizabeth 18, Asa 16 (Farmer), Richard G.W. 14, James M. 10, Margaret 11, Jule H. 5, Sabry 1 p. 545-78
MARRIAGES (RHEA)
Asa Newport to Elizabeth Rodgers, 24 Oct 1821 (same), John Rogers Bm (A)
Mary A. Newport to Isaac Cline q.v.
Sally Newport to Alford Harris q.v.
Sarah Newport to A.J. Bowlinger q.v.
MISCELLANEOUS (RHEA)
Asa Newport: MG 1841-1850

- - - - - - - - - - - -

NEWTON

TAXES (RHEA)
1823 (Capt. Smith's Co.): Henry Newton 1 WP
1830 RHEA CENSUS
James Newton 00001 - 21001 p. 359
1850 RHEA CENSUS
Rachael Newton 27 (SC): see Riley Kersey
MARRIAGES (RHEA)
John S. Newton to Sally Davis, 26 Jan 1817, John Parker Bm (A)

- - - - - - - - - - - -

NICHOL / NICKLES

1840 MEIGS CENSUS
John Nickles 000000001 - 000000001 p. 242
1850 MEIGS CENSUS
John Nichol 63 (NC)(Miller), Mary 63 (NC) p. 781-531
[John Nichols married Sally Sharp on 15 July 1809 in Roane County]

- - - - - - - - - - - -

NICHOLASON

1850 MEIGS CENSUS
A.O.P. Nicholason 4, Naoma E. 1: see John Johnson

- - - - - - - - - - - -

NIMTON

MARRIAGES (RHEA)
Jeniva Nimton to James Fields q.v.

- - - - - - - - - - - -

NIPER

1840 RHEA CENSUS
Matthew Niper 1011 - 0001

- - - - - - - - - - - -

NOBLET / NOBLETT

TAXES (RHEA)
1808 (Jonathan Fine's List):
William Noblett 1 WP, 100a Piney River
1819 (Capt. Ramsey's Co.): William Noblet 1 WP, 172a
1830 RHEA CENSUS
Thomas Noblet 200002 - 0012001 p. 389
William Noblet 00101001 - 0012001 p. 389
MARRIAGES (RHEA)
Nancy A. Noblett to Thomas W. Murray q.v.
Peggy Ann Noblett to John Bowman q.v.
Thomas W. Noblett to Elizabeth Casey, 31 Jan 1827, Isaac H. Brown Bm (A)
MISCELLANEOUS (RHEA)
Caleb B. Noblett: Witnessed deed for land, 1834
Thomas W. Noblett: Bondsman for John Bowman, 1835
" " " Bondsman for Thos W. Murray, 1833
" " " Trustee, Sulphur Springs Presbyterian Meeting House, 1834
William Noblett: Deeded land for S.S. Presbyterian Church

- - - - - - - - - - - -

NOLAN

MISCELLANEOUS (RHEA)
Thomas Nolan: Bondsman for Robert Bell, 1813
" " Bondsman for Owen David, 1811
" " Bondsman for Joel McNutt, 1810

- - - - - - - - - - - -

NORMAN

TAXES (RHEA)
1823 (Capt. Wilson's Co.): Matthew Norman 1 WP
1830 RHEA CENSUS
Matthew Norman 1110001 - 0200001 p. 353
1840 MEIGS CENSUS
Clinton Norman 11001 - 0010101 p. 230
Henry Norman 10001 - 10001 p. 230
Matthew Norman 00020001 - 00001001 p. 238
Michel Norman 10001 - 00001 p. 238
1850 MEIGS CENSUS
Clinton Norman 37 (Farmer), Elizabeth 35, Mathew 17 (Farmer), William J. 14, Asbury 12, Mary Jane 10, Velina 2, Syntha VAUGHN 19 p. 742-237
Henry Norman 38 (Farmer), Louisa 34, John A. 13, Joseph C. 7, Manda Jane 5, Julinda 3, Louisa E. 1 p. 741-227
Matthew Norman 66 (NC)(Farmer), Cassaann 65 (Va), William 20 (Farmer) p. 765-407
William Norman 30 (Farmer) p. 765-408
MARRIAGES (RHEA)
Anna Norman to Stephen Faris q.v.

Clinton Norman to Elizabeth Jones, 4 Sept 1832 (10 Sept), Archibald F. Gerrel [Fitzgerald] MG, Benjamin Blankenship Bm (AR)
Julindian Norman to Aiden Bridwell q.v.
Lafayette Norman to Caroline Bryson, 8 June 1850 (9 June), J.W. Thompson MG (R)

MARRIAGES (MEIGS)
Hetty Ann Norman to Dillard L. McMillon q.v.
Yance Norman to Elizabeth Buckner, 27 July 1843 (28 July), Richard Simpson JP

MISCELLANEOUS (MEIGS)
Lafayette Norman: Mexican War (discharged)
Lafayette F. Norman: JP(?) 1845
Matthew Norman: Purchased Lot 81 in Decatur
Mitchell R. Norman: Cherokee Removal muster roll, 1836

- - - - - - - - - - - - -

NORRIS

1850 RHEA CENSUS
Elijah Norris 28 (Ga)(Farmer), Margaret J. 26, Luisa J. 2, Sarah M. 4/12 p. 632-631

- - - - - - - - - - - -

NORTON

1850 MEIGS CENSUS
Jonathan Norton 28 (Farmer), Louisa Jane 25, Elizabeth 2, James R. 1 p. 808-727

- - - - - - - - - - - - -

NORVILLE

MARRIAGES (RHEA)
Elizabeth G. Norville to Henry N. Whittenburg q.v.

- - - - - - - - - - - - -

OAKES

1840 MEIGS CENSUS
James W. Oakes 10001 - 00001 p. 235

MARRIAGES (RHEA)
James W. Oakes to Mary Ann Richardson, 25 June 1835 (27 June), D.L. Godsey MG, James B. Porter Bm (AR)

- - - - - - - - - - - - -

OBAR

MISCELLANEOUS (RHEA)
Robert Obar: Revolutionary War pensioner, 1835 list

- - - - - - - - - - - - -

ODEN

TAXES (RHEA)
1823 (Capt. Smith's Co.): Vincent Oden 1 WP

1830 RHEA CENSUS
Vincent Oden 11011 - 0001001 p. 384

MARRIAGES (RHEA)
Sally Oden to William Poynor q.v.
Vincent Oden to Levicey Lawson, 1 Jan 1822 (same), John Mitchell JP or MG (AR)

- - - - - - - - - - - - -

O'KELLY

1850 RHEA CENSUS
Benjamin O'Kelly 34 (NC), Cassander 35 (NC), Nancy E. 17 (NC), Martha J. 12, Mary S. 10, Kizziah E. 8, Francis M. 5, Clerissa A. 1, James D. 1 p. 623-565
Francis O'Kelly 63 (NC)(Farmer), Nancy 46 (NC), Thomas C. 17 (NC)(Farmer), Francis A. 15 (NC), Martha R. 12, Joseph M. 9, William H.H. 5, James S. 3, Julia A.C. 1, Mary DEAN 42 (NC), Martha R. DOBBS 22 p. 628-604

MARRIAGES (MEIGS)
Francis D. O'Kelly to Amelia F. Gerald [Fitzgerald], 14 Nov 1839 (same), B.F. McKenzie JP

MISCELLANEOUS (RHEA)
Charles O'Kelly: Bondsman for Henry Roach, 1834

- - - - - - - - - - - - -

OLDHAM

1830 RHEA CENSUS
John Oldham 101101 - 120001 p. 360

1850 MEIGS CENSUS
Sarah Oldham 35 p. 736-180

MISCELLANEOUS (MEIGS)
John Oldham: Common School Commissioner, Dist 6, 1838
" " On Circuit Court jury, 1836
" " House used to hold elections in District 6
" " Hiwassee District, Moore's Chapel area

- - - - - - - - - - - - -

OLINGER

1840 MEIGS CENSUS
Daniel Olinger 01021001 - 00102001 p. 228

1850 MEIGS CENSUS
Jacob Olinger 49 (Va)(Blacksmith), Margaret 40 (NC), Delilah 25, Mary 22, Elizabeth 20, Nancy 18, Rebecca 15, George 11, Joel 6, Jacob 5 p. 729-125

MARRIAGES (RHEA)
Mary Olinger to Abner Hughes q.v.

- - - - - - - - - - - - -

OLIVER

MARRIAGES (RHEA)
Polly Oliver to Edmund Howerton q.v.
Susan Oliver to James Gasque q.v.

- - - - - - - - - - - - -

O'NEAL / O'NEEL

1830 RHEA CENSUS
A. Oneel 311101 - 1011 p. 368

1840 MEIGS CENSUS
Abraham O'Neal 0222001 - 0010001 p. 227

MARRIAGES (MEIGS)
Blackburn O'Neal to Jane Lawson, 22 Nov 1845
John J. O'Neal to Mary Ann Moore, 23 July 1844 (30 July), Jessee Locke MG
Mary O'Neal to Washington Tims q.v.

- - - - - - - - - - - - -

ORME

MISCELLANEOUS (RHEA)
James Orme: Bondsman for William W. Pile, 1832

- - - - - - - - - - - - -

ORR / ORE

TAXES (RHEA)
1819 (Capt. John Lewis' Dist.): William Orr 1 WP
1823 (Capt. Lewis' Co.): William Orr 1 WP
1830 RHEA CENSUS
Sarah Orr 022200 - 0 [sic] p. 359
1840 RHEA CENSUS
John Orr 00021 - 0000201001
Sarah Orr 00021 - 0000201001 [sic]
MARRIAGES (RHEA)
John Orr to Emaline Majors, 16 Sept 1839 (19 Sept), William H. Bell MG, Joseph Hicks Bm (AR)
Jane Orr to Solomon Dannel q.v.
Martin Orr to Manerva T. Riggle, 29 Mar 1847 (no return) (R)

- - - - - - - - - - - - -

OSBORNE

1830 RHEA CENSUS
Mary Osborne 0001 - 000001 p. 362

- - - - - - - - - - - - -

OUTLAW

1830 RHEA CENSUS
Reddie Outlaw 12101 - 00001 p. 373
MISCELLANEOUS (RHEA)
Alexander Outlaw: Bm for Mathew W. McClellan, 1814

- - - - - - - - - - - - -

OVERSTREET

MARRIAGES (RHEA)
John Overstreet to Elizabeth Henry, 13 Sept 1810, Robert Neely Bm (A)
MISCELLANEOUS (RHEA)
John Overstreet: Bondsman for Samuel Sherrill, 1810

- - - - - - - - - - - - -

OWEN / OWENS

TAXES (RHEA)
1819 (Capt. Wm McCray's Co.): Henry Owen 1 WP
1823 (Capt. Howerton's Co.): John Owen 1 WP
1830 RHEA CENSUS
Alexander Owen 30001 - 0000101 p. 392
Henry Owens 12000001 - 01010001 p. 391
J. F. Owens 1021001 - 110001 p. 378
John Owens 22001 - 00101 p. 365
Jno Owens 31001 - 01001 p. 389
1850 RHEA CENSUS
John Owens 43 (Ga)(Farmer), Rebecca 22, Nancy 2 p. 569-215

1850 MEIGS CENSUS
Aaron Owen 28 (SC)(Farmer), Lucinda 40 (SC), John WALLEN 47 (SC)(Farmer), Love Ann 10, Martha E. 8, Mary C. 4 p. 764-400
George P. Owen 42 (Farmer) p. 792-616
Jesse Owen 36 (Farmer), Mary 34, Mary E. 17, Nancy L. 15, Margaret 13, George A. 9, Eliza Ann 8, Cyntha C. 6, William M. 5 p. 791-610

MARRIAGES (RHEA)
Andrew Owens to Dardant Majors, 12 Mar 1834 (15 Mar), John Pardee MMEC, Orville Paine Bm (AR)
Charlotte Owens to Isaac Lewis q.v.
Clarassy Owens to Allen Blevins q.v.
Eliza Owens to John Swafford q.v.
James H. Owens to Catherine Moore, 4 May 1809, Daniel Swan Bm (A)
John Owens to Peggy Thompson, 9 Dec 1819 (same), Jonathan Fine JP, Absolom Burns Bm (AR)
Jonathan Owens to Betsey Knox, 3 Nov 1819, John Knight Bm (A)
Phebe Owens to James Rogers q,v,
Polly Owens to John Knight q.v.
William Owens to Nancy Gear or Lear, 12 Sept 1812 (16 Sept), William Long JP, Richard Philpot Bm (AR)

MARRIAGES (MEIGS)
Dicy Ann Owen to Samuel Jones q.v.
Elizabeth Ann Owens to Ezekiel Marshall q.v.
James M. Owens to Susanna Reynolds, 14 Aug 1849 (16 Aug), Jesse Locke MG
John Owens to Rebecca Yonas, 7 Jan 1847, "Executed as directed and returned to office" Thos V. Atchley JP, Drury L. Godsey Bm
John Owens to Rebecca Yonas, 13 Jan 1847 (same) [the above record was listed thusly and may represent the date it was returned to the office]

MISCELLANEOUS (RHEA)
Alexander Owens: Bondsman for James Rogers, 1831
Andrew Owens: Bondsman for Dickenson Jennings, 1834
John Owens: Indicted by first Grand Jury
Thomas Owens: Bondsman for John Armstrong, 1819

- - - - - - - - - - - - -

PACE

1850 RHEA CENSUS
Hardy Pace 72 (NC)(Hatter): see Solomon Henry

- - - - - - - - - - - - -

PAGE

TAXES (RHEA)
1819 (Capt. John Ramsey's Co.): John Page 1 WP
MARRIAGES (RHEA)
Ann Ivy Page or Payne to Alexander M. Robeson q.v.
Woodson Page to Martha Clifton, 16 Sept 1830, John Parker Bm (A)

- - - - - - - - - - - - -

PAINE / PAYNE

TAXES (RHEA)
1819 (Capt. John Lewis' Co.): Orville Paine 1 WP, 200a
1823 (Capt. Lewis' Co.): Orville Paine 1 WP, 201a
Walter Payne 1 WP
(Capt. Brown's Co.): Thomas D. Paine 1 WP
1830 RHEA CENSUS
Orville Paine 100011 - 00011 p. 394
1840 RHEA CENSUS
Orville Paine 1110201 - 110001
1840 MEIGS CENSUS
James M. Payne 0001 - 1001 p. 244
Joseph Payne 1211001 - 3202001 p. 244
1850 RHEA CENSUS
Orville Paine 50 (Farmer), Elvira 40, Horatio 20 (Student of Medicine), Flavius J. 18 (Farmer), Orpha J. 16, Evelina 14, Hanibal 11, Mary 7, Angelina 4, Alfred 2 p. 596-379
MARRIAGES (RHEA)
Ann Ivy Payne or Page to Alexander M. Robeson q.v.
Altimira Payne to Cornelius Moyers q.v.
Emmaline Paine to George W. Rice q.v.
Minerva Paine to James Bean q.v.
Nancy Paine to John C. Simpson q.v.
Orville Paine to Elvira Locke, 19 Oct 1828, Samuel R. Hackett Bm (A)
[Orville, son of William and Orpha Paine; Elvira, dau of John and Mary J. Moore Locke]
Walter R. Paine to Peggy Chambers, 16 Oct 1822 (17 Oct), John Rice JP, Jacob Brown Bm (AR)
MARRIAGES (MEIGS)
Matilda T. Paine to William Eawin or Erwin q.v.
MISCELLANEOUS (RHEA)
Bird Paine: Bondsman for John S. Evens, 1838
" " Doctor; bro of Orville
Orville Paine: Bondsman for William Hope, 1825
" " Bondsman for Andrew Owens, 1834

\- - - - - - - - - - - -

PANNEL

1830 RHEA CENSUS
Thomas Pannel 21001 - 20001 p. 376

\- - - - - - - - - - - -

PANTHER

1830 RHEA CENSUS
Joseph Panther 2100001 - 0110001 p. 387

\- - - - - - - - - - - -

PARDO / PARDOE / PARDEE

1830 RHEA CENSUS
John Pardo 100001 - 2000001 p. 389
1840 RHEA CENSUS
John Pardoe 00100001 - 00020001
MISCELLANEOUS (RHEA)
John Pardee: MMEC 1831-1836

\- - - - - - - - - - - -

PARE

MISCELLANEOUS (MEIGS)
John A. Pare: Private, Mexican War

\- - - - - - - - - - - -

PARISH / PARRISH

1840 MEIGS CENSUS
Phillip P. Parish 100001 - 10001 p. 235
MISCELLANEOUS (MEIGS)
Stephen Parrish: Tanner in Decatur

\- - - - - - - - - - - -

PARKER

TAXES (RHEA)
1819 (Capt. McGill's Co.): Elijah Parker 1 WP
(Capt. Bradley's Dist.): John Parker 1 WP, 1 Town Lot
John S. Parker 1 WP
1823 (Capt. Howard's Co.): Elisha Parker 2 BP
(Capt. Brown's Co.): John Parker 1 WP, 2 Town Lots
(Capt. Smith's Co.): William Parker 1 WP
1830 RHEA CENSUS
Alvice [Alvia] Parker 120001 - 001001 p. 362
Berry G. Parker 00001 - 001 p. 361
Eli Parker 110001 - 10001 p. 369
Francis Parker 1011 - 011101 p. 363
G. G. Parker 10001 - 00001 p. 363
Hannah Parker 01 - 10000001 p. 383
John Parker 0011302 - 02002 p. 383
John H. Parker 10001 - 10001 p. 361
Johnsey Parker 10001 - 20001 p. 361
Solomon Parker 00001001 - 00000001 p. 362
Thomas Parker 00001 - 0001 p. 361
William Parker 0000001 - 0021001 p. 361
1840 RHEA CENSUS
John H. Parker 210001 - 011001
Thomas Parker 000001 - 11001
1840 MEIGS CENSUS
Eli Parker 0120001 - 101001 p. 246
1850 RHEA CENSUS
Eli Parker 51 (NC)(Farmer), Prudence 42, Greenbury G. 25 (School Teacher), Margaret J. 22, William J. 21 (Farmer), Daniel 17 (Farmer), Eleanor 12, Elizabeth 9, Malinda 6, Prudence 4 p. 557-148
MARRIAGES (RHEA)
Armenta Parker to Joseph Dyer q.v.
Benjamin G. Parker to Susannah Hudson, 24 Feb 1830 (2 Mar), Beal Gaither JP, Thomas Parker Bm (AR)
Elisha Parker to Patsy James, 26 Sept 1818 (27 Sept), F. David JP, Henry Airheart Bm (AR)
Elizabeth Parker to James Reese q.v.
Greenberry J. or G. Parker to Catherine Rice, 7 May 1827 (20 May), Beal Gaither JP, Isaac Baker Bm (AR)
Harriet Parker to Wiley McCoy q.v.
James H. Parker to Mary Miller, 8 Mar 1842, Hughlett W. Smith Bm (A)
John Parker to Polly Dearmon, 19 Aug 1819 (same), John Moore JP, John Robinson Bm (AR)
John Parker to Sally Reney or Revely, 24 Oct 1827 (25 Oct), John Cozby JP, Charles Revely Bm (AR)

Johnsey Parker to Mahulda Chastain, 26 July 1824 (same), William Gamble JP, Jonathan Fry Bm (AR)
Mary Parker to John Hughs q.v.
Nancy Parker to Pulaski Poe q.v.
Philip Parker to Catherine A. Jenkins, 23 Sept 1834, Edward Goad Bm (A)
Philip Parker to Rhoda Crawford, 29 Sept 1840 (same), Jacob Gwin JP (A)
Priscilla Parker to Jacob Plowman q.v.
Sarah Ann Parker to William H. Williams q.v.
Thomas Parker to Nancy Chastain, 9 Mar 1830 (9 Mar or 3 May), Beal Gaither JP (AR)

MISCELLANEOUS (RHEA)

Bassel Parker: Bondsman for Thomas Gaither, 1833
Benjamin Parker: Bondsman for William C. Bell, 1831
" " Clerk, Fellowship Baptist Church of Christ, 1828-29
Harriet Parker: Member, Fellowship Church, 1828-29
Huldah Parker: Member, Fellowship Church, 1828-29
John Parker: Purchased Lot 11, Town of Washington
" " Bondsman for John Harris Smith, 1815
" " Bondsman for John S. Newton, 1817
" " Bondsman for Alexander Sapp, 1818
" " Bondsman for George W. Acre, 1822
" " Bondsman for Robert Stockton, 1824
" " Bondsman for John H. Beck, 1825
" " Bondsman for Woodson Page, 1830
" " Bondsman for Laben B. Rowden, 1831
" " Bondsman for James Engledow, 1831
" " Bondsman for Henry Griffith, 1832
" " Bondsman for Pleasant Manner, 1832
John H. Parker: Member, Fellowship Baptist Ch, 1828-29
Johnsey Parker: Member, Fellowship Baptist Ch, 1828-29
" " Bondsman for John Chastain, 1828
Solomon Parker: Member, Fellowship Baptist Ch, 1828-29
Thomas Parker: Bondsman for Benjamin G. Parker, 1830
" " Member, Fellowship Baptist Ch, 1828-29

MISCELLANEOUS (MEIGS)

Eli Parker: Common School Commissioner, Dist 5, 1838
Elisha Parker: Hiwassee District, Moore's Chapel area
John Parker: Hiwassee District, Concord area
Solomon Parker: Hiwassee District, Pinhook Ferry area

- - - - - - - - - - - - -

PARKS

TAXES (RHEA)

1819 (Capt. John Lewis' Dist.): Robert Parks 1 WP, 220a
1823 (Capt. Lewis' Co.): Robert Parks 1 WP, 100a

1850 RHEA CENSUS

Joseph Parks 1: see George W. Short

MARRIAGES (RHEA)

Eliza Parks to George W. Short q.v.
Margaret Parks to Allison Howard q.v.
Mariah Parks to Mansion Howard q.v.
Mary Parks to Josiah Smith q.v.
Miller E. Parks to Manerva Vanpelt, 31 Mar 1846 (same), Jesse P. Thompson JP (R)

MISCELLANEOUS (RHEA)

John Parks: Bondsman for Henry Tuttle, 1814
Joseph Parks: Mexican War

- - - - - - - - - - - - -

PARKHILL

TAXES (RHEA)

1819 (Capt. McGill's Co.): David Parkhill 1 WP

MISCELLANEOUS (RHEA)

David Parkhill: Lot 1, Town of Washington, 1814

- - - - - - - - - - - - -

PARKSDALE

MARRIAGES (RHEA)

Nathan Parksdale to Rebecca Birdwell, 31 Oct 1833 (same), John Randles JP (R)

- - - - - - - - - - - - -

PARMER

MARRIAGES (RHEA)

William Parmer to Visey Hardin, 21 Mar 1829 (25 Mar), Beal Gaither JP (AR)

MISCELLANEOUS (MEIGS)

Everett Parmer: Cherokee Removal muster roll, 1836

- - - - - - - - - - - - -

PARSONS

MARRIAGES (RHEA)

Nancy Parsons to Thomas Stokes q.v.

MARRIAGES (MEIGS)

Emanuel Parsons to Rebecca McDowell, 27 Nov 1843, James McDowel Sur(?)
Joseph M. Parsons to Partena Crawford, 12 Aug 1843 (14 Aug), John Seabern JP, David Lewis Sur(?)

MISCELLANEOUS (RHEA)

Enoch Parsons: Lot 2, Town of Washington

- - - - - - - - - - - - -

PASS

1850 RHEA CENSUS

James H. Pass 26 (NC)(Millwright), Eleanor 26 (NC), William W. 5 (NC), Emily F. 3 (NC), Martha A. 1 (NC) p. 600-408

- - - - - - - - - - - - -

PASSENGER

1830 RHEA CENSUS

George Passenger 10100001 - 00110001 p. 385

- - - - - - - - - - - - -

PATE

1850 MEIGS CENSUS

Iredell Pate 30 (Farmer), Elizabeth 27, Samuel 19, Frances C.J. 8, Mary Ann 4, John W. 1 p. 785-572

- - - - - - - - - - - - -

PATTEN

1830 RHEA CENSUS
Uriah Patten 002000001 - 0001001 p. 379

- - - - - - - - - - - - -

PATTERSON

TAXES (RHEA)
1808 (James Campbell's List): Robert Patterson 1 WP
1840 MEIGS CENSUS
James Patterson 011101 - 211001 p. 239
1850 RHEA CENSUS
Alexander T. Patterson 43 (Cabnetmaker), Leah 38, James D. 21 (Farmer), Jane R. 19, Flora E. 15, Flavius J. 13, Octavas 11, Esther E. 8, Nathaniel E. 5, Cornelius E. 2 p. 586-340
1850 MEIGS CENSUS
James Patterson 48 (NC)(Farmer), Mary 45 (Va), William W. 25 (Farmer), Newton A. 22 (Farmer), Tursey A. 18, Martin L. 15 (Farmer), Elizabeth S. 13, Kissiah Jane 10, Mary M. 4, James M. 1 p. 800-676
Washington Patterson 33 (SC)(Farmer), Mary Ann 27 (NC), Cynthia Ann 7, Wilson 6, Asbury 5, Julian 3, George 1 p. 765-409 [Washington married Mary Ann Collier on 13 Sept 1838 in McMinn County]
MARRIAGES (RHEA)
Alfred N. Patterson to Mary M. Gamble, 1 Apr 1828 (same), James McDonald JP, John Patterson Bm (AR)
Polly Patterson to Terry Riddle q.v.
MISCELLANEOUS (RHEA)
John Patterson: Bondsman for Alfred W. Patterson, 1828
Robert Patterson: Bondsman for John Carroll, 1810
" " Bondsman for Terry Riddle, 1819
" " On Board of Commissioners for Town of Washington, 1812-1813
" " Purchased Lot 83 in Town of Washington
MISCELLANEOUS (MEIGS)
James Patterson: Common School Com., Dist 7, 1838
" " JP 1838-1841

- - - - - - - - - - - - -

PAUL

TAXES (RHEA)
1819 (Capt. Wm McCray's Co.): Moses Paul 1 WP, 230a
1823 (Capt. Howerton's Co.): Archibald D. Paul 1 WP
James Paul 1 WP
Moses Paul 230a Piney Ri

1830 RHEA CENSUS
A. D. Paul 00001 - 31001 p. 389
James A. Paul 21001 - 01001 p. 391
Moses F. Paul 00001001 - 00000001 p. 391
Thomas G. Paul 00001 - 00001 p. 391
W. Paul 100001 - 20001 p. 377
1840 RHEA CENSUS
Archibald D. Paul 1000001 - 0032101
Martin E. Paul 301001 - 1001
1840 MEIGS CENSUS
James S. Paul 210001 - 010001 p. 246
1850 RHEA CENSUS
Archibald D. Paul 50 (SC)(Farmer), Cyntha 47, Cyrena M. 24, Myra W. 23, Calista E. 19, Narcissa E. 17, Nancy C. 14, Vaun A. 12, Saphrona A. 9, Amanda F. 5 p. 557-143
1850 MEIGS CENSUS
James Paul 87 (Va): see John L. Aikman
James S. Paul 51 (Farmer), James W. 18 (Farmer), Martha Jane 17, Benjamin J. 14, Mary Ann 8, John H. 1 p. 817-800
MARRIAGES (RHEA)
James Paul to Ann Brown, 5 Sept 1821 (6 Sept), Jonathan Fine JP, Archibald D. Paul Bm (AR)
John Paul to Elizabeth Hornsby, 19 Apr 1832, John F. Paul Bm (A)
Margaret J. Paul to Nicholas H. Long q.v.
Martin E. Paul to Martha Cruese, 18 July 1829, John F. Paul Bm (A)
Thomas Paul to Sarah Ervin, 10 July 1830, John F. Paul Bm (A)
MISCELLANEOUS (RHEA)
Archibald D. Paul: JP 1837-40, 1845-46; Hiwassee Dist.
" " " Bondsman for James Paul, 1821
John F. Paul: Bondsman for Richard Haynes, 1829
" " " Bondsman for Martin E. Paul, 1829
" " " Bondsman for Thomas Paul, 1830
" " " Bondsman for John Paul, 1832
" " " Bondsman for Henry Garrison, 1834
Martin E. Paul: MG (EPD) 1839-40

- - - - - - - - - - - - -

PEAK

1840 MEIGS CENSUS
Jacob Peak 13041 - 000001 p. 244
Luke Peak 000101 - 00001 p. 246
Newton Peak 00001 - 0001 p. 239
1850 MEIGS CENSUS
Jacob Peak 49 (Farmer), Kissiah 43, James 20 (Farmer), William C. 18 (Farmer), Luke 16 (Farmer), Standerfer 11, Mary Jane 8, Charlotte 6, Sarah E. 5, Margaret 1 p. 788-589
Luke Peak 42 (Farmer), Malinda H. 36, Lucinda Jane 8, Thomas J. 7, James K.P. 5, William D. 3, Mary B. 2 p. 788-593
MARRIAGES (MEIGS)
Newton Peak to Netty Ann McCollon, 15 Nov 1839 (16 Nov), Pryor Neal JP or MG
MISCELLANEOUS (MEIGS)
Jacob Peak: Trustee, Decatur Academy, 1840
" " Owned store at Pinhook Landing

- - - - - - - - - - - - -

PEARSON / PIERSON / PERSON

TAXES (RHEA)
1819 (Capt. McGill's Co.): John Pierson 1 WP, 71a
Sarah Person 41a
MARRIAGES (RHEA)
John Person or Pearson to Susanna Ellis, 21 or 27 Jan 1817 (same), Jonathan Fine JP, Jas C. Mitchell Bm (AR)
Polly Pearson to John Campbell q.v.
Sarah Pearson to James Steen q.v.

MISCELLANEOUS (RHEA)
Edward Pearson or Edmond Pierson: JP or MG 1826-27
John Pearson: Bondsman for John Campbell, 1816

- - - - - - - - - - - - -

PEARCE / PIERCE / PEIRCE

TAXES (RHEA)
1823 (Capt. Lewis' Co.): Cimmy Pierce 1 WP
(Capt. Jackson's Co.): Robert Pierce 1 WP, 2 BP
1830 RHEA CENSUS
William Pierce 0100001 - 200010001 p. 369
1840 RHEA CENSUS
James Pierce 00221001 - 2001201
John Pierce 210201 - 230001
1840 MEIGS CENSUS
James Pierce 00010001 - 003 p. 228
Lovina Pierce 1101 - 012001 p. 233
Robert Pearce or Pence 101001 - 211001 p. 226
William H. Pierce 20001 - 00001 p. 228
1850 RHEA CENSUS
James Pearce 61 (Farmer), Rachael 57, Eliza J. 31, William D. 29 (Farmer), James C. 27 (Farmer), Samuel D. 25 (Student), Leander 21 (Farmer), Elbert D. 19 (Farmer), Viney 15, Juli E. 12 p. 600-407
Joseph Pearce 20 (NC)(Apprentice Tanner): see Jas J. Able
Margaret Pearce 48 (Va), James 28 (School Teacher), John 26 (Farmer), Sarah S. 17, Susannah S. 16, Thomas S. 14, Robert J. 11, Margaret P. 9 p. 630-616
1850 MEIGS CENSUS
Elizabeth Pearce 40, Racheal 22, James 20, Jane 12, Vanburen 10, William C. 8, Joseph 6, Sarah 4 p. 726-105
James Pearce 68 (Va)(Farmer), Mary 60 (NC), Sarah 26 (NC) p. 748-281
Stephen Pearce 40 (Va)(Farmer), Elizabeth 37 (NC), James M. 17, Martha C. 14, Thomas 12, Mary Jane 9, Margaret 7, Wm 5, Alfred 3, Daniel 1 p. 747-280
William H. Pearce 39 (Va)(Farmer), Nancy 34, Moses 10, Catharine 7, Stephen 6, Mary 3 p. 753-327
MARRIAGES (RHEA)
Mahala E. Pierce to Alfred Collins q.v.
Melisa Pearce to Anderson Cooper q.v.
Sarah Pearce to Thomas F. Jack q.v.
Sarah A. Pearce to John Morgan q.v.
Susannah Pierce to David Campbell q.v.
William Pierce to Louvina or Lovina Gillespie, 6 May 1819 (same), John Moore JP, Thomas Kelly Bm (AR)
MARRIAGES (MEIGS)
Elizabeth Pearce to Frederic T.C. Ford q.v.
Franklin Pierce to Sarah Herrid, 28 Aug 1845 (same), B.F. McKenzie JP, Thomas Leuty Sur(?)
James Pearce to Mary Day, 25 Jan 1841 (4 Feb), B.F. McKenzie JP, Jesse Taylor Sur(?)
James P. Pierce to Mrs. Katherine Day, 19 Sept 1843 (same), B.F. McKenzie JP, John K. Edds Sur(?)
July Ann Peirce to Harvey McKenzie q.v.
Philip Pierce to Elizabeth Mahon, 19 Feb 1845 (20 Feb), M.C. Atchley MG
Prudy Ann Peirce to John Edds q.v.
Sarah M. Peirce to Henry M. Miller q.v.
Sariah Peirce to Moses H. Edds q.v.
William F. Pierce to Eleanor Hill, 15 Sept 1846 (16 Sept), James Pierce MG
MISCELLANEOUS (RHEA and MEIGS)
Arthur Pierce: Bondsman for Squire Burton, 1822
Franklin Pierce: JP(?) 1844
James Pierce: MG 1846-49
Philip Pierce: JP(?) 1845
Robert Pearce: Blacksmith, Cherokee Removal muster roll, 1837
William Pierce: Purchased lot in Cottonport

- - - - - - - - - - - - -

PELFRY / PELPHRAY

1850 MEIGS CENSUS
Nathan Pelfry 30 (Farmer), Elizabeth 27, Louisa Jane 7, Mary Ann 4, William B. 3 p. 816-765
MARRIAGES (MEIGS)
Nathan Pelfrey to Elizabeth Ford, 9 July 1841 (11 July), Leroy Looney JP, Joseph Mosses Sur(?)
MISCELLANEOUS (RHEA)
Nathan Pelphray: Bondsman for Andrew Johnson, 1835

- - - - - - - - - - - - -

PENDERGRASS

1840 MEIGS CENSUS
John Pendergrass 120001 - 210111 p. 224
MISCELLANEOUS (MEIGS)
John Pendergrass: MG 1849

- - - - - - - - - - - - -

PENNINGTON

1850 MEIGS CENSUS
James Pennington 31 (SC)(Farmer), Jane 28, Jasper N. 2 p. 776-502 [James married Jane Vincent on 8 Nov 1842 in McMinn County]

- - - - - - - - - - - - -

PENNY / PINNY

MARRIAGES (RHEA)
Thomas M. Penny to Linda Garr or Lindsey Gan, 2 Nov 1822 (7 Nov), James McDonald JP (AR)
MARRIAGES (MEIGS)
Miles P. Penny to Mary Ann Bean, 26 Aug 1848 (31 Aug), William Johns JP, John M. Lillard Sur(?)
MISCELLANEOUS (RHEA)
Thomas Pinny: Bondsman for Finney Rawlins, 1812

- - - - - - - - - - - - -

PEPPERS

MARRIAGES (RHEA)
Eliza Peppers to Robert C. Johnson q.v.

- - - - - - - - - - - - -

PERCY / PURSEY / PEARCY / PIERCY

TAXES (RHEA)
1819 (Capt. John Lewis' Co.): James J. Pursey 1 WP
1830 RHEA CENSUS
James Pearcy 101001 - 11002 p. 393
1840 RHEA CENSUS
James Percy 01001001 - 10201001
1840 MEIGS CENSUS
Thomas Piercy 00001 - 0001 p. 233
MARRIAGES (RHEA)
Leney Percy to Jefferson Hughes q.v.
MISCELLANEOUS (RHEA)
Miller Percy: Bondsman for Henry Fisher, 1843

- - - - - - - - - - - - -

PERKINS

1830 RHEA CENSUS
Benjamin Perkins 000001 - 000101 p. 392
MISCELLANEOUS (RHEA)
Benjamin Perkins: Bondsman for Samuel Quinton, 1830

- - - - - - - - - - - - -

PERREMON

TAXES (RHEA)
1819 (Capt. McCray's Co.): John Perremon 1 WP, 200a

- - - - - - - - - - - - -

PERRIGIN / PEREGIN / PERIGIN

1840 RHEA CENSUS
Sarah Perigin 001 - 00011001
1850 RHEA CENSUS
James L. Perrigin 24, Faraby 20 (SC), Sarah E. 2, John H. 10/12 p. 621-551
MARRIAGES (RHEA)
J.W.L. Peregin to Fereby Tally, 3 July 1847, John S. Evens JP (R)
Sarah Perigin to Aley R. Houpt q.v.

- - - - - - - - - - - - -

PERRY / PERRIN / PERREN

1830 RHEA CENSUS
Betsy [Beaty?] Perrin 00001 - 20001 p. 389
1840 RHEA CENSUS
Beaty Perry 200001 - 022001
1850 MEIGS CENSUS
Allen Perry 25 (NC)(Farmer), Matilda 23, Sarah 5, Mary E. 4, Martha C. 2, James F. 1 p. 745-259
Noah Perry 22 (Farmer), Jane 18, Susannah 1, Ruth 66 p. 746-265
MARRIAGES (RHEA)
Beatty Perren to Betsey Thompson, 18 Dec 1823 (same), Fred Fulkerson JP (AR)
Beaty Perrin to Betsy Thompson, 18 Dec 1824 (same), James Thompson Bm (A) [NOTE: this record was listed twice by Allen, but with different years]
MARRIAGES (MEIGS)
Celia Perry to Levin S. Coffey q.v.
Mary Perry to Thomas C. Stokes q.v.
Noah Perry to Jane Mavity, 25 Sept 1847, T.C. Stokes JP(?)
MISCELLANEOUS (RHEA and MEIGS)
Eli Perry: Hiwassee District
James Perry: Lot 3 in Town of Washington
Noah Perry: Private, Mexican War
Rufus Perry: Surety for Edmond Lawson, 1850

- - - - - - - - - - - - -

PETERS

TAXES (RHEA)
1819 (Capt. W.S. Bradley's Dist.): Joseph Peters 100a
1823 (Capt. Brown's Co.): Bruten Peters 1 WP
1830 RHEA CENSUS
Aggy Peters 11001 - 122201 p. 365
1840 RHEA CENSUS
Aggy Peters 00101 - 0203001
1850 RHEA CENSUS
Agness Peters 55 (Va), Nancy 32, Elizabeth 28, Cyntha 22, Benjamin F. 19 (Farmer) p. 583-329
MARRIAGES (RHEA)
C.I. Peters to A.P. Caldwell q.v.
Catharine Peters to William Rector q.v.
Harriet I. Peters to William Hounshell q.v.
Mary A. Peters to Linsey McCary q.v.
MISCELLANEOUS (RHEA and MEIGS)
Bruten Peters: Bondsman for Richard Manly, 1822
John Peters: Hiwasssee District
Joseph Peters: Married Margaret McGill of Soddy
Joseph B. Peters: Bondsman for William W. Lea, 1840

- - - - - - - - - - - - -

PETERSON

1830 RHEA CENSUS
Joseph Peterson 1210001 - 101201 p. 366
1840 RHEA CENSUS
Joseph Peterson 01211001 - 0010101
1850 RHEA CENSUS
Joseph Peterson 62 (NC)(Farmer), Mahala 54 (NC), Luisa 18 (Ala), John 16 (Farmer) p. 613-450
Parmelia H. Peterson 22, John I. 2, Hannah J. 3/12, Robert 21 (Apprentice Blacksmith) p. 613-449
1850 MEIGS CENSUS
Thomas Peterson 22 (Farmer), Sarah Ann 21, Mahala 1 p. 770-451
MARRIAGES (RHEA)
Charles W. Peterson to Permelia I. Murphy, 28 June 1845 (same), J.S. Evens JP (AR)
Elizabeth Peterson to Stephen Thompson q.v.
Louisa Peterson to Russell A. Thompson q.v.
Thomas Peterson to Sarah Poe, 21 Sept 1848 (same), James H. Locke JP (R)
MISCELLANEOUS (RHEA)
C. W. Peterson: Bondsman for James T. Nanny, 1845
Lewis Peterson: Bondsman for John Acre, 1819
Thomas Peterson: Private, Mexican War

- - - - - - - - - - - - -

PETTIT / PETTET / PETIT

1830 RHEA CENSUS
Sarah Pettet 0101 - 211101 p. 377
1840 MEIGS CENSUS
James Petit 10001 - 00001 p. 227
Sarah Petit 0001 - 10212001 p. 227
1850 MEIGS CENSUS
Sarah Pettet 50 (NC), Sally Jane 34 (Ky), Susan 7, Gideon 4, Charlotte 4, Joseph 2 p. 731-140
MARRIAGES (RHEA)
Betsy Petet to Levy Garen q.v.
Eliza Pettit to Charles Johnson q.v.
MARRIAGES (MEIGS)
Eliza Pettitt to Charles McCarroll q.v.
James Pettit to Martha Stout, 1 Dec 1841 (2 Dec), A. King MG, Benjamin F. Locke Sur
Polly Pettitt to Martin Lawson q.v.
Susanna Petitt to James Burtz q.v.
MISCELLANEOUS (MEIGS)
Gideon Petitt: Ocoee District
James Petitt: Ocoee District

- - - - - - - - - - - - -

PHARIS / PHARRIS / PHARISS / PHEARIS

TAXES (RHEA)
1823 (Capt. Piper's Co.): James Pharis 1 WP
John Pharis 1 WP
Robert Pharis 480a
Samuel Pharis 1 WP
1830 RHEA CENSUS
Isaac Pharis 120001 - 101101001 p. 359
John Pharis 20001 - 111001 p. 359
Robert Pharis 20401001001 - 00010201001 p. 358
1840 MEIGS CENSUS
Hugh L. Phariss 20001 - 00001 p. 241
James Phariss 212001 - 011101 p. 242
John Phariss 1311001 - 101011 p. 241
John L. Pharess 3010001 - 0211 p. 229
Robert Phariss 022022002 - 4000030011 p. 241
Stephen Phariss 20001 - 10001 p. 224
MARRIAGES (RHEA)
Hetty Pharis to Abraham Brown q.v.
Hugh Pharris to Peggy Sears, 23 Dec 1834 (24 or 25 Dec), James Willis MG, Abraham Brown Bm (AR)
James Pharris or Phearis to Elizabeth Brady, 29 Mar 1822 (31 Mar), John Farmer MG, Saml Pharis Bm (AR)
Nancy Pharis to Peter L. Pharis q.v.
Peter L. Pharis to Nancy Pharis, 25 Mar 1835, Timothy F. French Bm (A)
Rachel Pharis to Robert Doak q.v.
Rebecca Pharis to Bethwill Gaddy q.v.
Sidney Pharris to Robert Kellison q.v.
MARRIAGES (MEIGS)
Doctor Pharis to Eliza Ledbetter, 16 Feb 1842 (7 Feb), Jas H. Hague JP, William Cudgenton Sur(?)
Francis M. Phariss to Charity Bunch, 4 Mar 1843 (same), D.L. Godsey MG, Martin Bunch Bm or Sur
Nancy Pharis to William Crudjungton q.v.
Rebecca Faress to Stephen Maner q.v.
William Phariss to Elizabeth Goalden, 18 Jan 1840 (same), James Patterson JP, J.H. Cudgington Sur
MISCELLANEOUS (RHEA and MEIGS)
Hugh Pharis: Bondsman for John Buster, 1833
John Pharis: Hiwassee District, Moore's Chapel area
John L. Pharis: Cherokee Removal muster roll, 1836
Peter Pharis: Bondsman for Archibald McKissick, 1834
Robert Pharis: Hiwassee District, Moore's Chapel area
Samuel Pharis: Bondsman for James Pharris, 1822
" " Hiwassee District
S. Phariss: Elder, Concord Baptist Church of Christ, 1824
Stephen Phariss: Employed in Navigation according to 1840 Meigs Census

- - - - - - - - - - - - -

PHILLIPS / PHILIP

TAXES (RHEA)
1808 (John Henry's List): Benonley Phillips 1 WP
1840 MEIGS CENSUS
Elihu Phillips 00001 - 0001 p. 239
Jacob Phillips 230001 - 140001 p. 245
Martha Phillips 0 - 101001 p. 240
Reuben Phillips 121001 - 110101 p. 232
Reuben Phillips 11130001 - 2020001 p. 239
[1 may have been marked through]
1850 MEIGS CENSUS
Elihu Phillips 34 (Farmer), Lucinda 10, Margaret 8, Mary Ann 6, Sarah E. 3 p. 798-668
James Phillips 22 (Farmer), Margarett 24, Nancy C. 0 p. 748-282
Martha Phillips 45 (NC), Manda M. 12, Jane DAVIS 60 (NC) p. 802-689
Reuben Phillips 60 (Farmer), Alma 52, Kissiah Jane 14, Martha M. 12, Columbus 11 p. 798-667
MARRIAGES (RHEA)
Mary Phillips to Elijah M. Hall q.v.
Milley Phillips to John Carroll q.v.
Polly Phillips to Alfred Danby q.v.
Reuben Phillips to Anny Fike, 21 Nov 1835, William Crow Bm (A)
William Phillips to Martha Davis, 15 July 1826 (17 July), Wm C. Wilson JP, Robert Jordan Bm (AR)
MARRIAGES (MEIGS)
Drucilla Phillips to William Mabary q.v.
Elihu Phillips to Elizabeth Fyke, 7 Jan 1840, John Bower MG
Elizabeth J. Phillips to William Fitch q.v.
James Phillips to Margaret Day, 2 Oct 1849 (4 Oct), James Pierce MG
Mary Phillips to John Reed q.v.
MISCELLANEOUS (MEIGS)
Elihu Phillips: JP(?) 1844
Reuben Phillips: Ocoee District

- - - - - - - - - - - - - -

PHILPOT / PHILPOTT

1830 RHEA CENSUS
Alexander Philpot 1100101 - 20020101 p. 371
1840 MEIGS CENSUS
Alexander Philpot 00100001 - 00002 p. 229

MARRIAGES (RHEA)
Elizabeth Philpot to James Johnson q.v.
Hanson Philpot to Elizabeth Mahan, 25 Dec 1829, James Blakely Bm (A)
Patsey Philpot to Cain Gentry q.v.
MARRIAGES (MEIGS)
M. Philpot to Henry J. Hodge q.v.
Mary Philpott to Thomas Sparks q.v.
MISCELLANEOUS (RHEA and MEIGS)
Alexander Philpot: Hiwassee District, Burkett Chapel area
" " Purchased property in Cottonport
Barton Philpot: JP(?) 1838
Hanson Philpot: Bondsman for Thos D. McKeowin, 1834
Reubin Philpot: Bondsman for Robert Collison, 1816
Richard Philpot: Bondsman for Hiram Mahaffy, 1809
" " Bondsman for William Owens, 1812
" " Hiwassee District, Moore's Chapel area
- - - - - - - - - - - - -

PICKARD

1850 RHEA CENSUS
Luisa Pickard 37, Luisa T. 6, Lurena E. 3: see William H. Snodgrass
Nicholas Pickard 8: see Dudley Dismany
MARRIAGES (RHEA)
Lucinda Pickard to Eli Coulter q.v.
- - - - - - - - - - - - -

PICKETT

1830 RHEA CENSUS
Charles Pickett 0011 - 002001 p. 394
1840 RHEA CENSUS
Cassanda Picket 0 - 00010001
James Picket 00001 - 00001
1850 RHEA CENSUS
Passen M. Pickett 26 (NC)(Farmer), Eliza 21, Mary C. 7, Lewis R. 5, John W. 3, James F. 3/12 p. 638-676
MARRIAGES (RHEA)
Tomase J. Pickett to Elias H. Morgan q.v.
MISCELLANEOUS (RHEA)
James Pickett: Bondsman for John Jewell, 1832
- - - - - - - - - - - - -

PICKLE

MARRIAGES (MEIGS)
John H. Pickle to Sarah S. Winton, 11 Aug 1845 (14 Aug), James Sewell MG, Hugh Goddard Sur(?)
[1850 Bledsoe Census: John H. Pickle 26, Sarah S. 26, William C. 2]
- - - - - - - - - - - - -

PILE

1840 RHEA CENSUS
William W. Pile 010101 - 200001
MARRIAGES (RHEA)
Ceedem or Cedren Pile to Elizabeth Seamore, 27 June 1838 (28 June), Henry Collins JP, Cyrus Waterhouse Bm (AR)
Thomas C. or J. Pile to Elizabeth E. Jenkins, 10 Oct 1836 (10 Nov or 10 Oct), S. Dyer JP (AR)
William W. Pile to Mary Ann Merriott, 6 Dec 1832, James Orme Bm (A)
William W. Pile to Emely B. Holland, 17 Mar 1842, Allen Holland Bm (A)
MISCELLANEOUS (RHEA)
Cedron Pile: Bondsman for William Ferrell, 1835
" " Bondsman for Decatur K. Sykes, 1841
- - - - - - - - - - - - -

PINKERTON

1840 MEIGS CENSUS
Thomas Pinkerton 10001 - 00001 p. 235
- - - - - - - - - - - - -

PIPER

TAXES (RHEA)
1823 (Capt. Piper's Co.): William Piper 1 WP
1830 RHEA CENSUS
James Piper 00001 - 022001 p. 383
William Piper 0011001 - 000201 p. 359
1840 RHEA CENSUS
Richard Piper 00110001 - 210101
MARRIAGES (RHEA)
James Piper to Margaret Armstrong, 23 --?-- 1821, Flemming Manley Bm (A)
Nancy Piper to James Johnson q.v.
Thomas Piper to Polly Harwood, 19 or 25 Oct 1819, "Found in the papers of D. Walker JP", Benjamin Johnson Bm (AR)
MISCELLANEOUS (RHEA and MEIGS)
Chase Piper: Bondsman for Martin Ferguson, 1828
William Piper: Hiwassee District
- - - - - - - - - - - - -

PITMAN / PITTMAN

MARRIAGES (RHEA)
Eldridge Pitman to Hetty Weese, 22 Mar 1833 (same), Daniel Walker JP, James Poe Bm (AR)
Moses Pittman to Sally Clark, 4 Nov 1829, Allen Hilbourn Bm (A)
Rebecca Pitman to William Putnam q.v.
Thomas M. Pitman to Gilley Clifton, 12 or 27 July 1833 (28 July), Danl Walker JP, Eldridge Pitman Bm (AR)
MISCELLANEOUS (RHEA)
Eldridge Pitman: Bondsman for Thomas M. Pitman, 1833
- - - - - - - - - - - - -

PITTS

TAXES (RHEA)
1823 (Capt. Howard's Co.): William Pitts 1 WP
- - - - - - - - - - - - -

PLOWMAN

MARRIAGES (RHEA)
Jacob Plowman to Priscilla Parker, 31 Aug 1822 (1 Sept), John Rice JP, Joseph McMillian Bm (AR) [1850 Hamilton Census: Priscilla Plowman 62, Thomas 31, Thurzia 31]

- - - - - - - - - - - - -

PLUMLEE / PLUMBLEE / PLUMLY / PLUMER

1850 RHEA CENSUS
Daniel Plumlee 56 (Unk)(Farmer), Amanda 45 (Unk), Sarah 5, Margaret IVY 7 p. 638-673 [Daniel Plumly married Amanda Cuningham on 23 Jan 1845 in McMinn County]
1850 MEIGS CENSUS
J. C. Plumblee 33 (School Teacher), Elizabeth 36, James R. 13, Adaline 11 p. 805-711 [Jackson C. Plumlee married Elizabeth Manning on 2 Mar 1848 in Roane County]
MISCELLANEOUS (MEIGS)
Daniel Plumer: Hiwassee District, Euchee area

- - - - - - - - - - - - -

POE

TAXES (RHEA)
1823 (Capt. Brown's Co.): Jesse Poe, 1 WP, 159a Tenn Ri
(Capt. Smith's Co.): Pulaski Poe 1 WP
1830 RHEA CENSUS
James Poe 110001 - 21001 p. 385
Jesse Poe 0300001 - 101001 p. 376
P. Poe 000001 - 2010001001 p. 376
1840 MEIGS CENSUS
Poleskie Poe 1000001 - 1111001 p. 238
William Poe 200101 - 110001 p. 224
1850 RHEA CENSUS
Asabel R. Poe 18: see Daniel J. Rawlings
1850 MEIGS CENSUS
Pulaskie W. Poe 59 (Va), Rebecca J. 25, Sarah A. 0 p. 771-457
MARRIAGES (RHEA)
Jesse Poe to Isabella Rhea, 1 Oct 1819, John Stubbs Bm (A)
John Poe to Dorothy Gouge, 4 Feb 1812 (same), Abraham Howard JP, Josiah Gouge Bm(?) (AR)
John Poe to Rebecca Hinkle, 20 Oct 1819 (7 Nov or 20 Oct), John Rice JP, John Rawlings Bm (AR) [1850 Hamilton Census: John Poe 65, Rebecca 49, James 28, Nancy 26, Sarah 21, Francis 19, Larkin 17, Jesse 12, Rebecca 10]
Kisiah Poe to Jacob Kinchlow q.v.
Lucy Poe to John Rawlings q.v.
Phereby Poe to James Miller q.v.
Pulaski Poe to Nancy Parker, 27 or 29 Sept 1822 (28 or 29 Sept), John Rice JP, Jesse Poe Bm (AR)
Sarah Poe to Thomas Peterson q.v.
MISCELLANEOUS (RHEA)
James Poe: Bondsman for Richard Clifton, 1833
" " Bondsman for Eldridge Pitman, 1833
Jesse Poe: Bondsman for Pulaski Poe, 1822
" " Hiwassee District, Concord area
John Poe: Bondsman for G.W. Derossett, 1836
Pulaski Poe: Bondsman for G.W. Selvidge, 1831
" " Hiwassee District, Concord area

- - - - - - - - - - - - -

POLLARD

1830 RHEA CENSUS
Thomas Pollard 00000000 - 00000001 p. 391
MISCELLANEOUS (RHEA)
William Pollard: Bondsman for Richard Cooper, 1829

- - - - - - - - - - - - -

POPE

MISCELLANEOUS (RHEA)
Fielding Pope: MG 1830-31 [1850 Blount Census: Fielding Pope 50, Theressa 53, Thomas 23, etc.; Fielding Pope married Theresa C. Meigs on 24 Mar 1829 in McMinn County]

- - - - - - - - - - - - -

PORTER

1830 RHEA CENSUS
John H. Porter 01010001 - 2210001 p. 375
1840 MEIGS CENSUS
John Porter 21200001 - 00001001 p. 244
Nicholas D. Porter 200001 - 023001 p. 227
Pleasant Porter 00001 - 00001 p. 241
1850 RHEA CENSUS
Nancy A. Porter 35, Mary L. 8: see James Wilson
1850 MEIGS CENSUS
N.C. Porter 47 (Farmer), Lavina 45, Nancy 22, Sarah 21, Mariah 19, Martha Jane 17, Thomas 14, Eliza 9, Tennessee 1 p. 727-114
Pleasant M. Porter 39 (Va)(Farmer), Charlotte 40, Thomas W. 8, David H. 6, James K. 4, George 2, Daniel 1 p. 725-97
MARRIAGES (RHEA)
John Porter to Mary Ann Hoyal, 5 Mar 1834 (16 Mar), Jas Wilson JP, John Davis Bm (AR)
Nicholas C. Porter to Lavina Miller, 24 Feb 1825 (same), John Rice JP, John Clack Bm (AR)
Sally B. Porter to James C. Wilson q.v.
MARRIAGES (MEIGS)
Mary Ann Porter to David C. Dempsey q.v.
Sarah Porter to T. J. Leonard q.v.
MISCELLANEOUS (RHEA and MEIGS)
James B. Porter: Bondsman for James W. Oakes, 1835
Pleasant M. Porter: Cherokee Removal muster roll, 1836

- - - - - - - - - - - - -

POSEY / PUSEY

MARRIAGES (RHEA)
Sarah Pusey to Henry Fisher q.v.
MISCELLANEOUS (RHEA)
Benjamin Posey: MG 1834

- - - - - - - - - - - - -

POSTON

1830 RHEA CENSUS
William Poston 011001 - 210001 p. 392

- - - - - - - - - - - - -

POTEET / POTEETE

TAXES (RHEA)
1823 (Capt. Brown's Co.): William Poteete 1 WP
MARRIAGES (RHEA)
James Poteet to Jane Brown, 1 Jan 1810 (same), Abraham Howard JP, Jacob Sands Bm (AR)

- - - - - - - - - - - - -

POTTER

1830 RHEA CENSUS
James Potter 231001 - 0110010001 p. 354
1850 MEIGS CENSUS
William Potter 44 (Ky)(Blacksmith), Margaret 38 (Ky), Andrew 18 (Ky)(Blacksmith), Charles 15 (Ky), Elizabeth Jane 13 (Ky), Sanford 9 (Ky), George W. 7 p. 730-125

- - - - - - - - - - - - -

POWELL / POWEL

TAXES (RHEA)
1808 (John Henry's List): James Powell 1 WP
1819 (Capt. John Robinson's Co.): James Powell 1 WP
1823 (Capt. Wilson's Co.): James Powell 1 WP
(Capt. Jackson's Co.): Scott Powell 1 WP
1830 RHEA CENSUS
James Powell 2020001 - 0011001 p. 386
Scott Powell 110001 - 10001 p. 377
1840 MEIGS CENSUS
Mary Powel 001 - 0000001 p. 233
1850 MEIGS CENSUS
John Powel 26 (Farmer), Mary 18 p. 739-210
Scott Powel 51 (Va) (Farmer), Mary 46 (Va), Robert 21 (Farmer), Narcissa 17, Daniel 15 (Farmer), Jacob 12, James J.P. 6, Thomas H.B. 4 p. 739-207
MARRIAGES (RHEA)
Green Powell to Peggy Hunter, 6 July 1815 (same), James Small Bm (A)
Nicholas Powell Jr. to Jane Robinson, 8 Dec 1810 (same), James Powell Bm (AR)
MARRIAGES (MEIGS)
John Powell to Mary J. Butler, 8 Dec 1849 (9 Dec), William Johns JP
MISCELLANEOUS (RHEA and MEIGS)
James Powell: Bondsman for Nicholas Powell Jr., 1810
Scott Powell: Hiwassee District
Thomas Powell: Hiwassee District, Cottonport area

- - - - - - - - - - - - -

POWERS / POWER

TAXES (RHEA)
1823 (Capt. Jackson's Co.): John Powers 1 WP
1830 RHEA CENSUS
John J. Powers 00100 - 0000001 p. 370
1840 MEIGS CENSUS
John J. Powers 00001001 - 00100001 p. 226
Robert S. Powers 00001 - 001
[1 written over 2 or vice versa]
1850 MEIGS CENSUS
Malinda Power 39, Sarah C. 10 p. 723-77
[Robert S. Powers married Malinda McDowel on 9 Feb 1839 in McMinn County]
MARRIAGES (RHEA)
Mark Powers to Mary Harp, 2 Aug 1834, Joshua Harp Bm (A)
MISCELLANEOUS (RHEA and MEIGS)
Mark Powers: Bondsman for Joshua Harp, 1834
Robert Powers: Cherokee Removal muster roll, 1836
Robert S. Powers: Cherokee Removal muster roll, 1837

- - - - - - - - - - - - -

POYNOR

MARRIAGES (RHEA)
William Poynor to Sally Oden, 7 Oct 1821, Daniel Holladay Bm (A)

- - - - - - - - - - - - -

PRATER / PRATOR

1840 MEIGS CENSUS
Charles Prator 10001 - 00001 p. 242
MARRIAGES (MEIGS)
Charles Prater to Mary Holmes, 15 Sept 1838 (18 Sept), William Green MG, John W. Smith Sur(?)

- - - - - - - - - - - - -

PRENTICE

MISCELLANEOUS (RHEA)
James Prentice: Bondsman for Moses Wyatt, 1820

- - - - - - - - - - - - -

PRESLEY

1850 RHEA CENSUS
Gillum Presley 48 (NC)(Farmer), Barbary 48 (SC), James W. 19 (Farmer), Matilda C. 14, Luisa 7 p. 631-623
Mary Presley 36 (NC), Jacob 15, Nancy J. DEAN 16 p. 578-274
William R. Presley 22 (Farmer), Mary A. 21 p. 631-624
MARRIAGES (RHEA)
Mary Ann Presley to William Martin q.v.
William R. Presley to Mary Ann Hughes, 9 Oct 1849 (same), Jesse Locke MG (R)

- - - - - - - - - - - - -

PRESOCK / PRYSOCK

1840 RHEA CENSUS
Frederick Presock 1200100001 - 0112101
MARRIAGES (RHEA)
Frederick Prysock to Betsey Corder, 10 Aug 1834 (same), John McClure JP, Frederick Hoover Bm (AR)

MISCELLANEOUS (RHEA)
Frederick Prisock: Bondsman for Isaac Goldsby, 835

- - - - - - - - - - - - -

PRESTON

TAXES (RHEA)
1819 (Capt. John Ramsey's Co.): James Preston 1 WP, 2 BP, 250a, 1 Stud Horse (tax, $2.00)
1823 (Capt. Howerton's Co.): George Preston 1 WP
(Capt. McCall's Co.): James Preston 1 WP, 3 BP, 250a Whites Creek
1830 RHEA CENSUS
George Preston 0100001 - 21001 p. 362
James Preston 0102001 - 0020001 p. 388
1840 RHEA CENSUS
James Preston 000012001 - 000000001
1850 RHEA CENSUS
Rector Preston 47: see Margaret Roddye
MARRIAGES (RHEA)
Elizabeth Preston to Charles H. Royster q.v.
George Preston to Anney Roddye, 10 Sept 1821 (no return) (R)
Nancy Preston to James T. Stockton q.v.
Sarah M. Preston to Michael L. Woods q.v.
MARRIAGES (MEIGS)
William G. Preston to Louisa E. Price, 5 Oct 1841 (7 Oct), Leroy Looney JP, James Kelly Sur(?)
MISCELLANEOUS (RHEA)
George Preston: JP 183-38
" " Bondsman for Wm T. Gillenwaters, 1819
James Preston: Bondsman for Isaac Baker, 1817
" " Hiwassee Dist, Fooshee & Hardwick Islands area
Rector Preston: Bondsman for Michael L. Woods, 1835

- - - - - - - - - - - - -

PRESSWOOD / PUSWOOD

TAXES (RHEA)
1823 (Capt. Braselton's Co.): Thomas Puswood 1 WP
1850 MEIGS CENSUS
Elizabeth Preswood 23, Minerva C. 5, Nancy S. 1 p. 777-511
MARRIAGES (MEIGS)
Miles V. Presswood to Barbara A. Tillery, 26 Feb 1845 (29 Feb), Daniel Cate JP, Wm P. Tillery Sur(?)
Pleasant M. Presswood to Elizabeth Tillery, 24 Sept 1844 (26 Sept), John Huff Esq., Leonard Huff Sur(?)

- - - - - - - - - - - - -

PREWITT / PREWET / PRUETT / PRUITT / PRIVETT

1830 RHEA CENSUS
Micajah Privett 00001 - 001 [Micajah Prewitt married Permelia Jane Hammons on 20 Jan 1848 in Roane County; living in Roane Co in 1850]
1850 MEIGS CENSUS
Andrew Pruett 23 (Farmer), Susannah 24, John 1 p. 781-538
Mary Prewet 32 (NC), Julett 12, Susannah 10, Matilda 8, Maranda 6, Obediah 5, Lean (f) 1 p. 714-13
MARRIAGES (RHEA)
Lewis Pruitt to Rhoda Crawford, 5 June 1830 (26 June), James A. Darwin (R)
MARRIAGES (MEIGS)
A.J. Prewitt to Susan Stephens, 30 May 1846 (31 May), Thos V. Atchley JP
Mary Ann Prewitt to Solomon Harden q.v.

- - - - - - - - - - - - -

PRICE

TAXES (RHEA)
1808 (James Campbell's List): William Price 1 WP
1823 (Capt. Wilson's Co.): Isaac Price 1 WP
Jacob Price 1 WP
James Price 1 WP
Samuel Price 1 WP
Sion Price 1 WP
Thomas Price 1 WP, 281a Sewee Cr
William Price 560a Sewee Creek
1830 RHEA CENSUS
Jacob Price 33001 - 00101 p. 364
Thomas Price 1122000101 - 10200010001 p. 364
1840 RHEA CENSUS
Biddy or Beddy Price 011 - 000100001
James M. Price 00001 - 00011
1840 MEIGS CENSUS
Andrew J. Price 10001 - 11001 p. 235
Dorsey Price 2410001 - 3231201 p. 236
Jacob Price 01330001 - 0000001 p. 243
James Price 11111 - 01030101 p. 244
John Price 00001 - 00001 p. 235
1850 RHEA CENSUS
Elizabeth Price 9, William L. 7: see William Gipson
John C. Price 29 (School Teacher), Avesta A. 20, Jeston E. (f) 8/12 p. 570-222
William C. Price 26 (Wagonmaker), Rachael 25, Jacob 4, Catharine E. 2, Thomas E. 2/12 p. 582-306
1850 MEIGS CENSUS
Dorcy Price 54 (Farmer), Mary 55, Racheal 23, Henry 25 (Farmer), Martha 13, James 12, Betsy Ann 2 p. 767-428
Isaac N. Price 23 (Farmer), Margaret 20, John 2, Sarah 1 p. 784-558
Jacob Price 60 (Farmer), Catharine 59, Elizabeth 27, James P. 28, Samuel P. 22, Thomas H. 20, Doctor 17, Jacob P.B. 10 p. 787-587
James T. Price 38 (Farmer), Pricilla 45 (Va), James 24, Jesse 17, Charles 11 p. 783-553
John Price 29 (Farmer), Rebecca 25, Emily J. 9, Sarah E. 7 p. 767-429
Mary Price 35, James 18 (Tanner), Elizabeth 16, Thomas 12 p. 725-99
Samuel Price 25 (Farmer), Mary Ann 22, Mary Ann 5, Louisa 4, John D. 1 p. 777-509
MARRIAGES (RHEA)
Elizabeth Price to Joel Bledsoe q.v.
James M. Price to Judith Gibson, 8 May 1840 (no return), Zebeedee Brewer Bm (AR)
John Price to Vesta A. Creede, 29 Mar 1848 (no return) (R)
Margaret Price to Alexander Rice q.v.
Moses Price to Catharine Seybolt, 15 Jan 1814 (same), Moses Seybolt Bm (AR)

MARRIAGES (RHEA) continued
Moses Price to Peggy McClanahan, 19 Oct 1819 (21 Oct), John Rice JP, Henry Price Bm (AR)
Rebecca Price to Thomas Price q.v.
Sarah Price to Elijah Cruson q.v.
Solomon Price to Betsy Leach, 17 June 1819 (same), "I certify I married the persons in these returns" Jonathan Fine JP, Walter Edwards Bm (AR)
Thomas Price to Rebecca Price, 6 June 1829 (7 June), John Farmer MG, Welcom Wilhelms Bm (AR)

MARRIAGES (MEIGS)
James T. Price to Priscilla (Pricey) Mapes, 16 Jan 1847 (same), Daniel Cate JP, D.L. Godsey Sur(?)
John Price to Rebeccah Rhineheart, 28 June 1838 (same), A.J. McGee MG
Louisa E. Price to William G. Preston q.v.
Mary Ann Price to Cage Low q.v.
Minerva Price to Joseph Mapes q.v.
Nancy Price to William Buster q.v.
Samuel Price to Polly Ann Langford, 7 May 1844 (9 May), T.B. McClure JP
Sarah Price to A. Sweatman q.v.
Thomas J. Price to Mary Mapes, 19 Oct 1846 (25 Oct), Ezekiel Ward JP

MISCELLANEOUS (RHEA)
Dorsey Price: War of 1812
Henry Price: Bondsman for Moses Price, 1819
Isaac Price: Bondsman for Ceder Murphree, 1819
Thomas Price: JP 1821-24
William Price: Bondsman for James McAllister, 1814
" " On Board of Commissioners to construct new jail, 1825-26

MISCELLANEOUS (MEIGS)
Dorany Price: Purchased Lot 10 in Decatur, 1836
Henry Price: Private, Mexican War
Jacob Price: JP 1838-39, 1841
" " Chairman of County Court, 1840
Jas T. Price: Common School Commissioner, Dist 6, 1838
John Price: Private, Mexican War
Josiah [John] Price: Hiwassee District
Reuben W. Price: Private, Mexican War
Samuel Price: Hiwassee District; Private, Mexican War
Stephen Price: Private, Mexican War
Thomas Price: Revolutionary War pensioner(?)
" " Hiwassee District
" " Cherokee Removal muster roll, 1837
William Price: Hiwassee District

\- - - - - - - - - - - - -

PRIDDY / PREDY

1850 MEIGS CENSUS
David Predy 42 (Farmer), Eliza 34, John 14, Elizabeth 12, Martha 10, Burk 5, James 3, Nancy 4/12 p. 722-75
MARRIAGES (RHEA)
Judy Priddy to David Varner q.v.
MISCELLANEOUS (RHEA)
William Priddy: Bondsman for David Varner, 1812

\- - - - - - - - - - - - -

PRILLAMON / PRILLAMAN / PRELEMON / PRELIMAN

1830 RHEA CENSUS
Jacob Preliman 10110001 - 21301 p. 367
MARRIAGES (RHEA)
Jacob Prillamon to Desdamony Gorman, 23 Sept 1833, "Executed" V.H. Giles JP (R)
John Prillaman to Margaret H. Jack, 7 Jan 1839 (10 Jan), Bryan R. McDonald JP, Vaden H. Giles Bm (AR)
Polly Prillamon to Henry Martin q.v.
Sarah Prillamon to Vaden H. Giles q.v.
MISCELLANEOUS (RHEA)
John C. Prillamon: Bondsman for Vaden H. Giles, 1834

\- - - - - - - - - - - - -

PROWELL

MARRIAGES (RHEA)
Sampson Prowell to Fanny Hunter, 15 Sept 1827 (same), Thomas Cox JP & Bm (AR) [1850 Polk Census: Sampson H. Prowell 49, Frances 58, Mary A.P. 10, Sampson H. 13, Minerva 16, John EVANS 13]

\- - - - - - - - - - - - -

PRYOR

MARRIAGES (RHEA)
Betsy Pryor to Jesse Boulton q.v.

\- - - - - - - - - - - - -

PUCKETT

1830 RHEA CENSUS
James Puckett 00001 - 000001 p. 380
MARRIAGES (RHEA)
John S. Puckett to Martha Clough, 2 Mar 1835 (same), William Smith JP, Greenberry Casteel Bm (AR)

\- - - - - - - - - - - - -

PUGH

MARRIAGES (RHEA)
Flemming C. Peugh or Pugh to Sarah Allen, 7 Sept 1876 (same), Thomas Cox JP, John Allen Bm (AR)

\- - - - - - - - - - - - -

PURDON

MARRIAGES (RHEA)
John Purdon to Polly Howerton, 18 Feb 1809, John Graham Bm (A)

\- - - - - - - - - - - - -

PURDY

1850 MEIGS CENSUS
Elizabeth Purdy 52 (NC), Nancy 15 (NC), Mathew 10, Joseph 14, Franklin 12 p. 761-398
Thomas Purdy 21 (Farmer), Elizabeth 22 p. 764-399

MARRIAGES (MEIGS)
Thomas Purdy to Elizabeth C. Melton, 14 Aug 1850, Garrow Denton Sur

- - - - - - - - - - - - -

PURSER / PERSER / PINCER

TAXES (RHEA)
1823 (Capt. Lewis' Co.): James Purcer 1 WP
1850 RHEA CENSUS
James Purser 66 (SC)(Farmer), Elizabeth 64 (SC), Rebecca 21, William B. 20 (Farmer), Polly A. 14, Sarah GOAD 70 (SC), Ruth GOAD 66 (SC) p. 593-360
Pleasant M. Purser 30 (Farmer), Ruhaney 30, Darcus P. 4, William T. 1 p. 688-351 [Pleasant married Reuhany Fisher on 22 Jan 1843 in McMinn Co]
MARRIAGES (RHEA)
Eliza Perser to James M. Thompson q.v.
James Pincer to Molly Little, 2 Apr 1812 (same), Thomas Goad Bm (A)
James Purser to Elizabeth Goad, 28 Mar 1811 [bond]

- - - - - - - - - - - - -

PUTMAN / PUTNAM

TAXES (RHEA)
1823 (Capt. Braselton's Co.): Moses Putnam 1 WP
Wilson Putnam 1 WP
1830 RHEA CENSUS
Benjamin Putman 21001 - 10011 p. 364
Moris Putman 01001 - 21001 p. 386
Rebecca Putman 0111 - 01111001 p. 386
Winsey(?) Pitman [probably Wilson Putnam] 00021 - 0102001 p. 386
MARRIAGES (RHEA)
Benjamin Putnam to Polly Buchannon, 7 Jan 1823 (8 Jan), John Farmer MG, Jesse Atwood Bm (AR)
Eleanor Putman to Joseph Rush q.v.
Polly Putnam to David Lions q.v.
Wilson Putnam to Rebecca Pitman, 20 Oct 1830, Robert Lyons Bm (A)
MARRIAGES (MEIGS)
C. Putnam to John Walling q.v.
MISCELLANEOUS (MEIGS)
Norris Putnam: Hiwassee District, Pinhook Ferry area

- - - - - - - - - - - - -

PYOTT

1850 RHEA CENSUS
Edward Pyott 36 (Va)(Farmer), Margaret 33 (Va), John E. 10 (Va), Joel 8, James C.H. 5, William W. 3, Samuel A. 2 p. 555-130
MISCELLANEOUS (RHEA)
Edward Pyott: Trustee, Mars Hill Academy, 1850

- - - - - - - - - - - - -

QUALLS

1830 RHEA CENSUS
Hubert Qualls 100001 - 0001 p. 368
James Qualls 0001 - 1001 p. 387
Robert Qualls 1011001 - 1121 p. 367
1840 RHEA CENSUS
Berry Qualls 110001 - 01001
Hubbard Qualls 121001 - 10001
Rebecca Qualls 001 - 001110001
1840 MEIGS CENSUS
Nathan Qualls 00011001 - 01113001 p. 231
1850 RHEA CENSUS
Benjamin Qualls 13: see Mary Bean
Mary Qualls 22: see William Lowry
1850 MEIGS CENSUS
George Qualls 26 (Farmer), Nancy 25, William 6, Margaret 4, Infant (f) 0 p. 744-252
Nathan Qualls 60 (Va)(Farmer), Nancy 24, Mary 40, Martha 29, Talitha 20, James M. 9, George W. 6, Francis M. 3, Preston T. 3, Sarah E. 2, Infant (m) 0 p. 744-253
MARRIAGES (RHEA)
Lucretia Qualls to Ellet Johnson q.v.
Nancy Qualls to Lewis Willson q.v.
Robert G. Qualls to Elizabeth Snow, 13 Dec 1846 (same), J.J. Cervin MG (R)
Russell Qualls to Betsy Wilhelms, 9 Apr 1835, Thos Snow Bm (A)
MARRIAGES (MEIGS)
George W. Qualls to Nancy L. Miller [Lockmiller], 23 Mar 1844 (24 Mar), Thomas V. Atchley JP, William T. Armstrong Sur(?)
Nathan Qualls Jr. to Matilda L. Miller [Lockmiller], 3 Feb 1844 (5 Feb), Thos V. Atchley JP, James Wilhelm Sur(?)
MISCELLANEOUS (RHEA and MEIGS)
Berry Qualls: Bondsman for Ellet Johnson, 1839
Nathan Qualls: JP(?) 1843

- - - - - - - - - - - - -

QUEENER / QUINER

1850 MEIGS CENSUS
George W. Quiner 43 (Farmer), Racheal 28, Susan 6, John 4, Caroline 2 p. 783-554
[George W. Queener married Rachel Lattimore on 3 Jan 1839 in McMinn County]
MISCELLANEOUS (MEIGS)
Jacob Queener: Private, Mexican War

- - - - - - - - - - - - -

QUICK

1830 RHEA CENSUS
Eoli Quick 0001 - 11001 p. 375

- - - - - - - - - - - - -

QUIET / QUIETT / QUIOT

MARRIAGES (RHEA)
Cyrus Quiet to Sarah Cox, 8 July 1825 (same), Wm Smith JP, Maradith Cox Bm (AR)
Eslie Quiett to Fanny Shaffer, 26 Feb 1828 (same), Joseph McCorkle JP, William S. Russell Bm (AR)
MARRIAGES (MEIGS)
Caroline Quiett to Anderson Blevins q.v.
Cyrus Quiett to Nancy Underwood, 17 Apr 1842 (same), D. L. Godsey MG, Abraham Cox Jr. Sur(?)

Elinder Quiett to John M. McDaniel q.v.
MISCELLANEOUS (MEIGS)
A.J. Quiett: Surety for John M. McDaniel, 1850
Andrew Quiett: Private, Mexican War
Cyrus Quiet: Hiwassee District, Cottonport area
Thomas Quiett: Private, Mexican War

- - - - - - - - - - - - -

QUILLIAN

1850 MEIGS CENSUS
Thomas Quillian 60: see Benjamin L. White

- - - - - - - - - - - - -

QUINTON

1830 RHEA CENSUS
Alsey Quinton 00201 - 00010001 p. 364
MARRIAGES (RHEA)
Arty M. Quinton to William Srader [Swader?] q.v.
Samuel Quinton to Rhoda Harwood, 10 Nov 1830 (same), Beal Gaither JP, Benjamin Perkins Bm (AR)
MISCELLANEOUS (RHEA)
Samuel B. Quinton: Bondsman for William Srader, 1830

- - - - - - - - - - - - -

RAFFITY

TAXES (RHEA)
1819 (Capt. Robinson's Co.): Richard Raffity 1 WP, 330a

- - - - - - - - - - - - -

RAGAN

MARRIAGES (RHEA)
Aggebis Ragan to Henry Myers q.v.
Sally Ragan to Sanford Parkey or Turley q.v.
MISCELLANEOUS (MEIGS)
Joseph A. Ragan: Ocoee District

- - - - - - - - - - - - -

RAGLAND / RAGLIN

TAXES (RHEA)
1823 (Capt. Piper's Co.):
Gideon Ragland 1 WP, 3 BP, 160a [Ten Mile]
1830 RHEA CENSUS
Gideon Ragland 0000001 - 0100001 p. 360
1840 MEIGS CENSUS
Gideon Lagland [sic] 00000001 - 00010001 p. 239
1850 MEIGS CENSUS
Gideon Ragland 66 (Va)(Farmer), Artamisa 65 (Va) p. 800-679 [Gideon, 1784-1874, son of Gideon Ragland; Artamesia, 1785-1862, dau of John Wilson; sister of Wm C. and James Wilson; married 5 Mar 1808 in Pittsylvania Co., Va.; at least three daus: Nancy H., Mary F., and Elizabeth W.]
MARRIAGES (RHEA)
Mary Raglin to James Griffith q.v.
Nancy H. Ragland to Robert Stockton q.v.
MARRIAGES (MEIGS)
Elizabeth W. Ragland to Nelson C. Redman q.v.
MISCELLANEOUS (MEIGS)
Gideon Ragland: Hiwassee District, Ten Mile Stand area
" " Common School Com., District 7, 1838

- - - - - - - - - - - - -

RAGLE

1850 RHEA CENSUS
Mary A. Ragle 43: see Michael Hassler

- - - - - - - - - - - - -

RAGSDALE / RAGSDELL

TAXES (RHEA)
1819 (Capt. McGill's Co.): David Ragsdale 1 WP
1823 (Capt. Howard's Co.): David Ragsdale 1 WP, 150a
1830 RHEA CENSUS
David Ragsdell 3210101 - 011001 p. 394
1840 RHEA CENSUS
David Ragsdale 11321001 - 0001001
1840 MEIGS CENSUS
Jane Ragsdale 0 - 000001001 p. 242
1850 RHEA CENSUS
David Ragsdale 60 (SC)(Farmer), Cyntha 50 (NC), James M. 26 (Clerk), John N. 23, George H. 20 (Farmer), Dewitt C. 15, Thomas H. 11, Sarah CRANMORE 81 (NC) p. 625-581
MARRIAGES (RHEA)
Aggy Ragsdale to Samuel L. Miller [Lockmiller] q.v.
Harriet Ragsdale to Benjamin Suddath q.v.
Jane Ragsdale to Vardaman Anderson q.v.
Sarah E. Ragsdale to Leander Wilson q.v.
William F. Ragsdale to Sarah Garwood, 2 Nov 1848 (same), Leander Wilson MG (R) [1850 Hamilton Census: William Ragsdale 31, Sarah 26, James P. 1, Ann GARWOOD 14, James M. RAGSDALE 25]
MISCELLANEOUS (RHEA)
David Ragsdale: JP 1844-46
James M. Ragsdale: Private, Mexican War
William F. Ragsdale: Bondsman for Leander Wilson, 1842
" " " Bondsman for Thos K. Munsey, 1845
William H. Ragsdale: Private, Mexican War

- - - - - - - - - - - - -

RAINS / REINS

MARRIAGES (RHEA)
Hiram Rains to Catherine Davis, 8 Apr 1834, John Clingan Bm (A)
MARRIAGES (MEIGS)
Martha Reins to F.M. Moore q.v.
MISCELLANEOUS (MEIGS)
James H. Rains JP(?) 1843-44

- - - - - - - - - - - - -

RAMSEY / ROMSEY / RAMEY / RAMY

TAXES (RHEA)
1819 (Capt. W.S. Bradley's Co.): George Ramsey 1 WP
William Ramsey 1 WP, 1000a
(Capt. John Ramsey's Co.): John Ramsey 1 WP
1823 (Capt. Smith's Co.): George Ramey 1 WP

1840 MEIGS CENSUS
John Ramsey 20001 - 00001 p. 232
Sarah Ramsey 01 - 001201 p. 227
1850 RHEA CENSUS
John S. Ramsey 35 (Farmer), Barbery S. 24, Catharine E. 32, William B. 2, Samuel S. 11/12 p. 565-187
1850 MEIGS CENSUS
Sarah Romsey 60, Nancy 21 p. 729-28
MARRIAGES (RHEA)
Jane Ramy to John Farmer q.v.
John Ramsey to Sally Brooks, 15 Jan 1824 (18 Jan), Thomas Cox JP, Leonard Brooks Bm (AR)
John L. Ramsey to Barbrie F. Frazier, 11 Nov 1846 (12 Nov), Wm H. Bell MG (R)
[this record was listed twice: #77 & #252]
MARRIAGES (MEIGS)
Daniel R. Ramsey to Lydia F. Day, 2 Feb 1841 (same), Richard Simpson MG and Sur(?)
Elizabeth Ramsey to James Fox q.v.
Milla Ramsey to Stephen J. McClannahon q.v.
Sarah Ramsey to William Farbank q.v.
MISCELLANEOUS (RHEA and MEIGS)
John Ramsey: Bondsman for George W. Allen, 1817
" " Hiwassee District, Moore's Chapel area
George Ramsey: Hiwassee District
William Ramsey: Early resident in Town of Washington
" " Security for John Moore, 1812
" " Signed petition to move Indian Agency

- - - - - - - - - - - - -

RANDLES / RANDAL / RANDLE

TAXES (RHEA)
1823 (Capt. Wilson's Co.): John Randles 1 WP, 160a
1850 MEIGS CENSUS
William A. Randles 31, Frances 31, James G. 8, Jane 6, Caroline 4, Ellen 2, Tennessee 1 p. 753-324
MISCELLANEOUS (RHEA and MEIGS)
John Randles: JP 1833-35; Trustee, 1836-40
" " Hiwassee District; Lot 67 in Decatur
James F. Randals: Cherokee Removal muster roll, 1836

- - - - - - - - - - - - -

RANDOLPH

TAXES (RHEA)
1823 (Capt. Brown's Co.): Wm Randolph 1 BP, 200a TR
1830 RHEA CENSUS
Mary Randolph 0001 - 0000201 p. 385 [widow of John Marriott and William Randolph]
1840 RHEA CENSUS
Mary Randolph 00001 - 000000001
1850 RHEA CENSUS
Mary Randolph 71 (Pa) p. 603-443
MARRIAGES (RHEA)
Martin H. Randolph to Peggy Walker, 8 Oct 1817, "I married these parties" William Randolph, Elder and Bm (AR)
MISCELLANEOUS (RHEA)
Martin Randolph: Bondsman for Thompson Hide, 1817
William Randolph: Elder 1817-21
" " Bondsman for Martin H. Randolph, 1817

- - - - - - - - - - - - -

RANSOM

TAXES (RHEA)
1823 (Capt. Lewis' Co.): George Ransom 1 WP
1830 RHEA CENSUS
George Ransom 000001 - 321001 p. 392
MISCELLANEOUS (RHEA)
George Ransom: Bondsman for Stephen Mayfield, 1826

- - - - - - - - - - - - -

RAWLINS / RAWLINGS / ROLLENS / ROLLING

TAXES (RHEA)
1808 (John Henry's List): Daniel Rollens 2 WP, 2 BP, 500a E Fork, Richland Creek
1819 (Capt. Bradley's Dist):
Asael Rawlings 1 WP, 1 BP, 210a
D. & Rezin Rawlings 1 WP, 1 BP, 1075½a
(Capt. J. Ramsey's Co.): Daniel Rawlings 1 WP
1823 (Capt. Brown's Co.): Resin Rawlings 1 WP, 8 BP, 369a Pleasant Valley, 150a near town, 6½a Southern Liberties, 17a near town, 236a mouth Clear Cr
1830 RHEA CENSUS
Resin Rawlings 0101001 - 01111 p. 384
1840 RHEA CENSUS
Viney Rawlings 0 - 0 [sic]
1850 RHEA CENSUS
Adam Rawlings 65 (NC)(Farmer)(black), Viney 65 (Va) (black) p. 612-438
Daniel J. Rawlings 37 (Merchant), Eliza J. 28, Elisha K. 6, Bella 8, Asabel P. POE 18 (Farmer) p. 613-446
Phillip T. Rawlings 24 (Farmer), Caroline E. 22, Anderson KELLY 15 p. 613-444
MARRIAGES (RHEA)
Finney Rawlins to Jane Gowing, 24 Dec 1812 (same), William Long JP, Thomas Pinny Bm (A)
John Rawlings to Lucy Poe, 14 Apr 1812, Palatiah Chilton Bm (A)
Mary Rawlings to Thomas Blackburn q.v.
Mary K. Rawlings to Vreckinburg Thompson q.v.
Mary K. Rawlings to Robert M. Hooks q.v.
Rezin Rawlings to Polly Ann Kennedy, 6 Sept 1808 (same), Abraham Howard JP (R)
Rezin Rawlings to Viney Miller, 3 Aug 1826 (same), Matthew Donald MG, James Berry Bm (AR)
MISCELLANEOUS (RHEA)
A.S. Rawlings: Early merchant in Town of Washington
Asahel Rawlings: Circuit Court Clerk, 1810-21
" " Bondsman for Carlisle Humphreys, 1816
D.N. Rawlings & Co.: Early store in Washington
Daniel Rawlings: County Court Clerk, 1808-1823
" " Lot 22, Town of Washington
" " Secretary, Board of Commissioners, 1813
" " Signed Petition to move Indian Agency
" " JP for new county 1808
John Rawlings: Bondsman for John Poe, 1819
Rezin Rawlings Bondsman for Jacob Manice, 1809
" " Bondsman for William Ferguson, 1822
" " Bondsman for Thomas Jack, 1818
" " Signed Petition to move Indian Agency

- - - - - - - - - - - - -

RAYDER

1830 RHEA CENSUS
William Rayder 00001 - 000001 p. 383
- - - - - - - - - - - - -

REACER / REECER

MARRIAGES (RHEA)
Easter Reacer to Abraham Hughes q.v.
MISCELLANEOUS (RHEA)
John Reecer: Bondsman for Andrew Casteel, 1829
- - - - - - - - - - - - -

RECTOR

TAXES (RHEA)
1808 (Jonathan Fine's List):
Morgan Rector 1 WP, 130a Piney River
1819 (Capt. John Ramsey's Co.):
Cumberland Rector 1 WP, 350a
1823 (Capt. McCall's Co.):
Cumberland Rector 350a Whites Creek
(Capt. Braselton's Co.):
Landon Rector 1 WP, 150a Piney River
1830 RHEA CENSUS
Cumberland Rector 0102001 - 0001 p. 388
Landon Rector 200011 - 01011 p. 387
1840 RHEA CENSUS
Cumberland Rector 000001001 - 0
James Rector 10001 - 0001
Jessee Rector 0100001 - 220001
Landon Rector 2011101 - 20101
William Rector 110001 - 1
1850 RHEA CENSUS
Jesse Rector 54 (Va)(Farmer), Sarah 45, Mary A. 18, Susan E. 17, James E. 16, Martha J. 14, Sarah C. 12, Jesse S. 9, Luisa E. 7, Washington S. 4, Salina E. 2 p. 594-369
Landon Rector 52 (Farmer), Mary 47, Charles 24 (Farmer), John 21, Melvina 19, Elvira 16, Houston 14, William 11, Landon 6 p. 547-90
Sarah Rector 60 (Va), Malissa BOXLEY 21 p. 557-147
MARRIAGES (RHEA)
Charlotte Rector to William H. Stockton q.v.
Eliza B. Rector to Henry Whittenburg q.v.
Elizabeth Rector to John Baker q.v.
Emily Rector to Sterling Holloway q.v.
James F. Rector to Susan Adkins, 20 July 1839 (21 July), A.D. Paul JP, Jefferson Jackson Bm (AR)
John W. Rector to Melvina Barton, 22 Oct 1849 (8 Nov), Snelson Roberts MG (R) [living with Landon and Mary Rector in 1850]
Landon Rector to Polly Wasson, 31 Aug 1822, "I certify that I married them" Jesse Thompson JP, Byrum Breeding Bm (AR)
Mahala Rector to Pleasant W. Miller q.v.
Malinda Rector to Hezekiah McPherson q.v.
Mary Louisa Rector to Russell Duncan q.v.
Presley Rector to Seibby Johnson, 19 Sept 1812, Thomas Anderson Bm (A)
Sely Rector to George W. Riegle q.v.
Wm Rector to Catharine Peters, 2 Feb 1841 (no return) (R)
MARRIAGES (MEIGS)
Cumberland Rector to Sarah Buster, 19 Aug 1841 (same), Jacob Price JP, David Buster Sur(?)
Sarah Ann Rector to James Hany q.v.
MISCELLANEOUS (RHEA)
Charles Rector: Bondsman for James T. Stockton, 1833
George W. Rector: Bondsman for Robert Hogan, 1824
Jesse Rector: Bondsman for Robert Beard, 1841
" " JP 1843, 1848
Landon Rector: Erected a forge about 1825
" " Bondsman for John Baker, 1821
- - - - - - - - - - - - -

REDMAN / REDMOND

TAXES (RHEA)
1823 (Capt. Piper's Co.): John Redman 1 WP, 160a
1830 RHEA CENSUS
Nancy Redmond 003001 - 01001 p. 357
1840 MEIGS CENSUS
William Redman 10001 - 10001 p. 236
1850 MEIGS CENSUS
John P. Redman 31 (Farmer), Artamissa B. 21, Almira C. 16, William 3, Robert 1 p. 800-674
Nelson C. Redmon 31 (Farmer), Elizabeth 27, John G. 7, Mary A. 5, Joseph N. 3, Nancy E. 1 p. 798-671
William Redman 48 (NC)(Farmer), Elizabeth 50 (NC), Mahala 18, Nancy 12, George 7 p. 782-544

MARRIAGES (RHEA)
William Readmon or Redmond to Rebecca Click, 30 or 31 Aug 1839 (3 Sept), John Condley or John Cozby JP, Jesse Eaton Bm (AR)
MARRIAGES (MEIGS)
John P. Redmon to Artimisa B. Stockton, 6 Jan 1845, "Within January 1845" William Green MG, John L. Baldwin Sur(?)
Nelson C. Redman to Elizabeth W. Ragland, 14 Oct 1841 (same), Mark Renfrow JP, Wilbern Davis Sur(?) [Elizabeth, dau of Gideon and Artamisa Wilson Ragland]
William Redmon to Mary Robeson, 19 Apr 1838 (same), John W. Witten MG
William Redmon to Betsy West, 12 Sept 1843, "Solemnized the within rites and returned in due time" Thomas V. Atchley JP, John Blanton Sur(?)

MISCELLANEOUS (MEIGS)
John Redmon: Hiwassee District
N.C. Redmond: JP(?) 1838
W.H. Redman: JP(?) 1840
Wilson Redmon: Cherokee Removal muster roll, 1836
William H. Redmon Cherokee Removal muster roll, 1836
- - - - - - - - - - - - -

REDWINE

MARRIAGES (RHEA)
Sally Redwine to James Bundren q.v.
- - - - - - - - - - - - -

REED / REID / READ

TAXES (RHEA)
1808 (James Campbell's List): Hamilton Reed 1 WP
Robert Reed 1 WP
1819 (Capt. Bradley's Dist.): James C. Reed 1 WP, 2 lots
Samuel R. Reed 1 WP
1840 RHEA CENSUS
Zebulon Reed 000000001 - 00010001
1840 MEIGS CENSUS
William Reed 00230001 - 2200101 p. 239
1850 RHEA CENSUS
Gilbert Reed 30 (Unk)(Ditcher), Mary A. 27, Catharine 6, Charles 5, John M. 3, Nathan 1 p. 535-16
1850 MEIGS CENSUS
Blackstone Reid 33 (Farmer), Jane 27, Raymond 9, Julius 8, James 6, Hanah 4, Susan 2 p. 804-706
Farley Reid 26 (Va), James 8, Mary Jane 2 p. 742-231
William Reed 60 (NC)(Farmer), Nancy 48 (Ky), Matilda 24 (Ky), Tempa 11, Nancy 12, Julian 15 p. 797-662
MARRIAGES (MEIGS)
John Reed to Mary Phillips, 6 Dec 1844 (12 Oct), William Green MG, Elihu Phillips Bm
Judy Louisa Reed to James Neil q.v.
Lones Reed to William Myers q.v.
Nancy A. Reed to Charles Gamble q.v.
Sarah A. Reed to Samuel Deatherage q.v.
MISCELLANEOUS (RHEA)
James Reid: Bondsman for Ransom Murphree, 1816
James C. Reed: Bondsman for James Butler, 1819
" " " Lots 14 & 27, Town of Washington
Jesse Read: Bondsman for Aron Marr, 1824
Samuel Reid: Bondsman for Isham S.E. Hardin, 1816

- - - - - - - - - - - - -

REESE / REECE / REASE / REES / RECE

TAXES (RHEA)
1819 (Capt. John Lewis' Dist.): Jesse Rees 2 BP
Roger Rees 2 BP, 200a
1823 (Capt. Howerton's Co.):
Rodger Reece 165a Vans Spring Creek
1840 RHEA CENSUS
Joseph Rease 000001 - 31001
Mary Rease 0 - 10001 [age 25, pensioner]
Roger Rease 020110001 - 0100001
1850 RHEA CENSUS
Benjamin Reese Unk (Farmer), Mary 30 (NC), Betsy J. 13, Mary A. 6, Lucy G. 4, Letha 3, Thomas B. 2 p. 541-51
Clerk Reese 17: see Rufus M. Crews
Jane Reese 20: see John Usry
Joseph Reese Unk (Unk)(Laborer), Sally 42 (Unk), Nancy 16, Lyda 14, Polly 12, Rebecca 10, Ishum 9, Jane 7, James F. 5, William R. 2 p. 549-111
MARRIAGES (RHEA)
Anny Reese to William Lamond Jr. q.v.
Benjamin Reece to Polly Reece, 27 July 1841 (31 July), E.E. Wasson JP, Maxwell Damport [Davenport?] (R)
Betsey Reese to Aron Marr q.v.
Blancey Reese to Aaron Rhea q.v.
Henry Reece to Polly Jeffries or Jeffers, 5 or 3 Nov 1836 (6 Nov), A.G. Wright JP (AR)
Henry Reece to Alley Runnels, 12 Feb 1828 (same), Matthew Hubbard JP, William Gwin Bm (AR)
Isham Reese to Mahala Thompson, 15 Dec 1830 (16 Dec), James Swan JP, Isaac H. Eddington Bm (AR)
James Reese to Elizabeth Parker, 23 Apr 1824, John Cozby JP, William Forbes Bm (AR)
Polly Reece to Benjamin Reece q.v.
Sally Reese to John Lemmons q.v.
Susannah Reese to John Woodward q.v.
MISCELLANEOUS (RHEA)
Henry Reese: Bondsman for Joseph Foard, 1829
Isham Reece: Bondsman for William Thompson, 1833
" " Witness for Caleb B. Noblett, 1834
Jesse Reece Sr.: Hiwassee District, Pinhook Ferry area
Joseph Reese: Bondsman for John Lemmons, 1832
Mary Reece: Revolutionary War pensioner, 1841 list
Roger Reece: Hiwassee District, Pinhook Ferry area
William H. Reece: Bondsman for Bentley Atkins, 1835
" " " Hiwassee District, Pinhook Ferry area

- - - - - - - - - - - - -

REMLEN

MARRIAGES (RHEA)
Sally Remlen to Martin Shults q.v.

- - - - - - - - - - - - -

RENFRO / RENROE / RENTFRO / RENFROW

1830 RHEA CENSUS
Joshua Renfro 2001 - 00001001 p. 363
Mark Renfrow 311 - 00112001 p. 363
1840 MEIGS CENSUS
Joshua Renfro 0011120001 - 000010001 p. 247
Mark Renfro 202001 - 220001 p. 247
Mary Renfro 03 - 110001 p. 247
1850 MEIGS CENSUS
Mark Rentfro 38 (Farmer), Sarah 40, Joshua 22 (Farmer), John 21, Elizabeth 20, Enaretha (f) 17, Niama 16, James M. 15, Anas 13, Robert 12, Nancy 10, Thomas J. 9, Martin V. 7, Mary Jane 5, Susan E. 2 p. 806-718
Robert Rentfro 27 (Farmer), Lydia 30, Sarah E. 4, William M. 2, Eliza p. 801-679
Thomas Renfro 35 (Farmer), Louisa 28, William 9 p. 806-715
MARRIAGES (MEIGS)
Joshua Renfroe to Elizabeth Rowden, 4 Mar 1850, Leroy Looney JP or Sur
Polly Renfrow to Samuel Baker q.v.
Robert Renfrow to Lydia Daniel, 22 Dec 1845 (same), Leroy Looney JP
Thomas Renfrow to Eliza Ford, 13 Dec 1844 (same), Mark Renfrow JP
MISCELLANEOUS (MEIGS)
John Rentfrow: Cherokee Removal muster roll, 1836
Joshua Renfroe: Hiwassee District
Mark Renfrow: JP 1839-41, 1844; Circuit Court jury, 1836
Thomas Renfrow: Circuit Court jury, 1836; JP(?) 1844
" " Cherokee Removal muster roll, 1836

- - - - - - - - - - - - -

RENOWE / RENOE

MARRIAGES (RHEA)
Eli Renowe to Rebecca Kirksey, 26 Nov 1821 (29 Nov), John Farmer MG, William Banks Bm (AR)
MARRIAGES (MEIGS)
Lavina Renoe to James Hancock q.v.

- - - - - - - - - - - - -

REPPITO / RIPPETO

1840 MEIGS CENSUS
James M. Reppito 11001 - 11001 p. 227
MISCELLANEOUS (MEIGS)
James M. Rippeto: Ocoee District

- - - - - - - - - - - - -

REVELY / REIVLEY / RIVLEY / RIEVLY

TAXES (RHEA)
1823 (Capt. Brown's Co.):
Hugh, Sally, & Farry Revely 350a Tenn River
1840 RHEA CENSUS
Charles Revely 200001 - 11001
1850 RHEA CENSUS
Charles Reevely 40 (Potter), Cyntha 42, Elizabeth L. 16, John E. 13, Nancy L. 12, James M. 10, William J. 8, Hugh P. 6, Robert H. 3 p. 633-641
MARRIAGES (RHEA)
Charles Revely to Cinthy Lauderdale, 12 Jan 1822 (same), John Cozby JP, William B. Cozby Bm (R)
James K. Reevly or Reivly to Polly Walker, 18 July 1822 (same), Matthew Donald MG, Francis Rievley Bm (AR)
Sally Revely to John Parker q.v.
MISCELLANEOUS (RHEA)
Charles Revely: Bondsman for John Parker, 1827
Charles Reiveley: Bondsman for John C. Simpson, 1821
Francis Riveley: Bondsman for James K. Rievly, 1822

- - - - - - - - - - - - -

REVIS

1850 MEIGS CENSUS
James Revis 22 (Farmer), Mary 15 p. 748-283
MARRIAGES (MEIGS)
James Revis to Mary Miller, 16 Jan 1850, John Dabney Sur
MISCELLANEOUS (MEIGS)
James Revis: Private, Mexican War

- - - - - - - - - - - - -

REW

MARRIAGES (MEIGS)
Elizabeth Rew to Samuel Woody q.v.

- - - - - - - - - - - - -

REYNOLDS / RENALDS / RUNNOLDS / RUNNALDS / RUNNELS

TAXES (RHEA)
1819 (Capt. Wm McCray's Co.): John Reynolds 50a
1823 (Capt. Howerton's Co.): Elijah Renalds 1 WP
(Capt Wilson's Co.): Henry Runnels 1 WP
(Capt. Brown's Co.): Jacob Reynolds 1 WP

1830 RHEA CENSUS
Elijah Reynolds 200001 - 11001 p. 365
Jacob Reynolds 0000010001 - 210101 p. 383
Jas or Jos Reynolds 00010001 - 001001 p. 369
John Runnles 011011 - 21101 p. 358
Henry Runnolds 1001011 - 2311001 p. 393

1840 RHEA CENSUS
Elijah Reynolds 21200001 - 101101
Michael Reynolds 020001 - 000001
Sarah Reynolds 0001 - 01111001

1840 MEIGS CENSUS
William Reynolds 00001 - 00001 p. 233

1850 RHEA CENSUS
Michael Reynolds 41 (Farmer), Nelly 42, Henry 17 (Farmer), Thomas 15, Sarah 14, Polly A. 12, Jane 11, Martha 9, James R. 7, Orpha 6, William 4, Fanny 2 p. 595-376
Nancy Reynold 74: see David G. Scragins

1850 MEIGS CENSUS
Thomas Reynolds 48 (NC)(Farmer), Nancy 46, William 21 (Farmer), David 19 (Farmer), Samuel 18, Nathan 17 (Farmer), Benjamin 13, Thomas 10, James M. 5 p. 728-118

MARRIAGES (RHEA)
Alley Runnels to Henry Reece q.v.
Elijah Runnels to Betsy Majors, 6 Aug 1823 (same), James Holloway Bm (A)
Elizabeth Reynolds to Thomas H. Dearing q.v.
Jacob Reynolds to Margaret McAndles or McCandless, 27 Mar 1821 (same), John Rice JP, Richard A. McCandless Bm (AR)
Matilda Runnels to Thomas Majors q.v.
Michael Runnels to Nelly Good, 5 Nov 1830 (same), James A. Darwin JP, Henry Reynolds Bm (AR)
Rachael Reynolds to John Woodward q.v.

MARRIAGES (MEIGS)
Matilda Reynolds to Isaac McKeown q.v.
Susanna Reynolds to James M. Owens q.v.
William A. Reynolds to Frances Houser, 28 May 1840 (1 June), William J. Russell and Joseph McCorkle Bm
William D. Reynolds to Martha A.E. Vernon, 6 Aug 1849 (9 Aug), Jesse Locke MG, John Seabourn Sur

MISCELLANEOUS (RHEA)
Dennis Reynolds: Bondsman for John Woodward, 1819
Elijah Runnals: Bondsman for Isaac Brown, 1826
Henry Reynolds: Bondsman for Michael Runnels, 1830

- - - - - - - - - - - - -

RHEA / RAY

TAXES (RHEA)
1808 (Jas Campbell's List): Hugh Rhea 1 WP, 150a
Jesse Rhea 1 WP
Joseph Ray 1 WP
1819 (Capt. J. Robinsn's Co.): Hugh Rhea 1 WP, 1 BP
(Capt. Bradley's Dist.): John Rhea Esq. 1 Lot, 1202a
(Capt. John Lewis' Co.): Robert Rhea 1 WP, 125a
(Capt. Wm McCray's Co.): Warren Ray 1 WP
1823 (Capt. Howerton's Co.): Aaron Rhea 1 WP
Robert Rhea 1 WP, 100a Piney R
(Capt. Braselton's Co.): Hugh Rhea 1 WP
(Capt. Brown's Co.): John Rhea 1 Town Lot, 1000a below Piney River (NC Grant)
(Capt. Lewis' Co.): William Rhea 1 WP
1830 RHEA CENSUS
Aron Rhea 00001 - 10001 p. 391
Henrietta Rhea 1001 - 0001201 p. 362
Hugh Ray 11012001 - 110011 p. 387
1840 RHEA CENSUS
Aaron Rhea 220001 - 010001
1840 MEIGS CENSUS
Thomas Ray 10001 - 0001 p. 227
William Ray 10001 - 12001 p. 240
1850 RHEA CENSUS
Aaron Rhea Unk (SC)(Farmer), Blanche 40, Warren 21 (Farmer), John 19 (Farmer), Henry 15, Hugh 12, Blanche J. 9, Aaron 5 p. 555-131
James Rhea 26 (Farmer), Jane 24, Wright 2, James 3/12 p. 567-197
Pleasant Rhea 31 (Farmer), Mariah 36, Eliza J. 14, John 11, Mary A. 8, William 6, Orlena T. 4, Robert 2, Lucinda 5/12 p. 572-237
Sarah J. Rhea 14: see James J. Floyd
1850 MEIGS CENSUS
John Ray 23 (Farmer), Mary Jane 21 p. 797-661
Melissa Del Ray 1: see David H. Sharp
William Ray 27 (Farmer), Rhoda 36, Stephen F. 0 p. 808-728

MARRIAGES (RHEA)
Aaron Rhea to Blanchy Rease, 16 May 1822 (17 May), William Kennedy JP, Jacob Garrison Bm (AR)
David Rhea to Elizabeth Crow, 28 Feb 1835, Harmon Gaddy JP(?) (A)
Hugh Rhea to Betsy Beck, 28 Sept 1818, "Found among papers of D. Walker JP" (AR)
Isabella Rhea to Jesse Poe q.v.
James Rhea to Louisa Jane Smith, 5 Feb 1847 (no return) (R)
Jane Rhea to Wesley Hare q.v.
Margaret Rhea to William Davenport q.v.
Peggy Rhea to Robert Hill q.v.
Pleasant Rhea to Mariah Killough, 21 Feb 1840 (same), Richard Waterhouse JP (AR) #1624
Polly Rhea to Hiram Spencer q.v.
Polly Ann Rhea to Thomas Lemmons q.v.
Rachel Rhea to James Doughty q.v.
Rebecca Rhea to Squire Burton q.v.
Reuben or Robert Rhea to Matilda Gibson, 7 June 1828 (10 June), Danl Briggs MG, John Johnston Bm (AR)
Vinney Rhea to Joseph Marr q.v.
Warren Rhea to Elizabeth Marr(?), 23 Feb 1819 (same), Jonathan Fine JP, Aaron Atkins Bm (AR)
William Rhea to Mary R. Edington or Eddington, 9 Sept 1833 (12 Sept), John Pardee MMEC, Jefferson Riggle Bm (AR)
MARRIAGES (MEIGS)
Annes Ray to William Hair q.v.
Jacob Rray [sic] to Abagail Guron, 30 Oct 1838, M. Shaver JP(?)
John Ray to Mary J. Winton, 2 Mar 1849 (6 Mar), S.B. Harwell MG(?), John Seabourn Sur(?)
Richardson Rhea to Elizabeth Davis, 13 May 1846 (14 May), D.L. Godsey MG, Isaac Benson Sur
Thomas Rhea to Mary McNutt, 30 Aug 1838 (6 Sept), William Lea JP, Thomas Leuty Sur
William Ray to Rodey McWinton, 27 Dec 1848 (29 Dec), James Sewell MG, John Seaburn Sur
MISCELLANEOUS (RHEA)
A. Ray: Elder, Concord Baptist Church of Christ, 1824
Abner Ray: Cherokee Removal muster roll, 1837
Pleasant Ray: Bondsman for David Robinson, 1838
MISCELLANEOUS (MEIGS)
Aaron Ray: Private, Mexican War
Abner Ray: Hiwassee District, Ten Mile Stand area
Pleasant Rhea: Private, Mexican War

- - - - - - - - - - - - -

RHODES / RODES / ROADS

TAXES (RHEA)
1819 (Capt. Bradley's Co.): John H. Rodes 2 Town Lots
1823 (Capt. Brown's Co.): John H. Roads 2 Town Lots
1840 MEIGS CENSUS
Andrew Rhodes 22000000 - 000001 p. 226
1850 RHEA CENSUS
Hiley Rhodes 49 (Va), Joseph 18 (Ky)(Farmer), James B. 12, Caroline 9/12 p. 619-539
Tinsley Rhodes 32 (NC)(Blacksmith), Frances 30 (NC), Sarah J. 12, William S. 10, Elizabeth 8, Martha A. 5, Caswell 2 p. 553-117
MARRIAGES (MEIGS)
Louisa Rodes to Benjamin Cash q.v.
MISCELLANEOUS (RHEA)
John H. Rodes: Signed Petition to move Indian Agency

- - - - - - - - - - - - -

RICE / RISE / REICE / RICER

TAXES (RHEA)
1819 (Capt. Bradley's Dist.): John Rice 1 WP
Rice & Mitchell 2 Town Lots
1823 (Capt. Brown's Co.): Joseph Rice 1 WP
1830 RHEA CENSUS
Aaron Rice 00001 - 0 p. 365
Alexander Rice 20001 - 00001 p. 370
Henry Rice 10011 - 000001 p. 391
Jesse Reice 000002001 - 00000001 p. 364
John Rice 211001 - 011001 p. 352
John Ricer 1001 - 00001 p. 378
Margaret Ricer 0003 - 100121 p. 378
Roge Rice 0211001 - 210001 p. 364
Roger Rice 01001001 - 0000101 p. 391

William Rice 200011 - 00011 p. 377
[1 very dim; may have been erased]
William Rice 00101001 - 0122001 p. 377
William Ryce 300101 - 0220001 p. 369

1840 RHEA CENSUS

Alexander Rice 210001 - 000001

1840 MEIGS CENSUS

Jesse Rice 0010001 - 22101 p. 234
Richard Rice 00001 - 00001 p. 227
William S. Rice 10001 - 20001 p. 231

1850 MEIGS CENSUS

Alexander Rice 43 (Va)(Farmer), Lucinda 36, Amedia 18, Alexander 15, George W. 9, Almira 7, Mary M. 6, Martha 5, Andrew J. 4, Celia J.C. 1, Mary TAYLOR 44 p. 760-378 [Lucinda and Mary Taylor, daus of Robert and Catharine Sevier Taylor]

Calvin Rice 23 (Farmer), Eliza Jane 21, Sarah Ann 3, Jesse V. 2, Nancy E. 1 p. 762-389

Jesse Rice 53 (NC)(Farmer), Sarah 29, Elizabeth 19, Mary 16, Lackey (f) 13, Mahala 8, John H. 6, Thomas J. 3 p. 762-388

Richard Rice 30 (Farmer), Olivia 30, William 9, Eliza Jane 7, Miles F. 5, Racheal P. 3 p. 731-141

MARRIAGES (RHEA)

Alexander Rice to Margaret Price, 27 Oct 1825 (same), John Robinson JP, David Leuty Bm (AR)

Alexander Rice to Lucinda Taylor, 26 Nov 1840 (27 Nov), D.L. Godsey MG (A)

Ann Rice to John P. Hays q.v.

Catherine Rice to Greenberry G. Parker q.v.

Elijah C. Rice to Sally Rowden, 17 Apr 1833 (same), Matthew Hubbert JP, William Lewis Bm (AR)

George W. Rice to Emaline Paine, 11 Dec 1827 (same), John Henninger MG, Thomas McCallie Bm (AR) [Emaline, dau of William and Orpha Paine] [1850 Marion Census: George W. Rice 43, Emiline 42, Mary P. 21, Louisa 19, Caroline 16, Patrick 14, Andrew 10, Orphy 6]

Jane Rice to Christian Corell q.v.

Joseph Rice to Mary Miller, 16 Dec 1819, Benjamin Johnson Bm (A)

Joseph Rise to Elizabeth Lewty [Leuty?], 21 Dec 1847 (23 Dec), Jesse Locke MG (R)

Miranda Rice to John McClanahan q.v.

Polly Rice to Welcome Wilhelm q.v.

Susan Rice to James A. Mahan q.v.

William Rice to Elizabeth or Eliza Francis, 26 Sept 1824 (same), John Robinson JP, Hugh Crozier Bm (AR)

MARRIAGES (MEIGS)

Amedia Rice to Emily Taff, 1 Oct 1850, David Gennoe Sur

Calvin Rice to Eliza J. Richardson, 5 Nov 1845 (6 Nov), D.L. Godsey MG, David Gennoe Bm

Richard Rice to Angeline Collins, 9 Aug 1838 (same), Mathias Shaver JP, Robert Pearce Sur

Susan Rice to William H. Dearmon q.v.

MISCELLANEOUS (RHEA)

Alexander Rice: Bondsman for John McClanahan, 1829
" " Bondsman for Charles M.K. Welch, 1834
Elijah Rice: Bondsman for William Barnett, 1822
Elijah E. Rice 2nd Bugler, Mexican War
James G. Rice: Signed petition to move Indian Agency
John Rice: Bondsman for Robert W. McMillen, 1819
" " Bondsman for John Robinson, 1822
" " Bondsman for Nathan Harwood, 1824
John Rice: JP 1819-25; hotel keeper in Washington
" " Signed petition to move Indian Agency
" " Lots 8,79,80 in Town of Washington
Rice, Humphrey & Co.: Early merchants in Washington
Samuel R. Rice: Lot 45, Town of Washington, 1814
William Rice: Bondsman for James A. Mahan, 1835

MISCELLANEOUS (MEIGS)

Alexander Rice: 3rd Sgt., Cherokee Removal muster roll
Calvin Rice: Surety for Samuel Hardy, 1850
Isaac Rice: Hiwassee District, Moore's Chapel area
Joel Rice: Hiwassee Dist, Cottonport - Moore's Chapel area
Richard Rice: Cherokee Removal muster roll, 1837

- - - - - - - - - - - -

RICHARDS

TAXES (RHEA)

1823 (Capt. Wilson's Co.): Curtis Richards 1 WP
James Richards 1 WP

1830 RHEA CENSUS

Carter Richards 0001 - 12101 p. 356

1840 MEIGS CENSUS

Curtis Richards 210001 - 000221 p. 245
James Richards 100001 - 1100101 p. 238

1850 MEIGS CENSUS

Curtis Richards 53 (NC)(Farmer), Edith 48 (NC), Charles 18 (Farmer), Joseph J. 16 (Farmer), Elijah D. 13, Semintha 9, Elizabeth 6 p. 810-744

Leodica Richards (f) 35, Luke 15, Angaline 8, Sapporia 4, Hannah ATCHLEY 61 p. 784-560

May Richards 45: see Farley Brady

MARRIAGES (RHEA)

Charles Richards to Mary Sapp, 23 July 1815, "I certify that I married Them" J. Fine JP, Jonathan Burns Bm (AR)

Curtis Richards to Edy Maynard, 9 Aug 1826 (10 Aug), Beal Gaither JP, Gross Scruggs Bm (R)

James Richards to Besey Atchley, 9 Mar 1829 (10 Mar), Beal Gaither JP (AR)

Joshua Richards to Tempy Rush, 12 Dec 1825 (13 Dec), John Farmer MG, Henry Jones Bm (AR)

Patsy Richards to Jonathan Burns q.v.

MARRIAGES (MEIGS)

Louesa J. Richards to James J. Floyd q.v.

Polly M. Richards to William Bolin q.v.

MISCELLANEOUS (RHEA)

Frederick Richards: Surveyor's list of land S of Tenn River

- - - - - - - - - - - -

RICHARDSON / RITCHERSON / RICHESON / RICHISON

1830 RHEA CENSUS

John Richardson 22101 - 000001 p. 360
Zedock Richardson 11001 - 110001 p. 375

1840 RHEA CENSUS

Thomas Richardson 1212001 - 10001

1840 MEIGS CENSUS

John Richeson 00001 - 10001 p. 235
Nancy Richeson 02 - 0020001 p. 235

1850 MEIGS CENSUS

John Richardson 25 (Va)(Farmer), Lucinda 26 (Va), Sarah E. 9, Paralee 7, Julia 4, Thos 2, Jas 1 p. 749-299

MARRIAGES (RHEA)
David Richardson to Jincey Jacobs, 2 or 7 May 1821 (9 May), John Cozby JP, Thomas Davis Bm (AR)
Hiram Richardson to Catherine Hoslin, 3 Sept 1843 (A)
Jinsey Richardson to Isaac W. Geren q.v.
Mary Ann Richardson to J.W. Oakes q.v.
William Ritcherson to Nancy Givens, 7 Sept 1847 (same), S.R. Hackett JP (R)
MARRIAGES (MEIGS)
Eliza J. Richardson to Calvin Rice q.v.
James Richardson to Nancy Moore, 29 Dec 1847 (same), D.L. Godsey MG
Nathan Richardson to Mary J. Rodgers, 23 Nov 1845 (27 Nov), D.L. Godsey MG, Wm P. Richardson Bm
William P. Richardson to July Ann Rogers, 4 Jan 1844 (same), D.L. Godsey MG, N. Richardson Bm
MISCELLANEOUS (RHEA)
Amos Richardson: Revolutionary War pensioner, 1835 list
Wm Richardson: Bondsman for Frederick Williams, 1844
" " Private, Mexican War
MISCELLANEOUS (MEIGS)
James Richison: Hiwassee District
Zedoc Richardson: Hiwassee District, Cottonport area

\- - - - - - - - - - - - -

RICHMOND / RICHMON

1830 RHEA CENSUS
John S. Richmon 11001 - 30001 p. 364
MARRIAGES (RHEA)
Jane Richmon to Jesse H. McFall q.v.
John S. Richmond to Mary Chastain, 22 May 1822 (same), John Farmer MG, Joseph Chastain Bm (AR)
Joseph Richmond to Ann Stacy, 24 July 1828, Daniel Smith Bm (A)
MISCELLANEOUS (MEIGS)
John S. Richmond: Hiwassee District, Pinhook Ferry area
Joseph Richmond: Hiwassee District, Pinhook Ferry area

\- - - - - - - - - - - - -

RIDDLE / RIDLE

TAXES (RHEA)
1808 (Joseph Brooks' List): James Riddle 1 WP, 150a
1819 (Capt. McCray's Co.): Jeremiah Riddle 1 WP, 150a
1823 (Capt. Howerton's Co.):
Jeremiah Riddle 150a Whites Creek
Samuel T. Ridle 1 WP
1840 MEIGS CENSUS
Thomas Riddle 110001 - 20001 p. 247
1850 RHEA CENSUS
Joshua I. Riddle 34 (Blacksmith), Martha 30, Milo 13, Arlena 11, James 9, Mahala A. 7 p. 639-679
1850 MEIGS CENSUS
Benjamin H. Riddle 26 (Farmer), Elizabeth J. 23 (NC), Thomas J. 1 p. 790-607 [Benjamin married Elizabeth H. Fairell on 3 Dec 1846 in McMinn County]
Thomas Riddle 42 (Farmer), Elizabeth J. 34, Elias 16 (Farmer), John 16 (Farmer), Catharine 12, Mary Ann 11, Jane 9, William 7, Elizabeth 4, Margaret 3, Harriet 1 p. 802-685

MARRIAGES (RHEA)
Amitta Riddle to Charles Morgan q.v.
Elizabeth Riddle to John Riddle q.v.
James Riddle to Rhoda King, 13 July 1833, Aron Miller Bm (A)
John Riddle to Elizabeth Riddle, 14 Feb 1824 (same), John McGill Bm (A)
Malinda Riddle to William McDowell q.v.
Peggy Riddle to Daniel Higgins q.v.
Terry Riddle to Polly Patterson, 15 or 14 Sept 1819 (same), Robert Patterson JP and Bm (AR)
MISCELLANEOUS (RHEA)
Jeremiah Riddle: Bondsman for Daniel Higgins, 1824

\- - - - - - - - - - - - -

RIGGS / RIGG

1830 RHEA CENSUS
Addison Riggs 10001 - 10001 p. 370
Martin Riggs 20101 - 00001 p. 370
Townsley Riggs 0010001 - 01010001 p. 370
1840 MEIGS CENSUS
Adison Rigg 211001 - 21101 p. 229
Martin Rigg 012001 - 210001 p. 224
Townly Rigg 0000000001 - 000020001 p. 229
William B. Rigg 00001 - 00001 p. 229
1850 MEIGS CENSUS
Martin Riggs 44 (Va)(Farmer), Delilah 45 (NC), Robert A. 21 (Farmer), William A. 19 (Farmer), Charlotte E. 17, Martha M. 15, Martin V. 10, Malinda C. 8, George W. 5, Margaret E. 3 p. 723-85
Tunley Rigg 80 (Md)(Farmer), Charity 73 (Va), Martha 3 (Va) p. 744-248
William Rigg 37 (Va)(Farmer), Claressa Ann 27 (Va), Mary 13 p. 731-139
MARRIAGES (RHEA)
Martin Rigg to Delila Blacke, 16 July 1825 (21 July), Thomas Hall MG, William Hunter Bm (AR)
Matilda Riggs to Samuel Gamble q.v.
Nancy Rigg to Isaac Clement q.v.
MARRIAGES (MEIGS)
Jane Rigg to James Collins q.v.
MISCELLANEOUS (RHEA and MEIGS)
Martin Rigg: Ocoee District
William B. Rigg: Bondsman for Tipton Wood, 1835

\- - - - - - - - - - - - -

RIGGLE / RIGLE / RIEGLE

TAXES (RHEA)
1819 (Capt. Ramsey's Co.): George W. Riggle 1 WP, 2 lots
Henry Riggle 2 BP, 1 lot
Jacob Riggle 1 WP
John Riggle 1 WP
1823 (Capt. McCall's Co.): George W. Riggle 1 WP
(Capt. Braselton's Co.): John Riggle 1 WP
1830 RHEA CENSUS
George W. Rigle 011001 - 00120001 p. 387
John Rigle 0102001 - 0210001 p. 387
1840 RHEA CENSUS
John Riggle 000010001 - 00021001

MARRIAGES (RHEA)
Ann Rigle to Burwell M. Harwood q.v.
Betsy Riggle to Martin Wyrick q.v.
Eliza Riggle to Wilson Davenport q.v.
George W. Riegle to Sely Rector, 24 Apr 1810, John A. Smith Bm (A)
Gilbert Riggle to Alethia West, 27 Feb 1837 (28 Feb), Jacob Gear JP, Rolly C. Miller Bm (AR)
Malinda Riggle to Joshua Bailey q.v.
Manerva T. Riggle to Martin Orr q.v.
Marial Riggle to Michael Davis q.v.
MISCELLANEOUS (RHEA)
George Riggle: Bondsman for Nicholas Starnes, 1816
Gilbert Riggle: Bondsman for William A. Chastain, 1836
" " Bondsman for Wilson Davenport, 1837
" " Bondsman for Michael Davis, 1838
Henry Riggle: Bondsman for Martin Wyrick, 1819
" " Signed petition to move Indian Agency
Henry Riggel: Lots 7,36,37 in Town of Washington
Jacob Riggle: Bondsman for James Moore, 1812
" " Bondsman for Hughlett W. Smith, 1836
" " Lot 15 in Town of Washington
Jefferson Riggle: Bondsman for William Rhea, 1833
Solomon Riggle: Signed petition to move Indian Agency

- - - - - - - - - - - -

RILEY / RILLEY

MARRIAGES (RHEA)
Catherine Riley to Andrew Lacy q.v.
James Riley to Jennie or Janney Shields, 20 Feb 1815 (no return) (AR)
Robert Willey or Rilley to Polly Dunlady, 20 June 1829 (21 July), John Farmer MG, Thomas Seay Bm (AR)

- - - - - - - - - - - -

RINEHART / RHINEHEART

1840 MEIGS CENSUS
Joseph Rinehart 02010001 - 0002 p. 232
1850 MEIGS CENSUS
Emanuel Rinehart 34 (NC)(Farmer), Mary Ann 27, Betsy Jane 4, Tennessee 2 p. 771-463
MARRIAGES (RHEA)
Rachel Rinehart to David Barnett q.v.
MARRIAGES (MEIGS)
Ann Rhineheart toWilliam Tharp q.v.
Emanuel Rhinehart to Polly Ingle, 17 July 1844 (same), D. L. Godsey MG, Chain Moore Sur
Rebecca Rhineheart to John Price q.v.

- - - - - - - - - - - -

RIPLEY

1830 RHEA CENSUS
Pleasant Ripley 01011 - 321001 p. 355
MARRIAGES (RHEA)
Pleasant Ripley to Sally Godby, 22 Oct 1831 (7 Nov), Heil Butram JP, James Ripley Bm (AR)
MISCELLANEOUS (RHEA)
James Ripley: Bondsman for Pleasant Ripley, 831

- - - - - - - - - - - -

RITCHIE / RICHEY

1850 RHEA CENSUS
Polly Ritchie 42 (NC), Dewsey 14, John 12 p. 559-157
MARRIAGES (RHEA)
James P. Ritchie to Mary Ann Gordon, 20 Mar 1832 (same), William Kerr JP, Adam Seybolt Bm (AR)
Margaret Richey to Elias J. Chapin q.v.

- - - - - - - - - - - -

RIVERS

1830 RHEA CENSUS
William Rivers 010001 - 10001 p. 377
1840 MEIGS CENSUS
William Rivers 1101001 - 1122001 p. 230
MARRIAGES (MEIGS)
Daniel Rivers to Emily J. Wade, 31 Dec 1846 (same), Thomas B. Mall(?) [1850 McMinn Census: Daniel Rivers 26, Jane 22, Mary J. 10/12]
Martha Rivers to Creed Walker q.v.
MISCELLANEOUS (MEIGS)
William Rivers: JP(?) 1840

- - - - - - - - - - - -

ROACH

MARRIAGES (RHEA)
Henry Roach to Polly Slagle, 28 Nov 1834 (no return), Chas O'Kelley Bm (AR)

- - - - - - - - - - - -

ROANE

TAXES (RHEA)
1819 (Capt. Bradley's Dist.): Archibald Roane 1000a
MISCELLANEOUS (RHEA)
Lewis Roane: Bondsman for Levy Chaney, 1819

- - - - - - - - - - - -

ROARK / ROWARK

TAXES (RHEA)
1823 (Capt. Piper's Co.): Thomas Roark 1 WP
180 RHEA CENSUS
Samuel Rowark 111001 - 111001 p. 362
Thomas Rowark 420011 - 20101 p. 362
1840 MEIGS CENSUS
John Roark 10001 - 1001 p. 248
Samuel Roark 0111001 - 0011101 p. 248
Thomas Roark 0341001 - 10021001 p. 239
1850 MEIGS CENSUS
Samuel Roark 28 (Carpenter) p. 818-805
Samuel Roark 51 (SC)(Farmer), Sarah 46 (SC), Mary Ann 22, James M. or W. 19 (Farmer), Thomas 15 or possibly 18 p. 819-810
Thomas Roark 54 (Farmer), Sarah 27, Gilford 16 (Farmer), Elizabeth 14 p. 818-804

MARRIAGES (RHEA)

James Roark to Jerusha Blythe, 24 Aug 1825 (1 Sept), Thomas Hall JP, Wm S. Leuty Bm (AR)
[1850 Hamilton Census: James Roark 52, Jeresalum 44, Wm 18, Martha 15, Joseph 8, Sarah 5]

Lewis Roark to Jane Frazier, 10 Feb 1821 (11 Feb or 12 Mar), J. Thompson JP, John Davis Bm (AR)

MARRIAGES (MEIGS)

Dicy Roark to Jackson West q.v.

Harvey Roark to Susan Manerd, 24 Mar 1847, John K. Brown JP

John H. Roark to Lutitia Witten, 18 Oct 1847 (21 Oct), Heil Buttram MG, D.L. Godsey Sur

Margaret Roark to William Knox q.v.

Mary Ann Roark to Grisley Hackler q.v.

Nancy Roark to Joshua E. Witten q.v.

Thomas Roark to Mary Daniel, 26 Aug 1844 (27 Aug), William Green MG

MISCELLANEOUS (MEIGS)

James Roark: Hiwassee District, Moore's Chapel area

Thomas Roark: Hiwassee District, Moore's Chapel area

- - - - - - - - - - - - -

ROBERTS / ROBERT

TAXES (RHEA)

1819 (Capt. Bradley's Dist.): H.D.F. Roberts 1 WP, 6 Lots

1850 RHEA CENSUS

Snelson Roberts 35 (NC)(School Teacher), Jemima 35, Martha J. 16, Edmund F. 15, Hugh L.W. 13, Balis P. 11, Ann S. 9, Josaphine 7, Homer V.M. 5, Alfred E. 3, John W.T. 1 p. 548-101

1850 MEIGS CENSUS

George W. Roberts 19 (Farmer), Lelia 18 p. 725-100
[George Roberts married Selita Sharp on 2 Mar 1848 in Roane County]

Hugh Roberts 65 (Farmer), Sarah 35, Hugh 23 (Farmer) p. 792-620

MARRIAGES (RHEA)

Thomas P. Robits or Roberts to Nancy Roddye, 27 July 1819 (same), John Rice JP, Thomas S. Jones Bm (AR)

John Roberts to Mahala Bolen, 1 June 1830 (2 June), Joseph McCorkle JP, William Blevins Bm (AR)

MISCELLANEOUS (RHEA)

Henry D.F. Roberts: MG 1818

Snelson Roberts: MG 1849-50

MISCELLANEOUS (MEIGS)

Peter Roberts: JP(?) 1840

- - - - - - - - - - - - -

ROBINSON / ROBERTSON / ROBERSON / ROBESON / ROBISON / REBESON

TAXES (RHEA)

1808 (John Henry's List): Tirey Robinson 1 BP
John Robertson 1 WP*
Miles Robinson 1 WP*
[*sons of Tirey]

1819 (Capt. Bradley's Dist.): Fleming Robinson 1 WP
(Capt. John Robinson's Co.):
John Robinson 1 WP, 1 BP, 1 Town Lot

1823 (Capt. Piper's Co.): Calvin Robertson 1 WP
Calvin Robertson 1 WP
(Capt. Lewis' Co.): John Robinson 1 WP, 40a

1830 RHEA CENSUS

Calvin Robertson 001001 - 001001 p. 359

J.F.K. Robertson 111101 - 10001 p. 384

Robert Robison 2101001 - 011201 p. 383

1840 RHEA CENSUS

Anthony Robinson 100001 - 20001

David Robertson 10001 - 00001

Edward Robertson 10001 - 10001

Harvey Robinson 10001 - 10001

James Robertson 110001 - 200001

John Robinson 110001 - 110001

John Robertson 110001 - 200001

Robert Robertson 00210001 - 0000101

Sarah Robertson 0001 - 001100001

1840 MEIGS CENSUS

Arthur Robertson 00101 - 1001 p. 241

Benjamin Robertson 001010001 - 1100100011 p. 241

1850 RHEA CENSUS

Anthony Robison 40 (Va)(Farmer), Malinda 38, Susan E. 14, William 13, Lutitia J. 11, Thomas H. 9, Semantha C. 7, John W. 3, George H. 1, Thomas LANE 20 p. 584-323

David Robison 36 (Farmer), Eliza 35, Benjamin B. 10, William R. 9, Mary A. 7, George W. 5, James W.G. 6/12 p. 572-238

Harvey Robeson 37 (Va)(Miller), Mahala 37, Thomas H. 9, Nancy A. 8, Elizabeth T. 5 p. 585-326

Hezekiah Robison 21 (Farmer), Elizabeth 25, Andrew J. 7/12, Martha HARWOOD 75 (SC) p. 573-241

James Robison 45 (Farmer), Elizabeth 40, Felix A. 19, Mary J. 15, Martha A. 12, James O. 9, Catharine E. 7, Thomas J. 3, David F. 9/12 p. 533-6

John Robeson 51 (Farmer), Hannah 41, Benjamin F. 18 (Farmer), Elbert E. 15, Brunetta A. 14, Eliza R. 11, Samuel P.C. 8, John M. 7, James A. 4 p. 541-56
[John married Hannah Earnest of Greene Co.; his brother, James, married Elizabeth Earnest. They were sons of Jacob Robinson]

Permelia Robeson 45 (Va), Harvey 17 (Farmer), George 14, Benjamin 13 p. 584-324

Samuel Robeson 39 (Wagonmaker), Mary 32, Mary E. 6, John W. 4, Thomas F. 2 p. 548-103 [Samuel, son of Jacob, married Mary McPherson]

Sarah Robison 60 (Pa), Sarah N. 28 (NC), William A. 25 (NC), Margaret J. 19 (NC) p. 586-339

1850 MEIGS CENSUS

Andrew Robertson 51 (NC)(Farmer), Frances 51 (NC), Andrew 19 (Ky)(Farmer), Mary Jane 16, Sarah C. 14, Zarina 10, Turner G. 7 p. 782-541

Calvin C. Robinson 23 (School Teacher), Martha L. 22 p. 772-470

Daniel Robertson 26 (Farmer), Susannah A. 18, Sarah E. 1 p. 811-748

James C. Roberson 25 (Farmer), Emetter 22, Mathis 3 p. 819-813

MARRIAGES (RHEA)

A.M. or Alexander M. Robeson to Ann I. Payne or Ann Ivy Page, 12 Aug 1839 (13 Aug), Jacob Gear JP (AR)

David Robinson to Eliza Harwood, 18 Oct 1838 (same), Jas Montgomery JP, Pleasant Rhea Bm (AR)

Edward M. Robertson to Susannah Robertson, 28 Dec 1837 (same), James Montgomery JP (R) [Allen shows the year as 1839 and the Bm as Harrison Barnett]
Elizabeth Robertson to James I. Duncan q.v.
Fanny Robertson to Lewis James q.v.
Hezekiah Roberson to Elizabeth Harwood, 20 Dec 1848 (21 Dec), Snelson Roberts MG (R)
Jane Robinson to Harrison Barnett q.v.
Jane Robinson to Nicholas Powell Jr. q.v.
John Robinson to Polly L. Lavender, 25 Jan 1822 (27 Jan), John Rice JP & Bm (AR)
Mark Robinson to Polly Spartin or Spurlin, 18 Sept 1813 (same), William Long JP (AR)
Mary Robinson to Richard M. Johnson q.v.
Milly Robinson to Jeremiah Hammond q.v.
Susannah Robertson to Edward M. Robertson q.v.
William Robinson or Robertson to Mary Compton or Crumpton, 4 or 2 Sept 1844 (5 Sept), John S. Evens JP, James C. Miller Bm (AR)
William E. Robinson to Harriett Harwood, 5 Oct 1849 (same), W.E. Colville JP (R)

MARRIAGES (MEIGS)

Arthur Robinson to Nancy Baker, 21 Aug 1838 (26 Aug), William Green MG, Nelson C. Redmond Sur
Calvin E. Robeson to Martha L. Guinn, 29 Apr 1850, Chas K. Smith Sur
Daniel Robertson to Susan M. Bell, 26 Oct 1848 (30 Oct), N.B. Briggs MG
Frances Robertson to George W. Ahart q.v.
James Robinson to Martha Maberry, 17 Aug 1842 (same), James M. Hague JP, William Mayberry Bm
James Madison Robeson to Emeretta Fairbanks, 2 Sept 1846 (3 Sept), D.L. Godsey MG
Mary Robeson to William Redmon q.v.
Temperance M. Robeson to John E. McAlpin q.v.

MISCELLANEOUS (RHEA)

David Robinson: Bondsman for John Moore, 1842
James Robinson: Trustee, Sulphur Springs Meth. Ch., 1841
" " Trustee, Mars Hill Academy, 1850
John Robinson: Bm for Thos Howerton or Hamilton, 1818
" " Bondsman for John Parker, 1819
" " JP 1822-26; Registerar of Deeds 1823-27
John Robertson: Bondsman for Lewis James, 1823
Robert Robertson: Bondsman for Wyatt Silcox, 1835

MISCELLANEOUS (MEIGS)

Alexander C. Robinson: Hiwassee Dist, Burkett Chapel area
Andrew Robertson: Surety for George W. Ahert, 1850
Calvin Robertson: Purchased Lots 51,52,57 in Decatur
M. C. Robertson: MG 1849

\- - - - - - - - - - - -

ROCKHOLD / ROCKHOLT

1850 MEIGS CENSUS

Alford Rockhold 46 (Farmer) p. 749-296
Tolbert Rockhold 29 (Doctor): see Ruth Blevins
William Rockhold 48, Nancy 25, Frances 9, Thomas 7, James 5, William 3, Tolbert 1 p. 749-298

MARRIAGES (RHEA)

Mary Rockhold to James Hall q.v.
Ruth (Mary) Rockhold to James Blevins q.v.

MARRIAGES (MEIGS)

William Rockhold to Nancy Melton, 17 Mar 1840 (19 Mar), Peach Taylor JP, W. Lillard Sur(?)

MISCELLANEOUS (MEIGS)

Thomas Rockholt: Purchased Lots 56 & 68 in Decatur
Thomas T. Rockholt: Cherokee Removal muster roll, 1837

\- - - - - - - - - - - -

RODDY / RODDYE / RODY

TAXES (RHEA)

1819 (Capt. McCray's Co.) Jesse Roddye 1 WP, 891½a
1823 (Capt. Howerton's Co.): James Roddy 1 WP
Jesse Roddy 1 WP, 883a

1830 RHEA CENSUS

Isaac Roddy 2100001 - 010001 p. 383
James Roddy 11001 - 20001 p. 389
Jane Roddy 1111 - 00101 p. 383
Jesse Roddy 000011001 - 00111001 p. 389
Jesse Roddy 00001 - 03001 p. 389
Jno Rody 1110001 - 0110001 p. 372
Rosanna Roddy 0101 - 0000001 p. 365

1840 RHEA CENSUS

Harvey Roddy 110110002 - 000110101
James Roddy 101101 - 122001
Jesse Roddy 000010001 - 0001
Jesse Roddy Jr. 11001 - 10001
Mary Roddy 0021 - 0110001

1850 RHEA CENSUS

David M. Roddy 40 (Farmer), Elizabeth B. 27, Wright S. 5, Mary J. 3, David M. 11/12, William COLEMAN 17 p. 535-14 [David, son of Jesse]
Harvey Roddy 33 (Farmer), Martha J. 29, Richard C. 10, John T. 8, Rachael J. 6, Edward 4, Peter G. 2, Jenkin DAVID 85, Elizabeth RODDY Unk, James RODDY 19 p. 605-472
Jesse Roddy 36 (Farmer), Susan 33, James 11, Lyda A. 9, Thomas 7, John 6, Jane 4, Margaret 9/12, Jesse RODDY 76 (Farmer) p. 546-85
Margaret Roddy 45, Jesse P. 26 (Farmer), William G. 24 (Farmer), Sarah 19, Mary 16, Susan 14, Elizabeth 12, George 10, Amanda STOCKTON 12, Rector PRESTON 46 (Farmer) p. 546-86

MARRIAGES (RHEA)

Anney Roddye to George Preston q.v.
Catherine Roddye to Robert Craven q.v.
Charlotte Roddy to Samuel T. Whittenburg q.v.
David M. Roddy to Elizabeth Smith, 2 Nov 1842 (same), Jesse P. Thompson JP (R)
Elizabeth Roddy to William P. Gillenwaters q.v.
Eliza Jane Roddy to Jacob K. Caldwell q.v.
Harry Roddy to Martha Jane Boulton, 19 July 1838 (same), Richard Waterhouse JP, John S. Evens Bm (AR)
James E. Roddy to Elizabeth I. Lewis, 28 Dec 1848 (same), William H. Bell MG (R)
Jesse Roddye to Susan Lea, 5 Sept 1836 (8 Sept), George Preston JP (AR)
Liddy Roddy to Allen Haley q.v.
Lucinda Roddy to Benjamin White q.v.
Mahala Roddy to Moses Farmer q.v.
Nancy Roddy to Thomas P. Roberts q.v.

MISCELLANEOUS (RHEA)
David M. Roddy: Bondsman for Thomas Hudleston, 1839
" " " Bondsman for Calvin C. Dudley, 1841
" " " Sheriff 1840-42
Isaac Roddye: Bondsman for Samuel F. Martin, 1827
" " JP 1831
James Roddye Bondsman for George W. Short, 1836
" " Bondsman for Charles Woolard, 1836
" " Postmaster at Kelly's Ferry (Cottonport) 1831
James E. Roddy: Private, Mexican War
Jesse Roddye: Bondsman for John Young, 1810
" " Bondsman for John Hampton, 1833
" " Bondsman for Moses Farmer, 1834
" " Bondsman for Russell D. Walker, 1841
" " Early resident, Town of Washington
" " Commission for Town of Washington, 1813
" " Signed petition to move Indian Agency
John Roddy: Laid out village of Cottonport, 1834
Phillip Roddye: Lot 28, Town of Washington
William T. Roddy: Signed petition to move Indian Agency
MISCELLANEOUS (MEIGS)
Edward Roddy: Sgt., Mexican War
Isaac Roddy: Hiwassee District, Cottonport area
James Roddy: Private, Mexican War

\- - - - - - - - - - - - -

RODRICK

TAXES (RHEA)
1823 (Capt. McCall's Co.): Samuel Rodrick 1 WP

\- - - - - - - - - - - - -

ROGERS / RODGERS

TAXES (RHEA)
1819 (Capt. McCray's Co.): James Rogers 2 BP, 288½a
(Capt. McGill's Co.): William Rogers 1 WP
1823 (Capt. Howerton's Co.):
James Rodgers 1 WP, 1 BP, 443½a
1830 RHEA CENSUS
Elijah Rodgers 111001 - 31101 p. 356
James Rogers 00110001 - 000110001 p. 388
John Rodgers 00001 - 00001 p. 356
William M. Rodgers 010001 - 11001 p. 356
1840 RHEA CENSUS
Ann Rogers 0 - 000000001
1840 MEIGS CENSUS
Sarah Rogers 11 - 01110001 p. 245
William M. Rogers 2011001 - 021101 p. 236
1850 RHEA CENSUS
John Rogers 44 (Va)(Farmer), Elizabeth 39 (Va), William M. 18 (Va)(Farmer), James A. 17 (Va)(Farmer), Henry T. 15 (Va), Mary A. 13 (Va), Nancy J. 11 (Va), David 9 (Va), Samantha S. 7 (Va), Mark A. 5 (Va), Emanuel B. 3 (Va) p. 550-114
1850 MEIGS CENSUS
Joseph Rogers 41 (Farmer), Mary 30, Elizabeth 17, Nancy 14, Mary 12, Annis 8, J.K.P. 6, Sarah 3, Margaret 1 p. 757-357
William M. Rodgers 54 (Surveyor), Mary 47, Mahala E. 19, Sarah E.T. 15, William W. 13, Franklin 11 p. 775-492

MARRIAGES (RHEA)
Benjamin Rogers or Robers to Permelle or Permealy Moyers, 5 Sept 1822 (same), John Cozby JP, James Smith Bm (AR)
Elizabeth Rodgers to Asa Newport q.v.
James Rodgers to Margaret P. Campbell, 22 Apr 1813, John Love Bm (A)
James Rogers to Phebe Owens, 20 Oct 1831, Alexander Owens Bm (A)
John Rodgers to Sarah Collins, 3 Sept 1829 (same), James A. Darwin JP, William Rodgers Bm (AR)
Margaret Rogers to William Gordon q.v.
Martha L. Rogers to Elias Majors q.v.
Mary Rogers to William Cox q.v.
William Rodgers to Nelly May, 14 June 1813 (no return), David Gentry Bm (AR)
William Rogers to Mary Lauderdale, 11 Aug 1814, Evan Evans Bm (A)
William Rogers to Ruth Garner, 28 May 1831 (29 May), Daniel Briggs MG, Avara Hannah Bm (AR)

MARRIAGES (MEIGS)
Dinely Rogers to Eli Colvin q.v.
July Ann Rogers to William P. Richardson q.v.
Mahala Rogers to A.R. Snider q.v.
Mary J. Rogers to Nathan Richardson q.v.
Matilda Rogers to James H. Locke q.v.
Nancy Rogers to John Tillery q.v.
Sarah Rogers to Frederick Wirick q.v.
Thomas R. Rogers to Elizabeth V. McClure, 12 Nov 1845 (15 Nov), D.L. Godsey MG, William Lillard Sur

MISCELLANEOUS (RHEA)
James Rogers: Bondsman for William Gorden, 1824
" " Early member Rhea County Bar
" " Lots 26 & 35, Town of Washington
John Rogers: Bondsman for Asa Newport, 1821
Jonathan Rogers: Bondsman for John McDonough, 1821
William Rogers: Bondsman for John Rodgers, 1829
" " Bondsman for Jeremiah Lillard, 1836
" " Lot 8, Town of Washington

MISCELLANEOUS (MEIGS)
John Rogers: Ocoee District
William M. Rogers: Hiwassee District, Moore's Chapel area
" " " County Surveyor, 1836; teacher
" " " County Court Clerk 1839-40

\- - - - - - - - - - - - -

ROLAND

MISCELLANEOUS (MEIGS)
Daniel Roland or Roland Daniel: Mexican War (died in service)

\- - - - - - - - - - - - -

ROLLSTON

1830 RHEA CENSUS
Betsy Rollston 0011 - 0002001 p. 394

\- - - - - - - - - - - - -

ROLOW

MARRIAGES (MEIGS)
Peter Rolow to Susan Britten, 7 Sept 1847 (9 Sept), Thomas H. Munsey MG (R)

- - - - - - - - - - - - -

ROMINE / ROMINES

TAXES (RHEA)
1823 (Capt. Braselton's Co.): Jasper Romines 1 WP
1830 RHEA CENSUS
Jacob Romines 000000001 - 01001001 p. 380
Latin Romines 012011 - 1201 p. 380
Mary Romines 02 - 0010001 p. 379
Samuel Romines 020000001 - 00000001 p. 379
Thomas Romines 010001 - 1001 p. 380
1840 RHEA CENSUS
Mary Romine 0 - 1000100001
Nicholas Romine 2001001 - 011001
1850 MEIGS CENSUS
Lydia Romines 35 (NC), George W. 17, James 9, Joseph 6, Susannah 4 p. 714-14
Solomon Romines 55 (NC)(Farmer), Susannah 55 (NC) p. 714-15
MARRIAGES (RHEA)
Allis Romines to Mahalieal Barnes q.v.
Nicholas Romines to Susan Weeks, 6 Mar 1835 (7 Mar), William Smith JP, James Smith Bm (AR)
Polly Romines to George Samples q.v.
Thomas Romines to Rebecca Hughes, 10 May 1821 (no return) (AR)
MARRIAGES (MEIGS)
Joseph Romines to Adeline Edwards, 17 Jan 1843 (18 Jan), John Seabourn JP, Martin Romines Bm
MISCELLANEOUS (RHEA)
Thomas Romines: Bondsman for Nathaniel Burns, 1828
MISCELLANEOUS (MEIGS)
Jasper Romines: Hiwassee District, Pinhook Ferry area
Jobe Romines: Private, Mexican War

- - - - - - - - - - - - -

ROSCOE

MISCELLANEOUS (MEIGS)
John W. Roscoe: Private, Mexican War

- - - - - - - - - - - - -

ROSE / ROWS

1830 RHEA CENSUS
Thomas C. Rose 02122001 - 112001 p. 394
1840 RHEA CENSUS
William Rose 0012001 - 02002
1850 RHEA CENSUS
Edmund Rose 40 (Farmer) p. 548-99
William W. Rose 53 (NC)(Farmer), Margaret 42, Nancy 31 (Ga), Edith 17, Columbus F.A. 8, John W. 6, James M. 3, Mary E. 1 p. 587-341
MARRIAGES (RHEA)
Martha I. Rose to Richard Godbyhere q.v.
Sarah Rose to Peter Ryan q.v.
William W. Rose to Margaret Maloney, 28 Nov 1840 (4 Dec), Martin E. Paul LPD (AR)
MISCELLANEOUS (RHEA)
David C. Rose: Private, Mexican War
Edmund Rose: Private, Mexican War
Joseph Rose: Private, Mexican War
W. W. Rose: MG CPC 1847-48

- - - - - - - - - - - - -

ROSER / ROZIER / ROSEN / ROPER

1830 RHEA CENSUS
David Roper 00112001 - 11100001 p. 373
1850 RHEA CENSUS
David Roser 58 (SC)(Hammerman), Nelly 68 (NC), David C. 12 p. 547-91
Dralow Rozier 32 (Unk)(Hammerman), Minerva 30 (NC), Thomas J. KERBY 17 (Working in Forge), Houston 14, Clerissa ROZIER 9, Britain 8, Frances 7, Rachael 3, Miller 1 p. 543-65
Eliza Roser 1: see Stephen Vollo
MARRIAGES (RHEA)
E. A. Rosen to William Morgan q.v.
MISCELLANEOUS (MEIGS)
David Roper: Hiwassee District
George W. Roper: Cherokee Removal muster roll, 1837

- - - - - - - - - - - - -

ROSS

TAXES (RHEA)
1819 (Capt. Bradley's Dist.): David Ross heirs 7655a
1830 RHEA CENSUS
Charles Ross 11001 - 20001 p. 381
1840 RHEA CENSUS
Charles Ross 1111001 - 101101
1840 MEIGS CENSUS
Mary Ross 0 - 1000101 p. 225
MARRIAGES (RHEA)
Lourana Ross to Joseph McDonald q.v.
Susanna Ross to Henry Nave q.v.
Templin W. Ross to Eliza Sevier, 16 May 1817, John Cozby JP, John Day Bm (A)
MISCELLANEOUS (MEIGS)
John Ross: Hiwassee District, Burkett Chapel area
Lewis Ross: Hiwassee District (Reservation)

- - - - - - - - - - - - -

ROTHWELL

1850 MEIGS CENSUS
Richard Rothwell 59 (Va), Lucy 58 (Va), Emelia Ann 18, Lucy 21 p. 775-497
Walter B. Rothwell 29 (Va)(Farmer), Charlotte 27, Malissa D. 6, Lucinda 5, William T. 3, George 1 p. 776-503 [Walter Rothwell married Charlotte Lawson on 21 Dec 1842 in McMinn County]
MARRIAGES (MEIGS)
Walter L. Rothwell to Annis M. Galloway, 6 Dec 1848 (7 Dec), D.L. Godsey MG, John M. Lillard DC [Deputy Clerk] [1850 McMinn Census: Walter L. Rothwell 26, Annis M. 20, William T. 6/12]

- - - - - - - - - - - - -

ROWDEN / RODDEN

TAXES (RHEA)
1819 (Capt John Ramsey's Co.): Abedaigo Rowden 1 WP
Asa Rwden 1 WP
1830 RHEA CENSUS
Abraham Rodden 10011 - 10001 p. 358
[Abraham Rowden married Anne Brandon on 26 Sept 1825 in Roane County]
Asil Rowden 202001 - 031001 p. 354
Samuel E. Rowden 00011 - 00001 p. 385
1850 MEIGS CENSUS
Alkana Rowden 47 (Farmer), Louisa E. 21, Thomas 17 (Farmer), Sarah A. 15, William E. 11, Mary M. 8, John H. 7, James N. 4 p. 806-716
[Alkanah Rowden married Catharine McKody on 7 Feb 1825 in Roane County]
Shadrick Rowden 24 (Farmer), Sarah 25 p. 806-717
[Shadrack Rowden married Sarah Utley on 11 Apr 1850 in Roane County]
MARRIAGES (RHEA)
Abenego Rowden to Catsey or Beatsey Hannah, 2 Dec 1815, "I certify that I married above parties" M.J. Fine JP, James Hannah Bm (AR)
Elijah Rowden to Selah Hughes, 29 Feb 1820 (same), Thomas McNabb Bm (A)
Laben B. Rowden to Jane Hubbert, 27 Mar 1831, John Parker Bm (A)
Millissant Rowden to William Lewis Sr. q.v.
Nancy Rowden to William Meyers q.v.
Nathaniel Rowden to Margaret McFarlin, 12 Dec 1828 (same), Stephen Winton JP (A)
Oledish or Obedience L. Rowden to John Logan q.v.
Prudence Rowden to John Clack q.v.
Sally Rowden to Martin Shultz q.v.
Sally Rowden to Elijah C. Rice q.v.
Samuel Rowden to Nancy Smith, 26 Sept 1829 (27 Sept), Matthew Hubbert JP, Gideon P. Thompson Bm (AR)
MARRIAGES (MEIGS)
Elizabeth Rowden to Joshua Renfroe q.v.
Josie Rowden to Mary Ford, 6 Jan 1848 (same), John Ford JP
Susan Rowden to Ewell Johnson q.v.
MISCELLANEOUS (RHEA and MEIGS)
Asa Rowden: Hiwassee District
Hardin B. Rowden: Hiwassee District, Moore's Chapel area
James Rowden: JP(?) 1839
Samuel E. Rowden: Bondsman for John Logan, 1828

\- - - - - - - - - - - - -

ROYAL / RAYL

MARRIAGES (RHEA)
Abner Royal to Rebecca Brown, 4 Jan 1815, "Executed by me 8 Jany 1815" William Long JP, Nicholas Nail Bm (AR)
MARRIAGES (MEIGS)
William Rayl to Nancy L. Cox, 12 Oct 1838 (21 Oct), John Taff JP, Luther B. Cox Bm

\- - - - - - - - - - - - -

ROYSTER / ROYESTER

1840 MEIGS CENSUS
Hardy M. Royester 0201001 - 0111001 p. 243
1850 MEIGS CENSUS
Joseph G. Royster 29 (NC)(Farmer), Phebe 22, John H. 2, Mary Jane 1, Elijah BUTTRAM 18 (Farmer), Micheal F. 16, Francis A. 14, William D. 11 [brothers of Phoebe] p. 788-591
MARRIAGES (RHEA)
Charles H. Royster to Elizabeth Preston, 13 Mar 1834 (same), M.S. Shaver JP, Frederick Hoover Bm (AR)
Lelitha Royster to Jonathan Collins q.v.
MARRIAGES (MEIGS)
Caroline Royster to Jonathan M. Collins q.v.
Elizabeth Royster to William A. Witt q.v.
John Royster to Artimissa M. Keeton, 30 Nov 1850, J.C. Wann Sur
Joseph G. Royster to Phebe Buttram, 15 May 1847, Thomas Atchley JP
MISCELLANEOUS (MEIGS)
J.G. Royster: JP 1849

\- - - - - - - - - - - - -

RUCKER

1840 MEIGS CENSUS
James E. Rucker 00001 - 1001 p. 224
MISCELLANEOUS (MEIGS)
James Rucker: Hiwassee District, Lower Goodfield area
James E. Rucker: Ocoee District
Wilford Rucker: JP 1836-38
" " Commissioner to lay off Decatur, 1836
" " Trustee, Decatur Academy, 1838-39

\- - - - - - - - - - - - -

RUDD

1850 RHEA CENSUS
Elijah S. Rudd 29 (Tailor), Eliza G. 23 (Va), Alex A.M. 8, Sarah E. 6, James C.J. 3 p. 627-594 [Elijah married Eliza Garland, 25 May 1841, McMinn Co]
MISCELLANEOUS (MEIGS)
Elijah L. Rudd: 1st Corp., Mexican War

\- - - - - - - - - - - - -

RUE

TAXES (RHEA)
1823 (Capt. Wilson's Co.): John Rue 1 WP
1850 MEIGS CENSUS
John Rue 54 (Farmer), Richard 20 (Farmer), Nancy 14, Samuel 13 p. 714-10

\- - - - - - - - - - - - -

RUMFELD

1850 RHEA CENSUS
John Rumfeld Unk (SC)(Carpenter), Peggy Unk (SC), Henry 19 (SC)(Farmer), Myra 17 (SC), Margaret 16 (SC) p. 618-525

William Rumfeld 28 (NC)(Farmer), Jane 23 (NC), John 4 (NC), Matilda 2 (NC), James 5/12 (NC) p. 598-395

- - - - - - - - - - - - -

RUNYON / RUNYAN / RUNNION

1830 RHEA CENSUS
John Runyan 10101001 - 1200001 p. 352
1840 MEIGS CENSUS
Tabner Runion 210001 - 10001 p. 236
MARRIAGES (RHEA)
John Runyon to Lorinda Lewis, 21 Apr 1833 (23 Aug), Joseph McCorkle JP (R)
Juda Runnions to Joel K. Bledsoe q.v.
Susan Runyon to Peter Neil q.v.
Tavenor Runyon to Jane Tillary, 8 Jan 1833 (same), D.L. Godsey JP, Thomas Tillery Bm (AR)
MISCELLANEOUS (RHEA and MEIGS)
Lar Runyon: JP(?) 1840
Simeon Runyan: Cherokee Removal muster roll, 1837
Tavernor Runyon: Bondsman for Joel Brooks, 1831
" " Bondsman for Thomas Tillery, 1832
" " Bondsman for Charles W. Lewis, 1833
Ware Runnian: Bondsman for John Atchley, 1826 or 1827
William Runyon: Bondsman for John Silcock, 1827

- - - - - - - - - - - - -

RUSH

TAXES (RHEA)
1823 (Capt. Howerton's Co.) Isaac Rush 1 WP, 38a Piney
William Rush 78a Piney Ri
1830 RHEA CENSUS
Isaac Rush 0002111 - 0020000101 p. 362
Lorenzo Rush 10001 - 20001 p. 362
1840 MEIGS CENSUS
Isaac Rush 00011001 - 000100001 p. 246
Lorenzo Rush 11101 - 131001 p. 245
1850 MEIGS CENSUS
Phebe Rush 74 (NC), Elijah L. 20 (Farmer), Hugh C. 18 (Farmer), Mary Ann 16 p. 818-802
MARRIAGES (RHEA)
Joseph Rush to Eleanor Putman, 10 Dec 1830 (12 Dec), James Wilson JP, Thomas Carter Bm (AR)
Lorenzo D. Rush to Hanny Harwood, 17 Oct 1826 (same), John Farmer MG, Thomas York Bm (AR)
Tempy Rush to Joshua Richards q.v.
MISCELLANEOUS (MEIGS)
Isaac Rush: Hiwassee District, Moore's Chapel area
John Rush: Hiwassee District, Moore's Chapel area
Lorenzo D. Rush: Hiwassee District, Moore's Chapel area
" " " Cherokee Removal muster roll, 1836

- - - - - - - - - - - - -

RUSS

1850 RHEA CENSUS
Thomas Russ 47 (Va*)(Farmer), Chrisa 42 (Va), Mary J. 19 (Va), William W. BUFFINGTON 17 (Va)(Farmer) p. 637-671 [*state may not have been Va; looks more like Ct]

- - - - - - - - - - - - -

RUSSELL

TAXES (RHEA)
1808 (Joseph Brooks' List): Andrew Russell 400a Sale Cr
John Russell 400a Sale Creek
John Russell 1 WP, 250a S C
1819 (Capt. McGill's Co.): John Russell 2 WP, 1 BP, 450a

1830 RHEA CENSUS
Samuel Russell 2001 - 001 p. 368
William B. Russell 0001 - 1001 p. 370
William S. Russell 10001 - 00011 p. 382
1840 RHEA CENSUS
Uriah W. Russell 110001 - 11001
1840 MEIGS CENSUS
William S. Russell 121001 - 010001 p. 233

1850 MEIGS CENSUS
William B. Russell 46 (Farmer), Jane M. 40, James C. 6, George W. 3 p. 740-220
William S. Russell 46 (Va)(Farmer), Susan 40, John T. 21 (Farmer), David A. 19 (Farmer), Felix G. 17 (Farmer), Susan 15, Thomas J. 13, Mary E. 7, Sarah R. 5 p. 752-315

MARRIAGES (RHEA)
Barshaba Russell to Alexander Thompson q.v.
E.M. Russell to H.M. Montgomery q.v.
James B. Russell to Ann Coulter, 5 Dec 1827 (6 Dec), Samuel M. Aston VDM, George Russell Bm (AR)
Jacob Russell to Jane Smith, 5 Mar 1814, David Rush Bm (A)
Matthew Russell to Ann Witt, 10 Aug 1818, Pleasant Barnes Bm (A)
Samuel R. Russell to Nancy Ann Gamble, 15 Jan 1827 (16 Jan), Edmond Pearson MG, Geo Russell Bm (AR)
William B. Russell to Jane Cowan, 23 Aug 1826 (same), Robert Bell Bm (AR)
William S. Russell to Susan Blevins, 5 Mar 1828 (6 Mar), Peach Taylor JP, Abraham Cox Bm (AR) [William, son of John and Sarah Rosana Sprowell Russell; Susan, dau of David and Sarah Torbett Blevins]

MARRIAGES (MEIGS)
Elizabeth A. Russell to Wright S. Miller q.v.

MISCELLANEOUS (RHEA)
George Russell: Bondsman for James B. Russell, 1827
" " Bondsman for Samuel R. Russell, 1827
S. R. Russell: MG 1831, 1834
William S. Russell: Bondsman for Amos King, 1827
" " " Bondsman for Archibald Taylor, 1827
" " " Bm for Jeremiah Bowling, 1828
" " " Bondsman for Eslie Quiett, 1828
" " " Bm for Pleasant M. Miller, 1829
" " " Bm for William Armstrong, 1834
William Russell: Purchased lot in Cottonport, 1834
MISCELLANEOUS (MEIGS)
John Russell: Private, Mexican War
William S. Russell: Sheriff 1845-51
" " " Common School Com., District 3, 1838

- - - - - - - - - - - - -

RUTHERFORD

MARRIAGES (RHEA)
William Rutherford to Elizabeth Moyers, 8 Mar 1816 (15 or 11 Mar), B. Catching JP (AR)

- - - - - - - - - - - - -

RYAN / RYON

TAXES (RHEA)
1819 (Capt. W.S. Bradley's Dist.): Charles Ryan 1 WP
1830 RHEA CENSUS
Abner Ryan 220011 - 121011 p. 363
Harris Ryon 10001 - 0001 p. 378
Thomas Ryon 000000001 - 030000101 p. 378
1840 RHEA CENSUS
Abner Ryan 0121001 - 2111001
Charles Ryan 000000001 - 000100001
Harris Ryan 1110010001 - 02001
James C. Ryan 00001 - 000001
1850 RHEA CENSUS
Harris Ryan 43 (Farmer), Patsy 41, Florena 17, Lucinda 16, Giles 14, Mary E. 12, Rebecca J. 7, Darius W. 3 p. 620-542
James C. Ryan 36 (NC)(Farmer), Sarah 42 (NC) p. 603-442
MARRIAGES (RHEA)
Delphia Ryon to Thomas Knight q.v.
Elizabeth Ryon to William Hutson q.v.
Eunita H. Ryan to Newton J. Edmonds q.v.
Florina Ryan to William Henderson q.v.
Harris Ryon to Martha Ryon, 16 May 1827, John Vanderpole Bm (A)
Judy Ryon to Elisha Moore q.v.
Lucinda Ryon to Samuel Frazier q.v.
Martha Ryon to Harris Ryon q.v.
Peter Ryan to Sarah Rose, 25 May 1844 (30 May), Washington Morgan JP, Alfred Hutchinson Bm (AR) [1850 Knox Census: Peter Ryan 28, Sarah 21, Henry 5, Nancy Jane 2, Elizabeth 4/12]
Polly Ryan to Silan Conley q.v.
Sarah Ann Ryan to Jacob George q.v.
Unity Ryon to George W. Brummet q.v.
MISCELLANEOUS (RHEA)
Charles Ryon: Bondsman for Elisha Moore, 1824
Harris Ryon: Bondsman for William Corvin, 1833
" " Bondsman for George W. Brummett, 1835
" " Revolutionary War pensioner, 1833 and 1841 lists

- - - - - - - - - - - - -

SABREL

MISCELLANEOUS (RHEA)
James Sabrel: Bondsman for Mulin Morris, 1839

- - - - - - - - - - - - -

SADLER / SADLERS

1840 RHEA CENSUS
James W. Sadler 100001 - 00002
MARRIAGES (MEIGS)
E.R. Sadlers to John Clifton q.v.

- - - - - - - - - - - - -

SALLY

MISCELLANEOUS (MEIGS)
Moses Sally: Hiwassee District, Moore's Chapel area

- - - - - - - - - - - - -

SAMPLES / SAMPLE / SAMPLY / SAMPLER / SAMPLEY

1830 RHEA CENSUS
Jesse Samply 00001 - 11001 p. 382
[Jesse Samples married Deborah Browder of McMinn County on 25 Dec 1832]
MARRIAGES (RHEA)
George Samples to Polly Romines, 16 Dec 1831 (17 Dec), William Smith JP, Timothy F. French Bm (AR)
Nelly Sample to Larkin Manes q.v.
MISCELLANEOUS (RHEA and MEIGS)
Charles Sampler: Purchased Lots 6 & 7 in Decatur
Jesse Sample: Revolutinary War pensioner, 1835 and 1841 lists
William Sampley: Purchased Lot 15 in Decatur

- - - - - - - - - - - - -

SAMS / SAM

1830 RHEA CENSUS
Warren Sams 00200001 - 0101101 p. 354
William Sam 0100001 - 11 p. 364
MARRIAGES (RHEA)
Braxton C. Sams to Susannah Casey, 23 Apr 1825, John Cole Bm (A)
Patsy Sams to Daniel McPhail q.v.
Polly Sams to Thomas Edmonson q.v.
MISCELLANEOUS (RHEA)
Warren Sams: On Surveyor's list of land S of Tennessee Ri

- - - - - - - - - - - - -

SANDERS / SAUNDERS

TAXES (RHEA)
1819 (Capt. John Robinsn's Co.): David Sanders 1 WP
1840 RHEA CENSUS
Shadwick Saunders 100010001 - 000030001
1850 RHEA CENSUS
Harvey Sanders 22 (Farmer), Loretta 25, Elias B. 1, David BELL 25 (Wagoner) p. 547-89
MARRIAGES (RHEA)
Elizabeth Sanders to William Henderson q.v.
Susan Saunders to Zeof Jackson q.v.

- - - - - - - - - - - - -

SANDFORD

1840 RHEA CENSUS
Henry C. Sandford 000001 - 22000101
Samuel C. Sandford 20001 - 20001

- - - - - - - - - - - - -

SANDS

MISCELLANEOUS (RHEA)
Jacob Sands: Bondsman for James Poteet, 1810

- - - - - - - - - - - - -

SAPP

TAXES (RHEA)
1819 (Capt. J. Lewis' Dist.): John Sapp 2 BP, 1 Lot, 439½a
MARRIAGES (RHEA)
Alexander Sapp to Frances Anderson, 3 Jan 1818 (same), "Married by me" William Randolph, Elder, John Parker Bm (AR)
John Sapp to Winny Anderson, 14 Dec 1814 (same), Alexander Ferguson Bm (A)
Mary Sapp to Charles Richards q.v.

- - - - - - - - - - - - -

SAPPINGTON

MARRIAGES (RHEA)
James M. Sappington to Anna Clark, 27 July 1826 (same), Thomas Cox JP, William Ingle Bm (AR)

- - - - - - - - - - - - -

SATTERFIELD

1850 MEIGS CENSUS
Sarah Satterfield 70 (NC): see Thomas Kaywood

- - - - - - - - - - - - -

SCHOOLFIELD

MARRIAGES (MEIGS)
Robert E. Schoolfield to Mary A. Hutcherson, 5 July 1849 (same), M.C. Robertson MG

- - - - - - - - - - - - -

SCOTT

1850 RHEA CENSUS
Lavina Scott 42 (Unk), William L. BURNETT 22 (Blacksmith), Thomas J. 20 (Farmer), James SCOTT 11, Lucinda 4 p. 539-42
1850 MEIGS CENSUS
Jane Scott 56, John 28 (Blacksmith), Elizabeth 23 p. 759-369
John Scott 46 (London, Eng)(Doctor), Eliza 30 (London), Horrace M. 6 (London), Edith M. 4 (London), Thomas 0 p. 799-676
MARRIAGES (MEIGS)
Mary Ann Scott to John Cox q.v.
MISCELLANEOUS (MEIGS)
John Scott: Surety for James Taylor, 1850
" " Private, Mexican War

- - - - - - - - - - - - -

SCROGGINS / SCRAGGINS / SCOGGIN

1840 MEIGS CENSUS
David G. Scoggin 0111001 - 111000101 p. 239
1850 RHEA CENSUS
Andrew J. Scroggins 22 (Ala)(Farmer), Juli 19, Martha A. 1/12 p. 565-181 [Jackson Scroggins married Julia Buttram on 20 Dec 1848 in McMinn County]
David G. Scraggins 52 (NC)(Farmer), Martha 56 (NC), Emeline 23 (Ala), Nancy 19, Noah 16 (Farmer), Luisa 14, Nancy REYNOLDS 74 (Va), Amanda DYAL 3 p. 540-50
Doctor F. Scroggins 25 (Ala)(Farmer), Margaret 19, Noah H. 3, David T. 2, Campbell Y. 7/12 p. 565-182 [D.F. Scroggins married Margaret Buttram on 17 Mar 1846 in McMinn County]
MISCELLANEOUS (RHEA)
David G. Scroggins: Trustee, Mars Hill Academy, 1850

- - - - - - - - - - - - -

SCRUGGS / SCRUGS

1830 RHEA CENSUS
Gross Scruggs 21001 - 121001 p. 386
1840 MEIGS CENSUS
Richard Scrugs 1321011 - 0112001 p. 231
MISCELLANEOUS (RHEA)
Gross Scruggs: Bondsman for Curtis Richards, 1828

- - - - - - - - - - - - -

SEABER / SEEBER

MISCELLANEOUS (RHEA and MEIGS)
Philip Seaber: Fellowship Baptist Ch of Christ, 1828-29
Philip Seeber: Hiwassee District, Moore's Chapel area

- - - - - - - - - - - - -

SEABOLT / SEYBOLT / CEBOLT

1840 MEIGS CENSUS
Adam Cebolt 0000000001 - 0 p. 229
David Cebolt 010001 - 221001 p. 229
MARRIAGES (RHEA)
Catherine Seybolt to Moses Price q.v.
David Sebolt or Seabolt to Mourning Singleton, 27 Nov 1825 (29 Nov), Thomas Cox JP, Starling Singleton Bm (AR)
Mary Seabolt to John Gordon q.v.
MISCELLANEOUS (RHEA and MEIGS)
Adam Seabolt: Hiwassee District, Burkett Chapel area
Adam Seybolt: Bondsman for James F. Ritchie, 1832
Moses Seybolt: Bondsman for Moses Price, 1814

- - - - - - - - - - - - -

SEABORN / SEABOURN / SEBORN / SIBOURN / CEBURN

TAXES (RHEA)
1819 (Capt. Bradley's Dist.): George Seaborn 1 Lot
1823 (Capt. Lewis' Co.): George Seborn 1 Lot

1840 MEIGS CENSUS
John Ceburn 112001 - 120001 p. 224
1850 MEIGS CENSUS
Andrew J. Seaborn 22 (Farmer), Lucinda 18 p. 723-84
John Sebourn 50 (Farmer), Hester 43, George W. 20 (Farmer), Nancy Ann 18, Eliza Jane 16, Nepolian 13, Elizabeth M. 10, Matilda C. 8, Martha A. 7, Malinda A. 3 p. 724-90
MARRIAGES (MEIGS)
Andrew J. Seabourn to Lucinda Frost, 18 July 1849 (21 July), John Pendergrass MG, John Seabourn Sur(?)
MISCELLANEOUS (MEIGS)
John Seabourn/Sebroun/Seaborn: JP 1838-49
" " County Court Clerk, 1848-52
" " Chairman of County Court, 1840, 1846
" " Trustee, Decatur Academy, 1840
" " Common School Com., District 1, 1838

\- - - - - - - - - - - -

SEAL

1850 RHEA CENSUS
Oliver Seal 26, Sarah J. 19, Emeline KNIGHT 8 p. 622-565

\- - - - - - - - - - - -

SEARS / SERES / SIERS

TAXES (RHEA)
1808 (Joseph Brooks' List): Bennett Seres 1 WP
1823 (Capt. Piper's Co.): William Siers 1 WP
1830 RHEA CENSUS
William Sears 120001 - 1111001 p. 358
1840 MEIGS CENSUS
William Sears 0012001 - 01230001 p. 241
MARRIAGES (RHEA)
Peggy Sears to Hugh Pharris q.v.
MARRIAGES (MEIGS)
Dicy Sears to William Smith q.v.
Frankey Sears to Leonard Huff q.v.
William R. Sears to Jane Bennett, 14 Jan 1845 (19 Jan), A. Fooshee JP

\- - - - - - - - - - - -

SEAY / SEA

1830 RHEA CENSUS
Thomas Seay 1111001 - 11111 p. 374
1840 RHEA CENSUS
William H. Seay 1210001 - 1101101
MARRIAGES (RHEA)
Eliza Seay to William P. Tillary q.v.
Huldah Seay to Daniel Lemons q.v.
Rachel P. Seay to Thomas Johnston q.v.
MARRIAGES (MEIGS)
Thomas H. Seay to L. Tillery, 14 July 1839 (15 July), Daniel Cate JP, Wm P. Tillery Bm
MISCELLANEOUS (RHEA and MEIGS)
Thomas Seay: Bondsman for Robert Willey, 1829
" " Hiwassee District, Sewee Creek area
Thomas Sea: Cherokee Removal muster roll, 1836
William F. Seay: Bondsman for James W. Duncan, 1832

\- - - - - - - - - - - -

SEGLAR

1840 MEIGS CENSUS
William Seglar Sr. 00001001 - 000001 p. 233
William G. Seglar 00001 - 10001 p. 233

\- - - - - - - - - - - -

SELF / SELPH

MARRIAGES (RHEA)
Betsey Self to Jacob Weir q.v.
Elijah Self to Polly Hanson, 10 May 1812, Jonathan Marlan Bm (A)
Rebecca Self to Solomon Hanson q.v.
William Self to Rebecca Wear, 14 July 1812 (no return), Solomon Hanson Bm (AR)
MARRIAGES (MEIGS)
Eliza Selph to William Moore q.v.

\- - - - - - - - - - - -

SELLERS

1830 RHEA CENSUS
Isiah Sellers 210001 - 10001 p. 354
Sampson Sellers 010001 - 211001 p. 356
William W. Sellers 2010001 - 13101 p. 368
MISCELLANEOUS (RHEA and MEIGS)
Cain Sellars/Sellers: Hiwassee District
Isiah Sellers: married Nancy Todd on 24 Oct 1822 in Roane Co; also Isaiah married Mary Gallant on 22 Oct 1840 in McMinn Co
Micah Sellers: Pastor, Concord Baptist Church, 1824
Micha Sellers: On Surveyor's list of land S of Tenn River
William Sellers: married Margaret Matheny on 21 Jan 1830 in Roane County

\- - - - - - - - - - - -

SELVIDGE

MARRIAGES (RHEA)
George W. Selvidge to Elzabeth H. Leuty, 30 Nov 1831 (same), Peach Taylor JP, Pulaski Poe Bm (AR)
MISCELLANEOUS (RHEA)
George W. Selvidge: Bondsman for William Smith, 1832

\- - - - - - - - - - - -

SEVIER / SIEVER / SENER

MARRIAGES (RHEA)
Eliza Sener or Sevier to Templin W. Ross q.v.
MISCELLANEOUS (RHEA)
Philip Siever: MG 1828

\- - - - - - - - - - - -

SEWELL / SEWEL

1850 MEIGS CENSUS
Francis M. Sewel 22, Mary Ann 30 (Va), Jessee M. 1 p. 743-241
MARRIAGES (MEIGS)
Francis M. Sewell to Mary Ann Mavity, 5 Oct 1848 (same), James Pierce MG, John M. Lillard DC

\- - - - - - - - - - - -

SEXTON / SEXON

1840 MEIGS CENSUS
James Sexon or Sesion 0000000001 - 01000001 p. 228
1850 RHEA CENSUS
Elizabeth Sexton 28 (Ga), John S. 14, William 5 p. 627-591
Holla Sexton (f) 48 (Ga), James 13, Mary A. 10 p. 627-592
John M. Sexton 2: see Elijah McGuire
Toliver Sexton 61 (SC)(Carpenter), Rebecca 56 (SC), Polly 32 (SC) p. 621-553
MARRIAGES (RHEA)
Elizabeth Sexton to James Bryant q.v.
Lewis Sexton to Jane Tims, 28 July 1830, Jacob Wells Bm (A)
Mahala Sexton to William Gross q.v.
Martin Sexton to Mary Tims, 1 Dec 1830, Jacob Wells Bm (A)
Rebecca Sexton to Jacob Wells q.v.

SEYMORE / SEAMORE / SEEMORE

TAXES (RHEA)
1808 (James Campbell's List): Henry Seemore 1 WP
William Seemore 1 WP
1819 (Capt. W.S. Bradley's Dist.):
William Seymore 1 WP, 2 BP, 2 Town Lots, 2a
1830 RHEA CENSUS
William Seymore 211001 - 01100001 p. 385
1840 RHEA CENSUS
William Seymore 01111001 - 0011001
MARRIAGES (RHEA)
E.C. Seymore to Abraham Graham q.v.
Elizabeth Seamore to Cedron Pile q.v.
Isaac H. Seymore to Mary Geer or Gear, 4 Mar 1841 (same), Richard Waterhouse JP, Wm Seymore Bm (AR)
Mary Ann Seymore to Decatur K. Sykes q.v.
Sarah Seymore to Richard Wilhelm q.v.
William Seymore to Sarah Lewis, 24 July 1810 (same), Jesse Lewis Bm (AR)
MISCELLANEOUS (RHEA)
David P. Seymore: Bondsman for Henry Minick, 1845
William Seymore: Bondsman for Jesse Lewis, 1809
" " Bondsman for Isaac H. Seymore, 1841
" " Purchased Lot 10 in Washington

SHADACK

1850 MEIGS CENSUS
Ezekiel Shadack 56 (NC)(Farmer), Telitha 56 (NC), Solomon S. 17 (NC)(Farmer), Elijah 15 (NC)(Farmer), Ezekiel 14 (NC), Elisha 12 (NC) p. 780-527

SHADWICK

MARRIAGES (RHEA)
Rebecca Shadwick to Hezekiah Burton q.v.

SHAMLIN / SHAMBLIN

1850 MEIGS CENSUS
A.B. Shamblin 29 (Farmer), Eliza Jane 17 ("married within year") p. 737-192
George Shamlin 50 (NC)(Farmer), Sarah 50 (NC), Arnold P. 27, Asheal E. 25, Sarah A. 16 p. 736-191

SHARP / SHARPE

TAXES (RHEA)
1823 (Capt. Piper's Co.): Elisha Sharp 1 WP, 160a

1830 RHEA CENSUS
Elisha Sharp 011121 - 22001 p. 360
1840 RHEA CENSUS
Richard Sharp 110011 - 11002
1840 MEIGS CENSUS
David Sharp 00000001 - 010010001 p. 239
Elisha Sharp 101101 - 012201 p. 241
William Sharp 002001 - 00001 p. 237

1850 MEIGS CENSUS
David H. Sharp 30 (Farmer), Jane 28, Ellen Jane 3, Judge J. 2, Melissa Del Ray 1 p. 798-669
Elisha Sharp 58 (Farmer), Ellender 49, James 25 (School Teacher), Mary 26, Levina C. 21, Sarah Ann 19, Thomas P. 11, Elisha F. 9, Lennard J. 5 p. 799-677 [Elisha, son of William, married Elender Huff, dau of John and Mary Carder Huff, on 24 Dec 1817 in Cocke(?) Co. Children not with parents in 1850: David H., John C., Mary, Jane, and Harriet C.]
John C. Sharp 29 (Farmer), Sarah Ann 19 p. 796-650

MARRIAGES (RHEA)
Eleanor Sharp to Jesse Matthews q.v.
Joel Sharp to Nancy McClenahan, 12 Aug 1833, John McClenahan Bm (A)
MARRIAGES (MEIGS)
David Huff Sharp to Mary J. Boggess, 30 July 1846 (6 Aug), J.B. McClure JP, D.L. Godsey Sur
Edward Sharp to Eliza Shelton, 16 Aug 1842 (same), B.F. McKenzie JP, Jefferson Matthews Bm
Harriet C. Sharp to Darius Waterhouse q.v.
Jane Sharp to Wright Smith q.v.
John Carder Sharp to Sarah Ann Boggess, 21 Oct 1849 (25 Oct), Wm L. Adams JP, J. Seabourn Sur(?)
Mary Sharp to Benjamin F. Locke q.v.
Rachel Sharp to Isah Homes q.v.

MISCELLANEOUS (RHEA)
Elisha Sharp: Bondsman for Bethwell Goddy, 1827
MISCELLANEOUS (MEIGS)
Elisha Sharp: Purchased Lots 3,4,11,12 in Decatur
" " Circuit Court jury, 1836
" " House used for elections, District 7
" " 2nd Lt., Cherokee Removal muster roll, 1836
" " Hiwassee District, Ten Mile area
Eli Sharp: Common School Commissioner, District 2, 1838
Jacob Sharp: Hiwassee District, Burkett Chapel area

SHAVER / SHAFER / SHAFFER

1830 RHEA CENSUS
Henry Shafer 00001 - 20011 p. 386
Mathias Shafer 01010101 - 10011 p. 374
Thomas Shafer 10001 - 10001 p. 372
1840 MEIGS CENSUS
Mathias Shaver 0011101 - 0010001 p. 236
1850 RHEA CENSUS
John Shaver 71 (Pa)(Millwright): see Thomas Williams
1850 MEIGS CENSUS
Mathias Shaver 52 (NC)(Farmer), Racheal 50, Calvin J. 20 (Carpenter), Rebecca R. 17, Jackson L. 2 p. 763-396
MARRIAGES (RHEA)
Fanny Shaffer to Eslie Quiett q.v.
Thomas Shafer to Sally Lewis, 20 Aug 1823, "Returned with papers of D. Walker JP" (AR)
MISCELLANEOUS (RHEA)
M. S. Shaver: JP 1834
Matthias Shaffer: JP 1832
MISCELLANEOUS (MEIGS)
Mathias Shaver: JP 1836-44; Registerar 1840-60
" " Chairman of County Court, 1836-37
" " On Circuit Court jury, 1836
" " Trustee for Decatur Academy, 1840
Sampson Shaver Purchased Lots 39 & 48 in Decatur, 1836

- - - - - - - - - - - - -

SHELL

MARRIAGES (RHEA)
Catherine Shell to William Benson q.v.
MISCELLANEOUS (RHEA and MEIGS)
Adam Shell: Bondsman for Peter Airheart, 1819
James Shell: JP(?) 1839, 1845

- - - - - - - - - - - - -

SHELTON

TAXES (RHEA)
1819 (Capt. McGill's Co.): Christian E. Shelton 200a
1823 (Capt. Howard's Co.): Crispin E. Shelton 1 WP, 168a
David Shelton 1 WP, 47½a
(Capt. Brown's Co.):
Palatiah Shelton 1 WP, 1 BP, 300a Tenn Ri
1830 RHEA CENSUS
C.E. Shelton 0111001 - 001101 p. 380
David Shelton 200011 - 21001 p. 382
Ezekiel Shelton 000001 - 0001 p. 378
1840 RHEA CENSUS
Sarah Shelton 00021 - 0000101
William H. Shelton 000111 - 00001
1840 MEIGS CENSUS
Bennet Shelton 00001001 - 0011001 p. 240
1850 RHEA CENSUS
Clever Shelton 26 (Farmer), Sarah 23, Margaret 3, William H. 2, Elizabeth 6/12 p. 631-620
1850 MEIGS CENSUS
Nancy Shelton or Melton 56 (Va), Anna 25 (Ky), Manuel 22 (Farmer), William 19 (Farmer), Riley 17 (Farmer), Zebodee 14, Louisa 12, Frances 10 p. 762-385
MARRIAGES (RHEA)
David Shelton to Elizabeth Witt, 6 Sept 1822 (same), A. David JP (AR) [David, son of Azariah and Sarah Holt Shelton]
Hezekiah Shelton to Margaret Love, 17 Apr 1828 (same), Wm W. Woods JP and Bm (AR) [Hezekiah, son of Azariah and Sarah]
Martha Shelton to Anderson Jones q.v.
William Shelton to Barbara Francis, 19 Dec 1816 (23 Dec), Jonathan Fine or John Rice JP, Asa May Bm (AR)
MARRIAGES (MEIGS)
Eliza Shelton to Edward Sharp q.v.
John Shelton to Lydia M. Shelton, 7 Apr 1841 (9 Apr), James Patterson JP, A.J. Shilbay Sur [1850 McMinn Census: John Shelton 31, Lydia 30, Bennet 8, Andrew 6, Powhattan 3, William 1]
Lydia M. Shelton to John Shelton q.v.
Martha Shelton to Joshua Lewis q.v.
Sterling Shelton to Miss [blank] Gregory, 10 Mar 1840, A.J. Baker Sur
MISCELLANEOUS (RHEA and MEIGS)
David Shelton: son of Azariah and Sarah
Hezekiah Shelton: Bondsman for William Clark, 1819
" " Bondsman for William James, 1821
James Shelton: Commissioner to lay off Decatur, 1836
Palatiah Shelton: Hiwassee District, Cottonport area

- - - - - - - - - - - - -

SHEPPARD / SHEPHARD

1830 RHEA CENSUS
Jno Sheppard 0001001 - 210111 p. 394
1840 MEIGS CENSUS
John Shephard 310001 - 011001 p. 237

- - - - - - - - - - - - -

SHERLEY

1850 RHEA CENSUS
Rufus B. Sherley 23 (Merchant), Malinda 24, Thomas SHROPEHER 18 (Student) p. 613-447

- - - - - - - - - - - - -

SHERRILL

TAXES (RHEA)
1808 (Jonathan Fine's List):
William Sherrill 1 WP, 300a Piney Ri
MARRIAGES (RHEA)
Samuel Sherrill to Fanny Carden or Cardin, 3 Dec 1810 (9 Dec), Wm Long JP, John Overstreet Bm (AR)
MISCELLANEOUS (RHEA)
George Sherrill: Bondsman for John McDonald, 1812

- - - - - - - - - - - - -

SHIELDS

1830 RHEA CENSUS
Daniel Shields 110011 - 11001 p. 358
MARRIAGES (RHEA)
Janney Shields to James Riley q.v.

- - - - - - - - - - - - -

SHIFLET / SHIFLETT

1840 MEIGS CENSUS
Austin Shiflet 211001 - 011101 p. 224
1850 RHEA CENSUS
John Shiflett 22: see Andrew Campbell
1850 MEIGS CENSUS
Austin Shiflet 49 (Va)(Farmer), Elizabeth 45 (Va), George W. 18, Austin C. 14, Benjamin F. 12, Andrew J. 9, Francis M. 7, Harriet E. 4 p. 716-27
MARRIAGES (MEIGS)
Mary Ann Shiflet to Joseph Cofer q.v.
Nancy J. Shiflett to John Cofer q.v.
Sarah Shiflett to Andrew Campbell q.v.

\- - - - - - - - - - - - -

SHILENGTON

TAXES (RHEA)
1823 (Capt. Howerton's Co.): William Shilengton 1 WP

\- - - - - - - - - - - - -

SHIPLEY

TAXES (RHEA)
1819 (Capt. McGill's Co.): Richard Shipley 1 WP
1850 MEIGS CENSUS
Enoch Shipley 20 (Farmer), Racheal 17, Mahala C. 0 p. 744-249
Mahaha Shipley 42, Samuel 17 (Farmer), Thomas 15, Susanna 13, Elizabeth Jane 10, Mary 5 p. 727-116

\- - - - - - - - - - - - -

SHOAT

MARRIAGES (RHEA)
Sylus Shoat to Esabella Brown, 9 July 1816, John Birdsong Bm (A)
MARRIAGES (MEIGS)
Elias Shoat to Elizabeth Fullington, 30 Oct 1844 (same), Mark Renfrow JP

\- - - - - - - - - - - - -

SHOEMAKER

TAXES (RHEA)
1819 (Capt. J. Robinson's Co.) Charles Shoemaker 1 WP
MARRIAGES (RHEA)
William Shoemaker to Mary Ann Moore, 28 Sept 1834, V. H. Giles JP, Thomas Hodges Bm (AR)

\- - - - - - - - - - - - -

SHORT

1840 RHEA CENSUS
George W. Short 20001 - 00001
1850 RHEA CENSUS
George W. Short 35 (Farmer), Eliza 27, Robert P. 10, Miller E. 9, Nancy R. 6, John H. 4, George G. 2, Joseph A. 2/12, Joseph PARKS 1 p. 543-66
MARRIAGES (RHEA)
George W. Short to Eliza Parks, 28 July 1836 (11 Aug), A. G. Wright JP, James Roddy Bm (AR)

\- - - - - - - - - - - - -

SHOUN

MARRIAGES (RHEA)
Polly Shoun to Thomas Jack q.v.

\- - - - - - - - - - - - -

SHROPHER

1850 RHEA CENSUS
Thomas Shropher 18: see Rufus B. Sherley

\- - - - - - - - - - - - -

SHUBIRD

1850 RHEA CENSUS
Mathew Shubird 22 (Farmer), Elizabeth 20 (Va), Sarah J. 1 p. 617-523

\- - - - - - - - - - - - -

SHUGART / SUGART

MARRIAGES (RHEA)
Lemuel Shugart or Sugart to Eliza Cozby, 10 Nov 1840 (same), Benj Wallace MG, J.H. French Bm (AR)

\- - - - - - - - - - - - -

SHULTZ / SHULTS

MARRIAGES (RHEA)
Jacob Shultz to Patsy Horton, 16 Nov 1812, John Shultz Bm (A)
Jacob Shultz to Betsy Colbough, 17 Dec 1815 (18 Dec), David Murphree JP (AR)
Martin Shultz to Sally Rowden, 23 Dec 1815 (24 Dec), David Murphree JP (A)
MISCELLANEOUS (RHEA)
John Shultz: Bondsman for Jacob Shultz, 1812
John R. Shultz: Lot 65, Town of Washington

\- - - - - - - - - - - - -

SHUMMON

MISCELLANEOUS (RHEA)
A.F. Shummon: MG 1849

\- - - - - - - - - - - - -

SILKIRK / SILCOCK / SELKIRK / SILCOX

1830 RHEA CENSUS
Eliza Selkirk 0 - 001000001 p. 382
John Silcock 00001 - 00001 p. 380
1840 RHEA CENSUS
John Silkirk 101001 - 211001001
Wiat Silcock 20001 - 00001

MARRIAGES (RHEA)
John Silcock to Nancy McFarland, 16 Sept 1826 or 1827 (17 Sept), Wm Smith JP, Wm Runyon Bm (AR)
Wyatt Silcox to Serena or Larena Ann Likins, 18 Nov 1835 (same), Carson Caldwell JP, Robert Robertson Bm (AR)
MISCELLANEOUS (RHEA)
John Silkirk: Bondsman for Hezekiah Burton, 1832
" " Bondsman for Andrew McFarland, 1839
Wyatt Silcox: Bondsman for Jonas Likins, 1836

SILVEY / SILLVEY / SIVELY / SILVA / SEVEL / SYLVA

1830 RHEA CENSUS
William Sillvey 101001 - 111011 p. 394
1840 RHEA CENSUS
William Sylva 1211001 - 00212
MARRIAGES (RHEA)
Anna Silvey to John Goad q.v.
Sally Silvey to John Hickey q.v.
Silas Sevely to Nancy Martin, 27 Apr 1827, Allen Hilburn Bm (A)
Solomon Sively to Dicy Brewer, 28 Dec 1838 (30 Dec), George Preston JP (AR)
William Silva or Silvey Sr. to Fanny Cunningham, 25 Sept 1839 (26 Sept), Henry Griffith or Griffett JP, John Goad Bm (AR) [NOTE: this record was listed twice in Courthouse records: as Silva in #36 and as Silvy in #87; Allen shows name as Silvey]

SIMCOX / SIMCOCK

1840 RHEA CENSUS
Thomas Simcock 00001 - 0001
MARRIAGES (RHEA)
Sarah Simcox to David Bell q.v.
Thomas J. Simcox to Jane Johnson, 11 Apr 1840 (12 Apr), A.D. Paul JP, West W. Johnson Bm (AR)

SIMMONS / SIMONS
(see also LEMMONS)

1840 MEIGS CENSUS
Jesse Simmons 111001 - 01001 p. 230
MARRIAGES (RHEA)
John Simmons to Jane Gann, 17 Jan 1820 (same), A. David JP, John Myers Bm (AR)
Sally Simons to Samuel Sullivan q.v.
Thomas Simons or Limons to Elizabeth Love, 21 Mar 1813, William McAllister Bm (A)

SIMPSON / SIMSON / SIMPTON

TAXES (RHEA)
1823 (Capt. Brown's Co.): John C. Simpson 1 WP
1850 RHEA CENSUS
Robert Simpson 40 (Unk)(Well Digger), Nelly 30, James 4, Harriet 1 p. 633-638
1850 MEIGS CENSUS
Richard Simpson 39 (Farmer), William 10, Thomas 8, John 6 p. 722-72
MARRIAGES (RHEA)
John C. Simpson to Nancey Paine, 11 Jan 1821 (same), John Cozby JP, Charles Reiveley Bm (AR)
Malinda Simpson to William R. Hassler q.v.
Paschal Simpson to Sally Burkhart, 5 Aug 1826 (6 Aug), John McClure JP, James P. Miller Bm (AR)
Robert Simpson to Mary Duncan, 5 Dec 1833, Matthew Limon Bm (A)
Sally Simpson to Montford Frazier q.v.
William Simpson to Jemima Casteel, 6 Aug 1833, Hugh H. Edington Bm (A)
MARRIAGES (MEIGS)
Eda Caroline Simpson to Martin H. Stephens q.v.
Lydia Simpson to Henry Sliger q.v.
Robert Simpson to Eleanor Moyars, 2 Apr 1846 (same), William Johns JP, Lukey Moore Sur
Sarah Simpson to Daniel McDowell q.v.
MISCELLANEOUS (RHEA and MEIGS)
John C. Simpson: Bondsman for Strother Blackwell, 1820
Richard Simpson: MG 1840-46; Ocoee District
Robert Simpson: JP(?) 1846

SIMS / SIMMS

TAXES (RHEA)
1808 (Jonathan Fine's List):
Littlepage Simms 400a Muddy Creek
1830 RHEA CENSUS
Vincent Simms 0110001 - 1111101 p. 380
1850 RHEA CENSUS
Thomas Sims 56 (SC)(Carpenter), Rebecca 42 (SC), John 20 (Farmer), George 16 (Farmer), Margaret J. 15, Lucinda J. 12, Hannah M. DOTSON 17 p. 631-619
William Sims 30 (Shoemaker), Nancy L. 29, Margaret J. 5, John B. 4, Juli A. 1, Elliott 24 (Shoemaker) p. 627-593
MISCELLANEOUS (RHEA)
William Sims: Bondsman for John Baker, 1841
MISCELLANEOUS (MEIGS)
Thomas Sims: Farrier, Mexican War

SINGENER

1830 RHEA CENSUS
Richard Singener 110001 - 110011 p. 376

SINGLETON / SINGLETIAN

1830 RHEA CENSUS
James Singleton 231001 - 1001 p. 364
John Singleton 2111101 - 03021 p. 379
1840 MEIGS CENSUS
David Singleton 010001 - 210001 p. 230
John Singleton 011110001 - 11022001 p. 236
Robert R. Singleton 00001 - 31001 p. 228
1850 RHEA CENSUS
David Singleton 46 (NC)(Farmer), Ruth Unk, Samuel 17, Jane 15, Rosiana E. 14, Viney 10, William 7, Eliza A. 6, Rebecca 4, Mary C. 2 p. 618-534
1850 MEIGS CENSUS
John Singleton 75 (Va)(Farmer), Elizabeth 60 (Va), Frances 36 (SC), Henry 33 (SC)(Farmer), Mary 25 (SC), William 23 (Farmer), Anne 22, Harris 18 (Farmer), Catharine 16, Eliza 13 p. 739-206
Nancy Singleton 23, Emeline 4, Henry 2 p. 737-196
MARRIAGES (RHEA)
David Singleton to Malinda Glenn, 5 Aug 1831 (18 Aug), John Cozby JP, Greenberry Casteel Bm (AR)
Juncey Singleton to George Weeks q.v.
John H. Singleton to Mary Johnson, 3 Jan 1838 (same), B.F. Jones JP, Gordon S. Templeton Bm (AR)
Mourning Singleton to David Seabolt q.v.
Robert E. Singleton to Jane Akin, 27 July 1833, William F. McCormick Bm (A)
William Singleton to Eliza Ward, 8 Dec 1819 (same), Jeremiah Howerton Bm (A)
MARRIAGES (MEIGS)
David Singleton to Rutha Moyers, 23 Nov 1838 (same), J. Frie JP
Nancy Singleton to A. B. Michals q.v.
MISCELLANEOUS (RHEA)
David Singleton: Bondsman for Jonathan Fry, 1825
" " Bondsman for Retten H. George, 1829
" " Bondsman for John W. Hughes, 1830
Starling Singleton: Bondsman for David Sebolt, 1825
MISCELLANEOUS (MEIGS)
David Singleton: Circuit Court jury, 1836
" " Hiwassee District
Henry Singleton: Cherokee Removal muster roll, 1836

\- - - - - - - - - - - -

SKEEN

1830 RHEA CENSUS
Eli Skeen 000000001 - 001001 p. 371

\- - - - - - - - - - - -

SKILLERN / SKILLEM

MARRIAGES (RHEA)
James Skillem or Skillern to Scotty Lewis, 13 Dec 1827 (same), John Henninger MG, William Skillern Bm (AR)
Luvana Skillern to Isaac A. Goolsby q.v.
MISCELLANEOUS (RHEA)
William Skillern: Bondsman for James Skillern, 1827

\- - - - - - - - - - - -

SLAGLE

MARRIAGES (RHEA)
Polly Slagle to Henry Roach q.v.

\- - - - - - - - - - - -

SLATER

1850 RHEA CENSUS
William T. Slater 30 (Saddler), Margaret E. 21, Mary E. 4 p. 612-440
MARRIAGES (MEIGS)
John Slater to Rebecca Swafford, 29 July 1842 (same), Robert Stockton JP, Alex Clark Sur(?)

\- - - - - - - - - - - -

SLAUGHTER

MARRIAGES (MEIGS)
Elizabeth Slaughter to John Henson q.v.

\- - - - - - - - - - - -

SLIGER

1830 RHEA CENSUS
John Sliger 00003 - 000001 p. 354
1850 MEIGS CENSUS
Jacob Sliger 44 (Farmer), Rebecca C. 44, Wyatt 23, Adam J. 21, Francis M. 19, Louisa 18, Plesant 16, Jacob L. 14, Thomas N. 12, Isabella 11, James D. 10, Samuel 5 p. 785-565
John Sliger 48 (Farmer), Hetty 48, Enoch 21, Catharine 18, Martha 17, Jackson 13, Hetty 11 p. 780-529
MARRIAGES (MEIGS)
Henry Sliger to Lydia Simpson, 22 Nov 1846 (same), T.B. McElwee JP, D.L. Godsey Sur(?)
Vilety Sliger to James Taylor q.v.
MISCELLANEOUS (MEIGS)
Thomas Sliger: Resident of District 6

\- - - - - - - - - - - -

SLOVER

TAXES (RHEA)
1823 (Capt. Smith's Co.):
Jacob Slover 1 WP, 160a Goodfield
MARRIAGES (RHEA)
Martha Slover to John Martin q.v.
Sally Slover to Benjamin Allen q.v.
MISCELLANEOUS (MEIGS)
Jacob Slover: Hiwassee District

\- - - - - - - - - - - -

SMALL

TAXES (RHEA)
1823 (Capt. Brown's Co.): Robert Small 1 WP
1850 MEIGS CENSUS
Wilson Small 30: see Andrew N. Snider
MARRIGES (RHEA)
Margaret Small to George Hunter q.v.
Polly Small to Joseph Cahill q.v.
Sarah Small to Elijah McPherson q.v.
MARRIAGES (MEIGS)
Henry Small to Hannah Wan, 9 Apr 1846 (same), William Green MG, John Small Bm
Jane Small to Frederick M. Johnson q.v.
John Small to Sarah Wan, 24 Sept 1845 (26 Sept), Dickerson Morris JP or MG, Jonathan C. Wan Bm
MISCELLANEOUS (RHEA and MEIGS)
James Small: Bondsman for Green Powell, 1815
" " Hiwassee District, Moore's Chapel area

- - - - - - - - - - - - -

SMALLEN

1850 MEIGS CENSUS
Solomon Smallen 34 (Farmer), Sarah 44, Martha 15, Robert A. 9, Benjamin L. 7, William D. 4, Benjamin 87 (Va) p. 719-48 [Solomon M. Smallen married Mrs. Sarah Pugh on 1 Sept 1840 in McMinn Co]

- - - - - - - - - - - - -

SMARTT / SMART

MARRIAGES (RHEA)
William C. Smartt to Elizabeth Waterhouse, 16 Nov 1827 (same), William W. Woods MG, Richard Waterhouse Bm (AR)
MISCELLANEOUS (RHEA)
John B. Smart: Drummer, Cherokee Removal muster roll, 1837

- - - - - - - - - - - - -

SMITH

TAXES (RHEA)
1808 (James Campbell's List): William Smith 1 WP
1819 (Capt. John Lewis' Dist.): James Smith 1 WP, 130a
(Capt. Robinson's Co.): John A. Smith 1 WP, 2 BP
Mumford Smith 1 WP, 177a
William Smith 1 WP
(Capt. McGill's Co.): Wm Smith 1 WP, 1 BP, 166a
1823 (Capt. Braselton's Co.): Anderson Smith 1 WP
Mumford Smith 1 WP, 177a
Randolph Smith 1 WP
(Capt. Brown's Co.): James Smith 1 WP
John Smith 1 Stud Horse (tax, $4.00)
(Capt. McCall's Co.): James Smith 1 WP
John Smith 1 WP
(Capt. Lewis' Co.): John Smith 1 WP, 3 BP
(Capt. Smith's Co.): John Smith 1 WP, 111a Tenn R
William Smith 1 WP
(Capt. Piper's Co.): Theophiles Smith 1 WP
(Capt. Howard's Co.): William Smith 2 BP, 110a

1830 RHEA CENSUS
Anderson Smith 200001 - 00001 p. 386
Charles Smith 02101 - 010001 p. 378
James Smith 210001 - 111001 p. 387
Jas or Jos Smith 0100001 - 0100001 p. 378
John Smith 111201 - 0310001 p. 366
John Smith 000001 - 0001 p. 362
Jno A. Smith 0113101 - 1100001 p. 376
Martha Smith 0002 - 12000001 p. 363
Mumford Smith 000000000001 - 0 p. 376
Mumford Smith 0001101 - 1211101 p. 386
Nathaniel Smith 11001 - 11001 p. 354
T. B. Smith 20000001 - 0100001 p. 393
Thephilius Smith 0121001 - 10001 p. 357
Washington Smith 111001 - 010101 p. 389
William Smith 00021001 - 02110001 p. 386
William Smith 0111100101 - 002001 p. 381
William Smith 10001 - 00001 p. 386
Wright Smith 0130001 - 0111 p. 385
1840 RHEA CENSUS
A. W. Smith 22011 - 11003001
Alexander Smith 000001 - 2001
Andrew Smith 000001 - 00001
Huling W. Smith 01001 - 30001
James Smith 0000001 - 0001001
James Smith Jr. 0220001 - 1012001
James Smith 000001 - 2001
John Smith 00111001 - 00120001
John Sith(?) 10001 - 0001
Mumford Smith 00000001 - 00131001
Nancy Smith 0221 - 0000001
Thomas Smith 000001 - 00001
William F. Smith 00001 - 0001
Wright Smith 11011001 - 211101
1840 MEIGS CENSUS
Abraham Smith 0021001 - 210001 p. 245
Henry Smith 10001 - 10001 p. 240
Isaac Smith 02001 - 10001 p. 240
Jiles Smith 10001 - 00001001 p. 231
John Smith 00001 - 1001 p. 240
John Smith 000101 - 1110011 p. 246
John W. Smith 221101 - 1 p. 237
Joseph Smith 001001 - 131001 p. 243
Margaret Smith 21 - 20001 p. 237
Pleasant Smith 00001 - 100001 p. 240
Sarah S. Smith 00001 - 001100001 p. 237
Thephilus Smith 00010001 - 00100001 p. 240
Thomas B. Smith 120001 - 11001 p. 242

1850 RHEA CENSUS
Albion R. Smith 22 (Clerk) p. 612-434
Alexander Smith 36 (Farmer), Malora 32 (NC), Harriet 12, Sarah A. 11, George 9, Charlotte 7, Elizabeth 5, Elijah 3, Emaline 4/12 p. 536-23
Alexander Smith 30 (Farmer), Sarah Unk, Eliza A. 3, Andrew 8/12 p. 565-185
Benjamin D. Smith 6: see Jesse Harwood
George M.J. Smith 17, Salina J. 15: see Isabella Kennedy
George W. Smith 10: see Sarah Hunter
James Smith 57 (SC)(Farmer), Nancy 56, Catharine 28, William G. 22 (Farmer), Thomas G. 19 (Farmer), James H. 17 (Farmer), Martha A. 10 p. 500-170
Loretta Smith 18, Sarah C. 6/12: see Elizabeth Mulvaney
Nancy Smith 61 (mulatto) p. 614-458

Nancy Smith 53 (Va), Charles D. 27 (Ala)(Farmer), William S. 16 (Farmer) p. 586-334
Nathaniel Smith 24 (Cabnetmaker), Elizabeth 19, Eliza J. 4, John W. 2 p. 613-455
Richard Smith 36 (Farmer), Eliza 36, Coleman 17 (Farmer), Dolly 15, William 13, John 7, Mary A. 4, James 3, Franklin 1 p. 561-176
Stephen D. Smith 40 (Farmer), Mary P. 40, Nancy E. 17, Nicholas A. 16, Josiah R. 12, Mary E. 6, James E. 1 p. 570-220
Thomas Smith 44 (Farmer), Lucy 45, Mary A. 24, Elizabeth 22, James C. 19, Thomas C. 16, William H. 15, George L. 13, Rebecca 10, Nathan S. 8, Robert B. 6 p. 637-667
William Smith 21 (Farmer), Nancy 31, Sarah E. 7/12 p. 608-497
William F. Smith 31 (Farmer), Margaret A. 29, Lorinda 8, John T. 6, Susannah M. 4, Sarah L.E. 1, Ruth HARWOOD Unk p. 574-250
Wright Smith 31 (Farmer) p. 576-265
Wright Smith 65 (SC)(Farmer), Zilphu 40, Benjamin D. 32 (School Teacher), Joseph D. 17 (Student), Priscilla 16, Adeline 14, Penelope 12, Pete A. 10, James J. 7 p. 573-244

1850 MEIGS CENSUS

Abram Smith 83 (Va), Elizabeth 62 (NC) p. 794-633
Banister Smith 51 (Farmer), Eliza 47 p. 764-405
Bryant W. Smith 30 (Farmer), Lucinda 30, Mary 3, Thomas 2 p. 788-594
Fanny Smith 40, James 20 (Farmer), Calvin 7 p. 741-224
James Smith 21 (Farmer), Sarah 23, Luke 16 p. 764-406
John W. Smith 41 (Farmer), Sarah 44, James 18 (Farmer), Thomas 16 (Farmer), Gideon 14, Rebecca 14, Joshua 7 p. 770-446
John W. Smith 30 (Farmer), Phebe 27, Nancy Jane 11, James W. 5, David I. 2 p. 814-779
Joseph Smith 45 (Farmer), Elizabeth 44, Rebecca 20, Hugh 18 (Farmer), Samuel 13, Malissa 10, Lacky (f) 6, Racheal 4, William 1 p. 792-619
Joseph Smith 25 (Farmer), Lucy 23, Thomas H. 7, William M. 5, Harriet 3, James P. 1 p. 752-320
Josiah Smith 25 (Farmer), Sarah 19, Elizabeth p. 759-372
Phillip Smith 50 (Farmer), Mary 48, Elizabeth 17, Jacob 14, Minerva 10 p. 816-766
William Smith 27 (Farmer), Dicy 26, Wright 3, Nancy Ann 1 p. 814-780

MARRIAGES (RHEA)

Alexander Smith to Maloney Brewer, 14 Sept 1836, R.N. Gillespie Bm (A)
Amanda C. Smith to Thompson Cash q.v.
Anderson Smith to Elizabeth Fulton, 26 Sept 1822 (29 Sept), Fred Fulkerson JP, Arthur Fulton Bm (AR)
Anney Smith to James Spencer q.v.
Betsy Smith to Farley Brady q.v.
Caroline C. Smith to William W. Lea q.v.
Catherine Smith to William Stinnite q.v.
Catharine A. Smith to Solomon Henry q.v.
Charity Smith to Joseph Dunham q.v.
Dolly Smith to Nelson M. Narimore q.v.
Eliza Smith to John P. Long q.v.
Elizabeth Smith to Daniel Holland q.v.
Elizabeth Smith to David Walker Jr. q.v.
Elizabeth Smith to David M. Roddy q.v.
George Smith to Anney Clower, 21 Feb 1829 (22 Feb), B. Winton JP (AR)
George W. Smith to Sarah Evans, 9 Jan 1836 (10 Jan), D.L. Godsey JP, Wm Smith Bm (AR)
H. M. Smith to Martha Williams, 30 Jan 1845 (same), Samuel Frazier JP, J.C. Gerin Bm (AR)
Henry Smith to Chonea (Cheny) Johnson, 10 July 1835 (12 July), John Pandale JP, S. Johnson Bm (AR)
Hughlett W. Smith to Elvira Miller, 31 Dec 1836 (1 or 2 Jan 1837), James McCanse JP, Jacob Riggle Bm (AR)
James Smith to Polly George, 25 Sept 1819 (same), John Cozby JP (AR)
James W. Smith to Louisa P. Campbell, 19 Mar 1834 (20 Mar), Benj Wallace MG, John P. Long Bm (AR)
Jane Smith to Jacob Russell q.v.
John Harris Smith to Lucy Battles/Bottles, 12 Dec 1815 (19 Dec), David Murphree JP, John Parker Bm (AR)
John W. Smith to Mariah Hunter, 14 Sept 1831 (15 Sept), Peach Taylor JP, Benjamin F. Locke Bm (AR)
Josiah Smith to Mary Parks, 10 May 1826 (11 May), James A. Darwin JP, William Lowry Bm (AR)
Leah E. Smith to Charles W. Ault q.v.
Louisa Jane Smith to James Rhea q.v.
Libby Smith to Samuel Bowman q.v.
Mary Smith to Nathan Dodson q.v.
Mary Smith to Jesse Harwood q.v.
Mary Ann Smith to Samuel B. Hackett q.v.
Mumford Smith to Mary Ann Blythe, 21 Oct 1841 (no return), Solomon Henry Bm (AR)
Nancy Smith to Samuel Rowden q.v.
Nancey Ann Smith to Harvey Montgomery q.v.
Phebe A. Smith to James H. Locke q.v.
Prudence Smith to James Carnahan q.v.
Rachel Smith to Warren West q.v.
Rebecca Smith to A.J. Covington q.v.
Riley Smith to Cintha Myers, 3 Mar 1826 (same), Thomas Cox JP, William Myers Bm (AR)
Thomas Smith to Scotty Walker, 21 Sept 1830 (23 Sept), John Condley JP, Anderson Walker Bm (AR)
William Smith to Molley Butler, 18 Aug 1820 (22 Aug), Arthur Fulton JP (AR)
William Smith to Susan Beck, 28 July 1828 (29 July), Matthew Hubbard JP, Mumford Smith Bm (AR)
William Smith to Mary Wheeler, 24 Sept 1832 (30 Sept), Matthew Hubbert JP, Thos H. Wheeler Bm (AR)
William Smith to Margaret Evans, 19 Dec 1832 (20 Dec), Mathias Shaver JP, George W. Selvidge Bm (AR)
William G. Smith to M.A. Ault, 15 Jan 1840 (16 Jan), John Condley JP (R)
Wright Smith to Zelphay or Zilpha Davis, 2 June 1831 (same), Jas Wilson JP, Saml R. Hackett Bm (AR)

MARRIAGES (MEIGS)

A. P. Smith to Mary Jane --?--, 18 Sept 1844 (same), R. Simpson MG, J.G. Tipton Sur(?)
Aaron Smith to Lucinda Walden, 29 Jan 1839 (30 Jan), Jacob Price JP, James Rowden Sur(?)
Elijah S. Smith to Mary J. Winton, 4 Apr 1844 (same), W.F. Forrest MG, Allen Haley Bm
James Smith to Sarah Guinn, 11 Apr 1850, Abner Guinn Sur
John Smith to Frances Snow, 22 Sept 1838 (23 Sept), Jacob Price JP, William Snow Bm
John W. Smith to Pheaby Moore, 15 Sept 1838 (5 Oct), James Patterson JP, Charles Prater Bm

John W. Smith to Sarah Little, 10 Feb 1842, D.L. Godsey MG, John Hunter Bm
Jordan Smith to Polly Snow, 12 Jan 1842 (same), James Moore JP, D. Beagles Bm
Katherine Smith to David Mitchell q.v.
Malindy Jane Smith to Abner Guinn q.v.
Margaret Smith to John Mitchell q.v.
Mary Smith to Thomas Cox q.v.
R. Smith to Margaret Breedwell, 15 June 1844 (20 June), D.L. Godsey MG, John Long Bm
Rebecca Smith to Lewis Benton q.v.
William Smith to Rebecca Hill, 14 Dec 1843 (same), John Huff Esq, Thomas J. Price Bm
William Smith to Dicy Sears, 24 Nov 1845 (26 Nov), William Green MG, Thomas McCallon Bm
Wilson C. Smith to Eleanor Blevins, 10 Mar 1841, "not written, found June 1, 1849", Joseph McCorkle and Wm Russell, Adms., William Rockhold Sur(?)
Wright Smith to Jane Sharp, 29 Nov 1843 (30 Nov), Wm L. Adams JP, James Gillespie Bm

MISCELLANEOUS (RHEA)

B.W. Smith: Bondsman for Nathaniel Layman, 1842
Benjamin D. Smith: Bondsman for Austin Evans, 1840
" " " Bondsman for John Hailey, 1840
" " " County Court Clerk, 1840-44
Charles Smith: Bondsman for James Boulton, 1837
Daniel Smith: Bondsman for Joseph Richmond, 1828
H. W. Smith: Bondsman for James H. Parker, 1842
Henry Smith: Bondsman for James Fields, 1835
James Smith: Bondsman for Benjamin Rogers, 1822
" " Bondsman for Isham Goff, 1831
" " Bondsman for Nicholas Romines, 1835
" " Bondsman for James F. Bolen 1836
" " JP 1848
James W. Smith: Bondsman for William B. Cozby, 1833
" " " Bondsman for John B. Stevenson, 1833
Joel Smith: Bondsman for William Thompson, 1834
John Smith: Bondsman for William W. Piles, 1835
John A. Smith: Bondsman for George W. Riggle, 1810
M.W. Smith: Bondsman for Davis Able, 1839
Mumford Smith: Bondsman for William Smith, 1828
Randolph Smith: Bondsman for John Davidson, 1818
Thomas Smith: Bondsman for Moses Eller, 1836
" " Bondsman for John Love, 1836
William Smith: Bondsman for George W. Smith, 1836
" " JP 1826, 1831-33
" " Commissioner to construct new jail, 1825
" " Lots 29-32 in Town of Washington
William F. Smith: Bondsman for Thomas Ault, 1839
William M. Smith: JP 1824, 1826, 1830
William R. Smith: Had mercantile business in Washington
Wright Smith: Bondsman for John Davis, 1841

MISCELLANEOUS (MEIGS)

Benjamin D. Smith: Private, Mexican War
C. R. Smith: Surety for William J. Abel, 1850
Charles Smith: Private, Mexican War
Charles K. Smith: Surety for Calvin C. Robeson, 1850
Daniel Smith: Hiwassee District, Pinhook Ferry area
Henry Smith: Cherokee Removal muster roll, 1837
Isaac Smith: Cherokee Removal muster roll, 1837
James Smith: Surety for Abner Gwinn, 1850
John Smith: Common School Com., District 8, 1838
" " Cherokee Removal muster roll, 1837
John A. [Jackson?] Smith: Hiwassee District, Sewee Cr area
John W. Smith: Constable, District 4, 1836
" " " Cherokee Removal muster roll, 1837
Joseph Smith: Common School Com., District 6, 1838
Martha Smith: Ocoee District
Nathaniel Smith: Hiwassee District
William Smith: Common School Com., District 4, 1838
Wilson C. Smith: Cherokee Removal muster roll, 1838

- - - - - - - - - - - - -

SNEAD

MISCELLANEOUS (RHEA)

Robert Sneed: MGBC 1834

- - - - - - - - - - - - -

SNELSON

TAXES (RHEA)

1808 (Jonathan Fine's List): James Snelson, 1 WP, 100a TR
1819 (Capt. John Ramsey's Co.): James Snelson 220a
1823 (Capt. McCall's Co.): James Snelsn 150a Tenn River
Samuel Snelson 1 WP
Thomas Snelson 1 WP

1830 RHEA CENSUS

James Snelson* 000030001 - 00001000 p. 387
[* Snelson written over Nelson or vice versa]
Samuel Snelson 221001 - 100001 p. 363
Thomas Snelson 11001 - 21002 p. 364

1840 RHEA CENSUS

John Snelson 000001 - 20001
William Snelson 000001 - 000001

1850 RHEA CENSUS

William Snelson 47: see Farley Brady

MARRIAGES (RHEA)

John Snelson to Melicia Miller, 1 Feb 1836 (7 Feb), William Green MG, Thomas Carter Bm (AR)
Samuel Snelson to Elizabeth Macay or Macoy, 2 Oct 1817 (same), Jonathan Fine JP, James Snelson Bm (AR)

MISCELLANEOUS (RHEA)

James Snelson: Bondsman for Moses Trimble, 1809
" " Bondsman for Samuel Snelson, 1817
Samuel Snelson: Member, Fellowship Baptist Church of Christ, 1828-29
" " Hiwassee Dist, Fooshee-Hardwick Is area
Thomas Snelson: Bondsman for John Burton, 1822
William Snelson: Bondsman for Shelby Munday, 1834

- - - - - - - - - - - - -

SNIDER

1850 MEIGS CENSUS

Andrew N. Snider 27 (Cotton Spinner), Mahala 19, Wilson SMALL 30 (Cotton Spinner) p. 819-818
[Andrew R. Snider married Mahaly Leamar or Lemore on 22 Oct 1847 in McMinn County]
Pascheal Snider 26 (Va)(Farmer), Sarah 27, Racheal 1 p. 796-651

MARRIAGES (MEIGS)

A. R. Snider to Mahala Rogers, 22 Oct 1850, J.C. Wann Sur

- - - - - - - - - - - - -

SNODGRASS / SNOTGRASS

1840 RHEA CENSUS
Elijah Snodgrass 1000101 - 0210001
George M. Snodgrass 00001 - 0001
1840 MEIGS CENSUS
Thomas Snodgrass 00001 - 00001 p. 230
1850 RHEA CENSUS
Elijah Snotgrass 52 (Farmer), Margaret 51, Amanda M. 17, Elijah F. 11 p. 568-209
George M. Snotgrass 27 (Farmer), Margaret 29, James A. 8, Andrew C. 2 p. 568-210
John A. Snotgrass 31 (Farmer), Nancy M. 33, Thomas J.K. P. 6, Alfred L. 4, Mary A. 2, Margaret E. 3/12 p. 606-477
William H. Snotgrass 38 (Farmer), Lucretia 28, Elijah G. 13, John J. 11, Luranda 7, William E. 5, James A. 3, Alexander 1, Luisa PIKARD 37, Lurena E. 3, Luisa T. 6 p. 606-478
MARRIAGES (RHEA)
Datsia A. Snodgrass to Alfred Collins q.v.
Elizabeth Snodgrass to John M. Holland q.v.
George M. Snodgrass to Elenor Maloney, 4 Nov 1839 (7 Nov), A.G. Wright JP (R)
George M. Snodgrass to Margarett Crumpton, 5 Aug 1847, W.W. Rose MG (R)
John A. Snodgrass to Nancy M. Holland, 29 Dec 1840 (same), Wm Stewart MG or JP, Andrew J. Thompson Bm (AR)
William Snodgrass to Mary Sykes, 12 Aug 1847 (13 Aug), Ezekiel Ward MG (R)
MISCELLANEOUS (MEIGS)
George M. Snodgrass: MG 1846-47

- - - - - - - - - - - - -

SNOW

1830 RHEA CENSUS
John Snow 213001 - 020001 p. 387
1840 MEIGS CENSUS
John Snow 10301001 - 2101001 p. 245
John U. Snow 00101 - 00001 p. 246
William Snow 10001 - 00001 p. 245
1850 RHEA CENSUS
Pleasant Snow 25 (Farmer), Nancy 22, Charlotte 2, Marion 5/12, Edy DOUGLASS (f) 12 p. 638-674
MARRIAGES (RHEA)
Albert Snow to Mary Ann Willson, 25 Nov 1848 (same), J.H. Locke JP (R)
Caroline Snow to Stephen Willson q.v.
Elizabeth Snow to Robert G. Qualls q.v.
Martha Snow to John Sykes q.v.
Pleasant Snow to Nancy Sykes, 6 Jan 1847, E. Ward MG (R)
Rebecca Snow to John Duckworth q.v.
MARRIAGES (MEIGS)
Frances Snow to John Smith q.v.
Polly Snow to Jordan Smith q.v.
Samuel Snow to Elizabeth Maberry, 28 Dec 1843 (same), T.B. McClure JP, Leonard Huff Bm
MISCELLANEOUS (RHEA)
Thomas Snow: Bondsman for Russell Qualls, 1835

- - - - - - - - - - - - -

SOLOMON / SOLLOMON / SAULMON

1840 RHEA CENSUS
John Saulmon 002010001 - 0001001
1840 MEIGS CENSUS
Ewin Sollomon 10001 - 00001 p. 225
1850 RHEA CENSUS
Elizabeth Solomon 21, Andrew J. 6, Martha L. 4, George W. 10/12 p. 542-61

- - - - - - - - - - - - -

SPARKS / SPARKES

1850 MEIGS CENSUS
Absolum Sparkes 48 (SC)(Farmer), Sarah 23 (SC), Thomas 14, Mary Jane 12, William 7, Martha 5, Lucinda 3, George 2, James 0 p. 717-32
MARRIAGES (MEIGS)
Thomas Sparks to Mary Philpott, 1 May 1843 (same), Benjamin F. McKenzie JP, Joseph Bracket Bm

- - - - - - - - - - - - -

SPARLEN / SPARLIN / SPURLING

TAXES (RHEA)
1808 (John Henry's List): John Sparlen 1 WP
MARRIAGES (RHEA)
Polly Spurling or Sparlin to Mark Robinson q.v.

- - - - - - - - - - - - -

SPENCE

1840 RHEA CENSUS
Stephen Spence 110201 - 111101
1850 RHEA CENSUS
John [James] Spence 30 (NC)(Farmer), Mahala 37, Myra A. 1 p. 616-511
John Spence 27 (Farmer), Tennessee 19 p. 618-533
Stephen Spence 49 (NC)(Farmer), Martha 49 (NC), Jane 21, Stephen 18 (Farmer), Mary 14, Franklin 12, Sarah 8, Gerge M.D. 6 p. 616-509
MARRIAGES (RHEA)
Elizabeth Spence to Thomas J. Hail q.v.
James Spence to Mahala Hale, 2 Feb 1848, Edward Childress MG (R)
John Spence to Tennessee Knight, 1 May 1850 (same), J.A. Mitchell JP (R)
MISCELLANEOUS (RHEA)
Stephen Spence: Bondsman for Thomas Knight, 1839

- - - - - - - - - - - - -

SPENCER

1830 RHEA CENSUS
James Spencer 10001 - 00001 p. 355
1840 MEIGS CENSUS
James Spencer 011001 - 010001 p. 224
MARRIAGES (RHEA)
Hiram Spencer to Polly Rhea, 18 Nov 1828 (20 Nov), Philip Siever MG, John Spencer Bm (AR)
James Spencer to Anney Smith, 16 Oct 1824 (same), Johnson Winton Bm (A)

MISCELLANEOUS (RHEA)
John Spencer: Bondsman for Hiram Spencer, 1828
" " Private, Mexican War
L., H., J., and W. Spencer: Members, Concord Baptist Church of Christ, 1824

- - - - - - - - - - - - -

SPRADLING

1850 MEIGS CENSUS
Mordica Spradling 34 (Va)(Farmer), Levina 30, Tyro (m) 10, Polly Ann 9, Nancy E. 7, Richard 5, Charlotte 4, Hugh H. 2, Mortimore 1 p. 776-504 [Mortimer Spradlin married Louvicy Lawson on 29 Oct 1838 in McMinn Co]

- - - - - - - - - - - - -

STACY

1830 RHEA CENSUS
Mark Stacy 0121101 - 0101101 p. 392
1840 RHEA CENSUS
Mark Stacy 00000001 - 0012001
1850 RHEA CENSUS
Sarah Stacy 25: see Stephen Breeding
MARRIAGES (RHEA)
Ann Stacy to Joseph Richmond q.v.
Anna M. Stacy to Flemming H. Fulton q.v.
Levy or Levi Stacy to Patsey Carrell, 18 Oct 1835 (19 Oct), John Pardee MMEC, Flemming H. Fulton Bm (AR)
Mark Stacy to Elizabeth Likens or Likins, 15 June 1839 (16 June), Martin B. Paul MG, Nathan S. Broyles Bm (AR)

- - - - - - - - - - - - -

STAFFORD

1830 RHEA CENSUS
Washington Stafford 2001 - 10001 p. 390
MARRIAGES (RHEA)
Thomas Stafford to Nancy Myrum, 19 Mar 1810 (same), Alexander Forbes Bm (A)

- - - - - - - - - - - - -

STANLY / STANLEY

TAXES (RHEA)
1823 (Capt. Smith's Co.): Jonathan Stanley 1 WP
1830 RHEA CENSUS
Jonathan Stanley 11001 - 2001 p. 369
1840 MEIGS CENSUS
Nancy Stanly 0011 - 0122001 p. 231
1850 MEIGS CENSUS
Nancy Stanly 50 (Va), Alkana 29 (Farmer), Lucinda 22, John L. 20 (Farmer), Nancy C. 19 p. 734-171
MARRIAGES (MEIGS)
Lidia Ann Stanly to William M. Childress q.v.
Mary Stanley to Sanford Adkins q.v.
Susan Stanley to Jonathan Isom q.v.
MISCELLANEOUS (MEIGS)
Cain Stanley: Private, Mexican War
John Stanly: Surety for Sanford Adkins, 1850

- - - - - - - - - - - - -

STANNER

MARRIAGES (MEIGS)
Thomas E. Stanner to Elizabeth A. Edds, 19 Sept 1849 (same), Nathaniel Barnett MG

- - - - - - - - - - - - -

STAPLES

1830 RHEA CENSUS
David B. Staples 000001 - 000001 p. 352 [David married Sally Kimbreal on 30 Dec 1824 in Roane County]

- - - - - - - - - - - - -

STAPLETON

1840 MEIGS CENSUS
Thomas Stapleton 300001 - 120001 p. 230
MARRIAGES (MEIGS)
Thomas Stapleton to Anna Lawson, 15 May 1841, James Comson Sur(?)

- - - - - - - - - - - - -

STARBUCK

MARRIAGES (RHEA)
Martha J. Starbuck to Owen Fisher q.v.

- - - - - - - - - - - - -

STARK

MISCELLANEOUS (RHEA)
Samuel Stark: Bondsman for Francis Monday, 1822

- - - - - - - - - - - - -

STARNES / STURNS / STARNIS

1840 MEIGS CENSUS
Benjamin Starns or Sturns 1210001 - 2111001 p. 229
1850 MEIGS CENSUS
Sophia Starnes 35 (NC), Caroline 25 (NC), John 23 (NC), Joshua 21 (NC), Malinda 19 (NC), Frankland 17, Rebecca 15, Jane 13, Hannah 11, Roseanna 9 p. 742-232
MARRIAGES (RHEA)
Malinda Starnis to Elijah Clingon q.v.
Nicholas Starnes to Mary Ann Barry, 6 Sept 1816, George Riggle Bm (AR)
Nicholas Starnes to Barbara Winters, 10 Oct 1816 (same), J. Fine or J. Rice JP, Thomas Johnson Bm (AR)
MARRIAGES (MEIGS)
John Starnes to Elizabeth Chapman, 6 Dec 1844 (same), William Johns JP, Elias Moore Sur(?)
Sarah Starns to Owen Martin q.v.
Sarah C. Starnes to P. J. Deane q.v.
MISCELLANEOUS (MEIGS)
Joshua Starnes: Private, Mexican War

- - - - - - - - - - - - -

STARR / STEARR

TAXES (RHEA)
1808 (Jonathan Fine's List):
Henry Stearr 1 WP, 100a Piney River
1830 RHEA CENSUS
Jas or Jos Starr 0020000011 - 001000001 p. 367

STAUNTON

TAXES (RHEA)
1823 (Capt. Wilson's Co.): Thomas Staunton 1 WP
MARRIAGES (RHEA)
Rebecca Staunton to Elijah Camron q.v.

STEEL

MISCELLANEOUS (RHEA)
Elmore Steel: Private, Mexican War

STEEN

MARRIAGES (RHEA)
James Steen to Sarah Pearson, 20 or 10 Sept 1820 (no return), George Gothard Bm (AR)
MARRIAGES (MEIGS)
James M. Steen to Sarah Ford, 10 Aug 1846 (13 Aug), Leroy Looney JP

STEPHENS / STEVENS

TAXES (RHEA)
1823 (Capt. Wilson's Co.): John Stephens 1 WP
1830 RHEA CENSUS
Burt S. Stephens 201001 - 120001 p. 390
William Stephens 2000100001 - 000001 p. 392
1850 MEIGS CENSUS
Haywood Stephens 21, Caroline 20 ("Married within year") p. 815-783
Haywood Stephens 23 (Farmer), Caroline 21 p. 781-537
Henry J. Stephens 26 (NC)(Farmer), Dicy Ann 20 (NC), Nancy Jane 1 p. 781-539
Sylvana Stephens (m) 47 (NC), Emaly Jane 23, Benjamin F. 18 (Farmer), Sarah 15, Lovrick 15, George W. 12, Martin V. 10, William M. 6 p. 814-777
MARRIAGES (RHEA)
Elizabeth Stevens to Thomas Davis q.v.
MARRIAGES (MEIGS)
Martin H. Stephens to Eda Caroline Simpson, 13 Apr 1848, Thomas V. Atchley JP, John M. Lillard Sur(?)
Susan Stephens to A.J. Prewitt q.v.
MISCELLANEOUS (RHEA)
B. M. Stephens: MG MEC 1832
R. M. Stevens: JP 1835
William Stephens: Hiwassee District

STEPHENSON / STEVENSON

MARRIAGES (RHEA)
David Stephenson to Rosannah Benson, 13 May 1829, Robert Benson Bm (A)
John B. Stevenson or Stephenson to Elizabeth B. Ustick, 28 Feb 1833 (same), Benjamin Wallace MG, James W. Smith Bm (AR)

STEWART / STUART

TAXES (RHEA)
1819 (Capt. McCray's Co.): Edward Stuart 1 WP, 266a
(Capt. Lewis' Dist.): James Stuart 1 WP, 1 Lot, 100a
(Capt. Bradley's Dist.): Mercy Stuart 2 Town Lots
1823 (Capt. Howerton's Co.): Edward Stewart 1 WP, 1 Stud Horse (tax, $2.00), 266a Camp Creek
(Capt. Wilson's Co.): John Stewart 1 WP
(Capt. Smith's Co.): Samuel P. Stewart 1 WP

1830 RHEA CENSUS
Edward Stewart 00000001 - 222001 p. 389
Jas or Jos Stuart 0132001 - 1020101 p. 394
John Stourt 300001 - 21201 p. 352
Jno Stuart 2210001 - 0020001 p. 371
Layton Stewart 11001 - 10001 p. 391
Mercy Stewart 001 - 00100001 p. 383
Samuel Stuart 012001 - 400201 p. 373
1840 RHEA CENSUS
James Stuart 01010001 - 00101001
James H. Stuart 00011 - 20001
Mercy Stuart 0 - 30001001
Samuel Stuart 10001 - 00001
1840 MEIGS CENSUS
James Stewart 20000 - 120001 p. 233
John Stewart 3020001 - 020301 p. 236
Joseph Stewart 11001 - 110101 p. 232
Joseph Stewart 000210001 - 0001 p. 233

1850 RHEA CENSUS
Francis Stuart 35 (Farmer), Elizabeth 31, Hannah M. 7, Mary E. 5, John D. 3 p. 597-385
James Stuart 66 (Va)(Farmer), Sarah 64 (NC), Emeline 24, Jane TAYLOR 21, Elizabeth TAYLOR 19, Able McCARTER 23 (Farmer), Meredith 24 (Farmer), Moses 21 (Farmer) p. 596-382
Mercy Stuart 70 (Va), Clarissa TANNER 31, Mary J. TANNER 11 p. 611-426
Samuel Stuart 34, Elizabeth 36, Thomas C. 10, Mary E. 6, Mahala 4, Polly HALE 30 p. 596-383
1850 MEIGS CENSUS
John Stewart 59 (Md)(Farmer), Lety 47, William 22, Richard 22, James 17, Lety 15, Tyra F. (m) 13, Mathew B. 11, Martin V. 9, Tennessee 6 p. 778-514
John G. Stuart 27 (Lawyer): see David Leuty
Joseph Stewart 39 (NC)(Farmer), Malinda 40, Caroline 17, John 15, Martha 10, Mary 7, Joseph 4 p. 733-156
Lety Stewart 20, Mahala 17, Rebecca C. 15, Margaret Jane 12: see Hiram Jolly
Luvana Stewart (f) 28, Willis 13, James 11, John F. 6 p. 742-236

MARRIAGES (RHEA)
Charles Stewart to Jane Cannon, 26 Dec 1828 (same), Robert Hall MG, Hamilton Stewart Bm (AR)
Emaline Stewart to Able McCarter q.v.
James Stewart to Dicy Adison, 7 May 1831, Thomas M. Harp Bm (A)
James H. Stewart to Lucinda Hill, 23 July 1835 (same), R. M. Stephens or Stevens JP, John Hoyal Bm (AR)
Jane Stewart to John Knight q.v.
Jerusha Stuart to William Hill q.v.
Katheine Stewart to James J. Alexander q.v.
Laban Stewart to Nancy Wells, 10 Sept 1823 (no return), Edward Stuart Bm (R)
Louisa Stewart to Edward P. Childers q.v.
Maryann Stuart to Henry Glass q.v.
Samuel Stewart to Elizabeth A. Hail, 9 Dec 1836 (12 Dec), H. Collins JP (R)
Thomas W. Stewart to Clarinda Tanesy or Lancry, 24 Aug 1832 (same), Peach Taylor JP
MARRIAGES (MEIGS)
Andrew Stuart to Lurenna Inman, 18 Feb 1843 (19 Feb), B.F. McKenzie JP, William Lillard and Thomas Leuty Bm
Joseph Stuart to Ara King, 11 Sept 1839 (12 Sept), B.F. McKenzie JP, Jacob Nideffer Bm
Joseph Stuart to Huldah Jones, 10 Feb 1842 (same), B.F. McKenzie JP, John Davis Bm
M. Stuart to P. Miller q.v.
MISCELLANEOUS (RHEA)
Edward Stewart/Stuart: Bm for Nathaniel Gillon, 1822
" " Bm for Leban Stewart, 1823
Hamilton Stewart: Bondsman for Charles Stewart, 1828
James Stewart: Bondsman for Thomas C. Wroe, 1829
" " Bondsman for Abraham T. White, 1832
" " Bondsman for Reuben Hickson, 1845
" " Bondsman for William Walton, 1824
" " Security for Reuben Freeman
" " Early resident in Washington; built a trip forge on Richland Creek for making iron by water power
William Stewart / Stuart: MG 1840. 1841
MISCELLANEOUS (MEIGS)
Andrew Stewart: Pvt., Mexican War (died in service)
John Stewart: Hiwassee District
" " House used to hold elections, District 4
" " Common School Com., District 4, 1838

\- - - - - - - - - - - - -

STIFF

MISCELLANEOUS (RHEA)
William S. Stiff: Bondsman for John W. Cranmore, 1836

\- - - - - - - - - - - - -

STILL

MARRIAGES (RHEA)
John Still to Peggy Killough, 10 May 1831 (15 May), John Condley JP (R)
MISCELLANEOUS (RHEA)
Elijah Still: JP 1838

\- - - - - - - - - - - - -

STINNETT / STINNITE

MARRIAGES (RHEA)
William Stinnett or Stinnite to Catharine Smith, 17 Jan 1820 (20 Jan), William Kennedy JP (AR)
Sally Stinnett to Richard Witt q.v.
MISCELLANEOUS (RHEA)
Henry Stinnett: Bondsman for Richard Witt, 1812

\- - - - - - - - - - - - -

STOCKTON

TAXES (RHEA)
1823 (Capt. Wilson's Co.): Clayton Stockton 180a
James Stockton 1 WP
(Capt. Piper's Co.): Daniel Stockton 1 WP, 80a
(Capt. Smith's Co.):
Daniel Stockton 1 WP, 1 Stud Horse (tax, $1.50)
1830 RHEA CENSUS
Clayton Stockton 001110001 - 010000001 p. 356
D. M. Stockton 2000001 - 112001 p. 358
David Stockton 10001 - 000001 p. 358
J. P. Stockton 011000001 - 000000001 p. 377
James Stockton 01001 - 2020001 p. 358
Joseph Stockton 210001 - 211 p. 375
Robert Stockton 10001 - 11001 p. 360
William H. Stockton 00001 - 0001 p. 359
1840 MEIGS CENSUS
James T. Stockton 21001 - 1 p. 246
Robert Stockton 110001 - 001001 p. 239
Thomas Stockton 00001 - 0001 p. 240
W. H. Stockton 010001 - 020001 p. 243
1850 RHEA CENSUS
William H. Stockton 42 (Ky)(Farmer), Emeline 27, Thomas 18, Mary 14, Edweny 7, Mathias 5, Letta A. 3, Robert STOCKTON 45 (Ky)(Stock Jobber), Nancy 42 (Va), Richard 14 p. 556-136 [Wm H. and Robert, sons of Robert and Nancy Blakey Stockton of Kentucky; Emeline, Wm's 2nd wife, was dau of Matthias and Barbara Lotspeich Broyles; Wm and Emeline were married 2 May 1842]
1850 MEIGS CENSUS
Hugh Patton Stockton 21 (Farmer), Elizabeth 17 p. 754-338
Amanda Stockton 12: see Margaret Roddy
MARRIAGES (RHEA)
David D. Stockton to Mary Hawl or Howe (Polly Hall), 26 May 1827 (same), J. Collins JP, Daniel M. Stockton Bm (AR)
James T. Stockton to Nancy Preston, 26 Aug 1833 (5 Sept), James Wilson JP, Charles Rector Bm (AR)
Jane Stockton to James Hughes q.v.
Joseph P. Stockton to Martha Moore, 7 Mar 1831 (same), Robert Cooley JP and Bm (AR)
Mary Stockton to Hiram Gibson q.v.
Nancy Stockton to Elisha Kirklin q.v.
Robert Stockton to Nancy H. Ragland, 9 Aug 1824 (10 Aug), John Farmer MG, John Parker Bm (AR) [Nancy, dau of Gideon and Artimisa Wilson Ragland]
William H. Stockton to Charlotte Rector, 29 Nov 1828 (9 Dec), James Wilson JP (AR)

MARRIAGES (MEIGS)
Artimisa B. Stockton to John P. Redmon q.v.
H. P. Stockton to Elizabeth Crew, 25 July 1850, A.G. Godsey Sur
Samuel Stockton to Sarah Ernestine Stockton, 29 May 1850, William Benson Sur
Thomas P. Stockton to M.E. Boggess, 19 June 1839 (same), William Wan Jr. Bm
MISCELLANEOUS (RHEA)
D. Stockton: Elder, Concord Baptist Church, 1824
Daniel M. Stockton: JP 1827-31
" " " Bondsman for Adam Humbolt, 1827
" " " Bm for David D. Stockton, 1827
" " " Bondsman for William Moyers, 1831
Isaac D. Stockton: Bondsman for Leroy Bedwell, 1830
MISCELLANEOUS (MEIGS)
D. Stockton: Hiwassee District, Sewee Creek area
Daniel M. Stockton: Hiwassee District, Ten Mile Stand area
Clayton Stockton: Hiwassee District, Sewee Creek area
James T. Stockton: JP 1839
" " " Common School Com., District 8, 1838
Robert Stockton: JP 1842-43, 1847

STOKES

TAXES (RHEA)
1819 (Capt. Bradley's Dist.): Isaac Stokes 1 WP
1823 (Capt. Brown's Co.): Isaac Stokes 1 WP
1830 RHEA CENSUS
Edwane Stokes 000111001 - 001010001 p. 373
Levin Stokes 122001 - 211001 p. 394
1840 MEIGS CENSUS
Edward Stokes 01001 - 30001 p. 237
George Stokes 100001 - 11001 p. 238
Larken M. Stokes 0000200001 - 2000200001 p. 234
Leven Stokes 0110101 - 1211101 p. 235
1850 MEIGS CENSUS
Cealy Stokes 84: see Thomas Coffee
Edward L. Stokes 40 (NC)(Farmer), Nancy 34, William P. 14, Malinda Jane 13, Mary E. 11, Eliza Ann 9, Sarah Ann 8, Washington L. 5 p. 751-314
George Stokes 46 (NC)(Farmer), Mahala 37, Sarah 28, David C. 13, Celia 12, James 10, Racheal 8, Catharine E. 6, Manda E. 4, Infant (m) 0 p. 767-426
Levin Stokes 50 (NC)(Farmer), Mary Ann 45, Mary Ann 24, James C.C. 21, Celio 17, Richard A. 14, Martha Jane 11, Rufus S. 3, Sara Gorda 1 p. 761-382
MARRIAGES (RHEA)
Edward S. Stokes to Nancy Evans, 24 Dec 1833 (26 Dec), James Blevins JP, John T. Blevins Bm (AR)
Larkin M. Stokes to Sarah Blevins, 2 Feb 1836, Violet Eaves Bm (A)
Samuel Stokes to Nancy Bishop, 4 Nov 1818 (5 Nov), John Cozby JP (R)
Thomas Stokes to Nancy Parsons, 26 Sept 1827 (same), Joshua McClure JP, Joseph Evans Bm (AR)
MARRIAGES (MEIGS)
Mary Stokes to Isaac Hutchinson q.v.
Thomas C. Stokes to Mary Perry, 15 Jan 1846 (same), B.F. McKenzie JP, Leven S. Coffey Bm
William Stokes to Matilda Coxey, 13 Nov 1845 (same), M.C. Atchley MG, Maradith McInturf Bm

MISCELLANEOUS (RHEA)
Edward S. Stokes: Bondsman for David Fairbanks, 1832
George Stokes: Bondsman for Samuel Blevins, 1833
" " Bondsman for Moses Blevins, 1834
Larkin M. Stokes: Bondsman for Hezekiah Lucus, 1833
Leven Stokes: Bondsman for James Lay, 1830
MISCELLANEOUS (MEIGS)
George Stokes: Constable, District 3, 1836

STONE / STON

MARRIAGES (RHEA)
Eliza Stone to William Bell q.v.
MARRIAGES (MEIGS)
Jane L. Stone to Jonathan K. Chastain q.v.
MISCELLANEOUS (RHEA)
John Ston: On Surveyor's list of land south of Tenn River

STONECIPHER

MISCELLANEOUS (MEIGS)
Jesse Stonecipher: Private, Mexican War

STONER / STINER

TAXES (RHEA)
1823 (Capt. Brown's Co.): Michael Stiner 1 WP
1830 RHEA CENSUS
Michael Stoner 001*01 - 000101 p. 279
[* blurred, either 2 or 3]
MARRIAGES (RHEA)
Eliza Stoner to James Engledow q.v.
MISCELLANEOUS (RHEA)
Michael Stoner: Bondsman for William Harris, 1816
" " Purchased Lot 17, Washington

STORY

1850 RHEA CENSUS
John Story 12: see John Ives
MISCELLANEOUS (RHEA)
John Story: On Surveyor's list of land south of Tenn River

STOUT

TAXES (RHEA)
1819 (Capt. Bradley's Dist.): Benjamin C. Stout 2 Lots
1823 (Capt. Brown's Co.):
Benjamin C. Stout 1 WP, 1 BP, 4 TL
1850 MEIGS CENSUS
John Stout 39 (Farmer), Eliza Ann 32, William D. 12, Mary Ann 10, James L. 9, Lenias M.A. 7, John W. 5, Thomas K. 4, Caswell T. 2 p. 721-64

MARRIAGES (RHEA)
Benjamin C. Stout to Jane C. Hazelrigg, 4 June 1818, Sam Houston Bm (A)
Jemimah Stout to John Alexander q.v.
Mary Ann Stout to William Whittenburg q.v.
Sally Stout to John McDaniel q.v.
MARRIAGES (MEIGS)
Martha Stout to James Pettit q.v.
MISCELLANEOUS (RHEA)
Benjamin C. Stout: Bondsman for Jesse Coffie, 1817

- - - - - - - - - - - - -

STOVER

1830 RHEA CENSUS
Patsy Stover 1012 - 1000001 p. 375

- - - - - - - - - - - - -

STRAIN

TAXES (RHEA)
1808 (John Henry's List): John Strain 1 WP

- - - - - - - - - - - - -

STRASNER

TAXES (RHEA)
1808 (Jonathan Fine's List): Mykel Strasner 1 WP [Michael Straisner married Elizabeth Brashir on 20 Apr 1807 in Roane County]

- - - - - - - - - - - - -

STREBECK

1850 RHEA CENSUS
George H. Strebeck 36 (Md)(House Joiner), Eleanor 33 (Md), Harriet E.D. 13 (Md), Owen W.J. 9 (Md), Mary F.R. 5 (Md), Olonzo W. 2 (Md) p. 618-527

- - - - - - - - - - - - -

STUBBS

MISCELLANEOUS (RHEA)
John Stubbs: Bondsman for Jesse Poe, 1819

- - - - - - - - - - - - -

STULTS / STUTT / STUTTS / STUTS

1840 RHEA CENSUS
James Stults 1112001 - 201001
1840 MEIGS CENSUS
Abner Stults 20211 - 021001 p. 239
Abraham Stults 310001 - 000011 p. 234
1850 RHEA CENSUS
George J. Stults 28 (Miller), Eleanor E. 28, Jacob J. 1, Elizabeth 6/12 p. 571-228
James Stutts 52 (Va)(Farmer), Frances 46, Emeline 16, James 13, Elizabeth 11, Joana 9, Lewis F. 4 p. 541-53 [James Stolts married Fanny Davis on 12 Dec 1820 in Roane County]

MARRIAGES (RHEA)
Caroline Stults to James Mathis q.v.
Elizabeth Ann Stuts to Richard Manley q.v.
George J. Stults to Ellen E. Gear, 1 Sept 1847 (2 Sept), Ezekiel Ward MG (R)
MISCELLANEOUS (MEIGS)
Absolem Stults: Cherokee Removal muster roll, 1836
George I. Stults: Private, Mexican War
John Stults: 4th Corp., Mexican War

- - - - - - - - - - - - -

STURGESS

1850 MEIGS CENSUS
James W. Sturgess 50 (Pa)(Carpenter), Eliza 36, Columbus L. 18 (Farmer), James M. 17 (Farmer), Sarah 15, Martha Jane 13, Thomas H. 11, Nancy 9, Eliza 7, Isaac 4, John E. 2 p. 793-628

- - - - - - - - - - - - -

STYRES

MARRIAGES (RHEA)
Anna Styres to Moses Trimble q.v.
Elizabeth Styres to Abraham Atchley q.v.

- - - - - - - - - - - - -

SUDDITH / SUDDATH

1840 RHEA CENSUS
Benjmin Suddath 101001 - 10001
1850 RHEA CENSUS
Benjamin Suddith 40 (NC)(Farmer), Harriet 33, Francis 14, Mary E. 11 p. 624-571
MARRIAGES (RHEA)
Benjamin Suddath to Harriet Ragsdale, 12 Apr 1832 (same), William Smith JP, Samuel P. Hackett Bm (AR)

- - - - - - - - - - - - -

SULLINS

MISCELLANEOUS (RHEA)
Timothy Sullins: MG MMEC 1835-36

- - - - - - - - - - - - -

SULLIVAN / SILLIVAN

TAXES (RHEA)
1823 (Capt. Howard's Co.): John Sillivan 146a
Samuel Sillivan 1 WP
William Sillivan 1 WP
(Capt. Jackson's Co.): William Sillivan 1 WP
1830 RHEA CENSUS
John Sullivan 0001010001 - 00223001 p. 381
William Sullivan 000001 - 20001 p. 381
1840 MEIGS CENSUS
William W. Sullivan 00200001 - 02122001 p. 231
1850 MEIGS CENSUS
Ezekiel T. Sullivan 31 (SC)(Carpenter), Nancy 38 (SC), William H. 8, Sarah R. 5, Mary L. 2 p. 735-175

William Sullivan 61 (SC)(Farmer), Sarah 61 (SC), Polly T. 28, Robert B. 24 (Farmer), John H. 21 (Farmer), Permelia E. 19, Cisley S. (f) 17, Younger P. (m) 10, David W. 6 p. 735-179

MARRIAGES (RHEA)

Dempsey Sullivan to Sally Mildham, 20 Sept 1825 (same), Matthew Donald MG, Lewis Morgan Bm (AR)

Jonathan Sullivan to Matilda Clingan, 16 June 1821, William W. Sullivan Bm (A)

Jonathan B. Sullivan to Sarah Gibbs, 2 Mar 1831 (6 Mar), Wm Smith MG or JP, Allen Kennedy Bm (AR)

Samuel Sullivan to Sally Simmons, 3 July 1823 (4 Jan)[sic], A. David JP, Allen Henderson Bm (AR)

MARRIAGES (MEIGS)

Elizabeth Sullivan to Delaney Trusler q.v.

Martha Sullivan to Martin Cunningham q.v.

Milbery Sullivan to Elisha Moore q.v.

MISCELLANEOUS (RHEA and MEIGS)

Robert B. Sullivan: Private, Mexican War

Wm W. Sullivan: Bondsman for Jonathan Sullivan, 1821

- - - - - - - - - - - - -

SUNDAGIRE

1830 RHEA CENSUS

John Sundagire 110011 - 1100010001 p. 353

- - - - - - - - - - - - -

SURGUINE

1840 MEIGS CENSUS

Edward E. Surguine 110011 - 11101 p. 227

- - - - - - - - - - - - -

SUTHARD

MISCELLANEOUS (RHEA)

Aaron Suthard: Bondsman for Wm B. Johnson, 1840

Robert B. Suthard: Bondsman for Peter Neil, 1835

- - - - - - - - - - - - -

SUTHERLAND

MARRIAGES (RHEA)

Elizabeth Sutherland to Moses Atchley q.v.

MARRIAGES (MEIGS)

Eliza Sutherland to James McNutt q.v.

MISCELLANEOUS (RHEA and MEIGS)

Eli S. Sutherland: Elder, 1835-36

John Sutherland Jr.: Hiwassee District

- - - - - - - - - - - - -

SUTTON

TAXES (RHEA)

1819 (Capt. McGill's Co.): Buck Sutton 1 WP
(Capt. John Robinson's Co.): Dempsy Sutton 1 WP

1830 RHEA CENSUS

Jeremiah Sutton 001001 - 11001 p. 371

John Sutton 0000100001 - 000100001 p. 357

1850 MEIGS CENSUS

Elizabeth Sutton 82: see Thomas P. Davis

MARRIAGES (RHEA)

Dempsy: see Dempsy Sullivan

Jesse Sutton to Frances Clement, 6 July 1825 (7 July), John Walker JP or MG, Allen Gentry Bm (AR)

Mary Sutton to Peter M. Joquess q.v.

MISCELLANEOUS (RHEA and MEIGS)

Jesse Sutton: Bondsman for Isaac Clement, 1825
" " Bondsman for Allen Gentry, 1825

John Sutton: Revolutionary War pensioner

- - - - - - - - - - - - -

SWADER / SRADER

1830 RHEA CENSUS

Christian Swader 0002 - 00000001 p. 364

Francis Swader 10001 - 10001 p. 364

MARRIAGES (RHEA)

William Srader to Arty M. Quinton, 10 July 1830, Samuel B. Quinton Bm (A)

- - - - - - - - - - - - -

SWAFFORD

MARRIAGES (RHEA)

Howard Swafford to Nancy Narremore or Narrimore, 8 or 6 Apr 1823 (8 Apr), A. David JP, John Swafford Bm (AR) [1850 Bledsoe Census: Howard Swafford 50, Andrew J. 24, John 22, Manerva 20, Nancy J. 18, George 18, Howard 16, Eliza A. 13]

John Swafford to Eliza Owens, 6 June 1840 (11 June), Samuel Frazier JP (AR)

MARRIAGES (MEIGS)

Rebecca Swafford to John Slater q.v.

MISCELLANEOUS (RHEA)

John Swafford: Bondsman for Howard Swafford, 1823
" " Bondsman for John Clark (Clack), 1835

- - - - - - - - - - - - -

SWAGERTY

TAXES (RHEA)

1808 (Jonathan Fine's List): Thomas Swagerty 1 WP

- - - - - - - - - - - - -

SWAN / SWANN

TAXES (RHEA)

1819 (Capt. John Robinson's Co.): Daniel Swan 1 WP
(Capt. Ramsey's Co.): James Swan 1 WP, 100a
(Capt. Wm McCray's Co.): John B. Swan 100a
(Capt. Bradley's Dist.): Moses H. Swan 1 WP, 1 Lot
1823 (Capt. Braselton's Co.): James Swan 100a Wolf Cr
(Capt. Howerton's Co.): John B. Swan 100a Muddy Cr
Samuel Swan* 1 WP
Thomas B. Swan 1 WP
[* Samuel married Nancy McElwee on 21 Dec 1819 in Roane County]

1830 RHEA CENSUS

James Swan 0101101 - 221211 p. 366

John B. Swan 000010001 - 000000001 p. 391

Thomas B. Swan 20001 - 000001 p. 391
[Thomas married Margaret H. Cravens on 17 Mar 1825 in Roane County]

MARRIAGES (RHEA)
Isaac N. Swan to Rebecca Love, 14 Sept 1836 (15 Sept), Benjamin Wallace MG, Samuel Hogue Bm (AR) [1850 Polk Census: Isaac N. Swann 41, Mary R. 29, Martha M. 7, Charles C. 2, Wells A. 3/12]
Sarah Swan to James S. Thompson q.v.
MISCELLANEOUS (RHEA and MEIGS)
Daniel Swan: Bondsman for James H. Owens, 1809
" " Lot 9, Town of Washington
James Swan: JP 1828-31
William Swan: Hiwassee District, Pinhook Ferry area

- - - - - - - - - - - - -

SWART

MISCELLANEOUS (RHEA)
Chapman Swart: Member, Goodfield Baptist Church, 1827

- - - - - - - - - - - - -

SWEATMEN / SWETMAN

1850 MEIGS CENSUS
Sarah Sweatman 24, Lea (m) 8, Jackson 5, Almira Jane 2 p. 772-472
MARRIAGES (MEIGS)
A. Sweatman to Sarah Price, 10 Aug 1847 (same), D.L. Godsey MG
MISCELLANEOUS (MEIGS)
Augustus Swetman: Private, Mexican War

- - - - - - - - - - - - -

SWICKLER

MISCELLANEOUS (RHEA)
J.W. Swickler: Private, Mexican War

- - - - - - - - - - - - -

SWISHER

MISCELLANEOUS (MEIGS)
S. G. Swisher: MG 1847

- - - - - - - - - - - - -

SYKES / SIKES

TAXES (RHEA)
1823 (Capt. Brown's Co.): Drury Sykes 1 WP
1830 RHEA CENSUS
Drury Sikes 0001001 - 21001 p. 367
1840 RHEA CENSUS
Dempsey Sikes 2220001 - 101101
1840 MEIGS CENSUS
Drury Sykes 01000001 - 00200001 p. 231
1850 RHEA CENSUS
James A. Sykes 11: see Beriah Frazier
Margaret Sykes 15: see William Bell
1850 MEIGS CENSUS
Dempsey Sykes 55 (NC)(Farmer), Charlotte 49 (NC), William 20 (Farmer), Smith 18, Joseph 13, Anna 11, Zadock 10 p. 734-166

MARRIAGES (RHEA)
Decatur K. Sykes to Mary Ann Seymore, 13 May 1841 (same), Jacob Gear JP, Cedron Pile Bm (AR)
Eli Sykes to Mary Blacks, 28 May 1831, Nicholas G. Frazier Bm (A)
Elizabeth Sykes to Henry Johns q.v.
Jane Sykes to David Casteel q.v.
John Sykes to Martha Snow, 5 Feb 1848 (6 Feb), John S. Evens JP (R)
Mary Sykes to William Snodgrass q.v.
Nancy Sykes to David Johns q.v.
Nancy Sykes to Pleasant Snow q.v.
MISCELLANEOUS (RHEA)
Eli Sykes: Bondsman for David Johns, 1831

- - - - - - - - - - - - -

SYLVESTER

1850 RHEA CENSUS
John Sylvester 7: see Thomas Knight

- - - - - - - - - - - - -

TABER

TAXES (RHEA)
1823 (Capt. Lewis' Co.): John H. Taber 1 WP

- - - - - - - - - - - - -

TAFF / TOFFE / TAP

TAXES (RHEA)
1823 (Capt. Smith's Co.): John Taff 1 WP
1830 RHEA CENSUS
Jno Tap 221101 - 00102 p. 375
1840 MEIGS CENSUS
John Taff 01121001 - 220001 p. 232
1850 MEIGS CENSUS
Calvin R. Toffe 27 (Farmer), Nancy 24, Margaret 24, Alexander W. 2, John MARSHALL 54 (NC)(Farmer), John P. 23 (NC)(Farmer), Mary Ann 16 (Deaf and Dumb), Milly Jane 14 p. 767-430
John Taff 62 (Va)(Farmer), Jane 47 (NC), Asbury 25 (School Teacher), Emaly 19, Cyntha Jane 17, John 15, Margaret 13, Sarah Ann 11, Mary 9, Emaline 7, Margaret HOUPT 27 p. 763-397
MARRIAGES (RHEA)
John Taff to Jane Houpt, 10 Jan 1831 (13 Jan), D.L. Godsey MG (R)
MARRIAGES (MEIGS)
Calvin R. Taff to Nancy Collins, 27 Sept 1847 (30 Sept), D.L. Godsey MG
Emily Taff to Amedia Rice q.v.
Martha E. Taff to Rice Hughes q.v.
MISCELLANEOUS (MEIGS)
John Taff: Hiwassee District, Lower Goodfield area
" " Common School Com. in District 3 1838
" " Purchased Lots 50,65,74 in Decatur, 1836
" " War of 1812; JP 1836-42

- - - - - - - - - - - - -

TALLENT / TALANT / TALTON

1840 MEIGS CENSUS
Enoch Talton* 120001 - 101001 p. 225
[* last name also looks like Fallon]
1850 MEIGS CENSUS
Enoch Talant 46 (Farmer), Catharine 48, Mary Ann 21, Richard 18, David 15, Sarah 12, James 11, John 8 p. 718-44
MISCELLANEOUS (MEIGS)
Jeptha Tallent: Private, Mexican War

- - - - - - - - - - - - -

TALLY / TALLEY

1830 RHEA CENSUS
David Tally 01001 - 010011 p. 378
William Tally 000001 - 0001 p. 360
1840 MEIGS CENSUS
William Tally 3000101 - 0000110001 p. 241
1850 MEIGS CENSUS
William Tally 54 (Va)(Farmer), Stacia 48, Alexander A. 12 p. 807-724
MARRIAGES (RHEA)
Ferety Tally to J.W.L. Peregin q.v.
William Talley to Stacy Bryant, 29 Aug 1821 (same), Jesse Thompson JP (AR)
MARRIAGES (MEIGS)
Edy Talley to James Fitch q.v.

- - - - - - - - - - - - -

TANKERSLY / TANKSLY

1830 RHEA CENSUS
Paddle(?) Tankersly 0001 - 110011 p. 359
MARRIAGES (RHEA)
Zorobable Tanksly to Cynthy Garner, 3 July 1828 (same), John Farmer JP, Berryman Kimbrel Bm (AR)
MISCELLANEOUS (RHEA)
Zarabelle Tankarsley: Bm for Washington Atchley, 1831

- - - - - - - - - - - - -

TANNER

1850 RHEA CENSUS
Clarissa Tanner 31, Mary J. 11: see Mercy Stuart

- - - - - - - - - - - - -

TATE

MARRIAGES (RHEA)
Rebecca Tate to Bird Atchley q.v.
MISCELLANEOUS (RHEA and MEIGS)
James Tate: Bondsman for Thomas Bicknell, 1835
" " Buglar, Cherokee Removal muster roll, 1837
Mitchell Tate: Cherokee Removal muster roll, 1836-37

- - - - - - - - - - - - -

TAYLOR

TAXES (RHEA)
1819 (Capt. Bradley's Dist.) Robert Taylor 100a
1823 (Capt. Brown's Co.): James Taylor 1 WP, 74a Hi Dist
Robert Taylor 1 WP, 107a
Robert Taylor 100a Tenn River
(Capt. Jackson's Co.): John Taylor 1 WP
1830 RHEA CENSUS
A. Taylor 20001 - 1000101 p. 375
Darcas Taylor 11 - 10001 p. 380
Jas Taylor 12001 - 201 p. 376
Jno Taylor 0111001 - 211001 p. 374
P. Taylor 10001 - 10001 p. 376
Robert Taylor 030000001 - 00022001 p. 384
Sealon Taylor 1200001 - 210001 p. 395
William Taylor 100001 - 11001 p. 382
1840 RHEA CENSUS
Catharine Taylor 0011 - 000011001 [widow of Robert]
Darhey Taylor 0 - 110001
1840 MEIGS CENSUS
Jesse Taylor 01001 - 10001 p. 236
John Taylor 110001 - 110001 p. 236
Peach Taylor 210001 - 011001 p. 237
Sarah Taylor 0101 - 0021001 p. 232
William Taylor 21001 - 120001 p. 227
1850 RHEA CENSUS
Darcus Taylor (f) 40, Luisa 18, Harriet 10, Amanda 5 p. 623-568
Jane Taylor 21, Elizabeth 19: see James Stuart
1850 MEIGS CENSUS
Mary Taylor 44: see Alexander Rice
Peach Taylor 49 (Farmer), Mary 43, Mary Ann 18, John 16 (Farmer), Franklin 13, James O. 8, Manda T. 3 p. 769-442
Sarah Taylor 65 (Va), Lorinda 28, Ruth 21, William L. 19 (Carpenter), Sarah 10 or 16 p. 773-479
Stephen Taylor 52 (Doctor), Serenah 36, James 23, Jane 21, Richard 19, William 15, Ellen 12, John 10, Infant (m) 0, Adaline CUMMINGS 17 or 77 p. 761-380 [Stephen married Serenah Hail on 18 Feb 1849 in McMinn County]
Stephen Taylor 26 (Farmer), Elizabeth C. 26, Oliva A. 4, William 2, John H.L. 1 p. 757-356

MARRIAGES (RHEA)
A. or Archibald Taylor to Margaret Looney, 4 Mar 1827 (5 Mar), Thomas Cox JP, Wm S. Russell Bm (AR) [1850 Bradley Census: A.R. Tailor 48, Margaret 51, Cynthia 21, Sarah 17, Hugh 14; Archibald, son of Robert and Catharine; Margaret, dau of Samuel Looney]
Charles A. Taylor to Patsey Walker, 19 Dec 1816, "I have joined them together as husband and wife" Wm Randolph, Elder, Roswell Hall Bm (AR)
Cinthia Taylor to John Thompson Marriott q.v.
Isabella Taylor to Thomas Godbyhere q.v.
James Taylor to Nancy Lillard, 26 July 1821 (same), John Rice JP, Thomas Kelly Bm (AR)
John Taylor to Hulda Haskins, 31 Jan 1811 (same), William Taylor Bm (A) [see 1850 Lincoln County Census]
John Taylor to Polly Lea or Leagins, 13 or 11 Dec 1826 (13 Dec), Thomas Cox JP, Thos Wommack Bm (AR)

Jonah Taylor to Eleanor Clayton, 28 Jan 1811 (same), Wm Taylor Bm (A)
Louisa Taylor to Larkin Gothard q.v.
Lucinda Taylor to Alexander Rice q.v.
Margaret Ann Taylor to Hezekiah James q.v.
Nancy Taylor to Moses Blevins q.v.
Nancy Taylor to James C. Airhart q.v.
Peach Taylor to Mary Blevins, 14 Sept 1824 (16 Sept), John Rice JP, John Hutson Bm (AR) [Allen shows date as 1823] [Peach, son of Robert and Catherine; Mary, dau of David and Sarah Torbett Blevins]

MARRIAGES (MEIGS)
James Taylor to Vilety Sliger 14 Dec 1850, John Scott Sur
Lively Taylor to Henry McVey q.v.
Lorinda Taylor to John Kelly q.v.
Sophia Taylor to William Childress q.v.

MISCELLANEOUS (RHEA)
Peach Taylor: JP 1826-34
Philip Taylor: Bondsman for John Gorden, 1812
" " Bondsman for Richard Gravely, 1812
William Taylor: Bondsman for Jonah Taylor, 1811
" " Bondsman for John Taylor, 1811

MISCELLANEOUS (MEIGS)
Andrew I. Taylor: Cherokee Removal muster roll, 1837
Archibald Taylor: Hiwassee District, Concord area
Peach Taylor: JP 1841-45
" " Chairman of County Court, 1840-43
" " Hiwassee District, Concord area
Richard Taylor: Reservation, Tenn River near Cottonport

- - - - - - - - - - - - -

TEAGUE

1850 RHEA CENSUS
Isaac N. Teague 30 (NC)(Tailor) p. 627-595

MARRIAGES (MEIGS)
Peggy Teague to Philow Corvin q.v.

- - - - - - - - - - - - -

TEASSTALLER

1850 MEIGS CENSUS
Sally Teasstaller 23, William H. 5, Rossetty E. 3 p. 813-770

- - - - - - - - - - - - -

TEDDER

1850 RHEA CENSUS
Spencer J. Tedder 28 (Farmer), John ANDERSON 25 (mulatto) p. 561-173

- - - - - - - - - - - - -

TEDFORD

MISCELLANEOUS (MEIGS)
Ralph E. Tedford: MG 1844

- - - - - - - - - - - - -

TEFFORD

1830 RHEA CENSUS
John Tefford 10001 - 21001 p. 355

- - - - - - - - - - - - -

TEMPLE

1830 RHEA CENSUS
John Temple 100001 - 01001 p. 387

- - - - - - - - - - - - -

TEMPLETON

TAXES (RHEA)
1823 (Capt. Jackson's Co.): Edmund Templeton 1 WP

1830 RHEA CENSUS
Ed Templeton 2111011 - 111101 p. 371

1840 RHEA CENSUS
John H. Templeton 10001 - 00001

1850 RHEA CENSUS
John H. Templeton 35 (Ky)(Farmer), Mary 33, James S. 11, Sarah 6, William A. 4, Mary J. 6/12, James B. 25 (Student), Lucinda WATERMAN 21 p. 624-577

MARRIAGES (RHEA)
Mahala Templeton to Isaac Masoner q.v.

MISCELLANEOUS (RHEA and MEIGS)
Edward Templeton: Hiwassee District, Burkett Chapel area
" " Bondsman for Isaac Masoner, 1828
Gordon S. Templeton: Bm for John H. Singleton, 1838

- - - - - - - - - - - - -

THOMAS

TAXES (RHEA)
1819 (Capt. W.S. Bradley's Dist.): Jack Thomas 1 WP
(Capt. Wm McCray's Co.): William Thomas 1 WP
(Capt. Ramsey's Co.): William Thomas 1 WP, 101a
1823 (Capt. Howerton's Co.):
William Thomas 1 WP, 100a Muddy Cr

1830 RHEA CENSUS
Jonathan Thomas 0101001 - 03121 p. 374
Lewis Thomas 10001 - 00001 p. 366

1840 MEIGS CENSUS
Abraham Thomas 0012211 - 0110201 p. 225
Lucretia Thomas 1 - 10001 p. 232 [widow of Henson W.]

1850 RHEA CENSUS
William Thomas 25 (NC)(Farmer), Amand 24 (NC), Joseph D. 8 (NC), Minerva 5 (NC), Elizabeth 60 (unk), Sarah Unk (NC) p. 546-84

1850 MEIGS CENSUS
Casandra M. Thomas 30: see William A. Godsey
John Thomas 20, Daniel C. 5, Thos H. 1: see Alfred Cate
Sarah Thomas 14: see John T. Blevins

MARRIAGES (RHEA)
Henson W. Thomas to Lucretia Blevins, 1 Jan 1834 (2 Jan), James Blevins JP, Moses Blevins Bm (AR) [Lucretia, dau of David and Sarah Torbett Blevins]
Irena Thomas to Thomas Tillery q.v.
James Thomas to Elizabeth Lancaster, 19 Sept 1820 (same), William Thomas Bm (A)
John Thomas to Elizabeth Magones or Mageres, 25 Sept 1822 (no return) (AR)
Polly Thomas to William Cannon q.v.
Sally Thomas to John Dinkins q.v.
Thomas C. Thomas to Jane Marr (or Man), 20 Feb 1828 (21 Feb), James McDonald JP, Wm R. Black Bm (AR)

MARRIAGES (MEIGS)
Elizabeth Thomas to Moses Blevins q.v.
Julia Thomas to William Godsey q.v.
Lucretia Thomas to William W. Lillard q.v.
Nancy Thomas to Alfred Cate q.v.
MISCELLANEOUS (RHEA)
William Thomas: Bondsman for James Thomas, 1820

THOMASON

1830 RHEA CENSUS
Arnold Thomason 00210001 - 0011001 p. 373

THOMPSON

TAXES (RHEA)
1819 (Capt. McCray's Co.): James Thompson 1 WP, 100a
Jesse Thompson 1 WP, 200a
John Thompson 320a
Thomas Thompson 1 WP, 217a
(Capt. Ramsey's Co.):
Moses Thompson 1 WP, 1 BP, 156a
1823 (Capt. Howerton's Co.):
James Thompson 1 WP 100a Muddy Creek
Jesse Thompson 1 WP, 620a W Fk Whites Cr
John Thompson 200a Vann's Spring Creek
Moses Thmpson 1 WP, 1 BP, 155a Muddy Cr
(Capt. Piper's Co.): John Thompson Jr. 1 WP, 50a
Joseph Thompson 1 WP, 160a
(Capt. McCall's Co.):
Thomas Thompson 1 WP, 1 BP, 210½a Piney River
(Capt. Brown's Co.): Thompson & Kennedy 2 WP, 1 BP, 2a Southern Liberties
1830 RHEA CENSUS
J.B. Thompson 00001 - 00001 p. 384
James Thompson 02131001 - 0100001 p. 389
Jesse Thompson 1110101 - 120201 p. 390
John Thompson 000000001 - 000200001 p. 361
Josiah Thompson 21001 - 00001 p. 390
Jno Thompson 000001 - 000001 p. 389
Joseph Thompson 1111001 - 0021001 p. 365
Margaret Thompson 0 - 00001001 p. 389
Mary Thompson 01 - 0100001 p. 365
Moses Thompson 1102001 - 0210001 p. 389
Moses R. Thompson 20001 - 110012 - 390
Polly Thompson 21001 - 00001 p. 390
Thomas Thompson 1112301 - 1120101 p. 389
1840 RHEA CENSUS
A.J. Thompson 10011 - 20011
Absolom S. Thompson 10001 - 10001
E.M.D. Thompson 00001 - 00001
James Thompson 002210001 - 01001001
Jane Thompson 01102 - 0111201
John O. Thompson 1000001 - 11111
Mary Thompson 0001 - 0000101
Moses Thompson 00111001 - 00211
Russell Thompson 21001 - 00001
Thomas Thompson 001010001 - 00111
William Thompson 00011 - 21001
William A. Thompson 20001 - 10001

1850 RHEA CENSUS
Absalum S. Thompson 40 (Farmer), Malinda 36, Sarah C. 10, Margaret A. 8, Jesse A. 5, Thomas K. 4 p. 553-120 [Absolem S. Thompson married Malinda Gibbons on 24 Sept 1835 in Roane County]
James M. Thompson 22 (Farmer), Luisa M. 25 p. 588-352
Jesse P. Thompson 32 (Sheriff), Sarah 23, Amanda 21, Francis M. 18 (Farmer), Houston DEAN 20 p. 534-10
John L. Thompson 21 (Farmer), Lucilla S. 20 (SC) p. 534-11
John Thompson 25 (Farmer), Frances 23, Mary A. 6, James A. 5, William A. 2 p. 583-316
John A. Thompson 53 (NC), Elender 40 (Va), Sarah 15, William 10 p. 545-77
John S. Thompson 32 (Farmer), Nancy 20 (NC), Margaret J. 1/12 p. 554-128
John W. Thompson 25 (Methodist Clergyman), Harriet 31 p. 599-402
Maranda Thompson Unk: see Elijah Farmer
Moses Thompson 67, Kitsy B. 42, Jane 27, William R.S. 25 (School Teacher), James E.F. 21 (Farmer), Van Buren 16 (Farmer) p. 538-38
Moses C.R. Thompson 36 (Farmer), Cyrena 27, Frederick R. DYAL 7 p. 537-32
Moses R. Thompson 48 (NC)(Wagonmaker), Catharine 54 (Va), Benjamin T. 18 (Wagonmaker), Richard W. 17 (Blacksmith), Sarah 16, Andrew H. 12 p. 600-410
Polly Thompson 61: see Daniel Broyles
Russell Thompson 37 (Farmer), Margaret A. 13, John H. 12, James A. 11, Cyntha V. 9, Syrena 7, Asbury C. 5, William R. 4, Zachary T. 1 p. 609-500
Thomas Thompson 69 (School Teacher), Margaret 31, Thomas K. 29 (Farmer), Priscilla 24, Nancy 22 p. 554-129
Uriah Thompson 28 (Farmer), Elizabeth 40, William H. 1 p. 577-272
William Thompson 18: see Doctor W. Horner
William Thompson 41 (Farmer), Cyntha 41, Holly E. 15, Elizabeth C. 13, Eliza J. 11, Addison F. 9, William M. 7, John L. 2, James R. YOUNG 23 (Ky) (Blacksmith) p. 608-499
William Thompson 21 (Farmer), Margaret I. 16, Barbary HIGHT 62 p. 594-369
William A. Thompson 39 (Farmer), Elizabeth 35, William F. 12, Priscilla S. 14, Thomas J.C. 10, John S. 8, Joseph N. 6, James W.E. 3, Epps G. 1 p. 550-112 [William A. Thompson married Elizabeth Gibbon on 26 Nov 1834 in Roane County]
1850 MEIGS CENSUS
Alfred Thompson 19: see James Burchum
Sally W. Thompson 49, Elizabeth 33 p. 797-656
MARRIAGES (RHEA)
A. Thompson to West W. Johnson q.v.
Abraham L. Thompson to Susan West, 24 Oct 1834 (1 Nov), Matthew Hubbert JP, Absolom S. Thompson Bm (AR)
Alexander Thompson to Bershaba Russell, 23 Oct 1835 (same), James McCanse JP, Miles T. Thompson Bm (AR)
B.F. Thompson to Sarah P. Miller, 24 May 1850 (same), John O. Torbett JP (R)
Barbara Ann Thompson to Joseph A. Broyles q.v.

MARRIAGES (RHEA) Continued

Betsey Thompson to Beatty Perren q.v.

Gideon B. Thompson to Myra Waterhouse, 11 May 1830 (same), Fielding Pope MG, Thomas McCallie Bm (AR)

Harriet Thompson to Daniel Broyles q.v.

Holly E. Thompson to James Young q.v.

Jackson S. Thompson to Patient Holland, 10 Apr 1835 (23 Apr), Matthew Hubbert JP, William B. Miller Bm (AR)

James M. Thompson to Eliza Perser, 1 July 1848 (9 July), J.P. Collins JP (R)

James S. Thompson to Sarah Swan, 18 Jan 1836 (same), John Pardoe MMEC, Jackson Thompson Bm (AR)

James W. Thompson to Ann Givin, 28 or 25 July 1832 (28 or 27 July), Carson Caldwell JP, Anson Dearmon Bm (AR)

Jemimah Thompson to Jeremiah Lillard q.v.

Jane Thompson to Henry McCary q.v.

Jane Thompson to James Majors q.v.

John Thompson to Elizabeth Green, 12 Feb 1817, James Thompson Bm (A)

John Thompson to Frances McFalls, 27 Oct 1842 (no return) (R)

John L. Thompson to Nancy Brown, 22 June 1849 (8 July), M.S. Thompson JP (R)

John W. Thompson to Harriet Hausie (Haws), 29 Aug 1849 (same), A.F. Shummon MG (R)

Joseph or Josiah Thompson to Nancy Thompson, 20 Sept 1820 (24 Sept), Arthur Fulton JP, Moses Thompson Bm (AR)

Larkin F. Thompson to Artimes Majors, 9 Jan 1836, John Hoyal Bm (A)

Lucinda Thompson to Beaty Breeding q.v.

M.D. Thompson to Sarah C. Baldwin, 16 or 10 Mar 1840 (no return), James Holloway Bm (AR)

Mahala Thompson to Isham Reese q.v.

Malinda H. Thompson to Isaac Edington q.v.

Margaret Thompson to Levi H. Knight q.v.

Margarett J. Thompson to William B. Young q.v.

Mary Thompson to James Johnston q.v.

Moses Thompson to Catherine Hite, 18 Sept 1824 (same), Fred K. Fulkerson JP, Hezekiah Haite Bm (AR)

Moses C.R. Thompson to Syrena Dudley, 7 Nov 1846 (17 Nov), Daniel Broyles JP (R)

Nancy Thompson to Josiah Thompson q.v.

Peggy Thompson to John Owens q.v.

Rachel Thompson to Jesse Majors q.v.

Russell A. Thompson to Louisa Peterson, 18 Dec 1850 (21 Dec), John Wyott JP (R)

Sally Thompson to William McCormick q.v.

Squire Thompson to Serena Davis, 12 Dec 1831, William Thompson Bm (A)

Stephen H. Thompson to Elizabeth Peterson, 7 Oct 1837 (8 Oct), Azariah Barton JP, Wm Thompson Bm (AR)

Susey P. Thompson to James Johnson q.v.

Susannah Thompson to Hiram Mahaffy q.v.

Sarah Thompson to Sherrell Dudley q.v.

Fredinburg or Vreckunburg Thompson to Mary K. Rawlings, 28 Nov 1822 (same), Matthew Donald MG, G.W. Kennedy Bm (AR)

William Thompson to Sally Nelson, 15 Jan 1825, "Executed by me" William Gamble JP, John Moore Bm (AR)

William Thompson to Cinthia Cooper, 6 May 1833 (9 May), Matthew Hubbert JP, Isham Reese Bm (AR)

William Thompson to Mary Crammer, 4 Sept 1834, John Cozby JP, Joel Smith Bm (AR)

William M. Thompson to Margarett E. Furguson, 25 Dec 1847 (11 Jan 1848), Samuel Frazier JP (R)

MARRIAGES (MEIGS)

Katharine Thompson to James Burcham q.v.

Rebecca S. Thompson to Calloway Gresham q.v.

MISCELLANEOUS (RHEA)

Absolom Thompson: Bondsman for John Looney, 1830

Absolom S. Thompson: Bondsman for Abraham L. Thompson, 1831

Andrew J. Thompson: Bm for John A. Snodgrass, 1840

Esquire [Squire] L. Thompson: Bondsman for Isaac Edington, 1829

Gideon B. Thompson: Bondsman for Edmund Bean, 1828
" " " Bondsman for Oliver Miller, 1828
" " " Bondsman for Jas H. Blain, 1829
" " " Bm for Samuel Rowden, 1829

Jackson Thompson: Bm for James S. Thompson, 1835

Jacob Thompson: Cherokee Removal muster roll, 1836

Jesse P. Thompson: JP 1820-1848
" " " Registerar of Deeds, 1829-1836
" " " Trustee, Mars Hill Academy, 1850
" " " Private, Mexican War
" " " Hiwassee District, Sewee Creek area

James Thompson: Bondsman for John Thompson, 1824
" " Bondsman for Beaty Perrin, 1824

John W. Thompson: MG 1849-50

Joseph Thompson: Hiwassee District

Moses Thompson: Bondsman for Joseph Thompson, 1820

Moses B. Thompson: Bm for Alexander Thompson, 1835

Moses W. Thompson: Bondsman for Jesse Majors, 1830

W.R. or M.R.S. Thompson: JP 1848-49

William Thompson: Bondsman for Robert Moore, 1825
" " Bm for Squire Thompson, 1831
" " Bm for Stephen H. Thompson, 1837

THORNBERRY / THORNBURY

1830 RHEA CENSUS

Jno Thornberry 0022001 - 11101 p. 370

1840 MEIGS CENSUS

Peter Thornbury 00101 - 00001 p. 227

MARRIAGES (RHEA)

Lewis Thornberry to Susan Anderson, 23 Dec 1835, William Long Bm (A)

MARRIAGES (MEIGS)

Mary Thornberry to James Hobbs q.v.

Peter Thornberry to Mary Gody, 20 July 1839 (23 July), John Seabourn JP, L. Thornberry Bm

----

THORNHILL

MARRIAGES (RHEA)

Minerva Thornhill to Joshua Harp q.v.

THORNTON

1830 RHEA CENSUS
Joseph Thornton 0001 - 21001 p. 366
MARRIAGES (RHEA)
Joseph Thornton to Polly Henry, 1 Jan 1823 (2 Jan), John Moore JP, William Locke Bm (AR)
MISCELLANEOUS (RHEA)
Joseph Thornton: Bondsman for Hiram Henry, 1833

- - - - - - - - - - - - -

THORP / THARP

1830 RHEA CENSUS
John Tharp 0000000101 - 00000001 p. 357
1850 MEIGS CENSUS
Alexander Tharp 28 (Farmer), Dicy Ann 20, Andrew 5, Margaret E. 1 p. 815-790
Amos Thorp 30, Elizabeth B. 28 (NC), Joseph C. 18 (Farmer), Nancy E. 13, Conrad C. 10, Caswell H. 8, James M. 4 p. 748-290
Michael Thorp 10: see Plesent M. Miller
Sally Thorp 33, Vanburen 7 p. 781-534
William Thorp 51 (Va), Anna 45 (NC), Joseph 17, Martha 14, Conrad A. 8, Nancy 10 p. 778-515
MARRIAGES (MEIGS)
Alexander Tharpe to Dicey Ann Jones, 24 Feb 1849 (25 Feb), J.L. Aikman JP, John Seabourn Sur(?)
William Tharp to Ann Rhineheart, 21 Sept 1841 (1 Jan 1849), "Returned not written on", Joseph McCorkle & William Russell, Adms., John Ingle Sur(?)

- - - - - - - - - - - - -

THRAILKILL

TAXES (RHEA)
1823 (Capt. Wilson's Co.): Joseph J. Thrailkill 1 WP
1830 RHEA CENSUS
Joseph Thrailkill 10001 - 210001 p. 352
MARRIAGES (RHEA)
Joseph J. Thrailkill to Cissie Atchley, 28 Mar 1821 (30 Mar), John Farmer MG, John Bennett Bm (AR)
Patsy Thrailkill to John Bennett q.v.
MISCELLANEOUS (RHEA)
Joseph J. Thrailkill: Bondsman for Michael Wilson, 1825

- - - - - - - - - - - - -

THURMAN

1850 RHEA CENSUS
Alfred Thurman 34 (SC)(Farmer), Matilda 28, William H. 8, James J. 6, Thomas A. 4, Mary 11/12 p. 606-479
Henry Thurman 43 (Va)(Farmer), Matilda 39, Minerva J. 18, Eliza A. 16, Samuel A. 14, John W. 12, Margaret E. 7, Marlin M. 5, Benjamin F. 3, Elizabeth C. 1, William H. 10 p. 582-305
Jackson Thurman 23: see Allen Holland
MARRIAGES (RHEA)
Frederick Thurman to Jane C. Carnahan, 19 Oct 1824 (21 Oct), Wm Kennedy JP, Wm Carnahan Bm (AR) [1850 Bledsoe Census: Frederick 46, Jane 46, James 17, Jane 13, John 11, Mary 6, Charles 19]
Jackson Thurman to Martha M. Holland, 14 Mar 1850 (15 Mar), E.P. Childers MG (R)
William Thurman to Martha McFalls, 3 Nov 1849 (8 Nov), William Ganaway MG (R)

- - - - - - - - - - - - -

TIGNER

MARRIAGES (RHEA)
Elizabeth Tigner to Joseph Adams q.v.

- - - - - - - - - - - - -

TILLERY / TILLORY

TAXES (RHEA)
1823 (Capt. Smith's Co.):
Samuel Tillery 1 WP, 160a Goodfield
(Capt. Wilson's Co.): William Tillery 1 WP
1830 RHEA CENSUS
Ann Tillery 11011 - 20101 p. 375
William Tillery 011001 - 221001 p. 352
1840 MEIGS CENSUS
Ann Tillory 01 - 00011001 p. 235
Coffel T. Tillery 120001 - 10001001 p. 238
Hugh Tillory 00001 - 0001 p. 235
Thomas Tillery 11001 - 01 p. 235
William Tillery 0110101 - 111101 p. 236
1850 MEIGS CENSUS
Jacob Tillery 26 (Farmer), Sarah 23, William 4 p. 819-812
William Tillery 47 (Farmer), Barbary Ann 45 (Va), Coffell 18 (Farmer), Elender 16, Neoma 14, Isaac R. 9 p. 777-510
William P. Tillery 25 (Farmer), Eliza Ann 37, Racheal P. 13, Mahala E. 11, Hugh 10, Louisa L. 7, William T. 5, John L. 1 p. 783-557
Thomas Charles* Tillory 32 (Farmer), Martha 32, John W. 14, Permelia 9, Jennetta 9, Rebecca 6, Richard 1 p. 714-16 [*Charles was written above Thomas Tillory, so may have been his first name]
MARRIAGES (RHEA)
Cowfield T. Tillery to Irena Brooks, 24 Aug 1830 (25 Aug), D.L. Godsey JP, Richard S. Murphy Bm (AR)
Jane Tillary to Tavernor Runyon q.v.
Polly Tillary to Charles W. Lewis q.v.
Thomas Tillery to Irena Thomas, 6 Sept 1832 (same), Joseph McCorkle JP, Tavnor Runyon Bm (AR)
William P. Tillary to Eliza Seay, 22 Jan 1835, Charles W. Lewis Bm (A)
MARRIAGES (MEIGS)
Barbara A. Tillery to Miles V. Presswood q.v.
Coffield Tillery to Nancy Fuller, 14 July 1838, Tavnor Runyan -?- [NOTE: this record was on page with others from 1839]
Elander A. Tillery to Thomas Elsay q.v.
Elizabeth Tilley to Pleasant M. Presswood q.v.
Hugh Tillery to Belinda Brooks, 5 Feb 1840, Thomas Tillery Bm(?)

John Tillery to Nancy Rogers, 1 Feb 1845 (same), Daniel Cate JP
Margaret Tillery to Joseph H. Cate q.v.
MISCELLANEOUS (RHEA and MEIGS)
Samuel Tillery: Hiwassee District, Sewee Creek area
Thomas Tillery: Bondsman for Tavenor Runyon, 1833
William Tillery: Hiwassee District, Sewee Creek area

- - - - - - - - - - - - -

TIMBERLAKE

MISCELLANEOUS (RHEA)
Richard Timberlake: Bm for Philemon K.W. Estell, 1828

- - - - - - - - - - - - -

TIMMONS / TIMONS

1840 MEIGS CENSUS
Mathus Timmons 0020001 - 000021001 p. 226
1850 MEIGS CENSUS
George W. Timons 28 (Farmer), Caldena 24, William H.H. 10, Mary Ann 6, Cealy B. 4, George W. 2 p. 784-564

- - - - - - - - - - - - -

TIMS

MARRIAGES (RHEA)
June Tims to Lewis Sexton q.v.
Mary Tims to Martin Sexton q.v.
MARRIAGES (MEIGS)
Washington Tims to Mary O'Neal, 19 Aug 1848 (20 Aug), Wm Johns JP [1850 Hamilton Census: Washington Tims 25, Mary 28, Sarah 1, Eliza O'NEAL 19]
MISCELLANEOUS (RHEA)
Washington Tims: Private, Mexican War

- - - - - - - - - - - - -

TINDLE / TINDAL

TAXES (RHEA)
1823 (Capt. Lewis' Co.): Joshua Tindle 1 WP, 200a
1830 RHEA CENSUS
Jeremy Tindle 10001 - 00001 p. 353
1840 RHEA CENSUS
William Tindle 10001 - 1001
1840 MEIGS CENSUS
John Tindle 00001 - 00001 p. 243
MARRIAGES (RHEA)
John or Jeremiah Tindal to Polly Hill, 3 Aug 1826 (same), Daniel Briggs MG, William Tindal Bm (AR)
William Tindle to Sally Wilhelms, 19 Aug 1823 (21 Aug), Thomas Cox JP, Joshua Tindle Bm (AR)
MARRIAGES (MEIGS)
Jno Tindel to [blank] Wilhelms, 2 Sept 1839 (12 Sept), E.E. Cooper JP or MG, Jacob Wilhelms Bm
MISCELLANEOUS (RHEA and MEIGS)
Jeremiah Tindell: Bondsman for Welcome Wilhelm, 1830
" " Bondsman for John Myers, 1831
Joshua Tindle: Bondsman for William Tindle, 1823
William Tindle: Bondsman for John Knight, 1829
" " Bondsman for John/Jeremiah Tindal, 1826

- - - - - - - - - - - - -

TINER

1850 RHEA CENSUS
Anderson Tiner 51 (Farmer), Eliza A.E. 35 (Pa), Cyntha S. 24, Elizabeth M. 22, Sidnah P. 20, Cassander S. 17, James M. 39 p. 570-224
MARRIAGES (RHEA)
Lewis Tiner to Annie Johnson, 28 Aug 1818 (same), John Cozby JP (AR)

- - - - - - - - - - - - -

TIPTON

1830 RHEA CENSUS
Rebecca Tipton 0 - 000000001 p. 393
1850 MEIGS CENSUS
Isaac H. Tipton 35 (Farmer) p. 732-144
MISCELLANEOUS (MEIGS)
J.C.* Tipton: Ocoee District [*probably should be I.G.]

- - - - - - - - - - - - -

TOBAT

TAXES (RHEA)
1808 (James Campbell's List): George Tobat 1 WP

- - - - - - - - - - - - -

TODD

TAXES (RHEA)
1823 (Capt. Wilson's Co.): Williamson Todd 1 WP
1830 RHEA CENSUS
William Todd 121001 - 1010001 p. 364
MARRIAGES (MEIGS)
M.N. Todd to E.R. Chattin q.v.

- - - - - - - - - - - - -

TOLIVER

1850 MEIGS CENSUS
John Toliver 31 (Va)(Farmer), Martha Ann 30 (Va), George W. 6, Martha E. 2, William 1 p. 739-209

- - - - - - - - - - - - -

TOLLET

MARRIAGES (RHEA)
Nancy Tollet to John R. Young q.v.

- - - - - - - - - - - - -

TOMISON [THOMISON]

1850 RHEA CENSUS
William P. Tomison 36 (Va)(Farmer), Nancy 34 (Va), Elizabeth 12, John 10, Rhoda 8, William P. 7, Zachary T. 3, Sarah 2, Harriet 8/12 p. 603-461
MARRIAGES (RHEA)
William Tomison or Tomason to Nancy Guthrie or Guttery, 22 Mar 1824 (same), John Farmer MG, William Brashiers Bm (AR)

- - - - - - - - - - - - -

TORBETT / TORBET

1850 RHEA CENSUS
John O. Torbett 33 (Va)(Farmer), Eveline C. 32, Hugh M. 9, Sidnah E. 7, Sarah K. 5, Lewis S. 3, James G.T. 1, Lucinda K. TRIM 14 p. 580-289 [John married Eveline C. Trim on 18 Dec 1839 in McMinn Co]
Sarah B. Torbett 57 (Va), Susan J. 32 (Va), Mary E. 20 (Va), Sarah 22 (Va), Rush B. 20 (Farmer), Thomas F. 19, Virginia T. 16 p. 579-284
MISCELLANEOUS (RHEA and MEIGS)
John O. Torbett: JP 1848-50
Augustus Torbet: Cherokee Removal muster roll, 1837

\- - - - - - - - - - - - -

TOWNSBY

MARRIAGES (RHEA)
Rebecca Townsby to James Farlis Jr. q.v.

\- - - - - - - - - - - - -

TOWNSLEY

1830 RHEA CENSUS
John Townsley 000000001 - 00000001 p. 358

\- - - - - - - - - - - - -

TRAVIS

1850 RHEA CENSUS
Joseph I. Travis 50 (Farmer), Viney 48, Samuel 20, Nathaniel 14, Rachael 13, Vance 12, Elizabeth 10, Elvira 8, Caroline 5, John 3 p. 598-392

\- - - - - - - - - - - - -

TRAYNOR / TRAVNOR

MARRIAGES (RHEA)
John D. Traynor to Mary Ann Cozby, 10 Apr 1834 (same), Benjamin Wallace MG, G.W. Hill Bm (AR)
MISCELLANEOUS (MEIGS)
John D. Travnor: Purchased lot in Cottonport

\- - - - - - - - - - - - -

TREDWAY

MARRIAGES (RHEA)
Edmund Tredway to Rachel Mainard, 14 July 1822 (18 July), T. Price JP, Jesse Mainard Bm (AR)

\- - - - - - - - - - - - -

TRENTHAM

1850 RHEA CENSUS
James M. Trentham 32 (Farmer), Mariah 30, Absalum 11, Nancy J. 10, Sophia 7, William M. 5, Andrew J. 3, James M. 1 p. 602-684
MARRIAGES (RHEA)
Nancy Trantham to John Fout q.v.

\- - - - - - - - - - - - -

TRESITHAN

1840 RHEA CENSUS
James A. Tresitham 10001 - 10001

\- - - - - - - - - - - - -

TRIM

1850 RHEA CENSUS
Lucinda K. Trim 14: see John O. Torbett

\- - - - - - - - - - - - -

TRIMBLE / TRAMBLE

TAXES (RHEA)
1808 (John Henry's List):
David Tramble 1 WP, 100a E Fk Richland Cr
(Jonathan Fine's List): Richard Trimble 150a Piney
MARRIAGES (RHEA)
Moses Trimble to Anna Styres, 25 Jan 1809, James Snelson Bm (A)

\- - - - - - - - - - - - -

TRIPLET

1830 RHEA CENSUS
Abner Triplet 021001 - 110001 p. 39

\- - - - - - - - - - - - -

TRUE

1850 MEIGS CENSUS
William M. True 33 (NC)(Blacksmith), Milly M. 23 (Ga), Barnet M. 7, Sarah L. 4, Martha L. 1 p. 792-622

\- - - - - - - - - - - - -

TRUETT

MARRIAGES (RHEA)
Betsy Truett to John Brown q.v.

\- - - - - - - - - - - - -

TRUSLER

MARRIAGES (MEIGS)
Delaney Trusler to Elizabeth Sullivan, 25 Feb 1846 (26 Feb), Jesse Locke MG, Ezekiel Sullivan Bm

\- - - - - - - - - - - - -

TUCKER

1830 RHEA CENSUS
Samuel Tucker 000020001 - 01011001 p. 384
MARRIAGES (RHEA)
Woodson Tucker to Easter McGaffy or McGuffa, William Kennedy JP, Spilsby Dyer Bm (AR)

\- - - - - - - - - - - - -

TUELL

1850 MEIGS CENSUS
John W. Tuell 45 (SC)(Tailor), Mary 39, Joseph A. 20 (Farmer), John R. 15 (Farmer), Vincent H. 7, James A. 3, Millissa E. 2, Infant (f) 1 p. 796-653 [John married Polly Rose on 22 Aug 1832 in Roane Co]

- - - - - - - - - - - - -

TURBYVILLE

TAXES (RHEA)
1823 (Capt. Howard's Co.): John Turbyville 1 WP

- - - - - - - - - - - - -

TURNER

1830 RHEA CENSUS
Nathan Turner 10001 - 1010101 p. 364
1850 MEIGS CENSUS
Jacob Turner 69 (Va)(Farmer), David C. 28 (Farmer) p. 721-62
MARRIAGES (MEIGS)
Elijah Turner to Mary M. McCollon, 26 Feb 1840 (28 Feb), Prior Neil JP, Newton Locke Sur(?)
MISCELLANEOUS (RHEA)
E. Turner: Elder, Concord Baptist Church, 1824

- - - - - - - - - - - - -

TURNEY

MARRIAGES (RHEA)
Hopkins L. Turney to Teressa Francis, 24 May 1826 (same), John Henninger MG, James J. Campbell Bm (AR)

- - - - - - - - - - - - -

TUTTLE

MARRIAGES (RHEA)
Henry Tuttle to Mrs. Polly Hopkins, 22 Dec 1814 (no return), John Parks Bm (AR)
MISCELLANEOUS (RHEA)
Henry Tuttle: Signed petition to move Indian Agency

- - - - - - - - - - - - -

TYSON / TISON

TAXES (RHEA)
1823 (Capt. McCall's Co.): Jessee Tison 1 WP, 98a Piney
1830 RHEA CENSUS
Jesse Tyson 00010001 - 0010001001 p. 387
1850 RHEA CENSUS
Nancy Tyson 56 (SC): see Charles Woodward
MARRIAGES (RHEA)
Jesse Tyson to Nancy McAvery or McCary, 10 Sept 1823 (11 Sept), John Bollison or Robinson JP (AR)

- - - - - - - - - - - - -

UNDERWOOD

TAXES (RHEA)
1823 (Capt. Smith's Co.): John Underwood 1 WP [John married Cintha Bandy on 17 Dec 1822 in Roane County]
1830 RHEA CENSUS
John Underwood 11001 - 2001 p. 394
1840 RHEA CENSUS
John Underwood 1201001 - 212001
1840 MEIGS CENSUS
Samuel Underwood 1100000001 - 010001 p. 232
Samuel Underwood 10001 - 10001 p. 234
William Underwood 20001 - 00001 p. 232
MARRIAGES (RHEA)
Alexander Underwood to Jamima H. Harvy, 23 July 1831, Allen Harvy Bm (A)
July Ann Underwood to Hugh Crumbliss q.v.
Lethy (Aletha) Underwood to J.N. Cook q.v.
Mary A. Underwood to Samuel Bowers q.v.
Rachel Underwood to David W. Knight q.v.
Samuel Underwood to Martha Dake, 10 Dec 1835, Benjamin Harden Bm (A)
MARRIAGES (MEIGS)
Nancy Underwood to Cyrus Quiett q.v.
MISCELLANEOUS (RHEA)
Calvin Underwood: Bondsman for Hugh Chumbliss, 1843
John Underwood: Bondsman for John McDaniel, 1828

- - - - - - - - - - - - -

UPTON

TAXES (RHEA)
1819 (Capt. Wm McCray's Co.): James Upton 1 WP, 160a
MARRIAGES (RHEA)
Jane Upton to James Majors q.v.
MISCELLANEOUS (RHEA)
James Upton: Bondsman for Edmond Vaughn, 1815

- - - - - - - - - - - - -

URSERY / USRY / USERY

1840 RHEA CENSUS
John Usery 020001 - 100001
1850 RHEA CENSUS
John Usry 36 (Farmer), Catharine 32, Alexander 18 (Farmer), Thomas 16 (Farmer), Margaret A. 13, Jacob 8, Jane REESE 20 p. 598-397
MISCELLANEOUS (RHEA)
John Usery: Bondsman for Newton J. Edmonds, 1839
" " 3rd Corp, Mexican War
Robert Ursery: Hiwassee District, Burkett Chapel area

- - - - - - - - - - - - -

USTICK

MARRIAGES (RHEA)
Elizabeth B. Ustick to John B. Stephenson q.v.

- - - - - - - - - - - - -

VANDEGRIFF / VANDERGRIFF

TAXES (RHEA)
1823 (Capt. Howard's Co.): Christopher Vandergriff 1 WP
1830 RHEA CENSUS
Lucretia Vandergriff 211 - 011001 p. 36
1840 RHEA CENSUS
Leonard Vandergriff 02200001 - 000001
MARRIAGES (RHEA)
Christina Vandagriff to Joseph Cookson q.v.
MISCELLANEOUS (MEIGS)
Thomas J. Vandergriff: Mexican War (died in service)

- - - - - - - - - - - - -

VANDERPOOL

MISCELLANEOUS (RHEA)
John Vanderpool: Bondsman for Harris Ryon 1827

- - - - - - - - - - - - -

VANDEVER

1840 MEIGS CENSUS
Jacob Vandever 11110001 - 0110001 p. 228
MARRIAGES (RHEA)
Hollingsworth Vandever to Polly House, 24 Apr 1810, Adam House Bm (A)

- - - - - - - - - - - - -

VANDIKE / VANDYKE

MARRIAGES (RHEA)
Israel A. Vandike to Nancy Evans, 9 Feb 1831 (no return), William McElrey Bm (AR)
Missouri VanDike to William McElroy q.v.
MISCELLANEOUS (RHEA)
Letitia VanDyke: Lot in Southern Liberties

- - - - - - - - - - - - -

VANOY / VANHOY

1850 RHEA CENSUS
David Vanhoy 43 (NC)(Farmer), Ruth 35 (NC), Asabel 16 (NC), Minerva 14 (NC), Joshua 11 (NC), Martha 9 (NC), Lena 8, Lucinda 4 p. 638-675
1850 MEIGS CENSUS
Isam Vanoy 23 (Farmer), Mary 17, William M. 1 p. 794-639

- - - - - - - - - - - - -

VANPELT

1850 RHEA CENSUS
John Vanpelt 67 (School Teacher): see John Howard
MARRIAGES (RHEA)
Manerva Vanpelt to Miller E. Parks q.v.

- - - - - - - - - - - - -

VANZANT

MARRIAGES (MEIGS)
Henry C. Vanzant to Nancy McKown, 28 Feb 1848 (29 Feb), D.L. Godsey MG

- - - - - - - - - - - - -

VARNELL

TAXES (RHEA)
1823 (Capt. Wilson's Co.): William Varnel 1 WP
MARRIAGES (RHEA)
James Varnell to Viney Nelson, 13 Oct 1824 (same), Daniel Walker JP, Merryman Kimbree Bm (AR)
MISCELLANEOUS (RHEA)
John Varnell: Bondsman for Zachariah Nelson, 1824

- - - - - - - - - - - - -

VARNER / VERNER

TAXES (RHEA)
1819 (Capt. McGill's Co.): James Varner 1 WP
(Capt. John Lewis' Co.): Solomon Varner 1 WP
1823 (Capt. Brown's Co.): Edward Varner 1 WP
1830 RHEA CENSUS
Henry Varner 20101 - 00001 p. 377
1850 MEIGS CENSUS
Jacob Varner 24 (Blacksmith), Nancy 23, Mary 3, John 1 p. 805-709 [Jacob married Nancy Gallian on 16 July 1846 in Roane County]
Jacob Varner 22 (Blacksmith), Jane 30, Nancy 1 p. 805-710
MARRIAGES (RHEA)
David Verner to Judy Priddy, 23 Apr 1812 (same), William Priddy Bm (A)

- - - - - - - - - - - - -

VAUGHN

1830 RHEA CENSUS
Jno Vaughn 11001 - 20101 p. 374
Margaret Vaughn 001 - 0100001 p. 377
1840 MEIGS CENSUS
Alexander Vaughn 0001001 - 10001001 p. 238
John Vaughn 001001 - 01301 p. 238
1850 MEIGS CENSUS
Cyntha Vaughn 19: see Clinton Norman
Nathan Vaughn 21: see Miles V. Lillard
MARRIAGES (RHEA)
Betsy Vaughn to Joseph Evans q.v.
Edward or Edmond Vaughn to Polly Bobbett, 15 Dec 1815, "Executed the 16 Dec by me" William Long JP, James Upton Bm (AR)
Sally Vaughn to Nicholas Neal q.v.
MARRIAGES (MEIGS)
John Vaughn to Sarah Melton, 25 Feb 1840 (same), D.L. Godsey MG
Mary Vaughn to Milton E. Jameson q.v.
Murphree H. Vaughn to Mahala Webb, 31 Oct 1849 (1 Nov), Leroy Looney JP [1850 Roane Census: Murphey 29, Mahaly 29]
MISCELLANEOUS (RHEA and MEIGS)
James Vaughn: Bondsman for John R. Blythe, 1829

- - - - - - - - - - - - -

VERNON

TAXES (RHEA)
1823 (Capt. Smith's Co.):
Miles Vernon 1 WP, 160a Goodfield
(Capt. Lewis' Co.): Solomon Vernon 1 WP

1830 RHEA CENSUS
Miles Vernon 122211 - 2100001 p. 375
1840 MEIGS CENSUS
James Vernon 11100001 - 112101 p. 225
James H. Vernon 110002 - 11001 p. 236
1850 MEIGS CENSUS
James H. Vernon 41 (Farmer), Julian 41 (SC), Nancy H. 15, Reuben V. 13, Frances A. 10, Mary E. 8, Susan E. 4, Plesant M. 1 p. 757-359

MARRIAGES (RHEA)
James H. Vernon to Julia Ann McKenzie, 18 Feb 1834 (20 Feb), Joseph McCorkle JP, Wm Coleman Bm (AR)
James W. Vernon to Harriet McCaleb, 25 Feb 1845, Wm A. Whitten Bm (AR)
Mary Vernon to John Elder q.v.
MARRIAGES (MEIGS)
Martha A.E. Vernon to William D. Reynolds q.v.
MISCELLANEOUS (RHEA)
Ann Vernon: Member, Goodfield Baptist Church, 1827
Harrison Vernon: Lot 11 in Town of Washington
Miles Vernon: War of 1812
" " Deacon, Goodfield Baptist Church, 1827
" " Board of Commissioners to supervise constuction of new jail, 1825-26
MISCELLANEOUS (MEIGS)
Miles Vernon: Hiwassee District
" " Capt., Cherokee Removal muster roll, 1836
" " Com. to lay off Decatur Courthouse, 1836
" " Purchased Lots 34 and 45 in Decatur, 1836
" " Representative to General Assembly (House) 1829-33; (Senate) 1833-37

\- - - - - - - - - - - -

VICKRY / VICORY

1850 RHEA CENSUS
William R. Vickry 22 (NC)(Farmer), Minerva 19, John R. 9/12 p. 568-206
MARRIAGES (RHEA)
Lavicy Vicory to Bartholomew Lawson q.v.
Nancy Vicory to John Cline q.v.
W.R. Vicory to M. Boxley, 4 July 1848 (no return) (R)

\- - - - - - - - - - - -

VICKY

1850 RHEA CENSUS
Alfred Vicky 32 (NC)(Farmer), Racheal 27 (NC), John A. 12, Joseph H. 10, Martha A. 7, Daniel G. 5, Aaron H. 1, Sarah VICKY 44 (NC), Edmond 20, Mary 18, Caroline 9 p. 593-359

\- - - - - - - - - - - -

VINCENT / VINCEN / VINSEN

1830 RHEA CENSUS
John Vincent 2000001 - 210001 p. 364
Woodson Vincent 200001 - 10001 p. 364
1850 MEIGS CENSUS
Caleb Vincent 30 (Farmer), Margaret 28, Ann WEST 30 p. 786-579 [Caleb Vinson married Margaret Vinson on 29 Jan 1842 in McMinn County]
Jonathan Vincent 50 (Farmer), Cyntha 52, Malinda 26, Moses 21 (Farmer), John 18 (Farmer), Elile (m) 16 p. 776-501
Reuben Vincent 44 (Farmer), Leah 46 (Ky), Isaac M. 19 (Farmer), Mary Ann 17, Jacob J. 15, Serepta C. 10, Malinda L. 7, Charles W. 5, Ephram S. 3, Sarah D. 3 p. 790-608
MARRIAGES (RHEA)
Hamlen Vincen or Vinsen to Susanna Lasen or Jackson, 17 Apr 1824 (18 Apr), John Farmer MG (AR)
Nancy Vincent to John Hilburn q.v.
Patsy Vincent to Allen Hilburn q.v.
MISCELLANEOUS (RHEA and MEIGS)
Hamilin Vincent: Bondsman for John Milburn, 1824
John Vincent: Hiwassee District, Pinhook Ferry area
Wood Vincent: Hiwassee District, Pinhook Ferry area

\- - - - - - - - - - - -

VINES

1830 RHEA CENSUS
Jno Vines 01-010101 p. 376
MARRIAGES (RHEA)
Alexander Vines to Mary Ann Grantem, 15 Sept 1830 (17 Sept), Peach Taylor JP, Garrett Christopher Bm (AR)
Fanny Vines to Edward Clingham q.v.
Mary Ann Vines to Garrett Christopher q.v.
MISCELLANEOUS (RHEA)
Alexander Vines: Bondsman for Garrett Christopher, 1831
" " Bondsman for John Brady, 1835

\- - - - - - - - - - - -

VOLLO

1850 RHEA CENSUS
Stephen Vollo 39 (Ky)(Farmer), Elizabeth 40, Joseph 14 (Ill), Nancy A. 12, William 11, Elizabeth 9, Mary 7, John 6, Clark 3, Jeremiah 2, Eliza ROSER 1, Nancy VOLLO 74 (Va), James L. 3/12 p. 543-69

\- - - - - - - - - - - -

WADE

1850 MEIGS CENSUS
Martin Wade 48 (Va)(Farmer), Nancy 47, Hampton 18 (Farmer), Elizabeth 14, Crockett 10, James D. 7 p. 735-176
MARRIAGES (MEIGS)
Emily J. Wade to Daniel Rivers q.v.

\- - - - - - - - - - - -

WALAND / WADLAND

1830 RHEA CENSUS
Stephen Waland 00002 - 11011 p. 372
MISCELLANEOUS (RHEA)
S.A. Wadland: MG 1849

- - - - - - - - - - - - -

WALDEN / WALDON / WALDREN / WALDING

1840 MEIGS CENSUS
John Walden 00001 - 01001 p. 243
Thomas Waldon 000000001 - 000000001 p. 243
MARRIAGES (RHEA)
Mildry Waldren to John Young q.v.
MARRIAGES (MEIGS)
Lucinda Waldren to Aaron Smith q.v.
Mary Walding to Elias Crisp q.v.

- - - - - - - - - - - - -

WALDRUP / WALDROP

MARRIAGES (RHEA)
Catherine Waldrup to Cornelius Butram q.v.
MISCELLANEOUS (MEIGS)
Richard Waldrop: Hiwassee District

- - - - - - - - - - - - -

WALKER

TAXES (RHEA)
1819 (Capt. Robinson's Co.): Daniel Walker 2 BP, 200a
George Walker 4 BP, 3 Lots
Halton Walker 1 WP
(Capt. John Lewis' Dist.): Richard Walker 82a
(Capt. McCray's Co.): Robert Walker 1 WP, 223a
1823 (Capt. Braselton's Co.):
Daniel Walker Esq. 2 BP, 200a Yellow Cr
John Walker 1 WP
(Capt. Wilson's Co.): George Walker [no other data]
Hatten Walker 1 WP
John Walker 1 WP
John Walker 1 WP Dry Fork
(Capt. Howerton's Co.):
Robert Walker 1 WP, 230a Camp Cr
1830 RHEA CENSUS
Anderson Walker 10101 - 0001 p. 385
Daniel Walker Jr. 000001 - 0001 p. 385
Daniel Walker Sr. 100100001 - 010100001 p. 385
John Walker 1110101 - 110001 p. 355
John Walker 110001 - 2000001 p. 385
Jesse Walker 0 - 00000000001 p. 383
Tobitha Walker 12202 - 101321 p. 389
William Walker 0 - 0 p. 385
1840 RHEA CENSUS
Anderson Walker 021001 - 200001
Cssa Walker (free colored) 2 - 101
Daniel Walker 220001 - 0100100001
Richard Walker 201001 - 12101
Richard Walker 201001 - 12101 [sic]
1840 MEIGS CENSUS
James Walker 00100001 - 00120001 p. 233
John Walker 01001 - 20001 p. 232
John Walker 01101001 - 0001001 p. 239
William Walker 00001 - 0001 p. 234
1850 RHEA CENSUS
Byrd Walker 39 (Va), Frances 34 (Va), William 14 (Va), Nancy 15 (Va), Watson 12 (Va), George 10 (Va), James 9 (Va), John 8, Newton 6, Martha 4, Sarah 2 p. 621-555
Cassa Walker (f) 45 (SC)(mulatto), Lilburn H. 18, Merida G. 16, Sarah A. 13, Amanda J. 9, Thomas M. 6 p. 614-457
James R. Walker 21 (Farmer), Evaney 21 (NC) p. 596-384 [James married Evanna Turnmeir on 24 Feb 1848 in McMinn County]
John Walker 56 (NC)(Farmer), Rus 52 (NC), Sarah 24, Penelope A. 13, Nancy J. 3 (Ga) p. 547-93
Joseph Walker 27 (Farmer), Ibba 23, Samuel H. 4, John N. 2, Sarah J. 1 p. 547-96
Richard Walker 80 (Va)(Farmer), Mary 51, Margaret A. 22, Daniel B. 22 (Farmer), Mary 20, Lavina 18, Flavius J. 14, Jesse 14, Tennessee 11, Eunice 9 p. 533-2
[Richard married Mary Broyles on 1 Sept 1825]
1850 MEIGS CENSUS
David Walker 31 (Farmer), Nancy 31, Samuel 7, Eldridge 5, William L. 3, Brackston 0 p. 795-642
John H. Walker 40 (Va)(Farmer), Racheal 30, Marshall H. 16 (Farmer), Nancy F. 14, Sarah Jane 12, Tempy E. 8, Ruth 7, Isah (m) 5, Eliza Ann 3, Elizabeth 1 p. 756-348
John S. Walker 63 (Farmer), Elizabeth 61 (NC), Henry 22 (Ediot), Sarah G. 21 p. 795-643
Thomas Walker 33 (Farmer), Charity 32, William 11, Mary Jane 10, Sarah C. 8, Thomas N. 6, Charity A.D. 4, Louisa B. 2, Joseph M. 0 p. 730-132
MARRIAGES (RHEA)
Anderson Walker to Elizabeth Hines, 21 Jan 1829 (22 Jan), James Swan JP, John Walker Bm (AR)
David Walker Jr. to Elizabeth Smith, 27 Feb 1830, John Walker Bm (A)
Elizabeth Walker to Andrew Anderson q.v.
Elizabeth Walker to Michael W. Bustard [Buster] q.v.
Elizabeth Walker to John Davidson q.v.
John Walker to Reway Guffee, 18 Aug 1822 (same), John Cozby or Cox JP, John Marshal Bm (AR)
John Walker Jr. to Emily S. Meigs, 10 Jan 1824 (same), Thomas Cox JP, J. Meigs Jr. Bm (AR)
Leah Walker to Martin Murphree q.v.
Mariah Walker to Allen White q.v.
Mary Walker to Ransom Murphrie q.v.
Patsey Walker to Wilson Kilgore q.v.
Patsey Walker to Charles A. Taylor q.v.
Peggy Walker to Martin H. Randolph q.v.
Polly Walker to James K. Reivley q.v.
Rachel Walker to John Hampton q.v.
Russell D. Walker to Margaret Mahaffy, 27 Dec 1841 (28 Dec), Joseph Chastain MG, Jesse Roddy Bm (AR) [1850 Overton Census: Russell Walker 23, Margaret 29, James 8, Susan 6, Martha 4, Mary 3]
Sarah Walker to Zachariah Nelson q.v.
Scotty Walker to Thomas Smith q.v.
Telitha Walker to Richard Wallard q.v.

Tilda Walker to John Murphrie q.v.
Viney Walker to William Brocke q.v.
William Walker to Jane Campbell, 21 May 1818 (no return) (AR)
William Walker to Nancy Manley, 27 Apr 1825 (no return), Zachariah Nelson Bm (AR)

MARRIAGES (MEIGS)

Creed Walker to Martha Rivers, 6 July 1840 (7 July), B.F. McKenzie JP, William Rivers Sur(?) [1850 McMinn Census: Creed Walker 30, Martha 25, Philip 7, Narcissa 4, Nancy 4/12]
David Walker to Nancy Edgeman, 20 Dec 1841 (23 Dec), Jesse Locke MG
John Walker to Rachel Cox, 5 June 1839 (6 June), B.F. McKenzie JP, Luther B. Cox Bm
Nancy Walker to Ganium Brightwell q.v.

MISCELLANEOUS (RHEA)

Anderson Walker: Bondsman for Thomas Smith, 1830
" " Bondsman for Isaac Chamberlain, 1838
" " Bm for Nathan Chamberlain, 1845
Andrew Walker: Bondsman for Thomas Malony, 1824
Charles Walker: Bondsman for Michael W. Bustard, 1812
Daniel Walker: JP 1816, 1824, 1829-33
" " On first Grand Jury
" " Com. to establish Washington, 1812-13
" " Bondsman for Jesse Day, 1825
" " Signed petition to move Indian Agency
George Walker: Signed petition to move Indian Agency
Henry Walker: On Surveyor's list of land S of Tenn River
John Walker: JP 1819
" " Bondsman for Anderson Walker, 1829
" " Bondsman for David Walker Jr., 1830
John W. Walker: Bondsman for Pleasant Davis, 1839
Richard Walker: Lot 41, Town of Washington
Robert Walker: Bondsman for Michael S. Jones, 1815
William Walker: On Surveyor's list of land S of Tenn River

MISCELLANEOUS (MEIGS)

Isaac Walker: JP(?) 1841
John Walker: Hiwassee District, Sewee Creek area
John S. Walker: War of 1812
William Walker: Hiwassee District, Sewee Creek area

- - - - - - - - - - - -

WALLACE

1850 RHEA CENSUS

Nancy Wallace 76: see John Gray

MARRIAGES (RHEA)

Jane Wallace to Andrew Johnson q.v.
Robert Wallace to Rebecca Montgomery, 9 Sept 1819 (same), Ralph B. Locke Bm (A)

MISCELLANEOUS (RHEA)

Benjamin Wallace: MG 1832, 1842, 1850

- - - - - - - - - - - -

WALLARD

MARRIAGES (RHEA)

Richard Wallard to Telitha Walker, 10 Dec 1834 (1 Jan 1835), Jesse Thompson JP, William T. Gillenwaters Bm (AR)

- - - - - - - - - - - -

WALLEN / WALLING

1850 MEIGS CENSUS

Catharin Wallen 38, Sarah 6, Elizabeth 2, Hugh 5 p. 787-584
John Wallen 47, Love Ann 10, Martha E. 8, Mary C. 4: see Aaron Owen

MARRIAGES (MEIGS)

John Walling to C. Putnam, 27 June 1840, John Atkinson JP(?)
Samuel Wallen to Delpha Keenum, 27 June 1839 (30 June), Prior Neil JP, William Atkinson Sur(?)

- - - - - - - - - - - -

WALLENDEN

1830 RHEA CENSUS

William Wallenden 10001 - 0001 p. 361

- - - - - - - - - - - -

WALLS
(see also WELLS and WILLS)

TAXES (RHEA)

1823 (Capt. Howerton's Co.): James Walls 1 WP

- - - - - - - - - - - -

WALTERS

TAXES (RHEA)

1819 (Capt. McGill's Co.): George Walters 1 WP

- - - - - - - - - - - -

WALTON

TAXES (RHEA)

1819 (Capt. Lewis' Dist.): Henry Walton 1 WP, 140a
1823 (Capt. Lewis' Co.): Henry Walton 1 WP, 141a, 1 Stud Horse (tax, $4.00)
Henry Walton 1 WP, 140a
(Capt. Wilson's Co.): James Walton 1 WP, 90a T R

MARRIAGES (RHEA)

William Walton to Delila Henderson, 3 Feb 1824 (same), James Stewart Bm (A)

MISCELLANEOUS (RHEA and MEIGS)

James Walton: Bondsman for Barry Hogg, 1821
" " Hiwassee District, Pinhook Ferry area

- - - - - - - - - - - -

WANN / WAN / WANS

TAXES (RHEA)

1823 (Capt. Piper's Co.): William Wan 1 WP

1830 RHEA CENSUS

David Wan 0010001 - 0110001 p. 379
William Wann 1001101 - 122101 p. 359

1840 MEIGS CENSUS

William Wan 01110001 - 1012201 p. 242

1850 MEIGS CENSUS
Jonathan C. Wan 26 (Doctor) p. 774-484
William Wan 30 (Farmer), Elizabeth 27, Lorinda C. 4, Mary Jane 2, Infant (f) 0, Ann 64 (Va) p. 814-778

MARRIAGES (RHEA)
Joshua Wans to Lydia Collins, 5 Aug or 26 May 1820 (5 Aug), Thomas Price JP, Jonathan Collins Bm (AR)
Nancy Wann to Elbert E. Cooper q.v.
Robert Warren or Wann to Nancy Cole, 22 July 1834 (21 Aug), John Randles JP (AR) [see also WARREN]
MARRIAGES (MEIGS)
Daniel Wan to Sarah J. Hague, 13 May 1839 (6 June), Wm Wan Jr. Bm
Elizabeth Wan to Michael W. Buster q.v.
Hannah Wan to Henry Small q.v.
Jan Wan to Albert Hix q.v.
Jane Wan to Benjamin Hutson q.v.
Sarah Wan to John Small q.v.
William Wan to Elizabeth Gibson, 23 Jan 1845 (7 Apr), Thomas V. Atchley JP, D.L. Godsey Sur(?)

MISCELLANEOUS (RHEA)
Robert Wan: Bondsman for Jonathan Collins, 1834
William Wann: Bondsman for James Hughes, 1825
" " Bondsman for Elbert E. Cooper, 1833
MISCELLANEOUS (MEIGS)
Daniel Wan: Cherokee Removal muster roll, 1836
Jonathan C. Wann: Surety for A.R. Snider, 1850
" " " Surety for John Royster, 1850
William Wann: Sheriff, 1836-1840
" " Rep. to Gen. Assembly (House), 1839-45
" " Purchased Lots 38 & 58 in Decatur
" " Trustee, Decatur Academy, 1838-1840
" " Common School Commissioner, 1838
" " Hiwassee District, Ten Mile Stand area
William Wan Jr.: JP(?) 1839, 1841, 1843-44

- - - - - - - - - - - - -

WARD

TAXES (RHEA)
1823 (Capt. Howerton's Co.): Benjamin Ward 36a Piney Ri
(Capt. Wilson's Co.): Nicholas Ward 1 WP, 1 BP
1830 RHEA CENSUS
Celey Ward 0 - 000000001 p. 352
Nicholas Ward 10001 - 00001 p. 352
Wesley Ward 100001 - 0001 p. 362
1840 MEIGS CENSUS
Nichodemus Ward 0001001 - 22000100001 p. 244

1850 RHEA CENSUS
David Ward 35 (Ky)(Wagonmaker), Jane 28 (Ky), George W. 9 (Ky), James P. 6 (Ky), William F. 3 (Ky), Elizabeth M. 2 (Ky), Mary J. 1/12 (Ky) p. 637-669 [David Ward married Jane Marlow on 29 Feb 1839 in McMinn County]
1850 MEIGS CENSUS
Ezekiel Ward 60 (Va)(Farmer), Mary 70 (Va), Ezekiel 21 p. 782-545
Nancy Ward 23, William 21 (Farmer), Mary 20, Celia 18, Elizabeth 15, Martin 7, John 5, Julia 3 p. 779-519

MARRIAGES (RHEA)
Benjamin Ward to Dianah Hicks, 10 Nov 1824 (same), Thomas Price JP, Duke Ward Bm (AR) [1850 McMinn Census: Ben Ward 45, Dianna 50, Henry 18, Martha 16, Henry 14, Polly 12, Elizabeth 8]
Betsy Ward to Thomas Marlow q.v.
Eliza Ward to William Singleton q.v.
Nancy Ward to Samuel Hicks q.v.
Susan Ward to Reuben Marlow q.v.
MARRIAGES (MEIGS)
James H. Ward to Irena Gerl, 14 Apr 1842 (7 June), John T. Blevins JP, Wm W. Lillard Sur(?)
Nicodemus Ward to Nancy Isley, 29 May 1843 (12 July), Ezekiel Ward MG, George Isley Sur
Polly Ward to William Jolly q.v.

MISCELLANEOUS (RHEA and MEIGS)
Benjamin Ward: Bondsman for Robin Marlow, 1824
Duke Ward: Bondsman for Samuel Hixs [Hicks], 1824
" " Bondsman for Benjamin Ward, 1824
" " Hiwassee District, Sewee Creek area
Ezekiel Ward: MG 1843-1849

- - - - - - - - - - - - -

WARICK / WARRACK / WIRICK / WYRICK

TAXES (RHEA)
1819 (Capt. Ramsey's Co.): Martin Wyrick 1 WP
1840 RHEA CENSUS
James Wirick 11001 - 11001
1840 MEIGS CENSUS
Frederick Wirick 3310101 - 1010101 p. 245
Riley Warrack 0 - 00001 (free colored in household: 1-001)
1850 RHEA CENSUS
Andrew Wyrick 57 (Va)(Farmer), Catharine 59 (Va), William H. 25 (Va), Solomon 23 (Va)(Farmer), Adam 18 (Va)(Farmer), Alfred 16 (Va)(Farmer) p. 581-294
MARRIAGES (RHEA)
James Wyrick to Rachel West, 6 July 1839 (7 July), John Condly JP, John Wheeler Bm (AR)
Martin Wyrick to Betsy Riggle, 13 Jan 1819 (21 Jan), Jonathan Fine JP, Henry Riggle Bm (AR)
Pheby Wyrick to John Winfrey q.v.
S. Wyrick to M.E. Martin, 24 May 1831, Jesse Eaton Bm (AR)
Susan Wyrick to Jesse Eaton q.v.
MARRIAGES (MEIGS)
Frederick Wirick to Sarah Rogers 5 Oct 1841 (same), James M. Hague JP
Mary Ann Warick to .J. Brooks q.v.

- - - - - - - - - - - - -

WARNER

1830 RHEA CENSUS
John Warner 20120001 - 0221001 p. 367

- - - - - - - - - - - - -

WARREN

1840 RHEA CENSUS
James Warren 1001 - 0001
Robert Warren 00011 - 0100001
1850 RHEA CENSUS
James Warren 26 (NC)(Farmer), Franky 22, Isaac 12, Syrena 7, Catharine 6, Robert 4, Jane 1 p. 566-189
Robert Warren 40 (NC)(Farmer), Nicey 26, Elizabeth 4 (Deaf and Dumb), John A. 3, James T. 1, Mourning 62 (NC), Catharine 18 p. 566-190
MARRIAGES (RHEA)
Jesse Warren to Hannah Bowman or Boman, 29 Aug 1838 (20 Aug), Samuel Frazier JP, Elias Ferguson Bm, Wm R. Henry, Clerk (AR)
John Warren to Eliz Dean, 19 Jan 1841 (20 Jan), A.G. Wright JP (R)
Robert Warren or Wann to Nancy Cole, 22 July 1834 (21 Aug), John Randles JP (AR)
Robert Warren to Nicy Durham, 29 June 1844 (23 July), Jesse P. Thompson JP (R)
MISCELLANEOUS (RHEA)
Jesse Warren: Bondsman for Robert Mitchell, 1837

- - - - - - - - - - - - -

WASHAM

TAXES (RHEA)
1823 (Capt. Brown's Co.): Jeremiah Washam 1 WP
1850 RHEA CENSUS
Clabourn Washam 48 (Tailor), Eleanor C. 42, Leroy 18, James N. 13, Edward L. 11, Samuel C. 7 p. 612-439
MARRIAGES (RHEA)
Jeremiah Washam to Lucinda Francis, 22 July 1824 (same), John Henninger MG, Hugh Crozier Bm (AR)

- - - - - - - - - - - - -

WASSON / WASSUM / WASSEN

TAXES (RHEA)
1819 (Capt. Robinson's Co.): Jacob Wassum 1 WP
(Capt. Wm McCray's Co.): Jacob Wassum 820a
Jones Wassum 1 WP
1823 (Capt. Lewis' Co.): Andrew Wassum 1 WP
Jacob Wassom 1 BP, 820a
John Wasson 1 WP, 104a
Jonas Wasson 1 WP
(Capt. Brown's Co.): David Wasson 1 WP
Jacob Wassum 2 BP, 500a
Mount Verde Rd
1830 RHEA CENSUS
Andrew Wassom 010001 - 31001 p. 367
Jacob Wassom 000010001 - 00100001 p. 367
1840 RHEA CENSUS
E. E. Wassen 200011 - 02001
Jacob L. Wassum 1000011 - 11111
John Wassen 002000001 - 02110001
John A. Wassen 10001 - 0001

1850 RHEA CENSUS
Edward E. Wasson 46 (Farmer), Sarah 34 (Ky), Jeremiah C. 13, John H. 11. Alexander S. 8, Sarah H. 5, Safrona R. 1, John 74 (NC)(Farmer), William 21 p. 555-132
Jacob L. Wassum 43 (Farmer), Myrum 35 (SC), Mary J. 11 (SC), Jacob L. 9 (SC), Malissa C. 7 (SC), Zachary T. 2 (SC), Cyrus WATERHOUSE 13 (SC), Isabella COOPER 56 (SC) p. 578-276
Vesta Wasson 19: see Rufus M. Crews

MARRIAGES (RHEA)
Alexander Wasson to Nancy Atchley, 14 Sept 1835 (24 Sept), Matthew Hubbert JP, Wilson Kilgore Bm (AR)
Andrew Wassum or Wasson to Esther Erwin, 1 May 1819 (2 May), William Kennedy JP, Samuel Frazier Bm (AR) [1850 Jackson Census: Andrew Wasson 50, Hester 50, Andrew 28, Polly 18, Benjamin 14, Jacob L. 12, Hetty M. 9]
Caroline Wasson to William J. Holland q.v.
Edward E. Wasson or Wassum to Sarah Chapman, 1 Jan 1832 (3 Jan), Matthew Hubbert JP, Henry McCary Bm (AR)
Elizabeth Wasson to Thomas V. Atchley q.v.
Elizabeth Wasson to Joel McNutt q.v.
Elizabeth Wasson to John Dunlapp q.v.
Elijah Wasson to Cassa Garrison, 3 or 5 Mar 1840 (5 Mar), Charles Mitchell MMEC (AR) [1850 Jackson Census: Elijah Wasson 32, Cassa 29, Pleasant 9, Julia 8, Sarah 6, Nancy 5, Lydia 2, Elijah 11/12]
Jacob L. Wasson to Miriam Ferguson, 6 Nov 1845 (same), Charles Cox JP/Bm (AR)
John A. Wasson to Elizabeth Nelson, 14 Jan 1839 (15 Jan), A.G. Wright JP, Thomas R. Holland Bm (AR)
Malinda Wasson to Burton W. Holloway q.v.
Mary Wassum to John Love q.v.
Mary Ann Wassum to Pryor Barton q.v.
Mira W. Wassum to Rufus W. Cruese q.v.
Polly Wasson to Lander Rector q.v.
Rebecca Wassum to Lewis Knight q.v.
Sarah Wasson to James Fergueson q.v.
Sarah E. Wassum to Samuel Ferguson q.v.

MARRIAGES (MEIGS)
Elizabeth Wasson to Enoch Collins q.v.
Nancy Wasson to B.F. Huff q.v.

MISCELLANEOUS (RHEA)
Andrew Wasson: Bondsman for Benjamin Erwin, 1834
Edward E. Wasson: JP 1833, 1836, 1841, 1843, 1845
" " " Registerar of Deeds, 1836-1848
" " " Trustee, Mars Hill Academy, 1850
" " " Deeded land for Sulphur Springs Methodist Church, 1841
Jacob L. Wassum: Bondsman for Robert H. Dyer, 1827

MISCELLANEOUS (MEIGS)
Andrew Wassom: Hiwassee District, Moore's Chapel area
Jacob Wassom: Hiwassee District, Pinhook Ferry area
John A. Wasson: Cherokee Removal muster roll, 1837
Joseph E. Wasson: Cherokee Removal muster roll, 1837

- - - - - - - - - - - - -

WATERHOUSE

TAXES (RHEA)
1819 (Capt. Bradley's Dist.): Richard G. Waterhouse 1 WP, 2 BP, 5000a "inclusive of a variety of grants under which he numbers in his return for the claim as set forth together for year 1817"
1830 RHEA CENSUS
Blackstone Waterhouse 00002 - 0001 p. 383
1840 RHEA CENSUS
Richard Waterhouse 120111 - 00101
1850 RHEA CENSUS
Cyrus Waterhouse 13: see Jacob L. Wassum
Darius Waterhouse 35 (Physician), Harriet C. 23, Vesta E. 2, Elisha T. or F. 2/12 p. 614-460
Franklin Waterhouse 26 (Farmer), Lorinda 28, Vesta J. 8, James E. 5, Elvira 11/12 p. 533-4
[Franklin married Lorinda Thompson]
Myra Waterhouse 14: see David Leuty
Richard Waterhouse 45 (Farmer), Mary L. 36, Richard 17 (Clerk), John 15, Byron 11, James 9, Eglentine 7, Mary 2, Catharine 2 p. 612-441
[Richard married Mary Lane of McMinn County]
Susan Waterhouse 36, Susan 16: see Pitser M. Bailey
MARRIAGES (RHEA)
Elizabeth Waterhouse to William C. Smart q.v.
Euclid Waterhouse to Ann Eliza Campbell, 1 Sept 1836 (same), Timothy B. Sullins MMEC (AR)
Mary L. Waterhouse to Pitser M. Bailey q.v.
Myra Waterhouse to Gideon B. Thompson q.v.
Nancy Waterhouse to Jacob Garrison q.v.
Richard G. Waterhouse to Elizabeth Hackett, 1 Jan 1816 (same), Daniel Murphree JP (AR)
MARRIAGES (MEIGS)
Darius Waterhouse to Harriet C. Sharp, 4 May 1846 (7 May), William L. Adams JP, Aaron King Bm
[Harriet Caroline Sharp, dau of Elisha and Eleanor Huff Sharp]
MISCELLANEOUS (RHEA)
Cyrus Waterhouse: Bondsman for Cedrem Pile, 1838
Darius Waterhouse: Circuit Court Clerk, 1836-1856
" " Bondsman for Sherrell Dudley, 1837
Richard Waterhouse: Bondsman for Wm C. Smart, 1827
" " Bondsman for Brinkley Hornsby, 1828
" " Bondsman for Isaac Garrison, 1828
" " JP 1838-42; Lot 2 in Washington
" " Signed petition to move Indian Agency
" " Com. to supervise construction of new jail, 1825-26
" " Purchased land in Cottonport
" " Capt., Mexican War
Richd G. Waterhouse: Bondsman for Aaron Ferguson, 1821
" " " Large landowner in Rhea County

\- - - - - - - - - - - -

WATERS

TAXES (RHEA)
1808 (Jonathan Fine's List): John Waters 1 BP
John A. Waters 1 WP
Samuel Waters 1 BP

\- - - - - - - - - - - -

WATKINS / WADKINS

1830 RHEA CENSUS
P. Watkins 220001 - 12101 p. 367
MARRIAGES (MEIGS)
Harriet J. Wadkin to William Johnson q.v.
Mary E. Watkins to G.W. Mathews q.v.

\- - - - - - - - - - - -

WATSON

1830 RHEA CENSUS
Peggy Watson 10001 - 0000001 p. 364
1840 MEIGS CENSUS
Nathaniel Watson 111001 - 20000101 p. 247
William Watson 2021001 - 220001 p. 239
1850 RHEA CENSUS
William Watson 54 (Farmer), Elizabeth 52, Joseph 22 (Farmer), Calloway 21 (Farmer), Wesley 19 (Farmer), Mary 18, Ourey C. 16, Marion 14, Emeline 12, Charlotte 10 p. 566-194
1850 MEIGS CENSUS
Agga Watson (f) 60 (Va), Elizabeth 12, James 10 p. 782-549
Nathan Watson 42 (Farmer), Sarah 32, John 16 (Farmer), Betsy Jane 12, James C. 10, Nathan 5, Martha Ann 3 p. 813-275
William Watson 21 (Farmer), Sarah 20, Lucy Ann 1 p. 783-551
MARRIAGES (RHEA)
George Watson to Elizabeth Casey or Cassey, 26 Jan 1835 (same), Benj Wallace JP, James Cassey Bm (AR)
Joseph Watson to Agnes Good, 28 Apr 1810 (same), Woodson Francis Bm (A)
Nathaniel Watson to Eliza Massey, 3 Apr 1833 (7 Apr), I. Baker JP, John Massey Bm (AR)
MARRIAGES (MEIGS)
Nathaniel Watson to Sarah McRennels, 28 Sept 1847, John K. Brown JP
William Watson to Sariah Mapes, 9 Aug 1849 (same), E. Ward MG
MISCELLANEOUS (MEIGS)
George Watson: Ocoee District

\- - - - - - - - - - - -

WATTENBARGER / WHITTENBARGER

1830 RHEA CENSUS
Benjamin Whittenbarger 020001 - 200001 p. 369
Peter Wattenbarger 000001 - 20001 p. 354
[see 1850 McMinn County Census]

\- - - - - - - - - - - -

WATTS

MARRIAGES (RHEA)
William Watts to Rebecca Wood, 14 Jan 1834 (same), John Cozby JP, John Glenn Bm (AR)

\- - - - - - - - - - - -

WAYMIRES / WAYMOYERS

1840 MEIGS CENSUS
James Waymires 01001 - 010001 p. 231
MISCELLANEOUS (MEIGS)
David Waymoyers or Waymires: Cherokee Removal muster roll, 1836-1837 [last name spelled differently on the two lists]

- - - - - - - - - - - - -

WEATHERLY

1830 RHEA CENSUS
Abner Weatherly 010001 - 22101 p. 355

- - - - - - - - - - - - -

WEAVER

1830 RHEA CENSUS
John Weaver 000001 - 000001 p. 369
MISCELLANEOUS (RHEA)
Joseph C. Weaver: Bondsman for James Doughty, 1834

- - - - - - - - - - - - -

WEBB

TAXES (RHEA)
1819 (Capt. John Lewis' Dist.): Hiram Webb 1 WP
Jonathan Webb 1 WP
1840 RHEA CENSUS
Jesse Webb 0010101 - 101001
Josiah Webb 0011001 - 212001
William Webb 20001 - 00101
1840 MEIGS CENSUS
Matilda Webb 112001 - 010002 p. 226
Ritty Webb 0 - 0101 p. 230
William Webb 201001 - 020001 p. 225
1850 RHEA CENSUS
Ritter Webb 48 (Ohio), Emeline 18 p. 619-537
1850 MEIGS CENSUS
Ritter Webb (f) 40, Elender 20 p. 753-325
Marshall M. Webb 40 (NC)(Farmer), Nancy 40 (NC), John 18 (Farmer), Manda 17, William 13, Maddison 12, Susan 10, Lewis 8, Sarah 5, Lelio or Celio 2 p. 722-73
William Webb 48 (NC)(Farmer), Margaret 42 (NC), Columbus R. 20 (Farmer), Nancy 17, Elizabeth 15, William 12, John 10, Mary 7, Barton H. 4 p. 717-38
MARRIAGES (RHEA)
Jacob Webb to Elender Brookshire, 13 Feb 1828 (21 Feb), Jesse Thompson JP, Benjamin Webb Bm (AR)
Jesse Webb to Elizabeth Henry, 10 Feb 1842 (no return), Jesse Harwood Bm (AR)
Senthy Webb to William Knox q.v.
MARRIAGES (MEIGS)
Mahala Webb to Murphree H. Vaughn q.v.
MISCELLANEOUS (RHEA and MEIGS)
Andrew Webb: Bondsman for Noah Williams, 1834
Benjamin Webb: Bondsman for Jacob Webb, 1828
Gideon Webb: Hiwassee District, Hiwassee River area
Hiram Webb: Bondsman for John Dinkins, 1819
Julias Webb: Hiwassee District, Hiwassee River area
William Webb: Hiwassee District, Ten Mile Stand area

- - - - - - - - - - - - -

WEEKS / WEAKS

TAXES (RHEA)
1823 (Capt. Brown's Co.): George Weaks 1 WP
William Weaks 1 WP
1830 RHEA CENSUS
Thomas Weeks 21001 - 10001 p. 381
W. W. Weeks 310001 - 11001 p. 379
1840 MEIGS CENSUS
Gemwell Weeks 00001 - 0120001 p. 237
Jane Weeks 0011 - 0101001 p. 230
1850 RHEA CENSUS
Jane Weeks 48 (SC), Thomas A. 21, Mary A. 18 (Ala), John O. 15 (Ala) p. 620-548
MARRIAGES (RHEA)
George Weeks to Jincy Singleton, 15 Dec 1821 (18 Dec), John Cozby JP, Abraham Hughes Bm (AR)
Susan Weeks to Nicholas Romines q..v.
MISCELLANEOUS (RHEA)
George Weeks: Bondsman for Abraham Hughes, 1821
" " Bondsman for Robert Martin, 1822

- - - - - - - - - - - - -

WEEMS

MISCELLANEOUS (RHEA and MEIGS)
Washington Weems: Bondsman for John Fitgerral, 1826
" " Hiwassee Dist., Burkett Chapel area

- - - - - - - - - - - - -

WEESE

1840 MEIGS CENSUS
Abraham Weese 02001 - 10001001 p. 245
Henry M. Weese 200101 - 111111 p. 228
Samuel Weese 00110001 - 01110001 p. 245
MARRIAGES (RHEA)
Hetty Weese to Eldridge Pitman q.v.

- - - - - - - - - - - - -

WEIR / WEAR

1840 MEIGS CENSUS
Elias L. Weir 00001 - 1001 p. 229
MARRIAGES (RHEA)
Jacob Weir to Betsy Self, 18 Aug 1813 (no return), Jonathan Marlan Bm (AR)
Rebecca Wear to William Self q.v.
Sally Wear to Abraham Grimmett q.v.
MARRIAGES (MEIGS)
Elias L. Wier to L.J. Mathes, 22 Nov 1838 (23 Nov), J. Frie JP
L. L. Wear to M.H. Hounshell, 19 July 1840, Thomas C. Jorden Sur(?)
MISCELLANEOUS (RHEA and MEIGS)
John Wear: Hiwassee District, Burkett Chapel area
Samuel Wear: Lot 16, Town of Washington

- - - - - - - - - - - - -

WELCH

1840 MEIGS CENSUS
Charles M.K. Welch 200001 - 10001 p. 247
1850 MEIGS CENSUS
McMinn Welch 24 (Merchant) p. 745-257
MARRIAGES (RHEA)
Charles M. K. Welch to Nancy J. Condley, 3 Apr 1834, V.H. Giles JP, Alexander Rice Bm (AR) [Allen shows last name as Weldi]
C. M. K. Welch to Elizabeth Evit, 28 Dec 1843 (29 Dec), Samuel Frazier JP (A) [1850 Bledsoe Census: Charles Welch 39, Elizabeth 35, Susannah 13, Ephraim 11, Lavina 6, Edmond D. 4, Edy 1, Nancy J. EVITT 14, Thomas 13, William 40]
MARRIAGES (MEIGS)
C. M. K. Welch to Sarah Ann McClaron, 25 Dec 1841 (26 Dec), James Moore JP, Uriah Huff Sur(?)

- - - - - - - - - - - - -

WELKEN

MARRIAGES (RHEA)
John P. Welken to Sarah Bryson, 4 Jan 1849 (7 Jan), John W. Thompson MG (R)

- - - - - - - - - - - - -

WELLS

1840 RHEA CENSUS
Jacob Wells 110001 - 000001
1850 MEIGS CENSUS
Elizabeth Wells 23, William 6, George W. 5, Mary 1 p. 781-535
MARRIAGES (RHEA)
Jacob Wells to Rebecca Sexton, 12 Apr 1833, Wm Hughs Bm (A)
Nancy Wells to Laban Stewart q.v.
Polly Wells to Richard Fields q.v.
MISCELLANEOUS (RHEA)
Jacob Wells: Bondsman for Lewis Sexton, 1830
" " Bondsman for Martin Sexton, 1830

- - - - - - - - - - - - -

WEST

TAXES (RHEA)
1819 (Capt. John Lewis' Co.): Isaac West 1 WP, 550a
(Capt. John Ramsey's Co.): William H. West 1 WP
1823 (Capt. Lewis' Co.): Isaac West 1 WP, 550a
(Capt. Smith's Co.): James West 1 WP
(Capt. Piper's Co.): William H. West 1 WP
1830 RHEA CENSUS
Mary West 01001 - 021101 p. 366
W. W. West 11001 - 100001 p. 382
Warren West 00001 - 00001 p. 366
1840 RHEA CENSUS
Mary West 01101 - 00020001 [widow of Isaac]
Willis W. West 01000001 - 210101
1840 MEIGS CENSUS
Elizabeth West 0 - 102111 p. 245
1850 RHEA CENSUS
Jeffrey West 30 (Farmer), Orlinda 30, Leah A. 6, Warren 4, Napolean 3/12 p. 601-414
John West 15: see Isaac S. Hutcheson
Mary West 52 (Va), Francis A. CASH 23 (Farmer), Eliza 25, Eli EDGING 19 (Farmer) p. 579-285
1850 MEIGS CENSUS
Ann West 30: see Caleb Vincent
Jackson West 30 (Farmer), Juda Ann 30, William D. 7, Samuel H. 5, John T. 3 p. 802-684
Jerry West 80: see David Buster
Robert West 31 (Farmer), Elizabeth 24, Mary Jane 4, Mitchell 3 p. 733-164
MARRIAGES (RHEA)
Alethia West to Gilbert Riggle q.v.
Eliza West to F. A. Cash q.v.
Matilda West to John R. Barnett q.v.
Rachel West to James Wyrick q.v.
Susan West to Abraham L. Thompson q.v.
Warren West to Rachel Smith, 20 Dec 1827, John Logan Bm (A)
MARRIAGES (MEIGS)
Betsy West to William Redmon q.v.
Jackson West to Dicy Roark, 21 Mar 1843, Samuel M. Blythe JP(?)
MISCELLANEOUS (RHEA)
Warren West: Bondsman for Joseph Ford, 1837
William West: On Surveyor's list of land S of Tenn River

- - - - - - - - - - - - -

WHALEY / WHALY

TAXES (RHEA)
1823 (Capt. Brown's Co.): John Whaley 1 WP, 3 Lots
1830 RHEA CENSUS
John Whaly 22001 - 100101 p. 382
1840 RHEA CENSUS
John Whaley 212201 - 110001
1850 RHEA CENSUS
John Whaley 59 (Ky), Mary 47, Missouri H. 15, Tennessee C. 13, Theodore E. 11, Sarah A. 9, James O.A. 5, William F. 1, Adeline CLARK or CLACK 13 (mulatto), Alexander 9 (mulatto), Anderson 7 (mulatto) p. 625-580
Thomas Whaley 22 (Farmer), Mary A. 23, John T. 9/12 p. 615-501 [Thomas F. Whaley married Mary A. Howel on 5 Apr 1849 in McMinn County]
1850 MEIGS CENSUS
Albert Whaley 22 (Farmer), Elizabeth 25 (NC), Joseph A. 1 p. 747-276
Charles Whaley 30 (NC)(Farmer), Rebecca 21 p. 746-268
Jeremiah Whaley 67 (NC) (Farmer), Sarah V. 50 (NC), Cyntha 24 (NC), Adaline 22 (NC), Mary 20 (NC), Vilet 17, Jane 15, Martha 13 p. 746-267
Joseph Whaley 30, Sarah L. 24, Martha 6, William 3, Sarah Jane 1 p. 746-266 [Joseph L. Whaley married Sarah L. Huddleston on 1 June 1846, McMinn Co]
MARRIAGES (RHEA)
Hercelin Whaley to Emily Frazier, 18 July 1850 (same), John W. Thompson JP (R) [1850 Hamilton Census: Hurcules Whaley 25, Julia E. 28]
John Whaley to Polly Airheart, 16 July 1823 (17 July), A. David JP (A)

Mariah H. Whaley to James M. Caldwell q.v.
MARRIAGES (MEIGS)
Mary Whaley to John Jinkins q.v.
MISCELLANEOUS (RHEA)
John Whaley: Bondsman for William Hill, 1820
" " Bondsman for Edmund P. Childers, 1834
MISCELLANEOUS (MEIGS)
Henry Whaley: 1st Sgt., Mexican War
Hercules Whaley: 2nd Lt., Mexican War
John Whaley: Hiwassee District, Concord area

\- - - - - - - - - - - - -

WHEELER

1830 RHEA CENSUS
John Wheeler 000001 - 00001 p. 367
Mary Wheeler 00002 - 0002001 p. 392
1840 RHEA CENSUS
John Wheeler 2200001 - 000001
1850 RHEA CENSUS
John Wheeler 53 (Va)(Farmer), Virginia 43 (Ky), William M. 19 (Farmer), Samuel J. 16 (Farmer), John M. 14, Charles M. 10, Cyrena E. 4 p. 588-349
MARRIAGES (RHEA)
Margaret Wheeler to Thomas Lois q.v.
Mary Wheeler to William Smith q.v.
Rebecca Wheeler to David Hart q.v.
William Wheeler to Ruth Igou, 11 Mar 1836 (15 Mar), Matthew Hubbert JP (R)
MISCELLANEOUS (RHEA)
John Wheeler: Bondsman for James Wyrick, 1839
Thomas H. Wheeler: Bondsman for Wm Smith, 1832

\- - - - - - - - - - - - -

WHIPPLE

MISCELLANEOUS (MEIGS)
John M. Whipple: Private, Mexican War

\- - - - - - - - - - - - -

WHITE

1830 RHEA CENSUS
Daniel White 10001 - 00001 p. 375
1840 RHEA CENSUS
James White 00001 - 10001
Tollet White 010001 - 210001
1850 MEIGS CENSUS
Benjamin L. White 32 (Farmer), Eliza 30, Catharine H. 24, Alva 13, Caroline 10, Eliza 6, Jesse J. 4, Malissa Jane 1, Thomas QUILLIAN 60 p. 760-379
Jesse White 70 (Va)(Farmer), Gracy 67 (NC), Mathew A. 24, John L. 18 (Farmer) p. 757-355
Judge B. White 30 (Shoemaker), Elizabeth 17, Mary Jane 1 p. 766-421
MARRIAGES (RHEA)
Abraham T. White to Barbara Lasley, 6 Sept 1832 (same), R.M. Stephens MMEC, James Stewart Bm (AR)
Allen White to Mariah Walker, 19 Dec 1830 (21 Dec), Jesse Thompson JP (AR)
Barton White to Polly Butram, 9 July 1831, Alfred Carroll Bm (A)
Benjamin White to Lucinda Roddy, 2 Apr 1827 (6 Apr), Jesse Thompson JP, Edmund Bean Bm (AR)
Betsy White to John D. Jones w.v.
Elizabeth White to William A. Chastain q.v.
Robert White to Polly Mars, 21 Nov 1835, Jacob Jester Bm (A)
MARRIAGES (MEIGS)
Sarah J. White to William Jones q.v.
MISCELLANEOUS (RHEA and MEIGS)
Charles White: Hiwassee District, Ten Mile Stand area
George White: Lots 9 and 10 in Town of Washington
Hugh A.M. White: Hiwassee District, Cottonport area

\- - - - - - - - - - - - -

WHITEHEAD

MARRIAGES (RHEA)
Sarah Whitehead to Stephen Mayfield q.v.

\- - - - - - - - - - - - -

WHITESIDE

1830 MEIGS CENSUS
Jacob Whiteside 38 (NC)(Farmer), Jane 36 (NC), William T. 16, James B. 14, Sarah Jane 12, Andrew P. 3 p. 757-353
MISCELLANEOUS (MEIGS)
William Whiteside: Surety for Benson T. Johns, 1850

\- - - - - - - - - - - - -

WHITFIELD

TAXES (RHEA)
1819 (Capt. Bradley's Dist.): Wm Whitfield heirs 833⅓a
1823 (Capt. Brown's Co.): James Whitfield 1 Lot

\- - - - - - - - - - - - -

WHITING

MARRIAGES (RHEA)
Sally Whiting to John Bowdry q.v.

\- - - - - - - - - - - - -

WHITMOND

1830 RHEA CENSUS
Thomas Whitmond 100001 - 1211 p. 366

\- - - - - - - - - - - - -

WHITMORE / WHITMON / WHITEMAN

1830 RHEA CENSUS
Jesse Whitmore 000100001 - 001 p. 370
1840 RHEA CENSUS
Ann Whitmore 011 - 023211
1840 MEIGS CENSUS
Robert Whitmon 01001 - 30001 p. 224
1850 RHEA CENSUS
Henry C. Whitmore 5: see James Wilson

1850 MEIGS CENSUS

Howell Whitmore 39 (Farmer), Nancy 46, Louisa 18, Mary 16, Elizabeth Ann 14, John H. 8, Margaret Jane 6, Charles D. 3 p. 744-250

John Whiteman 93: see Joseph H. Cate

MARRIAGES (RHEA)

Eliza Whitmore to Robert B. Earles q.v.

Howel Whitmon or Whitmore to Nancy Gamble, 10 Feb 1830 (12 Feb), Thomas Cox JP, John W. Gamble Bm (AR)

Milly Whitmore to James Aikens (Eaken) q.v.

Sallyan Whitmore to A.W. Derosset q.v.

MISCELLANEOUS (MEIGS)

Howell Whitmore: Ocoee District; Sheriff, 1842-45

" " 1st Lt., Cherokee Removal muster roll, 1836-37

- - - - - - - - - - - - -

WHITNEY / WHITNER

1830 RHEA CENSUS

Joseph Whitner 10001 - 30001 p. 360

MARRIAGES (RHEA)

Sally Whitney to John Bowdry (Bowdins) q.v.

MISCELLANEOUS (RHEA)

Sally Whitney: Bm for John Gulfrd Burris (Burns), 1818

- - - - - - - - - - - - -

WHITSON

MARRIAGES (MEIGS)

Sariah Whitson to Isaac McDowell q.v.

- - - - - - - - - - - - -

WHITTENBERG / WHITTENBURG

1840 RHEA CENSUS

Christopher Whittenberg 000001 - 210001

Henry Whittenberg 10001 - 00001

John Whittenberg 00000001 - 0000001

Ralph Whittenberg 120001 - 000001

William Whittenberg 000001 - 000001

1850 RHEA CENSUS

Christopher I. Whittenburg 46 (Farmer), Mary 44, Nancy E. 17, Luisa J. 15, Margaret A.C. 13, Minerva F. 8 p. 587-346

Henry Whittenburg 31 (Farmer), Eliza D. 29 (Va), Jesse M. 10, William E. 8, Ira N. 4, Prudence M. 2 p. 587-343

John Whittenburg 75 (NC)(Farmer), Sarah 66, John W. 25 (Farmer), Nathan 34 (School Teacher), Ira M. 23 (Farmer) p. 587-344 [Sarah, dau of John Christopher and Barbara Hartley Lotspeich]

Ralph S. Whittenburg 41 (Farmer), Luretta 41 (Va), John D. 18 (Farmer), William W. 17 (Farmer), Henry H. 11, Sarah H. 8, Nancy E. 5, Ira S. 2 p. 587-338

S. T. Whittenburg 35 (Farmer), Charlotte J. 23, Margaret 6, Sarah J. 5, William 2, James H. 1, Abagail E. HARNER 17 p. 544-73

Samuel Whittenburg 35 (Farmer), Sarah H. 25 (Va), William A. 4, Timothy N. 1, Mary E. BROYLES 25 p. 587-342

William Whittenburg 43 (Farmer), Mary A. 41, Sarah F. 7, John A. 5, Stephen P. 3, Amos F. 1, Egletine A. BROYLES 21 p. 587-345

MARRIAGES (RHEA)

Daniel Whittenburg to Mary Ann Hill, 31 Oct 1832 (1 Nov), Matthew Hubbert JP, Christopher I. Whittenburg Bm (AR)

Henry Whittenburg to Eliza B. Rector, 13 Mar 1839 (14 Mar), Wm Bowers JP, Wm Whittenberg Bm (AR)

Henry N. Whittenburg to Elizabeth G. Norville, 1 May 1839 (same), Samuel Frazier JP, Ralph Whittenburg Bm (AR) [1850 Roane Census: H.N. Whittenburg 32, Elizabeth G. 41]

Samuel T. Whittenburg to Charlotte Roddy, 1 Feb 1843, Isaac S. Binyon Bm (A)

William Whittenburg to Mary Ann Stout, 31 Dec 1839 (3 Jan 1840), William Bowers or Barnes JP (AR)

MISCELLANEOUS (RHEA)

C.I. Whittenburg: Trustee, Sulphur Springs Methodist Church, 1841

" " " Bondsman for Daniel Whittenburg, 1832

Christopher Whittenburg: Bm for Ira D. Broyles, 1831

Henry Whittenburg: Bondsman for Robert D. Earles, 1840

Ralph Whittenburg: Bm for Henry N. Whittenburg, 1839

William Whittenburg: Bm for Henry Whittenburg, 1839

- - - - - - - - - - - - -

WICE

(see also BICE and RICE)

1830 RHEA CENSUS

John Wice 21100001 - 220201 p. 385

William Wice 00001 - 0001 p. 385

- - - - - - - - - - - - -

WICKLIFFE

1830 RHEA CENSUS

John Wickliffe 31001 - 10001 p. 356

- - - - - - - - - - - - -

WICKS

MARRIAGES (RHEA)

Nancy Wicks to Thomas M. Bolin q.v.

- - - - - - - - - - - - -

WIDOWS

MARRIAGES (MEIGS)

Isaac Widows to Barbary Keneda, 26 Dec 1850, W.M. Benson Sur

- - - - - - - - - - - - -

WIGGENTON / WIGGINTON

MARRIAGES (RHEA)

Jeremiah Wiggenton to Catherine Mitchell, 5 July 1830, Peter Fine Bm (A)

Mary Wigginton to Calvin Dean q.v.

Rhoda Wigginton to Lewis Acre q.v.

- - - - - - - - - - - - -

WILDS

MARRIAGES (RHEA)
Emiline Wilds to Thomas Bingham q.v.

- - - - - - - - - - - - -

WILHELM / WILHELMS / WILLHELMS / WILHIM

1840 RHEA CENSUS
Jacob Wilhelms 20001 - 010001
1850 MEIGS CENSUS
James Willhelm 30 (Farmer), Abigail 34, Elizabeth WILLHELMS 77 (Va) p. 787-583
MARRIAGES (RHEA)
Alemintar Wilhim to William Bice q.v.
Betsy Wilhelms to Russel Qualls q.v.
Jacob Wilhelms to Cecile Blackwell, 27 Mar 1833 (29 Mar), Daniel Briggs MG, Dennis C. Murphy Bm (AR)
Pleasant L. Wilhelms to Jane N.L. Miller [Lockmiller?], 29 Sept 1835, Samuel Miller Bm (A)
Richard Wilhelm to Sarah Seymore, 30 Dec 1809 (no return), William Kennedy Bm (AR)
Welcome Wilhelm to Polly Rice, 20 Jan 1830, Jeremiah Tindell Bm (A)
MARRIAGES (MEIGS)
James Wilhelms to Abegail Atchley, 25 Jan 1843, Thomas V. Atchley Esq., Nathan Qualls Bm
Miss [blank] Wilhelms to John Tindel q.v.
MISCELLANEOUS (RHEA)
A. Wilhelms: Signed petition to move Indian Agency
Andrew Wilhelm: Lots 18,19,54,76,77,78 in Washington
Pleasant L. Wilhelms: Bm for Saml L. Miller [Lockmiller], 1835
Welcome Wilhelms: Bondsman for Thomas Price, 1829
MISCELLANEOUS (MEIGS)
Elizabeth Wilhelms: Hiwassee District

- - - - - - - - - - - - -

WILHITE

1850 RHEA CENSUS
John F. Wilhite 35 (Farmer), Phebe 26, Thomas 8, David 7, Lewis 5, James 2, Jonathan 6/12 p. 604-467

- - - - - - - - - - - - -

WILKERSON / WILKINSON

TAXES (RHEA)
1819 (Capt. McCray's Co.): Lewis Wilkerson 1 WP, 150a
1823 (Capt. Howerton's Co.):
Lewis Wilkerson 1 WP, 150a Vann's Spring Cr
MISCELLANEOUS (RHEA)
John Weir Wilkerson: Lot 56, Town of Washington
" " " Bm for Samuel Bowman, 1812

- - - - - - - - - - - - -

WILKEY

1850 RHEA CENSUS
Samuel Wilkey 33 (Farmer), Cyntha 26, Christopher C. 8, Rhoda A. 6, Sylvester L. 3, Kizziah 1 p. 574-252 [Samuel Wilkey married Cyntha Hartley on 2 June 1840 in Roane County]

- - - - - - - - - - - - -

WILLIAMS

TAXES (RHEA)
1808 (John Henry's List): George Williams 300a
1819 (Capt. McGill's Co.): Jonathan Williams 1 WP
(Capt. Robinson's Co.):
Joseph Williams 1 WP, 308a
1823 (Capt. Lewis' Co.): David S. Williams 1 WP, 50a
(Capt. Howard's Co.): Jonathan Williams 1 WP
(Capt. Braselton's Co.):
Joseph Williams 1 WP, 308a
1830 RHEA CENSUS
Danil Williams 01001 - 00001 p. 390
John D. Williams 0100001 - 0 p. 373
1840 RHEA CENSUS
Elijah Williams 000001 - 24201
William Williams 112001 - 211001
William H. Williams 10001 - 00001
1840 MEIGS CENSUS
Elizabeth Williams 0001 - 00000001 p. 243
Frederic Williams 001100001 - 000010001 p. 244
Isaac Williams 00003 - 0011 p. 227
John D. Williams 111200001 - 0100001 p. 229
Joseph Williams 020001 - 20001 p. 244
Robert Williams 00001 - 10001 p. 245
Ruth Williams 111 - 111001 p. 226
William Williams 11110001 - 1211001 p. 226
William Williams 210001 - 00001 p. 245
1850 RHEA CENSUS
Mathias Williams 61 (NC)(Carpenter): see Peter Minick
Thomas Williams 31 (Carpenter), Recta M. 21 (Canada), Enoch M. 5, John SHAVER 71 (Pa)(Millwright) p. 571-230
1850 MEIGS CENSUS
John D. Williams 75 (Va)(Farmer), Sarah 56 (NC), William G. 17, Jacob L. 12 p. 746-261
Ruth Williams 34, Shadrick 21 (Farmer), Racheal 19, John 17 (Farmer), Mary 15, Jacob 13, Abigal 11 p. 721-66
MARRIAGES (RHEA)
Betsy Williams to Robert Kimbrell q.v.
Cinthia Williams to Josiah Moore q.v.
Elizabeth Williams to John Henry q.v.
Elizabeth Williams to Henry Minick q.v.
Frederick Williams to Nancy Casteel, 30 July 1844 (1 Aug), James Hooper JP, William Richardson Bm (AR)
James Williams to Uphama Fulton, 29 Dec 1828 (30 Dec), Jesse Thompson JP (AR)
James Johnson Williams to Lucy Howerton, 25 Dec 1810 (29 or 25 Dec), Abraham Howard JP, Jackson Howerton Bm (AR)
Jonathan Williams to Polly Milesham, 14 May 1814, William Bice Bm (AR)
Martha Williams to H.M. Smith q.v.

Noah Williams to Cynthia Corder, 12 May 1834, Andrew Webb Bm (A)
Rachel Williams to Peter Minnick q.v.
Syntha Williams to Nathan Neely q.v.
William H. Williams to Sarah Ann Parker, 30 June 1835 (5 July), William Green MG, Wm Williams Bm (AR)

MARRIAGES (MEIGS)
Anna Williams to Michael W. Coffey q.v.
Charles Williams to Katherine Buckner, 2 Mar 1843, Thomas V. Atchley JP, Thomas Mayberry Sur
Hosea H. Williams to Sarah Farmer, 19 Apr 1838, Daniel Briggs MG
Mary Williams to Reuben E. Bandy q.v.
Nancy Williams to Thomas Moore q.v.
Shadrack Williams to Nancy M. King, 18 Oct 1850, John N. Craighead Sur

MISCELLANEOUS (RHEA)
James S. Williams: Bondsman for James C. Wilson, 1829
Joseph Williams: Bondsman for James M. Nelson, 1822
" " Completed new jail in Washington, 1826
" " Early resident of Town of Washington
Thomas Williams: Bondsman for John Bennett, 1824
William Williams: Bondsman for Wm H. Williams, 1835

MISCELLANEOUS (MEIGS)
Isaac Williams: Ocoee District
John W. Williams: Private, Mexican War
" " " Surety for Gainum Brightwell, 1850
" " " Surety for Jonathan Isom, 1850
William Williams: Common School Com., District 5, 1838

- - - - - - - - - - - - -

WILLIAMSON

1830 RHEA CENSUS
John Williamson 0021001 - 001001 p. 389

- - - - - - - - - - - - -

WILLIS

1830 RHEA CENSUS
James Willis 20110001 - 0110001 p. 362
MISCELLANEOUS (RHEA)
James Willis: MG 1834

- - - - - - - - - - - - -

WILLS / WILES

1850 MEIGS CENSUS
David Wills 36 (Farmer), Levina 32, Amazana (f) 13, Christopher 12, Elijah 11, Sarah Ann 8, David H. 6, John Taylor 2 p. 786-576
MARRIAGES (RHEA)
William A. Wiles to Emeline Mitchell, 22 Feb 1835 (same), C. Caldwell JP, John Smith Bm (AR)
MISCELLANEOUS (MEIGS)
David D. Wills: JP(?) 1843

- - - - - - - - - - - - -

WILSON / WILLSON

TAXES (RHEA)
1819 (Capt. Robinson's Co.): James Wilson 1 WP
James Wilson 1 WP, 1 BP, 180a
(Capt. McCray's Co.): John Wilson 1 WP
1823 (Capt. Wilson's Co.): Asa Wilson heirs 480a Sewee Cr (returned by Wm C. Wilson)
James Wilson 8 BP, 320a
William C. Wilson 1 WP, 3 BP
(Capt. Braselton's Co.): James Wilson 180a Yellow Cr
1830 RHEA CENSUS
Eliza Wilson 1 - 201001001 p. 358
James Wilson 30010001 - 0011001 p. 358
James Wilson 00001 - 20001 p. 381
James Wilson 11110001 - 0011001 p. 386
N.W. Wilson 100001 - 0201001 p. 368
P.W. Wilson 00011 - 20001 p. 358
1840 RHEA CENSUS
Ann Wilson 001 - 00000001
1840 MEIGS CENSUS
David Wilson 000020001 - 001010001 p. 226
1850 RHEA CENSUS
James Wilson 44 (Wheelwright), Sarah 41 (NC), Dearana 19, William 17 (Farmer), John A. 15, Dealthea J. 13, Margaret J. 11, James W. 7, Sarah E. 5, Nancy E. 6/12, Henry C. WHITMORE 5 (mulatto), Hiram EVANS 32 (Wheelwright), Nancy A. PORTER 35 (NC), Mary L. PORTER 8 p. 575-260
1850 MEIGS CENSUS
Elizabeth Wilson 57, Wiley O. 14, James H. 2 p. 732-154 [NOTE: the household number, 154, actually was next to Wiley's name, making it appear as though Elizabeth was a member of the previous household of Elgin Brightwell]
George M. Wilson 35 (Farmer), Elizabeth 30, David W. 7, William H. 5, David WILSON 75 (Va) p. 724-93
Hugh L. Wilson 47 (Farmer), Maranda 41, James E. 21, Sarah 20, Samuel J. 17, Daniel J. 14, Richard C. 12, John T. 7, Ezekiel S. 6, Thomas C. 4, Martha Ann B. 2 p. 793-627 [Hugh married Marinda C. Clark on 12 Nov 1827 in Carter County]
William J. Wilson 71 (Eng)(Farmer), Anna 48 (SC)(Ediot) p. 736-189

MARRIAGES (RHEA)
Betsy S. Wilson to Hugh L. Baldwin q.v. [Betsy, widow of William C.; dau of Robert and Nancy Blakey Stockton of Kentucky]
Dealtha Willson to Alvin Hornsby q.v.
Isabella Willson to William M. Clack q.v.
James Wilson to Dicey Ellis, 18 June or Jan 1820, "Returned to office in papers of D. Walker JP" (AR)
James Wilson to Jemimah Wright, 24 Oct 1832 (same), John Farmer MG, James Mayo Bm (AR) [James, son of John and bro of Wm C.; James moved to Mo prior to 1850]
James W.C. Wilson to Sally (Sarah) B. Porter, 19 Jan 1829 (20 Jan), Daniel Walker JP, James S. Williams Bm (AB) [James Woods Cozby Wilson, son of James M. and Anna Cozby Wilson]
Leander Wilson to Sarah E. Ragsdale, 13 Sept 1842, William F. Ragsdale Bm (A)

Lewis Willson to Nancy Collins, 12 Mar 1850 (no return) (R)
Mary Ann Willson to Albert Snow q.v.
Michael Wilson to Mahala Atchley, 9 Nov 1825 (10 Nov), John Farmer MG, Jos J. Thrailkill Bm (AR)
Nathaniel W. Wilson to Sarah Miller, 19 or 17 Apr 1827 (19 Apr), Daniel Briggs MG, Avara Hannah Bm (AR) [Nathaniel, son of James and Mary Lynch Wilson]
Stephen Willson to Caroline Snow, 10 Sept 1848 (17 Sept), Washington Morgan JP (R)

MARRIAGES (MEIGS)

Clemenza L. Wilson* to Amos Broyles q.v.
Elenor C. Wilson* to Nile M. Broyles q.v.
Emily Wilson* to Moses Kennedy q.v.
[*daus of Wm C. and Elizabeth Stockton Wilson]
Jane Wilson to Henry Barnhart q.v.

MISCELLANEOUS (RHEA)

Betsy S. Wilson: Postmistress at Ten Mile Stand, 1831
George Wilson: Early resident, Town of Washngton
James Wilson: JP 1827-34
Leander Wilson: MG 1848
William Wilson: Bondsman for Rufus Anderson, 1844
William C. Wilson: JP 1826
William D.(?) Wilson: Bm for Carlisle Humphreys, 1814

MISCELLANEOUS (MEIGS)

Asa Wilson: Hiwassee District, Ten Mile area [died before moving from Kentucky; bro of Wm C. Wilson, James Wilson, and Artimisa Wilson Ragland]
James Wilson: Hiwassee District, Ten Mile area [married three times: to Mary Lunch, to Nancy Blakey Stockton (widowed mother of Elizabeth Stockton Wilson), and to Jemimah Wright; the Wilsons and Stocktons moved from Ky to Tenn about 1820]
Leander Wilson: MG 1849
Mark H. Wilson: JP(?) 1841,1845
[son of Wm C. and Elizabeth]
Michael Wilson: Common School Com., District 1, 1838
William Wilson: Hiwassee District
William C. Wilson: Hiwassee District, Ten Mile Stand area

\- - - - - - - - - - - - -

WINFIELD / WINDFIELD

1840 RHEA CENSUS

Joseph Winfield 20001 - 01001

MARRIAGES (RHEA)

Joseph Winfield to Rebecca Brewer, 28 Mar 1834 (1 Apr), Samuel Lisle MG, Samuel R. Hackett Bm (AR)

MISCELLANEOUS (RHEA)

Joseph Winfield: Bondsman for Lewis Brewer, 1845

\- - - - - - - - - - - - -

WINFREY

1850 RHEA CENSUS

John Winfrey 28 (Ga), Phebe 22 (Va), Eliza J. 7/12 p. 580-293

MARRIAGES (RHEA)

John Winfrey to Pheby Wyrick, 3 May 1847 (6 May), Daniel Broyles JP (R)

\- - - - - - - - - - - - -

WINTERS

MARRIAGES (RHEA)

Barbara Winters to Nicholas Starnes q.v.

\- - - - - - - - - - - - -

WINTON / WINTAN

TAXES (RHEA)

1819 (Capt. Robinson's Co.): George Winton 1 WP, 121a
1823 (Capt. Piper's Co.): Stephen Winton 1 WP, 160a

1830 RHEA CENSUS

Stephen Winton 10011001 - 1221001 p. 360

1840 MEIGS CENSUS

Stephen Winton 112010001 - 21023001 p. 241

1850 MEIGS CENSUS

Stephen Winton 70 (Pa)(Farmer), Nancy H. 35, Stephen C. 21 ("married within year") p. 797-660

MARRIAGES (RHEA)

Rhoda Winton to Nelson Battle q.v.

MARRIAGES (MEIGS)

Martha W. Winton to Hugh Goddard q.v.
Mary J. Winton to Elijah S. Smith q.v.
Mary J. Winton to John Ray q.v.
Sarah S. Winton to John H. Pickle q.v.

MISCELLANEOUS (RHEA)

George Winton: Signed petition to move Indian Agency
James A. Winton: Bondsman for James C. Alford, 1835
Johnson Winton: Bondsman for James Spencer, 1824
Stephen Winton: JP 1826-1835

MISCELLANEOUS (MEIGS)

Stephen Winton: JP 1841; Coroner, 1836
" " Com. to lay off County into Dists., 1836

\- - - - - - - - - - - - -

WISEMAN

1850 RHEA CENSUS

Nancy Wiseman 15: see William D. Everett

\- - - - - - - - - - - - -

WITT

TAXES (RHEA)

1819 (Capt. McGill's Co.):
Jesse Witt & Wm Baldwin 3 WP, 200a
1823 (Capt. Howard's Co.): Jesse Witt 1 WP, 200a
John Witt 1 WP

1830 RHEA CENSUS

Abner Witt 200011 - 11001 p. 382
Elijas Witt 211001 - 0203001 p. 359
Jesse Witt 00101001 - 11011 p. 382
John Witt 10001101 - 11 p. 382

1840 RHEA CENSUS

John Witt 3210401 - 00111

1850 MEIGS CENSUS

John (Joseph?) N. Witt 24 (School Teacher), Charity A. 16 ("married within year") p. 722-68
William A. Witt 28 (NC)(Farmer), Elizabeth 27 (NC), Jackson 18, Melissa A. 20, Frances M. 7, James E. 5, John A. 2 p. 785-569

MARRIAGES (RHEA)

Abner Witt to Ann Airheart or Airhart, 8 May 1824 (9 May), John Henninger MG, Samuel Frazier Bm (AR)
Ann Witt to Matthew Russell q.v.
Charles Witt to Jane Holt, 27 Mar 1831, Thomas W. Munsey Bm (A) [1850 Hamilton Census: Charles Witt 45, Jane 35, Jesse 16]
Delphia Witt to Charles Grigsby q.v.
Elizabeth Witt to David Shelton q.v.
John Witt to Leta Griffith, 31 May 1827 (same), James A. Darwin JP, Henry Griffith Bm (AR)
Margaret Witt to Andrew J. Bryson q.v.
Margaret Witt to Thomas W. Munsey q.v.
Mary Witt to Thomas Adams q.v.
Richard Witt to Sally Stinnett, 12 June 1812 (no return), Henry Stinnett Bm (AR)

MARRIAGES (MEIGS)

Joseph N. Witt to Charity A. Gamble, 18 Aug 1849 (23 Aug), J.M. Miller MG
Matilda Witt to Avery Hannah q.v.
William A. Witt to Elizabeth Royster, 30 July 1842 (31 July), John Gourley JP, Jane Collins Sur(?)

MISCELLANEOUS (RHEA)

Abner Witt: Bondsman for David Holt, 1835
Charles Witt: Bondsman for Allen Dalyrimple, 1828
" " Bondsman for Thomas W. Munsey, 1831
John Witt: Early merchant in Washington
" " Bondsman for John Acre, 1819
" " Bondsman for Joshua S. Green, 1821

MISCELLANEOUS (MEIGS)

John A. Witt: Cherokee Removal muster roll, 1836
Joseph Witt: Ocoee District

- - - - - - - - - - - - -

WITTON / WITTEN / WHITTEN

1840 RHEA CENSUS

William A. Witton 121001 - 010001

1840 MEIGS CENSUS

Sarah Witten 1210001 - 0110001 p. 242

MARRIAGES (MEIGS)

Joseph E. Witten to Nancy Roark, 26 Nov 1846 (30 Nov), Heil Buttram MG, D.L. Godsey Sur(?)
Lutitia Witten to John H. Roark q.v.

MISCELLANEOUS (RHEA)

James Witten: MG 1831
Thomas Witten: MG 1847
William A. Witten: Bondsman for James W. Vernon, 1845

MISCELLANEOUS (MEIGS)

James Witten: MG 1841
John W. Witten: MG 1838-39
Thomas Witten: MG 1847

- - - - - - - - - - - - -

WOMAC / WOMMACK / WAMOCK / WAMACK / WAMMACK / WARMAC

TAXES (RHEA)

1823 (Capt. Jackson's Co.): Jacob Wammac 1 WP

1830 RHEA CENSUS

Jacob Womac 20001 - 100001 p. 370
Jacob Warmac 00001001 - 000100001 p. 377
Thomas Wommack 10001 - 0101 p. 376

1840 MEIGS CENSUS

Jacob Wommack 0120001 - 2110001 p. 230
Thomas Wammack 011001 - 22001 p. 235

1850 MEIGS CENSUS

Jacob Wamack 52 (Va)(Farmer), Nancy 53 (Va), David 24 (Farmer), Sarah 21, Daniel 20 (Farmer), Mary 18, John 16, Susan 14, Jane 12, Elizabeth 10 p. 741-223
Jacob Wamock 19 (Farmer), Catharine 17 p. 749-295 [Jacob married Catherine Beavers on 21 Feb 1849 in McMinn County]
John Wamock 49 (Va)(Farmer), Mary 46, Melisa Ann 9, James W. 7 p. 746-270

MARRIAGES (RHEA)

Narcissa Wammack to Thomas Lucas q.v.
Sally Wammack to James Elder q.v.

MARRIAGES (MEIGS)

John Wommack to Polly Looney, 7 Nov 1840 (1 Jan 1841), Joseph McCorkle & Wm S. Russell, Adms
Mary Wammack to John C. George q.v.
Sarah Wammack to Thomas J. Bonner q.v.

MISCELLANEOUS (RHEA)

Jacob Wammack: Bondsman for James Elder, 1826
Thomas Womack: Bondsman for John Taylor, 1826

MISCELLANEOUS (MEIGS)

Jacob Womack: House used to hold elections, District 2
" " Hiwassee District, Burkett Chapel area

- - - - - - - - - - - - -

WOOD / WOODS

1830 RHEA CENSUS

Jas or Jos Woods 12100001 - 00100001 p. 378
Jno Woods 00001 - 00001 p. 378
Jno W. Woods 101001001 - 10101 p. 374
William Wood 00002 - 20001 p. 364

1840 MEIGS CENSUS

Harrison Wood 1011 - 00001 p. 224
John W. Wood 0011001 - 2301001 p. 236
Rachel Wood 00011 - 00001001 p. 224

1850 RHEA CENSUS

John Wood 40 (NC)(Farmer), Jemima 38 (NC), Martha M. 15 (NC), Susan M. 14 (NC), William T. 12 (NC), Mary 9 (NC), John H. 7 (NC), Humphrey P. 5 (NC), Sarah J. 3 (NC), Rebecca 1 (NC) p. 586-381

1850 MEIGS CENSUS

John Wood 40 (Farmer), Telitha 36, George 11, William 6, James 4, Racheal R. 2 p. 795-644
John W. Wood 50 (Va) (Blacksmith), Elizabeth 50 (Md), Nancy 19 ("married within year"), Celia 15, Racheal 13, William S. 12, Sally 10, Lorinda 7, James S. 7 p. 773-482
Samuel O. Wood 29 (Farmer), Mary 22, William 1 p. 714-11
Samuel W. Wood 30 (Va) (Wagonmaker), Nancy E. 26 (NC), Thomas F. 8, Martha Jane 6, Rebecca H. 5, Elizabeth 3, George M. 1 p. 773-476
William Wood 30 (Farmer) p. 720-58

MARRIAGES (RHEA)

Michael L. Woods to Sarah M. Preston, 14 Jan 1834, Rector Preston Bm (A)
Rebecca Wood to William Watts q.v.

Samuel O. Woods to Mary Hickman, 27 July 1848 (same), H. Douglas MG (R)
Tipton G. Woods to Anna F. Gerald [Fitzgerald?], 4 May 1835, William B. Rigg Bm (A)

MARRIAGES (MEIGS)
E.E. Woods to William R. Jenkins q.v.
John Wood to Telitha McAdams, 1 Oct 1839 (3 Oct), John Whitten MG, Archibald McCaleb Sur(?)
Jonathan Wood to Louisa E. Browder, 16 Nov 1850, W.C. Johnson Sur
Jonathan Wood to Nancy A. Hounshell, 23 May 1844 (same), Ralph E. Tedford MG
Mary A. Woods to George Hall q.v.
Nancy E. Woods to Richard Binyon q.v.
S.W. Woods to Nancy E. Brown, 28 Jan 1841 (same), D.L. Godsey MG, John W. Woods Sur(?)

MISCELLANEOUS (RHEA)
John Wood: Bondsman for David Casteel 1828
John W. Wood: Bondsman for David Bandy, 1828
William W. Woods: MG 1827-28
" " " Bondsman for Hezekial Shelton, 1828

MISCELLANEOUS (MEIGS)
Harrison Wood: Ocoee District
James Wood: Hiwassee District
John W. Wood: JP 1841-48
" " " Chairman of County Court 1850-51
M. A. Wood: Surety for W.C. Hutchison, 1850
Michael Woods: Hiwassee District, Sewee Creek area
Samuel Wood: Ocoee District
Solomon O. Wood: 2nd Corp., Cherokee Removal muster roll, 1836
W. Wood: Ocoee District

- - - - - - - - - - - - -

WOODBY

1850 RHEA CENSUS
Elizabeth Woodby 12: see Polly Bingham
K. P. Woodby 12: see Cain Able
Nancy A. Woodby 12: see John Wyatt

- - - - - - - - - - - - -

WOODWARD / WOODWOOD

TAXES (RHEA)
1819 (Capt. Lewis' Dist.):
John & Charles Woodward 2 WP, 175a
Thomas Woodward 120a
William Woodward 1 WP, 140a
1823 (Capt. Lewis' Co.): James Woodward 1 WP
John & Charles Woodward 2 WP, 175a
Thomas Woodward 120a
William Woodward 1 WP, 140a

1830 RHEA CENSUS
Chas Woodwood* 1000001 - 21000101 p. 393
Wm Woodwood* 200001 - 11001 p. 393
[*clearly written Woodwood]
Jas or Jos Woodward 100001001 - 111101

1840 RHEA CENSUS
Charles Woodward 00100001 - 0122001

1850 RHEA CENSUS
Charles Woodward 61 (Farmer), John E. 25 (Farmer), Margaret 22 (Idiot), Dorthala 18, Elizabeth 53, Nancy TYSON 56 (NC) p. 584-321
Esther Woodward 85 (Va): see Robert Mitchell

MARRIAGES (RHEA)
Ann Woodward to Robert Mitchell q.v.
Catherine Woodward to James Mitchell q.v.
Charles Woodward to Sally Collins, 6 Oct 1821 (same), H. Collins JP, William Collins Bm (AR)
James Woodward to Elizabeth Montgomery, 24 Sept 1829 (same), Matthew Hubbert JP, Robert Mitchell Bm (AR)
John Woodward to Susannah Reice or Reece, 28 July 1818 (29 July), H. Collins JP, John Day Bm (AR)
John Woodward to Rachel Reynolds, 14 Nov 1819, Dennis Reynolds Bm (R)
Margaret Woodward to William Gwin q.v.
Marjora Woodward to Daniel R. Kennedy q.v.
Polly Woodward to Matthew Hubbert q.v.
Susan Woodward to Isaac Binyon q.v.
William Woodward to Jane Logan, 30 May 1822 (same), William Kennedy JP, Robert Mitchell Bm (AR)

MISCELLANEOUS (RHEA)
Thomas Woodward: Coroner 1808

- - - - - - - - - - - - -

WOODY

1830 RHEA CENSUS
Joseph Woody 10001 - 20001 p. 377

1850 MEIGS CENSUS
Nicholas Woody 64 (SC)(Farmer), Martha 57 (SC), Jane 24, Catharine 22, Emaline 20, Riley 20 (Farmer), James 17, John 14, David 12, Racheal 10, Manda 9, Martha 8, Hugh A. 2 p. 713-4
Thomas Woody 32 (SC), Elizabeth 30 (SC) p. 713-5

MARRIAGES (RHEA)
Washington Woody to Polly Gooldsby, 29 June 1830 (1 July), John Cozby JP, Jos F. Woody Bm (AR)

MARRIAGES (MEIGS)
Samuel Woody to Elizabeth Rew, 3 Apr 1850, Nicholas G. Givens Sur

MISCELLANEOUS (RHEA)
Joseph F. Woody: Bondsman for Washington Woody, 1830

- - - - - - - - - - - - -

WOOLARD / WOOLLARD

1840 RHEA CENSUS
Charles Woolard 10001 - 10001

MARRIAGES (RHEA)
Charles Woolard or Woollard to Elizabeth Conner, 1 Dec 1836 (4 Dec), A.G. Wright JP, James Roddy Bm (AR) [1850 Hamilton Census: Charles Wollard 34, Ellen 31, John 12, James 8, Martha 5, Rufus 3, Charles 8/12]

- - - - - - - - - - - - -

WOOLAVER

1840 MEIGS CENSUS
George Woolaver 21001 - 01001 p. 232

- - - - - - - - - - - - -

WORLEY / WORLY

TAXES (RHEA)
1808 (John Henry's List): George Worley 1 WP, 500a
1840 MEIGS CENSUS
John Worly 20001 - 020001 p. 240
MARRIAGES (RHEA)
Edmund Worley to Susan E. Land, 13 Sept 1833, William K. Gray Bm (A)
Nancy Worley to William Hill q.v.
MISCELLANEOUS (RHEA)
George Worley: On first Grand Jury, 1808

WORMAN

MARRIAGES (RHEA)
Anne Worman to Thomas Holloway q.v.
MISCELLANEOUS (RHEA)
Joseph Worman: Bondsman for Thomas Holloway, 1833

WORTHINGTON

MARRIAGES (RHEA)
Levi Worthington to Maria Kennedy, 9 Dec 1833 (10 Dec), B. Wallace MG, William Kennedy Bm (AR)

WRIGHT / RIGHT

1830 RHEA CENSUS
Jimimah Wright 0 - 000101 p. 364
1840 RHEA CENSUS
A. G. Wright 001101 - 001001
1850 RHEA CENSUS
Abraham G. Wright 47 (Farmer), Ann 46, William T.G. 25 (Farmer), James M. 24 (Farmer), Caroline MAJORS 27, Mariah 35, Thomas DEAN 15 p. 534-7
1850 MEIGS CENSUS
William R. Wright 22 (Farmer), Lucinda 27 (Ky), William M. 10 p. 763-390 [Wm R. Wright married Lucy More on 6 Apr 1844 in McMinn County]
MARRIAGES (RHEA)
Jemimah Wright to James Wilson q.v.
Minerva Right to Robert Elder q.v.
Sarah Jane Wright to Masterson Mitchell q.v.
MISCELLANEOUS (RHEA)
Abraham G. Wright: Bm for Flemming H. Fulton, 1831
" " " JP or MG 1836, 1839-41, 1849
Charles Wright: Bondsman for Joseph Edington, 1811
Jeremiah Wright: Hiwassee District, Pinhook Ferry area

WROE

1850 RHEA CENSUS
Angeline Wroe 20: see S. Evens
MARRIAGES (RHEA)
Thomas C. Wroe to Mary Evans, 4 May 1829 (6 May), James A. Darwin JP, James Stewart Bm (AR)
MARRIAGES (MEIGS)
Jane F. Wroe to Jesse C. Derrick q.v.

WYATT / WIAT / WIATT / WIETT

TAXES (RHEA)
1823 (Capt. Wilson's Co.): Moses Wiat 1 WP
1830 RHEA CENSUS
John Wiatt 0001101 - 1120001 p. 361
Moses Wiett 01001 - 20001 p. 355
1850 RHEA CENSUS
John Wyatt 43 (Cabnetmaker), Amelia 43, Nancy A. WOODBY 12, Elizabeth MILLICAN 16 p. 613-454
MARRIAGES (RHEA)
Moses Wyatt to Polly Atchley, 30 Dec 1820, James Prentice Bm (A)
MISCELLANEOUS (RHEA)
Elijah Wyatt: Hiwassee District, Moore's Chapel area
John Wyott: JP 1848-50

WYLER

1830 RHEA CENSUS
Robert Wyler 00001 - 00001 p. 355

WYTHAM

1830 RHEA CENSUS
Elizabeth Wytham 0111 - 00110001 p. 353

YATES / YEATES

1830 RHEA CENSUS
John Yates 201001 - 21001 p. 379
1850 RHEA CENSUS
Embeistow Yates 26 (Unk)(Farmer), Amy 24 p. 542-58
MARRIAGES (RHEA)
John Yeates or Yates to Susan Luterall or Litterell, 7 Jan 1829 (25 Jan), Matthew Hubbert JP, William Litterall Bm (AR)
Martha Yates to Nathaniel Marlow q.v.
MISCELLANEOUS (RHEA)
John Yates: Cherokee Removal muster roll, 1836

YONAS / YOONISS

MARRIAGES (RHEA)
Nancy Yooniss to Joseph McClure q.v.
MARRIAGES (MEIGS)
Nancy Yonas to Bartly Lawson q.v.
Rebecca Yonas to John Owens q.v.

YORK

TAXES (RHEA)
1823 (Capt. Piper's Co.) Josiah York 1 WP
Thomas York 1 WP
MARRIAGES (RHEA)
Thomas York to Sally Looney, 11 May 1811, Joseph Lacey Bm (A)
MISCELLANEOUS (RHEA)
Thomas York: Bondsman for Lorenzo D. Rush, 1826

- - - - - - - - - - - - -

YOUNG

1840 MEIGS CENSUS
Carter Young 10001 - 00001 p. 225
John Young 011110001 - 0010101 p. 225
Reuben Young 10001 - 11011 p. 225
1850 RHEA CENSUS
James R. Young 23: see William Thompson
William B. Young 26 (Ky)(Blacksmith), Jane 20, James C. J. 2 p. 589-357
1850 MEIGS CENSUS
Absolem Young 28 (Farmer), Harriet 29, Nancy Ann 4, Louinda Jane 1 p. 719-46
Carter Young 30 (Farmer), Margaret 30, James E. 11, Malinda E. 6, Rhodah Jane 3, Eliza C. 1, Mary Ann 21 p. 719-47
John Young 73 (Va)(Farmer), Eliza 30, Rufus 24 (Farmer), Mary 9 p. 719-45
Thomas Young 20 (Farmer), Margaret 21, Cyntha Jane 0 p. 769-439
William Young 24 (Va)(Farmer), Margaret Jane 22, Elizabeth F. 4, Aron C. 2 p. 750-301
William J. Young 23, Darcus E. 18 p. 719-49
MARRIAGES (RHEA)
James Young to Holly E. Thompson, 30 Dec 1850 (same), John O. Torbett JP (R)
John Young to Mildry Waldren, 24 Jan 1810, Jesse Roddye Bm (A)
John R. Young to Nancy Tollet, 5 May 1847 (same), Noah Haggart MG (R)
Thomas Young to Mary Leonard, 26 Feb 1836, Reuben Young Bm (A)
William B. Young to Margarett J. Thompson, 23 Sept 1847 (24 Sept), Charles Cox JP (R)
MARRIAGES (MEIGS)
Carter Young to Peggy Grissum, 26 Sept 1838 (27 Sept), Wilford Rickner JP, Reuben Young Bm
Eliza Jane Young to William Collins q.v.
John Young to Eliza Emeline Helton, 7 Dec 1847 (9 Dec), Jesse Grisham JP
Thomas Young to Margarett Mariah Carrell, 20 Oct 1849 (21 Oct), Thomas Hunter JP
W. J. Young to Larky Elkin, 1 Aug 1850, Jesse Grisham Sur
MISCELLANEOUS (RHEA)
James M. Young: Lot 1, Town of Washington, 1812
Reuben Young: Bondsman for Thomas Young, 1836
MISCELLANEOUS (MEIGS)
William B. Young: Private, Mexican War

- - - - - - - - - - - - -

ZEIGLER / ZIGLER

TAXES (RHEA)
1823 (Capt. Smith's Co.): William Zeigler 1 WP
1850 MEIGS CENSUS
Jacob Zigler 32 (Va)(Farmer) p. 754-332
William F. Zigler 34 (Va)(Farmer), Delilah 32, Martha C. 11, Jacob 8, William 6, Rebecca 3, John 1 p. 753-331
MISCELLANEOUS (MEIGS)
Jacob F. Zeigler: 1st Sgt., Mexican War
William Zeigler: Member, Goodfield Baptist Church of Christ, 1827

- - - - - - - - - - - - -

REFERENCES

ALLEN, Penelope J.
1932 Marriage Records, Rhea County, 1808-1845. Typed copy in Chattanooga Public Library [transcribed from original bonds in Barnes Collection]

ALLEN, V. C.
1940 "Rhea and Meigs Counties in the Confederate War" in: ***Records of Rhea*** by T.J. Campbell

BOYER, Reba Bayless
1964 ***Marriage Records of McMinn County, Tennessee, 1820-1870.***

CAMPBELL, Thomas J.
1940 ***Records of Rhea: A Condensed County History.*** Rhea Publishing Company, Dayton, Tennessee

CURTIS, Mary Barnett
"The Rhea County, Tennessee, 1808 Tax List and 1819 Tax List" in: ***Early East Tennessee Tax Lists.*** Arrow Printing Company, Ft. Worth, Texas.

HUTCHERSON, Willis, and Marilyn McCluen
1973 ***Marriage Records of Roane County, Tennessee, 1801-1855.***

LILLARD, Stewart
1975 ***Meigs County, Tennessee.*** University Press, The University of the South, Sewannee, Tennessee.

MEIGS COUNTY
---- ***Marrige Records of Meigs County***: Vol. I, 1838-1846, and Vol. II, 1846-1857 (the latter copied from licenses and bonds, records destroyed by fire of 1902). Typed copy in McClung Room, Knoxville Public Library.
---- ***Marriage Records***: Microfilm of Courthouse records obtained from Tennessee State Archives, Nashville.
---- ***Report of County Commissioners, 1836-1840.*** Typed copy in McClung Room, Knoxville Public Library (Historical Records Project No. 65-44-1478).

RHEA COUNTY
---- ***Marriage Records of Rhea County.*** Microfilm of Courthouse records obtained from Tennessee State Archives, Nashville.
---- ***Minutes of the Commissioners of the Town of Washington, Rhea County, Tennessee, 1812-1833*** (incomplete). Typed copy in Chattanooga Public Library (donated by David H. Gray, October, 1978)

SISTLER, Byron and Barbara Sistler
1974 ***1850 Census Tennessee.*** Vol. 1 - Vol. 8. Evanston, Illinois.

THORNTON, Mable H.
1964 "Rhea County, Tennessee, 1823 Tax List" in: ***Ansearchin News***, Vol. XI, No. 1, pp. 9-20.

U.S. BUREAU OF THE CENSUS
1830 ***Tennessee Population Schedule, Rhea County.*** Microfilm M 19-175
1840 ***Tennessee Population Schedule, Meigs County.*** Microfilm M 704-528
1840 ***Tennessee Population Schedule, Rhea County.*** Microfilm M 704-535
1850 ***Tennessee Population Schedule, Meigs County.*** Microfilm M 432-890
1850 ***Tennessee Population Schedule, Rhea County.*** Microfilm M 432-893

WATERHOUSE, Carmck
1974 ***Certain Topics on the Ingham, Waterhouse, and Allied Families.*** Knoxville, Tennessee.

APPENDIX A

HEADS OF HOUSEHOLD ON 1850 CENSUS

RHEA COUNTY

The 1850 Rhea County census was recorded in eight Districts and the Town of Washington (in District 6). The household numbers do not always run consecutively; therefore, the list below will follow the original listing by districts and page numbers (followed by the household number). In most cases, one or more blnk pages were left between the districts.

DISTRICT 1

533- 1 James Holloway
533- 2 Richard Walker
533- 3 William D. Ellison
533- 4 Franklin Waterhouse
533- 5 William S. Johnson
533- 6 James Robison
534- 7 Abraham G. Wright
534- 8 Rebecca Keywood
534- 9 Riley Karsey
534- 10 Jesse P. Thompson
534- 11 John L. Thompson
534- 12 William Majors
534- 13 Allison Howard
535- 14 David M. Roddy
535- 15 Major Holloway
535- 16 Gilbert Read
535- 17 John Lemmons
535- 18 Thomas Lemmons
536- 19 William J. Meeks
536- 20 William Fullington
536- 21 Elijah Brewer
536- 22 Pleasant Monday
536- 23 Alexander Smith
536- 24 James H. Hays
536- 25 Lorenzo D. Harris
536- 26 William Gipson
536- 27 James Hays
537- 28 Thomas Harris
537- 29 Francis Monday
537- 30 Jane Hill
537- 31 Hiram Mathes
537- 32 Moses C.R. Thompson
537- 33 Milton Hammons
538- 34 Elizabeth Harris
538- 35 Margaret Greenler
538- 36 W.O.T. Harris
538- 37 Merril Brady
538- 38 Moses Thompson
538- 39 John McClendon
539- 40 John Garrison
539- 41 John Dunlap
539- 42 Lavina Scott
539- 43 William Lemmons
539- 44 John Boyd
540- 45 Austin Evans
540- 46 Isaac Morris
540- 47 Rufus M. Crews
540- 48 John F. Ford
540- 49 William Floyd
540- 50 David G. Scraggins
541- 51 Benjamin Reese
541- 52 Henry Cleek
541- 53 James Stutts
541- 54 Jacob Garrison
541- 55 Azariah Barton
541- 56 John Robeson
542- 57 Elcany Hammons
542- 58 Embislow Yates
542- 59 Elias Majors
542- 60 Larkin Majors
542- 61 Elizabeth Solomon
542- 62 Elizabeth Long
542- 63 Mary Bean
542- 64 Dawson Harris
543- 65 Dralow Rozier
543- 66 George W. Short
543- 67 Isaac Campbell
543- 68 John Holloway
543- 69 Stephen Vollo
544- 70 Henry Lowry
544- 71 William Gipson
544- 72 Josiah Hughs
544- 73 S.T. Whittenburg
544- 74 Allen Lemmons
544- 75 Andrew Bolinger
544- 76 William Lowry
545- 77 John A. Thompson
545- 78 Asa Newport
545- 79 Isaac P. Cline
545- 80 Frederick Bolinger
545- 81 Joel Dodson
545- 82 John C. Matlock
545- 83 Thomas Dodson
545- 84 William Thomas
546- 85 Jesse Roddy
546- 86 Margaret Roddy
546- 87 George Bowls
546- 88 Adam Harner
547- 89 Harvey Sanders
547- 90 Landon Rector
547- 91 David Roser
547- 92 David J. McAlpin
547- 93 John Walker
547- 94 Starling Holloway
547- 95 Pleasant Hollaway
547- 96 Joseph Walker
548- 97 Shiloh Crew
548- 98 James Fletcher
548- 99 Edmund Rose
548-100 Alexander Fletcher
548-101 Snelson Roberts
548-102 Thomas E. Ellison
548-103 Samuel Robeson
548-104 Elijah Farmer
549-105 Benjamin Bingham
549-106 William Fords
549-107 Jefferson Ingle
549-108 John Harrison
549-109 Garrett Garrison
549-110 Nathaniel Gillum
549-111 Joseph Reese
550-112 William A. Thompson
550-113 Pleasant Majors
550-114 John Rogers
550-115 James Majors
550-116 John L. Marsh

DISTRICT 2 (10 Sept 1850)

553-117 Tinsley Rhodes
553-118 Hesekiah Hale
553-119 Charles Lewis
553-120 Absalum S. Thompson
553-121 Joseph Gimsley
553-122 Francinah Mitchell
553-123 Calvin G. Dudley
554-124 William Bingham
554-125 John Grimsley
554-126 James I. Cash
554-127 Baty Breeding
554-128 John S. Thompson
554-129 Thomas Thompson
555-130 Edward Pyott
555-131 Aaron Rhea
555-132 Edward E. Wasson
555-133 Susan Mahaffy
555-134 William Hickey
555-135 Alexander McAlpin
556-136 William H. Stockton
556-137 Nile M. Broyles
556-138 Dennis McClendon
556-139 Thomas Breeding
556-140 Stephen Breeding
556-141 Hardy Cox
556-142 Charles Brady
557-143 Archibald D. Paul
557-144 Abraham Farmer

557-145 Burrell Boxley
557-146 Hesekiah McPherson
557-147 Sarah Rector
557-148 Eli Parker
558-149 Micajah Clack
558-150 Thomas Miller
558-151 James J. Floyd
558-152 William R. Miller
558-153 Robbin Miller
558-154 William Monday
558-155 Nathaniel Dodson
559-156 Archibald McCaleb
559-157 Polly Ritchie
559-158 David Foust
559-159 Andrew Emery
559-160 George W. Fullington
560-161 Samuel Dotson
560-162 Thomas J. Gillespie
560-163 David E. Gillespie
560-164 Andrew McCaleb
560-165 Samuel Allen
560-166 Thomas Bingham
560-167 William Fullington
560-168 David Hanks
560-169 Abraham Embree
560-170 James Smith
560-171 Mary Butler
560-172 Andrew J. McCuiston
561-173 Spencer J. Tedder
561-174 John Johnson
561-175 Sarah McCoy
561-176 Richard Smith
561-177 Alfred Brackins
561-178 Farley Brady
562-179 Addison C. Day

DISTRICT 3 (18 Sept 1850)

565-180 Thomas Ault
565-181 Andrew J. Scrogins
565-182 Doctor F. Scroggins
565-183 Henry Minick
565-184 Deaialthea W. Hornsby
565-185 Alexander Smith
565-186 John McAlpin
565-187 John S. Ramsey
565-188 Andrew Lowe
566-189 James Warren
566-190 Robert Warren
566-191 John Ford
566-192 Mary Harwood
566-193 Thomas J. Harwood
566-194 William Watson
566-195 Claudius Hale
567-196 George Hale
567-197 James Rhea
567-198 Edward E. Jones
567-199 William Dotson
567-200 Rufus M. Harwood
567-201 Esther Blye
567-202 Mary Blye
567-203 William T. Foust
568-204 Warner E. Colville
568-205 William M. Clack
568-206 William R. Vickry
568-207 Jonathan Chattean
568-208 Jesse Harwood
568-209 Elijah Snodgrass
568-210 George M. Snodgrass
568-211 Henry Eaton
568-212 Nathan Chamberlin
569-213 Joshua Good
569-214 Martha Clack
569-215 John Owens
569-216 Hiram Johnson
569-217 Thomas J. Kerr
569-218 Thornton J. Creed
569-219 John Chapman
570-220 Stephen D. Smith
570-221 Josiah Eaton
570-222 John C. Price
570-223 Fountain Dotson
570-224 Anderson Tiner
570-225 Nancy Martin
570-226 John Jolly
570-227 Samuel Moore
571-228 George J. Stults
571-229 George W. Barnett
571-230 Thomas Williams
571-231 Thomas Moulton
571-232 Peter Minick
571-233 Willie H. Cunningham
572-234 Elizabeth Henry
572-235 Susannah Ault
572-236 Aldridge Clifton
572-237 Pleasant Rhea
572-238 David Robison
572-239 George Henry
572-240 Solomon Henry
573-241 Hesekiah Robison
573-242 Isaabella Kennedy
573-243 Nimrod Moore
573-244 Wright Smith
573-245 Elizabeth Gear
573-246 Hyram Henry
574-247 William Collins
574-248 Alfred Collins
574-249 William Campbell
574-250 William F. Smith
574-251 Pincney Collins
574-252 Samuel Wilkey
574-253 James Deatherage
574-254 Ishner Lowry
574-255 Adam Ahart
575-256 John Brown
575-257 Daniel Carr
575-258 William W. Cash
575-259 Margaret Hartley
575-260 James Wilson
576-261 Bailey Clifton
576-262 John Compton
576-263 Zachariah Compton
576-264 Mary Leuty
576-265 Wright Smith

DISTRICT 4

577-266 John Essex
577-267 James Essex
577-268 Isaac Essex
577-269 Joshua Collins
577-270 John Ferguson
577-271 Peter W. Miller
577-272 Uriah Thompson
578-273 Henry McFall
578-274 Mary Presley
578-275 Daniel McFalls
578-276 Jacob L. Wassum
578-277 Andrew J. Collins
578-278 Jesse Eaton
578-279 Calvin R. McFall
578-280 Mary Houpt
579-281 Sanders D. Broyles
579-282 Abigail Ferguson
579-283 Nicholas Keith
579-284 Sarah B. Torbett
579-285 Mary West
579-286 Jonathan McCully
580-287 Charles W. Ault
580-288 Joseph Carr
580-289 John O. Torbet
580-290 Yancy Loy
580-291 William Essex
580-292 Henry H. Miller
580-293 John Winfrey
581-294 Andrew Wyrick
581-295 Nancy Collins
581-296 Kimbro Collins
581-297 Robert Ferguson
581-298 Levi W. Ferguson
581-299 Samuel B. Ferguson
581-300 Shadrack Hays
581-301 Joseph Garrison
581-302 Elijah Barton
582-303 Allen H. McFall
582-304 Jacob Garrison
582-305 Henry Thurman
582-306 William C. Price
582-305 William H. Thurman
582-307 James D. McFall
582-308 John Ellison
582-309 William Morgan
582-310 Abraham Howard
582-311 Addison Locke
583-312 Thomas C. Darwin
583-313 Samuel Hollaway
583-314 Joseph P. Hollaway
583-315 Samuel Dudley
583-316 John Thompson
583-317 Elizabeth Casy
584-318 Wesley Casy
584-319 Lindsey McCary
584-320 Pryor Barton
584-321 Charles Woodward
584-322 Daniel Broyles
584-323 Anthony Robison
584-324 Permelia Robeson
584-325 Anthony Logan
585-326 Harvey Robeson

585-327 John Bonham
585-328 John Howard
585-329 Agness Peters
585-330 Isaac S. Binyon
585-331 Alfred Marsh
585-332 Thomas R. Holland
586-333 Samuel Frazier
586-334 Nancy Smith
586-335 Sibella Godsbehere
586-336 Henderson Fisher
586-337 Thomas Godsbehere
586-338 Ralph S. Whittenburg
586-339 Sarah Robison
586-340 Alexander T. Patterson
587-341 William W. Rose
587-342 Samuel Whittenburg
587-343 Henry Whittenburg
587-344 John Whittenburg
587-345 William Whittenburg
587-346 Christopher I. Whittenburg
588-347 James F. Morrison
588-348 David Malone
588-349 John Wheeler
588-350 James Mathis
588-351 Pleasant M. Purser
588-352 James M. Thompson
588-353 James C. Ferguson
588-354 William T. Gass
588-355 Henry Collins
589-356 Russel Dunkin
589-357 William B. Young
589-358 Mary Mason

DISTRICT 5 (10 Oct 1850)

593-359 Alfred Vicky
599-360 James Purser
593-361 James M. Mitchell
593-362 William Compton
593-363 Thomas Dyal
593-364 William Gannaway
593-365 William K. Gonerway
593-366 John F. Gonerway
594-367 James P. Collins
594-368 William Thompson
594-369 Jesse Rector
594-370 Noah Fisher
594-371 Charles N. Fisher
594-372 Eli Coulter
594-373 Dudley Dismany
595-374 James Mathis
595-375 Harvey Millican
595-376 Michael Reynolds
595-377 Garlington Bramlett
595-378 [number skipped]
596-379 Orville Paine
596-380 Cornelius Broyles
596-381 John Wood
596-382 James Stuart
596-383 Samuel Stuart
596-384 James R. Walker
597-385 Francis Stuart
597-386 Jacob Byerley
597-387 John Day
597-388 James F. Ladd
597-389 Thomas F. Barnett
597-390 William H. Bradley
598-391 William Ives
598-392 Joseph I. Travis
598-393 Nicholas Nanny
598-394 James T. Nanny
598-395 William Rumfeld
598-396 Sarah Coulston
598-397 John Usry
599-398 Wilson Kilgore
599-399 Pleasant Masener
599-400 James M. Cunningham
599-401 Thomas Haws
599-402 John W. Thompson
599-403 James A. Darwin
599-404 Micajah Howerton
599-405 William H. Bell
600-406 Joseph Hicks
600-407 James Pearce
600-408 James H. Pass
600-409 Benjamin Allen
600-410 Moses R. Thompson
600-411 Joseph A. Broyles
600-412 Catharine Mathis
601-413 James R. Barnett
601-414 Jeffrey West
601-415 Polly Bingham
601-416 Amos Carr
601-417 Johnson Edgeing
601-418 William R. McCarter
601-419 Jane Coulter
601-420 Robert Mitchell
602-682 Elizabeth Dunn
602-683 Josiah Harden
602-684 James M. Trentham
602-685 Berryman G. Mathis

DISTRICT 6

603-421 Charles Cox
603-422 Adam Hasler
603-423 Robert C. Montgomery
603-424 Margaret Barnett
603-442 James C. Ryan
603-443 Mary Randolph
603-444 Phillip T. Rawlings
603-461 William T. Tomison
603-462 Albert W. Beddo
603-463 William N. Merriott
604-464 Newton J. Edmonds
604-465 Thomas Ives
604-466 James Hooper
604-467 John F. Wilhite
604-468 James Mayo
605-469 Audley P. Caldwell
605-470 Edward G. Childers
605-471 Benjamin Crow
605-472 Harvey Roddy
605-473 John Gearing
606-474 David Gearing
606-475 Allen Holland
606-476 John Holland
606-477 John A. Snotgrass
606-478 William H. Snotgrass
606-479 Alfred Thurman
607-480 Penelope Edmonds
607-481 John Gunter
607-482 Mary Eves
607-483 James H. Locke
607-484 James O. Jones
607-485 James A. McNutt
607-486 John Ives
607-487 Malinda Childers
608-488 Michel Hassler
608-489 Elijah Butram
608-490 Ruth Frazier
608-491 [see 614-491]
608-492 Bailey Minick
608-493 Newton Locke
608-494 Edmund Bean
608-495 Franklin Locke
608-496 Mariah Clawson
608-497 William Smith
608-498 George Minick
608-499 William Thompson
609-500 Russell Thompson

TOWN OF WASHINGTON

611-425 Robert N. Gillespie
611-426 Mercy Stuart
611-427 Joseph T. Frisby
611-428 William Cowan
611-429 John W. Chambers
611-430 Joseph S. Evens
611-431 John S. Evens
612-432 John H. Colville
612-433 James W. Gillespie
612-434 Albion E. Smith
612-435 Pitser M. Bailey
612-436 Jacob Kelly
612-437 John Hoyle
612-438 Adam Rawlings
612-439 Clabourn Washam
612-440 William T. Slater
612-441 Richard Waterhouse
613-445 John D. Chattin
613-446 Daniel J. Rawlings
613-447 Rufus B. Sherley
613-448 John B. Murphy
613-449 Permelia J. Peterson
613-450 Joseph Peterson
613-451 William Guinn
613-452 Luisa N. Harrison
613-453 Robert Lankford
613-454 John Wyatt
613-455 Nathaniel Smith
613-456 Mary A. Killough
614-457 Cassa Walker
614-458 Nancy Smith
614-459 Daniel Houston
614-460 Darius Waterhouse
614-491 David Leuty

DISTRICT 7

615-501 Thomas Whaley
615-502 McCassey Largen
615-503 James A. Mitchell
615-504 John Crawford
615-505 Levi Griffith
615-506 Henry Fisher
615-507 Jacob George
615-508 Thomas Knight
616-509 Stephen Spence
616-510 Anoneseeus Fondren
616-511 John Spence
616-512 Valentine Allen
616-513 Thomas M. Bolen
616-514 Hubbard Y. Cate
617-515 Thomas Knight
617-516 Jefferson Hale
617-517 John Campbell
617-518 George W. Horner
617-519 Beriah Frazier
617-520 Abner W. Frazier
617-521 William S. Dotson
617-522 James M. Dotson
617-523 Mathew Shubird
617-524 Doctor W. Horner
618-525 John Rumfeld
618-526 Hannah M. Frazier
618-527 George H. Strebeck
618-528 Thomas George
618-529 John George
618-530 Thomas O. George
618-531 Andrew Knight
618-532 Elizabeth Mulvany
618-533 John Spence
618-534 David Singleton
619-535 James M. Hale
619-536 Delany Freisby
619-537 Ritter Webb
619-538 William J. Ferrel
619-539 Hiley Rhodes
619-540 John Bolen
619-541 John W. Hughes
620-542 Harris Ryan
620-543 James F. Bolen
620-544 Jonathan Bandy
620-545 Andrew J. Covington
620-546 Thomas Conley
620-547 Jane McConney
620-548 Jane Weeks
621-549 Jacob Foust
621-550 Solomon Cate
621-551 James L. Perrigin
621-552 Joseph H. French
621-553 Toliver Sexton
621-554 Elijah McGuire
621-555 Byrd Walker
622-556 Nancy Lauderdale
622-557 Daniel Hodges
622-558 William McDonald
622-559 Margaret Jones
622-560 James Lea
622-561 Lewis Morgan
622-562 Elias Morgan
622-563 Oliver Seal
622-564 Elihu McKinney
623-565 Benjamin O'Kelly
623-566 James D. Allison
623-567 John M. Ferguson
623-568 Darcus Taylor
623-569 James Mitchell
623-570 Lyda Allison
624-571 Benjamin Smith
624-572 John Jewell
624-573 Bryant McDonald
624-574 Owin David
624-575 Washington Morgan
624-576 Thomas Jack
624-577 John H. Templeton
625-578 William B. Johnson
625-579 John Nash
625-580 John Whaley
625-581 David Ragsdale
625-582 Thomas Allison
626-583 John Jack
626-584 Thomas Largen
626-585 Elijah Largen
626-586 [skipped]

DISTRICT 8

627-587 [see 609-587]
627-588 Andrew Brittin
627-589 Andrew J. Bryson
627-590 Abraham Bryson
627-591 Elizabeth Sexton
627-592 Holla Sexton
627-593 William Sims
627-594 Elijah S. Rudd
627-595 Isaac M. Teague
627-596 John C. Davis
627-597 William C. Hollins
627-598 Thomas C. Johnson
628-599 James J. Able
628-600 Cain Able
628-601 James R. Able
628-602 C. Whitehouse Able
628-603 Eliza Dane
628-604 Francis O'Kelly
629-605 Phillip T. Foust
629-606 James J. Kelly
629-607 Charles D. Bean
629-608 John Foote
629-609 James Bradbury
629-610 James Montgomery
630-611 Robert P. Able
630-612 Stephen Gray
630-613 Catharine Martin
630-614 Elias Hickman
630-615 Margaret Munsey
630-616 Margaret Pearce
630-617 John Baker
631-618 Thomas Davis
631-619 Thomas Sims
631-620 Clever Shelton
631-621 Jefferson Moore
631-622 Alfred Hutcheson
631-623 Gillum Presly
631-624 William R. Presly
631-625 John Hughs
632-626 William Hughs
632-627 William Clingham
632-628 Alexander Hickman
632-629 Henry Hickman
632-630 William Martin
632-631 Elijah Norris
632-632 Jack Durham
632-633 Simon McCarroll
633-634 William McCarroll
633-635 Charles McCarroll
633-636 John W. Foust
633-637 Joseph McDonald
633-638 Robert Simpson
633-639 Elisha Moore
633-640 Samuel E. Foust
633-641 Charles Reevely
633-642 Anderson Jones
633-643 William Byce
634-644 Robert W. Byce
634-645 Phillip Foust
634-646 Emeline Gothard
634-647 John Moore
634-648 Allen Gothard
634-649 Jack Foust
634-650 Charles Morgan
635-651 Martin Morgan
635-652 Calvin Morgan
635-653 John C. Gothard
635-654 George Gothard
635-655 John Burwick
635-656 Norris Burwick
635-657 William Morgan
635-658 George W. Brown
636-659 John Harvey
636-660 Joshua S. Green
636-661 William A. Green
636-662 Henry Griffith
636-663 Andrew Campbell
636-664 Nichademus Marlow
636-665 Abner Hughs
637-666 Isaac S. Hutcheson
637-667 Thomas Smith
637-668 John Gray
637-669 David Ward
637-670 William Nash
637-671 Thomas Russ
637-672 Margaret Foster
638-673 Daniel Plumlee
638-674 Pleasant Snow
638-675 David Vanhoy
638-676 Passen M. Pickett
638-677 Washington Morgan
638-678 Lewis Morgan
639-679 Joshua I. Riddle
639-680 John Knight
639-681 William D. Everett
-682
through
-685 [see 602-682 through
602-685

APPENDIX B

HEADS OF HOUSEHOLD ON 1850 CENSUS

MEIGS COUNTY

Unlike the 1850 Rhea County Census, the enumerator for Meigs County did not list the citizens by districts. Based on the names, the list begins in the southern part of the County and ends with the northern portion.

713- 1 Avery Hannah
713- 2 Mary Miller
713- 3 Thomas Miller
713- 4 Nicholas Woody
713- 5 Thomas Woody
713- 6 George W. Allison
713- 7 Stephen Farris
713- 8 George Kincannon
713- 9 Emanuel Lipford
714- 10 Jane Rue
714- 11 Samuel O. Wood
714- 12 John Breedwell
714- 13 Mary Prewet
714- 14 Lydia Romines
714- 15 Solomon Romines
714- 16 Thomas Charles Tillary
714- 17 John F. Harvy
715- 18 William Brackett
715- 19 Mary Gilbreth
715- 20 Morgan Brackett
715- 21 Thomas Brandon
715- 22 Judah Lawson
715- 23 Zadack Lawson
715- 24 William Boucher
716- 25 Elisha Boucher
716- 26 John T. Miloway
716- 27 Austin Shiflet
716- 28 John King
716- 29 Joshua E. King
716- 30 Edward H. Brown
716- 31 Zachariah Ambers
717- 32 Absolem Sparkes
717- 33 William Grisham
717- 34 Drury Jones
717- 35 John Dunning
717- 36 Thomas Humphrey
717- 37 Mahala McDuffee
717- 38 William Webb
718- 39 Joseph Cofer
718- 40 James T. Cofer
718- 41 John Cofer
718- 42 Thomas Brown
718- 43 H. Davis
718- 44 Enoch Talant
719- 45 John Young
719- 46 Absolem Young
719- 47 Carter Young
719- 48 Solomon Smallen
719- 49 William J. Young
719- 50 Ervin Grisham
719- 51 Jesse Grisham
720- 52 George Francisco
720- 53 John A. Francisco
720- 54 Jacob Good
720- 55 Wiley Lewis
720- 56 C. T. Johnson
720- 57 William Hutcherson
720- 58 William Wood
720- 59 David Gregory
721- 60 George Gregory
721- 61 Joseph Morrison
721- 62 Jacob Turner
721- 63 John Hall
721- 64 John Stout
721- 65 Richard M. Johnson
721- 66 Ruth Williams
722- 67 Joseph J. Johnston
722- 68 John N. Witt
722- 69 John Campbell
722- 70 James W. Campbell
722- 71 Isaac McIntuff
722- 72 Richard Simpson
722- 73 Marshall M. Webb
722- 74 Mary Craighead
722- 75 Davis Predy
722- 76 Nancy McDowell
723- 77 Malinda Power
723- 78 Elizabeth Corvin
723- 79 Henry Coulter
723- 80 William Casey
723- 81 William H. Hunter
723- 82 Samuel Hunter
723- 83 Nicholas Frost
723- 84 Andrew J. Seaborn
723- 85 Martin Riggs
723- 86 John McAnally
723- 87 James E. Collins
724- 88 J. H. W. Fowler
724- 89 George Childres
724- 90 John Sebourn
724- 91 William Hunter
724- 92 David Lewis
724- 93 George M. Wilson
725- 94 Aqualla Farmer
725- 95 John B. Eldridge
725- 96 Elias Lane
725- 97 Pleasant M. Porter
725- 98 Isaac McDowell
725- 99 Mary Price
725-100 George W. Roberts
725-101 Easterly Curton
726-102 Hugh Baker
726-103 Richard Hobbs
726-104 Bob Martin
726-105 Elizabeth Pearce
726-106 Samuel Gamble
726-107 Jacob Gross
726-108 Darcus Mathis
726-109 Jehue McClanahan
726-110 Mason McClanahan
727-111 Josiah Lock
727-112 H. W. Horn
727-113 Joseph Lock
727-114 M. C. Porter
727-115 W. S. Miller
727-116 Mahala Shipley
727-117 Jesse Lock
728-118 Thomas Reynolds
728-119 Lesley Myres
728-120 Christopher Myers
728-121 Elza Lunsford
728-122 Henry Lunsford
728-123 William Micles
728-124 Benjamin Johnston
729-125 Jacob Olinger
729-126 James Doughty
729-127 Andrew Fox
729-128 Sarah Ramsey
729-129 James Fox
729-130 Zachariah Martin
730-131 Burton Holman or Halman
730-132 Thomas Walker
730-133 Louis Browder
730-134 Thomas Edmonson
730-135 William Potter
730-136 Thomas Mitts
731-137 Andrew Ladd
731-138 George R. Ladd
731-139 William Rigg
731-140 Sarah Pettitt
731-141 Richard Rice
731-142 John Gamble
731-143 Rhoda Lock
732-144 Isaac G. Tipton
732-145 Henry Munger
732-146 Samuel Goforth
732-147 Wilie O. Martin
732-148 Eliza Martin
732-149 Luther B. Cox
732-150 Ruth Cox
732-151 Marideth Cox
732-152 Jane Martin
732-153 Mary Falls
732-154 Elgin Brightwell
733 Elizabeth Wilson
733-155 Wiley O. Wilson

733-156 Joseph Stewart
733-157 Nancy Harverson
733-158 Rufus Harverson
733-159 Johnes or James Johns
733-160 Isaac Cookson
733-161 Sanford Askins
733-162 Elisha Moore
733-163 William L. Armstrong
733-164 Robert West
734-165 George Gross
734-166 Dempsey Sykes
734-167 Mary Snodgrass
734-168 Newton Lawson
734-169 Henry Askins
734-170 James A. Bowman
734-171 Nancy Stanly
735-172 Edward R. Chattin
735-173 Stephen J. Godsey
735-174 John Chattin
735-175 Ezekel T. Sullivan
735-176 Martin Wade
735-177 Henry M. Cinningham
735-178 Wesley Cranmore
735-179 William Sullivan
736-180 Sarah Oldham
736-181 Eli Corvin
736-182 Philo Corvin
736-183 James Corvin
736-184 William Gibbons
736-185 Thomas Corvan
736-186 Elijah Clingan
736-187 Lewis Moore
736-188 William J. Dodson
736-189 William J. Wilson
736-190 William Cate
736-191 George Shamblin
737-192 A. B. Shamblin
737-193 John W. Eaton
737-194 John Matherly
737-195 John Moore
737-196 Nancy Singletian
737-197 Berry Mooreland
737-198 Duncan Corvin
738-199 David Fox
738-200 David Johns
738-201 Grimes Bankston
738-202 James Davis
738-203 Nancy Myres
738-204 Abigail Moore
738-205 William Johns
739-206 John Singleton
739-207 Scott Powel
739-208 Samuel Lockmiller
739-209 John Toliver
739-210 John Powel
739-211 James Crew
740-212 Horatio Lennard
740-213 Robert Adams
740-214 James A. R. Cowan
740-215 Elizabeth Cowan
740-216 William Collins
740-217 Reuben C. Collins
740-218 Robert Moore
740-219 Abner Myers
740-220 William B. Russell
740-221 Charles Gamble
740-222 John H. Cowan
741-223 Jacob Womack
741-224 Fanny Smith
741-225 Joshua Gwin
741-226 William Jones
741-227 Henry Norman
741-228 Julian Breedwell
741-229 Calvin Atkinson
741-230 William Myres
742-231 Farley Reid
742-232 Sophia Starnes
742-233 Josiah Houser Jr.
742-234 James Houser
742-235 John Davis
742-236 Luvana Stewart
742-237 Clinton Norman
743-238 Nicholas Gibbins [Givens]
743-239 Benjamin F. McKinsey
743-240 Eldred Grubb
743-241 Francis M. Sewel
743-242 Isaac Masoner
743-243 James McCowan
743-244 James McCowan
744-245 Thomas H. Kincanon
744-246 Elizabeth Kincanon
744-247 Malinda Johnson
744-248 Tunley Rigg
744-249 Enoch Shipley
744-250 Howell Whitmore
744-251 John Gamble
744-252 George Qualls
744-253 Nathan Qualls
745-254 Joseph Cowan
745-255 Jane Malone
745-256 Dicy Mason
745-257 McMinn Welch
745-258 Thomas J. Mathis
745-259 Allen Perry
745-260 Reuben Bandy
746-261 John D. Williams
746-262 Levin Coffy
746-263 William Coffee
746-264 Jessee Maverty
746-265 Noah Perry
746-266 Joseph Whaley
746-267 Jeremiah Whaley
746-268 Charles Whaley
746-269 Henry McCroy
746-270 John Womack
747-271 John George
747-272 James Haney
747-273 Isaac V. Haney
747-274 James M. Grice
747-275 Nancy Brightwell
747-276 Albert Whaley
747-277 Riley Garner
747-278 Alexander Moore
747-279 Hiram Miller
747-280 Stephen Pearce
748-281 James Pearce
748-282 James Phillips
748-283 James Revis
748-284 James Moore
748-285 Chaney Moore
748-286 Ira Hanes
748-287 Phillip Adams
748-288 Ury Neaves
748-289 Ruth Blevins
748-290 Amos Thorp
749-291 Hannah Conly
749-292 Martin Milton
749-293 Sarah Lawson
749-294 Henry Colbough
749-295 Jacob Wamock
749-296 Alford Rockhold
749-297 William Ingle
749-298 William Rockhold
749-299 John Richardson
750-300 Samuel Looney
750-301 William Young
750-302 Jessee Martin
750-303 Elizabeth Blevins
750-304 Thomas Blevins
750-305 Eliza Blevins
750-306 David Bolin
750-307 Catherine Lawson
750-307 Phillip Blevins
751-308 James Blakely
751-309 John James
751-310 John W. Blankenship
751-311 William Allen
751-312 Thomas Blankenship
751-313 E. L. Higdon
751-314 Edward L. Stokes
752-315 William S. Russell
752-316 Elizabeth Blevins
752-317 Susan Lawson
752-318 Nancy Armstrong
752-319 Britton H. George
752-320 Joseph Smith
752-321 Horatio Ford
752-322 Benjamin McKenzie
753-323 Harvy McKenzie
753-324 William A. Randles
753-325 Ritter Webb
753-326 Elza Butram
753-327 William H. Pearce
753-328 Edward T. Burgess
753-329 James Dabney
753-330 Plesent M. Miller
753-331 William F. Zigler
754-332 Jacob Zigler
754-333 Issaac Cranfield
754-334 John McMullen
754-335 Robert J.D.W. Allen
754-336 Leander M. Wilson
754-337 Drury L. Godsey
754-338 Patten Stockton
754-339 Uriah Denton
755-340 Josiah Houser
755-341 Ganum Brightwell
755-342 John P. Hays
755-343 James Jinkins
755-344 Ebenezer Houser
755-345 William R. Miller
755-346 James Way [or Clay]

756-347 Bolen Isum
756-348 John H. Walker
756-349 Caswell Hughs
756-350 Judy Isam
756-351 George C. McCorkle
756-352 Christinia McCorkle
757-353 Jacob Whiteside
757-354 George Culbough
757-355 Jessee White
757-356 Stephen Taylor
757-357 Joseph Rogers
757-358 Robert Melton
757-359 James H. Vernon
758-360 Billy Malone
758-361 John S. Emmett
758-362 William Maynerd
758-363 Jacob Emett
758-364 John Hix
758-365 Asbury Lillard
759-366 William W. Lillard
759-367 Micajah Low
759-368 Jehue E. Cox
759-369 Jane Scott
759-370 Thomas Kaywood
759-371 John T. Blevins
759-372 Josiah Smith
759-373 Thomas Cox
759-374 Mathew Buckhanon
760-375 Dillard McMillian
760-376 James McDaniel
760-377 Abraham Cox
760-378 Elexander Rice
760-379 Benjamin L. White
761-380 Stephen Taylor
761-381 John McClanahan
761-382 Thomas Stokes
761-383 Levin Stokes
761-384 Robert Allen
762-385 Nancy Shelton
762-386 William R. Elder
762-387 William Buster
762-388 Jessee Rice
762-389 Calvin Rice
763-390 William R. Wright
763-391 Abbey McDaniel
763-392 Elizabeth Clack
763-393 Reuben McKinzie
763-394 George W. McKenzie
763-395 Robert Cooley
763-396 Mathias Shaver
763-397 John Taff
763-398 Elizabeth Purdy
764-399 Thomas Purdy
764-400 Aaron Owen
764-401 John Atkinson
764-402 John Benton
764-403 John Davis
764-404 Jonathan Franklin
764-405 Banister Smith
764-406 James Smith
765-407 Mathew Norman
765-408 William Norman
765-409 Washington Patterson
765-410 Wilson Collier
765-411 William Davis
765-412 Martha Ginno
765-413 James Jenoe
765-414 Isaac Benson
765-415 Mathias Benson
765-416 John Gorely
766-417 Clarissa Lewes or Leuven
766-418 John Helton
766-419 William Howard
766-420 Juda Breedwell
766-421 Judge B. White
766-422 David Jones
766-423 John W. Blevins
766-424 Hardin Blevins
766-425 Samuel Blevins
767-426 George Stokes
767-427 John Bowlen
767-428 Dorcy Price
767-429 John Price
767-430 Calvin R. Taff
768-431 Thomas Coffee
768-432 Robert Elder
768-433 William Davis
768-434 George Keynum
768-435 John R. Neil
768-436 James Branham
768-437 Dorcus Evans
769-438 Christian Carrell
769-439 Thomas Young
769-440 Benjamin Brewster
769-441 Violet Eaves
769-442 Peach Taylor
769-443 Ann Blevins
769-444 Andrew Hunter
770-445 Sarah Hunter
770-446 John W. Smith
770-447 Elizabeth Collins
770-448 John Dearmond
770-449 William H. Dearmond
770-450 Mary Long
770-451 Thomas Paterson
770-452 Lenias Lock
770-453 Lewis Gunter
770-454 Thomas J. Lock
770-455 Harrison W. Mahin
771-456 William A. Godsey
771-457 Pulaskie W. Poe
771-458 John McKinley
771-459 John M. Neal
771-460 Martan Long
771-461 John Hunter
771-462 John Ingle
771-463 Emanuel Rhinehart
771-464 John Lillard
771-465 Thomas Luty
772-466 Sarah Gwin
772-467 Rebecca Hamilton
772-468 David Jinoe
772-469 A. W. Hodges
772-470 Calvin C. Robinson
772-471 Michael Ayrehart
772-472 Sarah Sweatman
772-473 E. D. Gilbert
772-474 Miles Forester
773-475 Nancy H. Davis
773-476 Samuel W. Wood
773-477 Haywood Haney
773-478 William Marshall
773-479 Sarah Taylor
773-480 Maddison S. Benson
773-481 George W. Hales
773-482 John W. Wood
774-483 William Abel
774-484 Jonathan C. Wan
774-485 Alman Gwin
774-486 James Lillard
774-487 Martha Jane King
774-488 William Gallaway
774-489 Joseph McKorkle
774-490 Wm H. Baldin [Baldwin]
774-491 Wm Baldin [Baldwin]
775-492 William M. Rogers
775-493 Thomas Cox
775-494 Ishmeal A. Godsey
775-495 Nancy McAdoo
775-496 Thomas Galloway
775-497 Richard Rothwell
775-498 Mary Godsey
775-499 George Lock Miller
776-500 Absalem Gwin
776-501 Jonathan Vincent
776-502 James Pennington
776-503 Walter B. Rothwell
776-504 Mordica Spradling
776-505 James E. Fike
777-506 William Lillard
777-507 Daniel Cate
777-508 Joseph Achly
777-509 Samuel Price
777-510 William Tilary
777-511 Elizabeth Preswood
778-512 Plesant M. Miller
778-513 Alfred Cate
778-514 John Stewart
778-515 William Thorp
778-516 Susan Fine
778-517 James Massingell
778-518 Hiram Jolly
779-519 Nancy Ward
779-520 William Jolly
779-521 David Davis
779-522 Hiram Brandon
779-523 Noah Burchum
780-524 James Burchum
780-525 Pryor Neil
780-526 Robert R. Davis
780-527 Ezekeal Shadack
780-528 Hiram Gibson
780-529 John Sliger
781-530 George Isely
781-531 John Nichol
781-532 Elizabeth McCain
781-533 Thomas Harvey
781-534 Sally Tharp
781-535 Elizabeth Wells
781-536 Thomas S. Farmer
781-537 Haywood Stephens
781-538 Andrew Pruett

781-539 Henry J. Stephens
781-540 Jesse Brown
782-541 Andrew Robertson
782-542 William Mabry
782-543 William Mabry
782-544 William Redmon
782-545 Ezekiel Ward
782-546 Lewis Benton
782-547 Susannah Hill
782-548 Jeremiah Mapes
782-549 Agga Watson
783-550 Thomas Hackler
783-551 William Watson
783-552 Gadi Bocher
783-553 James T. Price
783-554 George W. Quinn or Quiner
783-555 Benjamin Baker
783-556 Jane Hoyl
783-557 William P. Tillery
784-558 Isaac B. Price
784-559 Rebecca Dake
784-560 Leodica Richards
784-561 Bird P. Atchly
784-562 John Davis
784-563 Abner Gwin
784-564 George W. Timons
785-565 Jacob Sliger
785-566 Richard D. Gaddy
785-567 Luke Carroll
785-568 Jonathan M. Collins
785-569 William A. Witt
785-570 Hannah Bishop
785-571 Ceala Newman
785-572 Iredell Pate
786-573 Eli F. Munsey
786-574 John Kitchen
786-575 David Buster
786-576 David Wills
786-577 William Lockmiller
786-578 John Lockmiller
786-579 Caleb Vincent
786-580 Samuel Grigsby
787-581 Benjamin F. Grigsby
787-582 Samuel Buster
787-583 James WillHelm [sic]
787-584 Catherine Wallen
787-585 Edward Farrar
787-586 Ruth Marshall
787-587 Jacob Price
788-588 Christenia Achley
788-589 Jacob Peak
788-590 Ezekeal Marshall
788-591 Joseph G. Royster
788-592 Elizabeth Achly
788-593 Luke Peak
788-594 Bryant W. Smith
789-595 Sarah Ford
789-596 Samuel Hutsell
789-597 Adam Cole
789-598 Caleb Moore
789-599 Squire Ford
789-600 John Ford
789-601 Edward W. Davis
790-602 Elizabeth Massey
790-603 Richard Nelson
790-604 George W. Achly
790-605 Richard Curington
790-606 Elizabeth Ferrell
790-607 Benjamin H. Riddle
790-608 Reuben Vincent
790-609 Luke Lockmiller
791-610 Jessee Owen
791-611 Thomas Edington
791-612 Eliza Jane Cook
791-613 James Cofer
791-614 Jessee Clark
791-615 Charles D. Franklin
792-616 George P. Owen
792-617 Thomas B. McElwee
792-618 William C. McLinn
792-619 Joseph Smith
792-620 Hugh Roberts
792-621 Wesly Martin
792-622 William M. True
793-623 Sarah Herd
793-624 George W. Bradley
793-625 Abijah Boggess
793-626 Daniel M. Clark
793-627 Hugh L. Wilson
793-628 James W. Sturgess
793-629 John Fitch
-630 [skipped]
794-631 Charity Dyer
794-632 John Fitch
794-633 Abram Smith
794-634 Isaac E. Fitch
794-635 Isaac Fitch
794-636 Noble N. Molton
794-637 Sarah McAllen
794-638 Thomas Bottom
794-639 Isam Vanoy
795-640 William C. McGinnis
795-641 Samuel Edgman
795-642 David Walker
795-643 John S. Walker
795-644 John Wood
795-645 Delilah McAdams
795-646 Nancy Green
795-647 John McAllen
796-647 James B. McAllen
796-648 George M. Clemison
796-649 Benjamin F. Locke
796-650 John C. Sharp
796-651 Pascheal Snider
796-652 Joseph T. Bryan
796-653 John W. Tuell
796-654 Harriet Butler
796-655 Levi H. Knight
797-656 Sally W. Thompson
797-657 John R. Foshee
797-658 Winny Atwood
797-659 Samuel Detherage
797-660 Stephen Winton
797-661 John Ray
797-662 William Reed
797-663 Hiram Munsey
797-664 Nancy Lawson
797-665 Rotan Green
798-666 David Bell
798-667 Reuben Phillips
798-668 Elihue Phillips
798-669 David H. Sharp
798-670 James McAdams
798-671 Nelson C. Redmon
798-672 Thomas Edgmon
799-673 Phillip L. Davis
799-674 Thomas P. Davis
799-675 Abner Deatherage
799-676 John Scott
799-677 Elisha Sharp
800-678 Isaac Aiken
800-679 Gideon Ragland
800-680 John L. Balden [Baldwin]
800-671 John Green
800-672 Jacob Green
800-673 William Harvy
800-674 John P. Redman
800-675 Thomas Green
800-676 James Patterson
801-677 James Griffith
801-678 John Gardner
801-679 Robert Rentfro
801-680 Joab Blackwell
801-681 Thomas Conduff
801-682 William H. Blythe
801-683 Samuel M. Blythe
802-684 Jackson West
802-685 Thomas Riddle
802-686 Simon McGinnis
802-687 Abijah F. Boggess
802-688 Hannah Green
802-689 Martha Phillips
802-690 William Fitch
802-691 Elizabeth Maples
802-692 Peter Allison
803-693 John Nelson
803-694 Hance Nelson
803-695 William Montgomery
803-696 Elizabeth Lawrence
803-697 Frances Crabtree
803-698 Gabriel Medaris
803-699 Thomas C. Jordan
804-700 Anderson Jones
804-701 Edmond Ford
804-702 William D. Ford
804-703 Polly Ford
804-704 Andrew Mee
804-705 Julius Hackler
804-706 Blackstone Reid
805-707 Riley Bise
805-708 Josiah Darwin
805-709 Jacob Varner
805-710 Jacob Varner
805-711 J. C. Plumblee
805-712 James Brown
805-713 Joseph Moss
806-714 Henderson Bowlen
806-715 Thomas Rentfro
806-716 Alkana Rowden
806-717 Shardick Rowden
806-718 Mark Rentfro
806-719 Phebe Butler

807-720 Tyri Kelly
807-721 James Hembro
807-722 Sarah George
807-723 Samuel Baker
807-724 William Tally
807-725 Enoch Ladd
807-726 Joseph Brown
808-727 Jonathan Norton
808-728 William Ray
808-729 Dolly Allen
808-730 Sarah Floyd
808-731 Leroy Loony
808-732 Jane Baker
808-733 John Baker
808-734 William Baker
809-735 William Blackwell
809-736 John Daniel
809-737 James Massy
809-738 Alexander McCall
809-739 Mary Massy
809-740 Judy Cash
810-741 Sarah Cash
810-742 Ruth Brown
810-743 Stephen Ford
810-744 Curtis Richards
810-745 James Milligan
810-746 Robert Murphy
810-747 Alexander D. Alford
811-748 Daniel Robertson
811-749 Enoch Collins
811-750 Jeremiah Chapman
811-751 William Green
811-752 William Johnson
811-753 Eliza Bell
811-754 William Lawson
811-755 Nathan B. Briggs
812-756 James D. Briggs
812-757 Randolph Gibson
812-758 Benjamin Hutson
812-759 Alfred Blackwell
812-760 Absolem Foshee
812-761 Jacob Gibson
[missing numbers on page 816]
813-768 Alfred Gibson
813-769 Lydia Jones
813-770 Sally Teasstaller
813-771 Daniel Green
813-772 Archibald Mariat
813-773 McMinn Lillard
813-774 Silas G. Latham
813-775 Nathan Watson
814-776 Elbert Blalock
814-777 Sylvan Stephens
814-778 William Wan
814-779 John W. Smith
814-780 William Smith
814-781 James Moore
814-782 James W. Moore
815-783 Haywood Stephens
815-784 Louis Huff
815-785 Joseph Buckhanen
815-786 John Huff
815-787 B. F. Huff
815-788 Miles V. Lillard
815-789 Benjamin Blalock
815-790 Alexander Thorp
815-791 Catharine Curington
815-792 Christinia Bennett
815-793 Caleb H. Hare
816-762 Wesly Miller
816-763 James J. Mathes
816-764 John Johnson
816-765 Nathan Pelfry
816-766 Phillip Smith
816-767 John Duckworth
817-794 Alexander Brown
817-795 William Brown
817-796 John K. Brown
817-797 John Alford
817-798 Mary Fleming
817-799 David D. Holcomb
817-800 Elizabeth ???
817-800 James S. Paul
817-801 Plesent Holoman
818-802 Phebe Rush
818-803 Thomas V. Achly
818-804 Thomas Roark
818-805 Samuel Roark
818-806 John L. Aikman
818-807 Claton Hoyl
818-808 William Knox
818-809 George M. Black
818-810 Samuel Roark
819-811 Joseph H. Cate
819-812 Jacob Tillery
819-813 James C. Roberson
819-814 Samuel Adams
819-815 Porter Crabtree
819-816 Jeremiah Miller
819-817 William L. Adams
819-818 Andrew N. Snider
819-819 R. H. McGinnes

[Last date: 29 October 1850]

APPENDIX C

STATISTICS FROM 1830, 1840, AND 1850 CENSUS

The total number of residents in Rhea and Meigs counties as reflected by the census records may be of interest to some researchers. Any comments that accompanied the census also are included in this appendix.

1830 RHEA CENSUS

"The number of persons Within My division consisting of 3828 males, 3709 females, 313 black males, 332 black females making a total of 8182 as appears on the foregoing Schedule Subscribed by Me this 27th day of Nov. eighteen hundred and thirty."

[signed] Jno Lea
Assistant to the Marshall
E. district of Tennessee

"We hereby certify this is a Correct copy of the above Schedule signed by the said John Lea, Assistant &c, has been set up at two of the most public places within the division for the inspection of all concerned"

[signed] R. B. Locke
B. F. Locke

- - - - - - - - - - - - -

1840 RHEA CENSUS

"The number of Persons within My Division Consisting of Three Thousand Nine Hundred and Ninty Nine [3999] appears in the foregoing Schedule Subscribed by me this 20th day of October in the year One Thousand Eight Hundred and Forty."

[signed] Jacob H. Love

"We hereby Certify that a Correct Copy of the above Schedule has been set up Signed by the said Jacob H. Love at Gilberts Store Sulphur Spring Rhea County Tennessee open to the inspection of all Concerned this 20th October 1840." [signed] John Cook
E. E. Wasson

"We hereby Certify that a Correct Copy of the Within Schedule has been Set Signed by the Said Jacob H. Love at the Court House in Washington Rhea County open to the inspection of all Concerned this 20th October 1840."

[signed] David Leuty
Edmund Bean

Whites

Age	Males	Females	Age	Male	Females
0-5	366	383	40-50	88	98
5-10	307	277	50-60	69	71
10-15	253	202	60-70	48	32
15-20	210	221	70-80	12	13
20-30	284	301	80-90	5	2
30-40	178	158	90-100	1	1

Free Colored males		Free colored females	
0-10	6	0-10	6
10-24	3	10-24	2
24-36	2	24-36	1
36-55	2	36-55	2

[NOTE: The Rhea County slave population by age was not copied because the microfilm did not include the entire list]
[The following miscellaneous information was included with the 1840 Rhea County census]

Numbers of Persons in each family employed in:

Mining	0	Manufacture and trade	69
Agriculture	1,180	Navigation	0
Commerse	7	Learned Professions	12

	age	(white)	(colored)
Deaf and Dumb	0-14	1	0
	14-25	0	0
	25+	2	0
Blind		2	1
Insane at public charge		0	0
Insane at private charge		1	0

Pensioners for Military Service and age in 1840

Daniel Broile 80	Thomas McKeddy 86
James Furgison 81	Harris Ryan 76
Thomas Hamilton 80	Mary Peace 23

- - - - - - - - - - - - -

1840 MEIGS CENSUS

"I do sollemnly swear that the number of persons set fourth in the return made by me agreeably to a provision of an act entitled an act to provide for taking the sixth census or enumeration of the inhabitants of the United States have been assertained by an actual inquiry at every dwelling house on a personal inquiry of the head of every family in exact conformity with the provisions of said act and that I have in every respect fulfilled the duties required of me by said act to the best of my abilities and that the return aforesaid is correct and true according to the best of my knowledge and [black ink blob] and belief and that I have carefully copied all the work of John W. Witten Deceased as found on his census Book which appears correct save small errors on page 16, Except this tenth day of October One Thousand Eight Hundred and Forty."

[signed] James Patterson

"Be it remembred that on this tenth day of October 1840 came before me James Patterson a resident in the County of Meigs district of East Tennessee an assistant to the Marshall of the district of East Tennessee for performing the duties prescribed by the Act of Congress to provide for taking the Sixth census or innumeration of the inhabitants of the United States and for other purposes and took and in my presence subscribed the above oath."

[signed] James Moore [seal]
Justice of the Peace for Meigs County

"We hereby certify that a correct copy of the above schedule signed by the said James Patterson has been set up at two of the most public places within the division, open to the inspection of all concerned October 10th 1840"

[signed] Wm Wan
James Moore
Citizens of Meigs County

age	whites males	whites females
0-5	445	425
5-10	432	385
10-15	345	226
15-20	269	250
20-30	328	331
30-40	187	238
40-50	124	134
50-60	83	67
60-70	35	44
70-80	21	23
80-90	1	4
100+	1	0
Totals	2271	2127

free colored	males	females
under 10	2	1
10-24		2
24-36	1	2
36-55		1
55-100	2	2

slaves age	males	females
0-10	43	53
10-24	56	50
24-36	22	19
36-55	14	19
55-100	4	4
	139	145

Total: 4,398 (2,869 taken by John W. Witton; 1,902 taken by James Patterson)

"The number of persons within my division consisting of 4771 Meigs County appear in the foregoing Schedule Subscribed By me this October ninth day in the year of our Lord 1840."

[Miscellaneous information from the Meigs County Census]

Numbers of Persons in Each Family Employed in

Mining	0	Manufacture and trade	69
Agriculture	1,172	Navigation	9
Commerce	0	Learned Professions	16

Pensioners for Revolutionary or Military services 2
[no names included]

	(white)	(colored)
Deaf and Dumb	2	0
Blind	0	0
Insane-Idiots at public charge	3	3
Insane-Idiots at private charge	2	0

Schools and Education:

Primary and common schools	14
Number of Scholars	245
Number of Scholars at public charge	432
Number of white persons over 20 years of age in each family who cannot read and write	613

- - - - - - - - - - - - -

1850 RHEA CENSUS

No summary page followed the 1850 Rhea County census, but the following tabulations appeared at the bottom of each page (added by Districts):

District	White M	White F	Colored M	Colored F	Mulatto M	Mulatto F	Total
1	405	341				1	747
2	187	194			1		382
3	256	233		1	1		491
4	262	257			1		520
5	194	207				1	402
6	132	137		2			271
Town	70	80	1	2	2	5	160
7	236	237			2	1	476
8	266	251	4	1		2	524
						Total*	3,973

[* This total differs from that given by the enumerator because mistakes were made in addition in three districts]

- - - - - - - - - - - - -

1850 MEIGS CENSUS

A very short summary appeared at the end of the 1850 Meigs County census that was signed by Creed Roper or Roser on 24 February 1851:

Dwellings 819 Families 819

White		Colored		Slave	
Males	2,284	Males	1	Males	190
Females	2,199	Females	0	Females	205
Totals	4,483		1		395

Grand Total: 4,879 Deaths 68

- - - - - - - - - - - - -

SUMMARY

1840 RHEA CENSUS 8,182

1840 RHEA CENSUS 3,999
1840 MEIGS CENSUS 4,771
Total of both counties in 1840 8,770

1850 RHEA CENSUS 3,986
1850 MEIGS CENSUS 4,879
Total of both counties in 1850 8,865

- - - - - - - - - - - - -

www.ingramcontent.com/pod-product-compliance
Lightning Source LLC
Chambersburg PA
CBHW080416270326
41929CB00018B/3050
* 9 7 8 0 7 8 8 4 9 1 2 2 1 *